For Julius and Gertrude
With affection and esteem
Abe

1972

Also by Abram L. Sachar

A HISTORY OF THE JEWS
(1938; Fifth Edition, Revised, 1965)

SUFFERANCE IS THE BADGE
(1939)

These are Borzoi Books
published in New York by Alfred A. Knopf

THE COURSE OF OUR TIMES

ABRAM L. SACHAR

THE COURSE OF OUR TIMES

NEW YORK

Alfred A. Knopf

1972

THIS IS A BORZOI BOOK
PUBLISHED BY ALFRED A. KNOPF, INC.

Manufactured in the United States of America

Library of Congress Cataloging in Publication Data:
Sachar, Abram Leon, 1899–   The course of our times.
Includes bibliographical references.
1. History, Modern—20th century. I. Title.
D421.S23 1972   909.82   72–2232
ISBN 0–394–47442–2

FIRST EDITION

for Howard, Edward,
and David

CONTENTS

CONTENTS

PREFACE

WHEN I BECAME PRESIDENT OF BRANDEIS UNIVERSITY, I WELCOMED THE
opportunity to teach an advanced course in contemporary affairs.
This provided continuity with an earlier incarnation when I was part
of the history faculty at the University of Illinois. For that matter,
teaching also offered occasional relief from the surfeit of adminis-
trivia. When my incumbency as president of Brandeis was completed
in 1968, Hartford Gunn, Jr., the director of the Greater Boston educational station, WGBH, suggested that the "classroom" would be
substantially extended if the course were put on the air. The temptation to reach an impressively diverse viewing audience was irresistible.
Fifty-two telecasts relative to the period since World War I were
prepared. This volume is a revision and expansion of those telecasts.

The lectures do not, of course, represent basic research. It would
have been sheer arrogance on my part to attempt to cover the last
half century with all of its complicated developments—and that in
the role of specialist. I have relied upon the patient scholarship of
others and attempted an overview, in the hope of providing an introduction to the complexities of contemporary affairs. For the events
that explode all about us are not happenings; they are consequences.
Kierkegaard aptly summarized the confluence of past and present
when he wrote: "Life must be lived forward, but can only be understood backwards." Without explanatory background, one can hardly
make sense of the rupture in the relations of the Soviet Union and
Red China, the American quagmire involvement in Vietnam, the

[xi]

civil war in Ireland, the turbulence in Black Africa, the passionate India-Pakistan hostility, the impasse in the relations of Israelis and Arabs in the much-Promised Land, and the host of other developments that bewilder us.

Since the core material in this volume comes from the Brandeis course and from the telecasts, the informal lecture format has been retained. But I have edited the scripts to eliminate repetitive sections that were necessary to maintain the interconnection for what was inevitably a changing audience. I have also added to each chapter some of the material it had been necessary to eliminate because of the time schedule of television programming. In developing the telecasts, it had been painful to omit illustrative or supporting data simply because the tyrant in the studio, watching the second hand of the clock, decreed "cut." Now I have the satisfaction of outwitting her and restoring much of the excised material.

In both the scripts and this volume, I have tried to apply whatever scholarly discipline I could command to achieve accuracy in fact and data. But judgments on actions and events, and biographical evaluations, are inevitably subjective. The vigorous, spirited, and often indignant mail response to the treatment of such controversial themes as the Spanish Civil War, the dictatorship in Greece, *apartheid* in South Africa and Rhodesia, the Castro phenomenon, the Lyndon Johnson years, has been a chastening experience. The historian is rarely ensconced in an ivory tower; he finds himself more often in an ivory foxhole.

I wish to acknowledge my thanks to the number of friendly critics who have written or called after the telecasts. Many of them, especially the academic and government figures, offered suggestions that have considerably improved the original drafts. I am even more indebted to members of the Brandeis faculty, whose specialized competence was invaluable when they took the time to review individual chapters. They include Dr. Rudolph Binion, Dr. Morton Keller, Dr. Marvin Meyers, Dr. Eugene C. Black, Dr. Roy C. Macridis, Dr. Joseph Berliner, Dr. Robert Szulkin, Dr. Ludovico Borgo, Dr. Nahum Glatzer, Dr. John Roche, Dr. John Schrecker, Miroslav Krek, Dr. I. Milton Sacks, Dr. Jack S. Goldstein, Dr. Ruth Morgenthau, Dr. Milton Vanger, and Dr. Donald Hindley. I am also indebted to the late Hans Sante, the West German Consul-General of New England; to his associate, the present Consul-General, Paul Kurbjuhn; and to Dr. Claus Duisberg of the diplomatic staff of the West German Embassy in Washington, for their views of the Adenauer period. Maurice Samuel, whose volumes on contemporary Jewish life are models of lucidity and eloquence, reviewed the chapters on Israel, Egypt, the reaction to genocide, and the moral dilemma of the collaborators. The section on the Irish uprising was checked by Mrs. Carmel Heaney, the Irish Consul in Boston. Of course, none of these friendly critics is to be held responsible for the chapters as they finally emerged, nor for the inadequacies or shortcomings that have remained.

As a novice in television, I am especially grateful to Miss Margaret MacLeod, the producer of *The Course of Our Times*. Her insistence on clarity without sacrificing accuracy went beyond the techniques of good telecasting.

Special thanks go to my editor, Ashbel Green, who shepherded me through the manuscript revision, and to my publisher, Alfred A. Knopf, a cherished friend of half a century, who suggested the volume and retained a continuous interest in it.

The processing of the telecasts and the validation of references for the volume demanded unusual conscientiousness, and I owe warm thanks to Mrs. Eleanor Charter and Mrs. Marjory Supovitz, members of my staff. It will be noted that I have not attempted to offer citations for well-known or easily accessible quotations.

The acknowledgment to my wife leaves all too much unsaid. In the preparation of the television programs and in the editorial work for the volume, she was the most patient and discerning of critics. She offered the saving grace of perspective when personal life was continuously complicated as television and writing had to be wedged into the demanding regimen of public service. I could speak with more relaxation in the studio, and could see this volume through the press with more confidence, because encouragement and candid judgment were delicately balanced by her with such skill.

ABRAM L. SACHAR

Brandeis University
Waltham, Massachusetts

THE COURSE OF OUR TIMES

1

THE SUNSET YEARS
OF THE OLD WORLD

ONE OF THE MOST WIDELY DISCUSSED BOOKS OF THE PERIOD JUST PRE-
ceding World War I was Norman Angell's *The Great Illusion*. It
was published in 1910, and quickly became an international best-
seller. It was translated into more than twenty languages, and passed
through many editions, the sales reaching millions. It prompted the
organization of hundreds of study groups in major universities and
the establishment of foundations and societies whose object it was to
bring the lessons of the volume before students and the public.

Angell's thesis was that modern warfare had become so destructive
there could be no victors. "The inescapable economic chaos resulting
from war," he wrote, "makes economic benefit from victory impossible." He was perceptive enough to realize that the passions and
ambitions of peoples often override rational considerations and that
they take no count of prudent self-interest. He tried to make this
clear and advocated a system of collective security that would enforce
the peaceful settlement of disputes. "Arm the law," he wrote, "not
the litigants." But to Angell's profound chagrin, the solid evidence
that he marshaled to prove the utter folly of war was equated by an
uncritical public with the conclusion that war had therefore become
automatically impossible. For, since war could bring no benefits,
even in triumph, then surely it had become as obsolete as the vindication of honor by the duel, the torturing of witnesses in law courts,
and the burning of nonconformists at the stake.

The intellectual stir created by Angell's volume was not limited to dreamers and doctrinaires. It was hailed as a decisive refutation of many of the axioms that underlay modern statecraft. Enthusiastic reviews appeared in the most influential journals, and Angell's thesis was gravely explored by cabinet ministers on both sides of the Atlantic. The German Ambassador in London made it the text of a diplomatic announcement. A French critic was certain that Angell's *Great Illusion* would rank with Darwin's *Origin of Species*. The King of England sent copies to all of his ministers. Lord Esher, who had been appointed chairman of the British Committee on Imperial Defence, adopted Angell's logic in toto, and foretold that it would exert an influence not inferior to Mahan's classic volume on *Sea Power*. In his address at the United Service Club in Britain, with Sir John French, Chief of the General Staff, presiding, he argued, a few weeks before the greatest conflict in history began, that, since Angell had invalidated the premise that economic prosperity depends on national power, neither Britain nor France had any further reason to fear German aggression. Angell was later awarded the Nobel Peace Prize.

In retrospect, the furore over the Angell thesis can be interpreted as a widespread case of wishful thinking. Yet its intellectual appeal to the prewar world was understandable. Since Waterloo in 1815, there had been no general war that threatened the stability of the social order. For a full century there had been steady material progress. An uninterrupted industrial advance had raised living standards for the peoples of the western world. Medical discoveries had revolutionized health patterns and had lengthened life expectancy. Schools had multiplied and illiteracy had been steadily reduced. Slavery had been abolished along with the slave trade; even benighted Russia had freed its serfs. Inventions increasingly freed men from successive areas of menial labor. Women were emancipated from age-old restrictions, and penal codes were humanized. Was it not inevitable, then, that with the passing of time, and not too much time, most of the evils that had so long bedeviled the world would be eliminated? Herbert Spencer wrote: "Progress is not an accident, but a necessity. . . . Always toward perfection is the mighty movement, toward a complete development and a more unmixed good." This too was the heart-warming vision of Louis Pasteur when he was honored at the Sorbonne by his fellow scientists on his seventieth birthday. "And you delegates from foreign nations," he declared in his ringing peroration, "bring me the deepest joy that can be felt by a man whose invincible belief is that Science and Peace will triumph over Ignorance and War, that nations will unite, not to destroy, but to build, and that the future will belong to those who will have done most for suffering humanity."

The faith in progress was, of course, not universally held. There were voices throughout the nineteenth and the early twentieth century that spoke a more somber language. The novels of Dostoyevsky were filled with bitter hatred of the complacent western civilization. Nietzsche despised the materialism and sentimentalism of his age with its stifling rationalism and its idolatry of science. One could not read Zola and his pessimistic determinism and still believe that man enjoyed any freedom of action. There were others who represented divergencies—Pareto and Kafka and Proust and, of course, the mighty Freud. Even the incorrigible imperialist, Rudyard Kipling, felt it necessary in *Recessional* at the celebration of the sixtieth year of Victoria's reign to sound a warning:

> Far-called our navies melt away
> On dune and headland sinks the fire
> Lo, all our pomp of yesterday
> Is one with Nineveh and Tyre!

But these dissonant voices barely penetrated the prevailing mood of high expectation. Faith in the inevitability of progress could not be shaken.

Then, in the summer of 1914, came the war, a world war, with shattering consequences in every continent. It was not fought with the savagery of World War II, where no sanctions were to be respected. But it loosed enough horror to belie every civilized value. There were submarine sinkings without warning, and poison gas, and blockades that starved millions of women and children and added their toll to the casualties on the battlefield. The carnage was unbelievable, ten million dead, twenty million wounded, countless millions uprooted, opening out the era of the homeless, unwanted man. There were no accurate figures on the material treasure that was destroyed, but it was estimated that it could not have been less than 330 billion dollars.

More disastrous than the fury of destructiveness were the spiritual consequences: man's loss of faith in himself, and of confidence in reason as the touchstone of progress. Valéry wrote in 1922, after summarizing the material losses of the war, "The Mind itself has not been exempt from all this damage. The Mind is in fact cruelly stricken; it grieves in men of intellect, and looks sadly upon itself. It distrusts

[5]

itself profoundly." Rebelling against the dictates of reason, D. H. Lawrence became the center of a cult that exalted passion and feeling in its place. "My great religion," he wrote, "is the belief in the blood, in the flesh, as being wiser than the intellect. We can go wrong in our minds, but what our blood feels and believes and says is always true. The intellect is only a bit and a bridle. All I want is to answer to my blood, direct, without fribbling intervention of mind or morals or whatnot."* The sense of ethical directive disappeared. Philosophy, literature, and the arts began to glorify meaninglessness, and offered a complete re-evaluation of the place of man. Spengler brooded, with gloomy satisfaction, over the inevitable triumph of Caesarism. Walter Lippmann wrote of the malaise of man in the repudiation of the faith of the fathers:

Man, when he considers his civilization, has a dusty taste in his mouth. He may be busy with many things, but he discovers one day that he is no longer sure they are worth doing. He has been much preoccupied; but he is no longer sure that he knows why. He has become involved in an elaborate routine of pleasures, and they do not seem to amuse him very much. He finds it hard to believe that doing any one thing is better than doing any other thing, or, in fact, that it is better than doing nothing at all. . . . Surveying the flux of events and the giddiness of his own soul, he comes to feel that Aristophanes must have been thinking of him when he declared that "Whirl is King, having driven out Zeus."†

For Santayana, all that was left of his Catholic faith was its aesthetics. "There is no God, and Mary is His Mother." He was reconciled to the fate that life is not a festival or a feast. It is a predicament.

But on the brink of the cataclysm, in the summer of 1914, the sun shone brightly on an England dedicated to progress as irresistible destiny. Europe was still the center of the world, and Britain the center of Europe. Geographically, it was insignificant, a mere blob when seen on the globe. But its power reached to the ends of the earth, and controlled a far-flung Empire. It was rich and arrogant, and its rulers remembered with pride the toast of Horace Walpole: "You can burn all of your Greek and Roman books. They're just the histories of little people." The boast did not seem extravagant. Most countries set their clocks by Greenwich time, the pound was an impregnable $4.86, and many of the world's currencies were in the

* Cited in Quincy Howe, *The World Between the Wars* (New York: Simon & Schuster, 1953), p. 181.

† Walter Lippmann, *A Preface to Morals* (New York: The Macmillan Company, 1929), p. 4.

sterling orbit. The rich gloried in their ostentation.* Britain's ships dominated the seas and kept watch over its trade and its finance. "The sun never sets on the British Empire" was the haughty claim. The crown was intermarried with all of Europe, its princes and princesses were on almost every throne, and portly Edward VII was a kind of obese epilogue to the Victorian Age, literally the Uncle of Europe. It was sunset, but few yet knew it.

Then came the pistol shots at Sarajevo and what Rilke called "the dreary human muddle of trumped-up doom." Nothing was ever the same again.

* "The Edwardian age was probably the last period in history when the fortunate thought they could give pleasure to others by displaying their good fortune before them." James Laver, *Edwardian Promenade* (Boston: Houghton Mifflin, 1958), p. 4.

2

"STAGGERING AND BLUNDERING" INTO WORLD WAR

WHEN WORLD WAR I BEGAN, THE BRITISH FOREIGN MINISTER, SIR Edward Grey, red-eyed and bent with exhaustion, stood at the window of his office and made the sober comment to the editor of the *Westminster Gazette* that the lamps were going out all over Europe, and that they probably would not be lit again in their lifetime. One of the soldiers in the trenches put it more prosaically. The war, he said, would last a hundred years, five years for fighting, and ninety-five to wind up the barbed wire. Both forecasts were fulfilled, each in its way. The war lasted four years, and was followed, a generation later, by an even more horrendous conflict which spawned social upheaval and revolution reaching into the far future. The dangers of the past were compounded because the newly contrived instruments of destruction now menaced the very fabric of civilization.

The tragedy seemed to be, and was, a senseless one. There was no inevitability about it, and yet it all happened as if inevitably. There had been recurrent national feuding since the beginning of the century, but it had always been contained. The confrontations of 1914 began as so many preceding ones had, in a remote corner of Europe, and the issues seemed to be manageable. This time they exploded. The study of the climactic crisis and the ensuing conflict that drew in all the continents is a sorry catalogue of reckless adventurism, diplomatic immaturity, appalling callousness, and plain stupidity.

There is now an extensive literature on the origins of the war, and on the war guilt. The history of its history reflects the political climate in which the studies were made. The first interpretations, from the Allied side, were influenced by the emotions of the war. There was an uncomplicated simplicity about all of them. Germany was solely responsible; it had long held the ambition to dominate the continent, and ultimately the world. *"Deutschland über Alles"*— "Germany Above All"—the national anthem, was as much claim as boast. The German General Staff had planned the war carefully and had looked for excuses to launch it. And since this was so, when the Allies convened at Versailles in 1919 to draw up the treaties, they insisted upon including an article (231) which compelled defeated Germany to accept the total responsibility "for launching the war and for causing all the loss and damage."

After 1920, and the general disillusionment with the fruits of peace, a school of revisionists tried to modify what they condemned as distorted judgment. A series of secret treaties had come to light, triumphantly released by the Communists when they came to power in Russia. These made it clear that the Allies had not undertaken a moral crusade in defense of democracy; they had been as eager to pursue aggressive national interests as the Germans had been. At the Versailles Conference, John Maynard Keynes, the British economic expert, not only pointed up the lunacy of the reparations imposed upon Germany; he also excoriated the Allies for cant and hypocrisy. The United States, increasingly isolationist, repudiated Wilson and his dreams of a new world order, and came to regret participation in the war. There were scholars and publicists who laid responsibility for edging the United States into the war upon the giant ammunitions firms; "merchants of death," one best-seller labeled them. Others argued that America entered the war to save the billions in credit that had been extended to the Allies by Wall Street and the bankers. Senator Gerald Nye persuaded Congress to pass strong neutrality acts that would, in the future, prevent any business with belligerents, to make certain that the United States would not again become involved in foreign wars.

After the rise of Hitler and the carnage that accompanied his triumphs and his downfall, the revisionist views were again revised, and historians were once more reading back into the past some endemic quality in the German people that made them a perpetual menace to their contemporaries. There were highly respected German scholars who supported this conclusion and linked the launching of the war to the recklessness of German diplomacy. Professor

Fritz Fischer came to a sorrowful *nostra culpa* as he assigned prime responsibility for the war to the General Staff, who were confident that quick victory would at last give Germany its place in the sun.*

Three generations have now passed since the watershed period of World War I, and there still is no scholarly consensus. But, the judgment of guilt aside, the major forces that were pushing the nations into conflict and that required the firm control of mature statesmanship are more easily identified.

To begin with, there was the dangerously combustible nationalism already present before the beginning of the century. It was present in Britain where, indeed, the term "jingo" originated, entering the language from a music-hall song during the British-Russian crisis of 1878:

> We don't want to fight
> But by jingo if we do
> We have the men, we have the ships
> We have the money too.
> The Roosians shall not have Constantinohhhple!†

The banked fire burned in France too, fed by the resolve to recover Alsace-Lorraine, which had been annexed by the Germans after the war of 1870. It was there in Poland, which had lost its independence in the eighteenth century and been divided up between Russia, Prussia, and Austria. It was there in Germany, where Pan-Germanism had been preached by the chauvinists of the nineteenth century, aided and abetted by the Kaiser and the military. It was there in Russia, where Pan-Slavism envisaged a vast confederation under Russia, to include all of the Slavic peoples. Above all, it was there in the polyglot Austrian Empire, mainly controlled by the Germans and the Hungarians, but with many oppressed nationalities—Serbs, Croats, Czechs, and Slovaks—ever more restive, planning and plotting to compel the Empire to concede autonomy. There were unremitting quarrels in the Balkans, escalating into the wars of 1912 and 1913, that hovered on the brink of larger catastrophes. Extreme nationalism, then, was the witch's cauldron that could easily burst asunder and overwhelm Europe and the world.

Unbridled colonial rivalry was another factor that contributed to the climate of war. The base of the European states had become inadequate for their modern needs and for the protection of their

---

* Fritz Fischer, *Germany's Aims in the First World War* (New York: W. W. Norton, 1967).
† The lyricist was G. W. Hunt, 1878.

expanding standards of living. They exploited the cheap labor of their possessions in far-off continents to obtain required raw materials, and they disposed of the manufactured products at high levels of profit. In Asia, Britain had large sectors of the continent in its trade orbit. So did France and, by the irony of history, Holland, with a Dutch Empire a hundred times bigger than the Motherland. In Africa, Britain and France had moved in early, and had pre-empted the most advantageous areas; and here, Belgium had taken over the Congo, nearly eighty times its own size. Always the rationale was the "white man's burden," the responsibility to civilize the savage and to bring him the blessings of Christianity, usually at 25 percent return. The natives complained that "once the whites had the Bible and we had the land, and now we have the Bible and the white men have the land."

The latecomers were Germany and Italy, who did not achieve modern statehood until after the middle of the nineteenth century.* They were determined that they would have a fair share, too, of colonial advantage, and they seized every opportunity to press for redistribution. To the German Kaiser it was a case of *Weltmacht oder Niedergang* (World Power or Ruination), and when there were no outlets in Africa, he turned for fulfillment to the Balkans and the Near East and challenged the monopoly of Britain, France, and Russia.

Above all, there was the precarious balance of power. Since there was no international authority, with a compelling sanction to bring disputes to the conference table, a system of alliances developed, a kind of European gang system. The major states chose up sides. The Triple Alliance brought together Germany, Austria, and Italy: the Triple Entente brought together Russia, England, and France. There were solemn assurances that an attack upon any one member of a military kinship would be treated as an attack on all of them.† Thus no issue could be insulated. A threat against Austria meant that Germany must respond. A threat against Russia meant that France must respond. A threat against France meant that England, though not required, would be expected to respond.

The expansion of armies and ships and planes on one side quickly compelled parallel expansion on the other, and defense budgets ate

---

* The historian Helmuth Plessner ascribed many of Germany's problems to its tardy national fulfillment and aptly titled his volume *Die Verspätete Nation* (The Belated Nation) (Stuttgart: W. Kohlhammer, 1959).

† Some of the pacts called for neutrality in case of attack by only one country.

into the vitals of national life. Norman Angell could write eloquently and convincingly that no state, however well prepared, could any longer win in a war; the ultimate cost was too high. But since Europe was so sensitively balanced, reason could not restrain pride, nor could logic restrain fear. Indeed, the statesmen of Europe found fascination in the dangerous manipulations of diplomacy. Winston Churchill wrote,

Nations and Empires crowned with princes and potentates rose majestically on every side, lapped in the accumulated treasures of the long peace. All were fitted, and fastened—it seemed securely—into an immense cantilever. The two mighty European systems faced each other glittering and clanking in their panoply, but with a tranquil gaze. A polite, discreet, pacific, and on the whole sincere diplomacy spread its web of connections over both. A sentence in a dispatch, an observation by an ambassador, a cryptic phrase in a Parliament seemed sufficient to adjust from day to day the balance of the prodigious structure. . . . The old world, in its sunset, was fair to see.*

But how long could fate be tempted? A day came when the sentence in the dispatch and the cryptic phrase in Parliament were not sufficient, when the cantilever was pushed too hard and could no longer maintain its balance.

Years before, Bismarck had grimly prophesied that if a world war was ever launched, it would begin over "some damned foolish thing in the Balkans." Now his foreboding was borne out. The war did begin in the Balkan cockpit of Europe, with a political assassination that was intended to challenge the control of Austria-Hungary, a heterogeneous Empire ruled by the aged Emperor Franz Josef, now in the twilight of a sixty-six-year reign. The heir to the throne was his grand-nephew, the Archduke Francis Ferdinand, who had hoped that he could ameliorate the problem of nationalist discontent through an ingenious trialism, a triple federation with considerable autonomy for the Germans, the Hungarians, and the Slavic bases of the ethnic groups, all united within the Empire and bound by common economic interests. There had been too much opposition from all sides to his plan and he had reluctantly abandoned it. Now he favored political and civil equality for all subjects of the Empire, and had undertaken a state visit to Sarajevo, the capital of the province of Bosnia, to demonstrate his conciliatory objectives. But if he inherited

* Winston Churchill, *The World Crisis* (New York: Charles Scribner's Sons, 1931), p. 97.

the throne and carried through such a reform, it would, of course, put an end to the strivings of the Serbs, who wanted no reform, no amelioration, nothing short of complete independence. The extremists were pledged to eliminate the Archduke before he came to power.

The Serbian irredentist leadership was centered in the Black Hand Society, dedicated to the union of all Serbians. Its technique was frankly stated: "This organization prefers terrorist activity to intellectual propaganda." Its headquarters were in Belgrade and it had cells in many cities and towns heavily inhabited by Serbs. The guiding spirit was the chief of military intelligence at the Serbian war office. When the announcement was made that the Archduke and his morganatic wife were to visit Sarajevo, the plot was hatched to assassinate them. The responsibility for action was placed in the hands of youngsters whose background pointed up the utter irresponsibility of the venture. They were school dropouts, ne'er-do-wells. One had been expelled for slapping his teacher. Another, aged seventeen, failing mathematics and suspended, contemplated suicide and looked upon the plot as a patriotic way of achieving his purpose.

The royal car came into Sarajevo on June 28, and when it passed the point where one of the assigned conspirators was stationed, he threw his bomb. It fell into the open car, but the Archduke threw it out before it exploded. Yet the royal couple went on to the mayor's reception, insisting that the ceremonies be continued, as if some kind of baleful compulsion drew them to their fate. After the ceremonies, the Archduke and his wife went back to their car, with unaccountably inadequate protection. The assassin, Gavrilo Princip, fired point-blank at the royal couple and both died within a few minutes of being struck. The entire visit of the Archduke and his wife, from entry to death, had lasted about seventy minutes, the length of a short film. But the shots were destined to set off chain reactions which, more than half a century later, have not yet been expended.*

For the Austrian government and its military arm, the issue admitted of only one interpretation, that the assassination had been plotted by the Serbian government, abetted by Russia. It was therefore an unconscionable challenge to the integrity of the Austrian Empire. It

---

* Ten years after the beginning of World War I, the Minister of Education at the time of the assassination, Ljuba Jovanovich, wrote that the Prime Minister of Serbia had known of the plot to kill the Archduke and had taken no precautions to prevent it. The revelation created a sensation in 1924 and added to the ammunition of the revisionist historians. Hamilton Fish Armstrong, *Peace and Counterpeace* (New York: Harper & Row, 1971), p. 352.

could neither be dismissed as the action of irresponsible malcontents nor condoned as a blunder on the part of a stupid officialdom. Actually, it supplied Austria with a providential opportunity to press for a showdown that would, once and for all, eliminate the dangers of nationalist disruption. The Austrian Foreign Minister, Count Leopold Berchtold, in drawing up an ultimatum, said frankly to the cabinet that a purely diplomatic victory, even if it ended with the humiliation of Serbia, would be worthless. He therefore insisted that the demands presented to Serbia must be so far-reaching that their rejection would be a foregone conclusion. Though the Serbian government did yield on virtually all of the demands, Austria refused to accept its assurances of punitive action unless Austria itself were authorized to track down the conspirators, even on Serbian soil. When the Serbians would not permit the violation of their sovereignty, Austria declared war.

Within the next few days, each of the other great powers had been drawn into the maelstrom; Russia to keep faith with her little Slav brother, Serbia; Germany to honor the blank check that was given to Austria at the outset of the crisis. When France mobilized, the Kaiser interpreted it as "irresponsible provocation," and declared war on France. In order to knock out France quickly, Germany attacked through neutral Belgium, and this helped to bring Britain into the war. Incidentally, but not too incidentally, England's declaration astonished the German Foreign Minister Bethmann-Hollweg. He had justified the invasion of neutralized Belgium on the grounds of "necessity." He promised that amends would be made for "the technical wrong," once the military aims of Germany had been fulfilled. Bitterly he told the British Ambassador that he could not understand the British action "just for a scrap of paper." It was a phrase that was to haunt the Germans thereafter and to have ideal propaganda value for Britain.

Thus, all the alliances had been honored. The cantilever that Churchill had so eloquently described had crashed, and all of its parts were irretrievably broken. A few pistol shots in a little-known land transformed the fate of a whole generation, even as quarrels in another era—in the jungles of Vietnam, in the hills of Kashmir, on the twilight frontiers of China—would affect the lives of myriads of families who were in no way related to the initial stages of conflict.

The scholars, with the wisdom of hindsight, and with access to once restricted documents, have ever since been analyzing the causes and the responsibility for the tragedy, meticulously exploring the might-have-beens and the ought-to-haves. Since there was clearly some right in the case of each nation and, as clearly, many errors and misjudgments, the verdicts are still as far apart as ever. If there is any consensus, it is that the real culprit was the international anarchy whereby the world was divided into belligerent alliances, with no power, above the alliances, to initiate collective action for the preservation of peace. This is why Woodrow Wilson fought so strenuously to salvage the League of Nations. With all of its limitations, he insisted, it would identify aggression and compel a cooling-off period. But in 1914 a decisive role was open to individual judgment, or lack of judgment, and there was no international deterrent to restrain impulsive action and to keep negotiations going.

Who were the men in whose hands fate placed such awesome power? There was the histrionic Kaiser Wilhelm, always striking belligerent poses, craving attention, as he had done from childhood when he went into tantrums of exhibitionism. He was a dangerously impulsive man, who once slapped the Czar of Bulgaria on the backside in the presence of the entire court. He came to every problem with a completely open mouth. Resplendent in uniform, he spoke of *Ich und Gott*, and God was usually the junior partner. There was the Russian Czar, a puppet of his mentally unbalanced Empress, constantly reneging on promises and convictions. In the heart of the war crisis, this was the entry in the Czar's diary: "During the morning we played tennis—the weather was magnificent," and then petulantly, "I was constantly being called to the telephone." There was King George V of Britain, amiable, well-meaning, but a total nonentity. It was Queen Mary who was dominant, even as the Czarina dominated in the Romanoff family. The phrase went that the King was George the Fifth, but Mary was the other four-fifths. Foreign policy was the responsibility of Sir Edward Grey, a placid, phlegmatic aristocrat, whose one passion seemed to be trout fishing and who twisted and turned in his inability to come to clear decisions. All through the frantic diplomacy that preceded the declaration of war, the German General Staff could not be sure whether Britain would or would not stand by France. And there was a host of lesser characters, supernumeraries, Von Moltke, Bethmann-Hollweg, Conrad von Hötzendorf, Sazonov, Viviani—little people coping with gigantic issues, their perverse decisions affecting the fate of the world.

The actions of these men not only committed their nations to war, but influenced the wantonness with which lives and values were squandered. Two examples will suffice. There was the incredible dictum of a German general, during the violation of Belgian neutrality, in justifying the destruction of priceless national shrines. In the march through Belgium, Louvain was reduced to ruins and the beautiful cathedral of Rheims shattered. This was the moment chosen by the general to rationalize the action: "We owe no explanation to anyone. Germany stands the supreme arbiter of her own methods. It is no consequence whatsoever if all the monuments ever created, all the pictures ever painted, all the buildings ever erected by the great architects of the world, be destroyed, if by their destruction we promote Germany's victory. War is war, and our troops must achieve victory—what else matters?"*

The Germans had no monopoly on callousness. In 1916 came the incredible bloodletting at Passchendaele and the Somme. The Allied armies were under the command of General Douglas Haig, another of the Colonel Blimps who fought the war by the outmoded manuals of previous campaigns. He developed his strategy according to his lights but, as Liddell Hart, the military commentator, noted, his lights were dim. He was described as a "beautifully groomed mediocrity, brilliant to the top of his boots." He sacrificed four hundred thousand men for a gain of four miles of mud and stink and barbed wire.

> Wire, barbed wire!—A dour
> And monstrous serpent round our lives,
> And we're like creatures mesmerized . . .†

Passchendaele and the Somme were responsible for the death or mutilation of between two and three million men. In his postwar Memoirs, Lloyd George wrote: "The tale of these battles constitutes a trilogy illustrating the unquenchable heroism that will never accept defeat and the inexhaustible vanity that will never admit a mistake. It is the story of the million who would rather die than own themselves cowards—even to themselves—and also of the two or three individuals who would rather the million perish than that they as leaders should own—even to themselves—that they were blunderers.‡

Of course, the men who made such tragic decisions had no realization that the consequences would be so costly. Lloyd George said that

* Major General von Disfurth. Cited in Quincy Howe, *A World History of Our Own Times* (New York: Simon & Schuster, 1949), Vol. 1, p. 445.

† R. H. Sauter in Brian Gardner, ed., *Up the Line to Death* (New York: C. N. Potter, 1967), pp. 63–4.

‡ Lloyd George, *War Memoirs* (Boston: Little, Brown, 1933–7), Vol. 4, p. 320.

"they staggered and blundered into war." They hoped always that they could resolve each issue in its own private corner, and keep it from spreading. In the heart of the Sarajevo crisis, when all the nations of Europe began to get involved, there was the plaintive cry of the Austrian diplomat: "Why couldn't we have been left to fight out our own little war in peace?"

The British had so little fear that the imbroglio in the faraway Balkans would possibly affect them that on the day the war was declared the attention of the public remained focused on the heavy-weight championship fight between Georges Carpentier and Gunboat Smith. In the first months of the war the mood in every capital was more euphoric than somber. The inability to understand that death was abroad was the clue to the parades when war was declared, the lightheartedness of the families who saw their sons leave for the front as if they were off to vacation or adventure.

There were cheers in the plaza of the Winter Palace at St. Petersburg, and in Unter den Linden in Berlin, and in the Champs Élysées in Paris, and in Trafalgar Square in London. Kelen, the gifted Hungarian cartoonist, wrote:

The night war was declared on Serbia, the streets were decked with flowers and flags . . . and we rushed about, shouting at the top of our lungs. . . . We just followed the brass band, picked up the hurrahs where we found them . . . shouted and shrieked, and did what youngsters do, demonstrated without knowing, because it was fun to be noisy in crowds. Only at night, in bed, I curled myself up in fright, and wondered what would happen next.*

It was because the war was so little understood that none imagined it could last long—perhaps till Christmas, perhaps a few months longer. Among the "men of action," Lord Kitchener, the War Minister, was regarded as out of his mind when he, alone of them all, warned of a long ordeal that might go on for two years, or even more.

Within a few months the full horror dawned upon all the nations of where their actions, so blithely launched, had led. Austria had gone in to clean out "the nest of Serbian robbers and assassins," and the Empire fell apart. The Russian army expected to be in Berlin quickly; it was shattered at Tannenberg, and the Russian Empire crashed. The German timetable called for the capture of Paris in forty days; at the Battle of the Marne the vaunted armies bogged

* Emery Kelen, *Peace in Their Time* (New York: Alfred A. Knopf, 1963), p. 8.

down in the nightmare of trench warfare, and the Empire ultimately was abolished. France expected to recover the coal and ore of Lorraine that had been wrested from her in 1870, and by the end of the war had suffered more casualties than the total male population of Lorraine. Britain hoped to eliminate the German navy quickly as a prime power so that it could regain the mastery of the seas. But it was soon fighting for survival in a deadly land war that destroyed the flower of its youth. In wrestling, the term "dog-fall" is used to indicate the point in the match when both participants are so completely drained and exhausted that they fall down and cannot go on. After the opening battles of World War I, where each participant imagined that the issues would be quickly and not too expensively settled, the dog-fall point was reached, and the stalemate set in.

For more than four years men died at the rate of six or seven thousand every day. The toll reached ten million dead, twenty million wounded, the youngest, the most vital, the promise of the future. In the wars of the sixteenth century, one in twenty had been casualties; in the wars of the eighteenth century, one in seven; in World War I, one in three. A large part of the capital wealth that had been painfully accumulated over the centuries disappeared in smoke and ruin and debris. International trade was a shambles, currencies were hopelessly inflated and lost most of their purchasing power. Above all, civilized Europe had revealed itself to the subjugated races of Asia and Africa in all of its weakness and its moral nakedness. Rudyard Kipling composed the epitaph, as if he were in the graveyard:

> If any question why we died
> Tell them, because our fathers lied.*

* Cited in Gardner, ed., *Up the Line to Death,* p. 150.

3

WOODROW WILSON
AND THE LEAGUE

IN MARCH 1920 THE U.S. SENATE REFUSED TO RATIFY AMERICAN PAR-
ticipation in the League of Nations. History rode on the decisive vote
which destroyed the dream of Woodrow Wilson to create an international mechanism that would substitute "a community of power" for
"a balance of power." In the bitterness of his frustration, Wilson
prophesied that within a generation the world would be again
plunged into bloody conflict and his melancholy forecast was all too
soon fulfilled.

Through the half century that followed Wilson's commitment to
the League, his reputation oscillated between the extremes of adulation and disparagement. During World War I, as the head and front
of the coalition to smash the German menace and to establish an
enduring peace, Wilson had been idolized as were few men in all
history. The despairing peoples of the enemy nations placed as much
hope on his aspirations as did the peoples of the western alliance. As
he toured the Allied capitals after the armistice, there were fervent,
almost hysterical, demonstrations, and the huge crowds often kneeled
when he passed. His pictures were displayed along with those of
Jesus and the saints, streets were renamed for him, statues erected. Sir
Harold Nicolson of the British delegation wrote that when he first
saw Wilson at Versailles, he felt that he was meeting the prophet,
and then he added: "We were journeying to Paris, not merely to
liquidate the war, but to found a new order in Europe. We were

preparing not only Peace, but Eternal Peace. There was about us the halo of some divine mission."*

After the angry bargaining and the unpopular compromises of the Peace Conference, when the halo was askew and often tarnished, Wilson came under the most violent abuse. The idealists were disappointed by the concessions that he granted; the hard-liners were outraged by the windy rhetoric that he applied to borders and finance. The judgment was expressed that he was a fuzzy intellectual, a rigid doctrinaire, naïve in worldly diplomacy and therefore at the mercy of the more experienced negotiators. John Maynard Keynes, attending the Peace Conference as a British financial expert, was very rough on him, identifying him as a "blind and deaf Don Quixote." He added:

What chance could such a man have against Mr. Lloyd George's unerring almost medium-like sensibility to everyone immediately around him? To see the British Prime Minister watching the company with six or seven senses not available to ordinary men, judging character, motive, and subconscious impulse . . . and compounding with telepathic instinct the argument or appeal best suited to the vanity, weakness, or self-interest of his immediate auditor, was to realize that the poor President would be playing "blind man's bluff" in that party.†

The novelist Ben Hecht described Wilson at Versailles as "a long-faced virgin trapped in a bawdy house and calling in valiant tones for a glass of lemonade."‡

The passing of the years has modified the panegyrics and softened the asperities. Wilson emerges neither as demigod nor ninny bamboozled by the slick diplomats of Europe. He emerges as a brilliant, scholarly liberal who made compromises at the Peace Conference to win international assent for a League of Nations, but who was inflexible at home when the attempt was made to weaken the League or to lessen the responsibility of the United States for its enforcement power. He was defeated by the political and economic complexities of a Europe so disrupted that it defied the statesmanship of even the ablest diplomats. He was defeated also by his own frailties, and a

* Harold Nicolson, *Peacemaking* (New York: Harcourt, Brace & Co., 1939), pp. 31–2.

† John Maynard Keynes, *Economic Consequences of the Peace* (New York: Harcourt, Brace & Co., 1920), p. 41.

‡ Ben Hecht, *Erik Dorn* (New York and London: G. P. Putnam's Sons, 1921), p. 300.

desperate illness that sapped his strength when the battle for the League reached the turning point.

Wilson was the son of an austere, imperious Presbyterian minister, born, as he wrote, "between the Bible and the Dictionary." Some psychiatrists have interpreted his dogmatic defense of his own ideas to the point of obsessive stubbornness as a reflection of his continuous competition with his father, living and dead. At college he immersed himself in the writings of his British mentors, Burke and Bagehot, and above all, Gladstone, with whose morals in politics he identified completely. He could not understand the party stalwarts who bantered about ideals or ridiculed absolutes. The British cynic Henry Labouchère used to say of Wilson's hero, Gladstone, "I don't object to Gladstone always having the ace of trumps up his sleeve, but merely to his belief that God Almighty put it there."* To Wilson this was not only insulting and irreverent but betrayed a lack of commitment to moral truth. "Politics," he insisted, "is a war of causes, a joust of principles."

Young Wilson was determined to make the study of politics his career. But first there was a teaching stint at Bryn Mawr, where he met and married Ellen Louise Axson, also the daughter of a Presbyterian minister. It was the happiest of marriages. Ellen knew intuitively how to manage her sensitive, easily wounded, highly principled husband, who needed someone entirely trustworthy to share his religiously oriented views and to adore him. He lost her through her early death, and his later triumphs were shared by a second wife.† But the influence of Ellen never disappeared.

In 1890 Wilson joined the politics department of Princeton for a long and influential part of his career, teaching until 1902, when he was appointed president of the university. It was then mainly a gentlemen's college, and the admissions emphasis was on family background and social prestige. Wilson immediately set himself to transform its image. He fought hard to eliminate the club system that was equivalent to the fraternity and sorority tradition on other American campuses. He proposed an alternative Quadrangle Plan, with its "comradeship of studies," inviting young, unmarried faculty to live with the students and to democratize campus life. He won faculty support, but Princeton's conservative alumni were not ready

* H. Pearson, *Labby* (New York and London: Harper & Brothers, 1937), p. 194.

† A year after Ellen's death, in 1914, Wilson married Edith Bolling Galt, the charming and vivacious widow of a Washington jeweler.

for such reforms. One of them complained that "Princeton is getting to be nothing but a damned educational institution." Eventually the alumni resistance compelled Wilson's resignation.

Meantime he had much impressed the Democratic leaders of the state, whose political machine had fallen into disfavor. In 1910 they were seeking a gubernatorial candidate whose integrity and conservatism would create attractive window dressing. Wilson had written and spoken eloquently of freedom from influence in politics, ideal courtship sentiments for a candidate. The Jersey City boss, "Little Bob" Davis, was asked whether, with such views, Wilson could possibly make a good governor. He replied, as bosses do, "How the hell do I know whether he'll make a good governor? He'll make a good candidate, and that's the only thing that interests me."* Wilson was nominated and elected governor of New Jersey, and then, to the consternation of his sponsors, he repudiated them and their views. He served as an efficient and progressive governor, curbing many dubious business practices and, to their horror, sponsoring the establishment of a direct popular primary. Before his term was over he was a national figure, the darling of the liberals.

In 1912 his name was proposed as a candidate for the presidency of the United States. The Democratic nominating convention struggled through forty-five ballots in a deadlock between Wilson and Champ Clark of Missouri, who had a long record of service as the Speaker of the House of Representatives. Wilson's manager clinched the nomination on the forty-sixth ballot when the Illinois and Indiana party managers, without Wilson's knowledge, were offered future favors in return for the votes of their swing delegations. Wilson placidly accepted the victory and assigned the credit for it to the fulfillment of God's will. He told his exhausted campaign manager, "You know, McCombs, I am a Presbyterian and I believe in predestination. It was Providence that did the work at Baltimore." McCombs said glumly that a chill ran through him. "Sure it was Providence, on the forty-sixth ballot." Since the Republican Party had been hopelessly split by the vendetta between Theodore Roosevelt and William Howard Taft, Wilson easily won the presidency.

His early presidential years were a *tour de force*. He labeled his reform program "The New Freedom," and under its banner he encouraged legislation that was intended to check the monolithic

* Ray Stannard Baker, *Woodrow Wilson* (Garden City, N.Y.: Doubleday, Page & Co., 1927–39), Vol. 3, p. 73.

hold of big business on the American economy. He was considerably influenced by a brilliant Boston lawyer, Louis Brandeis, whom he later elevated to the Supreme Court and whose philosophy was distilled in his work entitled *The Curse of Bigness*. Wilson's domestic record included the creation of a Federal Trade Commission, a Federal Reserve Board, the Clayton Anti-Trust Law, and the first important reduction in the tariff since the Civil War.

During his first term, the European war had widened to global proportions and Wilson, the domestic reformer, was soon called upon to set the limits of American foreign involvements. His policies moved through three stages. At the outset, the fighting abroad was regarded simply as the traditional struggle for national advantage by irresponsible political factions. Wilson spoke with smugness and self-righteousness about America's superior virtue. He cautioned his people, as a composite nation with many relationships to Europe, to resist the temptation of partisan involvement. But by 1916, as Britain and its Allies were clearly in danger of defeat, Wilson was enough of a realist to understand the consequences to the United States if imperial Germany achieved naval dominance. With Britain in control of the seas, it had not been necessary to build American military strength. If British protection were lost, the United States would have to create its own defense, perhaps with military conscription and exorbitant budgets for armaments. Officially, Wilson kept to his neutral resolves, and continued to lecture the belligerents. He had to be careful not to raise fears in the country that there was any likelihood of American involvement. He based his campaign for re-election in 1916 not only on his progressive achievements but on the claim that he had kept the country out of war. He was narrowly re-elected and undoubtedly this slogan was a factor in his victory.

Once elected, his neutrality was tipped in favor of the Allies. The year 1917 was disastrous for them. Russia had suffered catastrophic defeats, and its military forces were immobilized. Italy was almost knocked out of the war, after the stunning rout at Caporetto. The Allied attempt to penetrate the defenses of the central powers through the Dardanelles and the soft underbelly of the Balkans had been a costly failure. The German U-boats were sinking millions of tons of British shipping monthly. Yet it might still have been impossible to unite the American people in a rescue effort for the Allies; the population of Irish origin had no love for the British, nor did the Germans. The majority of Americans were resolutely opposed to military involvement and were not persuaded that there was any overriding American interest in the fate of either side. But Germany, with characteristic ineptness, virtually propelled the United States into the war and provided the unifying momentum for its vigorous prosecution.

Both the Allies and the Germans had been molesting American shipping, but Germany was much more aggressive in the violation of established neutral rights. Its attacks went beyond stopping neutral ships, searching them, and confiscating contraband. Its U-boats sank without warning whatever ships came into the war lanes. Then came the Zimmermann note, a diplomatic blunder that ranked with Bethmann-Hollweg's "just for a scrap of paper" indiscretion after the violation of Belgian neutrality. The note was sent by the German Foreign Minister to the Mexican President, encouraging an attack on the United States, with the promise of German aid and the return of Mexican land taken by the Americans in the past. The note was intercepted by the British, decoded, and forwarded to Wilson. It brought to a head the mounting resentment against German espionage in the United States, the huge sums spent on propaganda, the sabotage of ships carrying cargoes to the Allies. At a special session of Congress on April 6, 1917, Wilson called for a declaration of war against Germany. The peroration included idealistic overcommitments to the cause of global democracy that were later to haunt the President. "It is a fearful thing," he declared,

to lead this great peaceful people into war, into the most terrible and disastrous of all wars, civilization itself seeming to be in the balance. But the right is more precious than peace, and we shall fight for the things which we have always carried nearest our hearts, for democracy, for the right of those who submit to authority to have a voice in their own government, for the rights and liberties of small nations, for a universal dominion of right by such a concert of free peoples as shall bring peace and safety to all nations and make the world itself at last free.

All forecasts about a scholar serving as a war President were belied. The pacifist, the purveyor of words, turned out to be a superb coordinator, and he brought in teams of extremely able men to organize every area of the war effort. He concentrated on the morale of the enemy, seizing every opportunity to drive a wedge between the people and their leaders. His addresses, as much intended for the nations at war as for his own countrymen, were models of persuasion, and they reached their mark. In January 1918, he formulated the Fourteen Points as the war aims of America. Some appeared impossible of achievement: freedom of the seas, open diplomacy, abolition of trade barriers, the impartial adjustment of all colonial claims. But they held out to the enemy the hope of compassion. The British and the French war leaders shrugged off the Wilson rhetoric as fortunately harmless, but undoubtedly the morale of the enemy peoples was shaken.

The turn of the tide in favor of the Allies was largely the result of American participation. The huge supplies that poured in, the unending streams of manpower, deepened the defeatism of Germany and its allies. By the summer of 1918, the German High Command knew that the war was lost and they sued for peace. Later, the legend was spread by the Nazis that Germany had been stabbed in the back by the Socialists when the military was still strong and effective. This was nonsense, for it was the military leaders who sought escape and took the initiative to press for the armistice. The fighting ended on November 11, the central powers in complete collapse.

Now an exhausted and bankrupt world was to be put together again, and the task became one of the most imaginative opportunities ever offered to a statesman. Wilson eagerly accepted the mission, and he spoke with fervor of his determination to use unconventional approaches in order to rise above all party considerations and achieve lasting peace. "We're going to vote the proxies of millions of dead men," he proclaimed, "dead men who died in order that what we do now will make it impossible for the same awful sacrifice to be demanded of our children, and their children."

He should have remembered that any peace he recommended would need the approval of both Houses of Congress, and that Republicans as well as Democrats would have to be won over for American participation in the League of Nations. It was a disaster for Wilson and for the peace of the world that these elementary political precautions were disregarded. His debacle began when he insisted on personally leading the delegation to the Peace Conference. His chief adviser, Colonel House, tried in vain to dissuade him, reasoning that if Wilson remained in Washington he could act as a court of appeal after the issues were threshed out by his representatives. He would thus avoid the attrition in dignity and authority that was inevitable in the day-to-day haggling.* Then, incredibly, Wilson named no Republican of stature to share in the peace negotiations, bypassing men of the caliber of ex-President Taft and former Secre-

* John Garraty, *Woodrow Wilson* (New York: Alfred A. Knopf), p. 135.

tary of State Elihu Root, and his opponent for the presidency, Justice Charles Evans Hughes. The five-man delegation that he did name had little distinction, and only General Tasker Bliss identified himself as a Republican. Wilson's critics said that he had named himself four times, along with a nonentity.* The danger signals were now loud and clear. In the national elections of November 1918, Wilson had appealed for a Democratic Congress as a vote of confidence in his policies. When the Democrats lost both Houses, Wilson realized that the tough bargaining that he was to endure at Versailles was no more of a problem than the mounting misgivings of his own people.

Before the Peace Conference opened, Wilson toured the major capitals of Europe, and few men in history ever had such tumultuous receptions. The parade down the Champs Élysées was witnessed by two million people, screaming the name of the Messiah, weeping in the ecstasy of the moment. The French Premier who rode with him said: "I do not think there has been anything like it in the history of the world!" The British reception in London was more restrained but as deeply moving, again with more than two million jammed into the streets from Hyde Park to Buckingham Palace. In Rome the crowds surpassed any in the history of the ancient capital. Men, women, children, and wounded veterans reached out to kiss his hand or touch his clothes. Herbert Hoover, who later succeeded to the presidency, wrote of the mass delirium that he witnessed: "To them no such man of moral and political power and no such evangel of peace had appeared since Christ preached the Sermon on the Mount!"†

All this near idolatry was interpreted by Wilson to mean that his opponents in the United States and the European political leaders did not realize how fervent was the desire for peace among all peoples. It buttressed his resolve to fight for a League of Nations that would guarantee the sanction of collective action to preserve the peace.

Ironically, while Wilson was being hailed with hosannas in mass demonstrations, the war leaders of Britain and France were stump-

---

* The judgment on General Bliss was outrageously biased. He was a brilliant student of history and his views were well worth considering. The editor of *Foreign Affairs* described him as "one of the elders who wears juniors down." Armstrong, *Peace and Counterpeace*, p. 449.

† Herbert Hoover, *The Ordeal of Woodrow Wilson* (New York: McGraw-Hill, 1958), p. 69.

ing their homelands with election pledges to make the Germans pay for the war and its sufferings. Lloyd George asked for a vote of confidence to fulfill the mandate "to squeeze the vanquished until you can hear the pips squeak."* Clemenceau pledged that he would obtain full security for his country so that there would never be another assault by the Germans.

Wilson's reply to the vengeance pledges of Lloyd George and Clemenceau was given in a little Scottish church, where he came to pay tribute to his grandfather, who had preached there, and to his mother, who had received Communion there before her emigration to America. He stressed a settlement without rancor to poison the future, a peace without victory. "We must now be drawn together," he said, "in a combination of moral force that will be irresistible."

The tours, the parades, the proclamations, were all preliminaries. The Big Four, representing the United States, Great Britain, France, and Italy, now turned to the task of reorganizing the shattered world. Wilson was in the very fast company that he had been warned against. The men he faced, and the scores of delegations from the remotest parts of the world who demanded hearings and consideration, had economic and security problems to meet that could not be brushed aside with sonorous phrases and slogans. Lloyd George, with his disarming Welsh charm, was at the peak of his effectiveness, brilliant in negotiation, sharp-witted, capable of instant decision. He kept insisting on sanctions other than the nebulous guarantees of a League to protect the provisions of the treaties that would have to be imposed upon the conquered.

Clemenceau, close to eighty, had waited for the day when he could square accounts with the Germans who had twice, in his own lifetime, invaded his Fatherland. Harold Nicolson wrote, "He had one illusion, France, and one disillusion, mankind." Clemenceau distrusted lofty rhetoric as a substitute for military guarantees and reparations. He believed that "eternal peace" lasts until next year—if until then. And Wilson's dreams of a world united by the rule of law left him completely bewildered. "Mr. Wilson," he said, "has lived in a world that has been fairly safe for democracy. I have lived in a world where it has been good form to shoot a democrat." Once he burst out: "Who is this man who comes to us with fourteen points?

---

* The phrase was used by Sir Eric Geddes, a cabinet colleague of Lloyd George.

Why, God Almighty never had more than ten!" Lloyd George noted that Clemenceau was "like an old watchdog keeping an eye on a strange and unwelcome dog who has visited the farmyard and of whose intentions he is more than doubtful."

The work of drafting the treaties dragged on for many weary months. Wilson's pious hope for "open covenants openly arrived at" was quickly snuffed. It was clearly necessary, in the bedlam of claims and counterclaims, for the leaders to achieve a meeting of minds behind closed doors, without exposing their own angry disagreements. What emerged bore the unmistakable stamp of deal and barter. The major decisions that validated new national sovereignties stood up well. They recreated Poland and emancipated the Baltic states; they brought into being Czechoslovakia; they united the Slavs and the Croats to form a powerful Yugoslavia, fulfilling the irredentism that had triggered the war itself. But there were other issues whose disposition left putrefying wounds: reparations from the defeated powers; the judgment on the war guilt; the punitive occupation of Germany; the obligation to honor secret treaties; the dubious claims of Italy and Japan; above all, the powers to be assigned to the League of Nations. Here there were long splenetic, fatiguing arguments, and several times they almost broke up the Conference. At one point Lloyd George was ready to assault Clemenceau. Wilson stepped in and prevented physical encounter. Lloyd George insisted on an apology and Clemenceau hotly replied, "You shall wait for it as long as you wait for the pacification of Ireland." Orlando of Italy left the Conference in a dudgeon when the Allies refused to fulfill the secret promises that were made to bring Italy into the war. Wilson was not sure how his own commitments would be honored when he returned to the United States. His party had been roundly defeated in the congressional elections and his political leverage crippled. In a diary notation, Nicolson analyzed Wilson's frustrating dilemma: "The ghastly suspicion that the American people would not honor the signature of their delegates was never mentioned between us; it became the ghost at all our feasts."*

Wilson's aides pleaded with him to conserve his strength for the battles ahead, and not to strain his constitution. Wilson replied, in one of the few flashes of humor that came from him, "Constitution —why, I'm already living on my by-laws!" After months of day and night sessions, exhausted by the claims and counterclaims, several

* Nicolson, *Peacemaking*, p. 108.

times quite ill, conscience-stricken by the concessions that were wrested from him, gravely worried about adverse political developments at home, he placed all his hopes in the League. Once that was established, he consoled himself, surely whatever wrongs were incorporated in the treaties could be righted, since at last there would be an international umpire to adjudicate the disputes that wracked the world. This was apparently the judgment of the Nobel Peace Prize jury that named Wilson for the 1919 award.

Wilson now returned to the United States for the battle of his life, to win the support of the Senate for a treaty that was bound up inextricably with the League of Nations. Judging by the polls, the treaty was acceptable to the American public. Congress too, at this stage, while not enthusiastic, was not hostile. There were private assurances from approximately three-fourths of the senators that they favored the treaty if some protective reservations were included.

But those who resisted any involvement with Europe, though small in number, were extraordinarily resourceful and articulate. They were led by Senator Henry Cabot Lodge, a Massachusetts Republican, who compounded his opposition with a blazing personal hatred of the President. He was a brilliant strategist. He did not oppose the treaty, nor did he oppose the League. He fastened on Article 10, which committed the signatory nations to stand together to resist aggression. Lodge interpreted this to mean that, unless there were explicit reservations that would give the United States the option to abstain from participation, America would be dragged into every European quarrel. "I shall never trade away American sovereignty," he vowed, "for the United States of the World which is the quixotic dream of the President." All of his arguments were shrewdly marshaled to appeal to sections of the country where there was a developing uneasiness that participation in the war had been a mistake. Wilson would accept no reservations. Apart from the ghastly prospect of a return to the conference table for renegotiation, he had no faith in the sincerity of his opponents. They were putting forward the reservations, he was sure, to drain out the vitality of collective security. "The potency of the League is basic," he declared. "If it were emasculated by reservations it would become just another pious hope."

The issues were drawn, and Wilson now planned to stump the country to save the League by a direct appeal to the American people. The campaign tour, by train, began on September 3, 1919, against the explicit advice of Wilson's physician, Dr. Grayson, who knew the

President was down to his last reserves in strength. Wilson was adamant, even though he had not fully recovered from the illness that felled him when he was in Paris. "I do not want to do anything foolhardy," he said to his doctor, "but the League is now at its crisis and if it fails I hate to think of what will happen to the world." Again, "Our boys in the trenches did not turn back, and I cannot turn back now." Thus began two and a half grueling months of campaigning, often as many as ten speeches a day, from railroad back platforms, in crowded auditoriums, in every kind of heat, shaking hands with tens of thousands, with little quiet, little rest, and the additional frustration of rebuttals from the irreconcilables who trailed his travels from city to city. His voice became a croak. Still he went on. "I am ready to fight," he declared, "from now until all the fight has been taken out of me by death, to redeem the faith and promises of the U.S." Even when his strength gave out completely, he would not quit. The train reached Pueblo, Colorado, where the President collapsed. The left side of his face paralyzed, his words no longer distinct, he mumbled, "Don't give up this trip. . . . Senator Lodge will call me a quitter." Mrs. Wilson now gave the word to cancel the remainder of the itinerary. She sat with her weeping husband, determined that she would wear a mask, not only to the public but, as she said, "to the one I love best in the world, for he must not know how ill he is, and I must carry on." Wilson was rushed back to the White House, where he suffered a stroke and, from this point on, became a broken invalid.

For the next two months the government was in the hands of a regency composed of his physician, a few trusted aides, and his wife, who made the final decisions. In effect, Mrs. Wilson was the first woman President of the United States. The seriousness of his illness was not revealed to the Wilsons, nor to the country. Perhaps the President's pathological resistance to any talk of compromise was part of his illness. The appeals to accept reservations that would not sacrifice essentials came to him from the staunchest advocates of the League. There would then be no problem in winning confirmation for the Treaty and the League, and the United States would add its indispensable strength and prestige to the guarantees against aggression. Even Mrs. Wilson begged him to yield. He replied grimly, "Better a thousand times to go down fighting than to dip your colors to dishonorable compromise." By now his illness had entirely transformed his personality, austere and stubborn to begin with. One of the most momentous decisions in modern history was to be determined by a fatally incapacitated man, whose ailment affected judgment, whose bitterness eclipsed all other considerations.

During Wilson's convalescence some of the Republican opposition insisted on visiting him to determine whether he was competent to continue as President. Senator Albert Fall of New Mexico, who was later sentenced to a prison term for fraud, was one of the committee. Wilson put on a brave show, summoning all his strength to receive them. As Fall left, he said, "Mr. President, we are all praying for you." "Oh? Which way?" Wilson asked.

The treaty and its provisions for the League came before the Senate. The Democrats, following Wilson's orders, repudiated the reservations; the Republicans opposed the treaty without them. The group of irreconcilables played politics shrewdly, maneuvering the Democrats to defeat the reservations, and then helping the Republicans to defeat the treaty.

And so the League was dead—"as dead as Marley's ghost!" Lodge exulted. Worse defeats were in store for the tired, repudiated invalid. In the national election of 1920, the Republicans put forward as their candidate for President a handsome, poker-playing nonentity, Warren Harding, senator from Ohio, who took fullest advantage of the postwar disillusionment. "America's need is not heroics but healing," his ghost writer declared, "not nostrums but normalcy." Harding was elected in the closest approach to a landslide in American history prior to 1964. The historian Samuel Eliot Morison noted that "World War I was the most popular war in our history while it lasted, and the most hated after it was over."* Wilson lived on for three more years, long enough to see all his dreams become ashes, as the country turned more and more to the isolationism of Harding and Coolidge.

His own generation could not, of course, judge his career. It was too close to the controversies of his mission and to the frailties of his personality. Those who shared his vision could not forgive the men who destroyed it. Those who opposed his convictions accused him of edging America into all the hatreds that had bankrupted Europe. His cause was not furthered by a temperament that could arouse the extremes of hatred and suspicion. James Kerney, the editor who had fought Wilson in New Jersey politics, wrote that he was not made for long honeymoons. Winston Churchill, who also endured the extremes

---

* Samuel Eliot Morison, *Oxford History of the American People* (New York: Oxford University Press, 1965), p. 886.

of popularity and adversity, said: "If Wilson had been either simply an idealist or a caucus politician, he might have succeeded. His attempt to run the two in double harness was the cause of his undoing."*

As the years passed the reactions to the chemistry of personality became less important. What counted was the tragic perceptiveness of Wilson's forecast that, without the League or some strong international instrument, girded with enforcement power, the peaceful resolution of international disputes would be impossible, and the world would be plunged into an ever more destructive struggle.

Yet the ideal of an international guarantee against aggression lived on. When the United Nations came into being in 1945 at San Francisco, under the leadership of the President of the United States, it seemed as if the spirit of Woodrow Wilson was present in the vast Assembly Hall. When the United Nations too bogged down because its veto provisions deprived it of effective enforcement power, the words of Woodrow Wilson, warning against the emasculation of an international peacekeeping instrument, served as undertone in the debates. Those who held to the faith that the world would ultimately, for its own salvation, have to rely upon collective security could find morale in the reaction of Wilson when his secretary brought him word that the League had been voted down by the Senate. He reached for the Bible and read from Second Corinthians: "We are troubled on every side, but we are not distressed and we are not defeated."†

* Winston Churchill, *The Aftermath* (New York: Charles Scribner's Sons, 1929), p. 125.
† Second Corinthians 4:8.

4

THE WEIMAR REPUBLIC

THE ARMISTICE THAT ENDED WORLD WAR I WAS GREETED WITH MIXED emotions by the defeated nations. There was enormous relief, of course, that the destruction of life and resources would cease at last, that the millions of men who had been conscripted would return to their homes and their families. But the joy was clouded with the gravest anxiety. It was inevitable that the victorious Allies should seek vengeance and reparations, and the social upheavals of the long struggle, exacerbated by defeat and unconditional surrender, threatened German civil war. Both fears were justified. The retribution that was imposed by the treaties, and the internecine struggles that wracked the country, dominated the postwar history of Germany.

Up to its final stages, the German nation had little warning that the war could possibly end in defeat; perhaps stalemate, perhaps compromise, but assuredly not defeat. Until the spring of 1917 the people had exulted in the reports that were fed to them of dramatic victories. The enemy was being battered on every front. The U-boats were sinking Allied shipping faster than it could be replaced. The Treaty of Brest-Litovsk, dictated to the Russians, had placed under German hegemony the Baltic states, Poland, and the huge Ukrainian breadbasket of Asia. Other immense resources in Europe and the rich booty of colonies were within reach. Except briefly on the eastern front, no Allied soldier had set foot on German soil save as a prisoner. To be sure, the stream of dead and wounded kept coming back in coffins and on stretchers. But these were the expected costs of war.

There was the certainty of victory to compensate for such necessary sacrifice.

The first misgivings began to creep in when the United States entered the war in April 1917. These were deepened when all the stunning victories of the summer and fall still did not result in a German breakthrough; when reserves began to run low even as the supplies that poured in from America seemed to be inexhaustible. After General Ludendorff's spring offensive of 1918 failed, anxiety turned to panic. All the defensive border areas began to crumble. Bulgaria, protecting the back door of Germany, collapsed. Turkey capitulated, and finally Austria. As the Allied armies were poised to invade Germany itself, the traditional discipline, which had not been tested by disaster, buckled. There were strikes and riots. Soldiers joined the demonstrations. Red flags were hoisted in the public squares. The scenes in the main German cities brought reminders of the disintegration that had preceded the Russian revolution.

Belated attempts were now made by the General Staff to bring in more acceptable leadership, since Wilson had declared that the Allies would deal only with a representative government. The generals broke the news to the Kaiser that he must abdicate. On November 10, 1918, the royal train of cream and gold sought sanctuary in Holland and the Hohenzollern throne was forfeit.

The German High Command did not participate in the surrender discussions. The Allies preferred to exclude them, refusing any dealings with the Prussian Junkers whom they blamed for the war and its ghastly toll. Hence the Socialists and the Catholic Centrists who formed the caretaker government negotiated the peace terms with the Allies. In later years, regret was expressed that the warlords had been permitted to play the role of *Nein Sagers*, and that the surrender had not taken place on German soil. Then it would have been emphatically brought home to the Germans that the military had lost the war.* It would also have refuted the ugly canard, spread by the High Command, and later by the Nazis, that it was the Socialists and the Jews who had betrayed the nation.

But in the ecstasy of the triumphant moment there was no thought among the Allies of how the other side might later present its case

---

* Even the Socialist Friedrich Ebert, the first President, believed that the military forces had not been defeated but had yielded when an honorable peace was promised. He greeted returning German troops at the Brandenburg Gate in Berlin with the tribute, "No foe has overcome you . . . you have protected the homeland from invasion."

to history. It was enough that the war had ended in victory, and that the old regime had been discredited and overthrown. The compelling task was now to cooperate with the successor government that was called upon to preserve the social order, and to protect it from the menace of Bolshevism.

Friedrich Ebert, a former saddlemaker, the son of a tailor, became the head of a provisional Social Democratic regime charged with the responsibility of taking the country through its heartbreaking interregnum. "I will serve," he told his colleagues. "I have already given two sons." He called for a general election and it was conducted in the most advanced democratic tradition. All adults of twenty or over, women as well as men, were eligible, and thirty million exercised their franchise. The parties that supported the Republic won a decisive mandate. The intransigent extremist parties, right and left, were at this stage just splinter groups, largely limited to street fighting. The capital was transferred to Weimar with its memories of Goethe and Schiller, far from the Junker citadel of Berlin.

And yet, the Weimar Republic was to last less than fifteen years. It was a paradigm of advanced democratic practice, but all its reforms were surface gimmicks. As the last imperial Chancellor, Max von Baden, sneered: "No one becomes a master of violin playing just because he is given a master violin." The social structure remained virtually unchanged. The industrialists who had supported and fueled the war, the Junkers of Prussia and their counterparts in the other provinces who controlled the landed estates, were very little affected. When pressure was mounted for major land redistribution, the specter of Bolshevism was projected to frighten the legislators. Karl Marx was always in the wings, and he was no forgotten pedant. His *Manifesto* echoed in every debate; its shadow fell across ledgers in banks, and trusts, and holding companies. The merchants, the farmers, the white-collar middle class, voted steadily against any radical reforms, fearful that basic changes would open the way to revolution.

Nor had the military High Command been substantially curbed. They had led the country into the disastrous war, they had resisted any talk of compromise, they had demonstrated their conception of security when they dictated the Treaty of Brest-Litovsk to the Russians. Yet their organization remained intact. No countervailing forces were substituted or added. In Russia, at the outset of their revolution, Lenin and Trotsky, refusing to be dependent upon the czarist military, had built a completely new army committed to the

Soviet Union and to its objectives. In the other revolutions of the contemporary world—in Africa, in Asia, in Latin America—the first thought of the new leaders was to be sure of the loyalty of the military. But the Weimar leadership made no move to disturb the military structure. The army remained Prussian to the core, and the defense of the Republic became the responsibility of men who hated its very existence. They never forgot Bismarck's contemptuous description of the Social Democrats as "vagabonds without a Fatherland." When Hugo Haase, one of the architects of the Weimar constitution, attempted to report on the subversive activities of some of the army leaders, he was shot by infuriated nationalists on the steps of the Reichstag as he came to present his evidence.

Above all, Weimar was born in defeat. The Social Democratic leaders had placed their signatures on the armistice agreement that sheared away sacred German territory. Dr. Matthias Erzberger, of the Catholic Centrist Party, asked what alternative he had but to yield when Germany was prostrate and the Allies were poised to begin military occupation. "Who among us would refuse to sign if a gun were pointed at his heart? . . . Duress knows no dishonesty." But his passionate protest was not remembered when the recriminations began, and he himself was assassinated by Free Corps extremists. Nor was the regime forgiven for accepting the reparations bills, amounting to billions, imposed by the Allies. They were steadily pared, the terms of payment modified, international loans provided to assist in financing. When all the accounts were totaled it was revealed that between 1920 and 1933 Germany had paid thirty-six billion marks in reparations. She had borrowed thirty-three billion and had repaid virtually nothing.* But Weimar could not shake off the alleged guilt of condemning the German people to "serfdom for generations to come." The term "reparations" was as much a rallying cry for the disillusioned as was the bloody shirt waved by the Republicans after the American Civil War.

Even before the first election, then, the Weimar government faced threats to its survival. A small minority of militant radicals were determined to follow the Russian pattern. Regarding Ebert as a German Kerensky they planned to convert Germany into a Soviet state. They were led by Karl Liebknecht, editor of *The Red Flag,* who took the name of Spartacus to link up with the tradition of rebellion of

---

* Cited in Richard M. Watts, *The Kings Depart* (New York: Simon & Schuster, 1969), p. 504.

a legendary Roman slave. His lieutenant was Rosa Luxemburg, a Polish émigré who had been in and out of revolution since childhood. The close collaboration with Russia became public when one of the diplomatic cases, addressed to the Russian Embassy and therefore not subject to inspection, broke open. It was filled with incendiary Communist propaganda for use in the election. During the campaign the Spartacists decided that the time was opportune to carry out their long-planned coup, and they called for a Communist uprising in the Lenin pattern. Ebert was in a dilemma. Since he had no people's army, he had to rely on the available military leadership, the Reichswehr, and he called upon it to meet the danger. The Reichswehr complied with enthusiasm and in the four days of intense fighting in mid-January of 1919, the Spartacists were completely routed. Liebknecht and Luxemburg were captured and summarily lynched.*

Meantime there were Red risings in other parts of the distraught country. In Bavaria, the long-reigning house of Wittelsbach was toppled by the Communists, who arranged for an alliance with Red Russia. The Soviet state was considered by Ebert as a dagger, "pointed at the heart of the new Germany." Here too, as with the Spartacists, the Reichswehr was sent into action, and the brief Soviet interregnum was ended. By May, the Red revolutions, wherever they still sputtered, were extinguished.

To the leftists Ebert and his government were traitors who had betrayed the Socialist cause by crushing proletarian objectives. But they were equally damned by the Nationalist right, who denounced them as the November Criminals who had "stabbed Germany in the back."† Ebert was quite concerned about the Free Corps, who were taking on all the lineaments of private armies, with an ever-growing record of terrorism and assassination that threatened the security of the state. He initiated action to contain their menace and undoubtedly it was because of the expectation that the Free Corps would be outlawed that a rightist rebellion was now undertaken. It had the prestige support of General Ludendorff himself. Under the leadership of a German-American civil servant, Dr. Wolfgang Kapp, a Free Corps brigade descended upon Berlin. It was a commentary on the

---

* Rosa Luxemburg never had much hope that her own generation of revolutionaries would triumph in Germany. She once remarked grimly, "We are dead men on furlough."

† In some histories, the phrase is attributed to Von Hindenburg. He did not originate it but seized upon it in 1919 when loosely used, and falsely attributed it to an English general.

parlous position of the Weimar government that the Reichswehr High Command refused to intervene, claiming that it could not fire on men who had so recently been brothers-in-arms against a common enemy. Kapp took over the chancellery and the government fled to take up residence in Dresden.

A general strike was now called by the Social Democrat members of the government. It was remarkably effective, closing down transportation, communication, the media of distribution, banks, virtually every enterprise. There was no water, no milk, no power, almost complete paralysis. The working force of Germany had responded with near unanimity, and within a few days the revolt was over. Kapp fled, in top hat and spats, to take refuge in Sweden.

Yet there was no punishment for the Free Corps brigade members who had participated in the putsch. Although they were defeated traitors, they were permitted to march out in formation, and, in turning a corner of the main boulevard, they fired into a crowd of civilian spectators, killing and wounding many of them. The leniency of the government astonished the rebels themselves. Some years later, Frau Ludendorff revealed her husband's contempt for the Social Democrats. She published a letter that he wrote when he returned from his self-exile in Sweden. "It would be the greatest stupidity for the revolutionaries to allow us all to remain alive. Why, if I ever come to power again, there will be no pardon. Then with an easy conscience, I would have Ebert, Scheidemann and company hanged, and watch them dangle."*

The problems posed by political malcontents were serious enough, but the lethal enemy was inflation, whose corrosive alchemy converted precious assets into worthless paper. There had been such confidence in a German victory during the war, with the expectation that reparations would be imposed on the losers, that little attempt had been made to provide for its enormous cost. No high taxes were ordered; few loans were floated. Now came the inevitable retribution. The war debt was astronomical and the reparations to the victors were piled on top of this obligation. Pensions had to be paid to the families of those who had died and to the wounded. The suppression of the revolts was a further serious financial drain. Since the Allied blockade had not been lifted with the armistice, commodities were scarce and prices sky-rocketed. The government could not meet its

---

* Cited in William L. Shirer, *The Rise and Fall of the Third Reich* (New York: Simon & Schuster, 1960), pp. 34 ff.

fiscal responsibilities and it resorted to the printing presses. There was a flight of gold, and soon the mark lost all value and meaning. In 1913 it had been four to the dollar, and there had been no sounder currency in Europe. Just before the war was over it was eight to the dollar. In 1921 it was forty-five, at the end of 1922 it went up to seven thousand. In 1923, as problems mounted, it went to a hundred thousand, then to a million, a billion, a trillion.*

It was a field day for the speculators, who anticipated the inflation and prepared for it. They acquired land and industries, and equity that had intrinsic stability, buying on long-term mortgage terms, expecting to repay their obligations with depreciated currency. The experience of Hugo Stinnes, a sorcerer who transmuted paper into gold, became legend. He had risen from pit boy in the mines to become a sea captain. He kept buying on loans, all through the war. By 1922 he had control of a sixth of the oil industry, he owned empires in the coal mines, steamship lines, newspapers, he headed major trusts, he employed more than a quarter of a million people. And then, as planned, he paid off his loans in worthless marks, and became one of the world's first billionaires, all on the misery of his people.

The inflation was the turning-point disaster in modern German history, for it systematically emasculated the usually stable middle class and liquidated its forty billions in savings. The thrifty Germans were ruined, not by Communist expropriation, but by a bourgeois government that was committed to free enterprise and the preservation of private property. The peasants were harmed very little, for their assets were in land that rose in value in relation to the currency. Labor had a measure of defense; it was well organized and its unions could fight back to adjust wages to living costs. But the middle class, the heart of the nation, lost savings, insurance, and its means of livelihood. This middle class, outraged and frustrated, became an easy prey for the Nationalists and Nazis, and the Communists, a natural reservoir for those who despised the new regime.

The government struggled valiantly with its problems and, since they were largely economic, it placed its hopes in the genius of

* The bizarre world that Germany had become was illustrated in the story of two brothers who shared a legacy. One was frugal and carefully managed his bequest. The other was a playboy and a drunkard, and he bought a wine cellar to drink himself into happiness. The inflation turned thrift into nonsense. The savings of the frugal brother evaporated. The drunkard, left with his champagne bottles, found that he was a millionaire.

Walther Rathenau, one of its most experienced statesmen. Rathenau came from an old Jewish family, inheriting the controlling interest in the General Electric Company of Germany. He early left the business world to enter government service. During the war, he undertook responsibility for organizing the national resources and was given credit for extending the German capacity to resist the economic stranglehold the Allies had imposed. He was a clear-minded realist, who believed that it was imperative to meet the world as it now existed, instead of ranting and protesting in idle gestures which solved nothing. He advanced "the policy of fulfillment," a program to cooperate with the Allies, to work out with them practical, sensible methods of adjusting reparations goals. He hoped that conciliation would bring together former enemies in the common tasks of reconstruction. In 1921, as Finance Minister, he concluded a treaty with France, and then next year, as Foreign Minister, he came to a high-level understanding with the Russians.

The Nationalist elements were apoplectic. Every attempt to fulfill an iniquitous treaty, they thundered, was an act of treason, every attempt to deal with the Russians a betrayal. But, they sneered, it was to be expected. Wasn't Rathenau a Jew, and therefore a secret Communist? He was marked for death. In June 1922, as he was getting into his car, a grenade was thrown at him that smashed his spine and all the patient work that he had built. When the Nazis came to power they honored the assassin as a national hero, and a memorial tablet was placed on the spot of the murder to extol his act of patriotism.*

The Rathenau murder was only one of a mounting succession of terrorist acts. The subversive groups multiplied and their toll of victims reached into the top echelons of government. As the wave of assassinations grew, an informant reported to Police President Pöhner in Bavaria, "Herr President, political murder organizations exist in the country." "I know," the Police President replied, "but there are too few of them."†

---

* Rathenau's aged mother wrote to the mother of the assassin: "In grief unspeakable, I give my hand to you, the most wretched of women. Tell your son that I forgive him, as may God forgive him, if he makes a full and frank confession before earthly justice and reports before heavenly justice. . . . If he had known my son, the noblest man that earth ever bore, he would have rather turned the murderers' guns against himself, than against him. . . ." Harry Kessler, *Walther Rathenau* (New York: Harcourt, Brace & Co., 1930), p. 381.

† R. G. L. Waite, *Vanguard of Nazism* (Cambridge, Mass.: Harvard University Press, 1952), p. 213.

The Free Corps and the Communists were involved in many of these assaults, and their continuous battles with each other added to the confusion and turbulence of the period. When they were not assailing each other, they tore away at the Weimar government. One of the uprisings in 1923 that was launched in a beer hall in Munich provided the debut, as a revolutionist, for Adolf Hitler. He was quickly captured, along with the ubiquitous Ludendorff, who flits in and out of the story of terror in this period. But, as usual, the participants were given light sentences and further opportunities to plan the destruction of the Weimar government.

Then, for a golden moment, came a respite. A new group of statesmen took the places of those who had seen their countries through the war. The relentless Raymond Poincaré was succeeded in France by Aristide Briand, an internationalist in outlook who was to win a Nobel Peace Prize for his efforts at reconciliation. In Britain a Labour government had come in, headed by Ramsay MacDonald who, as a pacifist, had opposed the war, and had been denounced and vilified throughout its course. In the United States, though the Republican old guard was in office, there was better understanding of the advantages of a sound economic internationalism. Such men began to have second thoughts about a sick Germany in the heart of Europe. With this infection at the center, how could Europe recover?

There was at last a favorable climate for German statesmanship in the conciliatory tradition of Rathenau. It was provided by Gustav Stresemann, who was to be either Chancellor or Foreign Minister from 1923 to 1929, an interregnum period in which Europe was given one more chance to find its way to disciplined peace. Stresemann came from a middle-class family, the son of a beer-hall proprietor. He earned a doctorate for a thesis on the bottled beer industry. He had early abandoned business for politics and was elected to the wartime Reichstag. He began as a rabid Pan-German, but mellowed considerably when he was confronted with the dissolution of order that followed the violence of the bully boys. He soon joined the moderates in the policy of fulfillment. Far from sacrificing Germany's future of greatness, he insisted, it would more speedily be assured if the obligations of the treaty were accepted, if confidence were restored, for then the oppressive features of the treaty would undoubtedly be modified by agreement.

When he became Chancellor in 1923, one of his first acts was to call off the passive resistance in the Ruhr so that France might be persuaded to end its occupation. He referred the vexing problems of inflation and currency reform to outstanding financial experts. They set up a new rentenmark, pegged at 4.2 to the dollar, and supported by the resources of the efficiently managed railroad system. This action stabilized the currency, which quickly became one of the soundest in all Europe. Later, when he became Foreign Minister, Stresemann worked out special arrangements with the United States so that the reparations payments could be fulfilled. But it was agreed to cover such payments through loans floated in the United States. The loans were not to be limited to reparations; they were advanced to subsidize roads and schools, and private and public buildings that were now rushed to completion. Indeed, the whole industrial plant of Germany was built up and made affluent by the victors, while the British and the French got little help to bring their own economy into a competitive position. This was quite an achievement for Stresemann. It gave rise to the jibe that any nation with severe economic problems ought to seek a war with the United States, lose it, and then relax while the victors rebuilt it and ushered in a boom.

Stresemann continued to clean out the pus pockets that infected Germany's relationships with other European countries. He worked stolidly and patiently, but with quiet resourcefulness. He and Briand of France sponsored the Locarno Conference of 1925, where the attempt was made to fashion a new Europe, built on confidence and mutual respect. There Stresemann pledged that Germany would accept the frontiers established with France, so that anti-aggression alliances and pacts need no longer be sought. The machinery for the arbitration of international difficulties was set up. The name "Locarno" entered the European diplomatic vocabulary and came to mean international understanding, the desire to accommodate, to settle disputes amicably. Perhaps the delegates at Locarno sensed the new spirit in a world grown weary of perpetual crises, as they watched Briand and Stresemann in a little open boat on the lake, the Frenchman rowing the burly little German.

In 1926, Germany was admitted to the League of Nations and made a member of the Permanent Council. When difficulties developed in the agreed reparations program, it was revised with enthusiastic American participation, and the American loans continued to flow. When Stresemann died, in 1929, almost literally of overwork, he could close his eyes in peace, for he had restored Germany as a respectable member of the family of nations, and his country's economic life had been extraordinarily strengthened. The reaction of the country was reflected in the elections of 1928, when the Social

Democrats considerably increased their membership in the Reichstag, and the Nazis and the Communists fared very badly.

As it turned out, the Locarno period was only an interlude. Within three weeks of Stresemann's death the stock market in Wall Street collapsed, the confidence in the financial structure of the capitalistic system was seriously undermined, and, in the terrible ordeal of a world depression, the old hatreds were released, the old ghosts reappeared, and once again civilized values were in jeopardy. The Nazis had been waiting in the wings, and this was their opportunity. Hitler raised the swastika, and as the crooked cross supplanted the symbols of Christian and democratic life, Weimar became a tragic memory.

5

MUSSOLINI'S ITALY

BENITO MUSSOLINI TOOK OVER THE GOVERNMENT OF ITALY IN 1922 and ruled the country as a Fascist dictator for more than twenty years. Few men had as baneful an influence on the history of their time. He swept away the democratic fabric of the country, which had been patiently created by Mazzini, Cavour, and Garibaldi, and established the corporative state, which was really no more than predatory capitalism plus terror. He smashed the trade unions and chained the workers to a debased standard of living. He was continually rattling the saber, compelling all Europe to build armaments that ate away billions needed by war-weary peoples for reconstruction. He based his foreign policy on the cannibal theory that nations, to live, must feed upon the bodies of their neighbors.

His career was a consistent record of inconsistency. He held nearly every political and social belief at one time or another; practically every policy repudiated previous pledges or principles. In his youth he was an ardent Socialist; he was named for Benito Juárez, the beloved Mexican emancipator. When he became Il Duce, he ridiculed liberalism as "a putrefying superstition of the decadent nineteenth century." As a Socialist he wrote of the God-given rights of workers. But one of his first acts, after the march on Rome in 1922, was to destroy their bargaining power. As editor, he was a committed pacifist, serving a term in prison for opposing the Italian-Turkish War of 1911 which he denounced as an insane carnival. A little more than a decade later, he was Europe's most brazen jingoist. He never tired of declaiming: "War is the most important thing in a man's life, as maternity is in a woman's."

Before he achieved power, Mussolini defended freedom of speech and thought. "Imagine an Italy," he wrote, "in which millions should all think the same . . . and you would have a madhouse." This was a far cry from the megalomaniac who used prison and stiletto, noose and revolver and castor oil, to destroy opponents and to force national conformity. He was an early foe of Hitler and personally detested him. But when the Fascist axis was formed, he fawned on Der Führer and arranged public love-fests. He sponsored Ethiopia as a member of the League of Nations, and then snuffed out its independence by bombardment and poison gas. He denounced anti-Semitism as barbaric and recalled that the Jews had lived in Italy for twenty centuries. When he became Hitler's colleague, he attempted to eradicate their influence in a country where their proportion of the population was one in a thousand.

It is fair to ask how such a sawdust Caesar could come to power and sustain his mastery for two decades. In truth, Mussolini never really fooled his people on essentials. They knew him as a mountebank and a poltroon. But it must be remembered how drained and broken the country was left by World War I, the enormous losses in dead and wounded of its youngest and most vigorous sons. The northeast of Italy had been overrun by the Austrians, blasted in battle and despoiled during occupation. There had been extravagant hopes that the Allied victory would provide reparations, but such claims were soon lost in the complexities of postwar international alignments. The bitterness deepened when the veterans returned and found that all too many of those who had stayed behind had the available jobs and that profiteering had brought advantage to those who had been canny enough to avoid service. The first postwar election in 1919 was fought with continuous violence, and though it brought back a Socialist majority, there were so many splinter groups that it was impossible to govern with decision. There were paralyzing national strikes along with waves of factory seizures by defiant workers and of uncultivated land by peasants and agricultural laborers. Terrorist activity mounted and a sizable contingent of the Socialists now advocated a Russian solution.

For two years a succession of cabinets wrestled with the problem of preserving order and preventing the collapse of the economic system. Landowners, industrialists, middle-class professionals, all went into panic. When they could get little protection from the law they turned to private armies made up largely of thugs and hooligans. They began to look favorably upon the growing Fascist movement which had been organized by Mussolini, and which had gladly taken the assignment to fight the Socialists, to intimidate their membership, and to break up their meetings. Subsidies began to flow to them for rifles and gasoline and trucks. New recruits joined and they included demobilized officers, unemployed veterans, alienated intellectuals, rootless youth groups. As Italy moved toward a totalitarian coup, the democratic parties still could not unite and their quarrels continued. In 1922, when a hack politician, Luigi Facta, an alloy of timidity and bewilderment, took over the premiership after the country had been without any government at all for several weeks, the hour was opportune for a coup, and Mussolini was there to execute it.

Benito Mussolini was born in 1883, and almost from the beginning he was involved in revolutionary activity. He was educated in a Catholic seminary from which he was expelled for stabbing one of the fellow students. He moved to Switzerland to avoid the draft, consorting there with Communists and anarchists, eking out a precarious livelihood in a succession of menial odd jobs. Dr. Angelica Balabanoff, an Italian aristocrat who had turned Socialist, and who knew Mussolini well in this period, described him as a "crude, loud-mouthed bully, dirty, unkempt . . . a vagrant who slept under bridges and cheated his fellows."* It was at this time that he began living with Rachele, the daughter of one of his father's many mistresses. She was to become the first lady when he became Il Duce.

Mussolini returned to Italy in 1904, still the unwashed hobo, still dreaming of glory. Once he was found asleep in a cemetery where he had been making speeches to the dead. Gradually he settled into journalism, where he demonstrated exceptional talent. But he would not give up his revolutionary agitation, and when he opposed the Italian war in Libya in 1911 and called the Italian flag "a rag to be planted on a dunghill," he was imprisoned. In 1912 he was made editor of *Avanti,* a worker's organ which kept oscillating between socialism and anarchism. He vigorously denounced the Italian entry into World War I and vilified the Allies for predatory imperialism. Suddenly he changed and became an ardent interventionist, explaining that he had had a dramatic conversion. His out-

---

* Angelica Balabanoff, *My Life as a Rebel* (New York and London: Harper & Bros., 1938), pp. 42–52.

raged comrades accused him of selling out to the French for a generous subsidy. This was never proved, but Mussolini managed to acquire enough capital to found a paper of his own, *Il Popolo d'Italia,* in which he promoted the case for intervention, and later it became the Fascist organ. He served in World War I, but his claim that he had been badly wounded in action was a fraud. He was accidentally hurt during grenade practice and took no part in any of the major battles. Nevertheless, he wrote to many friends and colleagues, "I am proud to have reddened the road to Trieste with my own blood in the fulfillment of my dangerous duty."

When the war ended he became a strike breaker, at the disposal of the industrialists and the landowners. In March 1919, he organized what became the Fascist Party, taking the old Roman fasces, the bundle of rods of the Roman lictors, as the symbol for unity and discipline. With the backing of the industrialists, he entered politics and stood for Parliament in the elections of 1919. He received only 5,000 votes out of 346,000, but as the strikes and lockouts mounted, and workers took over the factories, many of the industrialists turned to him as their strong-arm guarantee to protect the status quo. In 1921, he won his seat in the Chamber along with twenty-two other Fascists. He found his opportunity in the inability of the democratic forces to unite. Five cabinets rose and fell in the three years between 1919 and 1922. As in France and Spain, in Germany and Austria, where the moderate forces fought each other and opened the way for the extremists to achieve power, the Italian Catholic and Socialist parties also floundered their way to suicide. There was a significant episode in 1921, when one of the Fascists, during a debate, drew a revolver on the floor of Parliament and made an obscene threat. One of the cabinet ministers protested, and the Prime Minister, Giolitti, pulled him back in his seat, warning him not to take sides between the extremists in the developing civil war.

In the spring of 1922 Mussolini was ready for the kill. He boldly announced that, since there was now no leadership in Rome, he planned to provide it. He had come a long way from his vagrant days. He was now a sartorial model in his stiff butterfly collar and respectable spats. The King was a cowardly little man, mean and petty, and he was fearful that a royal cousin who had been groomed by the Fascists might seize the throne. He invited Mussolini to form a government, "to save the country from chaos." Even this call did not persuade the moderate parties to subordinate their quarrels.

Mussolini had crowed that he had contempt for the stinking corpse of liberty, but the democratic parties preferred to watch the avowed executioner take over, rather than close ranks to prevent the disaster. It should be added that Mussolini's march on Rome was as spurious as most of his other boasts. Forty thousand of his followers made the march. He waited in his editorial office in Milan until all was safe; then he made his way to Rome by Pullman car, still prepared for a quick exit to Switzerland if the coup did not succeed. He burst into the King's presence in Fascist garb, the histrionic fakery consistent: "Excuse my appearance, but I come from the battlefield." There was no opposition, and the drifter of yesterday was now, at thirty-nine, the master of Italy, the youngest Prime Minister in his country's history.

He began at once to consolidate his coup. He had no well-thought-out program. When asked what it was to be, he replied, "There are just too many programs already. What Italy now needs is men, men of will." He demanded an enabling act from the thoroughly cowed Parliament, so that the coup could have the imprimatur of legality; the pattern of seeking validation for unconstitutional acts was later imitated by Hitler. For two years Mussolini kept slicing away at parliamentary jurisdiction, transferring to himself and to his appointees all the levers of authority. Billboards throughout Italy proclaimed: "Duce, you are all of us." "In Russia and in Italy," he declaimed, "it has been shown that it is possible to govern outside, above, and against the whole of liberalism's ideology. . . . Fascism is not afraid to declare itself as anti-liberal. It has once passed, and, if needful, will turn to pass again, over the more or less decomposed body of the Goddess of Liberty. . . ." All but the Fascist Party were outlawed and those who resisted were set upon by Mussolini-trained gangs of *squadristi*.

Still the old democratic tradition died hard. In the election of April 1924, though the Fascists applied intimidation and were in complete control of balloting and the tallying of the votes, the final count included two and a half million who were courageous enough to defy the regime. In the next month one of the irrepressible liberals, Giacomo Matteotti, delivered a stinging rebuke in Parliament, stigmatizing as naked dictatorship all that the government was doing. When he completed his address, he turned to the delegates at his side and said, "Now you may write the eulogy for my funeral." He knew that he was courting quick reprisal. A few days later he was kidnapped and murdered by five hoodlums and his broken body found in a ditch. The tragedy stirred the civilized world, and there were demonstrations in the cities of many foreign lands. Mussolini treated them with contempt and when the King was appealed to for action, his querulous response was, "I'm not a judge. Why do you bring these matters to me?"* It took two years to place the murderers on trial, then some of them were given a nominal two months' sentence.

The dwindling opposition now foolishly played into Mussolini's hands. They decided to boycott the sessions of Parliament as a protest, but their absence enabled Mussolini more easily to complete the destruction of the last vestiges of the democratic tradition. The judicial system was changed so that all appointments were in Mussolini's hands. Trial by jury was abolished along with the habeas corpus. By January of 1925, his dictatorship was complete. His secret police, the OVRA, comparable to the OGPU and the Gestapo of Russia and Germany, began the final hunt for any opponents who remained. One of them who had been seriously wounded in World War I was fatally attacked and, as he lay dying, murmured, "The Austrians at least left me alive; it took the Italians to dispatch me." Fascist vindictiveness reached into foreign countries where prominent political exiles had sought asylum. In 1937 the Rosselli brothers, Carlo and Nello, whose brilliantly edited journal sought to keep democratic hopes alive, were assassinated in France by hired gangsters.†

One of Mussolini's priority tasks was to reorganize the economy and to guarantee order and security. Ever conscious that Clio was looking over his shoulder, he tried to provide a systematic rationale for his program that would be impressive in the textbooks of the future. But, since he was profoundly half educated, he had neither the originality nor the consistency to think through any valid system of politics or of economic thought. His references and quotations were a grab bag of allusions for the moment, often drawn out of context, intellectual hand-me-downs. He went from thinker to thinker, just as he prowled from woman to woman. Freud must have been horrified to be cited as an endorsement for Fascist realism,

---

* When a member of the opposition presented him with a document containing incriminating evidence against Mussolini, the King covered his eyes and stopped his ears, saying: "I am blind and deaf. My eyes and ears are the chamber and the senate." Laura Fermi, *Mussolini* (Chicago: University of Chicago Press, 1961), p. 241.

† Charles F. Delzell, *Mussolini's Enemies* (Princeton, N. J.: Princeton University Press, 1961), p. 159.

[49]

and William James probably turned over in his grave when his philosophy of pragmatism was offered as a rationale for Fascist action.

Whatever doctrinaire labels were assigned to Mussolini's edicts, they were all aimed to safeguard and tighten the control of the magnates in industry, commerce, and agriculture. Their enterprises—iron and steel, oil, chemicals, automobiles, and others—were organized into syndicates and they became the new voting units. The trade unions were similarly organized but their officers were named by the government, and their power was emasculated. Strikes were strictly forbidden. Perhaps this is why Mussolini's reforms had such appeal for Judge Gary of the United States Steel Corporation, who was in constant conflict with his unions. During his visit to Italy he said wistfully: "What our country needs most now is a man like Mussolini!" There were others who were equally impressed. Mussolini buncoed such sophisticated observers as *New York Times* correspondents Anne O'Hare McCormack and Arnaldo Cortesi, who puffed him as the saviour of Italy from the chaos of radicalism.*

Inevitably the standard of living in Italy declined. The caloric intake for the general population became the lowest in Europe. Many of the earlier social insurance programs were canceled, and a pittance was now spent on education and social welfare, in a country where the poverty level, especially in the south, was scandalous and where unemployment was aggravated by the high birth rate.

The ugly facts were shielded by huge programs of public works, with new roads and ostentatious structures that were meant to glorify the Fascist state and Mussolini. Experts were called in for a drainage program in the Campagna swamps and there was a campaign to provide low-cost housing. The beggars were taken off the streets of tourist centers. Subsidies were offered to the steamship companies and airlines, to bring Italian prestige to every part of the world. But none of these well-publicized programs received the priority that went to the budgets for police, military, and the swollen bureaucracy of Mussolini's own underlings.

The social realities were also screened by an aggressive foreign policy, where bluster was more common than diplomacy. From the moment of his incumbency, Mussolini never lost an opportunity to remind his subjects that they were Romans, descendants of an

* See J. P. Diggins, *Mussolini and Fascism: The View from America* (Princeton, N.J.: Princeton University Press, 1972).

imperial élite. He took to the balcony often, striking a histrionic pose. He bellowed: "We dream of a Roman Italy, wise and strong and disciplined. That which was the immortal spirit of Rome resurges in our Fascism. Roman are the lictors' rods, Rome our fighting organization, Rome our pride and our courage. Civis Romanus sum." On another occasion he blared out: "Not for nothing have I chosen for my motto in life 'Live Dangerously.' And I say to you, like the old warrior, if I advance, follow me, if I retreat kill me, and if I die, avenge me." He established a routine for receiving foreign diplomats, by having them walk past a long double column of black uniformed troops who held out daggers, at arms' length.

He never stopped posing. His publicity flunkies ground out the releases that described his feats as invincible horseman, death-defying speed driver, daredevil aircraft pilot, skillful violinist, prolific writer, and profound political philosopher. Above all, he was proud of his sexual prowess and boasted that he was ready at any hour of the day or night. Here too he was a barbarian; one of his mistresses complained that he did not even take off his boots. He rarely walked; he strutted, as if he were trailing a long purple cloak behind him. He once asked an ambassador, who came to report on varieties of poison gas, which was the most dangerous. "Oh, your excellency, incense, incense is the most lethal." Ugo Ojetti, an astute art critic, after watching Mussolini in one of his stage-managed performances, wrote, "I cannot help thinking when I see him, how much his face must ache at night when he retires."

Meantime he had an early opportunity to show his neighbors what meat the Caesar ate. In 1923 there was an incident in Greece, where Italian representatives on the League of Nations' Commission were attacked by bandits and several killed. Mussolini sought no redress through the League of Nations, or through peaceable procedures. He quickly sent an ultimatum, demanding fifty million lire in damages, punishment of the bandits, and an investigation in which the Italian military attaché would participate. The ultimatum might have been a carbon copy of the Austrian demand on Serbia that triggered World War I. Greece yielded on every point, except the challenge to its sovereignty, and Mussolini immediately bombed Corfu. The League intervened and settled the dispute peaceably, but the world was warned that a dangerous demagogue was loose.

Throughout the first decade of Mussolini's tyranny there was a steady tightening of the police state, and overt opposition virtually disappeared. Elections, referenda, and voting were all rigged, with more propaganda than legislative significance. In a 1929 referendum, when a flat yes or no was called for, the vote was 8½ million, yes, and 137,000, no. It took daring for these thousands to risk detection and punishment for their defiance. Apparently they were determined, at all costs, to keep the flame alive. One of the last of them was Lauro Debosis, a young poet who, in October 1931, wrote an eloquent denunciation of fascism and the degradation that it had brought into Italian life. He had hundreds of thousands of copies printed and loaded them into a plane which he had only just learned to fly. He took off from a base in Switzerland, planning to circle Rome and rain down the pamphlets in a paper snowstorm over the workers returning from the factories and the worshippers on their way back from Mass. The Fascist planes came up after him. When all of his pamphlets had been distributed, he turned the plane out to sea, dived down, and was gone in the waves. Ruth Draper was in Rome at the time, and she watched the plane rise. She wrote later that as it took off, it seemed as if it were ascending the thirty-nine steps. It was a spectacular martyrdom, to be remembered for the morale it offered in the tragic years ahead when the full cost of Mussolini was to be paid.

Still ahead were twelve years from 1933 to 1945 in which Mussolini joined with Hitler to blackmail the democratic world. He defied the League of Nations to snuff out the independence of Ethiopia. He helped to destroy a million lives in the Spanish Civil War. He dragged his people into World War II and brought such disaster upon them that it took all the next generation to shake off its evil effects. He himself was done to death, not by soldiers fighting against him but by his own people, who executed him and his mistress and hanged them by their heels in the public square of Milan.*

* These episodes in Mussolini's career and in the tragedy of Italy are included in later chapters.

6

BRITAIN BETWEEN
THE WARS

ONE OF THE MOST STARTLING DEVELOPMENTS OF THE INTER-WAR period was the fate of Britain, the diplomatic arbiter of the nineteenth and early twentieth century, now stumbling and bumbling its way, attempting pathetically to maintain its position, and yet having neither the strength nor the prestige any longer to play a decisive role. Like a once rich relative, fortune gone, Britain labored to keep up appearances, hiding shabbiness under ceremony, masking weakness under bustle and motion. The dominions slipped away one by one, some, like Ireland, cutting loose completely, others repudiating virtually all imperial control, so that after World War II, the Empire had become a tenuous federation. A time came in the thirties when, though Britain continued the charades of self-deception, it could not deceive a new breed of tough, cynical, buccaneering dictators who sensed early that even their most unconscionable blackmail would not be resisted.

There is wonder how Britain came in the first place to its fulcrum importance as a world power. It was as small as the state of Wyoming. Its soil was poor, and its natural resources, except for coal, very meager. It had to import most of its food, and the danger of starvation was a tugging fear if ever war should come and an enemy mounted a blockade. It had risen to world hegemony because of its fortunate geographical location astride the strategic trade routes, a location skillfully exploited by an enterprising people that had created a huge merchant marine, and a mighty fleet to protect it.

Its overseas Empire, the prime source of its prosperity, was held together by this unchallenged naval power.

The debilitation of Britain as a result of the war was catastrophic. Seven hundred and fifty thousand men were killed in action, and more than a million and a half were wounded. There had been no conscription but the response to the call for service came from every section of the population. The losses included a grandson of Prime Minister Gladstone, a son of Prime Minister Rosebery, two sons of Prime Minister Bonar Law, a son of Prime Minister Asquith, a son of Foreign Secretary Lord Lansdowne, a son of the Labour leader, Arthur Henderson, a son of Kipling. The sons of the farmers and the industrial workers, those who had not attended the fashionable schools, also willingly rallied to the colors and gave their full share of sacrifice. H. G. Wells wrote in 1915, even before the worst casualties had bled the nation: "All over England now, where the livery of mourning had been a rare thing to see, women and children went about in the October sunshine in new black clothes. Everywhere one met these fresh griefs, mothers who had lost their sons, women who had lost their men, lives shattered and hopes destroyed."* A generation later, the enfeebling impact of the hemorrhage became starkly clear when mature statesmanship was needed, and there were few survivors to offer it.

The mood of the country had changed drastically from the early crusade days. Siegfried Sassoon, one of the most gifted of the younger poets, had been proud that he was part of the war effort. He wrote lyrically of his commitment, and gloried in the Military Cross that came to him for bravery in action. But soon his verses were heavy with the futility and the meaninglessness of the bloodshed:

> . . . the war won't end for at least two years;
> But we've got stacks of men . . . I'm blind with tears,
> Staring into the dark. Cheero!
> I wish they'd killed you in a decent show.†

When the war ended he observed that its real tragedy had been "the exploitation of courage." John Buchan, in his revulsion against all that had happened, wrote: "To speak of glory seemed a horrible impiety." For D. H. Lawrence, "All the great words were cancelled

---

* H. G. Wells, *Mr. Britling Sees It Through* (New York: The Macmillan Company, 1917), p. 383.
† Gardner, ed., *Up the Line to Death*, p. 99.

out for that generation." The nation was moving into its victorious peace, with little to console itself for the fresh graves of its sons.

The exhaustion of the economy made it difficult to realize that Britain had fought a victorious war. The national debt had risen tenfold since 1914. The immense investments abroad that had made Britain the banker of the world had been liquidated to help pay, in part, for the costs of war. The basic industries were in the deepest trouble. Coal was a very sick area, the best seams now depleted, the machinery antiquated, the administration inefficient. New forms of power such as oil and electricity were needed to meet vigorous competition from abroad, but these required investment capital that was not available. Equally serious was the psychological paralysis that affected British entrepreneurship. The war that physically debilitated the country was all too often an excuse for inadequacy or failure. The obsession with "the good old days" of prewar operation often led to disastrous decisions. Appearances meant so much that the City of London made long-term commitments in Central Europe on the basis of short-term borrowing in the West. The United States, Japan, India, and other enterprising nations had substantially expanded their plant during the war period, and as they won over the markets that had long been a British monopoly, the proud British boast, "the workshop of the world," became a mocking memory.

The merchant fleet, too, indispensable source of export and foreign trade, had been fatally depleted during the war through the effectiveness of German submarine action. Seven million tons went to the bottom, 38 percent of the total merchant fleet of 1914. Here too there must have been inept management. For with nearly two-fifths of the fleet destroyed, Britain still had to contend with excess unused shipping capacity. It had been expected that reparations from Germany would retrieve some of these losses, indeed, that they would help to renovate industry. But, as in its relationship with France, Germany found every manner of excuse to avoid or to reduce reparations. Liberals in Britain, led by Maynard Keynes, encouraged the Germans in their intransigence, insisting that the reparations were immoral and ultimately self-defeating.* Meantime, four million veterans, many wounded, had to be absorbed, and an agonizing clash developed between them and the civilians whose gratitude to

---

* Keynes was strongly refuted on the damaging effects of reparations. See Étienne Mantoux, *The Economic Consequences of Mr. Keynes* (London, New York, etc.: Oxford University Press, 1946).

the men who had fought was now worn thin by their own anxieties. The tenacity with which British leadership insisted upon reparations came more from desperate need than from any desire for vengeance.

The postwar years were dominated by three men, each reflecting the rapidly shifting temper of the country. At the outset, of course, there was still David Lloyd George, more ebullient and dynamic than ever. Early in his career he had been the stormy petrel of the Liberal Party, his political subtlety, and his bewitching oratory, bringing him quickly to prominence. He had passionately opposed the Boer War as an immoral assault on a free people, and had courageously borne the abuse of the jingoists. He had fought the tariff bills of the Tories, using the irresistible appeal, "Hands off the people's food." In 1911, noting that a Duke cost as much to maintain as a battleship, he had broken the final veto power of the House of Lords after a battle that shook the titled Establishment to its foundations. He had pioneered the first programs of national health insurance; the workers who received the benefit assignments often referred to them as their "Lloyd George."

During World War I, the party chafed under Prime Minister Asquith's maladroit conduct of affairs, and, in 1916, when the war was going very badly, it turned to Lloyd George for leadership. His organizing genius blasted the bumbling routine at home and at the fighting fronts, and toppled those who bore the most hoary family names. He was completely unimpressed by the trappings of power and liked nothing better than to escape to a country retreat to dine on cold rice pudding. There he demonstrated his contempt for the Colonel Blimps when he imported manure for his farm, observing that this was the only use he ever had for the overdecorated British cavalry. His impatient perfectionism was the decisive factor in sustaining British morale in the darkest days of the war. Winston Churchill looked up to him as his peerless mentor; in his prime, he declared, Lloyd George's initiative and his political dexterity were unequaled. "He had the power of seeing, in moments when everyone was asking about the next step, the step after that." Someone chided Churchill for such extravagant praise. "You talk as if Lloyd George can do everything. But he isn't God Almighty!" Churchill chuckled, "Remember, he's still young."

At the Peace Conference, Lloyd George, always at his best in negotiation, mesmerized the Big Four. Maynard Keynes was an unfriendly critic, but he had to admit, after watching him in action as he coped with Clemenceau and Wilson, that the man was incomparable. "How can I convey to the reader, who does not know him, any just impression of this extraordinary figure of our time, this syre, this goat-footed bard, this half-human visitor to our age from the hag-ridden magic and enchanted woods of Celtic antiquity? . . . An instrument and a player at the same time which is played by the company and is played on by them too."* After the unconditional surrender of Germany, Lloyd George capitalized on the national mood to call for a general election, and he was returned by the keyed-up electorate with a resounding mandate. Now, in 1919, at the peak of his prestige, he was expected to lead Britain through the shoals of the postwar period.

But the wizardry that had buoyed spirits and scored diplomatic points was not as effective to cope with the niggling, grinding, wearisome tasks of peace. The years until 1923 were plagued with angry crises as the unemployed and their families demanded attention. Two million were now on the relief rolls, 22 percent of all insured workers. In the cotton, coal, and engineering-centered towns, half of the workers were idle. Since relief was costly, the benefits were steadily cut. The returned veterans paraded with banners that read: "Wanted in 1914, but not wanted now." Strikes were frequent, and these triggered the counteroffensive of lockouts. There was even a London police strike. The most serious labor disturbances came from the miners, whose situation had become unendurable. Their strikes were on and off intermittently for several years, and then, broken by government retaliation, the miners went back, sullen and bitter, to the collieries.

Lloyd George found himself in a trap where oratory was useless to provide escape. He could not get the capitalist employers to bend to reform—"squandermania," they termed his proposals—nor labor to exercise discipline in negotiation. He maintained his position as Prime Minister almost from day to day, by dizzying political acrobatics. But promises to everybody satisfied nobody. "Lloyd George," one of the Conservatives insisted, "has not sold his soul, but he did pawn it." A later Liberal Party leader, Jo Grimond, berated the opportunism of a man "who couldn't see a belt without hitting below it."

---

* John Maynard Keynes, *Essays in Biography* (New York: W. W. Norton, 1963), pp. 35–6.

Ironically, the issue that brought Lloyd George down concerned foreign policy. The Greeks had been encouraged by Lloyd George in 1922 to enforce the war treaties that had given them important concessions in Turkish Asia Minor. Their invasion ended in disaster. The Conservative component in the Coalition government rejected Lloyd George's judgment as "dangerous adventurism" and, in 1922, they withdrew. Lloyd George promptly resigned. He stayed on in politics for another fifteen years, but his effective career had ended. The Liberal Party had shriveled away during the Coalition years, and he no longer had a base from which to command. He remained only as a legend, but the legend was part of another age. His judgments did not stand the test of history. He regarded Hitler, in his rise to power, as a well-motivated statesman, a Teutonic Roosevelt. He opposed decisive measures to abort Mussolini's rape of Ethiopia. As late as 1936 he was still battling against independence for India. "Is it not strange that desire should so many years outlive performance?"*

After the fall of Lloyd George in 1923, there were three elections in one year for new Parliaments. A new force was emerging, the Labour Party, committed to democratic socialism and a welfare state. It had no resemblance to the totalitarian Marxism of the Soviet Union, but it was far to the left of the repudiated Liberals. In the third election of the year, no party could command a majority. But Labour had sufficient strength to earn its long-awaited opportunity to form a government, albeit by the sufferance of the almost decimated Liberals. A whole flock of new leaders now came to the fore, some drawn from the pioneers who had patiently built the party, and some from disenchanted Liberals who were uncomfortable as middle-of-the-roaders and preferred the challenges of the left.† The key men were a hard core of trade unionists and some brilliant intellectuals who were ready with blueprints to chart their brave new world. The King gave the seals of government to Ramsay MacDonald.

The runner-up, J. R. Clynes, wrote later: "As we stood waiting for His Majesty, amid the gold and crimson magnificence of the Palace, I could not help marvelling at the strange turn of Fortune's wheel which had brought MacDonald, the starveling clerk, Thomas the engine-driver, Henderson the foundry-labourer, and Clynes the

---

* *Henry IV, Part II*, Act II, Scene iv.

† The Liberals suffered most perhaps from being less definably a "class" party than either the Tories or the Labour Party.

mill-hand, to this pinnacle, beside the man whose forebears had been kings for so many splendid generations."*

The fact that a man of MacDonald's background could become Prime Minister of Britain made clear how much the country had been transformed by the war and its dislocations. MacDonald was the illegitimate son of a Scottish servant girl. He was raised in poverty and self-educated. He became secretary to one of the Liberal members of Parliament, and was brought into the animated circle of journalists, social workers, and Fabian idealogues; these experiences sharpened his apprenticeship in politics. His marriage to Margaret Gladstone, a great-niece of the noted scientist Lord Kelvin, created a society sensation. His private happiness was early dimmed when Margaret died in childbirth, leaving him with four very young children. He was a confirmed pacifist, and had opposed the Boer War. When the hostilities were imminent in 1914, he resisted British involvement, not because he condoned the German actions, but because he believed ardently that war settled nothing. As the fighting raged, he refused to remain silent and he was often howled down in debate, especially when he defended the objectives of the Russian revolution. He had no sympathy for communism in Britain, but he believed that it was justified in Russia as a means of eliminating czarist tyranny. In the hang-the-Kaiser election of 1918, Conservatives and Liberals both assailed him as a Communist sympathizer, and he lost his seat in Parliament. But he was back in the House in 1922, and there he led the fight for a capital levy—an assessment on wealth, outside of taxes, as a means of reducing the national debt. It was this obscurely born commoner, a committed pacifist, reviled for his sympathetic interpretation of the Russian revolution, a maverick in politics, who was now called to head up the first Socialist government in Britain, indeed, the first Socialist government in western Europe. It was little wonder that the dismayed property-oriented Conservatives were sure that revolution was imminent.

There need not have been so much concern. Labour was governing with a minority mandate, and held office only because of Liberal support. The party itself was in no sense revolutionary. It was pledged to significant reforms, but there were none that could not be absorbed within the total British tradition. The Liberals were not at all frightened. Asquith had said: "If a Labour government is

* John Robert Clynes, *Memoirs* (London: Hutchinson and Co., Ltd., 1937), p. 343.

ever to be tried in this country, as it will sooner or later, it could hardly be tried under safer conditions." Baldwin of the Conservatives on the eve of the Labour takeover spoke in sporting terms. "When the Labour Party sit on these government benches," he said, "we shall all wish them well in their efforts to govern the country."

MacDonald vindicated the amiable freedom from anxiety in his cautious approach to responsibility. When he was summoned to the palace to accept the seals of authority, King George noted in his diary, "I had an hour's talk with him; he impressed me very much. He wishes to do the right thing." Conscious of the historic turn of events, and thinking of Queen Victoria, the King added: "Today, twenty-three years ago, dear grandmamma died. I wonder what she would have thought of a Labour government." She probably would also have been quickly reconciled. The British get over such shocks with remarkable aplomb.

MacDonald soon dissipated whatever fears still troubled the old order. Tall, courtly, immaculately dressed at official functions, he was often the handsomest and most relaxed of all those present. Indeed, many of his colleagues resented what they regarded as undue deference to the élite silver-buckled society in which MacDonald now moved. And later, when he would not act with urgency for radical legislation, they regretted that they had selected a Labour chief who had never worked with his hands, instead of a no-nonsense trade unionist who knew from personal experience why the Labour objectives were visceral issues. Beatrice Webb scoffed, "MacDonald was a magnificent substitute for a leader."

In any case the Labour incumbency, at this stage, was a very short one. It was in office, but not in power. No attempt could be made to carry through the pledge for the nationalization of basic industries. The domestic program could go no further than more substantial subsidies to those on relief, or to those who required more insurance benefits. A major change did take place in foreign policy, but Conservative cooperation would have been offered anyway, since the diplomatic climate was mellowing throughout Europe. MacDonald served as his own Foreign Minister, and he was eager to work closely with Briand of France, who was also a strong advocate of conciliation with Weimar Germany. There was a more realistic recognition that Europe had to live with the Russian revolution, and MacDonald was able to draft treaties with the Soviet Union that established direct economic and diplomatic relationships. But with minority government so delicately balanced, so reliant on coalition support, MacDonald did not even attempt to press for the more radical provisions in the Labour platform. In less than a year of official responsibility, it was necessary to dissolve Parliament and await a new mandate.

The election late in 1924 was hard-fought. The Liberals suffered another disaster and could no longer be considered as a major party. The Labour vote was very much what it had been, but there was a heavy loss of seats. It was a landslide victory for the Conservatives who, with the exception of a brief innocuous Labour interlude in 1929, were to remain in power for more than fifteen years, until the outbreak of World War II and beyond.

This period was mainly dominated by Stanley Baldwin, who could model for the popular conception of John Bull, and whose speeches and actions were perfectly attuned to a people that was hungry for tranquility. They had been worn out by the erratic brilliance and flashy opportunism of Lloyd George. They had been frustrated by the indecisiveness of three successive general elections where the political balance was so sensitive that it produced stalemate. They therefore welcomed Stanley Baldwin, steady, reliable, with no vision of Utopia, but with the promise of sound, common-sense adminis-tration.

Baldwin had been educated at Harrow, where one of his teachers had said to him: "Baldwin, you'll never do anything wrong, you haven't got the brains. But you'll never do anything big either." From Harrow he went to Cambridge, and then into the century-old family empire, the Baldwin Iron and Steel Works. After a thorough apprenticeship in the business world, he entered politics and was elected to Parliament in 1908. He was given modest financial and trade assignments there by the Conservatives through the discourag-ing war years. Recognizing that he had been too old to serve actively in combat, he donated a fourth of his fortune to the government. But the gift was anonymous and the secret was not out until many years later. After the war the opportunities for leadership came quickly. In 1922, he led the British delegation to negotiate a debt settlement with the United States. When the Conservative Prime Minister Bonar Law became too ill to discharge his duties, the quiet, phlegmatic Baldwin took his place.

He interpreted his mandate to mean a low-keyed business administration, a balanced budget, a laissez-faire approach, the less government the better. He had been an ardent admirer of the eight-eenth-century Prime Minister Horace Walpole, who had operated on the principle that one should let sleeping dogs lie. In his first broadcast over the radio, just then coming into popular use, Baldwin spoke reassuringly on the theme, "You can trust me." One of his foreign policy speeches of 1923 could have easily been written by any man or woman in the street, and even by many of the children. "Four words," he said, "of one syllable each, are the words which contain salvation for this country and the whole world. They are faith, hope, love, work. No government in this country today which has not faith in the people, hope in the future, love for its fellowman, and which will not work and work and work, will ever bring this country through into better days and better times, or will ever bring Europe through or the world through."

Baldwin was not too much disconcerted by figures of more than a million unemployed. In a period of wars and turbulence this was to be expected. A program of modest unemployment relief and reliance upon the market laws of supply and demand would assuredly weather the country's economic crisis. Within a year he restored the gold standard, and brought the pound back to its prewar rate of $4.86. "The pound must look the dollar in the face!" he had decreed. The economists pleaded that raising the value of the pound would have disastrous effects. The trade unions fought vigorously against the decree, fearful that it must mean the loss of foreign markets. Baldwin persisted and prices rose just when the European countries were lowering theirs. The revaluation was particularly hard on the coal industry, already quite sick. Five hundred mines, employing more than a hundred thousand workers, closed down. A government commission concluded after study that, for the industry to compete, either the hours of work must be extended or there must be a pay cut. The unions refused to accept either alternative. "Not a penny off the pay, not a minute on the day." In 1926, they called for a general strike and the response involved the mines, transport, steel, chemicals, power, virtually all the basic industries. Three million workers laid down their tools, and the economic life of Britain ground to a halt. For a moment it appeared as if the country faced revolution.

The threat was never a real one. The general strike of 1926 was entirely an economic weapon to compel a better wage settlement. It was not meant to force revolutionary changes in the social structure. At the height of the confrontation, a soccer team of strikers in Plymouth played a team of police. To be sure, some violence

was inevitable in a crisis of such magnitude—attacks on strike break-
ers, sabotage in the plants, occasional clashes between the workers
and the police. But there was no loss of life, no substantial property
damage, and the workers were on the defensive from the outset.
They had used a technique that was alien to the British tradition,
and they won little support from the general public. A quarter of a
million men and women from all walks of life enlisted as constables
to keep order. Students from Oxford and Cambridge volunteered
to man the buses, to operate the trains, to unload the ships. For nine
days the general strike was maintained, and the workers steadily lost
ground. When Baldwin made a patriotic appeal for both sides to
rely upon his fairness while he sought a way out, his intervention
was sullenly accepted as a face-saving device by the strikers. He
recommended some minor concessions, but the basic issues that precipitated the strike were glossed over. It was a disastrous defeat for
Labour, and it left a train of bitterness.

Soon afterwards the Trades Disputes Act was passed as a government measure. It ended the threat of economic paralysis by banning
unions from participation in sympathy strikes. Supplementary legislation forbade compulsion on workers by their unions to collect fees
for political activity, even if its purpose was to finance a union's
bargaining power. It was a surprising piece of vindictive legislation
wholly uncharacteristic of Baldwin, who might have been obtuse or
shallow but was rarely mean or vicious.

The new general election in May 1929 came on the eve of the
world depression. Baldwin asked for a vote of confidence on the basis
of his solid business record. "Safety first," cried the posters, "trust
Baldwin." The appeal was not enough now. Declining production,
unemployment, inadequate relief provisions, class conflict, and
rancor were eating into the vitals of national life, and the Tories
lost more than a hundred seats. The Liberals were definitively
eliminated as a political force, and disintegrated into just another
little splinter group.

Labour, for the first time, emerged as the strongest party, but it
still could not command an absolute majority. MacDonald was
called back to the Prime Minister's post, but it was 1923 over again,
a government on sufferance which could make no headway with
basic reform. MacDonald egg-danced from one crisis to another,
trimming, maneuvering, conceding, surviving only because the
opposition groups were unwilling to assume responsibility without

authority. Churchill scornfully referred to MacDonald at this stage as "the greatest living master of falling down without hurting himself."

But MacDonald did hurt himself. For it was impossible to rely upon routine political jugglery to deal with the engulfing depression and with growing intransigence in the major colonial areas—in Egypt and India and Palestine. The situation on the continent had now also seriously deteriorated as Mussolini and Hitler were bullying their way to power. The times called for a submergence of partisanship, and the party leaders, MacDonald and Baldwin, began to talk of a national government, with a moratorium on conventional politics during the dangerous period of economic crisis at home and danger abroad.

The old guard of the Labour Party were outraged. They remembered what they regarded as the betrayals of the general strike, the defeat of the miners, the Trades Disputes Act, the cavalier attitude of the Tories to the problems of the workers. How can there be a partnership in good faith, they stormed, with such callous men, even in the face of danger from the dictators who are riding on their tigers? The quarrel split the Labour Party and left scars that were not healed all through the period when Britain needed strength and unity to contend with Hitler and Mussolini and a Japan on the march. MacDonald and the colleagues who followed him into the Coalition with Baldwin were denounced as party traitors, as prisoners of the passion to hold on to public office.

MacDonald was not diverted. He insisted that the crisis had now reached the dangerous point where the security of Britain superseded any class or party interest. The Coalition government assumed responsibility in 1929; with occasional changes in cabinet personnel, it was to hold office through the entire World War II period. The spirit in which it functioned and its invertebrate reactions to the dictators were largely influenced by the objectives that held the Coalition together. MacDonald had asked for a "doctor's mandate," and, as an astute historian noted, the phrase was significant. These were the days before antibiotics, and doctors habitually prescribed rest for most ailments, confident that it could be relied upon to assure recovery.*

Britain was much more severely agitated by an internal royal crisis than by the dangers from the intransigence of the dictators.

* A. J. P. Taylor, *English History, 1914–1945* (New York: Oxford University Press, 1965), p. 324.

King George V had died in 1935 and was succeeded by his son Edward who, as Prince of Wales, had lived a bohemian life, mainly in foreign resorts, indifferent to responsibility, usually in the company of a raffish coterie. Soon the gossip about his relationship with an attractive American divorcee, Wallis Simpson, became a serious political problem. For Edward was intent upon marrying her and making her his Queen. The explosive opposition was not limited to the more conservative forces who found it difficult to regard "the Simpson woman" as an appropriate Queen. Even those who were little concerned with the private lives of the couple believed that it was immoral to divide the nation in a time of grave peril when unity was paramount. Stanley Baldwin, now Prime Minister, was adamant in his opposition. He refused Edward's compromise to have Wally become a morganatic wife with none of the rights of a Queen. Baldwin took the view that the humblest in the nation had gladly made sacrifices in wartime when the national destiny was at stake. Was it too much to ask the King to set an example for his people by choosing duty above inclination when such action called for far less sacrifice? In this stance Baldwin was solidly supported by the cabinet, the church officials, and the leaders of the Commonwealth.

Edward on his side would not yield. He preferred abdication, and on December 11, 1936, his radio broadcast to all the world announced: "I have found it impossible to carry the heavy burdens of responsibility and discharge my duties as King as I would wish to do without the help and support of the woman I love." It was a moving speech; nothing in Edward's career matched the dignity of the moment when he declared that he was quitting public affairs altogether. One international correspondent was so far carried away in florid hyperbole as to label the royal romance and its climax as the greatest story since the Resurrection. The couple went into retirement to spend the rest of their lives pursuing the trivia of fashion and sports in the cosmopolitan café society.

The significance of the episode was not in any change in the British power structure. Edward's brother succeeded to the throne as George VI and gave it the stability and security that the British people craved. What was significant was the depth of feeling aroused by a maudlin melodrama in a period when the foundations of national life were threatened. For in facing the aggression of the dictators, Baldwin, and then Chamberlain, who succeeded him after the abdication, demonstrated none of the firmness and determination that they had mustered when they sternly laid down the law to their own King. Churchill drew the contrast in the nervelessness that was eroding the respect and the power of Britain. "The Court is august," he said. "The private lives of the members are beyond reproach. But for three years of classic futility, they have paltered, faltered, maundered and gibbered on the bench." The traditional role of Britain, as one of the arbiters of the destiny of the western world, quietly evaporated amidst Chamberlain's sonorous assurances that his policy of compromise and placation would bring "peace for our time."

7

THE IRISH UPRISING
AND ITS AFTERMATH

MEMORY FOR THE IRISH IS MUCH MORE A SOURCE OF SORROW THAN OF pride. They cannot shake off the impact of the long years of repression by the British, a bondage that reaches back into the twelfth century, when Ireland was overrun by Anglo-Normans and much of the native population was uprooted to make room for the invaders. Memory includes the tragedy of Drogheda, in the seventeenth century, by which time religious conflict had entered as a factor; the British had become Protestant, while the Irish had remained Catholic. Oliver Cromwell, in his fanatic zeal, authorized the massacre of the entire Catholic population: men, women, and children, some three thousand souls, and exulted afterwards: "It has pleased God to bless our endeavors at Drogheda. I wish that all honest hearts may give glory of this to God alone, to whom indeed the praise of this mercy belongs." The entire island from the sea to the Shannon was taken. All who resisted were slain and thousands of Irish girls were sent into slavery to the Barbados and Jamaica. Memory includes the exploitation of the impoverished peasantry, especially the rent gouging, often by absentee English landlords. What rankled as much as the enforced impoverishment was the insult that had to be borne, such contempt as Jonathan Swift's, who wrote,

> A servile race in folly nursed,
> Who truckle most when treated worst.

More recent memory brings back the horror of the famine of the mid-1840's, in which about a million Irish starved to death and another million fled in what were called "coffin ships" because so many died in them on their way from the wretchedness that had become unendurable. In six years, from 1845 to 1851, the population of Ireland declined by two million. From 1845 to 1945 more than six million of the most vital and ambitious, twice the total population of the island, migrated to the United States and Australia, there nursing a hatred of the British that affected the diplomacy of the generations ahead. Those who remained struggled in vain to rise above degradation and despair. Francis Hackett, recalling the glory of Ireland in its early promise, its leadership in the golden era of St. Patrick, wrote: "And its radiance dies, leaving Ireland cowered in the corner, horror in her eyes, the sickly moonlight on the wreckage of her feast, broken bread, spilled wine."*

In every generation the cause of Irish independence had been espoused by militant Irishmen. The English demonstrated genius in the development of their own political institutions but, by some fatal perversity, neither understood the Irish nor made more than halfhearted attempts to do so. Some of the difficulties came from their inability to cope with the Irish temperament, but most of them came from outright human greed. Disraeli, who could react intuitively to the nuances of pride and physical insecurity, knew that the rancor had deeply set emotional and substantive causes, the affront to Catholic dignity and the depressed economy, "the Pope and potatoes."

There was a hopeful development when, at long last, late in the nineteenth century, one wing of the Liberal Party, led by Prime Minister William Gladstone, joined with some of the more progressive Conservatives to champion the reforms that the Irish patriots of the past century had advocated. It was Gladstone's plan to offer Home Rule, a modified autonomy, by which Britain would retain control only of foreign policy and military security. These could not be relinquished, Gladstone said, for Ireland was at the back door of Britain, and the remembrance of the threat from the French in 1798 which had placed the country in mortal danger was ever present. Gladstone staked his political career on the issue of Home Rule. But the counties in the north, around Belfast, largely Protestant in population, resisted any program that would place them under the jurisdiction of the island's Catholic majority. The promised safeguards were considered inadequate. The cry went up that

* Francis Hackett, *Ireland, A Study in Nationalism* (New York: B. W. Huebsch, 1920), p. 394.

[68]

"Home Rule is Rome Rule" and "Ulster will fight and Ulster will be right." For more than three decades after Gladstone's overtures, until the eve of World War I, the issue of Irish Home Rule convulsed British political life. Then a bill that granted autonomy was passed, over the veto of the House of Lords, which took advantage of every technicality that the law permitted. But enactment was suspended, with the understanding that it would become operative when the war ended, and after further negotiations with the northeastern counties to assure protection for their Protestant population.

The long debates over Home Rule and the tortoise pace of negotiations inevitably gave strength to the extremist advocates who decried "half-measures." For the younger generation of Irish, Home Rule, a satisfying objective in the late nineteenth century, was now no longer acceptable. In 1905 young Arthur Griffith, later to become President of the Irish Parliament, the Dail Eireann, created a party that took the name of "Sinn Fein," "Ourselves Alone." Its adherents rejected any settlement short of complete independence. It was nourished by a renaissance of the Irish cultural tradition centered in the Gaelic League, founded by a Trinity College professor, Douglas Hyde. Every effort was made to resurrect Gaelic as the language of Ireland, to emphasize the beauty and significance of the Irish ancestral heritage. Gaelic never became a popular tongue. It was never intended to be. It was looked upon as an alternative to English which, for all its richness, was the language of the usurper. How could one champion Irish freedom in the accents of the oppressor, where the overlord was the ventriloquist? It was expected that at least the leadership would learn and use Gaelic, and it did indeed deeply influence the writing and the speech of the rarest spirits, Yeats and J. M. Synge, Lady Gregory and James Joyce, and the actress-patriot, Maud Gonne.

At the outbreak of the world war, Sinn Fein, committed to the severance of all ties with Britain, was still an inconsequential minority with little popular support. Most of the Irish, south as well as north, loyally supported the Allied cause. There were 150,000 volunteers from Ireland who joined the British forces, and an Irish contingent distinguished itself in the battles at Gallipoli. But the threat to British dominion was ever present. The extremists in the Republican group, operating on the age-old principle that "England's hour of need is Ireland's hour of opportunity," placed their nationalist objectives above the most urgent military needs of the British. Arthur Griffith declared that Britain was as much a foreign power as Germany, and that the Irish had no stake in the imperial quarrels that had erupted in war.

The early political nationalists were a heterogeneous band, in temperament, in experience, and in social station, but they were all united by their grim memories of British repression, and by their passionate hope for a new day in a free Ireland. There was tall, handsome, bearded Sir Roger Casement, who had served Britain with distinction as a Consul in the Congo, and had been knighted for the persistence with which he had confronted the conscience of the world as he exposed white brutality against the blacks. Upon his return from Africa, he watched the reluctant hem-haw inaction of the British in meeting the needs of his native Ireland, and sorrowfully concluded that Ireland's only recourse lay in a German victory, from which would surely come the recognition of Irish independence. Though he knew that any effort to promote this aim would be judged as treason, he made several secret trips to Germany, and worked among the Irish prisoners there, to persuade them to organize an Irish legion, armed and equipped by Germany, to fight against the British.

Then there was Pádraic Pearse, a moody romantic, who wrote of death in the cause of Irish freedom as if it were a required blood atonement. He came of an English family and was trained for the law, but he preferred literature and teaching, and edited the struggling little journal of the Gaelic League. He founded St. Enda's, a bilingual school where Gaelic as well as English was taught, a school that influenced many of the Irish revolutionary leaders. He brooded over the Irish fate that had so worn down Irish pride that only heroic martyrdom could bring redemption. In language that would be judged as artificial and pretentious in men less dedicated, he called to the youth of his generation "to turn their backs to the pleasant paths and their faces to the hard paths, to blind their eyes to the fair things in life, to stifle all sweet music in the heart, the low voices of women, the laughter of little children, and to follow only the faint, far call that leads them into battle or to the harder death at the foot of the gibbet."* It was this rhapsodic visionary, guided by the inward eye, who was named President of the Irish Republic by his devoted followers. They planned for a national uprising on the Easter weekend of 1916.

* Cited in Edgar Holt, *Protest in Arms* (New York: Coward McCann, Inc., 1960), p. 50.

Neither Pearse nor his amateur lieutenants had any hope that their uprising would bring down the Establishment. They knew how pathetically inadequate their military strength was against the might of the British. But they were convinced that a dramatic sacrifice would ignite the dispirited, the discouraged, the subdued. Pearse had written: "The old heart of the earth needed to be warmed with the red wine of the battlefields. . . . Life springs from death: and from the graves of patriot men and women spring living nations."* His was a call to a people who had been ground down for centuries, who could provide magnificent leadership wherever they migrated, but who were pariahs in their own land. What did it matter if the physical uprising failed, and if those who took part lost their lives, so long as their effort stirred the people and made them realize that courage and pride were not lost among the Irish?

Nothing seemed to go right in that Easter uprising, so that not even failure could be ordered with dignity. The Germans were to have sent arms, but very little got through. When Sir Roger Casement tried to land on the Irish coast in a German submarine, the plans had been so badly worked out that he was quickly caught, tried for treason, and executed, the only concession to his rank and earlier service being a rope of silk for the hanging. The revolutionary leaders did seize some of the main buildings of Dublin, but they could not hold them for long. They inflicted about five hundred casualties on the British, but the uprising was soon under control and most of the insurgents were captured, among them Pádraic Pearse.

It would probably have been maturer statesmanship for the British to have responded with a measure of leniency. The revolutionists were nearly all young, mostly in their twenties and thirties. They were impelled exclusively by their love for their country. There was wide admiration for their bravado, which was judged as irresponsible rather than as malevolently treasonable. Shaw wrote that they were young idealists who should be treated as prisoners of war. Even the former Prime Minister Asquith paid them the tribute of patriotic integrity: "They were young men; often lads. They were misled, almost unconsciously I believe, into this terrible business. They fought very bravely, and did not resort to outrage.† But it was not easy for the British to be lenient. There had been conspiracy

* Cited in Dorothy Macardle, *The Irish Republic* (New York: Farrar, Straus and Giroux, 1965), pp. 35–7.
† Macardle, *The Irish Republic*, pp. 187–8.

with a deadly enemy. The attack had come in a dreadful period, amid the sinking of millions of tons of Allied food supplies and crucial arms, the hemorrhage of blood at Verdun and the other battlefields, the costly stalemate in the war everywhere. And there had been five hundred British casualties.

The arrests ran into the thousands, including those where there was the slightest suspicion of complicity. Hundreds were sent to prison for long terms, hundreds of others packed off to internment camps. The main conspirators were tried by court-martial. Ninety-seven were condemned to death, of whom sixteen of the ringleaders were executed, a few a day. The pacing was an additional assault on overwrought emotions that exploded with each news bulletin. The executed included Pádraic Pearse, who now had his wish, "to warm the old heart of the earth" with his blood. "Do not remember my failure," he declared, "but remember this, my faith." The executed also included James Connally who, seriously wounded in the fighting, had to be carried on a stretcher to the execution point, leaving a wife and small children. And they included, of all people, Francis Skeffington, a modest, frail pacifist, an anti-vivisectionist who was rounded up as he worked with a peace patrol to prevent looting. In the last view of him, he was holding tenaciously to a lamppost, still arguing, "But, gentlemen, one further point before I go."

All these, and the others who went to death with them, now brought triumph to their failure. For, by history's ironic twist, the executions provided the turning point in the long revolutionary struggle. A group of starry-eyed unknowns became cherished martyrs, their Quixotic actions transforming resignation and impotence into a renewed national determination. Pearse was hailed as a national hero, and his words, yesterday just febrile phrases, were now read and recited with reverence. The impact on Constance Gore-Booth was typical. She was an Irish aristocrat who had married a foreign nobleman and was now the Countess Markievicz. She was imprisoned after the Easter uprising and the executions. As she carried the garbage pails up the stairs in jail, she found new meaning in what had been an aimless social round. She exulted in the prison comradeships, as she recited long passages in Italian from Dante's *Inferno,* working by the side of the gangster moll, Chicago May.

Yeats wrote:

> All changed, changed utterly:
> A terrible beauty is born.

"A terrible beauty." The phrase became the key to all that followed. He added:

O but we talked at large before
The sixteen men were shot.
But who can talk of give and take
What should be and what not,
While these dead men are loitering there,
To stir the boiling pot.*

The lovely Maud Gonne said, "What the uprising did was to ribbon with gold the rags of our life." And a British representative admitted, "I do not think that anything we do now could conciliate the Irish here. They have blood in their eyes when they look our way."

The moderates and the peacemakers were discredited. Up to the Easter week, Sinn Fein had been a minority movement. Now its dreams became an irresistible unifying force. Helena Malony said: "We felt in a very real sense we were walking with Ireland into the sun." A whole group of new militants stepped in, or rather, *marched* in, to control the planning for the future. The leader was Eamon de Valera, and he was to dominate almost all of the next half century of Irish history.

De Valera was a stern, austere nationalist, touched somewhat with a Messiah complex, rarely in a long life yielding, even slightly, once his way had been set and his principles decreed. His inflexibility was clear not only to the British in their tortuous negotiations with him, but also to the patriots who worked and fought and risked their all at his side, and on whom he did not hesitate to declare war and to fight without mercy, when they challenged him or deviated from his resolution. He could be a terribly exasperating man in his dogmatism but, like the biblical Isaiah, "clad with zeal as a cloak," he claimed that in moral issues there could be no half-measures.

His career had been a pattern of paradox. He was born in New York of a Spanish father who owned a Cuban plantation and who died when Eamon was only two years old. If Eamon's Spanish grandfather had arrived in New York on time to claim him, he might have been reared in Cuba, and become a Cuban revolutionary. But his Irish mother had completed arrangements with his Uncle Patrick to take him to Ireland for his schooling there. He evinced rare proficiency in mathematics and taught the subject in a

* W. B. Yeats, "Easter 1916."

number of Irish colleges. Before World War I he joined the more radical element of Sinn Fein and he was prominent in the Easter uprising, commanding a group of insurgents, the last to surrender. He was sentenced to death, but then it was discovered that he had been born in New York and could claim American citizenship. The British did not wish to risk further complications with the United States, where there was enormous sympathy for the cause of Irish independence. Hence, though many of his comrades-in-arms faced the firing squads, his sentence was commuted. Inside the prison he was the natural leader, and his word was also the command in the country itself for the strategy of continued revolution.

Through the remainder of the war period, Sinn Fein strengthened its hold on the loyalty and respect of the Irish nation. Its new-found political power was dramatically demonstrated in the first general election, in December 1918, immediately after the armistice. Many of the Sinn Fein leaders were in prison, a large part of the country was under martial law, the polling booths were monitored by the military, and the raids and arrests never relaxed. Yet the Sinn Feiners won every seat except two in the counties outside Ulster, and even there they won ten seats. The Unionist historian Ronald McNeill (Lord Cushendun) summarized the results of the General Election of 1918: "The general election revealed that the whole of Nationalist Ireland had gone over with foot, horse, and artillery, with bag and baggage, from the camp of so called Constitutional home rule, to the Sinn Feiners, who made no pretence that their aim was anything short of complete independent sovereignty for Ireland. . . ."*

By prearrangement, the seventy-three Sinn Fein representatives did not take their seats in the British Parliament. Those who were not in prison convened in the Dublin Mansion House in a Parliament of their own, the Dail Eireann. There, on January 21, 1919, they read out the Declaration of Independence.† At this historic session De Valera was elected President of the Irish Republic. He received the news in his prison cell. Soon after, he escaped and began a triumphant tour of the United States, winning influential encouragement and major financial support.

Prime Minister Lloyd George, the master of realism, now attempted some overtures to establish a climate of reconciliation.

---

* Ronald McNeill, *Ulster's Stand for Union* (New York: E. P. Dutton & Co., 1922), p. 4.

† Curiously enough it was read in English and in French, but not in Gaelic.

He amnestied all political prisoners. As they emerged from their jails, they were hailed as national heroes, while Dublin lit up in joyous demonstrations. But since the British offers were not accompanied by any pledge to recognize Irish independence, Sinn Fein stepped up its defiance. It called upon the Irish to refuse to recognize any British jurisdiction in the newly established Irish state, to stop paying taxes, to set up their own courts. They warned that any who cooperated in the slightest with the British would be regarded as collaborators and punished. When the British sent in new legions to enforce their authority, defiance flared into open war. The Republicans resorted to guerrilla activity and terror, and there was a wave of assassinations of public officials and members of the constabulary, most of whom were Irish. Britain, just emerging from more than four exhausting years of war, virtually every family in mourning for its dead sons, the economy dangerously shaken, now had a major uprising on its hands. It was no Easter diversion; it was the defiance of a nation, solidly united in the determination to end seven hundred years of subjection.

These were the anguished months of the Black and Tans, so named because the reinforcements sent in by the British wore makeshift black hats and khaki uniforms. The fighting was brutal and relentless on both sides. The assassinations could rarely be legally punished, since no witnesses wished, nor could be induced, to give evidence, and no jurors, even when empaneled, would dare to convict. Where arrests were made the prisoners often resorted to long hunger strikes that won international headlines, especially in the United States. One that added another hero to the martyrs' roster was Terence MacSwiney, the mayor of Cork, who died on the seventy-fourth day of his hunger strike.

The British, increasingly frustrated by the arson, the ambushes, the murders, decreed collective responsibility and reduced whole neighborhoods where it was judged that there had been connivance in the acts of terror. The Sinn Feiners responded with more daring raids and reprisals that included even military garrisons. Observers from foreign lands reported that Ireland had become an occupied country, with soldiers and military cordons everywhere. One correspondent wrote that the British could no longer govern Ireland: they could only prevent Ireland from governing itself.

Meantime, a new Home Rule bill, the Government of Ireland Act of 1920, was adopted by the British Parliament and it guaranteed autonomy to both the north and south. There was still a basic reservation in the interest of national defense; Britain was to retain control of key military bases and ports. There was also a provision that six of the nine counties of Ulster would have the option to choose any mutually agreed arrangement with the south, or to remain linked integrally with Britain. The northeast counties quickly accepted Home Rule within the framework of the British Commonwealth. On June 22, 1921, King George V, despite great personal risk, journeyed to Belfast to open the new Parliament of Northern Ireland. He used the occasion for a fervent plea to end the senseless bloodshed: "I appeal to Irishmen to pause, and to stretch out the hand of forbearance and conciliation, to forgive and forget, to join in making for the land they love, a new era of peace, contentment, and goodwill."

The appeal broke the stalemate, and negotiations were opened. De Valera, who had been a hunted fugitive with a price on his head, was prevailed upon to come to London. He was warmly received by Lloyd George, and the two Celtic statesmen, Irish and Welsh, sat down together to attempt the resolution of one of Britain's most exacerbated problems.

All the Lloyd George charm could not soften De Valera. He remained adamant in the position that nothing short of complete independence was acceptable, nor would he yield on any partition of Ireland. But the parleys did not break off and after De Valera returned to Ireland he sent back two of his most trusted deputies, Arthur Griffith and Michael Collins, to continue the discussions. For two difficult, wearying months, they also held firm. Then Lloyd George insisted that the choice had to be made: either the Free State, with all of the dignity and protection of a Dominion, or else war and, this time, total war that would mean the reconquest of the island. Collins and Griffith were convinced that this was not a bluff, that Britain had now gone as far in compromise as it would. They concluded that Ireland could build upon the substantial foundations of virtual independence while it continued to work for the final concessions later. Early in December 1921, over De Valera's angry objections, they signed the treaty with Britain, certain that they had relinquished only shadows and symbols, but had won for their country the freedom and independence that had been the dream of all the past generations. They were confident too that this judgment would be upheld by a people that was sick to death of terror and bloodshed.

[76]

The treaty loosed a new, more violent storm in Ireland, this time setting Irishman against Irishman. De Valera and the hard-line Republicans refused to accept the settlement. They held firm for a complete break with Britain and they would not consent to any partition of Ireland. The Collins-Griffith forces pleaded that the settlement provided all the substance of the nation's long-deferred hopes and that, in time, all the rest of the objectives would be attained. Griffith said that Ireland was not precluded from asking for more. It had won the freedom to achieve full freedom. "England is going beyond where she is at present. All nations are going beyond where they are at present. And, in the meantime, we can move on, in comfort and peace, to the ultimate goal." For the moment, Griffith added, he had fulfilled the dream "of getting one of England's hands off Ireland's throat, and the other out of Ireland's pocket." After the stormiest of debates, the treaty was narrowly passed in the Dail, by 64 to 57. De Valera at once resigned. In the general election that followed, the action of the Dail was much more decisively confirmed, and the new Free State came into being. The nation turned with gratitude to the unfulfilled tasks of peace.

But, as so often in history, nothing fails like success. The radical wing of the Republicans, led by De Valera, refused to accept the nation's verdict and its fury, so long directed at the British, was now redirected against the new order and its advocates. Civil war is so often more unrelenting than any other, and so it was here. The fighting of 1922 and 1923 was shocking in its ruthlessness and implacability. The state that had been conceived in violence was now baptized in blood, and the blood was all Irish. The sunny Irish nature turned tense and gloomy. V. S. Pritchett wrote: "Irish laughter is without mirth. It is a guerrilla activity of the mind."* The terror was so great that one veteran commented in grief that every Irish mother thanked God when she saw the light of morning. There was no restraint, nor even reverence, for Irish shrines. The Republicans destroyed historic old buildings with priceless records that reached back to the Middle Ages. They burned the home of Sir Horace Plunkett, who had fought and bled for the Free State, and all of his precious paintings and manuscripts. At one point the Irish Republican Army occupied the main buildings of Dublin and it took more than two months of hard fighting to dislodge them.

* *New York Review of Books*, Jan. 27, 1972, p. 4.

There were continuous forays which cut down men who had gone through all the trials of the years of British occupation. These included Michael Collins himself, perhaps the most promising of the men who were to have fashioned the Irish future. Collins was assassinated by the bullets of the men he had trained to resist the common enemy. All he could say before he died was, "Forgive them." The government forces struck back, not only to save the Free State from anarchy, but to even scores with men who had turned so savagely on their comrades-at-arms. There were three times as many executions in this fratricidal tragedy as the British had ordered during the years of their control.

At last, early in 1923, De Valera, who had again gone underground but had disavowed the acts of terror, used his influence to terminate the civil war. He determined to carry his fight forward through parliamentary forms, as the assassinated Collins and Griffith, now dead too, had pleaded for him to do. He organized a new party, the *"Fianna Fail"*—Soldiers of Destiny—whose platform included all the items that the treaty had postponed for the sake of peace.

For the ten years that followed, as Ireland slowly recovered from the wars against the British and against itself, De Valera kept up the offensive, waiting in the wings for the moment of destiny when he would be recalled as the nation's spokesman. And the moment came, in 1932, when the Fianna Fail won its mandate. After ten years in the political wilderness, the once-hunted revolutionist condemned to death, the prison escapee with a price on his head, the strategist of the civil war against the government itself, was now the officially recognized Prime Minister.

Within the framework of peace which Griffith and Collins had established, De Valera began chipping away virtually every restriction that had loomed so large in the heat of the struggle. The oath of loyalty to the British sovereign was quietly abolished. The new constitution in 1937 made no reference to King or Commonwealth. The port facilities and the military bases, which Britain had been so determined to retain for its security, were all relinquished. During World War II, Ireland remained neutral, and its ports were barred to the craft of all the belligerents, including Britain. Unobtrusively, without fanfare, Ireland became a completely independent state. All the Irish saints must have rejoiced in Heaven as Douglas Hyde, venerable scholar and founder of the Gaelic League, became the first President of Ireland under the constitution of 1937. He was joined by Eamon de Valera, as the first Prime Minister under the new constitution.

Both sides now sought every opportunity to promote better relations as time began to mellow the ancient animosities. There were trade pacts for mutual commercial benefit, and the Irish currency was tied to the British monetary system. Tourism in both directions was encouraged. When the railroad between Dublin and Belfast foundered financially, the governments cooperated to buy out its stock, and electric facilities were similarly underwritten as a partnership venture.

At least two problems remained to prevent the permanent peace both sides sought as they faced the future. The Irish Republic had hoped that some day partition would be ended, and the island would become one. But the passing years deepened the determination of Ulster to retain its close ties to Britain. It had important manufacturing interests—linens, shipping, and other valuable trade assets that made the British relationship indispensable. And it was mortally afraid of becoming part of any Irish federation, however structured, which could tax the north, heavily subsidized by Britain, for the benefit of the south.

The other problem, not at all academic, was the status of the strong Catholic enclave in the Ulster counties. The Catholics never ceased protesting that they were being treated as a depressed minority, with none of the cultural and economic autonomy that they craved. They were outraged by continuous discrimination in matters of housing, employment, and police and judicial policy.* Their resentments simmered beneath the surface, but occasionally they burst into protest and riot, as they have done down to our own day.

Long before, in one of his best-loved plays, Yeats had portrayed Countess Cathleen, the traditional symbol of Ireland, who wandered into an Irish village in the guise of a poor old woman. She expressed the hope that some day, with the help of good friends, the strangers would be put out of her house. As the play ends, one of the villagers is asked if he saw an old woman going down the path. "I did not," he replied, "but I saw a young girl, and she had the walk of a queen."†

---

* Report of the Cameron Commission, on "Disturbances in Northern Ireland," appointed by the Governor of Northern Ireland, September, 1969.

† W. B. Yeats, *Cathleen ni Houlihan.*

8

THE AGONY OF FRANCE

THE STABILITY OF THE NEW EUROPE THAT EMERGED FROM WORLD War I depended on the strength of the democratic tripod—the United States, Great Britain, and France—the victors who were committed to protect the treaty settlements and to compel adherence to their provisions. But it turned out that the tripod was too wobbly for sustained support, and later there was no tripod at all. The United States receded into isolationism, repudiated the League, and refused to join the Allies in signing a treaty with Germany. Britain, impoverished by the war, no longer had the resources to support a great power role. It steadily detached itself from continental involvements, even to the point of seeking rapprochement with Germany, if only to extricate itself from expensive military commitments. France was even more seriously crippled by the war than Britain, and the responsibilities for the enforcement of the treaty provisions that it undertook became too burdensome to bear. It had no effective enforcement reserve, and its authority was continually challenged by the enemy who only yesterday had been so decisively defeated. It was ironic that the two powerful European democracies which had won such stunning victories, resulting in unconditional surrender, should so soon be faced with problems of actual survival.

To understand the tragic dilemma of France between the wars, it must first be stressed how narrowly it escaped complete disaster. It had been almost eliminated as a military factor in the first weeks of the German sweep to the outskirts of Paris, and was saved only by the miracle of the Battle of the Marne. The territory that had been conquered by the Germans represented only a small part of the country, but it was the highly industrialized sector, and it fed a substantial part of the economy. It contained 80 percent of the iron ore and 70 percent of the coal. Four thousand municipalities had been occupied by the Germans, and most of the others had been despoiled. Agriculture had been stripped by systematic expropriation of the livestock. Transportation was in chaos. Two million men, the youngest, the most vigorous, the ablest, had been killed or wounded, and many more millions had been drawn from peaceful pursuits and normal family life. There was not a single survivor in the 1914 class of St. Cyr, the French West Point. Fifteen years after the peace treaties, one could still see in the Paris subways the seats especially reserved for wounded veterans. During the war, there were 1,400,000 more civilian deaths than births, in a country where the falling birth rate was already a deep source of anxiety. In 1911, females outnumbered males by 2 percent; in 1920, the disproportion was 15 percent. All of these problems were compounded by the forfeit of French markets during the war. Other countries had seized the opportunity to take over what had been cherished French monopolies. A cartoon in *The New Yorker* portrayed two American women inspecting a bottle of wine. One asked the other: "Do the French *also* make Burgundy?"

It was virtually an obsession then, in the first years after the war, to anchor down security. Though the Germans had been decisively beaten, their country had escaped invasion and they had remarkable recuperative capacity. Their industrial plant had not been damaged, their population was much more numerous and steadily increasing. But sonorous words about reconciliation and the olive branch, treaties not backed by ironclad guarantees, were no safeguard; the remembrance was keen that there had been two German invasions in the span of a lifetime. Clemenceau was exasperatingly obdurate during the peace negotiations because he distrusted the assurances of diplomats. Even if their pledges were made in good faith, were they not subject to the vagaries of politics and would they later be in power?

The pressure was therefore unremitting for Germany to meet the reparations that had been imposed. The German leaders twisted and squirmed, and found every reason for avoiding fulfillment. The reparations, they argued, were astronomical, unrealistic, they lamed the German capacity for recovery, and if recovery were thwarted, how could there be any payments at all? Britain supported their case and scolded the French for their implacability and their unworthy passion for vengeance. The French leaders noted sarcastically that Britain was striking virtuous poses of compassion, but only after its own reparations had been collected in full. It had taken over all the German colonies, had destroyed the German navy and its threat to British seapower, and had confiscated all German holdings held abroad. Britain was safe. All France got was the return of its own Alsace-Lorraine, and the satisfaction of removing the mourning draperies from the statue of Strasbourg in the Place de la Concorde.

From the United States too came scathing criticism that France was jeopardizing the return to peace by its rapacity. The French interpreted the infuriating nobility of the Americans to mean the application of an old Roman adage: "Spare the conquered, and humble the proud." They suggested that the principle of bygones be bygones ought to be adhered to by all, and not just by France with its two million dead and wounded. "Let the United States forego payments on the war debts," they said, "and France could then afford to forego its reparations." President Coolidge bristled, "They hired the money, didn't they?" The French responded, "They did the damage, didn't they? The cost will have to come out of somebody's pocket; why should it be out of the pocket of the victim?" Winston Churchill provided the summary: "France is left to lick her wounds, and to mourn her dead." Each French government, then, wrestled with the problem of reparations. It was not a political abstraction that had little relevance for the average citizen. Reparations were essential to supplement taxes, else there would be serious encroachment upon living standards. The devastated areas had to be rebuilt, the plant that was destroyed had to be renovated, war debts had to be paid, compensation to the widows and the veterans had to be disbursed.

When the Germans defaulted in 1923 on the delivery of timber and coal, the French and the Belgians, against the advice of the British and the Americans, marched their troops into the Ruhr to operate the mines and obtain their reparations directly. When the Germans resorted to passive resistance, the French made wholesale arrests and there were retributive executions. The impasse lasted two years, with intensified bitterness all around, neither the French nor the Germans harvesting anything but nettles. The British and the Americans continued to express condemnations from the sidelines.

The problem of reparations was complicated by the rigidity of the French tax structure. It was hopelessly antiquated, but those who profited most from its creaky operation fought strenuously against any reform, even in wartime. The peasants virtually escaped taxation; the rates had been set in the Napoleonic period and there had been no reassessments since, though land values had risen sensationally. Normandy had been a long barren stretch: by the twentieth century it had become one of the nation's richest agricultural areas, but there had been no revision of the tax base. Corporations and the wealthy families usually found avenues of tax avoidance. The successive governments therefore had no alternative but to keep raising taxes on consumable goods and this struck hardest at the urban worker and the salaried middle classes.

Because German reparations came with such disappointing slowness and in such niggardly volume, the heavy costs of reconstruction had to be drawn from the French treasury itself. The military budget kept mounting, since France could not dare to economize on defense. The Ruhr invasion further jeopardized solvency, for the resistance to it, though passive, made the costs of occupation prohibitive. There was then the usual resort to the printing presses, and with few assets to guarantee the currency, the franc was soon in a losing struggle to survive. Before the war it had been worth twenty cents to the dollar. It declined steadily until it struck bottom, at two cents, a loss of 90 percent in value. The ensuing crisis became so dangerous that Raymond Poincaré, the tough, firm wartime President of France, was called back to head a national coalition cabinet that included six former premiers. His surgery was drastic and the franc was established at 3.9 cents, but this represented only 20 percent of its prewar value, with the most serious consequences for the thrifty middle-class families who watched with anguish the attenuation of their life savings. Social changes often create a *nouveau riche* class, with the ugly characteristics of ostentatious vulgarity. The crisis in France created a *nouveaux pauvres*, frightened, resentful, with their faith in the democratic system undermined.

To cope with all of these problems—security, German intransigence, the strains among the Allies, the decline of the franc—would have been difficult enough in a strong and well-balanced political system. But national government in France, with its proportional representation and its multitude of splinter parties, seemed to be structured to guarantee political bedlam. Every government had to be a delicately balanced coalition. Between 1875, when the Republic was established by the margin of one vote, and 1920, there had been fifty-nine ministries; and from 1920 until 1939, even with the continuous threat of war, there were another forty-one. In some years the government changed six or seven times. In such a system there could be neither stability nor consistency. It took the adroitness of the tightrope walker or the bullfighter to survive politically in the frenetic politics of the 1920's and 1930's. The game of shuffle, feint, and dodge was fascinating for tourists and foreign observers but the cost came out of the living standards of the French people.

In the immediate postwar period, leadership had been entrusted to Georges Clemenceau, already past eighty but as durable as the Arc de Triomphe. He was trained as a physician but early turned his caustic style and fierce energies to politics, by way of journalism. He had lived through the Franco-Prussian War of 1870 and had seen the Germans invade his country and take the French capital. He had been the only deputy then who had refused to ratify the dictated German treaty. In the years that followed, he had been outraged by the sterile feuding of French politics. When he was credited with leadership in overthrowing nineteen cabinets, he barked, "Nineteen? No. Only one. They were all the same!" He was seventy-six when he became Premier in 1917, in the darkest period of the war. He became a hero to the soldiers in the trenches, where he appeared frequently among them to cheer them on in his crushed felt hat, with his drooping mustache, his racy, bawdy, biting humor, and his complete fearlessness. His appeal gave Winston Churchill a text in the travail that Britain faced in World War II: "I will fight before Paris, I will fight in Paris, I will fight behind Paris. . . . The Germans may take Paris, but that will not prevent me from going on with the war. We will fight on the Loire, we will fight on the Garonne, we will fight even on the Pyrenees. And if at last we are driven off the Pyrenees, we will continue the war at sea."* Clemenceau could not be moved at Versailles as he doggedly held out for a peace that would be protected by more than a dreamy collective security. He had seemed vengeful and implacable to Wilson and Lloyd George; but he had insisted on ironclad guarantees because he knew the Germans well and dreaded a resurgence of their power.

Yet in the grim postwar years even the Old Tiger's toughness was not considered tough enough, and he was criticized as "soft" in the

---

* Cited in Hampden Jackson, *Clemenceau and the Third Republic* (London: Hodder & Stoughton for the English Universities Press, 1948), p. 179.

Blue Horizon Chamber, which received its name from the uniforms of the many veterans who had been elected to it. Forced to the wall by Wilson and Lloyd George at the Peace Conference, Clemenceau had made a few concessions. These had been violently opposed by the commanding general, Marshal Foch, who insisted on the outright annexation of the Rhineland, and the dispute degenerated into an ugly vendetta. The Chamber now turned on Clemenceau for "coddling the hated Germans." During the war he had been affectionately dubbed *"Père la Victoire"*—"Papa Victory." Now, as disillusionment with the peace deepened, he became *"Perdre la Victoire"* —"Lost Victory." When the presidency was to be assigned, the Chamber denied him the final honor that he coveted to climax his long career.* His sunset years were filled with recrimination as Foch and he traded insults. General Tasker Bliss, one of the American representatives at the Versailles Peace Conference, remembering the role that each had played in the war period, wrote sadly: "It is as if Homer had left Achilles and old Nestor, after all the glorious memories of their association in the war of Troy, in the hero-haunted Asphodel Meadow of the Elysian Plain, forever snarling at each other in childish, unreasoning hate."†

Repudiating Clemenceau, the Chamber turned instead to another long-time political adversary, Raymond Poincaré, and gave him the onerous assignment to deal with the obstreperous Germans and to compel them to take seriously the reparations commitment. Poincaré countered the German resistance by sanctioning the occupation of the Ruhr and transferring the control of its mines and industries to French officials. This drastic action precipitated long months of German sabotage and violence, and compelled reprisal executions and almost open warfare.

Poincaré was heartily denounced by the British and the other Allies, who accused him of needlessly exacerbating the international situation by his punitive harshness. An Italian diplomat raged: "Even when Poincaré catches the right train, he misses the right station." There was no doubt however that Poincaré was reflecting the mood of his people, who would brook no concessions to the Germans so that the burden of crushing taxation could be amelio-

---

* At the height of his power, Clemenceau had derided the presidency as being mainly vestigial. "There are two useless organs," he said, "the prostate and the presidency of the Republic." The jibe, however, may have been evoked by his detestation of Poincaré, who held the post.

† Cited in Armstrong, *Peace and Counterpeace*, p. 205.

rated. In one of the Chamber debates, a leftist deputy had cried, "The rich must be made to pay." A rightist Deputy shouted, "No, the Germans must be made to pay." Poincaré's Finance Minister satisfied both by his statement: "It is not the rich who shall pay first. It is the enemy."

But by 1926, after years of bickering, the frustrated antagonists reached the conclusion that they must try other methods to adjust to the times. The French had gone as far as they could with threat and pressure and force. The Germans had exhausted the effectiveness of sabotage and boycott. Both sides, chastened by the futility of continuous confrontation, accepted the conciliatory statesmanship of new leaders. France tried to rise above victory; Germany tried to rise above defeat.

The call went out to Aristide Briand, one of France's most experienced statesmen, who had been in and out of office for twenty-five years and had thoroughly mastered the mediator's art. Early in his career he had been a Socialist, but had later turned conservative. Party labels meant little to him. His unfailing concern was to find a political solution for problems that seemed insoluble to the doctrinaires who resorted, with fine French logic, to dogma and principle. He had been eleven times Premier, a perennial in the succession of cabinets in France. He was a polished debater, supple in discussion, fuzzy when ambiguities would best serve his ends, but clear and lucid when decisions had to be reached. Clemenceau said, "Poincaré knows everything and understands nothing; Briand knows nothing, and he understands everything."

In 1925, he was assigned the Foreign Office, and he dominated foreign policy during the next four critical years. Hopes were high that the passions and resentments of World War I could now be muted and Briand's intuitions were welcomed for the period of experimental conciliation. He cooperated fully with his German counterpart, Gustav Stresemann, and a warm personal friendship developed. Together they piloted the Locarno agreement, which attempted to ease the tensions that prevented the convalescence of Europe, and they shared the Nobel Peace Prize in 1926.*

After Stresemann's untimely death in 1929 one of his statements, made in banter to the former Crown Prince, became public. It implied that in his negotiations with Briand, he had used the technique of "finesieren." The word had many nuances. It could mean

_____
* See Chapter 4.

that he had used finesse, the approach of subtlety, and this was of course most appropriate in a period when sensitive diplomacy was essential. But it also carried the connotation of deceit, used, as Bismarck had often done, to boast of his cynical realism. It was seized upon by those who had been suspicious all along that Stresemann had been leading Briand on, making agreements with no intention of honoring them, fighting for time until Germany, released from the restraints of the Versailles treaty, would be prepared to challenge France. The revelation reawakened the fears that were always beneath the surface of French reactions to Germany. They cost Briand the presidency in 1931, a reward that he fully expected after thirty years of faithful service to France. He too suffered the fate of Wilson and Clemenceau, and his last days were lived in political eclipse, ruminating on a people's ingratitude "sharper than a serpent's tooth."

But the change in French political and social life in 1929, when the storm clouds had become an ominous thunderhead, was due to more than the outrage over Stresemann's alleged deceptions, or even to disenchantment with the results of Locarno. A universal depression, set off by the stock market crash in Wall Street, shook the national economies in many parts of the world. The threat of disaster did not immediately affect the French; indeed, 1930 was still a fairly prosperous year. But when the storm reached France it had gathered powerful momentum and the shock was stunning. As unemployment grew, the workers demanded their promised social welfare benefits, but the business world, with no profits in sight, refused to cooperate. André Siegfried's judgment summarized the impasse: "The heart of the French bourgeoisie is on the left, but his pocket book is on the right." The class struggle, always latent, was once again overt. Right and left extremists were drawn into direct action, and the country was convulsed by strikes and lockouts and the riots they precipitated.

In such an atmosphere it was inevitable that the smallest spark would set off dangerous revolutionary activity. The spark was supplied by the Stavisky scandals of 1934, and they nearly destroyed the Republic. Serge Stavisky was a smooth, debonair crook who, for years, had been involved in devious transactions. His shady financing, always with the come-on of fabulous profits, finally caught up with him in December 1933, when a fraudulent bond issue was exposed and he either committed suicide or was murdered to prevent him from talking. Investigation revealed that his knavery had involved many members of the Chamber of Deputies who had accepted favors offered to gain their cooperation. The public prosecutor had done almost nothing to protect the investors, and, since he was a brother-in-law of the Premier, the episode burgeoned into a national scandal. The rightist groups had been waiting for an issue that would discredit the democratic structure, and here they struck pay dirt. The strong Fascist group, led by a decorated army officer, Colonel de la Rocque, had behind him not only the Croix de Feu, which had begun as a veterans' organization and had turned into a Fascist private army, but also the support of leading industrialists, who had longstanding scores to settle with the liberals and the leftists. Money poured into the coffers of the Croix de Feu from the cosmetics king, François Coty, and from Eugène Schneider, the munitions tycoon. When a monster demonstration, sponsored by de la Rocque and the Fascists, took place on February 6, 1934, and led to major riots, the leaders of the Republic were genuinely frightened. Hitler had already come to supreme power in Germany, and Mussolini was at the peak of his prestige in Italy. There were Fascist dictatorships up and down the Balkans, and in Poland. France too was now perilously close to a Fascist coup.

In this crisis the main parties of the center and the left closed ranks. They had at last learned the tragic lesson of other lands where, in the face of the Fascist peril, the opposing forces continued to fight each other. Now a Popular Front was organized and it was joined even by the Communists. Its power was demonstrated when six hundred thousand aroused citizens gathered on Bastille Day, 1935, at the site of the old Bastille, to pledge, as they sang the *"Marseillaise"* and the *"Internationale"*: "We solemnly swear to remain united, in order to disarm and dissolve the Fascist leagues, and to defend and develop democratic liberties." Polarization was complete. The election of 1936 was fought with showdown ferocity, the leftist groups being determined to prevent the establishment of a Fascist state in France.

The leader of the Popular Front was Léon Blum, a fastidious intellectual, a strange symbol for a proletarian mass movement. Daudet, the critic-novelist, called him the revolutionary with the pearl-gray gloves. His career marked the last stand of democratic France before it was desolated by the Nazi conquest.

Léon Blum came from an old Alsatian Jewish family, the son of a silk ribbon manufacturer. His reputation as a Croesus sans-culotte was very much exaggerated. The family business gave the children moderate comfort and the advantage of an excellent education. The chief influences on young Blum were a firebrand grandmother, blind for most of her life, who owned a little bookstore where she harangued her customers on current social issues; and a self-denying mother who, according to her adoring son, used to slice up the apples she gave her children so that they would all have equal shares. Blum was a brilliant student, specializing in philosophy and law, rising in the courts to the highest judicial post. He was primarily interested, early in his career, in belles-lettres, and he wrote Latin verse, scholarly reviews, and several critically acclaimed volumes, including two on Stendhal and Goethe. He was a literary man about town, enjoying the friendship of such titans as Anatole France, André Gide, and Paul Valéry. But he was no drawing-room dandy. His skill as a fencer, with wrists of steel, earned him great respect, and his writings were not soft or fluffy. He could trade hard blows, even when their force was encased in immaculate French prose.

He was drawn to politics by the Dreyfus case which convulsed France in the 1890's. It involved a Jewish army officer who was accused of selling military secrets to the Germans. The case reeked of anti-Semitism and it united the reactionary forces in the army, the church, and the entrenched aristocracy. The defense won the support of Émile Zola, Anatole France, and other liberals to whom the prosecution represented not merely the fate of a man but a renewed assault on Republican France. The vindication of Dreyfus tempered and revitalized the republican commitment. Blum was part of the Dreyfus battle, along with the towering Socialist leader, Jean Jaurès, who became his mentor. Together, they organized the Socialist *L'Humanité,* whose daily editorials came from the gifted pen of Blum. When the paper was acquired by the Communists, Blum began editing *Le Populaire,* which became the influential voice of French socialism. When Jaurès was assassinated on the eve of World War I, Blum moved directly into politics to fulfill the unfinished mission of his chief.

He held no office all through the war period and in the immediate years that followed, but he was the most eloquent interpreter of democratic socialism in France, and throughout western Europe. He was especially effective in negotiations with labor leaders, although it was astonishing that this could be, for he was the scholar in the midst of tub thumpers, the man of letters in the hurly-burly of the market place. When he met Anthony Eden on a diplomatic mission, the conversation lagged until the discussion turned on Proust, and then both men relaxed and were able to reach each other. On the hustings, Blum's voice was soft, his style completely devoid of any of the attention-arresting tricks of the party hacks; but after the first few moments he could hold his audience completely. They were fascinated by the lucidity of the argument and the beauty and relevance of his expression. John Gunther wrote, after an interview: "Blum had no shoulders, only antennae. The antennae brought sure and direct understanding." This was the reason that Blum could continuously represent the peasants and miners of Norbonne who made up the main segments of his southeast France constituency. It was Blum, then, who conducted the negotiations to create the Popular Front, working patiently with unions and middle-class leaders, intellectuals and professional men, and the ever-suspicious bosses of the Communist Party.

In the election of 1936, in which the stakes were so high, the rightists concentrated for target on Blum, his Jewish race, and his collaboration with the Communists. Charles Maurras, the leader of the French Fascists, never stopped attacking "this naturalized German Jew, or son of one, this monster of the democratic republic." A front-page editorial, before the election, raged: "He is a man who must be shot, but in the back." Some hatchet men responded to the call. They dragged Blum from his car and left him for dead, an artery in his neck severed by a license plate. He fought back to health, carrying on the campaign and directing its strategy from his hospital bed. Since all the anti-Fascist elements were now thoroughly alerted to their peril, the electoral response was massive and the Popular Front won decisively. Léon Blum took office as the first Socialist Premier of France.

Since he was also the first Jewish Premier, many of his political opponents were unwilling for him to take office without insult. The rightist deputy, Xavier Vallat, rose in the Chamber to decry the misfortunes of a Christian, Gallic, peasant state, with deep-set traditions, headed now by a man so alien. "To govern this peasant nation of France it is better to have someone whose origins, no matter how modest, spring from our soil than to have a subtle Talmudist."* The Chamber responded as a body to repudiate Vallat. The venerable Édouard Herriot, as presiding officer, insisted upon making the reply himself, appealing to the political opponents of the Popular

* Joel Colton, *Léon Blum* (New York: Alfred A. Knopf, 1966), p. 144.

Front, in a time of peril, not to repeat the tragedies of the Dreyfus case. "Now is not the chosen moment," he said, "when so many evils menace France, to divide Frenchmen."

It was indeed a dangerous moment. When Blum took office the country was paralyzed by a general strike, complicated by the first of the sit-ins, with virtually all activities suspended, transportation, communications, public services. At its peak, the strike idled more than a million workers.* Blum moved into negotiation at once, and after ten frantic, wearying days and nights, he had the workers back in their jobs. At a victory celebration the Minister of Interior, Roger Salengro, voiced the gratification of the government: "Not a machine has been broken, not a drop of blood has been spilled," although the country had gone through "the most formidable social upheaval that the Republic had ever known."†

The first ten weeks of Blum's incumbency rivaled the Hundred Days of Franklin Roosevelt's American New Deal in the speed and the thoroughness of the legislation that was passed and became operative. It included guaranteed collective bargaining and the forty-hour week, and the whole battery of fringe benefits that were part of a new labor charter. Private armies of the totalitarian groups were dissolved; the Bank of France, the symbol of financial control by two hundred French families, was democratized in its management. For the first time in French history, women were named to head up ministries. It was said that the best three men in the Blum cabinet were Irène, Cécile, and Suzanne.

How well France might have fared if the Blum program of reforms could have continued to remake the life of the country becomes purely speculative; the Popular Front had little opportunity to consolidate the social gains of the decade. Considerations of social welfare had to give way to military preparation, for Hitler and Mussolini were now well launched on their blackmail binge. The political divisions in France were serious enough to threaten national security. The reactionaries had more in common with German Nazis than they had with French leftists. Paul Reynaud noted with despair that patriotism had become conditional: one would fight for one's country, provided it were not under a leftist government. The dictators counted on such internecine warfare and they took fullest

---

* Someone put a sign by the Seine River that since the lifeguards too were on strike, it was positively forbidden to attempt suicide.

† Colton, *Léon Blum,* p. 155.

advantage of it. Hitler defiantly tore up the Treaty of Versailles. There could be no precautionary action since the British government was in the grip of appeasement and Chamberlain warned Blum that France could expect no assistance if "aggressive" diplomacy should lead to war. In June 1937, Blum's government fell and the great social experiments of the Popular Front were frozen. The events of 1938 and 1939 accelerated the steady retreat of the democracies in the face of the military boldness of the Fascists. Churchill's passionate protest was prophetic. He denounced the appeasement governments of Britain and France who had the choice between war and shame. "They chose shame, and they will get war too."

9

LENIN AND THE RUSSIAN REVOLUTION

THERE WERE MANY UNANTICIPATED CONSEQUENCES BROUGHT ABOUT BY World War I, among them the destruction of four empires, the emergence of the United States and Japan as world powers, the loosening of colonial ties on all continents. But perhaps no consequence was as momentous and as little foreseen as the triumph of the Communists in czarist Russia. The achievement defies credulity, for it is the story of a small, tightly disciplined group numbering, in 1917, a bare twenty thousand in a population of one hundred and forty million, that was able to take advantage of the complete chaos of war to seize control, to ward off enemies within and without, and to establish one of the most formidable concentrations of power in history. Though there was a body of Communist doctrine, a compendium of Marxian principles, and a planned technique, these were only occasionally followed. Indeed, Karl Marx expected the revolution to begin in a highly industrialized society such as Germany's. Instead, it began in a peasant economy, one of the most backward in Europe. It came with such stunning suddenness that Lenin, the architect of the revolution, was nowhere near Russia when the red flags went up. It was continuously wracked by inner purge as the leaders challenged each other. Yesterday's allies could be today's enemies. Yesterday's law could be today's treason. Very few who participated in the original revolution died in their beds. Sooner or later they were executed as traitors, or were murdered as enemies by the comrades who succeeded them.

Yet with all the violence and fear that were loosed by suspicion and subversion, the revolution succeeded in reorganizing the vast reaches of Russia, transforming its peasant economy, building a mighty new industrial base, destroying its long-dominant religious institutions, reorienting education, and accomplishing all of this in the midst of foreign and civil war, and of international isolation.

For more than half a century scholars, strategists, and officers of state have sought to understand the phenomenon. Even with the benefits of hindsight, there is wide divergence in judgment. Yet three factors are usually agreed upon in all interpretations. There was, first, the complete disintegration of authority in Russia during the calamitous defeats of World War I. This laid bare the fatal vulnerability of the czarist regime and opened the opportunity for the well-organized Communist group to appeal to the exploited and the dispossessed. Then because czarist Russia was dictatorially organized, with no lines of communication by which to channel grievances to the seats of authority, relief and redress could be expected only through active conspiracy. Finally, when the historic moment required a catalyst to speed up the chemistry of revolution, the man of destiny, Lenin, was there.

It was the war that exposed the creaking ineptness of the Russian government and the corruption and inefficiency of its leadership. Millions of men had been conscripted to fight, fifteen million by 1917, and the casualties among them became a national hemorrhage. If they had died or were wounded in a cause that called for such sacrifice, there would still have been a dangerous attrition of morale. But to be siphoned out of family life for a cause that was not understood or that was deeply resented, to be maimed or to succumb because of the bungling and the failures in managing supplies and munitions, the graft in the commissary, the quarreling among officers and bureaucrats, such criminal callousness could not be further borne or tolerated.

But what more could have been expected? The symbol of the majesty of Russia was Czar Nicholas II, upon whom weighed awesome responsibility, and who responded with tragic incompetence. Lenin said of him that he lacked insides. The threat of death was always in his thoughts. He never forgot the scene at the bedside of his grandfather, Alexander II, who had been fatally wounded by a terrorist bomb. There were nine Romanoffs in the room for the farewell, and all of them were to die by assassination or execution. Nicholas was married to Alexandra, a granddaughter of Queen Victoria. Though the Czarina was sickly, superstitious, and a victim of quacks and astrologers, she dominated Nicholas completely. The heir to the throne, Alexis, was condemned by hemophilia to continuing illness, and the royal parents, blaming themselves for transmitting such suffering, sought refuge in the hocus-pocus of mysticism. This was how Rasputin, one of the most sinister charlatans of the day, came into their lives. That such a man could attain ascendancy in the royal household and in the political structure demonstrated how far the dry rot had corrupted the government.

Rasputin came out of a Siberian village in the role of *starets*, quite common in the tradition of Russia, the wandering fakir who preyed on the credulity of the ignorant and the desperate. He had no formal education, no disciplined training for anything. He was unkempt, unwashed, and his long black beard was usually scraggly and dirty. He had abandoned a wife and children and elevated rakishness into a gospel. Much of his boorishness, his studied impudence, his contempt for the amenities, was part of the act of the confidence man in every land, who courted the masses with their just-plain-folks routine.

He tried his nostrums on little Alexis and, luckily, brought him out of one of his crises. The Czarina was ecstatic. Clearly Rasputin was "the humble man of God," "the Christ returned to earth," who had been sent to save her child. She confided in him and some of her messages to him carried Freudian overtones that were unmistakable. "I kiss your hands and lean my head on your blessed shoulder." "I only wish one thing: to fall asleep, to fall asleep forever, on your shoulders and in your arms."*

It soon became impossible for the top officials in state and church to conduct their affairs without clearance through Rasputin. Peter Stolypin, one of the few competent Prime Ministers, ordered him out. Rasputin saw death in the tea leaves and so forecast. Stolypin was dismissed and then murdered. The Czarina's confessor complained that Rasputin was a charlatan. The good father was promptly banished. In September 1915, with the war going disastrously against Russia, the Czar left for the front to be with his men, and the power of decision passed to his half-demented wife and to Rasputin, who dominated her completely.

As the military losses mounted, tens of thousands of the soldiers in rebellion against the war deserted. They wandered around the

---

* R. K. Massie, *Nicholas and Alexandra* (New York: Atheneum, 1967), p. 199.

country, afraid to return home for fear of arrest and court-martial. A military expert reported, "The largest army ever mobilized had become an enormous, exhausted, badly clothed, badly fed, embittered mob." In this crisis, Rasputin brought in as Prime Minister one Boris Stürmer, a shocking choice, for his whole background bespoke criminality.

Some of the more responsible members of the government decided to take matters into their own hands. In December 1916, when the war could not go worse, they arranged a murder and carried it out, as Trotsky wrote, "in the manner of a moving picture scenario designed for people of bad taste."* One of the princes invited Rasputin to his home. There he was served some heavily dosed poison cakes. He went through all of them with no apparent effect. He was then served Madeira wine, thoroughly saturated with potassium cyanide, and the Prince played the guitar, waiting for the poison to do its work. It made Rasputin a little more sleepy. He was then shot half a dozen times and, when even this treatment did not kill him, he was stabbed repeatedly with a steel drill. His body was dragged into a car and dumped in a river. But when it came up again he was still alive, and with weights attached, he was again submerged. At last he was dead, out of the government and out of the war. This amalgam of Richard III and Cesare Borgia could well symbolize the incubus that had fastened itself on the body of Russia. The blows that rained upon it could not, for long, shake it off. When it was at last dislodged, the body of Russia was bruised and broken and in collapse, a ready victim for a determined power group.

A second factor that played into Communist hands was the absence of effective communication for protest and the orderly disposition of grievance. The czarist government was not even a clearly defined despotism; it was a cabal. Churchill defined it as "autocracy, tempered by assassination." In the earlier czarist days, poverty and misery were borne more or less submissively. But in the new century advancing industrialization created concentrations of hostile and resentful workers in the cities. Since there were no strong, responsible unions for dialogue and negotiation, violence was virtually the only outlet for redress. In 1905, there was an uprising and the Czar reluctantly consented to the creation of a Duma and some token parliamentary institutions. Stolypin, very much influenced by western example, was eager to modernize the government and he initiated some modest

* Leon Trotsky, *The History of the Russian Revolution* (New York: Simon & Schuster, 1937), p. 74.

land reforms that would encourage the peasants to retain their faith in the Little Father. But Rasputin's enmity thwarted Stolypin at every turn, and then, when the Prime Minister was murdered, all hope for reform ended. At the outset of World War I, Russia was as much a police state as ever and an inevitable target for revolution, when the central government was paralyzed by military disaster.

At this historic juncture point came Lenin. In the light of his decisive influence, it is startling to remember that his whole public career as dictator in Russia ran for only five years. He came to power in 1917, and was laid low by a stroke in 1922. He lingered for two more years, but he could no longer command events. Until his accession to power, he had been in exile, a hunted revolutionist, living underground, endlessly matching wits with the police in many lands. After 1922 he was an invalid, watching with concern the developing deadly rivalry among those who strove for his mantle. In between were five years, brief years, but Lenin charged them with such demonic force that neither his country nor the world were thereafter the same.

Lenin was born in 1870, in Simbirsk, on the Volga, the son of an upper-middle-class family. His father was a provincial school superintendent, his mother the daughter of a doctor. Lenin, a gifted student, took fullest advantage of the opportunities in school and gymnasia. But his older brother, Alexander, was early drawn into student conspiracies against the government and he was convicted and hanged. The tragedy drove Lenin into undying hostility, not only against the Czar and his minions but against the whole contemporary social system. He enrolled in the law school in Kazan where his renewed involvement in revolutionary activity resulted in his expulsion. But he was later permitted to take the bar examination, which he passed in 1891. He practiced aimlessly for eighteen months, winning only one case. He was clearly not meant for the law, and with his jaundiced view of society, wanted no part of it. By now he was deep in the classics of Marx, Engels, and Plekhanov. He had very little in common with Michael Bakunin, one of the leaders of anarchism, but he fully shared his credo of self-abnegation: "The Revolutionist is a doomed man. He has no private interests, no affairs, sentiments, ties, properties, not even a name of his own. . . . His nature excludes all romance, all tenderness, all ecstasy, all love."

In 1892, when Lenin was twenty-two, famine engulfed his native province. It was characteristic of his thinking by now, and an insight to the Communist approach, that he denounced both the relief that was rushed in to alleviate the distress and those who offered the help. To him famine was the bastard child of an iniquitous system. Only when the social order was completely destroyed would such plagues as famines be eliminated. He therefore welcomed the famine in the belief that it would create such chaos that the revolutionary passion would destroy the social order which was the root cause.* In the light of Lenin's reasoning it is easier to understand why Communists and Fascists so often teamed up in their attacks on the moderates and the liberals. Each was primarily interested, not in reform, but in creating enough disorder to overturn the established government. The Communists fought the democratic Socialists more relentlessly than they fought the reactionaries. Amelioration staved off revolution which alone, Lenin insisted, could bring permanent solutions. At twenty-two, in these reactions, the authentic revolutionist had emerged.

By 1893, he was leading the full-fledged conspiratorial life, constantly on the move. His letters and articles were filled with technical advice on bomb making in the home, the uses of invisible ink, the techniques of street fighting. He was often arrested, and in 1897 was banished to Siberia, which was now a kind of university for the revolutionists. In the permissive tradition of czarist prison life, he had many opportunities for reading and writing. Nadya Krupskaya, whom he had met during his wandering days and married, followed him into exile, even as she shared all of his experiences.

When he was released, he began the long shadow life in Europe, shuttling from city to city, his main occupation the editing of *Iskra* —"the Spark"—whose onionskin sheets were smuggled across frontiers to spread the Communist doctrine. In 1902, he was working at the British Museum where, some decades before, Karl Marx had done the research for *Das Kapital*. At this stage Lenin was part of that strange internationale of alienated intellectuals, declassed, uprooted, at home nowhere.

On the eve of the revolution of 1905, Lenin was thirty-four, quite insignificant in appearance, short, dumpy, bald, shabbily dressed, no orator and with no pretense at being one. But his mind was sharp and though his addresses were unadorned, they were clear and decisive. Maxim Gorki said that his words always brought to mind the cold glitter of steel shavings. By his firmness of will, he commanded

---

* Cited in David Shub, *Lenin* (Garden City, N.Y.: Doubleday, 1948), p. 25.

the loyalties of the small but compactly organized Communists who responded to his sense of mission.*

The 1905 revolution brought in a Duma and a moderate, middle-class reform group eager to follow the western parliamentary model. Lenin treated the development as a fraud. He hoped that the czarist government would continue its resistance, so that despair could lead to revolt. His wish was partly fulfilled for, within a year, the Czar reneged on his promises, curtailed the Duma's hard-won concessions, and began a systematic harassment of the reformers. Lenin fled with many others who were on the blacklist, and the next tormented years, until 1917, were again given to underground life, with no dignity, no peace, in a movement whose adherents were regarded and treated as lepers.

How did such a group subsist? Even in the shabbiest underground, they required support to survive, to finance propaganda, to mount their terror. They went to every extreme, including stealing from the society that they hated, robbing banks, holding up trains. One of the most skillful of these bank robbers, using the bomb and strong-arm methods, came to Lenin's attention in 1907, and a friendship was forged that, by 1912, encouraged Lenin to bring him into the Central Committee. He went then by the alias of Koba; he was to be known in later history as Stalin. The more moderate Socialist parties were aghast at the defiant violence of the Bolsheviks and the evil name that they were fastening on the Socialist and Labor parties. Lenin spat on their embarrassment. In paying tribute to a comrade who had repudiated every conventional virtue, he wrote: "A Central Committee, to be effective, must be made up of gifted writers, able organizers, and a few intelligent scoundrels. I commend Comrade Victor and admire his total disregard of the bourgeois prejudices of honor and truth."†

World War I created exactly the conditions for which the rebel groups had waited. No longer was there any question of petty tinkering or of moderate reform. Fifteen million men, a substantial part of the country's working force, had been uprooted and despatched to

---

* In contrast with Stalin and virtually all the dictators of his generation, Lenin hated flattery and eulogy. On one of his birthdays he refused to come in time for the testimonial salutes. When he arrived he thanked his comrades for their greetings but, even more, for excusing him from listening to the anniversary speeches. His hostility to adulation is discussed in R. A. Medvedev, *Let History Judge* (New York: Alfred A. Knopf, 1971), pp. 149 ff.

† Cited in Howe, *A World History of Our Own Times*, Vol. 1, p. 576.

the battlefields. The losses in death and disability were appalling, and there seemed to be no end. The major task of the Bolsheviks therefore during the first two war years was to promote sabotage, desertion, and class warfare.

When the revolution itself came in March 1917, however, it was so swift and unexpected that few of the Bolsheviks, including Lenin, were ready. A series of strikes had degenerated into some minor rioting in Petrograd. The police were called out, but they would not act against the demonstrators. The garrison in Petrograd mutinied. Sir George Buchanan, the British Ambassador, reported: "Some disorders occurred today, but nothing serious." He was not being fatuous, since none of the best informed imagined that the regime was in danger. But when the angry crowds grew larger, with soldiers in the vanguard, and red flags came out, it became apparent that this was much more than a riot. The Czar, prodded by his advisers, reluctantly offered some concessions. But it was now much too late. The combustible ingredients were everywhere and the government was doomed. With dramatic suddenness, the Czar abdicated, and the Romanoff dynasty came to its ignominious end.

There began an eight months' struggle by a provisional government to preserve order and to maintain the rudiments of civilized life. Prince Lvov, an advocate of parliamentary democracy, had been installed as temporary Prime Minister, and he recalled the Duma to lay plans for a Constituent Assembly and new elections. There was the hope that Russia would now become a constitutional state on the western model. But, from the beginning, authority was fragmented. There was an official government, responsible to the Duma, and by its side a shadow government, a Petrograd Soviet, responsible to the workers and the soldiers. The Soviet took up headquarters just across the hall from the Duma, and an uneasy, wary cooperation was attempted, to take the country through its fiery critical period.

All too soon it was clear that this bicephalous arrangement would not work. The Duma had the technical, legal authority, and the confidence of the western world. But the Soviet could command the workers and the railroads, the vital organs of community life, and above all, the main sectors of the Petrograd army. For several months there were violent disputes over the reforms that were needed, and over the continuance of the war effort. The Duma government was drastically reshuffled, and a more radical group took charge, headed by Alexander Kerensky. He was a brilliant orator, and he advocated more fundamental reform; but he was committed to constitutional procedures and to the war effort, and was therefore completely unacceptable to the activist Soviet elements.

It was at this point that Lenin's leadership was decisive. At the outbreak of the revolution he had been in Switzerland. At first he had shrugged off the significance of the uprising in Petrograd. He wrote to a Communist comrade, Alexandra Kollontai, later the first woman Soviet Ambassador, that it was just another capitalist upheaval in which the bourgeois had consolidated the power they already held. But the Communists in Petrograd urged him to return and he began to plan ways of getting away "from this damned Switzerland." The Germans controlled the route to Russia. They now tried a bold gambit. Why not expedite Lenin's return? After all, he was intent on getting Russia out of the war. He would be the ideal agent to destroy the home war morale. Hence he and a number of his colleagues were placed in a sealed train and shipped through Germany, arriving in Petrograd, in Churchill's memorable phrase, as a "plague bacillus."*

Lenin at once began to plan for the overthrow of the provisional government, the complete withdrawal from the war, and the redistribution of land to the peasants. Only an insignificant minority of his party was ready at this stage to go so far, and his views were repudiated. He had to flee the country again. But he kept up the drumbeat—Peace and Bread! Peace and Bread!—Withdrawal from the war and redistribution of land. The refrain struck a responsive chord for a people sick of the war, and for peasants who needed little encouragement to take over the land. Kerensky made the pledge to urge the Allies to negotiate more strenuously for peace; he promised major economic and social reforms. But he refused to abandon allies whose support Russia would need after the war for the giant tasks of reconstruction. And he shrank from the precedent of confiscation.

Kerensky was now between Scylla and Charybdis. The Bolsheviks attacked him for his continuing commitment to the Allies. They stimulated the disintegration of order, and encouraged the Russian armies in the field to lay down their arms and desert. The conservative forces assailed Kerensky for yielding too much, and there was a counterrevolutionary uprising in Petrograd. The distraught Kerensky was obliged to ask for the cooperation of the soviets and their Red Army to crush it. The revolt was smashed but Kerensky, seeking

* Winston Churchill, *The Aftermath* (London: Macmillan's, Ltd., 1944), p. 63.

to mollify both extremes, had succeeded with neither, and he emerged altogether discredited. He never realized how useless it was to lecture to an earthquake.

In a recent analysis of Russia under Lenin and Stalin, former Ambassador George Kennan excoriated the Allies for their shortsightedness in urging Kerensky to continue fighting the war: "The Russian Revolution and the alienation of the Russian people from the Western community for decades to come were only a part of the staggering price paid by the Western people for their insistence on completing a military victory over Germany in 1917 and 1918."* He added that the Allied obsession with the German problem, even when it meant that Russia would bleed itself to death, played into Communist hands. Years later, Lord Beaverbrook asked Kerensky, who was living in exile, what he thought the result would have been if he had withdrawn from the war and concentrated on the domestic problems of Russia. Kerensky replied, "Of course, we would be in Moscow now."

All of this reconstruction was hindsight. Meanwhile, early in the morning of November 7, Lenin struck. The key points of the city were taken over and the provisional government was driven out. The deputies dispersed, "cadavers moving in a twilight," Lenin called them contemptuously. In the evening, the all-Russian Congress of Soviets, whose meeting had been timed for this planned revolution, received its mandate from the Petrograd Soviet, and declared that it was now the functioning government.

There was one more hurdle. Before the Bolshevik coup, all the parties in the Duma had agreed upon a general election, and it was too late to cancel the call. It was the last election held in Russia where there was a free choice, and it was an unmistakable repudiation of Lenin's extremists. Of 707, only 175 were Bolsheviks, and they came from the larger cities; 410 represented Kerensky's Socialist Party.

Lenin knew precisely what was now required. As the new Assembly made ready to convene, and the more moderate delegates began arriving in Moscow, they were met with every form of harassment. They were risking their lives as they passed into the building between Red Guards who were stationed along all the access points. But they came, even carrying food and candles for a possible siege by the Communists. Trotsky wrote with sarcasm, "Thus democracy entered upon

* George Kennan, *Russia and the West Under Lenin and Stalin* (Boston: Little, Brown, 1961), p. 33.

the struggle with dictatorship heavily armed with sandwiches and candles." Many were arrested on trumped-up charges, others were intimidated by threats of physical violence. Several were murdered. When the Assembly convened, on January 17, 1918, Bolshevik soldiers and sailors packed the galleries, where machine guns had been mounted. The din and the disorder were carefully stimulated, and the gavel was torn from the hands of the elected chairman. Lenin sat in the gallery watching and directing the bedlam. The next morning all entrances to the hall were barred, the Assembly was dissolved, and an all-Soviet congress was convened instead. It dutifully passed the enabling legislation that transferred all control to the Bolsheviks. The Red revolution had been completed, virtually by default. Lenin made a private note that was to serve as guide in the years ahead. "Revolutions are the locomotives of history. Drive them at full speed ahead, and keep them on the rails."

LENIN WAS DETERMINED NOT TO REPEAT THE BLUNDERS OF KERENSKY and the moderates in postponing the withdrawal from the war. One of his first moves was to reaffirm the proclamation that had been issued during his drive for power. He appealed to the peoples of Europe to carry through the same kind of sweeping revolution that had occurred in Russia. He authorized the publication of the secret treaties that were related to war aims so as to embarrass the Allied governments by exposing their "hypocrisy." He was sure that the workers of Europe would lose heart for continued warfare when the sordid reasons were revealed for which they were risking life and security. How literally Lenin wished to be taken was demonstrated when he dismissed the Commander in Chief of the Russian armies and gave the word to the soldiers that they could beat him to death, which they did with enthusiasm.

But it takes two to make a peace, and Germany had no intention of permitting Russia to leave the war without a very heavy price. On November 29, only three weeks after the Bolsheviks seized power, an armistice was arranged. But when treaty discussions began, the Germans made it clear that extensive annexations were planned. Negotiations were conducted at Brest-Litovsk, on the Russian-Polish border, near Warsaw, a name that, because of the Draconian treaty that was there imposed, was to become infamous. Germany announced that Poland and all the Baltic states would at once be separated from Russia, and that Germany would deal directly with them. These were non-Russian territories that had always been an unwilling, restless part of imperial Russia, hence the shock of the announced disposition passed quickly. But the Germans then declared that they planned to appropriate extensive areas of Russia itself, notably the Ukraine, the breadbasket of the empire. There were to be other major amputations of strategic territory that involved the Balkans. The Germans had in view a ring of border satellite states so that Russia would be permanently fenced in and contained. In all, sixty-two million people were to pass under German control, along with half of the Russian industry and a third of her croplands. The Russian Foreign Minister, Leon Trotsky, was so outraged by the German terms that he threatened to break off the talks. "We shall not continue the war," he said, with frustrated oblique logic, "but there will be no peace." The German commander brusquely turned aside all objections, noting that the future of Germany had to be adequately protected from aggression. He commented to his staff: "The only choice they have is as to what kind of sauce they shall be eaten with."

For a moment Lenin was tempted to call for renewed resistance. He even talked of appealing to the Allies for help. With his usual studied contempt, he wrote: "Comrade Trotsky should be authorized to accept the assistance of the brigands of French imperialism against the German brigands." But, after sober thought, he knew that he might jeopardize the revolution itself by continued resistance. Indeed, in the weeks of indecision, the Germans had resumed their advance and their terms had become more drastic. Brest-Litovsk was signed in April of 1918. The final defiant gesture of the Communists was to ignore the reading of the treaty, and for one of their delegates to blow pipe smoke into the face of the German commander. But the Germans were not disconcerted, for Russia had surrendered a third of its population, a fourth of its land, a third of its industry, and three-fourths of its coal and iron. Finland, Poland, the Baltic states, the Ukraine, and Bessarabia were all sliced away to become satellites of a resurgent Germany.

Lenin yielded not merely because there was no choice. He counted upon successful revolutions in the European countries, and, above all, in Germany. He was encouraged by the rising peace sentiment there. In July 1917, the Reichstag, over the opposition of the military, had passed a resolution calling for peace, with no annexations and no indemnities. Lenin expected, therefore, that the Treaty of Brest-Litovsk, however humiliating, would be only temporary, and would give Russia time to recover its strength. When the inevitable revolution swept the European countries, there would be complete revision.

He wrote: "We shall prove ourselves capable not only of heroic attack, but also of heroic retreat. . . . We shall know how to wait until the international Socialist proletariat comes to our aid. And we shall then start a second revolution, on a world scale."

Meantime Lenin was launched on his second promised objective, the nationalization of land and industry and commerce, the abolition of all private enterprise. The stream of decrees that poured out of the sessions of the Soviet Council had few parallels in history, and they were to affect every area of personal and communal life. The American correspondent John Reed, who was fascinated by the revolution, wrote: "The depths of Russia had been stirred, and it was the bottom which came uppermost now."* One decree eliminated the private ownership of land, and it applied to the extensive properties of the church. In most parts of Russia, the decree merely made official the sweeping confiscation that had been under way for many weeks. The peasants had already risen, killed off thousands of the landlords, and proceeded with rule of thumb distribution, usually supervised by the local soviets, on the basis of the capacity to work the land. In February 1918, the Council announced that all title would be vested in the state, a preliminary to a major collectivist reorganization. The peasants were soon to resist most strenuously the government's plan for enforced collectivization. But, for the moment, the hated landlords had been eliminated, and the age-old land hunger of the peasants was being relieved. They now had a precious stake in the success of the revolution.

The momentum of change extended to industry and commerce where private ownership was also repudiated. The stock market was abolished, the banks were taken over, and personal savings were confiscated. To the horror of foreign investors, especially the French, whose billions in loans had financed the Russian railroad system, all bond obligations were canceled. By 1920, the respect that had been accorded to private achievement had turned to contempt and opprobrium. Those who sang the "Internationale" were exultant that the refrain had so quickly become prophecy:

> The earth shall rise on new foundations,
> We have been naught, we shall be all.

It was not to be expected that the vested interests would supinely accept the revolutionary changes that cut so deeply into their welfare.

* John Reed, *Ten Days That Shook the World* (New York: Random House, 1960), p. 42.

There was grim resistance from the élite to avoid elimination, from the middle class to avoid ruin, and from the peasants, in the euphoria of ownership, to avoid regimentation. The Communists were to learn how frustrating was the gap between the promulgation of Marxist edicts and the efficient management of complicated enterprises. Production went into a tailspin. The industrial output of 1921 was reduced to one-sixth of what it had been in 1913. Coal production fell by 33 percent. Fuel was practically nonexistent. In the fairly typical metropolis of Odessa, the electric power station was closed, water service was suspended, and, for a mite of cooking oil, one needed to queue up for hours. The peasants reduced their plantings, refused to turn over to government stations all yield beyond their own needs, and slaughtered livestock rather than surrender them. The workers in industrial plants, finding that special effort earned little reward, dawdled and malingered. Primitive barter took the place of normal exchange. In 1920 and 1921, three million died of starvation, and perhaps six million more of disease.

The old guard took advantage of the mind-boggling chaos to raise the flag of counterrevolution. There was civil war in every part of the country. Whole provinces fell away and, for a while, the authority of the central government was limited to the areas around Leningrad and Moscow. There was a dangerous revolt at Kronstadt where the sailors, who had been among the first to strike against the czarist regime, now mutinied against Communist control. Though the mutiny was ruthlessly crushed, it was a further warning to Lenin that he could count on no undeviating loyalty anywhere.

In wrestling with his problems, Lenin was continuously plagued by the doctrinaire cast of mind of the bureaucrats who surrounded him. The revolution had brought to awesome authority many men who had lived on postulates and polemics, prating of realism on premises of unreality. Lenin shuddered at the prospect that, in the recurrent crises that filled each day, he would be trapped by the intense self-absorption and the Byzantine hair-splitting of these chair-borne fighters. "The histories of revolutions," he declared, "are full of these word-spinners, and what remains of them? Only smoke and a bad smell." He appreciated the cynical jest of his colleague, Nikolai Bukharin, that the history of mankind was divided into three periods: the matriarchate, the patriarchate, and the secretariate. He therefore gave short shrift to the theorists and the dialecticians. He wanted action—determined, decisive. It was significant that his proclamations and orders were so often couched in military language.

These were Lenin's most harassed days, but also his most effective. His will and his stamina, with the whole world caving in on him, were tested now to the utmost. His secret police, the Cheka, was hardened to a ruthlessness that became eerie. The casualness with which human life was dispatched was pointed up in an incident that involved the first chief of the Cheka, Dzerzhinsky. Lenin had sent a note to him to ask how many counterrevolutionaries there were in a particular prison. Dzerzhinsky wrote back that there were about fifteen hundred. Lenin read the note, and then placed an X by the figure. Dzerzhinsky left the room and within a few days all fifteen hundred had been executed. The secretary later explained that there had been a misunderstanding; Lenin was in the habit of writing an X simply to indicate that he had read a document and noted its contents.*

Such actions explained why there was no squeamishness in the decision to eliminate the entire czarist family. Nicholas, Alexandra, and the children had been hustled into captivity and shuttled from one point to another, ending up in Ekaterinburg, deep in the Urals. There were counterrevolutionary forces in the neighborhood as the civil war closed in, and it was feared that the Czar might become a dangerous rallying point. Hence, on July 16, 1918, the local guards herded all eleven members of the royal family, including the youngest children, into the basement, where they were shot to death in a mass execution. They were dumped into trucks and hauled to a mine shaft where their bodies were hacked to pieces, covered with benzine, and cremated, so that no surviving relics would remain for the faithful. When the dispatch reached Lenin he was outlining a routine report to his staff. He announced that the "royal bandits had been eliminated" and then he added impassively, "let us proceed with the reading of the report, point by point."

To the western powers, the developments in Russia brought the extremes of relief and dismay. At first, in the Kerensky phase with its commitments to constitutional procedures, there was every expectation that a democratic order would emerge. It had been a travesty, with czarist Russia as an ally, to justify the war as a crusade for freedom. A few weeks after the Kerensky coup, Wilson could declare exultantly in his message to Congress: "Does not every American feel that assurance has been added to our hope for the future peace of the world, by the wonderful and heartening things that have been

* Shub, *Lenin,* p. 309.

happening within the last few weeks in Russia?" But in October, when the Kerensky government collapsed and Lenin ordered the immediate withdrawal of Russia from the war, the Allies knew that they had suffered a major disaster. Apart from the elimination of pressure on Germany's eastern borders, the Russian defection made it possible to transfer a million battle-hardened German troops to the other contested theaters of war.

Equally terrifying was the thought of communism itself, with its dynamism of subversion, its challenge to all western values—the economic system, the social structure, religious faith. To the statesmen of Europe communism was a virus, and it could infect all mankind. For the Communists were determined to foment revolution in every country; they had party affiliates throughout Europe and the world who were masters of infiltration. Hence, expeditions were organized by the Allied powers to lend aid to the counterrevolutionaries in the hope of restoring, not the old czarist system, but a moderate form of government that would respect the values of the western world and the obligations that Russia had undertaken.

The Allied invasions, with their threat on every frontier and with the military assistance that they pledged to inner resistance, became Lenin's most immediate survival problem. The United States assigned forces to occupy Vladivostok on the Pacific, primarily to salvage valuable military stores that had been sent to the Kerensky government, and also to back up the Czech legions that were fighting their way across Russia to the Pacific to join the armies of the West. British and American forces also landed at the port of Archangel, and they joined the counterrevolutionary units that were threatening Petrograd. These dissentients had already killed the Petrograd Chief of the Secret Police, and had wounded Lenin in two assassination attempts. There were other anti-Soviet forces that operated in the Ukraine and in the Baltic. In western Siberia, Admiral Kolchak was temporarily successful in driving out the Communists and he announced himself the supreme ruler of Russia.

In November 1918 the Germans collapsed and surrendered unconditionally. The Allied intervention in Russia could no longer be justified as an effort to maintain an eastern front or to prevent supplies from falling into German hands. Continued intervention now had one purpose, to help overthrow the Red regime. There were expropriated émigrés and refugees in every European capital to encourage and promote this objective, and they usually had the ear of the Foreign Ministers. Soviet statesmen, in future years, kept recalling the intervention attempts, and remained suspicious that the West would be ready to resume them if frontiers became vulnerable or if other circumstances promised success. The western Allies countered by pointing to Lenin's ceaseless involvement in world revolution, in encouraging and financing subversion and infiltration. With all his internal problems, Lenin always seemed to have the resources and the energies for conspiracy and disruption. The long struggle between the Communists and the West was to dominate the international relationships of the decades ahead.

At the moment, however, it seemed as if the defeat of Germany would be followed by the collapse of the Red revolution. Shaken and weakened by civil war, by foreign intervention, by the tailspin of production, by the loosening of authority everywhere, survival for the Bolshevik regime seemed most doubtful. Foreign trade, with Russia in complete isolation, was virtually eliminated. Even the Red Cross staffs were evacuated. Yet, by 1922, the regime had righted itself and re-established its control. The men who were so war-weary when they fought in the Allied cause, who had deserted in regiments and divisions, "voting for peace with their feet," as Lenin said, now rallied to the Red cause, prepared to fight again.

Few would have believed that such a reversal was possible. It came about through the genius of another of Lenin's collaborators, Leon Trotsky, who built an indomitable Red Army out of shreds and patches. Stalin later turned him into a nonperson, and relentlessly hunted him until he accomplished his assassination in a Mexican exile point. But Trotsky's contribution was written in the survival of the Communist state, and the record of this achievement Stalin could not obliterate.

Trotsky came from a well-to-do Jewish home in Odessa but, at eighteen, he was already a confirmed revolutionist and had served prison sentences for sedition. At twenty-five he was involved in the 1905 revolution and had become the head of the St. Petersburg soviet. After the uprising was thwarted, Trotsky was again in and out of prisons, in and out of exile. He was earning a precarious livelihood as a fly-by-night journalist in New York when news of the 1917 revolution reached him. His comrades contributed to a fund that would quickly get him back to Russia. Like Lenin, Trotsky was not yet sure that the Communists were ready to assume responsibility for the disintegrating Russian state. But in the turmoil of the period he won the confidence of Lenin, and was entrusted with important missions by him. These included personal responsibility for the negotiations at Brest-Litovsk. When he returned he was made Commissar for War.

Trotsky had no military training, but his organizational ability, his resourcefulness, his extraordinary impassioned oratory, made him indispensable to Lenin. He was a caricaturist's dream, with his thick glasses, his unruly bushy hair, his routine of dashing about the country in an armored car, on this front today, on another tomorrow, exhorting, cajoling, threatening, somehow evoking an effective fighting esprit de corps when the Red fortunes were at their lowest. He was successful even with former czarist regiments. He amazed Lenin when he revealed that he had enlisted more than thirty thousand czarist officers who were now fighting, and fighting with fervor, under the Red banner.

The Soviet cause was further advanced by the lack of coordination among the counterrevolutionary forces. The commanding generals had no common objective and no integrated strategy. Some were determined to restore the old order; others fought to resist Communist regimentation. Some craved power or loot; some were committed to building anew, on the western model. Some were outright mercenaries who operated under the direction of various foreign powers. It was this last factor that was seized upon by the Reds and exploited for its patriotic appeal. Suddenly the Communists became the loyal Russians who were defending the Fatherland, pledged to save Russia from "the plundering brigands of the capitalist world."

Slowly the tide turned and one by one the foreign armies were withdrawn. The Americans were the first to quit. They had brought too little to be effective and too much to be later forgiven by the Reds. The French withdrew when there were mutinies of their men, who refused to fight for the aims that had been announced. The British were hampered by strikes in England, when trade unions refused to fuel and provision the ships that were to take the soldiers into Russia. By 1920 the last foreign armies were out, and the counterrevolutionaries, deprived of support from abroad, were eliminated. Their armies folded and many of the generals were captured and executed.

But the cost of victory against external and internal enemies was incalculable. Each year after the revolution was so filled with hardship and disaster that the average family hoped only for survival. The peasant refusal to relinquish surplus supplies to feed the cities had uprooted millions of urban dwellers who drifted out to the country foraging for food. When indispensable imports had to be cut off, a strange breed of bagmen appeared, itinerant peddlers with food and other essentials in their packs, moving from place to place, ready to sell, but at exorbitant prices. Disbanded military units wandered through the country, looting to make their way, and further disrupting city life. To cap the misery there was a crop failure in the spring and summer of 1921 in the Volga basin, and millions more died of starvation.

Lenin was enough of a realist to know that the time had come to compromise. Communism had to be treated as a long-range goal: there were too many hideous legacies from the past that could not be eliminated quickly and by fiat. "We have advanced too far too fast, and beyond our present strength," he admitted. "We must prove that we have the courage to retreat." In March 1921, he scrapped the system of war communism, and announced the New Economic Policy, which brought back the private trader, permitted individual holdings for the peasant, and restored a measure of private property. He still held to the principle that there must be no unusual profit for the entrepreneur, but there was leeway for men and skilled technicians to receive special compensation, so long as industry was operated for the welfare of the people. In the inner councils the pledge was renewed that the ultimate Marxian goal would not be abandoned; for the moment, however, there was no alternative but to announce the compromise.

Then, in May 1922, at the moment of the most urgent need for decisive leadership, Lenin suffered a cerebral hemorrhage. The power struggle for succession began at once, the battle especially vicious between Trotsky and Stalin, both of whom stood closest to Lenin. A second stroke in 1923 destroyed Lenin's powerful will and invalided him. His understanding remained clear, but he could no longer command. It was necessary to appoint an interim executive, and the conflict raged around the failing chief, with all the foreboding that the horrors of the civil wars were soon again to convulse the country. In the next year Lenin died, and the worst fears were realized, a long agony of internecine conflict and purges, trials and executions. Churchill always felt that Lenin's early death was a tragedy for the world. He believed that Lenin's penetrating realism and his capacity for decision would have saved Russia from the miasma of twisted loyalties and mindless tyranny that was to curse a whole generation, during which the Communist Party not only lost its way but its map and its compass. "Lenin alone could have found the way back to the causeway," Churchill wrote. "The Russian people were left floundering in a bog. Their worst misfortune was his birth: their next worst

—his death."*

It was a strange compliment but it was a perceptive one. Though many Red leaders rose to power after Lenin, none survived in the veneration of the people, neither Trotsky, who was destroyed by Stalin, nor Stalin, who was thrown out of his tomb by Khrushchev. Each of the successors had their moment of supreme power and then was eclipsed and disgraced. Only in the case of Lenin did the glory of his image remain.

Lenin's body was embalmed by some secret formula, and placed in a glass case which was consigned to a special mausoleum on the western side of the Red Square in Moscow. Since the day of death in January 1924, the body lay to be honored by those who filed by, four abreast, through the years for nearly half a century, an endless line, sometimes fifteen thousand a day, moving silently and solemnly between the white lines down into the tomb. Lenin had abolished God and Christ, the saints and their ritual. He had abolished the Bible, whose millions of copies were converted into cigarette paper. But Lenin himself was more venerated than God, and his literary remains won more respect than the sacred writings of Christendom. Perhaps this was because there was always the remembrance of what Russia had been before Lenin's day—its ignorance, its superstition, its exploitation. Who could forget Rasputin and the Czars and the pogroms and the crushing poverty of the moujiks and the senseless butcheries of the war?

There were years of intense suffering still ahead but, in time, the country emerged from its travail. It remained a police state, but its schools, its farms, its factories, its cultural life, were now shared by all the people, and there was hope again. A day came when it was no longer empty propaganda to speak of competition with the West, if not in comforts, then in military strength, in economic security and cultural achievement. In 1957 when Sputnik was launched, it was not merely a technical triumph to indicate that the Soviets were in the space race; it was an announcement to the world that backward, creaking, obsolescent Russia was no more, and that communism had a dynamic quality that had to be taken into account. So the multitudes came to the shrine of Lenin, and then a second generation, and a third, day and night, through the years, silently and reverently in grateful homage, filing by the casket that held the body of the father of the revolution.

* Churchill, *The Aftermath*, p. 66.

10

THE MIRACLE
OF CZECHOSLOVAKIA

WHILE THERE WERE ALL TOO MANY TRAGEDIES THAT CAME OUT OF
World War I, one of the most gratifying developments, bordering on
the miraculous, was the creation of Czechoslovakia, an ancient state
reborn after a thousand years of political subjection. In the heart
of the old Austrian Empire was Bohemia, populated mainly by
Czechs, cultured, steady, hardworking, resourceful people, whose
proud tradition was linked to a sovereign Bohemia which had
flourished in the early Middle Ages. But independence had been
lost to the Hapsburgs in the wars and the revolutions of the seventeenth century, and its lands had been gathered up into the potpourri
that made up the Hapsburg Empire. Their neighbors were the
Slovaks, kindred Slavs, who had also never relinquished their dream
of nationalist resurrection. Both peoples sensed their unique opportunity for fulfillment when World War I shook the Austrian Empire
to its foundations. All their sympathies were with their Slav brothers,
the Russians. They were therefore a dangerous and formidable problem to the Austrian state; when they were conscripted to fight against
Russia, their loyalty was inevitably suspect. They were usually distributed among many regiments and battalions so that they would
not comprise large homogeneous units to become an operating base
for disaffection.

All through the war period there was ferment. The main strategy
for achieving independence, or at least greater autonomy, had to be
directed from outside the country, but with every precaution so as not

to jeopardize the safety of the population within. This called for sensitive diplomacy of the highest order and it was supplied by two statesmen, Tomáš Masaryk and Eduard Beneš, whose genius again confirmed the decisive historic role of personality.

Tomáš Masaryk was born in 1850 of a Slovak father, a coachman, and a Moravian mother, a cook. In his Memoirs he noted that his life was shot through with paradox, and this was an understatement. He was the scholar who became the man of action, the pacifist who commanded armies before he had a country, the moralist who could match wits with the most hardened politicians. He was to live in the ancient Hradčány Palace, but his first employment was as an apprentice to a locksmith, then to a blacksmith. His precociousness brought him special educational advantages which included superb university training in philosophy and sociology, and he became one of the most popular and respected professors at the University of Prague. His impact went beyond teaching. Herman Bahr, the Austrian-German historian, wrote in 1909: "Masaryk's pupils have united the Serbs and Croats of Dalmatia and are now bringing that distracted province to have faith in the future—so strong is the influence of the lonely Slovak in Prague who seems to some a mixture of Tolstoy and Walt Whitman, to others a heretic, to others again an ascetic, and to all an enthusiast."*

Masaryk came to national notice because of his courageous, scholarly independence. Czech patriots had taken pride in a brace of epic and lyric poems which were purportedly written in the thirteenth century, and they were pointed to as validation of the antiquity of Bohemian cultural excellence. There was a school of scholarship that had misgivings about their authenticity, but it was considered as tantamount to treason to say this openly, for then a cherished Czech cultural claim would be challenged. Masaryk entered the controversy, "the battle of the manuscripts." He concluded that the poems were indeed forgeries, and he insisted that national traditions should never be built on falsehood. "It is a deliberate and discerning love of our nation that appeals to me," he declared, "not the indiscriminate love that assumes that everything be right and righteous merely because it bears a national label." This was heresy, and it affronted the superpatriots. But Masaryk withstood their onslaughts, and emerged with a reputation for unimpeachable integrity.

He added to his thorny laurels by his learned defense of a Jew who

* Cited by H. W. Steed in the introduction of Tomáš Masaryk, *The Making of a State* (London: Allen & Unwin, Ltd., 1927), p. 18.

was accused of ritual murder. He was pitted against Dr. August Röhling, a prominent professor of Hebrew at the university, who gave his name to the canard that plagued eastern Europe every few decades and exacerbated its anti-Semitism, that the murder of Christians for ritual purposes was part of the Jewish doctrine. Masaryk defended the accused and exposed the obscurantism of a whole scholarly enclave.

He was early concerned with the problems of the Austrian Empire and its relationship to the aspirations of its many peoples. Several times elected to the Reichsrat, he was the leader of a splinter party that sought a formula of autonomy that would not destroy the Empire, nourished as it was by so many economic and social blood vessels and nerves. Travel brought him many influential friendships and broadened his political maturity. In Russia he met Tolstoy, and the two men found that they were kindred spirits, though they did not share each other's convictions about the state of the world.* Masaryk lived for a few years in the United States where he lectured at the University of Chicago, and he was fascinated and deeply moved by its constitutional history. He was drawn closer to America and to its traditions when, again in Europe, he met Charlotte Garrigue, a young lady from Brooklyn, and their marriage was an intellectual partnership as well as a love match. "She was beautiful to look at," Masaryk wrote in his sunset years. "She had a magnificent intellect, better than mine." In character and temperament Masaryk was deeply religious. "Jesus," he said "not Caesar, is my ideal." In 1930, when his grateful countrymen raised a tribute fund in his name, he turned over the entire $600,000 for cancer research.

It was this ascetic, uncompromising scholar, to whom the primacy of truth was so fundamental that he was prepared to scuttle the most precious legends of his people, who was soon to be involved in the most perilous conspiracies, bravely undertaken in the interest of an independent Czechoslovakia.

When the world war burst upon Europe, Masaryk was convinced that its implications went far beyond the traditional struggle over the balance of power. To him, as to Woodrow Wilson, it was the providential opportunity for the release of many of the smaller peoples, the fulfillment of the doctrine of self-determination. He had no fear

---

* "With his doctrine of non-resistance I could not agree. I held that we must resist evil always and in everything. . . . In extreme cases, violence and assault must be met with steel and beaten off so as to defend others against violence." Masaryk, *The Making of a State*, p. 72.

of a congeries of warring states, the Balkanization of Europe. He believed that it was possible for the little peoples of Southeast Europe, through resourceful statesmanship, to protect their economic welfare by cooperative effort, and yet to enjoy the blessings of national and cultural individuality. For the Austrian government, struggling with problems of survival, such thinking was disruptive, and Masaryk was hunted as a dangerous rebel. He fled the country in December 1914 with a death sentence on his head. In the next four years, in a diplomatic tandem with one of his disciples, Eduard Beneš, he gave all of his energies to promote the goal of Czech independence. At one point when the tide was running heavily against him, he was tempted to return to Prague, to be shot by the Austrians as its most wanted man and thus to serve his country as a martyr.

His young collaborator, Eduard Beneš, was a trusted protégé who, like Masaryk, had also gone underground. He was born in 1884 in Bohemia, the son of a peasant truck farmer. He was a brilliant student at the University of Prague but, at this stage, his national fame came from his talent as an outstanding soccer star. Very early Beneš came under the influence of Masaryk and their careers merged. The subsequent story resembles an Ian Fleming thriller, alive with forged passports, hair-breadth escapes, disguises, and police traps. "We agreed upon our whole plan of campaign," Masaryk recalled later, "and also about our helpers at home and abroad. As long as possible Beneš was to remain at home and to organize communications with me after the fashion of the Russian Secret Societies."*

Beneš gave little impression of a cloak-and-dagger personality. When Harold Nicolson met him at the Peace Conference he found him to be just a "competent, plausible little man," and this image of the nondescript was perhaps assiduously cultivated by Beneš himself, to achieve greater anonymity for his chosen task. Though he remained a controversial figure, he counted it as his highest compliment when some of his colleagues in the League of Nations avowed that no man of his generation so completely embodied the European man. Both Beneš and his chief now worked unflaggingly in the Allied countries, where there were major settlements of Czechs and Slovaks, to coordinate their nationalist aspirations with the Allied war aims.

A unique opportunity existed in Russia, where more than seventy thousand Czechs were centered in the key cities of St. Petersburg, Moscow, Kiev, and Odessa. The Czechs were mainly skilled artisans

---

* Masaryk, *The Making of a State*, p. 45.

who had adjusted very well to Russian life, but they were solidly committed to the freedom aspirations of their blood brothers and were eager to be helpful. Delegations visited the Czar to petition for special war assignments that would help both the Allies and their Motherland. It was easy for the Czar to make promises because whatever the Czechs did to break down morale in the armies of Austria was welcome. A Czech legion was organized, officered by Russians, and it acquitted itself bravely in Galicia and on other fighting fronts. It also helped to stimulate defections from the armies of the central powers who either joined the legion or went into the war industries of Russia, where there were crucial manpower shortages. The legion grew to more than thirty-five thousand crack troops of highest morale.

When the first Russian revolution in March 1917 overthrew the czarist government, the legion pledged its loyalty to Kerensky and backed his determination to continue the war effort against the central powers. After the Communists seized power in November and withdrew Russia from the war, the legion, expanded now by many more thousands of recruits, determined to reach the western front, even though to accomplish this it had to fight its way eastward all around the world. It was an extraordinary anabasis, a trek sheer across a Russia in chaos, across Siberia and the Pacific to the United States, and then on to Europe to join the hard-pressed Allies. Churchill wrote: "The pages of history recall scarcely any parallel episode at once so romantic in character and so extensive in scale." The achievement of "the army without a country" was, of course, more symbolic than actual. But the Czechs knew how crucial it was to make a dramatic impression upon the Allied statesmen who would, if victorious, be the architects of the peace treaties.

In France the diplomatic battle on behalf of Czech independence could not be fortified by any substantial military contribution. The Czech colony was quite small, about three thousand in Paris, where there was an active Sokol society to stimulate the nationalist spirit, and a few thousand more who were scattered through the rest of the country. But many of them held high positions and provided valuable leverage, notably, Milan Štefánik, a former pupil of Masaryk, who had settled in Paris early in the century and became an astronomer of some distinction. He had accepted French citizenship, and fought gallantly in the French air service. He arranged for the French Foreign Minister, Briand, to meet with Masaryk and Beneš in 1916 when the war was in stalemate. Briand was won over completely, and he became one of the earliest advocates of complete independence for Czechoslovakia as an Allied war aim. It was tragic that Štefánik did not live to savor the glory of Czech independence. He was killed in a plane crash only a few weeks before Czechoslovakia became a sovereign state.

In Italy, where there was another small but compact Czech group, the negotiations to win the support of the government moved very slowly.* The Italian leadership had no wish to eliminate the Austrian Empire, but only to win from it some coastal districts that fulfilled Italian needs. The Italians feared that the destruction of Austria might mean the development of strong competing successor-states. Yugoslavia already loomed as one of these. Masaryk and Beneš needed special skill to persuade the Italians that there was more to gain from smaller states, securely centered and pledged to peace, than from continuous unrest in the Balkans and Central Europe, or from a resuscitated Austrian Empire, defeated this time but waiting grimly for another round. They were sufficiently successful to win approval for the organization of a special unit from among the Czechs who were being held as war prisoners. Ultimately the legion enlisted twenty-two thousand volunteers, and they were cited for bravery by the Italian generals in the major battles of 1917 and 1918. Their gallantry under fire was not forgotten when the Big Four sat to put the world together again.

In England, the diplomatic mission was undertaken by Masaryk who understood fully that, though there were very few Czechs in the country, the support of Britain would be crucial at the Peace Conference. Masaryk won the friendship of the historian Hugh Seton-Watson, whose writings on the Balkans and Central Europe were most influential, and of Wickham Steed, the editor of the powerful *Times*. He received welcome calls to lecture in the major British universities and he used these opportunities with calculated resourcefulness. The British delegation at the Peace Conference later enthusiastically supported the Czech claims.

Above all there was the United States, where more than a million and a half fervently loyal Czechs and Slovaks centered in such cities as New York, Chicago, and Pittsburgh. Since many of them had pros-

---

* "One episode I remember. When I visited the Italian historian Professor Lumbroso, he was taken aback, for he had heard that I had been knocked on the head in Prague at the beginning of the war, and, as a conscientious historian, he had published an article on my death. 'You will live long,' he said." Masaryk, *The Making of a State*, p. 59.

pered, they were able to provide considerable financial support through what became a kind of United Czech Appeal. Fund-raising meetings brought in hundreds of thousands of dollars that were crucial to subsidize the diplomatic ventures. Masaryk had sessions with Woodrow Wilson, and he briefed himself in advance, so that he could buttress his case for national self-determination by quoting from Wilson himself. They became fast friends, and Wilson later included the independence of Czechoslovakia as one of the Allied war aims.

Yet in 1916 it appeared as if all this skillful diplomacy might come to naught. There were many peace overtures, a major effort coming from Austria itself when the young Emperor Karl succeeded his venerable old uncle, Franz Josef. Masaryk and Beneš were appalled, for there could be no independence for Czechoslovakia unless the war were prolonged until the Austrian Empire collapsed. Here was another example of the curious ironies that influence destiny and flout the oversimplification of doctrinaires. Masaryk was a moralist in politics. His ethical code was austere. He would rather face a firing squad than deviate from the truth in personal matters. But the achievement of peace on a negotiated basis would undoubtedly preserve the Austrian Empire, and this would mean the end of the nationalist dream of independence. Hence, despite the mounting casualties, Masaryk and the patriots prayed for the war to go on, until the disruption of Austria was assured.

As it turned out, there was no need to fear an early negotiated peace. Germany was riding high through 1917. Revolution had taken Russia out of the war, and the treaty dictated by the Germans at Brest-Litovsk was a demonstration of the savagery that could be expected from a German victory. The Allies were more determined than ever to see the war through and, as American participation began to turn the tide, they set their aim at unconditional surrender. This in turn strengthened the resolve of the Germans not to yield, and the war dragged on. Masaryk and Beneš were reassured that their diplomatic objectives would not be thwarted by a premature peace.

For the moment, however, the situation in the homeland itself was most precarious. Austrian troops were in control, and open demands for Czech independence were naturally regarded as treason; there were many executions. Public pronouncements had to be carefully formulated and could go no further than the hope for a free Europe, with autonomy for the peoples within the Empire. In April 1917, there was a Writers' Manifesto, signed by the outstanding literary men of the country, which called for a democratic Europe and a free Czechoslovakia linked more or less tenuously to the Empire; it was presented as a petition to the Reichsrat. The manifesto was angrily received by the Austrian Foreign Minister, who denounced it as subversive and detrimental to the war effort. In April 1918, as the nationalists grew bolder, there was a monster demonstration in Prague, participated in by tens of thousands. The multitudes in the huge square repeated the solemn oath: "Faithful in work, faithful in our fight, faithful in the midst of our suffering and privation, faithful unto death, we shall endure, until we win, as win we must. We shall endure until our nation's freedom is in our grasp."

By the summer of 1918, the Austrian forces were in collapse and the national groups, scenting victory, were sensible enough to subordinate their differences, at least temporarily, and to close ranks. The Council for Liberation within the country was now working in closest cooperation with the National Council in Paris. The young Emperor tried to save the Empire from disintegration by offering major concessions. But it was much too late, for it was clear that the demise was near. The major Allies had already recognized the independence of Czechoslovakia. The Declaration of Independence, indeed, had been proclaimed in Washington, with the blessing of Woodrow Wilson.

On October 28, 1918, independence was announced in Prague itself, and the tricolor flag, with the Bohemian lion, raised in the capital square; the Slovak declaration of solidarity followed. Two peoples, separated by a thousand years of subjection, now came together as a new sovereign state, a miracle accomplished by scattered colonies of emigrants in every part of the world, by fighting legions in Russia and Italy and on the western front, drawn from prisoners and expatriates and volunteers, cemented by the astute diplomacy of roving ambassadors, and all carrying in their hearts the pledge: "We shall endure." It was one of history's most exultant days, often looked back upon in the frustration and the heartbreak of the sellout to the Nazis at Munich, and of the Communist subversion that followed World War II.*

---

* Beneš realized that the military contributions of his people, compared to those of the British, the French, and the Italians, were not considerable. "At the same time, our action in Siberia was certainly of great importance to the Allies. And the mere fact that we had three armies, that there were about 150,000 men who, of their own accord, were willing to sacrifice their lives for their ideals, must be regarded as having very significant implications." Eduard Beneš, *Memoirs* (Boston: Houghton Mifflin, 1954), p. 499.

The first sovereign government was quickly organized and the sixty-eight-year-old Masaryk was named as President. Beneš, who had so long served loyally with him, now thirty-four, became his Foreign Secretary. The extraordinary esteem in which the newly created state was held was demonstrated when Beneš was invited to the plenary session of the Supreme War Council on November 4, and participated in the armistice negotiations that ended the war.

Now came the titanic task of state building after centuries of political subservience. All around Czechoslovakia the new succession states, many wracked by civil war, succumbed to dictatorships, ostensibly to preserve order and to protect elementary living standards. Masaryk and Beneš refused to follow this trend. They insisted that there was sufficient vitality and strength in the democratic process to justify faith in it. The structure of the state was therefore planned to combine the best features of the British and the American systems, with the President, the Prime Minister, and the Parliament in association, instantly answerable to the electorate. The short-range objectives were given priority. The currency had to be stabilized, for the financial structure of the Empire at the end of the war had gone down in the welter of ruin. The Czech crown became the base for a revised monetary order and the most rigid austerity was urged. Within four years there was a balanced budget and an unchallenged currency that inspired confidence.

The government recognized that political democracy meant little without social foundations that were solid and secure. The old order had authorized exceptional privileges to an élite of landowners. In October 1919, the great estates were broken up, not by confiscation, as the Communists had directed in Russia, but by purchase, managed through bond issues. The land was offered for redistribution and the peasants encouraged, through long-term loans, to acquire their own holdings. There was a parallel industrial revolution to develop the rich resources of the country—its timber, pig iron, textiles, its glassworks and porcelain. The famous Skoda works, among the most efficiently managed in Europe, still concentrated on munitions. But highly specialized steel and iron products and precision instruments were also produced, and there was a ready market for them in every part of the world. Cooperatives on the Swedish model received considerable government support; 11 percent of the people were quickly enrolled in one or another of them. Simultaneously, an expanded program of social reform was inaugurated that included government housing, sickness and unemployment insurance, and an eight-hour day. What Masaryk had launched was a Central European New Deal, fifteen years before it was tried in the United States. The whole face of the economy and the social order was transformed, and the jeremiads of the prophets of doom were confounded.

To support and to safeguard the fledgling state, a small but well-trained army was created, with reserve support from the Sokol movement which combined health, sports, and defense features. The Sokol clubs, with a tradition that was older than the Olympics, flourished in every part of the country, and by 1938, there were 3,200 branches, comprising 800,000 men, women, and children.

Masaryk and Beneš recognized that the continued stability of the republic would depend upon staunch allies and guaranteed friendships. As Foreign Minister, Beneš therefore gave attention, in the crucial postwar years, to the creation of regional agreements that were to supplement the collective security guardianship of the League of Nations. France was the natural anchor ally since it had the most at stake in preserving the war settlements, and the Franco-Czech alliance was hailed as mutually beneficial. Clemenceau called it: "A length of barbed wire to contain Germany and Communist Russia."

The cornerstone in the defense system in Southeast Europe itself was the Little Entente, an alliance of Czechoslovakia, Yugoslavia, and Rumania. They had little in common in political philosophy, but they were drawn together by the need to resist attempts to repudiate the treaties of peace. Yugoslavia required protection from a defeated Hungary. Rumania was in mortal fear of Communist Russia. Beneš hoped that out of political and military collaboration there would some day emerge an economic union, some form of Common Market for the Balkans.

The main faith of Beneš, however, lay in the League of Nations. He was convinced that enforceable collective security was the prime guarantor of the smaller states, and that the peace of the world depended on the strength and prestige of the League. He became its general ambassador, the spiritual heir of Woodrow Wilson. He was a key figure on the diplomatic teams that wrestled with international disputes, and was as often in Geneva as in Prague. Czechoslovakia, though one of the lesser states, was given a seat in the Security Council. Beneš served as president of the League six times.

One intractable problem remained to defy the statesmanship of Masaryk and Beneš. For security reasons the peace treaties had included strategic territory in the Czechoslovak state where substantial minority groups had lived for centuries: a million Hungarians, half a million Ruthenians, three and a quarter million Sudeten-Germans. These ethnic enclaves had sentimental ties with the other countries of Hungary, Russia, and Germany. Even the Slovaks, who numbered two and a half million and who, by the terms of the Declaration of Independence, came into the union as equal partners, had developed different cultural and social patterns because of the thousand-year domination by Hungary. Masaryk and Beneš worked valiantly to set an example of enlightened stewardship. Every guarantee was given to the minority groups. In a sincere effort to promote cultural pluralism, the government encouraged them to develop their own languages, their own literature and folkways, and to maintain their own schools. Of course there were failures, inadequacies, and shortcomings. There were irritating instances of Czech tactlessness, and sometimes the minority group leaders demanded more than could be practically granted. But in comparison to the treatment of minorities almost everywhere else, Masaryk and Beneš demonstrated the kind of enlightened statesmanship which was scurvily repaid by ostensible friends whom they too blindly trusted.

There was no dangerous irredentism, even among the Sudeten-Germans, until the blight of Nazism spread out from Germany to the surrounding areas and Hitler's agents, within and without, began to stimulate dissension. The Nazis regarded the peoples of Southeast Europe, except the colonies of Germans, as *"Dingervölker,"* dung people, whose role it was just to fertilize the region. They had a special mission in mind for the Sudeten-Germans, *"Herrenvolk,"* a master élite. They seized upon the minority status of the Sudeten-Germans and every disputed issue was escalated into crisis proportions. Ultimately the Sudetenland was to become the focus for the international showdown, and World War II was spawned from the appeasement that destroyed Czechoslovakia. But for the twenty years from 1919 to the outbreak of World War II, Czechoslovakia was the model state in Europe, a tribute to the genius of its two main architects, Tomáš Masaryk and Eduard Beneš.

11

ATATURK AND
THE RESURRECTION
OF TURKEY

IN THE CRASH OF EMPIRES DURING AND AFTER WORLD WAR I, THE "pomp, rule and reign" of the proudest and oldest dynasties went "to earth and dust"—the Hohenzollerns of Germany, the Hapsburgs of Austria, the Romanoffs of Russia. The Turkish Empire and its ruling house were not spared. The Allies who had forced the Treaty of Versailles on the Germans, and St. Germain on the Austrians, dictated Sèvres for the Turks. The Ottoman dynasty was ignominiously terminated as the last Sultan fled to Malta to escape the wrath of his subjects.

In the sixteenth and seventeenth centuries, the Ottoman Empire had wielded world power and its very name struck terror. The Osmanli Turks had poured out of Asia, inundating almost every part of Southeast Europe and North Africa, all the way to the Straits of Gibraltar. Then the decline set in as the virility of the family was sapped in harem politics. Some of the sultans wore themselves out in dissipation. Others succumbed to assassination. All through the eighteenth and nineteenth centuries there was a steady attrition of strength and influence. One by one the subject peoples broke away —the Serbs, the Bulgars, the Rumanians, the Greeks. The great powers sliced off other huge sections, the French taking Algeria, the Russians the Crimea, the Italians Tunisia and Tripoli, the British Egypt, the Sudan, and Cyprus. Turkey was in alliance with Britain and France, but it was a commentary on the cold-bloodedness of imperialism that the friends took more than the enemies did. At the threshold of World War I, Turkey had been evicted from virtually all of Europe and North Africa, and was scornfully labeled "The Sick Man of Europe."

There were deeply resentful younger people who were humiliated by the decline. They recalled the days of glory, and they knew that there could be no hope for national health and vigor without basic reform. In 1908 some of the army officers, the "Young Turks," engineered a revolt, and compelled the Sultan and the old guard to eliminate some of the vestigial excrescences that retarded the country's welfare. But it was a superficial revolution, with all too little enduring result. The rot was too far advanced to respond to homeopathic treatment.

In World War I the Turkish rulers waited until 1915 and then, in another losing gamble, threw in their lot with Germany. Turkey now proved to be the soft underbelly through which the Balkan states were penetrated, then Austria, and ultimately, Germany. The creaking old governmental contraption came apart as the victorious Allies made ready to carve up what remained of the Empire.

Mohammed VI was now the Sultan, a nephew of the wily old blackguard, Abdul Hamid (The Damned). The defeated and discredited Young Turk leaders had fled. Mohammed sued for peace and promised to be a faithful vassal; under the protection of the Allies, his throne would be safe and his personal welfare guaranteed. He nourished the hope that soon the Allies would start quarreling among themselves and his opportunity to escape from their surveillance would return. In November 1918, the Allied fleet of sixty ships sailed past the now silent guns of the Dardanelles and anchored in the port of Constantinople. The Allied representatives assumed all military and administrative jurisdiction, with the Sultan as the legal façade. The French compounded the humiliation when their commanding general insisted upon leading a parade on his white horse down the main street of the ancient capital. One of the Young Turk officers, Mustapha Kemal, who had repulsed the Allies at Gallipoli, was there to watch the degrading spectacle and he burned with anger. The scene was all set for him to assume his role of one of the master builders of the twentieth century.

The blond, blue-eyed Mustapha Kemal was a complex character, strong, decisive, cynical in his judgments, passionately devoted to a redeemed Turkey. He liked his liquor hard, his women flashy, his poker wild and high; but when he turned to national reforms, he rose above sentiment and appetite. In 1926, when there was an attempt on his life, he hanged the entire opposition cabal, including several of the men who had shared his military hardships in the wars of liberation. He then went on to a champagne celebration at his farmhouse to which he invited the diplomatic corps. On their way home at dawn, they passed all the executed men hanging from their gibbets. He continually astonished the western world as he kept oscillating between responsible statesmanship and undisciplined orgy. He could work hard through the day on sensitive foreign relations. He would then play poker all night and drink his confreres under the table. He was warned by his doctor about his unrestrained tippling and carousing but outlived the doctor. He was defiantly dissolute and scarcely selective; he could sleep with a waitress or a duchess with equal satisfaction. He was once asked what quality he admired most in a woman, and he replied: "Availability." One of his loves was said to be the actress Zsa Zsa Gabor. She described her experience in a popular magazine article,* and when she married soon afterwards, it was to a Turkish diplomat. When Mustapha Kemal died and was succeeded by a low-keyed practical statesman, one of Mustapha's female admirers said, "Turkey has lost her lover, and must now settle down with her husband."

Yet, while Mustapha Kemal was cruel and vengeful, he could command sacrificial devotion and he was unsurpassed in charm when he was in the mood for thoughtfulness. He had a unique gift of self-mockery that chastened his arrogance. He cared nothing for worldly possessions and he willed his land holdings, the gift of the nation to him, back to his people. He needed all the qualities of decisiveness and courage and resourcefulness, for he had the problem of expelling invaders and exploiters, and then completely rebuilding a nation from its ruins.

He was born in Salonika in 1881 of a Turkish mother and an Albanian father. His mother, like Stalin's, hoped that he would become a priest. But he resisted and was trained in the military schools of the day. The corruption of the government drew him early into the revolutionary fellowship that agitated most of the barracks. He served a number of jail sentences for his rebel writings and speeches. Several trips out of Turkey, especially to Bulgaria, brought home to him in what backwaters his people were marooned. Bulgaria's capital, Sofia, was a pale imitation of Paris or Vienna, but its spirit and activity were a glaring contrast to the decay and pietistic

* "My Story," *McCall's* (August 1960).

superstition of his own country. He was fascinated by what he saw in the western world, its pragmatism, its casual living, its permissiveness, its emancipation from encrusted beliefs. He wrote later: "The Ottoman Empire was a place where the joys of heaven were reserved for non-Moslems, while Moslems were condemned to endure the shades of hell."* He knew already that, if Turkey were ever to rank with the great nations, it would have to free itself from the paralyzing thralldom of the Sultanate and all that it represented.

Mustapha Kemal became a seasoned officer in the wars of Tripoli and the Balkan wars of 1912 and 1913. He opposed Turkish entry into World War I on the side of Germany, but once it was launched, he proved his brilliance as a military leader. The disastrous rout of the British at Gallipoli was his achievement, and it was accomplished with ragged soldiers against the best equipped armies of Britain. He emerged from the war with the only untarnished national reputation. Turkey was decisively defeated, and Mustapha Kemal watched with contempt as the Sultan obsequiously obeyed every Allied command, hoping to save his throne at the expense of the national interest.

Both the Allies and the Sultan spotted Mustapha Kemal as a potential troublemaker. The attempt was therefore made to immobilize him by an appointment as inspector general of Turkish forces in remote East Anatolia, with the assignment to supervise disarmament and compliance with the provisions of the armistice. Even as he was given his orders, the dismemberment of European Turkey was under way, long-disputed areas cavalierly assigned to Greece, Italy, and France.

Instead of obeying orders to arrange for disarmament, Mustapha Kemal began rallying Turkish resistance, proclaiming that the Sultan was no longer a free agent and that his humiliating concessions to the Allies were wrung from him under duress. In July 1919, in a schoolroom in Erzerum, he brought together representatives from Anatolia and there resolutions were adopted to resist Turkish territorial dismemberment and foreign invasion. These became the nationalist campaign platform for the parliamentary elections that had been set for January 1920. Mustapha Kemal's program won a decisive mandate, and when the new Parliament convened in Constantinople it formally adopted what had become a national pact.

The Allies knew then that their own treaty arrangements would

---

* Lord Kinross, *Ataturk* (New York: W. Morrow, 1965), p. 30.

be nullified if the nationalists were permitted to control the government. They had the Sultan dissolve the Parliament and declare its actions null and void. They occupied the main buildings of Constantinople, and arrested and deported to Malta those of the Turkish dissentient leaders whom they could round up. In August, they compelled the Sultan to sign the Treaty of Sèvres which formalized the dismemberment of Turkey.

Mustapha Kemal escaped the net, and he called upon the 350 delegates who were still at large to convene in Ankara, deep in the interior of the country. There, on April 23, 1920, they declared their defiance of the Allies, and the great Turkish revolt had begun. Winston Churchill's description was classic: "In the tapestried and gilded chambers of Paris were assembled the lawgivers of the world. In Constantinople, under the guns of the Allied Fleets, there functioned a puppet Government of Turkey. But among the stern hills and valleys of the Turkish Homelands in Anatolia, there dwelt that company of poor men . . . who would not see it settled so; and at their bivouac fires at this moment sat in the rags of a refugee, the august Spirit of Fair Play."*

Mustapha Kemal's task was herculean. There was as yet very little Turkish nationalism to which he could appeal. The Young Turks had been ineffective and had been discredited. The war had left confusion and debris, and the climate was defeatist. There was no commissary, no medical corps, the most primitive sanitation. The officers were few, and many were still concerned about their sacred oath of loyalty to the Sultan. Mohammed had sent teams of religious zealots into the country to stir up the peasants. The Greeks, egged on by Lloyd George and the British, were moving inland from the coast. They were able to penetrate nearly 400 miles beyond Smyrna. Mustapha Kemal therefore faced both a civil war and a foreign invasion.

The battles, mainly against the Greeks, went on for more than two years in a land already sick to death of war and its toll. The military orders were curt and unequivocal: "Soldiers forward. Direction: the Mediterranean." The fighting was merciless, with atrocities on both sides, and the victims were women and children as well as the fighting men. Villages were burned, wells were poisoned, torture was common. Mustapha Kemal and his lieutenant, Ismet Pasha, who was later to succeed him, demonstrated genius in their ability to hold

* Churchill, *The Aftermath,* p. 390.

their forces together—peasants, merchants, intellectuals, landowners, forces that had conflicting interests and that had usually been rent by internecine quarreling. Even the women were called into action, and they performed feats of valor that became legend.

At last, in the historic Battle of Sakarya River which raged for twenty-two days, the longest battle until then in modern history, the Greeks were completely routed. The dream of continued Greek mastery in Asia Minor ended as the demoralized Greek forces collapsed and the great retreat began. When Smyrna fell, fifty thousand Christians, augmented by other tens of thousands of refugees, waited in terror to learn their fate. At first, reassured by Mustapha Kemal's pledge that order would be maintained, they hoped to remain; but when the Turks arrived to occupy the city and the rumor spread that massacres had begun, a frantic exodus to the wharves followed. Greek ships evacuated all the wretched families that they could save— forty thousand in one day alone. Then fire broke out in the Greek sections of Smyrna and Mustapha Kemal made no attempt to have them extinguished. After three days in which much of the ancient city, the "infidel Smyrna" part, had been leveled, Mustapha Kemal was able to say, pointing to the fire, "It is a sign that Turkey is purged of the traitors, the Christians, and of the foreigners, and that Turkey is for the Turks."

The Allies were too war-weary and too much bogged down in problems everywhere else to attempt military assistance to the Greeks. They now evacuated Constantinople, taking the cowering Sultan with them. Mustapha Kemal assumed the title of Gazi, the destroyer of the infidels. The Turkish republic was proclaimed, and Mustapha Kemal, hailed as liberator, became the President.

There were now sharp divisions among the Allies. Indeed, as they bickered over the provisions of the peace they could scarcely be called allies. There was no longer an effective coalition to enforce the old Treaty of Sèvres, which now had to be revised in the light of a totally new situation. Hence an international conference was convened at Lausanne and, after long deliberation, not completed until July 1923, the Turks retrieved most of what they had lost in Asia Minor during World War I. The Gazi's lieutenant, Ismet Pasha, negotiated with brilliance and even used his deafness as a diplomatic weapon; he could ignore proposals that he had no intention of accepting. The non-Turkish areas were not returned. Armenia remained independent, the Arab states and Palestine were given mandate status under the League of Nations. But all the degrading capitulations that had permitted foreigners to proclaim laws within Turkish jurisdiction were abolished. Constantinople, renamed Istanbul, and its outlying territory were confirmed as Turkish, and all the purely Turkish territory of Anatolia was restored. Lausanne was often described as the best treaty ever won by a defeated nation.

Since Greeks and Turks were so intermingled along the coast and in the east Mediterranean islands, a dramatic solution was now undertaken, a massive exchange of populations, supervised and financed by the League of Nations, and directed by a skillful negotiator, Dr. Fridtjof Nansen, a Norwegian diplomat who added to the enduring Scandinavian contributions to peace. Four hundred thousand Turks living in the territories that were under Greek control were returned to Turkish soil and re-established there; 1,300,000 Greeks, living as minorities in overwhelmingly Turkish areas, most of whom had already fled, were transferred to Greece and its islands. The exchange went on for seven years, from 1923 to 1930, by which time only two enclaves remained: the colonies of Greeks in Istanbul itself and an ancient cluster of Turks in western Thrace. The exchange of populations, one of the great mass movements in modern history, inflicted immense suffering during the interregnum of dislocation and resettlement. But, after the first shocks were absorbed, the solution was accepted as sagacious long-range statesmanship, for it prevented, or at least ameliorated, the passionate irredentist quarrels that would have convulsed the future.

Mustapha Kemal's task had only just begun. He interpreted the problem of reconstruction as much more than ridding the country of foreign control, or even of correcting specific abuses. He had no patience with the view that nationalism must find its roots in traditional forms and customs if these had become obsolete. He was convinced that the decline of Turkey and the lure for exploitation that it had continuously held out to foreign powers lay in the obscurantism and venality of the imams and the dervishes, and in what they called "religious faith." What the country had endured through the last shameful centuries was a far cry from the clean, wholesome, challenging Islam of the evangelical years. It was now a patchwork of graft and superstition that smothered every action in daily life, since there had been no separation of the secular and the sacred. It not only affected law and government, dress and cuisine, social life and education; it also stifled methods of thought and outlook. The first census of 1927 listed 29,000 mosques and 14,500 schools. It was therefore essential to break the suffocating control of the priests, from the common village kadi up to the Sultan-Caliph himself.

Mustapha Kemal's major objective then, even before the debris of the war had been eliminated, was to abolish the Caliphate. This was a revolutionary decision of the first magnitude, as sweeping as if it had been announced in the Christian world that the Papacy was to be eliminated. The Caliph was historically the successor of the Prophet Mohammed, and therefore the head of the Moslems of the world. No wonder the Assembly, however loyal to the Gazi, hesitated, and at one point sought a compromise by offering the Caliphate to Mustapha Kemal himself, a suggestion that he scornfully rejected. In March 1924, the fateful step was taken. All functionaries in the religious hierarchy, down to the muezzin who issued the calls to prayer, were now to be appointed by Mustapha Kemal, the President. Since all aspects of life had been governed by the Koran, Mustapha Kemal knew that any reform would be vulnerable unless this relationship were cut with surgical finality. He therefore set a panel of jurists to work, in collaboration with foreign experts, and in 1926 their recommendations became the basis for a modern code, nationalist and secular, which borrowed, without any inhibitions, from the experience of the western countries, German commercial law, Italian criminal law, Swiss civil law. In 1928 there were further constitutional changes which eliminated Islam as the official state religion, and oaths in the courts were no longer linked with Allah, but with the affirmation, "My honor as a Turk."

Such iconoclasm could not, of course, be accomplished without opposition. The old religious leaders threatened Mustapha Kemal with divine wrath, and the conservative lawyers found every variety of legal obstacle to effect delay. Other vested interests fumed and complained, but since they did not dare open opposition, they relied upon quiet sabotage. Mustapha Kemal was not diverted; whenever he came upon opposition, he was swift and relentless in punishment. His rationale was plain. "Surviving in the world of modern civilization," he said, "depends upon changing ourselves. . . . In an age when inventions and the wonders of science are bringing change after change in the conditions of life, nations cannot maintain their existence by age-old rotten mentalities. . . . Superstition and nonsense have to be thrown out of our heads."*

* Cited in Niyazi Berkes, *The Development of Secularism in Turkey* (Montreal: McGill University Press, 1964), p. 464.

In mid-nineteenth century the Japanese had concluded that if they were to control their destiny in an era when the West had mastered the tools and the armaments of power, they would have to imitate the pragmatism and the technology that had brought these about. The Gazi, refueled constantly by the ideas of others, took the lesson of the Japanese to heart. He insisted upon European clothes for men as well as for women, the elimination of veils and of the long, cumbersome, unsanitary robes, the Oriental stuffiness. He declared that men could no longer wear the fez, the traditional headpiece. It had no brim and it was therefore too easy to kneel and touch the earth with the forehead five times in daily prayer. There was a rush for new headpieces, anything with a brim. Since the supply at the beginning was limited, the most bizarre headgear appeared —old derbies, hastily made cloth caps, straw baskets, anything with a peak, to save one from prison, the bastinado, or the hangman's noose. Mustapha Kemal went into the villages in highly personalized visits, wearing a Panama hat, tearing off fezzes wherever he found them. "Had the King of England or the President of the United States appeared in a convict's uniform with broad arrows, they would have produced the same effect."* At a diplomatic reception Mustapha Kemal slapped the face of an Egyptian envoy who was gauche enough to wear the fez when he knew how it would irritate his host. The fez decree seemed to be aimed at superficialities; surely it was more important to change what went on inside the head than what was worn outside. But Mustapha Kemal thought primarily in terms of object lessons and the fez represented the past. In his own words: "It sat on our heads like a symbol of ignorance and fanaticism, of hatred against progress and civilization."

But of course there were more fundamental changes. Mustapha Kemal was concerned with the primitive health standards, the polluted water supplies and the open sewers, the ignorance of bacterial contagion. Again relying upon expert foreign help, he introduced large-scale health reforms. Steadily the incidence of disease and death was cut down, with gratifying progress in the curbing of infant mortality.

The pace of innovation quickened, constantly stimulated by Mustapha Kemal's frenetic impatience. He introduced the Gregorian calendar to eliminate still another reminder of the obscurantist past.

* Harold C. Armstrong, *The Grey Wolf* (New York: Capricorn Books, 1961), p. 241.

He decreed that all Turks must now take family names, and he acceded to the National Assembly's wish that his own was to be Ataturk—"Father of all the Turks." To accelerate literacy, he abolished the ancient Turkish alphabet, substituting the Latin, thus simplifying the Turkish language and severing another link with the religious tradition of the Koran that was sustained by the old script. He even introduced the western dances and, wearing the inevitable Panama hat, often led selected ladies out onto the floor and ordered the soldiers who were present to follow him in the foxtrot. At the outset a more uncomfortable group of people, stiffly prancing about the room with bewildered partners, could probably not be found.

Ataturk was realistic enough to know that none of these revolutionary and initially unpopular changes would survive if they were imposed by fiat, and this was another reason for his major concern with far-reaching reform in the educational system. He began by the appointment of a Minister of Education who was to have no relationship to the religious hierarchy. He invited the American educator, John Dewey, to study the pedagogical problems of Turkey and to make recommendations for reform. The education of the young was withdrawn from the jurisdiction of the religious schools and a whole network of modern secular schools established to take their place. The illiteracy of the country was abysmal. Only 8 percent of the thirteen and a half million people could read. Every effort was bent to hasten teacher training, curriculum reform, and school building. Ataturk himself undertook highly publicized visits to village public schools, and he stood before the blackboards, chalk in hand, to outline some of the lessons. Within two decades, 40 percent of all children between the ages of seven and twelve were in class, mainly co-educational now, another break with the past. He multiplied vocational and professional schools. He reorganized the University of Istanbul on a western model, and many foreign scholars were induced to come as visiting professors. He encouraged the graduates of high schools and gymnasia to round out their training in the colleges of Europe and the United States, and he welcomed fellowships from abroad, often supplementing them from government funds. He knew that those who returned would become ambassadors for his modernization program.

More difficult to achieve were fundamental changes in the pattern of living for the women. They had, until the war, led sheltered, secluded lives, marrying early, often at fourteen or even sooner, almost always in arranged matches. Schooling for them was considered sheer waste. When they appeared in public they wore veils and voluminous black clothes to conceal the figure. Ataturk knew that he could banish the fezzes of the men, but to introduce the fashions of the western world for the women would not be as easily achieved. He therefore resorted to psychology. He asked the wives of the army officers and of the ranking social families to set the styles of dress, hoping that it would be considered old-fashioned and dowdy to cling to the repudiated past. His strategy worked, and within a few years another major revolution had been accomplished. For from western dress, supplemented by the changes in the law codes that transformed marriage and divorce and property rights, the steps were inevitable to political rights and activity. By 1934 equal suffrage became the law, and in the next year, seventeen women were elected to the Turkish Assembly, including the lovely Halide Edib, the first woman of Turkey, who became the gifted and eloquent historian of the revolution.

Meantime, reforms were mounted in the rural areas. Here the pace had to be slower than for the middle and upper classes, who were mainly city dwellers. Life for the peasantry, the bulk of the country's population, had been quite primitive. The land was poor and only a small part was arable. The rural economy had been limited to the raising of tobacco, wheat, barley, figs, and raisins, and the yield per acre was so poor in the first year of independence that substantial imports were required to sustain the population. To achieve an agricultural revolution required redistribution of land, huge irrigation projects, credits, modern machinery, loans to make it available, and patient instruction in its use. Following the Russian example, therefore, Ataturk announced a five-year plan. But he added a spectacular innovation. He combined military service with agricultural apprenticeship, where those who were drafted were given training in modern techniques on model farms and with modern machinery. Agronomists from countries with advanced production techniques were invited to supervise instruction and experimentation. There was encouraging success when the sugar beet was introduced and became an important staple. Within six or seven years, the country was mainly self-sufficient and began to export its products.

Ataturk turned as vigorously to the industrial problems of the country. Turkey had scarcely moved into the twentieth century in its technology. There were a few cigarette factories, some textile and flour mills, and some cottage industries that produced rugs and carpets, and many of these establishments were foreign owned. Ataturk steered between the need for foreign capital and a determination to encourage investment from domestic sources. He introduced the policy of étatism, state support for private effort, drafting the banks to help in the modernization of established industry and in the expansion of new enterprise. At the end of a decade the economy included substantial developments in textiles, steel, and chemicals, and the entire communications and transportation complex—airlines, shipping, telephone, and telegraph—passed under government control.

In 1938, Ataturk died of cirrhosis of the liver, only fifty-seven years old, defying, to the end, the orders of his physicians to moderate his drinking and carousing. Later he was equated with some of the contemporary dictators. The comparison with Mussolini infuriated him. "It is said that I should stand beside that mountain of complacency, the hyena in jackboots, who could destroy the innocent Abyssinian savage without a moment's regret." As for Hitler, he reminded critics that the Turkish dictatorship freed an enslaved people while the Nazi dictatorship enslaved a free people. Ataturk's indignation was justified. He was authoritarian, but not Fascist. He was nationalist, but not racist. He was a soldier whose reputation had been won on the battlefield, but he would not strut in uniform and was almost always seen in civilian clothes. He was secularist, but with no animosity to civilized values. He was not fighting the traditions of a democratic state, nor the constitutional freedoms of a Weimar Republic. He was fighting an effete, corrupt, feudal, rotted-out anachronism, and he won his fight.

It was appropriate, therefore, for him to say to his government officials, his inner family, at the peak of his power: "There are two Mustapha Kemals. One is sitting before you, the Mustapha Kemal of flesh and blood, who will pass away. There is another whom I cannot call 'me.' It is not I that Mustapha Kemal personifies, it is you, all of you present here, who go into the furthermost parts of the country to inculcate and defend a new ideal, a new mode of thought. I stand for these dreams of yours. And my life's work is to make them come true."

It is curious that his body should have been buried in the Museum of Ethnography in Ankara, and that the statue to his memory should stand guard outside. For Ataturk was no museum piece. He had brought a new modern nation into being.

12

THE STALIN
DICTATORSHIP

THERE ARE SHARP DISAGREEMENTS IN THE EVALUATION OF THE CAREER of Stalin, who dominated the life of Russia for nearly thirty years and, by this domination, changed the map and the history of Europe and of the world. The disagreements are not over his tyranny. No one denies the tenacity of his hatreds nor the ruthlessness with which he struck, neither his bitter detractors, nor those who profited from the way he wielded power, nor even his daughter, Svetlana, who fled Russia and the desolate memories of her father's dictatorship. The disagreements are over the motives that drove this haunted, brooding man. Was it the savagery of a monster, who killed and afflicted more millions than anyone in history, save possibly Genghis Khan or Hitler? Or was the relentlessness the inevitable concomitant of a root-and-branch revolution where the stakes were the fate of all the generations ahead?

Those who saw him as a fiend cited his often expressed cynical motivation. Stalin said to Lev Kamenev, a comrade in the Politburo, "To choose one's victim, to prepare one's plan minutely, to stake an implacable vengeance, and then to go to bed, there is nothing sweeter in the world." Lenin's measured judgment, after watching his operations was, "His spite is a most evil factor in politics." There was a deadly realism in the jest that when Lenin's widow recoiled in horror because of the endless purges and vehemently protested, Stalin told her bluntly to shut up or he would make someone else Lenin's widow. Khrushchev, in his sensational denunciation of 1956 soon after Stalin's death, excoriated his predecessor as "a criminal murderer, a brutal, capricious despot, a sickly, suspicious slanderer." A modern Communist historian finds it impossible to forgive Stalin his senseless brutality because it perverted Lenin's doctrine and his mission and laid a stain on communism which almost destroyed it. Only by the exposure of Stalin's bloody arbitrary rule and his cult of personality could the political atmosphere of the Soviet Union "be cleansed of the filth of adventurism and despotism" and restored to the Leninist norm.* These references all added up to the judgment that Stalin killed with no more compunction than a hurricane, even when the murders reached into the millions, until humanity itself became an underground movement.

There were others, many others, who felt that such extreme judgments were rendered out of context. They too deplored the tragedy of purge and slave labor, of imprisonment and torture and execution. But they wondered how Russia, enmeshed in evils that had been endured for centuries, could have been brought out of its stifling medievalism without the most pitiless measures. The enemies without and within were so numerous, so implacable, so resourceful, that surely only the strongest actions, often sweeping away the innocent with the guilty, could cope with them. Ramsay MacDonald, the British Labour Prime Minister, said, when he reached an accord with Stalin: "The common people in history have been working through violence into politics and now that they have got there, I would be patient. Remember the Spartacus revolt, and Wat Tyler, and John Bull and Oliver Cromwell and the French Revolution . . . One will write similar sentences of the times we are going through."†

In a revealing speech in 1931, Stalin vowed, as he clawed his way to power, that Russian backwardness would never again play into enemy hands. "Old . . . Russia," he said grimly,

. . . was ceaselessly beaten for her backwardness. She was beaten by the Mongol Khans, she was beaten by the Turkish Beys, she was beaten by Swedish feudal lords, she was beaten by the Polish-Lithuanian *Pans,* she was beaten by Anglo-French capitalists, she was beaten by the Japanese barons, she was beaten by all—for her backwardness. For military backwardness, for cultural backwardness, for political backwardness, for industrial backwardness, for agricultural backwardness. She was beaten because to beat her was profitable and went unpunished. . . . We are fifty

* Medvedev, *Let History Judge,* p. xxvii.
† Ramsay MacDonald, *Socialism: Critical and Constructive* (London: Cassell, 1924), p. 264.

or a hundred years behind the advanced countries. We must make good this lag in ten years. Either we do it, or they crush us.*

This was one of Stalin's most eloquent moments and it pointed up, even if it did not condone, why he clung to ruthlessness with what seemed barbaric tenacity. He said, at the height of the purges of 1934, "You cannot make a revolution with silk gloves."

Most Kremlinologists are prepared to mesh the extreme judgments. They recognize the problems that Stalin faced when he seized the mantle of Lenin. There were continuous counterrevolutionary plots spawned by die-hard elements that never gave up in their attempts to undo the revolution. The thousand and one changes that communism demanded, especially the unpopular forced collectivization in agriculture, called for short-shrift suppression of such dissent, suppression, Stalin insisted, that could not be accomplished "with silk gloves." But this much having been conceded, Stalin was judged to have gone far beyond the compulsions of survival. Lenin too had to protect the revolution, but he resorted to violence with regret, and only so far as it seemed necessary. Stalin apparently had neither the need nor the regret. Somewhere along the way, the purges and the killings, feeding on each other, became altogether capricious. Unrelenting enmities, personal tragedies, the loss of wife and children that destroyed his family life, the endless assassination plots against him, physical deterioration, or all of these together, turned Stalin into the monster that he became. Trotsky quoted a Georgian émigré's belief that Stalin's entire personality changed after the early death of his first wife: "Beginning with the day he buried [her], he lost the last vestige of human feelings. His heart filled with the inexpressibly malicious hatred his merciless father had already begun to engender in him when he was still a child. He crushed with sarcasm his less and less frequently recurring moral impulses. Ruthless with himself, he became ruthless with all people."† ‡

* Isaac Deutscher, *Stalin* (New York and London: Oxford University Press, 1967), p. 328.

† L. Trotsky, *Stalin, An Appraisal,* edited by Charles Malamuth (New York: Stein & Day, 1967), p. 340.

‡ Another traumatic influence may have been the pitiable fate of his mother, perhaps the only human being he truly loved. Stalin visited her after an absence of many years, and the impact on him is described with rare insight by the novelist Mervyn Jones: "Her face was wrinkled, her complexion blotchy, her eyes rheumy, her hair grey. At thirty-six she looked like an old woman. At the same age, ladies of leisure were nurturing their beauty, dancing, having love affairs. Joseph could do nothing for his mother now, but he swore that there would be a reckoning for what had been inflicted on her." Mervyn Jones, *Joseph* (New York: Atheneum, 1970).

The debate will not be resolved no matter how much testimony and documentation are added. For each shift of authority in Russia brings reappraisal of the past and of its historic figures, and the reappraisal is related to the political climate of the moment. Stalin was vilified by his colleagues when he fought his way to supremacy. He was then deified by the sycophancy of those who stood in dread of him when he became dictator. He was denigrated and made into a nonperson after his death, and thrown out of the tomb that he had shared with Lenin. After the fall of Khrushchev he was gradually rehabilitated and de-Stalinization was reviewed and revised. In Russia, it is extremely difficult to predict the past.

Joseph Stalin was born in a small town near Tiflis, in the Russian province of Georgia, in 1879, of a family that had been serfs until the emancipation of the 1860's. His father was an obscure cobbler, his mother a peasant. Young Stalin bore a consuming hatred for his father who, especially when in his cups, often beat the boy, as he did the mother, so that Joseph grew up immune to cruelty. The mother, widowed early, was a deeply religious woman who had lost her first three children; only Joseph survived. She lived for him, supporting the family with laundry work and baking in the homes of the affluent. At seven, Joseph came down with smallpox, and was pockmarked for life. He was also injured, so that his left arm, badly bent, was three inches shorter than the right. He was ever conscious of the deformity, and when he surfaced as a public figure, all his photographs had to be touched up. He never stood near tall men, and always wore army boots to add two inches to a very short stature. His mother hoped that he would qualify for the priesthood, and he was enrolled in a seminary to prepare for it. But the seminaries of the day, much like the universities, were hotbeds of conspiracy and sedition, directed against the Romanoff despotism. Joseph led in this revolutionary activity and, at twenty, in 1899, he was expelled.

The next twelve or thirteen years, until he came into the senior echelons of the Communist Party, were filled with the usual harried, hunted, underground activity. He organized strikes, dodged the police, lived under a different alias every year, often captured, imprisoned, exiled to Siberia, escaping, captured again. He took part in scores of robberies to obtain funds for the work of the party, and his exploits included daring railroad holdups and the hijacking of payrolls. He early won the notice of Lenin, who regarded him as a loyal lieutenant, and ever-larger revolutionary responsibilities were assigned to him. It was in the intervals between prison and exile that he helped to found *Pravda,* which later became the Communist Party organ.

When the 1917 revolution overturned the czarist regime, Stalin was freed, with most of the other political prisoners, and, now almost forty, came to Petrograd to direct party activity until Lenin's return from foreign exile. As a member of the inner council, he helped to engineer the October revolution, and played a major role in the civil war that almost tore the country apart. He remained close to Lenin in these tempestuous years, and inched his way to the post of secretary of the party. Carefully, unobtrusively, he placed his men in high posts and, by 1922, he had a firm grip on the strategic administrative machinery of the party.

He was already in a deadly rivalry with Trotsky and the four or five leaders of the Communist inner group, all vastly superior in their intellectual vitality and depth, all contemptuous of his dull, colorless, superficial approach to Communist doctrine. But he had a rare animal cunning and a sure political sophistication that few of the others accurately appraised and, when Lenin had his first stroke in 1922, Stalin's hand was already on the crucial levers of power. Lenin was quite apprehensive now as he noted Stalin's conspiratorial ingenuity. After his second stroke, which almost killed him, Lenin expressed his concern. He wrote: "Stalin is too coarse, and this fault, though tolerable in dealings among us Communists, becomes unbearable in a General Secretary. . . . Therefore, I propose to the comrades to find some way of removing Stalin from his position and appointing somebody else . . . more loyal . . . less capricious."* But it was too late. Lenin's strength was gone, his messages were diverted, he was kept incommunicado, and soon afterward he died. Stalin, not yet in firm control, was at his best in pitting his most powerful colleagues against each other, using each group to destroy the other. By 1928 he had eliminated all his potential rivals and was at last master of Russia. He was ready now to undertake the root-and-branch changes that were to transform all the future.

One of Stalin's prime objectives, to which he turned at once, was the socialization of agriculture, the abolition of private farming. Individual peasant holdings were, to him, the strongholds of bourgeois capitalism. By liquidating them, not only would the philosophy of collectivization be sustained; there would be more effective state

---

* Cited in Robert Payne, *The Life and Death of Lenin* (New York: Simon & Schuster, 1964), p. 571.

control over the heartland of Russian life. This meant the repudiation of the New Economic Policy authorized by Lenin as a sop to encourage production, and it called for renewed war on the kulaks, the private owners. Stalin set a five-year collectivization goal at 50 percent of all farming. His determination launched what was virtually a new civil war. The peasants, having eliminated the feudal landlords in the first years of the revolution, refused to yield what they had so painfully achieved. They cared not a fig for the philosophy of communism where it threatened their humble patrimony. Rather than turn over to the state what was requisitioned, they burned their surplus, killed their livestock, and smashed their farm implements. Stalin responded to the defiance with no squeamishness. He mercilessly uprooted, imprisoned, exiled, executed; every village in the land bore the marks of his reprisal. Ultimately, there may have been five million kulak families who were deported to Siberia and the frozen north. Stalin vowed that though the entire present generation were sacrificed, he would persevere. By 1939 he had herded into collectives 96 percent of the peasant families that had survived. The cost was terrifying, but Stalin had no qualms. He had carried through as far-reaching a social and economic restratification as the 1917 revolution itself.

Paralleling the all-encompassing collectivist drive in agriculture, Stalin undertook a five-year plan for the accelerated industrialization of Russia. It was essential, he said, to free Russia from its dangerous dependence on the outside world. Nor could the agricultural revolution gather momentum without the tools and the mechanical power that were indispensable in a modern society. The country must become "metallic," one of his ministers urged, and Stalin made the challenge a fiat.

The need that drove Stalin may be better understood when it is remembered that in 1928 there were only seven thousand tractors in all of Russia, virtually no major power plants, and that the few that existed were inadequate and inefficient. Hundreds of technicians now went to work on their charts and, for the next few years, the energies of the nation were channeled to fulfill the deliberately unreasonable quotas for tractors, electrical equipment, oil cracking plants, blast furnaces, mines, railways. Giant dams and plants were built in the Ukraine and in the far-off Urals; there were new machine distribution centers at Stalingrad and Kharkov and Rostov, out of reach if war should come. Scores of new cities came into being, and many of the older ones burgeoned into metropolises. Everything was done frenetically, in a siege climate, in what was later termed "gigantomania." Stalin was determined to refute the snide comment of Nikolai Bukharin, whom he executed, about "snail's pace industrialization."

The lashed-up tempo exacted a terrifying cost; Russia became, in André Gide's phrase, "an anthill Utopia." But it had little of the anthill's precision and efficiency. For though the American and German experts who had been brought in at non-Communist high salaries to apply their capitalistic talents did all they could, the unskilled Russian workers could not quickly master the complexities of modern technology. There were continual operational breakdowns, excessive casualties in accidents and in overwork. An American observer noted that Russia's battle of ferrous metallurgy involved more casualties than the Battle of the Marne. Since the Communists had repudiated foreign debts, there was no credit line for Russia and payment for the sizable investments in modernization necessitated cruel reductions in consumer goods. Rationing compelled long hours of waiting in queues for scarce essentials. The cities were depressingly overcrowded and inadequate housing was a daily torment.*

Stalin admitted to Churchill at one of their later meetings in Moscow that the campaign for rapid industrialization and collectivization had probably cost ten million Russian lives, and represented as great a degree of sacrifice as the war against Hitler. But by 1939 both agriculture and industry were completely under party control, and the country was no longer dangerously dependent on the outside world for its weaponry and its industrial products. Stalin had telescoped into a decade what it had taken the western nations half a century to achieve.

No dictator walks free from the threat of assassination. In Stalin's case, the threat was considerably intensified because of the deadly enmities that were spun off among the families whose lives he had so callously disrupted. Stalin reacted with lethal malevolence to the hatreds that swirled about him. He was especially unforgiving when he suspected disloyalty or misgivings among those who were closest to him. His state of mind was not calmed as Hitler came to power, vowing the achievement of *Lebensraum* for Germany at the expense of Russia, and as Japan moved into Manchuria and menaced Russia's

---

* A story of the period described the visit of the ghost of Lenin to the office of Stalin. "How goes it?" Lenin asked. "Oh, excellent," said Stalin, "excellent. The people are all with me." "Ah," said Lenin, "another such five-year plan, and all the people will be with me."

long eastern flank. These were the years when the democracies were in the throes of appeasement and eager to turn the Fascist dictators against Russia.

For a man as moody and as intuitively vindictive as Stalin, all these dangers and hostilities converged to generate and multiply the orgies of murder and reprisal that ultimately drove him beyond control. Stalin's paranoid identification of an enemy went thus: "He may not have actually committed a crime, but had he the opportunity, he would. Therefore he is guilty." A typesetter was sent to his death for a misprint of the word "Stalin"—man of steel—which appeared as "Salin"—man of lard. Dark suspicion flashed for him as a reflex action. One is reminded of Metternich, who was endlessly concerned with motive. When he heard of the death of Talleyrand, he mused, "I wonder what he meant by that!"

Stalin further demonized his tyranny by a decree that an entire family would be held responsible for the treason of any of its members. Such reactions encouraged, indeed they compelled, treachery and betrayal, and they corrupted and poisoned family life. Stalin not only destroyed the living who, he imagined, menaced him, but also their place in history. The official encyclopedias and other records rewrote the past and distorted it. Trotsky's name disappeared altogether. The records of old Bolsheviks who were Lenin's closest allies either became obscure footnotes or were eliminated. Each revision was accompanied by ever more extravagant adulation of Stalin's own role.

As the terror spread the disaffection spread too, each nourishing the other. When Stalin's wife, Nadezhda, remonstrated with him and warned him that his ruthlessness had long ago reached the point of diminishing returns, he vilified her with such ferocity that she committed suicide. When, years later, her daughter, Svetlana, fled to the United States and revealed the poisoned climate of her household, it confirmed what had already become clear even to those who were not close to Stalin.

Stalin's chief lieutenant was Sergei Kirov, a brilliant and attractive product of the revolution and deeply loyal to its basic principles. He saw the danger in Stalin's capricious extremism, and there gathered around him the younger men who relied on him to calm down their chief. A Saul-David trauma of envy and suspicion must have begun eating into Stalin. In December 1934, Kirov was assassinated. The murderer had obtained extraordinarily easy access to Kirov's office and there is now very little doubt that Stalin was involved. Khrushchev corroborated the suspicion in his speech to the Communist Party notables after Stalin's death. "The deeper we study the materials connected with Kirov's death," he said grimly, "the more questions arise."* But Stalin presided at Kirov's funeral, shed tears over the death of his "beloved" protégé, and publicly kissed the body in its beflowered coffin. Then he took advantage of the murder to widen the purge, beginning with forty members of his own inner bodyguard. Tens of thousands were rounded up, then hundreds of thousands, arrested, deported, imprisoned, executed, in the villages, the cities, in the party, in the military forces, on and on and on, until the whole country was in a terror spasm. A Russian historian of the purge wrote: "These were not streams, they were rivers of blood, the blood of honest Soviet people. The simple truth must be stated: not one of the tyrants and despots of the past persecuted and destroyed so many of his compatriots."† The head of the secret police, Nikolai Yezhov, wired to a party chief: "You are charged with exterminating ten thousand enemies of the people. Report results by signal." Apparently it was not necessary to supply names or identify cases, but only to record numbers. Those who fled to foreign countries were hunted down relentlessly. Trotsky found refuge in Turkey, then in Norway, finally in Mexico, until a Stalinist agent, a young Spaniard, penetrated his retreat in 1940 and split his skull with an ice pick. The murderer was sentenced to twenty years in prison by a Mexican court, but on Stalin's order was awarded the title "Hero of the Soviet Union."‡

Between 1936 and 1938 the world was further astonished by a series of public trials where every form of treason was laid at the door of former trusted associates, the pioneers of the revolution, the men who had stood closest to Lenin and who were now accused of collaborating with imperialist America, Nazi Germany, and Fascist Japan. The victims included the top echelons of the military up to Marshal Tukachevsky himself, the hero of the Civil War. One result of the military purge was its influence on the timing of Hitler's invasion of the Soviet Union. He was warned by his generals in 1939 against attempting the attack. He told the chief of staff, Keitel, that the first-class high-ranking officers were wiped out by Stalin in 1937 and the new generation could not provide the brains for effective

* Nikita Khrushchev, *Khrushchev Speaks* (Ann Arbor, Mich.: University of Michigan Press, 1963), p. 438.
† Medvedev, *Let History Judge*, p. 239.
‡ *Ibid.*, p. 179.

resistance. He was proved right, and the early failures and tremendous losses of the Russians almost brought complete collapse.* The indicted included every former head of the secret police, from the days of Lenin to Stalin's own appointments. They had devised all the refinements of torture; now the penalties that they had ordered for others were applied to them. The judges who read the verdicts were not long spared for, in most instances, they themselves were soon added to the execution rolls.

The prosecution was conducted by a genius in vituperation, Andrei Vyshinskii. He excoriated the revered heroes of yesterday and identified them as "human scum," "swine," "Fascist wreckers." He concluded every denunciation with the cry: "Shoot the mad dogs." From the indictments and confessions of the accused, it appeared that the revolution had been carried out, and the Soviet regime established, by traitors with the aid of traitors. One of Stalin's most respected biographers wrote: "He struck at the very roots of the idea by which the revolution, the party, and the state had lived. He was destroying the birth certificate and the ideological title deeds of his own regime."†

The public trials went on for years, and the accused almost invariably confessed to every crime that the prosecutor listed. The courtroom scenes were out of Dostoyevsky and Kafka. Had the victims been brainwashed, and were they then trotted out to serve as examples to others? Had they succumbed to a Pavlovian torture that broke them down in a conditioned reflex? Were their families hostage and did they hope by confession to spare them threatened disaster? Were some so loyal to the Communist faith that their lives had no meaning as individuals and they therefore preferred to die rather than repudiate leadership, however unfair? Bukharin summed up this tragic dilemma when he cried out after his nightmare confession: "I do not want to be *I*, I want to be *We*." Trotsky had explained this psychological motivation: "One must not be right *against* the party. One can be right only with the party, and through the party, for history has created no other road for the realization of what is right."‡ All these motives for confession were undoubtedly involved in the eerie Communist world whose mental processes continued to baffle the West.

* *Ibid.*, p. 214.
† Deutscher, *Stalin*, p. 373.
‡ *Ibid.*, p. 278.

After Stalin's death, he was execrated by the men closest to him and reduced to a nonperson by his successors. But this retribution came many years later. In the interval he led Russia through World War II. The Czarist regime could not survive the test of war; Stalin's Russia did. He led Russia through the Cold War and into the spectacular successes of the nuclear age. With all the passions and hatreds that he loosed, he apparently commanded extraordinary loyalty. Hence, the question posed at the outset returns as the appraisal of his role is pondered. How much of the violence that flowed from him was the inevitable price of a revolution that brought a backward, benighted country to pre-eminence, and how much was exacted because of a tyrant's paranoia? George Kennan balanced personal frailty with historic necessity. He noted that revolutionaries

came to feel that in the unwillingness of many social idealists in the past to practice cruelty and to shed blood deliberately had lain the source of their political failure—that only through a ruthless callousness toward *individual* human life could the way be found to the elimination of such things as ruthlessness and callousness in their relation to *people in the mass*—that there was even a certain superior virtue and self-sacrifice involved in the employment of evil means for worthy ends: it meant that a few accepted the burden of guilt and unpleasantness in order that others might have the privilege of remaining guiltless. This was, in short, the classic Dostoyevskian dilemma.*

The judgment of Stalin's most perceptive biographer, B. D. Wolfe, was that he kept changing his objectives and his methods, and ultimately his personality too, to meet the revolutionary circumstances as they arose, and that, in his virtuosity, he became the supreme example of "a man who succeeded in inventing himself."†

Whatever the motives and the forces that they released, the years of Stalin were a nightmare, and many who lived through their terror must have thought of the disintegrating years in ancient Greece, and of the last words of Socrates after his condemnation. He said to his judges: "The hour of departure has arrived, and we go our ways, I, to die, and you, to live, and which is better, God only knows."

* Kennan, *Russia and the West Under Lenin and Stalin,* pp. 241–2.
† B. D. Wolfe, *Three Who Made a Revolution* (New York: Dial Press, 1948), p. 426.

13

HITLER AND
THE NAZIFICATION
OF GERMANY

AMONG THE MANY TRAGEDIES THAT DARKENED THE POST-WORLD WAR I period, not least was the wretched fate of Germany. Disastrously defeated, it tried to establish a democratic order, but the effort failed and it was engulfed by a dictatorship whose cruelty and barbarism disgraced the German name and its long tradition of honorable achievement. The question has haunted every historian of the period: How could this happen in a highly cultured nation, and in the enlightened twentieth century? There had been instances of ruthlessness in many parts of the world—in the Congo, in Turkey, in Russia. But more, much more, was expected from Germany, a nation where the arts flourished, where the sciences were the glory of the western world, where respect for law was counted the highest civic virtue. Germany had the largest proportion of Nobel Prize winners, the most envied university system which the elect of the earth sought out to fulfill their research and their advanced academic requirements. How was it possible for people with such a proud record of fulfillment to bring to power, not by coup but by a freely exercised franchise, the Nazis, whose pledges were written in blood and who had made it clear that, once in the seats of authority, they would repudiate all the values that Christianity had cherished?

As noted earlier, there were pressures on the German people after the defeat of World War I that would have weakened the morale of any people—the humiliations of a dictated peace treaty; the inflation that wiped out the savings of the thrifty middle class; the panic of

[147]

the vested interests that impelled them to offer support to the private armies; the internecine struggles among the democratic groups, who exhausted their vitality in fighting each other even when faced by enemies whose discipline was fused in the fires of hate.* None of these factors by themselves may have been sufficient to corrupt a whole nation. But in a tragic moment, tragic for Germany and for all the world, Fate spewed up, from the dark sewers of German alienation, a monster, Adolf Hitler, who fused all of these pressures and added to them the force of his own evil genius.

Adolf Hitler's father was a minor customs official. His mother was a third wife who had been a maid to the first. She was twenty-three years younger than her husband and, by all accounts, highly neurotic. Adolf grew up in poverty, devoted to his mother but despising his father. His early work was in masonry, bricklaying, and housepainting. He hoped for a career in art, but he did not qualify for admission to an art school. He could not adjust to the steadiness of any trade, and he tramped from one odd job to another, portering, shoveling snow, beating carpets, whatever provided bare keep. It might have been expected that such struggles for livelihood would send him into the proletarian ranks. But he had no faith in their unions, and he despised the kind of people that they represented. He lived at a hostel for derelicts and often had to frequent charity soup kitchens to stave off hunger. It was in Vienna that his morbid loathing of Jews became an obsession. The feeling was not contrived, as it was in the case of many of his Nazi collaborators, who manipulated it as scapegoat weaponry.

In World War I Hitler joined the German forces. He fought well, until wounded and gassed, and then spent months in a military hospital, festering with hatred toward those who, he believed, were responsible for the German defeat. It was during this hospital experience that he decided on a career in politics. He signed on as a spy for the Reichswehr and an early assignment led him into one of the first cells of the Nazi Party, a small group of rabid malcontents, described as "seven nobodies, lacking everything from a program to a typewriter." From this grubby, insignificant cell grew the movement that was to disrupt the whole world.

Hitler soon imposed his leadership, and he provided the program and the strategy that drew the first converts to his Cave of Adullam—

* See Chapter 4.

the troubled, the frustrated, the embittered. He brought no conventional oratory to his appeals. Albert Speer, who later worked most closely with him as Minister of Resources, described him as a shrieking and gesticulating fanatic in uniform. His content was mainly inflammatory bombast, but it ignited the masses who came for therapeutic reassurance. Speer added that the speeches were soon forgotten, but the mood remained and it had hypnotic persuasiveness.*

In November 1923, Hitler felt that he had sufficient support to risk an attack on the already stormy province of Bavaria. His Munich putsch was a harebrained attempted coup, but it had the support of General Ludendorff and it was hoped that the magic of the warlord's name would win over the army and the police. The putsch fizzled into little more than a riot, and the participants, more theatrical than competent, were quickly routed. It was a commentary on the naïveté of the Weimar government that Hitler, captured two days after the fiasco, received a mild sentence and actually served only six months. The police carefully avoided firing on General Ludendorff, and he marched straight forward into their ranks. He was respectfully welcomed and was not even reprimanded.

It was during Hitler's prison period, where he was given the widest latitude, that he wrote *Mein Kampf*, which, though it sold very little in the years when Hitler was in the political wilderness, gained best-seller rank after the Nazis won control. Then, it became politic for every German household to possess a copy, if only for display. The book was a mess of repetitious nonsense, but it covered the themes that were calculated to stir the deep-seated resentments of the little people, the *Kleinbürgertum*. It struck at the French, "African apes on European soil," at the "Diktat of Versailles" and its inequities, at the Jews, "the bacillus in the bloodstream of the world," at the Russian Communists, from whom must be wrested whole provinces of fertile land to provide living space, *"Lebensraum"* for the Germans. Churchill noted that its prose might be "turgid" and "verbose" and "shapeless," but it was "pregnant with its message."

When Hitler was amnestied he once again took command of the Nazi cadres. At first he made little headway; Europe, Germany included, was entering the Locarno phase, an interlude of rapproche-

---

* Albert Speer, *Inside the Third Reich* (New York: The Macmillan Company, 1970), p. 17.

ment and conciliation when economic and social conditions seemed to be improving. But when the world swooned into the Great Depression, and all the old social wounds were reopened, the effect on the Nazi drive for power was cumulative. Now Hitler's hypnotic oratory won him millions of adherents. He was a master of the psychology of frustration and he fed on the national passion for vengeance. There were thousands of rallies, sometimes sixty a day. In 1930 the Nazis won 108 seats in the Reichstag. At the end of the year they captured their first province, Thuringia, which passed into the control of Dr. Wilhelm Frick, one of Hitler's closest collaborators. Frick dismissed all members of the police force whose loyalty to Nazism he doubted, and he purged educational and cultural institutions. A daily morning prayer of hate was introduced into the schools so that youngsters could call upon God "to punish our nation's traitors and bless the deed that brings us liberty."

Frick was forced out within two years, but not until he had made plain what the new pagan totalitarianism would mean for all Germany if the Nazis ever reached national dominance. No one could say later that Hitler and his lieutenants had improvised his agenda for destruction. He had written it out plainly for all to read, and it had its trial run in Thuringia. "We shall enter Parliament in order to supply ourselves, in the arsenal of democracy, with its own weapons, to paralyze the Weimar sentiment with its own assistance. If democracy is so stupid as to give us free tickets for this purpose, well, that is its affair. We come as enemies; as the wolf bursts into the flock."*

As the face of Germany changed, there were two groups that were strangely silent even in the period before Hitler had come to supreme power, when their influence might still have been positively exerted. Most of the Christian churches, Catholic and Protestant alike, would not have their routine disturbed by the quarrels of the politicians. The communicants who accepted the new order were known as "German Christians" and they easily reconciled Christianity and National Socialism. Then there were the intellectuals, primarily centered in the university world. Virtually all of them not only acquiesced when Hitler made the educational institutions part of his propaganda arsenal; they joined in extolling the Nazi aims. Some of them were Nobel Prize winners—Philipp Lenard, who owed his

---

* *Der Angriff.* Cited in Abram Leon Sachar, *Sufferance Is the Badge* (New York: Alfred A. Knopf, 1939), p. 32.

training to his Jewish teacher, Heinrich Herz; Erwin Baur, the biologist; Martin Heidegger, the philosopher; Victor Burns, who attained world renown for his work in international law. Above all, there was the interpreter of Goethe, Gerhart Hauptmann, Germany's greatest playwright, who saw no disgrace in coming out on stage arm-in-arm with the Nazi Minister of Propaganda, Joseph Goebbels, and the president of the racially purged theater chamber, Hans Johst. Hauptmann's plaintive cry must have been echoed by most of his colleagues: "If only life would demand no more solutions from us." Thomas Mann, one of the few men of letters who preferred exile to dishonor, wrote to Ernst Bertram: "The last thing you can be accused of is having turned your coat. You always wore it the 'right' way round."* Archibald MacLeish has branded this pious verbalizing of the church and the universities as the gravest moral irresponsibility.†

The years 1930 and 1931 were the worst of the world depression, and the capitalist structure was in jeopardy everywhere, including Germany. When unemployment reached six million in 1932, the steel barons, the bankers, the landed magnates poured ever-mounting subsidies into the Nazi coffers, to sustain the counteroffensive against the Communists. There were two national elections during that year, one for President and one for the new Reichstag. In the first Hitler pitted himself against Paul von Hindenberg, the national hero.‡ Although Hitler lost, it was only by a small margin, and he polled more than eleven million votes. In the second, the Reichstag election, his total reached nearly fourteen million and he captured 270 seats, the largest of any party in the history of the Republic. His votes did not come from the unemployed; those went in largest measure to the Communists. His stunning total came primarily from the burghers of the middle class.

Von Hindenberg was outraged by the prospect of the chancellorship for Hitler. "That man for Chancellor?" he cried, "Why, I'll make him a postmaster, and then he can lick my backside, on stamps." But with an election total of fourteen million, Hitler could not any longer be bypassed and in January 1933, he was named Chancellor. The impossible had happened. Only yesterday Hitler

---

* Cited in Joachim Fest, *The Face of the Third Reich* (New York: Pantheon Books, 1970), p. 249.

† Archibald MacLeish, *The Irresponsibles* (New York: Duell, Sloan & Pearce, 1940).

‡ At this stage Von Hindenberg, eighty-five years old, was senile. Theodore Lessing called him Zero paving the way for Nero.

was regarded as a caricature, a tramp in Vienna, a frustrated corporal in World War I, a neurotic who had failed ingloriously in a beer-hall putsch, a pamphleteer whose words were scavenged from the garbage cans. Now, at forty-three, he was Chancellor of Germany. In Bullock's phrase, the street gangs had seized control of a great modern state, and the gutter had come to power.* Churchill, looking back, wrote: "Adolf Hitler had arrived at last; but he was not alone. He had called from the depths of defeat the dark and savage furies latent in the most numerous, most serviceable, ruthless, contradictory and ill-starred race in Europe. He had conjured up the fearful idol of all-devouring Moloch of which he was the priest, and incarnation."† What had happened was the repudiation by the German people of the faith in parliamentary institutions to deal boldly and effectively with social crisis and mass unemployment. As in so many other parts of Europe, they turned instead to authoritarianism and to a personal deliverer.

Now Chancellor, with a new Reichstag election in the offing, Hitler acted at once to consolidate his position. He took control of the police, and all opposition meetings were placed under the surveillance of an auxiliary force with proved Nazi allegiance. Just before the voting the Reichstag was burned down. It was apparently the deed of a half-crazed Dutchman, but it was immediately denounced as a Communist plot, and the panic word was skillfully spread that the Communists were planning a takeover. Hitler suspended all civil rights and the opposition leaders were rounded up and imprisoned. In the election, the Nazis polled seventeen million and, when the Communist vote was declared invalid, Hitler had a clear majority. The Reichstag met on March 23, 1933, to commit suicide. The ceremony took place in the old opera house, and the organ played music by Brahms, since it was not yet known that the composer had a Jewish grandfather. The deputies then passed the act that made Hitler supreme for the next four years. The Nazis rose to sing the Horst Wessel song, the flag of the Republic was abolished, and the German people passed under the dictatorship of the Führer.

Hitler brought in with him a most extraordinary cabal of lieutenants, and their personalities and backgrounds threw further light on the violence and fanaticism of the Third Reich. Closest to Hitler was the swashbuckling Hermann Göring, impulsive, flamboyant, forever

---

* Alan Bullock, *Hitler* (New York: Bantam Books, 1961), p. 229.

† Churchill, *The Gathering Storm* (Cambridge, Mass.: Houghton Mifflin Co., 1948), pp. 70–1.

primping in ostentatious uniforms, thoroughly pagan. He came from a good family and was well educated, but he never cleared the bloodshed of the war out of his system. He had been an ace aviator, his record of kills surpassed only by his commander, Manfred von Richthofen, the famous Red Baron. After the republican revolution destroyed his faith in Germany, he lived in Sweden, where misfortune continued to haunt him. His frail Swedish wife, who suffered from epilepsy, had become so ill that Göring applied to the courts to obtain custody of her son by a former marriage. This was denied, for he was by then a dangerous narcotics addict and was obliged to undergo treatment in a Swedish asylum. This restless, unstable man, toughened by war, utterly callous of human life, was Hitler's chief military aide. His interest was purely animal: "I didn't join the party because of any ideological nonsense."* When World War II was launched in September 1939, Göring was designated to succeed to the chancellorship if anything should happen to the Führer.

Then there was the crippled Dr. Joseph Goebbels, a Nazi Caliban, the outstanding intellect in the anti-intellectual Nazi Party. He was a subtle, polished orator, a match in debate for his ablest opponents, and he had consummate skill in the techniques of propaganda. Ironically, his post was entitled "Minister of National Enlightenment," and, according to his critics, he had impressive qualifications: chest measurement, 36, mouth measurement, 63. It took real genius to convert the "Horst Wessel Song" into a national anthem; Horst Wessel was a pimp who was killed in a brawl over a whore. Goebbels manipulated the national frustration with typical German thoroughness. "We must organize hate," he wrote, "with ice cold calculation. . . . Vengeance is a dish best enjoyed cold." He found in anti-Semitism an ideal weapon for forging his new Germany. He used it continuously, although his wife, Magda, was reared in a Jewish home, and her mother's second marriage had been to a Jew. His most important and influential teacher, when he took his doctorate at Heidelberg, had been the distinguished Jewish scholar, Friedrich Gundolf. Goebbels nevertheless gave the lead to anti-Semitic tirades that had no restraint. "The Jew," he wrote, "is the cause and the beneficiary of our national slavery. He has ruined our race, rotted our morals, corrupted our traditions, and broken our power. Who thinks German, must despise the Jews. The one implies the other."† At another time he wrote that he treasured a prostitute above a married Jewess.

* Cited in Fest, *The Face of the Third Reich,* p. 74.
† Cited in Sachar, *Sufferance Is the Badge,* p. 41.

Finally, there was Alfred Rosenberg, a Baltic German, the so-called philosopher of Nazism, whose prolific pen was employed mainly for windy bombast. Oscar Wilde's comment on the style of Hall Caine applied perfectly here: "He wrote at the top of his voice." In his *Myth of the Twentieth Century*, which Goebbels called an ideological belch, Rosenberg outlined the cult of paganism and racism for the Nazi faithful. His model was not Charlemagne, who had Christianized Germany, but Widukind, who had resisted. He demanded that Christianity be purged of its excrescences, the odious handiwork of the Jewish zealots Matthew and Paul and such Africans as Tertullian, and that the Old Testament be replaced by Nordic sagas. In this volume is the whole Nazi imperialist program, which was to culminate in the planting of the swastika on Russia's fertile plains. Rosenberg, who had been educated in Russia and had a degree in architecture from a Russian university, apparently had developed a hatred against everything Russian, and he took special pleasure later in ordering the desecration of its cultural monuments—the churches, the monasteries, the homes of Tolstoy and Tchaikovsky. To him the Aryan was civilization's choicest product, and the German its quintessence.

These four—Hitler, Göring, Goebbels, and Rosenberg—molded the Nazi doctrine and action, and together they inspired the underground definition of the perfect Aryan: Blond as Hitler, tall as Goebbels, thin as Göring, and his name is Rosenberg. Very few men were as underrated as was Hitler when he took over the seals of office. The old-line politicians had been sure that they could use him for their purpose when they cooperated to name him as Chancellor. Franz von Papen, who was central in the negotiations, said smugly to one of his friends, "In two months we'll have pushed him into a corner so that he'll be squeaking." The world still regarded Hitler as a buffoon whose wild statements were interpreted merely as bait to achieve power. Some went to the other extreme and sized up Hitler as a gifted statesman with a passion for peace. Prime Minister Stanley Baldwin reported a conversation with Arnold Toynbee, the historian who pontificated on every turn in the march of civilization. Toynbee had returned from an interview with Hitler "which lasted one-and-three-quarter hours. He is convinced of his sincerity in desiring peace in Europe and a close friendship with England."* Many agreed with

* Thomas Jones, *A Diary with Letters* (London and New York: Oxford University Press, 1954), p. 181.

the German folk adage: No soup is served as hot as it is cooked. Hitler belied every expectation. He demonstrated such unrestrained ruthlessness, linked with such unerring instinct in his timing, that soon no boast seemed irrelevant.

In August 1934 he ordered all officers and men in the military forces to take an oath of allegiance to him: "I swear by God this holy oath, that I will render unconditional obedience to the leader of the German Reich, Adolf Hitler, supreme Commander of the armed forces, and that, as a brave soldier, I will be ready at any time to stake my life for this oath." The far-reaching oath presented an agonizing moral problem in the years ahead to those who, in disenchantment, pondered the elimination of the Führer.

Hitler's plans were now ready, and, with a four-year lease on authority, uncurbed, unqualified, there was apparently no obstacle to prevent fulfillment. All parties were dissolved and their assets taken over. No political activity was permitted except within the Nazi framework. The industrialists who had subsidized his rise to leadership received the return on their investment. The advanced social legislation of half a century was invalidated. Trade unions were outlawed and their holdings confiscated. Instead, a labor front was created, a national company union, in which the industrial magnates regulated the conditions of labor and the workers were forbidden the right to strike. When some of the leftist Nazi leaders protested, they were murdered in a succession of purges, and these included Gregor Strasser, one of the Nazi pioneers, for whose twins Hitler had acted as godfather. Women were taken out of industry and bluntly ordered to concentrate on the three K's—*Kinder, Kirche, Küche*: children, the church, and the kitchen. "The drive for the emancipation of women," Hitler sneered, "has its roots only in Jewish intellectualism."

Nor did the religious Establishment escape the long reach of the Nazis. At first most Catholic and Protestant churchmen imagined that the persecution of the Jews was an unfortunate by-product of a necessary social revolution, and that Christian institutions would be spared. "Where wood has to be planed, there must be shavings," Göring had said. They were soon enlightened. Hitler saw himself as the Nietzschean Superman, clad in the armor of hardness and free of the meekness and degeneracy of Christianity. Nazi propaganda continued to emphasize the incompatibility of the swastika and the cross. Very early there were skirmishes over the control of education between the government and the "black moles," the Nazi term for the Catholic clergy. The quarrel deepened and it flared into open war with the Papacy. The Protestant leaders watched with dismay the government's encouragement of pagan ideals, the emphasis on the old Norse gods, and the attacks on the Testaments. The Lutheran pastor Martin Niemöller, an ex-submarine commander, protested in vain the Aryanization of Jesus as an unscrupulous attempt to purify his Saviour with a forged birth certificate.

The arts and the sciences were also "coordinated." There were book-burning orgies, and the Nazi censors were left to their own judgment as they set the torch to the work of dissidents and nonconformists. The theater, opera, literature, all became vehicles of propaganda, and the most famous authors were eliminated if they were not Aryan, or if they would not link their art to the exigencies of political loyalty. As for science, it was "cleansed" of alien influence, and it cost Germany the continued participation of Einstein and other trail blazers in contemporary thought who were now stigmatized as "cultural Bolshevists." The subordination of science to the interest of the state was made clear in an address by Dr. Bernhardt Rust, Minister of Science, Education, and National Culture, at the 550th anniversary festival of Heidelberg University. The value of a scientific work was to be measured, not by its intrinsic integrity, but by the blood in the scientist's veins. Is he pure Aryan? Who is his grandmother?* The proud boast of Terence had been adapted and reversed. It now read: "I am an Aryan. Nothing foreign is human to me."

There followed the complete purge of Jewish life in Germany. It began with boycotts; it was continued with expulsions from professional and business life; then, though for the moment short of massacre, it was climaxed by the Nuremberg Laws, which deprived all Jews and anyone with the taint of Jewish ancestry of citizenship and participation in any form of national life. This included the expulsion of Jews from societies for the blind. A special department was set up for research into racial purity and genetics. Jews were obliged to add the names of Israel and Sarah. All elements in German culture that had any Jewish identification were eliminated. Of

---

* A revised version of "Little Red Riding Hood" was whispered all over Germany, where there were frantic explorations into ancestral records. Little Red Riding Hood goes through the woods and she meets the wolf. "Where are you going?" she is asked. "Oh, I'm looking for my grandmother." "So am I," says the wolf, "aren't we all?" After reading a long article extolling Aryan blood and Aryan genius, one writer was ready to lay a wreath on the Tomb of the Unknown Aryan.

course, such sweeping proscription created special problems in the case of classical authors, notably Heinrich Heine. The solution was ingenious. Heine's works remained in the German school curriculum but the author was noted as "anonymous." In 1938, after a distraught young Jew whose parents had been uprooted and dumped into a field, assassinated a Nazi official, a national reprisal was authorized in which thousands of Jewish shops and homes were looted and more than five hundred synagogues were desecrated and burned. A fine of four hundred million dollars was levied on the Jewish community for living the kind of lives that had induced the riots.

The widening repression precipitated Jewish mass migration, even where the families had lived in Germany for many centuries. Those who left were compelled to sacrifice their possessions. When the eighty-two-year-old Dr. Freud was expelled from Austria and sought refuge in England, he declared: "The inmates of the asylums are now expelling their physicians." The horror of concentration camps, crematoria, and the systematic murder of millions of Jews—the Final Solution—were to come later, but already Germany itself had fulfilled a Nazi objective: it was virtually *Judenrein*—cleansed of Jews.

It was impossible, however, to delimit the effects of such a purge, and they were to leave their mark upon the whole German nation. The right of a regime to stimulate terror, to decree imprisonment, to confiscate and expel and execute, all beyond the law, could today be invoked against a despised minority. But tomorrow it could be applied against good Aryans, then against party members who dared to disagree, then against neighboring nations whose lands and resources were coveted, and finally against the whole world.* The foreign policy of Hitler became more and more belligerent, beginning with the repudiation of the Treaty of Versailles, but soon reaching out to menace and conquer new areas. By 1939, Hitler's hand was against every neighbor, and when his blackmail could no longer be endured, the whole world was plunged into war. The realm that he had vowed would endure a thousand years lasted twelve. But by the time he had committed suicide in a bunker under

---

* Gerhart Hauptmann's emotional odyssey was typical. His initial reaction to the Nazi assaults on the Jews had been: "Ah, those few Polish Jews! Good God, it's not all that important—every revolution starts off by bringing the dregs to the top." But by 1938, when all his world crashed about him, he mourned: "This dog's muck will cover the world with war; this miserable brown ham actor, this Nazi hangman, is pushing us into a world conflagration." Cited in Richard Grunberger, *The Twelve Year Reich* (New York: Holt, Rinehart & Winston, 1971), p. 24.

Berlin tens of millions of families everywhere mourned their dead. At the outset of Hitler's bloodless conquest, Marvin Lowenthal wrote prophetically: "The Jews are on the road back to the prison of the Middle Ages; but in the nature of such a journey, they cannot go alone. The Germans are on the same road. And while Israel chants Ab ha-Rahamim, the martyr's dirge written by their ancestors in the Rhinelands, the Germans can raise their own voices in a song from Beethoven's *Fidelio*, the prisoners' chorus."*

* Marvin Lowenthal, *The Jews of Germany* (New York and Toronto: Longmans, Green and Co., 1944), p. 406.

14

THE SPANISH CIVIL WAR

THE 1930's WERE A PERIOD OF CONTINUOUS APPEASEMENT AND RETREAT for the western democracies. Confronted by defiant dictators who refused to accept the world order that had been established by the Treaty of Versailles, they kept paying blackmail in Manchuria and Ethiopia, in Austria and Czechoslovakia, in the hope of postponing a dreaded showdown. But each concession further whetted the appetite of the dictators, who probed for soft spots and knew that they could strike with impunity. Those who were committed to the western tradition of democracy began to lose hope. A great fear clutched at their hearts that there was neither will nor stamina left among free men to resist the totalitarian threat.

This is why the Spanish Civil War, in which a victimized people rose at last and fought back gallantly against the most unfavorable odds, so moved the democratic world. To the aggressors it was a welcome rehearsal for a planned World War II, a chance to test their weapons and the mettle of their foes. But to the men who were dedicated to the democratic credo, and who tried to make meaningful the symbolism of the struggle, it was regarded as a final effort to raise the flag for a way of life that was in mortal danger of extinction. Maynard Keynes said of the young volunteers who poured in to support the Republican cause that they were nearest to those who joined the Crusades, who risked their all for the Reformation, who fought in the Great Rebellion, and who made civil and religious liberties their legacy for the generations that followed. Hemingway, in *For Whom the Bell Tolls,* took the Spanish Civil War for his theme, and he perhaps best pointed up why it was not just another struggle in a far-off country. He wrote:

You felt . . . something that was like the feeling you expected to have and did not have when you made your first communion. It was a feeling of consecration to a duty toward all of the oppressed of the world . . . authentic as the feeling you had when you heard Bach, or stood in Chartres Cathedral or the Cathedral at León and saw the light coming through the great windows, or when you saw Mantegna and Greco and Brueghel in the Prado. . . . It was something that you had never known before but that you had experienced now and you gave such importance to it and the reason for it that your own death seemed of complete unimportance. . . .*

It was a cruel and savage fight. It started as a civil war, the Republicans determined to eliminate an entrenched feudalism and the Nationalists seeking to destroy the newly elected government that had expelled the monarchy and threatened traditional values. Soon the civil war was hopelessly complicated by the intrusion of outside forces. The Italian Fascists moved in with between fifty and sixty thousand Black Shirts, and the Nazis with air power and skilled technicians to dramatize their identification with the Nationalists. The Russians moved in with highly trained personnel and, later, with military equipment to support the Republicans. The democratic states, Britain and France, adhered to the non-intervention pact to which all the great powers had subscribed, which forbade the sale of arms to any of the belligerents. They held to their pious resolution even though Mussolini, Hitler, and Stalin kept pouring in men and equipment to protect and further their own objectives.

The bloodletting went on for three years, from 1936 to 1939. Millions died or were maimed. The extremists among the Republicans justified class liquidation as legitimate in a civil war. The Nationalists were equally ruthless, especially when there were hostile cities or territories to pacify. When General Franco and the Nationalists won out there was little magnanimity or compassion. More than a hundred thousand of the defeated were executed as traitors and hostages. Another half million fled to France to live on hopelessly in wretched camps. Then the peace of death fell over the ravaged and exhausted land.

But even this was not the end. When World War II erupted,

---

* Ernest Hemingway, *For Whom the Bell Tolls* (New York: Charles Scribner's Sons, 1940), p. 235.

Franco openly sided with Hitler and Mussolini. He did not bring Spain into the war since his cause was better served if he posed as a technical neutral. But he congratulated Hitler fulsomely after each of his early victories, and he backed up his words by sending troops, under the guise of volunteers, to fight the Allies on the eastern front. All through the war he provided the Nazis with observation posts in Spanish Morocco to monitor Allied ship movements. When the war ended in Fascist defeat Spain became a primary refuge for leading Nazis and Quislings.

The Allies at first punished Franco's wartime conduct with quarantine treatment. Spain was kept out of the United Nations and its agencies. One of the first resolutions of the Big Three condemned Fascist Spain for "its origins, its nature, its record, and its close association with the aggressor states." But when the Cold War of the forties and the fifties created a harsh new climate, the Soviet Union emerged as the more formidable enemy. Hence alliances and their rationale again shifted sharply. Spain was now looked upon as a welcome bulwark against communism. The boycott of Franco was lifted and Spain was admitted to the United Nations. It became eligible for massive economic aid from the United States. The history of the Spanish Civil War was rewritten to conform to the transformation of yesterday's enemies into today's allies. In the revisionist version, Franco became the shining knight who had saved Europe from atheist communism, and, by skillful mutation, the monster target became the hero symbol. The reputations of those who had fought on the Republican side were now reviewed. Azaña, Zamora, Madariaga, Prieto, Negrín, the liberal reformers of the thirties, were now identified as Communists or fellow travelers. The young Americans who had volunteered to serve in the Republican forces were now suspect. There were American Congressmen who labeled such volunteers as "excessive, premature anti-Fascists." The families of those who had fought and died could not assuage the heartbreak of bereavement with the consolation of sacrifice for a noble cause. Their dead were the rebuked and the besmirched.

To understand the passions that were loosed in the Spanish Civil War, it must be remembered how late Spain entered the twentieth century. It was a poverty-stricken country, where most of the land and the natural wealth was in the hands of less than five thousand families in a population of twenty million. The Catholic church was all-powerful, but instead of helping to ameliorate social conditions, it was an arm of the élite, militantly against reform of any kind, including the reform of popular education. There was affection on the part of the common folk for the average parish priest and deep respect for the Catholic faith, but such affection and respect were not extended to the church Establishment and the high church officials, who were blamed for their alliance with a government that had little concern for the impoverished and the disinherited. In the upheavals of the civil war, popular resentment often took the form of violent anti-clerical activity.

Early in the century strikes were frequent, though they were usually unsuccessful, because the workers were not well organized and they had no resources with which to hold out. There was a brief respite during World War I, when Spain remained neutral and profited from the trade with both sides. But when the war was over, the economic reaction set in again, the old problems of poverty and corruption came back more menacingly, and the crisis mounted. In 1923 the King, Alfonso XIII, emulated the Mussolini dictatorship coup and called in a trusted confidant, Primo de Rivera, to establish an authoritarian corporative state.

De Rivera was a playboy figure, personally charming and courtly, and constantly in the news and fashion magazines with his sports, his women, and his rakish living. When he was asked by his wife whether he had been faithful to her, he replied, "Frequently." But his government did very little to ameliorate the persistent social and economic problems. Criticism and petition were treated as disloyalty and met with harsh punishment. The liberals and intellectuals were weeded out and newspapers heavily censored. De Rivera boasted that he was determined to eliminate what he called "the disastrous mania of thinking." Living standards were precarious and when the seismic waves of the world depression of 1929 reached Spain, nearly every working family was disastrously affected. The strikes triggered violence and the country was on the brink of revolution.

Since the corporative model dictatorship had not worked, Alfonso moved to belated placation and he promised constitutional reform. He dismissed De Rivera, who was packed off to Paris where, after a few weeks in nightclubs, he drank himself to death. The censorship was relaxed, some of the exiles were permitted to return, and the Cortes was recalled. It was too late. The municipal elections of 1931 were so manifestly a repudiation of the monarchy that the King's advisers broke the news to him that he could no longer govern; in April 1931, without any formal abdication, Alfonso went into unlamented exile. Spain became a Republic amid high hopes that a new era was to begin that would transform the unhappy country into a modern state.

The returns in the first election for the reactivated Cortes were an overwhelming Republican endorsement. In the light of later charges by Hitler and Mussolini that they had intervened to prevent Spain from becoming a Red bastion, it should be remembered that, of 470 members, only one Communist had been elected. The Republican majority was made up of liberals and socialists with a wide variety of party labels, but they were basically no more radical than the New Dealers of Roosevelt in the United States, or the Labourites of MacDonald in Britain. But there were excesses by extremists on both sides during the heat of the election campaigns, hoodlum tactics by the private armies of the reactionaries, and riots and the burning of churches by the militant leftists. The Republican leader, Azaña, did not help when he dragged his feet in punishing violence that desecrated churches and convents and killed priests and nuns. Nor did the Primate of Spain, Cardinal Segura, with his incendiary speeches, his threatened excommunications, his denunciation of the Republic as barbarous, anti-Spanish, and anti-Christian.

The next four years were a period of continuous tumult as both sides struggled with their adversaries. When the Republicans were in power they hammered through major reforms in the interest of the workers and the peasants, including insurance rights for the unemployed, the sick, the disabled, and the elderly, benefits that were taken for granted in many other parts of Europe. The unions were given legal status and fixed hours of labor were guaranteed. Ancient privileges long enjoyed by the church, the landed gentry, and the industrial captains were canceled. Then, when the coalition of the center and the right won a majority in the Cortes in 1933, they curtailed the reforms and restored the religious and social benefits that the Establishment had enjoyed. There was a thoroughgoing purge of leftists, among whom were included even moderate liberals. In the two years of rightist supremacy, more than thirty thousand such dissentients were jailed. The army was swept clean of any whose loyalty to the Nationalists was in doubt and every vital area was placed under the command of a general who was hostile to the survival of the Republic. It was clear, as both sides grew increasingly intolerant, that the power struggle would not be resolved at the polls.

The leader of the Republicans was Manuel Azaña, not so affectionately referred to as "Old Frog Face." He combined the scholar and the man of action who could appeal both to the intellectuals and the proletariat. His early years were spent in journalism, and he covered World War I on many fronts with the Allied forces. He was equally at home in belles-lettres, and his translation of George Borrow's *Bible in Spain* was a classic. His *Garden of the Monks* was compared to the early work of James Joyce. His style in writing and on the platform was vigorous and colorful, carrying strong conviction. From the outset Azaña was a committed Republican and he led the struggle against the entrenched Establishment. When the Republic was in danger later on, he addressed the monster rally in a field outside Madrid. The Nationalists would not permit him access to the bull ring and a quarter of a million people poured in from all over the country, coming by truck and train, by mule and on foot, to hear Azaña in one of the greatest mass demonstrations in Spanish history. For two hours they listened to the array of speakers, now united against the common enemy. All the liberal groups were represented—democrats, socialists, even Communists and Syndicalists. On that day the foundations of a Spanish Popular Front came into being.

The decisive election of 1936 was a bedlam of violence and shrill illiterature. Both sides knew that, whatever the official verdict, the losing side would not peacefully accept it. The Republicans won overwhelmingly, and, as expected, the Nationalists defied the mandate. The extremists among them flocked to the Fascist party, the Falange, which had been founded in 1934 by the son of the late dictator De Rivera, a son whose aim in life had become to vindicate the dictatorship established by his father. He adopted the insignia of the bundle of arrows and the slogan *"Arriba España"*—Spain Arise, and at every public function there were unruly demonstrations.

Already the Fascist powers announced their stake in the election by adding insult to contempt. At the inauguration of Azaña as President, the Italian representative came in a black shirt and high boots and gave the Fascist salute. The provocations multiplied. One of the Republican leaders was brutally assassinated by the Nationalists. The Republicans retaliated by kidnapping and murdering one of the most influential rightist leaders. Then the rebellion was launched, led by the top echelons of the army, who were determined to prevent the Republicans from destroying the character and tradition of their ancestral Spain. The rebel chief was Francisco Franco, who was to emerge as the Caudillo, the master of Spain, and the most durable of the twentieth-century dictators.

Franco was trained from the outset for the military, although he gave no early promise of special competence. He entered the army school at Toledo and graduated next to last in the class. But his father's influence brought him a transfer to garrison command as a lieutenant. He served in Morocco in the wars against the native Riffs, during which he was wounded. While convalescing, he wooed Carmen Polo, the beautiful daughter of a wealthy and aristocratic family. When they objected strenuously to the match, Franco joined the Foreign Legion, and it was there that he earned his reputation as a tough, callous, determined officer. There was a mutiny over the execrable food that was served, and after the angry legionnaires had demonstrated, Franco had them stand at attention with their mess bowls and the stew that had caused the riots. As Franco walked along the line, one of the legionnaires thrust forward his mess tin and some of the contents spilled on Franco's uniform, as the soldier cried out: "Do you expect us to fight on filth like this!" Franco brushed off his uniform and ordered a new meal for the men. Then he called the men back in formation, again walked down the line, picked out the soldier who had spilled the stew on his uniform, and had him shot. The incident was not lost on the men nor on the military Establishment.

In the continued warfare with the Riffs, Franco won some of the very few Spanish colonial victories, and he rose steadily in responsibility and rank. The family of Carmen Polo relented and the wedding was celebrated with King Alfonso in attendance. At thirty-three, Franco became the youngest general in Europe since Napoleon, and he was given charge of the military academy at Saragossa. When the Republicans came to power and there was disaffection in the army, Franco was in the forefront; and when the civil war was launched from colonial bases and the first in command was killed in the flight to Burgos, Franco took his place at the head of the rebellion.

In the years of the civil war and of the long repression that followed victory, Franco changed very little. He remained cool, cautious, undeviatingly loyal to his mission. His imperviousness to danger in war and to the continuous threats of assassination was rooted as much in Christian piety as in ancestral fatalism. "God has given me life," he said after an abortive assassination attempt, "and only God can take it away." During one of the battles a shot blew the cork of a thermos flask out of his fingers. He continued drinking the coffee and then he lifted the cup to the enemy encampment, exclaiming, "Let's see if you can aim better next time." After years of purges and executions, he became, to his enemies, Enaño Sangriento, the Bloody Dwarf; to his devoted followers he was the saviour of Christian Spain, the man who salvaged Paz Española, the long Spanish peace.

The lineup at the outset of the civil war was fairly even. The Nationalists had control of most of the army and the loyalty of the officers. They had the church, the last-ditch Monarchists, and, of course, the conservative old-line families who commanded the wealth of the country. They also had the Foreign Legion and the many private armies of the paramilitary groups, the Carlists and the Falange. The government, on the other hand, had the navy, which was solidly Republican, and the bulk of the air force. It had the peasants and the workers and the most industrialized part of Spain, the Madrid-Valencia-Barcelona triangle. The loyalties of the numerous middle class were not polarized and were fairly evenly divided.

There are differing opinions as to which side would have won out if the Spanish Civil War had been left to the Spaniards. But it is clear that the war would have been much more quickly settled, that the awful toll of death would not have been exacted. The query is academic, however; the war did not remain localized. Hitler sent in about ten thousand crack Luftwaffe men and hundreds of planes, plus tanks and artillery. He was apparently eager for his men to get actual training in the blitz tactics that he was to use so effectively in Poland and in World War II. Mussolini also sent reinforcements to the Nationalists. The Roman Fascist weekly boasted of the Italian intervention: between 50,000 and 60,000 soldiers, 40,000 tons of war materiel, 750 aircraft which carried out 5,300 bombing missions. Soviet Russia supported the Republican forces with technicians and substantial supplies as the civil war became an international showdown.

In this lineup a great deal depended upon the reaction of the western democracies, Britain and France and the United States. The British government was headed by Stanley Baldwin and, soon afterwards, by Neville Chamberlain. Appeasement of the dictators was at full tide. Chamberlain had no love for Franco, but he could be depended upon to protect British economic interests. He insisted on non-intervention, embargoing military supplies to either side. The sympathies of the French government and of most of the French people were with the Republicans. But Chamberlain warned Léon Blum, the French Premier, that, in any breach of the non-intervention agreement, France could expect no cooperation from Britain. Blum already had severe enough problems with the Axis powers and sorrowfully he joined the British in non-intervention. Actually these decisions meant that the Republican cause was immobilized. Men and supplies were available for the Nationalists through the intercession of Hitler and Mussolini, but they were denied to the Republicans until the last stages of the war when Stalin sent belated and unavailing help. The mockery of non-intervention was summarized in the widely publicized David Low cartoon where Hitler and Mussolini, dressed as Spanish matadors, stand with Franco, who asks archly, "Well, aren't we all Spaniards here?"

Meantime, the United States declared that its policy would be neutrality and non-intervention. Franklin Roosevelt's sympathies were with the Republicans, but 1936 was an election year and he could not afford to alienate large blocs of voters who sided with the Nationalists. He confided to his political associates that raising the embargo would mean the loss of millions of Catholic votes. His Secretary of the Interior, the blunt Harold Ickes, wrote in his diary, "This was the cat that was actually in the bag, and it is the mangiest, scabbiest cat ever."* The embargo was technically enforced but, strangely enough, oil in huge quantities, shipped by American companies, did manage to reach the Fascists to fuel their planes and their armor.

It was almost a miracle that the Republican rank and file, all but deserted, was able to maintain resistance for several years. The experience in Madrid was typical. The Nationalist General Mola attacked, savoring an easy victory. When he was told that the resistance was much more stubborn than expected, he indicated that the four columns converging on the capital from every side would be joined by secret supporters from within, an inner fifth column, and the term "fifth column," identifying disruptionists who bored from within, entered the vocabulary of the western world. But the Madrileños vowed: "*No pasaran*," and the siege went on for years.

Will and spirit were ultimately not enough when arms gave out. The Republicans in despair turned more and more to the Russians for virtually the only help that they could count upon. In turn, the Russians, supplying the arms, the food, and invaluable technical

* Harold L. Ickes, *The Secret Diary of Harold L. Ickes* (New York: Simon & Schuster, 1954), Vol. II, p. 390.

instruction, commanded ever-increasing influence. Gradually the more moderate leaders were bypassed and ousted—Prieto, Negrín, Azaña—and the Communist faithful took control, under Largo Caballero, the Spanish Lenin, who hoped to turn Europe Red at both ends. Stalin exploited the idealism of the Republicans as shamelessly and cynically as Hitler and Mussolini exploited the fealty of the Nationalists. His first act was to seize the Spanish gold reserve and to send in his own political police. Old scores with political enemies were settled when he ordered the massacre of Trotskyites. The slogan of the Communists was "Liberty." The slogan of the Fascists "Christianity." Both slogans were profaned, as neither liberty nor Christianity was honored.

The agony continued even when there seemed to be no more hope. The Republicans defended each province, then each city and town. Republican Toledo was invaded by the Moors; no prisoners were taken. Santander and Bilbao, the heart of the Basque country, fought to the end. In April 1937, German planes bombed Guernica, a Basque pilgrimage point for eight hundred years. Here civilians were the chief casualties, seven thousand men, women, and children. Picasso, then at the peak of his artistic genius, dramatized the tragedy of the first completely blitzed city in history, what the Germans cynically termed a "controlled vivisectional experiment in modern bombing tactics." Italian planes mowed down the long lines of refugees on the roads to France from the stricken cities of Spain.

By now there was no pretense of non-intervention. After the fall and destruction of Santander, Mussolini wired Franco: "While the brave legionnaires enter Santander in intimate collaboration with the Nationalist troops, obtaining, in the name of western civilization, one of the most brilliant victories of the war against Asiatic barbarity, I am gratified to be able to testify to your Excellency my pride at having these troops under my command and my sincere admiration for their fearlessness and capacity in realizing such rapid victory."

In one of his last speeches, the old gladiator, Lloyd George, placed the blame squarely on the British government for giving lip service to non-intervention while the Fascists poured in all the weapons of annihilation that Franco requested. "Bilbao, Santander, Gijon, the Asturias, were all defended by as brave men as ever went into battle . . . but they had no munitions; they had no guns. . . . Who is responsible for that? Non-intervention. Who is responsible for keeping non-intervention alive? His Majesty's Government. If democracy is beaten in this battle . . . if Fascism is triumphant, His Majesty's Government can claim that victory for themselves. . . ."*

Arthur Koestler wrote of his prison experience in Seville and of the execution of Nicolás, a poor bewildered peasant who symbolized all of his people.

Requiescat in pace, Nicolás. Let us hope it was all over swiftly and that they did not make you suffer too much. They chose a solemn day for your execution. I wonder what flags the consulates flew? Little you were, a little Andalusian peasant, with soft, slightly prominent eyes, one of the poor and humble; this book is dedicated to you. What good does it do you? You could not read it even if you were still alive. That is why they shot you; because you had the impudence to wish to learn to read. You and a few million like you, who seized your old firearms to defend the new order which might perhaps have taught you some day to read. They call it armed rebellion, Nicolás. They call it the hand of Moscow, Nicolás, they call it the instinct of the rabble, Nicolás. That a man should want to learn to read.†

Barcelona and Madrid were the last to fall. At the end, the fighting had been sustained with virtually no equipment, with old and rusty guns, with crude homemade bombs, the battle raging in the outskirts, then within the city, then street by street, and house by house, until the cities were in ruins, with tens of thousands dead and maimed. The workers perished in these last abandoned months, remembering the call of La Pasionaria, the heroine of the Revolution: "Better to die on your feet than to live on your knees!" They went into the hopeless battle singing "Death the Bride." At last the resistance ended, in Barcelona, in Madrid, in the ghost garrisons that had fired their remaining shots, and then the peace of death brooded over the land.

Though the years have passed, the toll of the civil war has not been accurately determined. The estimate of the most careful students is that about six hundred thousand Spaniards were killed on both sides, and, after the war, another hundred thousand were executed by the victorious Nationalists. Half a million more lived on as refugees in the camps that had been opened by the French on the other side of the Pyrenees.‡

* David Lloyd George, *Spain and Britain* (London: The Friends of Spain, 1937), p. 9.
† Arthur Koestler, *Dialogue with Death* (New York: The Macmillan Company, 1952), p. 164.
‡ Gabriel Jackson argues that there were many fewer casualties during the civil war, but many more after it had ended. Jackson, *The Spanish Republic and the Civil War* (Princeton, N.J.: Princeton University Press, 1965), p. 539.

The foreign legions, having gained invaluable experience, departed to carry on their wars elsewhere. The Spaniards were left with deep wounds that had not healed a quarter of a century later. For years there was a great quiet in the land, a kind of horror of peace, broken all too frequently by the sound of shots against the wall at dawn. A whole generation grew up where certain words could not be uttered—freedom, liberty, compassion. Auden wrote:

> The stars are dead. The animals will not look,
> We are left alone with our day, and the time is short, and
> History to the defeated
> May say Alas but cannot help nor pardon.*

But the western world did not come off easily either. A wave of despair and shame engulfed the liberals in the democratic lands. Koestler's words were taken to heart: "Spain had been the last twitch of Europe's dying conscience." It would not any longer be possible to work up enthusiasm or commitment for any great cause. A young reporter was present in a Villanueva church where the dead and dying were brought. He watched the doctors going among the men to give what help and comfort they could.

Afterward I went outside and was sick. I was not sick at the spectacle of pain, but because of the unaccepted sacrifice. That it would not be accepted by the western democracies, I foresaw, for not one of those governments had the courage even to dispense with hypocrisy. That the Spanish resistance was a sacrifice for more than Spanish freedom can be seen by anyone now. For had not nobleness gone out of the world and had we not been abandoned, the dictators would not have been encouraged to demand Czechoslovakia, and whatever else they next demand. . . .†

The war had indeed been a useful rehearsal for the Fascists and the Communists. It led directly to World War II. The Spanish river Ebro flowed on down to the Seine, and it stained the waters of the Thames. It found its way to the Volga and the Vistula, and later it washed the innumerable graves in the Arlington Cemetery by the Potomac. Hemingway was prescient as he quoted John Donne: "Never send to know for whom the bell tolls; it tolls for thee."

---

* W. H. Auden, *Spain* (London: Faber and Faber, 1937).
† Ralph Bates, "Of Legendary Time," *Virginia Quarterly Review* (Winter 1939).

15

THE ROAD
TO WORLD WAR II

IN THE PREFACE TO HIS WORLD WAR II MEMOIRS, WINSTON CHURCH-
ill told of a conversation with President Roosevelt in which he
was asked to suggest what the war should be called. Churchill replied
that it should be called the Unnecessary War, for "there never was
a war more easy to stop than that which had wrecked what was left
of the world from the previous struggle." Churchill noted how often
the dictators had probed for soft openings and how easy it would
have been, without too much risk or cost, to stop them short before
they made serious headway. As he looked back on the critical decade
of the thirties, he was astonished to contemplate that though the
Allies had won the greatest war in history and had reduced the
enemy to unconditional surrender, they retreated with timidity from
every crisis, abandoning every bastion, relying pathetically on appeasement. Yet each concession had further whetted the aggressors'
appetite, until there was no more that could be yielded, at which
point the once powerful democracies passed, in Churchill's phrase,
"from security to the jaws of death." None of this was 20-20 hindsight. Churchill's analysis and the call for preventive action came
before, not after, the dictators had struck.

The signal that the international order was under gravest threat
was first sounded in the Far East. A military clique in Japan, rapidly
moving toward control of imperial policy, was eager to take over
major areas in China before the Chinese could develop resistant
strength. The more moderate civilian government found itself

increasingly helpless to deal with the rampant militants. On the night of September 18, 1931, a small explosion took place on the Japanese-leased section of the South Manchurian Railroad, near Mukden, in northern China. It was clearly a manufactured incident; five minutes later a southbound express was able to get through, and newsmen were not permitted for five days to see the purported damage. At the war criminal trial years later, the confession went into the record that the military cabal had planned for some time to absorb all of Manchuria. The explosion was the excuse for action and the military, without the knowledge or approval of the cabinet, struck at once. In twenty-four hours the Japanese had taken Mukden and were on the way to the conquest of the entire province.

China could muster little defense. It was hopelessly fragmented, feudal warlords exercising their will and the inner Communist threat adding to the disintegration. The harassed Chinese government sought the assistance of the League of Nations, invoking the Kellogg Pact and other treaty obligations, and it appealed also to Britain and the United States. But Britain was immobilized by a serious financial crisis. In the very week of the Japanese attack it had been obliged to abandon the gold standard, and fifteen thousand sailors, in a protest against severe pay cuts, had refused to board their ships. The United States was bogged down in its worst depression. Banks were closing in every city and unemployment had climbed to more than seven million. President Hoover, sorely beset, refused to join in any call for sanctions against Japan. He told his cabinet that the treaty with Japan and the Kellogg Pact were meant solely as "moral instruments." The most, therefore, that the United States could do was to announce its "moral reprobation" by refusing to recognize any territorial changes that took place by force. The outraged Chinese scoffed that the doctrine of nonrecognition had "the head of a tiger and the tail of a rat."

The response of the League of Nations to the Chinese appeal was to send to the troubled area a fact-finding commission, headed by a distinguished Englishman, Lord Lytton. But the commission was not appointed for many weeks, it did not reach Mukden for months, and, by then, the Japanese forces had overrun nearly all of Manchuria, a province larger than Texas, with a population of forty million. When the Lytton Report was finally issued, condemning the aggression, Japan promptly resigned its membership in the League. But it retained the loot that it had acquired during the contrived delays of negotiation. In March 1932, it created the satellite state of Manchukuo, with the last Manchu Emperor as its puppet head. In the climate of the Japanese cabinet "moral persuasion" belonged with the recitation of classical poetry.

The attack on the international status quo was contagious. Mussolini had been dreaming of imperial glory and he coveted the ancient kingdom of Ethiopia, the one large African land that had not lost its independence during the colonial scramble. It did not deter him that Ethiopia had been a special protégé whose entry into the League of Nations Italy had sponsored, nor that a pact of friendship had been solemnly signed in 1928. The lure of easy conquest overcame all scruples and pledges. It would give substance to Il Duce's rhetoric and would avenge the humiliating defeat of 1896 when primitive Ethiopian tribesmen had routed an overestimated Italian army.

Mussolini had a choice of pretexts in the usual border incidents. The one he chose, in December 1934, was in a village of mud huts with the unlikely name of Ualual that was even difficult to locate on a map. The Emperor, Haile Selassie, who knew what Mussolini was about, appealed to the League of Nations. At this stage, after many rebuffs, climaxed by the defiance of Japan, the League was hardly an instrument that could offer effective protection. There were continued procedural postponements during Mussolini's overt preparations for aggression. As soon as the rainy season had ended, on October 3, 1935, Mussolini's invasion began.

The Italian action was condemned by the League quickly enough and sanctions were voted, but they were weak and full of loopholes. Though arms and planes were on the embargo list, neither oil nor coal was restricted. Yet the Italian military was motorized, and if oil had been included, the war could not have continued. Nor did the British close the Suez Canal; men and arms for the conquest continued to flow to the battle area without hindrance. Even nations that voted the sanctions managed to consign their goods to noncommitted states, from which they were transshipped to Italy and then to the staging areas in Ethiopia. The United States imposed a neutrality embargo, but its oil exports increased measurably and helped to fuel the Italian war machine.

Mussolini had counted on all of this. Among the major powers he was regarded as a humbug; his fleet was compared by a British admiral to a squadron of paper boats which start to sink if you blow on them. But against the Ethiopians he knew there was no risk. His lavishly medaled generals therefore bravely pushed ahead with an expeditionary force that included two hundred thousand troops, four hundred bombers, and all the equipment of modern warfare. These were pitted against about thirty-five thousand regular soldiers of Ethiopia, and nearly a million natives who were armed only with the weaponry of the forests. It was wood against steel, slings against tanks, arrows against long-range cannons, and there was no defense against air attack. The son of Mussolini, Vittorio, described one of his forays: "One group of horsemen gave me the impression of a budding rose, unfolding as the bomb fell in their midst and blew them up. It was exceptionally good fun." The fun was made more hilarious when the Italians used mustard gas against the bewildered and demoralized natives.

The diplomats of England and France tried to patch up some compromise. Samuel Hoare of Britain and Pierre Laval of France met secretly to work out an arrangement by which Ethiopia would cede two-thirds of its land in return for some concessions in neighboring Eritrea, with a corridor to the sea. The Hoare-Laval pact meant that a truncated Ethiopia would become an Italian satellite. When the details of the pact became public there was a storm of indignation in Britain and Hoare was obliged to resign. In reality, all the diplomatic by-play need not have been tried; Mussolini would not accept a compromise anyway. He confided to his colleagues that he was determined "not to be cheated out of a war." How else could he build the image of a modern Caesar?

As it turned out, the operation did not go as smoothly as Mussolini had so confidently expected. The Ethiopians stretched the Italian forces to the utmost. They lost quickly in the main engagements, but their guerrilla resistance exacted a heavy toll from the invaders. Ultimately half a million Italians were involved and the conquest took six months. Addis Ababa did not fall until May 1935. As the Emperor went into exile he warned the European powers that the fate of his betrayed nation would soon be shared by many others. It should be added that soon after the Italian conquest, Hoare was back in the British cabinet. The League recognized the de facto situation and canceled the sanctions that had been voted after a reassuring statement from Mussolini, who said, "Italy will consider it an honor to inform the League of Nations of the progress achieved in her work of civilizing Ethiopia."

Meantime, in March 1935, Hitler, riding the success of his preliminary defiance of the Allies, declared that Germany would no longer be bound by the provisions of Versailles which forbade conscription. His announcement merely confirmed the violations of the treaty that had been under way almost from the outset. Every ingenious method had been employed to circumvent the prohibitions for rearmament, and the German air force had been steadily augmented secretly. The story was current that one family, having ordered a baby carriage directly from a factory, found that, however many times it was put together, it always came out a machine gun.

In March 1936, Hitler took one of his longest gambles. He decided to send his Nazi troops into the Rhineland, the buffer that had been demilitarized by the Versailles Treaty to provide protection to France and Belgium against a repetition of the 1914 attacks. Here Hitler was acting against the counsel of his closest military collaborators, who were convinced that any mobilization reaction from France would end disastrously for Germany. As a concession to his generals Hitler agreed that the commander of the expedition should carry sealed orders to draw back at once if the French moved to resist. He confessed later that the eighteen hours after the reoccupation of the Rhineland were the most nerve-racking of his life. He added, "If the French had then marched into the Rhineland, we would have had to withdraw with our tails between our legs, for the military resources at our disposal would have been wholly inadequate for even a moderate resistance."*

The French Foreign Minister, Pierre-Étienne Flandin, aware of the long-range significance of Hitler's actions, hurried to England to negotiate for a coordinated policy. He was certain that the Germans would pull back if there were a concerted show of strength by the French and British. But Baldwin and Chamberlain, the spokesmen for the cabinet, were unwilling to take a hard line. Chamberlain said that he could not accept Flandin's judgment as a reliable estimate of a mad dictator's reactions, and Britain was in no position to risk a war. Lord Lothian wondered why there was so much dismay. After all, he said, "the Germans are only moving into their own backyard." He argued that Hitler was merely adding modest strength to Germany's economy and that the action could not possibly threaten the security of all-powerful France.

Hitler's audacity had paid off handsomely. He proceeded at once with the construction of the Siegfried Line, a chain of fortifications in depth along the entire rim of the Rhineland, to serve as a shield for the armament factories of the Ruhr. His gamble had been vindi-

---

* War Trial Proceedings. Cited by Shirer, *The Rise and Fall of the Third Reich,* p. 293.

cated against the cautious judgment of his military advisers and this hardened his resolve to keep relying on his own intuition. It also deepened his contempt for the Allies who, after Manchuria and Ethiopia, had once again crumpled in the face of decisive action.

Hitler now turned his attention to Austria, the most precious prize of all. To be sure, what had once been a majestic Empire of fifty-two millions had been reduced by the war settlement to a rump of six and a half millions, concentrated around one city, Vienna, too small to live, too large to die. After the war, the Austrians, in a plebiscite, had opted for *Anschluss*, union with Weimar Germany. At the time the Allies refused to permit the fusion. It would have greatly enlarged Germany and rewarded a defeated enemy. After the Nazis became the masters of Germany and demonstrated what a ruthless dictatorship meant, the very idea of *Anschluss* became a horror. The Austrians now clung passionately to their independence and they welcomed the Allied guarantee of protection. But Austria had both strategic and sentimental value for Hitler, and it was high on his agenda.

His first try came at the beginning of his incumbency, before conscription and rearmament had consolidated his position. The Nazi cells inside the country stirred discontent wherever their propaganda could penetrate. All through 1933 Dr. Engelbert Dollfuss, the diminutive Chancellor, fought back to prevent Austria from being absorbed. He denounced the Austrian Nazis as traitors, exiled their leaders, prohibited their uniforms, their flags, their swastikas, and then, in June, outlawed the party. In reprisal Hitler cut off trade relations and organized the Nazi Legion which was billeted on the frontier and drilled in preparation for a putsch.

In July 1934, 144 Nazis, disguised as state police, stole into the Palace in Vienna and murdered the Chancellor. The coup might have succeeded but Mussolini, fearful of a much-enlarged Germany on his frontier, rushed troops to the border and threatened to expel the invaders. At this stage Mussolini's bombast had not yet been exposed, and Hitler quickly disavowed the actions of the men as unauthorized and irresponsible. No one was taken in by the disavowal for, as Dollfuss lay on the sofa, bleeding to death just below a carving of a weeping Madonna, the first act of the conspirators had been a telephone call to the German dictator for further instructions.

Hitler learned from the fiasco to prepare more carefully, and to make sure of his ground. By 1937, Austria had lost its Italian protector. Mussolini had been outraged when Britain and France joined in the imposition of sanctions after the invasion of Ethiopia. The two democratic Allies were enmeshed in troubles of their own. How far the British were willing to go in avoiding offense to Hitler, however dangerous his actions, was demonstrated when Sir Nevile Henderson, the tall, gangling British Ambassador to Berlin, called upon his countrymen to stop criticizing the Nazis and to show more understanding for their "great social experiment." Hitler judged that he could try again in Austria and in 1938 he launched Operation Case Otto, which became a model in successful blackmail.

The initial design had been to contrive the assassination of the ubiquitous fixer, Franz von Papen, the German Ambassador to Austria, and to use the "outrage" as an excuse for intervention. Papen learned of the plan and hurried to Berlin to suggest that such a procedure, apart from its discomfiture to him, was not very sensible. Much better would be a personal conference between Hitler and the new Austrian Chancellor, Dr. Kurt von Schuschnigg, where an ultimatum, on penalty of certain extinction for Austria, would assuredly result in "voluntary" submission to any conditions that Hitler wished to set. Hitler agreed and Schuschnigg was summoned to Berchtesgaden. The Führer gave one of his most effective tantrum performances.

Hitler insisted upon the conversion of Austria into a German protectorate, with six Nazis in the cabinet and the Austrian Nazi leader as Chief of Police. The pressure on Schuschnigg was unrelenting all day and far into the night. At last, worn out by the third-degree ordeal, Schuschnigg promised to recommend to his cabinet the acceptance of the demands. But when he returned to Austria, he called for a plebiscite. Hitler interpreted the action as a repudiation of a "sacred promise" and demanded the cancellation of the plebiscite. As Schuschnigg went to the radio to tell his people what was happening, the invasion had already begun.

The Nazis took over Austria with no resistance by its people and no opposition from the western powers.* In the market place in Linz, the town where he was born, Hitler proclaimed the unification of Austria and Germany. Nazification followed at once. The purge was complete, from the President and Chancellor down to the humblest clerk and janitor. It "purified" the theater, the opera, the arts, the

* But how little Germany was prepared to meet military resistance from the Allies at this stage was pointed up when 70 percent of the invading transport broke down en route to defenseless Austria and the fulfillment of plans lagged considerably behind the prepared timetable.

press, the medical schools, the universities. It cut down liberals, democrats, socialists, intellectuals, and, of course, Communists. Every civil and military post went to the Nazis.

It was another bloodless victory for Hitler, whose proclamation began: "Austria is a province of the German Reich." He had added seven million subjects to the Reich, had taken control of the gateway to Southeast Europe, and had again demonstrated that there need be no further fear of Britain and France. Long before, Alexander Pope had outlined the steps by which evil becomes respectable:

> Vice is a monster of so frightful mien,
> As to be hated needs but to be seen;
> Yet seen too oft, familiar with her face,
> We first endure, then pity, then embrace.

Within a few weeks of the rape of Austria, Hitler called in his chief military advisers to prepare for "Case Green," the code name for the absorption of Czechoslovakia, another goal cherished from the day he came to power. In the Munich City Hall there was an impressive scroll with the emblazoned inscription, "God make us free," and on it were listed the "lost provinces," Schleswig-Holstein, Alsace-Lorraine, the Polish Corridor, and the Sudeten part of Czechoslovakia. Now that the Rhineland and Austria had been "redeemed," Hitler was ready to bring home the three million Germans of the Sudetenland along with, incidentally, but not too incidentally, the strategic areas that they inhabited, their invaluable coal and iron and the world-famous Skoda munitions works. The Nazi Party in Czechoslovakia had been busy for many years fomenting disruption, and its leader, Konrad Henlein, had instructions from Berlin that the demands were to be so extravagant as to assure rejection. This would provide the pretext for Hitler to make his bid, first for the cession of the Sudetenland, and then for Czechoslovakia itself.

Hitler's advisers again counseled caution. They were sure that though Hitler had bluffed his way into the Rhineland and Austria it would not be possible to go farther and he was playing recklessly with the likelihood of a European war for which Germany was as yet ill-prepared. Hitler, however, trusted his intuition more than he did the military judgment of his General Staff. He believed that while there would be strong protest the democracies were now so craven in spirit and so frightened of war that they would again yield. Apparently he had been given private assurance from some of the appeasement-minded British diplomats that Britain would not go to war over Czechoslovakia. In May 1938, speaking off the record at Lady Astor's, Chamberlain told American and Canadian journalists that Britain could not fight to defend Czechoslovakia's present boundaries. His dislike of the Czechs as a people was well known. "Not out of the top drawer, or even the middle," he said to a cabinet colleague. The British Ambassador had reported this judgment to Charles Lindbergh, the American air hero of the 1920's, who expressed the conviction that the German air force was more powerful than anything that the Allies could muster. Lindbergh ridiculed the decadent French and the so-called Russian strength, and counseled that it would be best for the Allies to concede to Hitler's demands and seek an alliance with Germany.* This was also the judgment of the American Ambassador to Britain, Joseph Kennedy. "Anyway," he said, "I cannot for the life of me understand why anyone should want to go to war to save the Czechs." On September 7, *The Times* (London), whose editor was in the confidence of Chamberlain, suggested that the Czech government ought seriously to consider ceding the disputed territory. "For then the Czech state, freed of an alien intransigeant population, would be strengthened by its healthier homogeneity."† Hitler, thus further encouraged, provoked riots in the Sudetenland that escalated almost to the point of armed rebellion. The Czech government declared martial law and began mobilizing its forces to protect its frontiers. The crisis was now in its most dangerous stage and a European war was threatened.

Russia, up to this point continually bypassed, strongly urged a conference to explore a common front against Hitler's blackmail. Roosevelt also made an offer, surprising in the light of the American isolationist mood, to participate in a European conference. But Chamberlain cavalierly disregarded the overtures. Instead, on September 13, he asked for a personal meeting with Hitler in the hope of working out some acceptable compromise. He was unwilling to include even the French Prime Minister, though France and Czechoslovakia were in a binding security treaty. When Daladier asked if he should come along, he was curtly brushed off.

The conference was held in Berchtesgaden, the Hitler headquarters. Nicolson wrote that Chamberlain undertook the mission "with the bright faithfulness of a curate entering a pub for the first

---

* Reported by Harold Nicolson, *Diaries and Letters, Vol. I, 1930–39* (New York: Atheneum, 1966–8), pp. 272, 343.

† Cited in Leonard Mosley, *On Borrowed Time* (New York: Random House, 1969), p. 41.

time . . . apparently he did not know the difference between a social gathering and a roughhouse." Hitler sized up Chamberlain quite realistically. He was sure that however high the demands went, Chamberlain would submit. His rage act went on for hours, returning always to the threat that unless the Czechs yielded to his demands at once, he would not hesitate to invade. Chamberlain was either bowled over by the Führer's frenzy or had already conceded to himself before the conference that he would offer no opposition. He agreed that the principle of cession was sound and that he would recommend it to Parliament, to France, and to the Czechs. He did not need too much persuasion for his own party leaders: they were as reluctant as he to run the risk of war over Czechoslovakia. The French leadership was harder to convince. Daladier knew well that capitulation on Hitler's demands would wreck the security of Czechoslovakia and would fatally weaken the Little Entente that had been patiently built in the years since the war. Besides, concession in Sudetenland would probably not satisfy Hitler anyway, judging by his record till now. But Chamberlain made it clear that if the French insisted upon the defense of Czechoslovakia, they would have to stand alone, for the British would not participate. Daladier reluctantly yielded, although in his heart he knew it was a recipe for war in the name of peace. Thus abandoned, the Czech government had no alternative but to agree to the cession of the territory. Chamberlain flew back, this time to Godesberg to meet again with Hitler and to work out the details for an international commission to set the new frontiers.

To Chamberlain's astonishment he found that Hitler's price had gone up considerably. The Führer now refused to leave it to an outside body to determine which areas were German enough to warrant cession, nor would he wait for a plebiscite. He planned to march his troops in at once, to take over what he deemed was adequate. Apparently he was unwilling to take "yes" for an answer. He insulted the British Prime Minister, called him the vilest names, and shouted that he would smash Czechoslovakia regardless of what Britain and France decided. During a lull in the thundersquall he made the pledge that, if he now had his way, there would be peace, for this was his last territorial claim in Europe.

Chamberlain was appalled. He returned to Britain in anger, and found his colleagues grim and bitter. All the fruits of appeasement were in full view. He admitted to the cabinet that the situation had deteriorated beyond repair. He gave the orders to prepare for war and to get the shelters and the barricades ready for the expected onslaughts. He went on the air and in a flat, tired voice, said, "How horrible, fantastic, incredible it is that we should be digging trenches, trying on gas masks here, because of a quarrel in a far away country, between people of whom we know nothing."

Suddenly, while he was in the middle of his speech in Parliament, word came dramatically that Hitler was prepared to postpone invasion until there had been another conference. Chamberlain gladly accepted and his over-eager reply included a sentence which destroyed whatever bargaining power he may have had: "After reading your letter, I feel certain that you can get all essentials without war, without delay." What Chamberlain did not know was that a number of the German generals had everything in readiness to overthrow Hitler if Chamberlain had stood firm and there was the slightest danger that Germany would be engulfed in war. At the Nuremberg criminal trials after the Nazi defeat, the senior German general Field Marshal von Keitel was asked, "Would the Reich have attacked Czechoslovakia in 1938 if the western powers had stood by Prague?", and he answered, "Certainly not. We were not strong enough militarily." The Czech Ambassador to Britain, Jan Masaryk, said to Lord Halifax and his aides: "If you have sacrificed my nation to save the peace of the world, I will be the first to applaud you. But if not, gentlemen, God help your souls."*

Chamberlain flew a third time to meet Hitler and at Munich the sellout was completed. Everything that Hitler demanded was yielded. The Nazis were to take over the entire Sudetenland, without any plebiscite restriction; the Czechs were to demobilize; and the territorial cession would include the entire system of fortifications that were among the strongest in Europe. Churchill noted that Chamberlain had thrown away a small democratic state "with an army only two or three times as large as ours, and munitions only three times as great as those of Italy."

Hitler had again carried off a bloodless coup, this one more successful than any of the others. He had maneuvered Britain and France to become the executioners of a sovereign state to whom both powers had given their guarantee. Chamberlain brought nothing back with him except his umbrella. For the present, however, he treated the agreement as a spectacular triumph. He had indeed sacrificed a faithful ally but it was a small country and little related to

* John Wheeler-Bennett, *Munich* (New York: Duell, Sloan and Pearce, 1948), p. 178.

British interests. He returned to cheering crowds, announcing to them jubilantly that he had brought back "Peace in our time." "See," he added, waving a document as if he had achieved a celebrity's autograph, "here is a paper that bears Hitler's name!" The next day he wrote to the Archbishop of Canterbury: "Some day the Czechs will see that what we did was to save them for a happier future." Some messages arrived from a few old ladies with the appeal that his umbrella be cut up so that the pieces could be sold as sacred relics.

There were realists in Britain and in the western world who were heartsick. Czechoslovakia had been the strongest and best-defended of the Central European states. Now it was lost to the Allies. A Czech editor wrote, "We wanted to sing with the angels; now we must howl with the wolves." The British Labour leader, Clement Attlee, denounced Munich as Britain's greatest diplomatic defeat, in which "a brave and democratic people had been betrayed and handed over to a ruthless despot." One British critic fumed that Chamberlain had turned all four cheeks to the German Chancellor. A member of Parliament kept whistling the tune "London Bridge Is Falling Down." Churchill added: "If you will not fight when your victory will be sure and not too costly, you may come to the moment when you will have to fight with all the odds against you and only a precarious chance of survival." He was, as usual, a good prophet.*

---

* After Chamberlain's humiliation at Munich, the story went the rounds of a fishing session that included Mussolini and Hitler. Chamberlain patiently paid out his line, lit his pipe, and two hours later hauled in a large catch. Mussolini jumped into the pond and grabbed a fat pike. Hitler simply ordered the pond to be drained and as the fish thrashed about helplessly on the dry bed, Chamberlain asked why they were not scooped up. Hitler replied, "They have to beg me first." Grunberger, *The Twelve Year Reich*, p. 333.

16

THE FRUITS OF APPEASEMENT

AT THE ANNUAL ANGLO-AMERICAN PRESS ASSOCIATION DINNER IN Paris, just before Christmas 1938, a playlet skit was presented that depicted an imaginary second Munich Conference. Chamberlain promised Hitler all of Africa "by 2:00 P.M. next Saturday." He then coyly inquired, "Adolf, what would you have said if I had answered 'no' when you asked for Sudetenland?" Hitler wept in his sleeve. "Ach, Mr. Chamberlain, then you wouldn't have been an English gentleman!" The skit took on shocking reality for Chamberlain, when, a few weeks after pledging his word of honor at Munich that, having acquired the Sudetenland, he had fulfilled his last territorial ambition in Europe, Hitler reached out for what remained of Czechoslovakia. His generals warned him again that this time, since he was moving far beyond so-called German territory and population, he could not come off without war. Hitler refused to be deterred. "Don't worry," he crowed, "I saw the worms at Munich. I saw them crawl. They are too cowardly to fight."

In March 1939, he called to Berlin Emil Hácha, the new President of the weakened and emasculated Czechoslovakia, and ordered him to sign a document that would turn the rest of the country into a German province. All day long the harassed and humiliated President tried to resist. A pen was forced on him for the signature. He was chased around the conference table. He fainted three times. At last, after all the pressure that gangsters apply to a hostage, he signed to save his country from the bloodshed of an invasion that Hitler had threatened. France, bound by treaty to Czechoslovakia, reacted with dismay bordering on demoralization. The astonishing statement of the Foreign Minister, Georges Bonnet, was perhaps the most accurate summary of the plight to which appeasement had brought the democracies. "It is too late to take military measures," he said, "just as it is too early, since we are still not ready."

Within a few days the Führer rode in triumph into Prague as still another country became part of the expanding Reich. Significantly, the first stop was the National Bank, where eighty millions in gold reserves were taken over. Polish forces invaded at once to appropriate the Teschen area. Hungarian troops crossed the frontier to take Ruthenia. The speed to share in the loot was appropriately called the Gadarene rush. All too soon the despoilers were themselves to be despoiled.

The immediate effect on Chamberlain and his inner circle was outrage and embarrassment. What shook them was not so much the tragedy of a gallant little people. It is clear from the documentation of the period that Chamberlain had been more irritated than concerned by the Czechs' refusal to entrust their fate to the good will of their guarantors. But he was a businessman and a bargain had been made. Hitler had promised at Munich that the settlement reached there had satisfied all his claims. Now the promise upon which Chamberlain had staked his reputation as a statesman, and a good judge of men, had been broken, crudely broken, and Chamberlain felt cheated. He had been exposed as a dupe and a simpleton. He had even lost the confidence of a large part of his own party, who threatened to repudiate his leadership unless he moved at once to prevent further attrition of British prestige. It did not salve Chamberlain's pride when word reached him, through diplomatic and journalistic channels, of the appraisals that Hitler and his confederates had offered during and after the negotiations. There Chamberlain had been dismissed as a ninny and a humbug; Hitler had shouted at Sir Horace Wilson, Chamberlain's special adviser, that Chamberlain was "a wicked old *Scheisshund*, an ass-licker, his tongue is hanging out."* Count Ciano reported a conversation with Mussolini, his father-in-law. "These men," said Il Duce, "are not made of the same stuff as Sir Francis Drake and the other magnificent adventurers who created the empire. They are, after all, the tired

---

* Cited in Mosley, *On Borrowed Time*, p. 59.

sons of a long line of rich men." Of France he said, "It is a nation ruled by alcohol, syphilis and journalism."

After the rape of Czechoslovakia, Chamberlain announced solemnly that his confidence had been "wantonly shattered" and he urged an acceleration of rearmament, to be better prepared if there should be new crises and new tests of strength. He had resisted such measures in the past, and when Eden had reminded him that he was dealing with tough gangsters, he had advised Eden to go home and take some aspirins. Churchill had warned that, in modern warfare, a second-best air force was like a second-best poker hand, but the warning had been resented. Now the laggard pace of aircraft production, tanks, and other armaments was urgently quickened. There followed almost panicky guarantees to a whole group of other threatened nations—Poland, Rumania, Greece, and even far-off Turkey—apparently on the assumption that a firm stand bravely announced might now at last deter Hitler, that a guarantee a day might keep the Führer away. It was ironic that democratic Czechoslovakia, committed, well armed, with magnificent strategic and economic assets, should have been abandoned and coerced into extinction, but that a pledge of instant support was now offered to the Poles who had participated in the dismemberment of Czechoslovakia. Most dangerous of all, Chamberlain was leaving it to Poland and its junta government of colonels to determine, in its reaction to Nazi claims, whether Britain was to have war or peace.

In all of these critical developments, the Soviet Union had been completely bypassed. The offer by Stalin of a united stand against Hitler to save Czechoslovakia had been ignored. Though the Soviet Union had a defense pact with Czechoslovakia, Stalin had not been invited to participate in the discussions leading up to the Munich settlement. Stalin's renewed offer, after Munich, to join with the democratic powers to prevent further aggression had again been dismissed. Indeed, Poland was adamant in its rejection of any such guarantees if they meant that Russian troops would then be authorized to march through Poland. What assurance would there be, the Polish Foreign Minister asked, once the Russian troops were there, that they would ever leave? The Poles were apparently more fearful of being rescued by the Russians than of being attacked by the Germans. This was a period when alliances had the consistency of sand, each signator distrusting all the others, with the sure knowledge that any shared military plans would probably immediately be relayed by spies, or by the negotiators themselves, to all the other chancelleries.

Hitler was already deep in his maps and his battle orders to settle old scores with Poland, in what he had termed "Operation White." His aim was to regain the ancient Hanseatic city of Danzig, and its principal port, Gdynia, through which Poland could reach the sea, but whose population was mainly German. He aimed also to eliminate the Polish Corridor, a long strip of land that the Treaty of Versailles had assigned to Poland, through which Germans had to travel to reach East Prussia and Berlin. We know now that, while these objectives were the public demands, Hitler was determined to destroy Poland altogether, to eliminate it as a potential second front and a threat to Germany's military position. In his briefing to the military he said: "I shall give a propagandistic reason for starting the war—never mind whether it is plausible or not. The victor will not be asked afterward whether he told the truth or not. In starting and waging war it is not right that matters, but victory. Poland is to be destroyed by a surprise attack and this has priority."* The Nazi air force staff were equally cynical. One of them said: "There have already been three partitions of Poland. So now there will be a fourth."

Hitler was sure that when he struck at Poland the British and the French would once again back down. The guarantees that had been announced for Poland he dismissed as sheer bluff. He could not imagine that such cravens as Chamberlain and his appeasement colleagues would find iron in their spines now, when there was none there in the crisis of Czechoslovakia. Even if Britain and France did intervene, he had nothing but scorn for their capacity. He gloated: "I'll cook them a stew they will choke on." To his generals he said, "While England may talk big, may even recall her Ambassador, perhaps put an embargo on trade, she is sure not to go to war." Thus he wrote off Britain and France.

Meantime, he initiated diplomatic overtures that seemed fantastic even for opportunists as cynical as Hitler and Stalin. He moved into negotiations for an alliance between Nazi Germany and Communist Russia, not only to assure neutrality, if either were involved in a war with the West, but to divide the spoils that such a war might bring. The spoils would include Poland and the Baltic states. To follow the diplomatic negotiations of the 1939 summer that led up to

---

* Cited in Shirer, *The Rise and Fall of the Third Reich,* p. 532.

the alliance is a dizzying experience. The record is studded with whodunit dramatics, secret sessions, midnight meetings, spies, broken codes, internal rivalries, sellouts, plots by Hitler's own generals to eliminate him, conspiracies in the foreign offices and the embassies to countermand the wishes of their chiefs. Day by day, hour by hour, the chancelleries buzzed with intrigue, while millions of apprehensive citizens in each country, the ultimate victims, listened to the rumors with dismay or terror. In this hour of destiny, the fate of whole nations was in the hands of a power-mad maniac, Hitler, a cynical monster, Stalin, a foolish mediocrity, Chamberlain. On the surface, there were compliments and threats, used as gambits in a game of Russian roulette; underneath the real sentiments were hidden, but not sufficiently guarded to prevent exposure. Stalin to Ribbentrop just as the Soviet-Nazi pact was signed: "I know how much the German nation loves its Führer and I should therefore like to drink to his health." Stalin to his inner corps: "What dirty bastards all of these Nazis are." Ribbentrop to Stalin: "Marshal, you know what they are saying in the streets; that Stalin may yet be persuaded to join the anti-Comintern pact!" Chamberlain to Stalin: "If we could only come to some agreement, we could save Europe and the world." Chamberlain in his diary: "I distrust Russia's motives which seem to me to be concerned only with getting everyone else by the ears." There were several especially juicy statements during the negotiations: Stalin's assurance to Ribbentrop, a guarantee that "the Soviet would never betray its word of honor"; Hitler's statement to a Swedish emissary, to reassure Britain, "Have I ever told a lie in my life?" Hitler in his public addresses, that he wanted only to correct the injustice of Versailles. But to his generals, "My only fear is that at the last moment some *Schweinhund* will submit a mediation scheme." It was Franklin Roosevelt who made the final desperate try, in a message to Hitler, but he admitted privately that it would have "about the same effect as a Valentine, sent to somebody's mother-in-law, out of season."

In the last week of September 1939, the pact between Communist Russia and Nazi Germany, an ideological monstrosity, was sealed and announced. Ribbentrop signed for Germany, wondering how long it would be before the Nazi attack on Russia would begin. Molotov signed for Russia, certain that it would not be kept. The old ruffian was at his best in this kind of diplomacy. Churchill described him, with his cannonball head, his Siberian winter smile, as the most perfect representation of a robot. The scene recalled Disraeli's reference to Robert Peel, "with a smile like the silver plate on a coffin."

The pact, though long rumored, was still one of the diplomatic bombshells of the century. The Nazis, who had spewed filth on Stalin and his supporters, who had endlessly manipulated the fear of communism in their bid for power, were now in alliance with their arch enemy. The Communists, to whom the Nazis were the ultimate evil, were now locked in embrace with them. Only a few years before, Stalin had slaughtered thousands of his ablest officers because they had been suspected of favoring a German detente. Yesterday's treason had become today's official policy. The cartoonist, David Low, summarized the bizarre development in a famous cartoon: Hitler tipping his hat to Stalin: "The scum of the earth, I believe," and Stalin tipping his hat in return: "The bloody assassin of the workers, I presume." But, for the moment, each dictator had warded off a danger. Hitler had secured his back door as he made ready to destroy Poland. Stalin had brought the Nazis and the western Allies closer to war, hoping that they would rend each other into exhaustion. During the mutual carnage, Russia would appropriate the Baltic states and large parts of eastern Poland.

Inevitably the Nazi-Soviet pact bewildered and unsettled the Communist parties and their fellow travelers throughout the world. They had never deviated from the official litany of anti-Fascist insult and abuse. The Nazis were always singled out as an especially predatory brand of the Fascist horror. Now they were allies. Millions could not bring themselves to take the sharp hairpin turn. They abandoned the Communist parties, carrying their disenchantment into the politics of their countries. Some of the most violent anti-Communist tracts of the 1940's came from disillusioned ex-Communists.

In the meantime, even after the pact had been announced, Chamberlain still hoped that he could avert a total war. He tried hard to badger Colonel Beck, the Polish Foreign Minister, into a compromise, pointing out that Poland did not have the strength to resist the Nazis, and that it would take some time before the British and the French military effort could have any appreciable impact on Germany. But Colonel Beck expressed confidence that his country had the capacity to resist until Britain and France, honoring their commitments, would provide effective deterrents.

While the Allies argued what they would or would not do, Hitler's planes roared out over Poland, hellbent for a quick victory. There would be none of the World War I strategy of attrition. Hitler relied on the blitz, lightning war, speed, deep penetration, the coordinated use of planes, and motorized transport and mobile artillery. "Our weapons," he boasted, "are mental confusion, contradictions of feeling, indecision, and panic." This strategy, to blast the enemy into impotence, had been thoroughly tested during the Spanish Civil War, where the casualties had nearly all been Spaniards. It was now applied in Poland and it was devastating. The Luftwaffe knocked out the diminutive Polish air force in two days. The tanks tore through the open flat countryside so that all resistance collapsed in three weeks. Chamberlain had sternly warned Hitler that his aggression would no longer be condoned. But as the Nazi planes and tanks pulverized the pathetic Polish resistance, he still hesitated and temporized, twisting and turning to gain time. He sent messages and emissaries, first to restrain the Nazis and then, after the blitz, to achieve some face-saving compromise that might satisfy Hitler and still salvage something for Poland. But Hitler was too flushed with victory, too certain of his strike at the jugular, to listen.

All the concessions that Chamberlain had made now rose up to haunt him. He had acquiesced as Germany rearmed, but had urged no countermeasures in Britain, not even conscription. He had permitted the Nazis to remilitarize the buffer Rhineland, to undermine and then annex Austria and Czechoslovakia. His contemptuous disregard of Stalin had eliminated the possibility of reliance upon Russia for a second front against Hitler. Now he was trapped in an all-out war in defense of Poland, the country which only a few months earlier had joined in the rape of Czechoslovakia. There were no options left and, with the Polish air force already destroyed, Chamberlain brought his country into war against Germany; France followed suit. He had been given a choice between two evils and had chosen them both. "Here was decision at last," wrote Churchill, "taken at the worst possible moment, and on the least satisfactory ground, which must surely lead to the slaughter of tens of millions of people."

Chamberlain's war broadcast of September 3, 1939, was an agony of dejection, the tired voice quavering: "Everything that I have worked for, everything that I have hoped for, everything that I have achieved during my public life, has crashed in ruins." Even here Chamberlain remained consistent in his mistiming and inappropriateness. The whining message, filled with self-pity, was little calculated to rally a people in the face of its mortal danger.

Relief could come to Poland only if there were an immediate strong offensive on Germany's west front to compel the diversion of troops. Hitler gambled that there would be no such attacks. He left only a small contingent to guard the west. His main force was thrown against Poland to eliminate it quickly, and he gambled with prescience. After the declaration of war, Chamberlain's main effort was spent in the attempt to persuade Hitler to call off his Luftwaffe and panzers. The British planes distributed propaganda leaflets over the German lines, a kind of confetti strategy. Churchill wrote: "We contented ourselves with dropping pamphlets to rouse the Germans to a higher morality."

To magnify the predicament of Britain and France, Russia struck hard from the east, both as a precaution against too deep a Nazi penetration that would menace the Russian frontiers, and also to secure the loot that had been promised in the secret Nazi-Soviet pact. Lithuania, Estonia, and Latvia were overrun and, to make sure that there would be no national revival, those political and intellectual leaders of the doomed countries who had not escaped were rounded up for liquidation.

Russia, invoking the law of security, had marked out Finland as well, to protect its flanks if there should ever be a confrontation again with Germany. Finland, however, refused to yield, and its resistance precipitated what became known as the Winter War. Finland's total population was three and a half million; it was hopelessly outnumbered by Russia's hundred and eighty million, but it astonished the world and stirred the deepest admiration by its efficient and stubborn resistance. The Russians had overwhelming air superiority and introduced new model 40-ton tanks. But the Finns made an ally of the terrain and the Arctic weather, and their ingenious guerrilla tactics forced the Russians to fight on for months. The odds were too heavily weighted, however, and when Russia threw in twenty-seven divisions against the three that were left to the Finns, surrender came at last. Molotov toasted the victory: "Another glorious page in Russian military history that showed that the springs of valor, self-sacrifice, and heroism among our people are inexhaustible." Stalin was sensible enough to offer fairly lenient terms to avoid the possibility, however remote, of bringing in long-range assistance from Britain and France. The frontiers were moved back about seventy miles westward, ostensibly to protect Russia from any future attack by way of the Baltic.

In the West, all through the winter, the war settled down into what was called the *Sitzkrieg*, the sitting war, a twilight period with very little action. The correspondents labeled it the "Phony War." Britain and France sat behind the Maginot line and the Germans consolidated and digested their conquests. Negotiations were continued to persuade Hitler to recognize the rule of law, but he dismissed all overtures unless the British and the French validated his conquests and returned all the German colonies that had been lost in World War I. Hitler welcomed the *Sitzkrieg* for the opportunity that it offered to tool up for the next strike, this time at Denmark and Norway, and, if necessary, Sweden. He was eager to obtain naval and air bases for the planned attacks on Britain and its commerce.

In April of 1940, Denmark was taken over in a lightning attack. The King and his family did not even have time to flee. Sweden yielded with no resistance and it was permitted the status of an independent neutral. But the Nazis interpreted this to mean that they had the right to use Swedish territory as a springboard for the attack on Norway.

Hitler planned his blitz there carefully. He made use of a valuable corps of Germans who, as children during World War I, starving and desolate, had been taken into Norwegian homes, and had been cared for with love and concern throughout the long war period. They had learned Norwegian and they knew the terrain of the country. Hitler now sent them back into Norway to ferret out strategic secrets and to facilitate the conquest. Their ready cooperation gave new credence to the old dictum that no good deed ever goes unpunished. The main airfields were swiftly captured and the absolute air supremacy that the Nazis thereby achieved kept the British naval units at bay. Within days, all of Norway fell. Hitler's official paper announced the conquest in screaming headlines: GERMANY SAVES SCANDINAVIA! He had usually counted on local Nazis to cooperate in conquest and in subsequent occupation. He found very few in Norway, but one odorous character, Vidkun Quisling, lent himself for the purpose and he was named as the puppet head of state.*

Having secured his northern flanks by immobilizing the Scandinavian countries, Hitler was ready to move against the western democracies, reserving the coup de grâce for Britain itself. On May 10 he struck at Holland and Belgium, even though every assurance had been given that their neutrality would be respected. Indeed, only a few years before, Belgium had given up its alliance with Britain and France and had opted for neutrality in the hope that the country could thus avoid being drawn into any war among the major powers. King Leopold, eager to avoid any provocation of the Germans, had refused even unofficial conferences with the British and the

---

* See Chapter 21.

French to explore contingency plans for a possible German attack. It was on the assurance that Belgian neutrality was to be scrupulously respected that no fortifications had been extended from France to the sea along the frontiers of Belgium. Hitler snorted when he was reminded that, once again, the treaty that protected Belgium had become just a "scrap of paper." The phrase had been used by Bethmann-Hollweg, the German Chancellor who had authorized the violation of Belgian neutrality in World War I. The announcement of the German invasion was now handed to the Dutch Ambassador by a nephew of the same Bethmann-Hollweg.

The conquest of Belgium followed. Major defenses fell like tenpins. Typical was the reputedly impregnable fortress at Eben Email, the strongest in Europe. It was seized by parachute troops and capitulated in a few hours. The other powerful bases and the main cities were simultaneously overrun. King Leopold was so demoralized that he yielded without even consulting his allies. His precipitate surrender and the terrifying problems that ensued for the trapped Allied armies were not forgiven either by the Allies or by his own people. After the war, he was not recalled until 1950, only to abdicate soon thereafter.

Holland too was easily overrun, although the Dutch offered brave initial resistance. They even opened the dikes, sacrificing huge areas of painfully salvaged land. But the enemy forces circled beyond the traditional obstacles, disrupting communications and reserves far to the rear. Spies and saboteurs who had already been skillfully infiltrated helped to seize the strategic bridges and to immobilize the airfields. Then came the terror demonstrations that the Nazis had perfected to demoralize the civilian population. Rotterdam was attacked by torrents of Nazi planes and the destruction of the core of the city, and the huge toll of dead and wounded, numbed civilized life in the stricken city. Fearing that similar disasters awaited The Hague, Utrecht, and Amsterdam, Holland gave up, and the Queen and her family sought refuge in London.

The catastrophe in Poland, the conquest of Denmark and Norway, and now the blitz of the Low Countries, with France and Britain obviously next on the Nazi timetable of destruction, brought the hapless incumbency of Neville Chamberlain to an end.* The British turned inevitably to Winston Churchill, who had never ceased warn-

---

* Chamberlain retired in bitterness; a few months later, as he lay dying of cancer, Nazi bombs fell within forty yards of his bedside.

ing his people that they must face up to the dictators. On the very day that Hitler struck at Belgium and Holland, he was called upon to become Prime Minister. "At last," he wrote, "I had the authority to give direction over the whole scene. I felt as if I were walking with destiny."* So did his nation and so did the western world, for whom the way back to security and freedom, however, was not to come except, in Churchill's own words, through "blood and toil and sweat and tears."

* Churchill, *Memoirs of the Second World War*, p. 227.

17

THE COLLAPSE
OF THE FRENCH THIRD
REPUBLIC

BY THE SPRING OF 1940 HITLER, WHOM THE FORMER FRENCH PREMIER, Léon Blum, called a "motorized Attila," had achieved the diplomatic and military victories on the European continent that nullified all the restrictive provisions of the Treaty of Versailles. Indeed, his conquests went considerably beyond the rectification of purported injustices. They were so extensive that he regarded himself as a more exalted Charlemagne. Only France and Britain remained to be disposed of in the West, after which he planned to settle his scores with Russia.

The French had ample warning that the Nazis represented a new force that could be resisted only by imaginative countervailing tactics. Hitler had taken Austria and Czechoslovakia bloodlessly by blackmail, but the blitz in Poland, in Denmark and Norway, in Belgium and Holland, which had destroyed opposition everywhere in a matter of days, should have alerted the French that they could not rely on reputation and traditional strategy. Yet, when the Nazis launched their assault on May 10, 1940, the French were caught by surprise. Many of the front-line units were off on target practice. Ranking staff officers were attending a play sponsored by the army theater. Anti-tank guns had been assigned to the training camps and were not available in time for defense. Ten to 15 percent of the front-line troops were on home leave. The military adhered to its relaxed and leisurely procedures even as Hitler was blasting and uprooting the old world.

The Nazi armor sliced through the French defenses, parachutists capturing strategic roads, bridges, and airfields, tanks penetrating and encircling whole divisions. They operated with such irresistible speed that General Rommel chuckled over the pun that they were enjoying a "tour de France." There was panic everywhere. Millions of refugees clogged the highways, trains, and buses as they fled from the cities of the north and west, further hampering the improvised attempts to maintain a semblance of order and protection. The Nazi Stukas kept screaming down from the skies to treetop level, strafing the hordes of bewildered families already desperate for food, water, and shelter. Young Charles de Gaulle, in command of a tank division, later wrote of the debacle that he witnessed: "At this spectacle of a lost people and a military rout, and from the reports of the scornful insolence of the Germans, I felt myself borne up by a limitless fury. . . . So were others, but the war was lost, almost at the beginning."*

What had happened to convert into a rabble a military establishment that was reputed to be one of the most powerful in modern history? How could the catastrophe come so quickly and with such finality? Apparently the French military leadership was not only inept, but had been enfeebled by moth and rust. The men in charge, Generals Maurice Gamelin and Maxime Weygand, leftovers from a romanticized past, still planned by the textbooks of World War I. They relied on the defensive strength of the Maginot line into which hundreds of millions had been poured. In William Shirer's phrase, "military sclerosis" had set in. And there was no pressure from the French people for daring and commitment to adjust to the dangers of the new world. They too clung to the status quo, unwilling to accept heavier taxes or modified living standards, to cope with an enemy that had long been feeding on outraged pride and the passion for vengeance. As far back as 1932, Churchill had noted in a House of Commons speech that France, "though armed to the teeth, was pacifist to the core."

Hence the blows fell with shattering force and no defense points could be held for long. The formidable Ardennes, a forest described by Caesar as "full of terrors," impregnable through the centuries, was expected to delay the German forces until the French regrouped and reorganized. It was penetrated in a day. On May 12, within forty-eight hours of the first major attack, there was a decisive break-

---

* Charles de Gaulle, *War Memoirs* (New York: Simon & Schuster, 1955–60), Vol. I, p. 39.

through at Sedan, as crushing a disaster as the Prussian victory in the same ill-fated city in 1870 that toppled Napoleon III's Second Empire. The road to Paris, eternal Paris, was open. Hitler was determined not to risk a repetition of the Marne defense that had turned the tide in World War I. Though he had the Allied forces trapped in a pocket at Dunkirk, he ordered a forty-eight-hour pause, slowing down the offensive there so as to make sure of capturing Paris. The respite gave the British the opportunity to evacuate more than 320,000 of the trapped army units, and Dunkirk became one of history's most spectacular naval rescue operations.*

Dunkirk was a major disappointment to Hitler, but he was certain that it would soon be retrieved, and meantime his forces swept toward Paris. Their momentum demonstrated how carefully they had prepared. The parachute troops performed at each new strategic objective with faultless precision. The necessary equipment, down to the rubber boats, was always in place and on time, as canals and rivers and bridges were crossed, as key points fell. The Maginot fortification, the reputed impregnable defense line, was taken from the rear, and four hundred thousand of the finest troops were encircled. Discipline cracked and the French forces disintegrated. The Nazis raced ahead, not even waiting to secure their flanks, for they were virtually unopposed. On June 14, only a few weeks after the first assault, the Nazis goose-stepped down the Champs Élysées and the swastika flew on the Eiffel Tower.

As the military situation deteriorated, the French cabinet and the generals went through the agonies of decision whether to surrender or to continue resistance from outside France. Paul Reynaud was now the Premier, having displaced the discredited Daladier, even as Churchill had displaced Chamberlain. But he had been elected by a majority of one vote, after wrangling and backbiting that boded ill for the unity required to face a formidable enemy. De Gaulle later described the sorry scene he had witnessed from a balcony: "The danger for the country, the need for a national effort, the collaboration of the new world, were invoked only to decorate the pretensions and the rancors."

Reynaud's role in the politics of the thirties had resembled Churchill's "lone wolf" role in Britain. Like Churchill he had the advantage of inherited wealth and family connections and, after a brilliant record in the university and the law, he entered the

* See Chapter 18.

[196]

Chamber of Deputies to make politics his career. Small in stature, trim, wiry, athletic, his detractors called him "the jockey." But he was more of a kinetic bantam cock, aggressive and innovative, impatient with red tape and obsolescence in governance and in weaponry. All through the appeasement period he had fought against concessions to the dictators. He was appalled by the sellout at Munich and had resigned from the Daladier cabinet in protest. Now, in France's most dangerous crisis, he tried to counteract the prevailing sense of doom as he demanded continued resistance. He reminded his demoralized colleagues that the French navy, one of the most powerful in the world, was a solid and reliable asset, and that there were loyal reserves in North Africa and the French colonies. To him, as later to Churchill, defiance was no cave of despair: it was a holding action until the spirit of the people, revitalized by brave and unconquered allies in the old world and the new, would regenerate France.

But among his colleagues in the cabinet there was little resolution to go on. Marshal Pétain, the hero of Verdun in World War I, now eighty-five, had been called back to leadership for the prestige image that he evoked. He had despised the Republic and its politics, upon which he blamed the enfeeblement of France. Though he distrusted the Germans, he argued that, by cooperating with Hitler, a new French state could arise, based on authoritarian principles which would eliminate the corruption of the liberals, the "godless Republicans," the Socialists, and the flapdoodle of Popular Front fantasies. General Weygand, while not sharing Pétain's extreme anti-democratic views, was convinced that the war was lost, that Britain would not hold out; indeed, that Britain would soon have its "neck wrung like a chicken," and that an accommodation quickly worked out with Hitler would save France endless misery. Even as the arguments continued, the Germans were closing in on Paris. It was declared an open city and was deliberately not defended in order to save both its people and its priceless treasures from the devastation that resistance would have inevitably produced. The cabinet fled, first to Tours, and then to Bordeaux.

It was at this juncture that Churchill attempted a final appeal to the French cabinet to re-establish the government of France in North Africa, and to consolidate the British and French fleets to add strength to their resistance. He advanced a breathtaking proposal, the union of Britain and France, as in the old Norman days, into one federated state, with common citizenship and pooled military and economic resources, not only to meet the current emergency but to influence the entire future. Reynaud declared himself strongly for the proposal and expressed his confidence in Britain's staying power. The alternative, he warned, was enslavement to the Germans and to the madman who led them. Addressing himself to Pétain, he said: "You take Hitler to be Wilhelm I, the old gentleman of 1870, who only pirated Alsace-Lorraine. But Hitler is a Genghis Khan!"

The appeal failed. The cabinet was shot through with defeatism and a mounting bitterness against Britain, whose every action was impugned as self-preservative. One minister accused Churchill of attempting to reduce France to the status of a dominion. Another derided his proposal as a maneuver to carry off the French colonial empire. Pétain argued that it was like proposing fusion with a corpse since Britain would soon be finished. The mood of the Chamber was to act upon the advice that Ernest Renan had offered in the tragedy of 1871: "France dies; do not disturb her agony." The decision was made to surrender. Reynaud resigned as Premier, and Pétain, who replaced him, immediately sued for an armistice.

Hitler took fullest advantage of the surrender to identify it as a dramatic retribution. He ordered the French representatives to appear before him in the forest of Compiègne, in the same railway coach where the French had humiliated the Germans at the end of World War I, and he performed an exultant jig before the cameras. The terms were not as harsh as some of the extremists, in the arrogance of victory, wished to go, a France half vegetable patch and half brothel. But they were harsh enough. The northeast of France was to be occupied by the Germans, along with the entire Atlantic coastline down to Spain. The rest of France would be governed as a satellite state, centered at Vichy. It was stripped of food, equipment, and livestock. All males and childless women under forty-five were conscripted for dictated service, and a million Frenchmen were shipped to Germany as a labor force, destined to bear the agony of captivity for five years. There were those who remembered that there had been no occupation of Germany after World War I, and no forced exile in a foreign land for males siphoned out for indentured labor. Yet the Germans had been whining for a generation that the Treaty of Versailles had been a *Diktat*.

The surrender terms brought sorrow and misery; Pétain, Laval, and the Vichy men added degradation by hewing to the Nazi line. They set up an authoritarian police state, based on an old world peasant economy, with press censorship, strict labor restrictions, and, somewhat later, the Nazi anti-Jewish laws. The Republican institutions, pioneered in France, the France that Thomas Jefferson had called "every man's second country," were scuttled. One of the conditions agreed to by Pétain obligated the French to turn over all anti-Nazi German refugees. Thousands of them, who had sought safety in France, were rounded up and deported to face the executioner's ax, and these included some of the most honored German Socialist leaders. There were five days between the submission of terms and the enforcement of the armistice. The Vichy officials could have facilitated the escape of the principal refugees, but the Minister of the Interior issued orders to track down those whom the Nazis had proscribed. De Gaulle directed his Free France broadcast to Pétain from London: "Did France need a man like you, Marshal—you, the Conqueror of Verdun—to negotiate and agree to the conditions of such a bondage? Anyone would have done."

Churchill was now determined at least to prevent the French fleet from falling into the hands of the Nazis, to be used against the British. Before the surrender he exhorted the French leaders to send the fleet units to British or American ports, or to the West Indies. Admiral Jean Darlan, who had created the fleet, was in the best position to influence the decision. He could have become the Free French leader by assuming the responsibility for continued resistance from outside the continent. Although he hated the Germans, he also despised the British, and he had no faith that they would have the stamina to hold out against sustained Nazi air bombing. Pétain joined him in the refusal to move the fleet to other ports, but pledged that it would not be used against the Allies. Churchill doubted their assurances that the Nazis, once the fleet was in their hands, would not press it into service. He therefore interned the warships that were berthed in British ports, and ordered the de-activation of the powerful squadron that was riding anchor at the British naval base in Alexandria. He insisted that the units at the French base at Mers-el-Kebir, in North Africa, either move to the French West Indies or be scuttled. Pétain flatly refused. "Mr. Churchill," he said, "is the judge of the interests of his own country, but not of ours. He is still less the judge of French honor." By his command, the French admiral prepared to resist any attempted British seizure. Churchill now had the heartbreaking task of attacking the fleet of his old World War I ally, "the most unnatural, painful decision," he wrote, "in which I have ever been concerned."

Virtually the entire squadron was sunk, with substantial loss of life, and the action almost drove the infuriated Vichy men to a declaration of war against Britain. But Churchill and the Free French were convinced that the great mass of the French people understood the tragic dilemma. In his Memoirs, Churchill told the story of two peasant families in a village near Toulon, each of whom had lost their sailor son by British fire at Oran. A funeral service was arranged and all the neighbors were asked to join. Both families requested that the Union Jack lie on the coffins, side by side with the Tricolor. Churchill added: "In this we may see how the comprehending spirit of simple folk touches the sublime."

But France itself was now in the hands of the collaborationists, who hated the old democratic order and who wished to join with the Nazis in building a new Europe. The cabinet had been completely reorganized by anti-Republicans, headed by Pierre Laval, who was named Premier. He issued his orders in closest collaboration with Hitler and the Nazis, behind the façade of the fast-fading Pétain. He declared, "We are paying today for the fetish which chained us to democracy and led us to the worst excesses of capitalism, while all around us Europe was forging a new world." He defined the new order: "Parliamentary democracy lost the war. It must give way to a new regime—audacious, authoritarian, social, national." As for foreign policy: "We have only one road to follow, and that is a loyal collaboration with Germany and Italy. We must practice it with honor and dignity. And I am not embarrassed to say so. I urged it during the days of peace." He told a cabinet meeting that he waited for the day when Britain would be toppled and Churchill, Eden, and Duff-Cooper would be lynched.* Vincent Auriol, who was to become President when France regained its independence, described Laval in these nadir days, when the Republic was being done to death: "Everything about him is black—his clothes, his face, his soul."

Meantime daily life in both occupied and Vichy France gradually stabilized. The millions of refugees returned to their homes, public services began again to function. Schools, universities, churches, bars, theaters, newspapers, the courts, trade, commerce, and professional life ground on in sullen routine and resigned docility displaced Gallic animation. The Nazi censorship was rigorous and the Gestapo infiltrated every part of community and personal life. Hope was not abandoned but the effort to keep the spirit of defiance alive had to be the responsibility of rare spirits who had gone underground. Their

---

* Geoffrey Warner, *Pierre Laval and the Eclipse of France* (New York: The Macmillan Company, 1969), pp. 197 ff.

resistance, however, was extremely difficult and dangerous and, at the outset, it was not even popular. For the collaborationist government was headed by Marshal Pétain, and the aura of his image as a World War I hero still clung to him and gave a measure of respectability to the regime.

But as the true intentions of the Nazis emerged, and as men like Laval and the other Nazi toadies increasingly overshadowed Pétain, recruits to the Resistance multiplied. Their activity was not yet coordinated. They followed local and regional leaders, some drawn from the trade unions, others from the demobilized military, still others from among the ranks of intellectuals and writers. They were mechanics and priests, concierges and teachers, farmers and students, aristocrats and taxi drivers. There were many factions among them, Catholics, Communists, Nationalists—and their long-range objectives were militantly diverse. But they were all united in their hatred of the Nazi invader and in their contempt for the men of Vichy.

The *maquis** of the Franc-Tireur movement included twenty-nine thousand committed veterans, with weapons parachuted to them by the Allies. The regular military had enlisted thirty thousand more. They comprised a secret army, invaluable later in their support of the Allied troops when the liberation landings began. Gradually national leadership emerged. There was Jean Moulin, the Monsieur X in the Resistance saga, a heroic figure who succeeded in coordinating most of the underground activities. He was ultimately captured by the Nazis and tortured until every bone in his body was broken, but he went bravely to his death, his lips sealed to the end. Appropriately, after the liberation, he was given a hero's burial in The Invalides. There was Georges Bidault, who came out of Christian Democratic politics and journalism and took over the mantle from Moulin. He gave broader meaning to the Resistance, linking it with the spirit of old Clemenceau who used to say, "Honor to the nation in which men speak out, and shame on the nation in which men are silent." He developed resourceful techniques of sabotage and harassment that played hob with the routines of the occupying forces.

In the Vichy years there was hardly an area without its underground network. They provided intelligence reports to the Allies, they helped to rescue Allied airmen shot down by the Germans, they managed the escape of Frenchmen who were to be deported for forced

---

* The term is of Corsican origin. The outlaws there took to the *maquis*—the bush—to carry on their vendettas against the law.

labor in Germany, they were quick with reprisals when the Nazis punished sabotage or executed hostages. They took special pleasure in tormenting the Vichy men, who began to receive parcels containing miniature coffins to remind them of the fate that awaited them when liberation came.

Outside France, there was another eloquent voice to remind the world that Vichy was not France. It was the voice of a young officer, Charles de Gaulle, who was to turn the cause of Resistance from a gallant but hopeless defiance to a mighty force for liberation. He appeared at first to be a most unlikely rallying point for, though a giant of a man, more than six and a half feet tall, irresistible in oratory, as brave as any Resistance hero had to be, he had neither warmth nor glow. He was coldly reserved, self-isolated, cantankerously arrogant. His integrity was unmistakable but it was a belligerent integrity. He repelled the Allied leaders, to whom he owed his opportunities, by an Olympian haughtiness and by what seemed a vainglorious truculence in identifying himself with eternal France. When General Edward Spears, Churchill's personal representative in France, first met him, he wrote, "Sitting at the table he dominated everyone else by his height . . . his heavily-hooded eyes very shrewd. . . . It was easy to imagine that head on a ruff, that secret face at Catherine de Medici's Council Chamber. . . ."* And one of De Gaulle's own colleagues said, "The trouble with this extraordinary man is that he is not a human being."

But De Gaulle was quite human in his driving ambition. All through the tragic years of French humiliation, his sense of mission became ever more obsessive, and he lived the part that he had conjured up for himself, scattering his sibylline utterances to sustain the mood. He wrote later that "those who aspire to command, *make* themselves ready. . . . They build in the secrecy of an inner life, the structure of their attitudes, their belief, their will. That is why, in times of tragedy, when the winds blow down convention and habit, they alone remain standing, and, consequently, they alone matter."

DE GAULLE CAME FROM AN ÉLITE FAMILY; HIS FATHER WAS A DISTIN-guished professor of Catholic philosophy at a Jesuit college, the home a citadel of conservative piety that ever emphasized the virtues of

* Edward Spears, *Assignment to Catastrophe* (New York: A. A. Wyn, 1954–5), Vol. 2, p. 139.

patriotism and frugality. He was educated at St. Cyr, the French West Point, where his build and height won him the name of "Big Asparagus." His military record in World War I was outstanding. He was wounded three times and was taken prisoner at Verdun in 1916. He attempted five escapes before his release when the armistice was declared. Quite early he began questioning the outmoded strategic concepts that dominated military thinking. He called for the repudiation of defensive tactics, the Maginot line mentality that was dangerous in the new era of mobile warfare. He was the first to advocate the coordination of expanded air power and the mass use of tanks. He dedicated his classic book on tank warfare to Marshal Pétain, his mentor, the godfather of his only son. Later, as their historic roles made them enemies, each condemned the other to death. In this early period virtually no one in France paid attention to De Gaulle's unorthodox military theories. This was not because of blindness or stupidity. It was primarily because the French leadership was tired and dispirited and intent on preserving peace at almost any price. But in Germany De Gaulle's imaginative approach was studied with deepest interest, and was applied in the rearmament program. France was to be disastrously defeated in World War II with the blitz concepts that De Gaulle had predicted would be the dominant strategy of the new age.

When France fell to the Nazis in the summer of 1940, De Gaulle escaped to England, carrying with him in his small plane, as Churchill said, "the honor of France." In London he established the headquarters of the liberation movement, appealing to Frenchmen everywhere to continue resistance in whatever way was possible. His first broadcast set the theme: ". . . the cause of France is not lost. The very factors that brought about our defeat may one day lead us to victory. . . . Whatever happens, the flame of French resistance must not and shall not die." At first the appeal evoked little response. De Gaulle was virtually unknown. He was pitted against a legal government in France headed by a national hero who denounced him as a lackey for the British, "Churchill's French butler." In the first shock of defeat most Frenchmen believed that it was wise to remain on the outskirts of allegiance and to follow the more passive counsel of the Vichy men.

When one considers De Gaulle's rise to eminence, operating as an absent surrogate, the achievement is spectacular. From June 1940, he did not set foot on French soil and was not seen by the French people until he returned for the liberation parade. He was just a radio voice that came out of Studio B2 in the British Broadcasting offices. Yet it may have been this very absence, during the horror of occupation, that created the mystique upon which he counted as a powerful unifying force. He shared the pain and degradation of the present, in what Churchill called the "hairshirt syndrome," but he also represented the hope for regeneration. At first it flickered feebly, but even the flicker lit up the gloom as De Gaulle reiterated the pledge that he would never waver in the task of restoring Gallic honor, "Pouring over the gulf into which the country has fallen . . . calling her, holding the light for her, showing her the way of rescue."*

By the end of 1942 the Allied forces had recovered sufficiently to take the offensive. They were now reinforced by the limitless reserve power of the Russians, whom the Nazis had wantonly attacked, and by the Americans, who entered the war after the Japanese strike at Pearl Harbor. Hitler's Russian gamble had turned into a disaster that devoured millions of the dwindling Nazi manpower. America poured in planes and tanks and ships, food and equipment, and whole armies under fresh and imaginative leadership. It was possible now to plan and carry through the counterattack. It was agreed that North Africa would provide the most promising base from which to re-establish beachheads on the beleaguered European continent. The Germans and the Italians had already been cleared out of the eastern end of the Mediterranean littoral. Now the invasions were mounted to pre-empt the western end, and, by mid-1943, Morocco and Algeria and Tunisia were reconquered. There was close coordination between the British, the Americans, and the Free French forces, and the French commander, General Giraud, was an integral part of the liberation team.

By September 1943 there were landings at the southern tip of Italy itself. It still required hard fighting to inch northward; the Germans exacted heavy costs before yielding ground. The Italians were trapped between the retreating Nazis and the advancing Allies. A starved and frozen people now paid heavily for Mussolini's perfidy when he drove the dagger into the back of his French neighbor. They realized what a bladder of wind Mussolini had been and he was toppled from power and later executed by his own Italians. The liberated parts of Italy began to fight at the side of the Free French, the British, and the Americans, and Churchill welcomed them as they "worked their passage home." On June 4, 1944, Rome was retaken, the first of the capital cities to be freed.

* De Gaulle, *War Memoirs,* Vol. 1, p. 302.

Through the winter and the spring of 1944 the buildup of the forces went forward on the British coast for the long-awaited landings in France. The Allied strength was now so formidable that the wags worried lest the British Isles sink beneath its weight. June 6 was D-Day and a mighty armada went into action against the German firepower, the Luftwaffe, the mines and underwater obstacles, and the barbed wire. Many of the great military names of the era were involved—Eisenhower as supreme commander, Montgomery, Bradley, Patton, and of course, De Gaulle.

Within a week, more than 325,000 men had been landed in France and had consolidated their positions. Here was Dunkirk in reverse, with all the exultation of retrieval and vindication. The reconquest eastward began, coordinated with the march up from the south, from Marseilles, and Nice, and the Rhone Valley. The waiting Resistance units came down from the hills, and out of the forests of central France. They rose up out of the basements and the alleys of Paris itself, clearing out strategic strong points in the city in preparation for the arrival of the armored French divisions. The German commandant, General von Choltitz, had been ordered by Hitler to reduce the city to ruins before evacuation, but he defied the Führer and the surrender was humane and civilized.

On August 26, 1944, De Gaulle arrived in Paris for the triumphant walk down the Champs Élysées from the Étoile to the Place de la Concorde. He made his way, with a long file of cars, through the cheering, weeping millions, to Notre Dame, for the special Thanksgiving service. He was still a target for last-ditch collaborationists, and there was a hail of bullets from the snipers on the rooftops as he arrived. In the midst of the ceremonies in Notre Dame there was further shooting. De Gaulle stood tall and erect at the altar, intoning the *Te Deum* as the bullets echoed through the cathedral.

Within the next few weeks Belgium, Holland, Luxembourg, and all of France were cleared of the Nazi invaders. The Allied troops and their planes and tanks were poised on the frontiers of Germany for the invasion that would bring down Hitler and the Nazi Reich. De Gaulle, in his first broadcast in exile, alone, reviled, under the Vichy sentence of death, had vowed: "Whatever happens, the flame of French resistance must not and shall not die." History did not always vindicate hope and patience so dramatically.

18

CHURCHILL
AND THE SALVATION
OF BRITAIN

AFTER THE FALL OF FRANCE, HITLER WAS MASTER OF THE CONTINENT up to the frontiers of Russia. With Britain itself threatened by the blitz and invasion, the country turned to Winston Churchill who, from the political wilderness to which he had been consigned, had continually warned the West against the apostles of destruction. He was now called, almost too late, to provide the leadership which made his eloquence prophetic when he declared that "if the Commonwealth were to last for a thousand years, men would say, 'this was their finest hour.'"

Churchill lived nearly ninety years. As a boy he heard Gladstone speak, and as the revered elder statesman of a grateful Commonwealth he exchanged greetings with President John Kennedy. He worked with and fought against giants and titans—Lloyd George, Wilson, Lenin, Stalin, Gandhi, Franklin Roosevelt, Truman, Hitler, De Gaulle. He had many shortcomings. He was terribly wrong on freedom for Ireland and on sovereignty for India. He completely misjudged Gandhi, whom he described as a half-naked fakir. He had little sympathy for the social welfare legislation that was demanded in the aftermath of World War II, and this failure of perspective was the reason that he lost the election after he had saved his country and the world from its greatest danger.

But in the crisis of war he was incomparable. He symbolized the spirit of unyielding resistance. Even more, he gave his people a sense of mission, the mission that they alone had the responsibility for the survival of freedom. And he had the genius to marshal courage in prose so felicitous that he won the Nobel Prize for literature. The citation noted that the prize had come to him for his mastery of historical and biographical description, as well as for the brilliance of the oratory with which he defended human values.* It was appropriate to speak so of his words and his style. For they were weapons. His verbs were marching orders. His adjectives were trumpets. Even the roll of a syllable could carry defiance. His deliberate mispronunciation of the word "Nazi," which came out as "Naaazi," transmitted the scorn and contempt that he felt for the enemy. His gutteral roar evoked the symbol of the British lion. He assessed his historic role on his eightieth birthday: "I have never accepted what many people have kindly said—namely that I inspired the nation. Their will was resolute and remorseless and it proved unconquerable. It fell to me to express it. It was the nation and the race dwelling all around the globe that had the lion's heart. I had the luck to be called upon to give the roar."

By technical standards his oratory was halting, florid. A speech impediment gave him a lisp. But his imagery was unforgettable, and he had a sure instinct for mood. After Dunkirk his afflicted people did not want rhapsodic delusion; hence he called them to sacrifice through "blood and toil and sweat and tears," and the appeal was minted into the languages of the western world. After the miraculous achievement of the RAF, which drove the Luftwaffe from the British skies, he noted his gratitude in words that every schoolboy treasured. "Never in the field of human conflict was so much owed by so many to so few." His political opponents ruefully confessed that he could pulverize with a phrase. Of Neville Chamberlain's fake concern for the poor: "Mr. Chamberlain loves the workingman. He loves to see him work." After a pompous party member asked Churchill how he liked his speech, in which he had rambled on for hours: "Very good," was the reply. "It had to be, to include every known cliché and platitude ever uttered, with the exception perhaps of 'please adjust your dress before leaving.'" When Stanley Baldwin's home was bombed during the Nazi blitz, Churchill, remembering Baldwin's appeasement which had helped to build the power of the Nazi war machine, observed, "How ungrateful of them." He could be exquisitely tender

---

* How he wrote was as important as what he wrote. He explained: "Writing a book was an adventure. To begin with it was a toy, an amusement; then it became a mistress, and then a master, and then a tyrant."

too. The diary reference to his bride "Clemmie" on their wedding day read: "September, 1908, when I married and lived happily ever afterwards."

Churchill was born in 1874, a direct descendant of the Duke of Marlborough, the illustrious soldier of Queen Anne's day who was rewarded for his victories with a dukedom and the estate at Blenheim. He was the son of Randolph Churchill, one of the meteoric characters in the Victorian galaxy that included Gladstone, Disraeli, Palmerston, and Rosebery. His mother was a ravishing American beauty, Jenny Jerome, one of the celebrated sisters whose father owned part of *The New York Times* and was one of the pioneers of the American turf, a racing king who went through several fortunes. Winston was born prematurely in a cloakroom during a royal ball at Blenheim Palace, which his grandmother, the Duchess, thought was "most unconventional." He was proud of his combined American and British ancestry and constantly referred to it in his negotiations with Roosevelt for American aid.* His lineage and its privileges made it equally possible for him to overcome adversity or to accept fame as his due.

His career would scarcely serve as a paradigm for those who prescribed discipline and application as a preparation for greatness. He was an intellectual truant, a pugnacious, redheaded, truculent little maverick whose baby face was most misleading. In school he was in constant trouble, remaining for three years in the lowest forms. Probably he found no fun in what he later called "purposeless monotony." He was admitted to the military academy at Sandhurst after failing the entrance examination twice. He could not qualify for the crack regiment that the family had counted on, and he was therefore assigned to the less socially acceptable cavalry. It did not bother him; he said that, anyway, he preferred riding to walking. He left Sandhurst before completing the training, and the next years were spent as a war correspondent attached to the fighting forces in many parts of the world—Cuba, India, the Sudan, and South Africa. He was wounded in the Boer War, captured, and then escaped. He always resented the fact that the reward for his capture was only £25 and that the police circular described him as nondescript in appearance, talking through his nose, and unable to pronounce the "s" without lisping. Years later, in his Irish negotiations, he was

* On his first American lecture tour, Mark Twain introduced him: "By his father, he is an Englishman; by his mother, an American. Behold, the perfect man!"

upbraided by the rebel leader, Michael Collins, who had a price of £5,000 put on his head. Churchill thought that Collins should feel honored, for after all he, Churchill, had been assessed at only £25. Churchill returned from his adventures as a war hero with an established reputation as a gifted correspondent.

He began his long parliamentary career as a Tory, but he bolted the party in 1906 and crossed the floor to the Liberal side when he concluded that the Tories were still anchored in the eighteenth century. This was his most "radical" period, when he enjoyed the esteem of Sidney and Beatrice Webb, the foster parents of the Labour movement, who were impressed by Churchill's emancipation from inherited shibboleths. Though he had Marlborough ducal blood in his veins, he was part of the battle to restrict the power of the House of Lords.

During World War I he entered the cabinet as a Coalition Liberal. He was constantly challenging established routines and was an early convert to the use of armored cars, the ancestor of the tank. In the Admiralty, he planned the disastrous Dardanelles campaign. It cost a quarter of a million lives and almost ended his scarcely launched public career. He always insisted that the campaign was poorly executed, but his colleagues did not agree and he wrote in 1915, "I am finished." He was in and out of Parliament, and in and out of office, until 1929, when, disenchanted with the Liberals, he returned to the Tory fold. He was rewarded as a prodigal son, or, as he put it, "for re-ratting," when Stanley Baldwin brought him into the cabinet as Chancellor of the Exchequer. But his intransigence and abrasiveness were no less vocal, and he was virtually disowned by the Tories for what the leadership condemned as "unreliability." He then spent ten long years, from 1929 to 1939, in a political wilderness, indulging his hobbies—bricklaying, with pride in his union card, painting, always in lush, vivid colors, avoiding the grays, the browns, the dull, the somber.

But he stayed on in Parliament, a scourge to the appeasers and the pacifists of the thirties. He was not unsympathetic to the German Weimar Republic; he advocated all possible help to buttress its strength so that the democratic parties there could establish stability. But if it was not to be helped, then it was suicidal to permit British defenses to lag while a resentful enemy girded for a day of reckoning. "All those bands of sturdy Teutonic youths," he warned, "marching through the streets and roads of Germany, with the light of desire in their eyes to suffer for the Fatherland, are not looking for status.

They are looking for weapons." His speeches were grounded on solid research. He drew heavily on the specialized knowledge of economic and military experts. A South African banker, Solly Zuckerman, helped him to analyze the progress of German aircraft by scrutinizing the reports of the German metallurgical industry. An Oxford professor, F. A. Lindemann, pored with him over figures of car loadings, budgetary expenditures, taxation, and national income, and deduced what this meant in hidden diversion of funds for rearmament.

By 1937, from his own unimpeachable sources, he knew that Britain was in gravest jeopardy. "The dictators are riding to and fro on tigers which they dare not dismount, and the tigers are getting hungry." When the Chamberlain government still refused to accelerate major armament, he gave full rein to his frustration: "I have watched this famous island descending incontinently, fecklessly, the stairway which leads to a dark gulf. . . . Future generations will never understand how it was that a victorious nation, with everything in hand, suffered themselves to be brought low, and to cast away all that they had gained by measureless sacrifice and absolute victory. . . ."

In March 1938, as Hitler followed his artichoke strategy, peeling off one leaf at a time, Churchill pounded away at the need for more adequate preparedness. The news that Austria had been engulfed came just as the Nazi Foreign Minister, Ribbentrop, was lunching with the British cabinet. Churchill was present and he remarked, "I suppose they asked me . . . to show him that, if they could not bite themselves, they kept a dog who could bark and might bite." Through 1938 Churchill was the alarmist, exposing British unpreparedness, warning that German rearmament would inevitably be used to rain death and destruction on the land. When Chamberlain returned from Munich, exulting that he had saved the peace, Churchill denounced the agreement as total and unmitigated defeat. Hitler, he said, "instead of snatching the victuals off the table, had been content to have them served to him by Chamberlain, course by course." He then sorrowfully saw the fulfillment of his prophecies when Hitler repudiated his pledges and destroyed the Czechoslovakian state.

When Hitler concluded the pact with Stalin in 1939, it was clear that there would soon be war and there was a virtually unanimous call for a National Coalition cabinet. In this emergency Churchill was invited to return to his old post in the Admiralty. "Winston is back," was flashed all over the seven seas. He loyally supported Chamberlain and the discredited leaders of the government. But when the war came and the disasters mounted and Hitler's legions ran amok, the demand for a leadership that was not tainted with appeasement and that could restore confidence brought Churchill to the Prime Minister's post. His introduction to his task was the fall of Holland and Belgium, and the entrapment of the British and French forces at Dunkirk. "Within six weeks," he recalled, "we were to find ourselves alone, almost disarmed, with triumphant Germany and Italy at our throats, with the whole of Europe in Hitler's power, and Japan glowering on the other side of the globe." Churchill wasted neither time nor energy on recriminations. "Although impatient for the morning, I slept soundly."*

Since the Luftwaffe was poised to strafe the exodus from Dunkirk, it was not expected that more than thirty or forty thousand of the half million men crowded on the beaches could be evacuated. The appeal went out to the British to make available anything afloat. A fleet of fishing vessels, yachts, rowboats, dinghies, launches, whatever could move on water, joined up with the ships and barges that were part of the regular military, a most extraordinary naval gallimaufry. Most of the evacuation had to be effected by night. The Royal Air Force offered the protective cover and took on the Luftwaffe. For five days and nights the battle raged in the skies as the hodgepodge craft made their trips back and forth across the Channel, some boats and their exhausted crews ferrying four times in one day under constant fire. Before the evacuation had been completed, hundreds of the Luftwaffe had been knocked out of the skies, and 215,000 British and 120,000 of the French were evacuated. They had to leave all their equipment behind, but the manpower was brought to safety to fight another day. Even more, the embattled island that had been read out as soon to be overwhelmed and dispatched had convincingly demonstrated its staying power. A few days later, Churchill reported the achievement and made clear that this was no mere despairing effort. To be sure, he did not treat Dunkirk as a victory. "Wars are not won by evacuations," he declared. But it was a test for the air force and, even more, for the soldiers of Britain. And then he added the famous peroration that was adrenalin for the anguished spirits of his countrymen:

We shall fight on the beaches, we shall fight on the landing-grounds, we shall fight in the fields and in the streets, we shall fight in the hills; we shall never surrender, and even if, which I do not for a moment believe,

* Churchill, *Memoirs of the Second World War*, p. 227.

this island or a large part of it were subjugated and starving, then our Empire beyond the seas, armed and guarded by the British fleet, would carry on the struggle until in God's good time, the New World, with all its power and might, steps forth to the rescue and the liberation of the Old.*

The voice, the spirit, the appeal to the best instincts of the British— these were as important as weaponry. They consolidated the nation and toughened its determination to bear any burden or sorrow.

But weapons were essential too. An entire armory had been left behind in the evacuation and it would take time, even without harassment, for British industry to retrieve the loss. It was here that American aid proved indispensable. Roosevelt had moved ever closer to identification with the Allied cause. He now made weaponry available in unlimited quantities and, within a few weeks, much of what had been abandoned had been replaced, even though it brought the American reserves down to an almost precarious level.

The successful evacuation of Dunkirk was a grave disappointment to Hitler but it was soon retrieved by the lightning victory over France. Hitler was now ready for the climactic attack on Britain, by air and by sea. There was strong hope that actual invasion would not be necessary if the air blitz could be sufficiently terrifying: a blitz not only on war objectives, but on industry, on civilians, on their stamina and their will. Hitler planned the blitz with a coordinated blockade of Britain that would add starvation as pressure for capitulation. It was not a far-fetched possibility. It was constantly in the mind of Ambassador Joseph Kennedy in London and Ambassador William Bullitt in Paris. Göring, who was given the assignment by Hitler for the sustained air attack, was confident that, after a taste of intense bombardment of London and other parts of Britain, the decadent British, having deteriorated from a courage culture to a creature comfort culture, would sue for peace. To demoralize the country, even before the blitz, the Nazis began dropping dummy parachute packs that contained radios and maps, to create the impression that a fifth column inside England was all prepared to cooperate with an imminent invasion.

* The American correspondent, Ed Murrow, had helped to prepare him for the radio address and he related that when Churchill reached the end of the "We shall fight on the beaches" peroration, he cupped his hand over the microphone and added: "We'll hit them on the head with beer bottles, which is all we have to fight with." Alexander Kendrick, *Prime Time: The Life of Edward R. Murrow* (Boston: Little, Brown, 1969), p. 199.

The Battle of Britain began early in August 1940, and it continued until the end of October, an agony of nearly three months that was to test to the fullest the resolution of the British common folk. The Luftwaffe, in squadrons of hundreds, was pitted against the Royal Air Force, a small band of well-trained pilots whose numbers had grown from about four hundred to seven hundred since the Polish blitz. The invading planes bombed London for eighty-two of eighty-five consecutive nights. They had come over Warsaw and Poland had collapsed at once. They had blasted Rotterdam and Holland had immediately yielded. The mere threat of what would happen to eternal Paris was sufficient to hasten the city's surrender. But England stood fast. The RAF struck back.* Each day the toll of Nazi planes mounted. But there was a toll from the RAF as well and the surviving pilots had to double their daily missions and then triple them. It was fortunate for the British that Hitler did not realize how close he came to victory. In the ten days from August 8 to 18, the RAF lost 154 pilots; their replacements were less than half that number, and these were raw and untried. On September 15 there was not a single squadron left in reserve when the last German aircraft turned for home.

There were seven million people in London, plain folk, not prepared or disciplined for the trials of elementary survival under such terror. A hundred and fifty thousand civilians were killed in the first few weeks of the blitz. One wonders whether New York could have taken this long travail, or Chicago, or Boston, or Los Angeles. But the English did, living with death and mutilation, with completely disrupted routines, shuttling between bombed-out homes and shops and air raid shelters, each family doggedly accepting protective duties that had been assigned—air raid wardens, fire fighters, national guard —the morale high, with no thought of accusation against leadership for this sorry pass, with no thought of surrender.† The mood was reflected in the oft-repeated story of the Cockney who chided his friend for complaining. "What are yer grousin' about? We're in the finals, h'ain't we? And we're playin' at home, h'ain't we?"

---

* It was a providential development that only a year earlier one of Churchill's science advisers, Sir Henry Tizard, helped to perfect radar, without which even the bravery and gallantry of the RAF would not have sufficed for victory.

† Not all English cities reacted with heroism. There were serious problems of morale, for example, in Liverpool.

The saga had many facets to illustrate the fortitude and the low-keyed emotional reaction of those critical days. One that Churchill selected as never to be forgotten dealt with the UBX, the Unexploded Bomb Squads. Hitler used large numbers of delayed-action bombs that were dropped and triggered for later detonation. It was necessary to assign special suicide squads to dig up the bombs and carefully defuse them. The volunteers were always there for the nerve-racking task. They were gaunt and haggard men and women, who went about their assignments with an eerie resignation. Some had records of twenty bombs before the explosion and death. Some reached twenty-five, even thirty. The Earl of Suffolk, his lady private secretary, and his elderly chauffeur, who called themselves the "Holy Trinity," had a record of thirty-four bombs dug up and defused with quiet efficiency. And then, on the thirty-fifth, they were blown to bits. Churchill wrote: "We may be sure that, even as for Greatheart, 'all the trumpets sounded for them on the other side.'" The Luftwaffe had the bad judgment to bomb Buckingham Palace and came within a few yards of hitting the King. Nothing could have helped more to solidify the resistance and to heighten morale. For the Royal family remained in London and regularly joined in the visits to the bombed-out sections.

In mid-November, Hitler sent five hundred planes over Coventry with hundreds of tons of explosives and thousands of incendiaries. The center of the ancient city was devastated, including the beautiful cathedral. Hitler vowed the "Coventrization" of scores of other cities, and he kept his promise in Plymouth and Manchester, in Leeds and Glasgow and Liverpool. But the rebuilding was begun as fast as the planes had finished dropping their destructive cargo, and the defiance went on. It did not matter, Churchill wrote, where the blow struck. "The nation was as sound as the sea is salt."

The most resolute symbol was Winston Churchill himself. He was everywhere, with his long cigar, his bulldog face, and his eloquent growl. Now in the tugboat, in the captain's plug hat and the pea jacket, the ancient garb of the Elder Brother of the Trinity House, one of the oldest of England's societies which had helped to establish seapower;* now at the controls in a four-engine bomber with the cigar tight in his mouth. As the V-2's, the long-range rockets, came over from emplacements across the Channel, Churchill was in a

---

* Someone suggested that Churchill's clothes were obviously hand-me-downs from a rhinoceros whose skin he also wore.

different part of the ravaged city each morning, picking his way through the broken glass and the other debris, cheerfully calculating that it would take ten years at the present rate to demolish just half of London. He watched air raids from the Air Ministry and members of his staff were apprehensive that he was tempting Providence. "My time will come when it comes," Churchill chuckled. "That may be," said a dejected voice from the corner. "But there's no need to take half a dozen of us with you."

By every logic Britain should have yielded, for the statistics of defeat were unanswerable. But Churchill was never good at statistics even when he was Chancellor of the Exchequer. "Those damned little dots," he grunted. Every day, at a different point, he was there with a new message that blended realism and hope. "Death and sorrow will be the companion of our journey," he said, "but we must be undaunted. We must be inflexible. Our quality and deeds must burn and glow through the gloom of Europe until they become the veritable beacon of its salvation."

Those who listened as the rain of death and havoc went on through the summer of 1940 knew how close the peril was. They knew that, if the Nazis won, it would not be a conventional military victory such as the textbooks recorded. The Nazis would not stop with Europe or Asia or Africa. They would be the *Herrenvolk*, the supermen, determined upon a biological screening of worldwide dimensions. Already the reports of their treatment of conquered people in labor battalions and concentration camps were trickling in from the fastnesses of Hell. What kind of a world would emerge from a Nazi victory became clear as more and more territory resounded to the marching boots of the conquerors. From captured documents the Nazis' exact plans for a vanquished England were revealed. They had been prepared with Prussian thoroughness. Ribbentrop was slated to become Vice Regent, Reichskomissar. The country was to be divided into six military commands. Able-bodied men between seventeen and forty-five were to be shipped off to the continent for slave labor, as was done with the Poles and the French. Raw materials, food supplies, industrial goods, were all to be routed to Germany. All of this was in prospect, immediately after the thorough purge of long lists of leaders selected for elimination and execution. These consequences were in the minds of the listeners as the defiant speeches of Churchill, more potent than weapons, came through.

The daily radio count of British and Nazi planes that went down was followed by the free world, to calculate what the chances of survival had now become. The RAF was decimated to the point where it was questionable if another week of resistance was possible. But the Luftwaffe too was cut to pieces, and the toll was ultimately too much to sustain. Then the incredible British took the initiative. They began bombing flights over Berlin, strategically not yet important, but psychologically a master stroke. For this was a massive blow to Hitler's ego. He had been crowing to his people that no bomb would ever fall on the capital. One raid occurred while Molotov was in Berlin for a conference with Ribbentrop. It was necessary to hurry into an air raid shelter. Ribbentrop kept boasting how England would soon be knocked out. Molotov asked, "If that is so, why are we in this shelter, and whose are these bombs which fall?"

Hitler's order to switch from strikes on British airfields and radar installations to massive bombing strikes on cities probably saved Britain and was largely responsible for Hitler's abandonment of the plans for invasion. It may be that he was also influenced by the psychological shock that came from the bombing of Berlin. In any case, he came to agree with the military staff that the British would not yield under the punishment of the blitz and that invasion would have to be postponed. He decided instead to turn to the East. After all, the solemn pact with Russia had been signed, tongue in cheek, to protect the German rear until the enemies in the West had been immobilized. Hitler had never lost his hatred of communism and his contempt for the Red leaders. He could settle his scores with Churchill and Britain later on. He therefore canceled Operation Sea Lion, the Channel invasion plans, and, on June 22, 1941, the invasion of Russia began.

It was again a moment of crucial decision for Churchill and the British. Perhaps Hitler's involvement in war with Russia was a way out. England could slow down its military activity and let the two totalitarian regimes tear each other to pieces, as the Russians had hoped Germany and the democracies would do. But Churchill did not hesitate for a moment. He resolved at once to join with the Russians with every possible resource for the ultimate defeat of Hitler. If to fight this scourge of mankind, he said, called for an alliance with the Devil, he would go down to Hell to conclude it. He told the House of Commons, "No one has been a more consistent opponent of Communism than I have been for the last twenty-five years. I will unsay no word that I have spoken about it. But all this fades away before the spectacle that is now unfolding. . . . We are resolved to destroy Hitler and every vestige of the Nazi regime." For, if Hitler were successful, he would change the whole world into "that bottomless pit of human degradation over which the diabolic emblem of the swastika flaunts itself. Can you doubt what our policy will be? . . ."

Here, then, we leave Churchill for the moment, at the turning point in the war, the greatest years of his career, when he had brought his country from the abyss and instilled it with the will to keep on fighting. There were still terrifying days ahead—the loss of Greece and Yugoslavia, the defeats in the Pacific where Japan mounted almost irresistible power, the attrition of the bloody campaigns in North Africa and Italy, the staggering losses at sea. Churchill never lost courage or patience or resourcefulness. Through sorrow, anguish, and sacrifice, he remained vivid, the symbol of resistance for all who fought: his uniforms, his hats, his V sign, his cigar, his walking stick, and, above all, the gravelly voice, the words carrying the defiant message: "We shall never surrender."

Nearly a century before, Macaulay had written of the ordeal of Chatham who had saved Britain from defeat by Napoleon: "The ardour of his soul had set the whole kingdom on fire. . . . He had imparted to the commanders who were at his side, his own impetuous, adventurous, and defiant character. They, like him, were disposed to risk everything, to play double or quits to the last, to think nothing done while anything remained undone, to fail rather than not to attempt." There could be no more appropriate summary of Churchill in *his* finest hour.

19

FDR: FROM ISOLATION
TO INTERVENTION

THE MAGNIFICENT RESISTANCE OF BRITAIN IN THE SUMMER OF 1940 compelled Hitler to postpone his plans for invasion. But the British spirit by itself would not have availed. The capacity to endure depended too on the range and scope of American assistance. Would the United States pledge its resources to help save the Allied cause, or would it limit its participation to sympathy and blessings and to what Britain could still afford to buy? Churchill, in his urgent appeals for massive aid, warned that Britain could not long survive without total American commitment. He argued that the British cause was basically the American cause too, because Hitler's victory would carry with it Nazi control of the Atlantic, and would place the United States at the mercy of a Nazi war machine made impregnable by the appropriation of its conquered loot. The man who had the deciding role was Franklin Delano Roosevelt, whose consummate political craftsmanship brought a nation that was determined to avoid any entangling alliances to all-out intervention in the most destructive war in history.

Roosevelt came from old Dutch stock that had been part of American life since colonial days. There were inherited fortunes from both sides of his family, so that he could be reared with all the privileges of wealth and social position: youth on the ancestral estate in Hyde Park, the right schools—Groton, Harvard, and Columbia Law—leisurely European travel, marriage to Eleanor Roosevelt, the godchild and favorite grandniece of former President Theodore Roosevelt.

Young Franklin practiced law briefly and then opted for a political career, beginning with an apprenticeship in the New York State legislature. There he became identified with the reforming mavericks who repudiated the Tammany leadership. His mentor was Woodrow Wilson, who had also broken with the party stalwarts, and when Wilson became President in 1913, he brought Franklin into the government as Assistant Secretary of the Navy.

The harassed President was not an easy chief in the strenuous days of World War I and the problems that it spawned, but young Roosevelt could be counted on for undeviating loyalty. In the election of 1920, he was the Democratic vice presidential nominee in the hopeless battle to save the League of Nations. The political defeat was not too serious. It gave the handsome, well-placed, eloquent young Roosevelt national visibility. But what *was* serious, well-nigh fatal, was the attack of polio in 1921 which permanently crippled him. He lost the use of his legs and was never again able to walk without heavy braces and crutches. His Pulitzer Prize biographer has a poignant description of Roosevelt's difficulties at a wartime summer conference in Morocco: "Servants made a chair with their arms and carried the President up the winding stairs, his legs dangling like the limbs of a ventriloquist's dummy."* Such incapacity would normally have spelled the end of a promising career, except for the devotion and tenderness of Eleanor and the perseverance that he demonstrated in the long battle with paralysis. He wrote later: "I spent two years lying in bed just trying to move my big toe." He fought his way back so effectively that few people ever thought of him as a cripple. The impression of the broad shoulders, made sturdy by frequent swimming exercises, the finely chiseled features, the magnificent voice, the radiant smile, the charm of manner, all combined to mark him as an inevitable possibility for highest national office.

He was elected governor of New York in 1928 at the lowest point in the fortunes of the Democratic Party, and he used the period to lay the groundwork in New York for the regenerative social legislation of the later New Deal. In 1932, with the Depression eating into the vitals of America, President Hoover discredited, and the nation in panic, avid for confident leadership, Roosevelt was a most attractive presidential candidate for the Democrats. He did not win the nomination easily, and there were some high shenanigans in the back rooms that called for trade and compromise. But in the election

---

* James MacGregor Burns, *Roosevelt: The Soldier of Freedom* (New York: Harcourt, Brace, Jovanovich, Inc., 1970), p. 324.

Roosevelt swept the country. On the day of his inauguration every bank in the country had closed and industry and commerce had ground to a halt. His ringing call, " . . . the only thing we have to fear is fear itself," became the working credo for his generation.

In the years ahead, there were few neutral reactions to Roosevelt. Those who disliked him and his policies usually detested him. Those who admired were enraptured, almost blindly loyal. The Roosevelt haters regarded him as a political madcap, a demagogue who had turned against his class to pander to the masses. Some could not forget his excoriation of them as "economic royalists," his vow to drive the money-changers from the temple. He was accused of brazen opportunism and deviousness. One irate industrialist compared him to Columbus: "When he started out he didn't know where he was going; when he got there, he didn't know where he was; when he returned he didn't know where he had been; and he did it all on borrowed money!"

But Roosevelt's admirers swore by him. For them, he could do no wrong. They were enthralled by his daring, his compassion, his concern for the underprivileged. Apparently he enjoyed crisis, and he was at his best at such a time, with a gaiety that, Justice Frankfurter said, was much too often unfortunately taken for jauntiness. His energy, like Eleanor's, seemed inexhaustible. The journalist Joseph Alsop explained: "It's just that damned extra Roosevelt gland." One of his biographers, Rexford Tugwell, wrote that "Roosevelt's political energy was a fiery flame and the head of steam that it generated allowed its containing vessel no rest, even in invalidism." And he was completely fearless. A correspondent who had covered the assassination-conscious world of Mussolini, Ataturk, and Hitler noted that Roosevelt never seemed to be in the slightest concerned about his personal safety. He always sat with a broad window at his back.

A whole generation away from the actions and passions of his career, more objective historical appraisals are possible. Undoubtedly the prod of responsibility expanded Roosevelt's awareness. When he was first elected to the presidency, the glib judgment was passed on him that he was just an amateur in statesmanship, superficial, flashy, unreliable. Walter Lippmann wrote that he was too eager to please. "He is not the dangerous enemy of anything." Mencken referred to him as "Roosevelt minor." He may have had a wide streak of opportunism in his make-up, and he could be very hard on friends and allies. But when the democratic way of life was at stake, he demonstrated how imaginative and decisive he could be. Taking office, in the words of his inaugural, as head of a "stricken nation in the midst of a stricken world," he saved the free enterprise system by eliminating some of the most glaring abuses that would have destroyed it. Very early, also, he recognized the global danger of predatory fascism and skillfully brought a once-burned-twice-shy people to commit its abundant resources to contain it.

Considering the isolationist climate of the time, Roosevelt *had* to be a political animal to fulfill such a mission. Dorothy Thompson said that every pore in Roosevelt's body was an ear. He worked remarkably well with Churchill, whom he admired above any contemporary statesman. He was not subservient to him, nor taken in by his eloquent blandishments. He did not hesitate to criticize Churchill's social conservatism and the tenacity of his imperialist commitments. In the five years of close association there were profound disagreements and frequent eruptions of temper, inevitable in the interplay of two such incandescent personalities. Once, when concern was expressed that Roosevelt seemed so tired after a long summit conference, he explained, "Of course I'm tired. So would you be if you had spent the last five years pushing Winston uphill in a wheelbarrow." But these were the consequences of sheer physical exhaustion under the stress of decisions that would influence all the future. In the rare moments of comparative serenity, Roosevelt was fascinated by Churchill and was proud to be associated with him. He once cabled him: "It's fun to be in the same decade with you!"

In his first term, Roosevelt devoted very little attention to foreign affairs. He was mainly concerned with the domestic crisis, and here the pace of reorganization was frenetic. The New Deal bills tumbled over each other as they were pushed through Congress. Some of them, especially for banking and the stock markets, were related to the emergency, and they helped to restore shattered confidence. Some of them—the major relief measures, the program of public works, bridges, roads, schoolhouses, airports—changed the face of the country even as they cut back the terrifying unemployment rolls. Most of them—social security, the Tennessee Valley Authority, agricultural reform—established the responsibility of government to protect the opportunity and the security of its citizens. Roosevelt said: "A government that cannot take care of its old, that cannot provide work for the strong and willing, that lets the black shadows of insecurity rest on every home, is not a government that can or should endure." Later this conception of government was to be taken for granted, even by the Republicans. But at this stage, it represented a revolutionary change from the unbending adherence to the "rugged individualism" of Coolidge and Hoover. In the election of 1936, which was in essence a referendum on the New Deal, Roosevelt's plurality was the largest in American history, and he lost only two states, Maine and Vermont.

It was after the electoral triumph of 1936 that Roosevelt was increasingly diverted from his concentration on domestic affairs. The dictators had sensed the weakness of the European democracies and they were determined to press as hard and as far as their bluster and threat would carry them. Roosevelt had the prescience to understand quite early the mortal danger of this Fascist aggression, not only to the European states but to the long-range welfare of America. He was no doctrinaire moralist; he worked very comfortably with dictators, just as he formed convenient alliances with party bosses in the metropolises of America. But he saw in Hitler an insatiable destructive force which threatened the whole world and its civilized values. The fate of Austria and Czechoslovakia had made it clear that to rely on appeasement to contain the Fascist dictators was tragically self-deceptive. He said, "No man can tame a tiger into a kitten by stroking it." Roosevelt's intuition was sound. We now know from the evidence offered in both the Nuremberg and the Japanese war crimes trials that as early as 1938 Hitler called upon his industrialists and generals for planes that could bomb New York, and that Hitler and Matsuoka had perfected the details for attacking the United States in both oceans.

But how could Roosevelt win support for his views from a people that was so inflexibly isolationist, that had genuine concern for the tormented victims of the dictators but would not risk war to bring decisive help? It was Roosevelt's task to persuade his people to authorize full support for the beleaguered democracies without losing their confidence that he was determined to avoid war. This called for rare political finesse and it was fascinating to watch Roosevelt on his whirligig while the destiny of his generation was at stake.

To begin with, he was inhibited by the rigid neutrality laws that had been passed to make certain that the United States could not directly or indirectly be drawn into war. These laws forbade the sale of arms to any belligerents, victims as well as aggressors, and there could be no loans extended to them. The only deterrent that the United States could resort to, in cases of clear aggression, was to refuse to recognize the conquests, and such a deterrent roused amused contempt rather than caution. The solace to the victims was dubious when they were in effect told during the Japanese invasion of Manchuria and the rape of Ethiopia: "Though we will not lift a finger to prevent your being attacked, be of good cheer. After you have been killed, we shall refuse to admit that you are dead."

In October 1937, Roosevelt sent up a trial balloon in a Chicago speech, where he warned that the actions of the dictators "could engulf states and peoples remote from the original scene of the hostilities." He therefore hoped that some means could be found "to quarantine" the aggressors. The word "quarantine" instantly set off the isolationist alarms, and they rang deafeningly. There was the most eloquent sympathy for the victims of the dictators, but for the United States to attempt even the most moderate form of quarantine was regarded as involvement. Roosevelt was rebuked in Congress and in most of the press, and he was warned to ride at anchor, even by members of his own cabinet. To his close adviser, Judge Samuel Rosenman, he remarked sadly, "It is a terrible feeling to be leading way out in front, and then to look and find that no one is following."*

The furthest that Roosevelt dared to go at this stage, in May 1937, was to include provision, in the renewal of the Neutrality Act, for what was termed Cash and Carry. The act permitted belligerents to buy nonmilitary supplies, such as steel, oil, cotton, and copper, for cash on the barrel, and the purchase would have to be transported in their own ships. The expectation was that this would favor the Allies since they still controlled the Atlantic sea lanes.

The ambivalence of American public opinion, and Roosevelt's problem in resolving it, came sharply into focus in several legislative battles early in 1938. Congress remained unshaken in its resolution to stay clear of involvements, no matter how serious the Fascist provocation. Yet there was widespread indignation and angry reactions because the political leadership in Britain and France preferred to placate the dictators rather than to face up to them. A bill was introduced in the House of Representatives by an Indiana congressman, Louis Ludlow, that war could not be declared, except if there were invasion, unless the action were first approved by a national referendum. Despite the most vigorous protests from Roosevelt and from congressional leaders of both parties that such mandatory

* Samuel Rosenman, comp., *The Public Papers and Addresses of Franklin D. Roosevelt* (New York: Random House, 1938–50), p. 115.

delays, in a world of blitz warfare, would play into the hands of the aggressors, the bill was very nearly passed.

Meantime Roosevelt appealed for accelerated rearmament, arguing that it was suicidal to remain as unprepared as Britain had been when the international climate had become so dangerous. He recommended a defense budget to include a two-ocean navy in order to counterbalance the expansion of German and Japanese strength in the Atlantic and the Pacific. The debate was acrimonious and, though the recommendation was adopted, the strength of the minority that resisted indicated that even defense expenditures were widely suspect. When early in 1939 an off-the-record judgment by Roosevelt leaked out that the American frontier was now in France and along the Rhine, the outburst was so vehement that Roosevelt had quickly to explain that he had been misquoted.

Hitler was, of course, kept fully informed by his diplomatic representatives and by a network of intelligence agents of the state of American public opinion. He was convinced that, though there would probably be increasing material support from the United States for the victims on his agenda, there was little risk that the powerful military potential of America would ever become available to the Allies. This conviction was reinforced when the Conscription Law that had been authorized for one year came up for renewal and was almost lost in the House. At the height of the European crisis, it passed by one vote, 203 to 202.

Roosevelt's plea to include munitions and arms in the Cash and Carry provisions of the neutrality laws remained bottled up in the Senate. Late in July 1939, on the eve of war, after a long session with the leaders of both parties of the Senate, the Vice President, John Garner, had to break the news to Roosevelt. "Captain," he said, "we may as well face the facts. You haven't got the votes." Roosevelt was obliged to reassure the nation: "There is no thought in any shape, manner or form, of putting the nation on a war basis."

In the end it was not Roosevelt but Hitler who completed the conversion of America from nonalignment to intervention. The Führer was undone by the malady which is endemic with most dictators, who rarely know when to stop. Hitler too at last overreached. In the spring of 1940, when Hitler engulfed all the neighboring neutral countries and then quickly conquered France, the American psychological climate was transformed. It was now clear that neutrality was no protection against limitless aggression. To Hitler, treaties and guarantees were all stratagems to be made and broken as national ambition dictated. Roosevelt judged that he could now go much further in resistance, and he moved quickly to make up for the long dialogue with the deaf. He warned the Nazis that there were ways to stop aggression by methods short of war. "To stop aggression short of war" was a phrase loaded with the sternest warning, and it had a fuse attached. The world had changed drastically since Roosevelt's quarantine speech had backfired. This time there was hearty endorsement of the explicit pledge that America would no longer limit its concern to protest and indirect aid.

Roosevelt obtained quick and virtually unanimous approval in Congress for a sharply accelerated military buildup to include conscription, and the appropriations now reached into the billions. After Mussolini ordered the attack on mortally wounded France on June 10, 1940, Roosevelt not only denounced the perfidious act, the stabbing of a neighbor in the back, but pledged that all the resources of the United States would be harnessed to help the victims of aggression. There followed the transfer of fifty destroyers to Britain for convoy duty and for the defense of the beleaguered island. In return, Britain leased to the United States six sites in the Caribbean as air and naval stations. The destroyer-bases exchange was interpreted to both peoples as mutually advantageous; in effect, it marked the end of American neutrality.

Nevertheless it was significant that in such actions Roosevelt had to bypass Congress and exercise executive authority. The hope was held that the defeat of Germany and her allies could be effected without actual American participation. In the presidential election campaign of 1940, Roosevelt found it politic to offer the assurance: "We shall not send our boys to take part in Europe's wars." But the reserves of Britain were now almost exhausted and, if its access to arms was to be limited to Cash and Carry, it would be unable to hold out much longer. In March 1941, after Roosevelt had been inaugurated for his precedent-shattering third term, he proposed the Lend-Lease Act that would empower the administration to provide all required help to any country whose defense the President deemed vital to the security of the United States. Roosevelt offered a homely analogy in a press conference on December 17, 1940. "Suppose my neighbor's house catches fire and I have the length of garden hose four or five hundred feet away. If he can take my garden hose and connect it up with his hydrant, I may help him to put out the fire."* There was still determined resistance. Senator Burton Wheeler warned, "The Lend Lease program is the New Deal's Triple 'A' foreign policy; it will plow under every fourth American boy." But the opposition could no longer command American policy. The Lend-Lease Act was passed, and, immediately thereafter, seven billions were voted to meet Churchill's appeal: "Give us the tools and we will finish the job." In this way the United States became "the arsenal of democracy." In the first week of 1941 Roosevelt could speak boldly to Congress. "We must be wary of those who with pounding brass and tinkling cymbal preach the 'ism' of appeasement."

Another decisive turn came in June, when Hitler launched the massive attack on Russia. Churchill announced at once that, since the supreme enemy was Hitler's Germany, Britain would stand by the side of Russia. Roosevelt had to be more cautious. It was a wrench for the American people to think kindly of Russia, especially after the Nazi-Soviet pact. But Russia quickly earned its place as an indispensable ally. It relieved the intolerable pressure on Britain as Hitler assigned most of the Nazi armored strength to the eastern front. The tenacious resistance of the Russians also provided precious time for America to build up its military resources. Within four or five months Roosevelt could toast some of the visiting generals in the White House and announce that, since Russia was vital to the security of the United States, it was eligible to receive Lend-Lease aid.

With Britain, of course, the collaboration was wholehearted and sustained. Its closeness was revealed when Roosevelt and Churchill and their advisers met in August on board ship off Newfoundland, where measures to provide all-out aid to Britain and to Russia were reviewed and perfected. The summit conference was climaxed with the dramatic announcement of an Atlantic Charter, wherein a new world was envisioned, freed at last from Nazi tyranny, with pledged access to opportunity and to better standards of living. The charter itself was vague and doctrinaire, but its spirit marked the 180-degree turn in American opinion from the days of its undeviating isolationism.

As Roosevelt edged closer to intervention a Nazi spokesman warned that his policy of "pinpricks, challenges, insults and moral aggression" had become "insupportable."* Hitler now threw over

---

* Burns, *Roosevelt*, p. 26.

all restraints and ordered retaliatory action. Several of the American destroyers that were escorting British ships through the Atlantic lanes were torpedoed by German submarines. Roosevelt immediately announced that if German submarines or vessels came into the shipping lanes, they would be fired upon on sight. In his fireside chat of September 11, 1941, he said: "When you see a rattlesnake poised to strike, you do not wait until he has struck, before you crush him." The public opinion polls of the next month indicated that 70 percent of those who were interviewed were now in favor of war, if necessary, to defeat the Nazis. It required little persuasion to have the provisions of the Neutrality Act repealed, so that American ships were free to transport any war cargo to the Allies and to receive armed protection from American escorts. The cycle of intervention was completed when, on December 7, the Japanese struck at Pearl Harbor and Hitler followed with a declaration of war against the United States.

As usual, it was Winston Churchill who offered the most cogent summary of the significance of this turning point in history. He realized, he said, that many disasters, immeasurable cost and tribulation, still lay ahead. But there was doubt no longer about the outcome. He concluded: "I thought of a remark which Edward Grey had made to me no more than thirty years earlier, that the United States is like a 'gigantic boiler.' Once the fire is lighted under it, there is no limit to the power it can generate."† His forecast was accurate. There were indeed four grievous years of bloodshed and destruction ahead, but the fire was at last under the gigantic boiler, and the power of the flame ultimately consumed the Nazis and their minions.

* Burns, *Roosevelt,* p. 26.
† Churchill, *The Grand Alliance,* pp. 607–8.

20

TITO AND
THE EMERGENCE OF
YUGOSLAVIA

MARSHAL TITO CAME OUT OF A SMALL BALKAN STATE BUT HE CHANGED the character and destiny of international communism. His career includes a long guerrilla struggle that subverted the power of the Nazi military machine and leadership in a pitiless civil war fought within an international war. Beyond all this, it includes the emergence of a new force, Titoism, which successfully challenged the monolithic Kremlin control of the Iron Curtain world.

Tito was born in 1892 as Josip Broz of a Croat-Slovene peasant family, one of fifteen children. His father had intended him to migrate to the United States to seek his fortune there, but even steerage fare was out of reach. Tito knocked about at many jobs—as a café waiter, a blacksmith, a mechanic—until he became a skilled metal worker and could join a union. He enlisted early in the conspiratorial movements that corroded the stability of the Hapsburg Empire. In World War I, young Broz was conscripted for the Austrian forces and sent to the Russian front, but he offered no loyalty to the Empire whose uniform he wore. In 1915 he was speared by a Cossack and taken prisoner and he spent many months in convalescence in a Russian hospital. When the Communist revolution swept over Russia in 1917 all prisoners were freed and Tito stayed on for several years to fight with the Red forces. He learned Russian, read widely in Communist literature, and fulfilled some modest chores for the party. When he was ready to return to his home community in Zagreb, he was listed in the Soviet records as a reliable Communist agent.

His native land had changed markedly during his years in Russia. Yugoslavia had come out of World War I a very much enlarged Balkan state, with a population of fourteen million. But it was pieced together from old Serbia and Montenegro and from other large chunks of the defunct Austrian Empire, a hodgepodge of races and religions, all with long histories of hostility. It was precariously held together by King Alexander, who lived from one crisis to another until a terrorist succeeded in penetrating the guard and assassinated him while he was on a diplomatic visit to France.

It was in this dangerous climate that Broz began on his assignment to undermine the fabric of the state and to establish a Communist enclave in the heart of the Balkans. He had to work adroitly because the royal government was alert to the continuous Communist danger. He lived the double life of the typical revolutionary, openly the impressive, dignified, smartly dressed engineer, underground, the indefatigable propagandist, the organizer of Communist cells in his union and in related labor organizations. It was probably in this period that he assumed the alias "Tito" for which many explanations have been offered. An amusing one is that he always gave peremptory orders—"You there," "Do this," and in the Serbo-Croat idiom it came out as *"Ti," "To."* Tito laughed at this explanation and said that his alias was really the Serb form of the Roman name, Titus. But if "You there," "Do this," was not the authentic origin of the name, it was an accurate summary of the arbitrary way in which Tito functioned.

The police again caught up with him and, in 1928, he was sent to prison for six years. This long confinement contributed new dimensions to his conspiratorial experience. He directed a flourishing Communist cell within the prison walls, and he was able to establish communication with the outside leadership and make his influence felt in policy strategy there. He continued with his reading and his study, and plowed his way through the Communist classics. He mastered six or seven languages and became most proficient in chess. He used to banter, "It was just like being at a university."* When he emerged in March 1934, now forty-two years old, he was the hardened, versatile revolutionist who was to have a major role in the shaping of his time.

He was now entrusted with international missions, the most important coming in 1936 when he established headquarters in Paris

---

* Fitzroy Maclean, *The Heretic* (New York: Harper & Bros., 1957), p. 44.

for the recruitment of volunteers to fight against Franco in Spain. But these assignments were dwarfed by the opportunities that opened when Hitler engulfed virtually all of Europe. Tito could come forward in patriotic resistance to the Nazis even as he planned and fought for social reconstruction. He was thus transformed from a hunted pariah into an authentic national hero.

Hitler demanded satellite subjection for Yugoslavia. The other Balkan kingdoms quickly yielded and they hurdled over each other in servility. But in Yugoslavia there was an explosion of wrath and obdurate resistance; no one underestimated what it would mean to accept the tutelage of the Nazis. The popular reaction was: "Better war than to submit. Better death than slavery." Hitler's enraged response was not long delayed.

Within a few hours the Nazi bombers were over Belgrade and seventeen thousand civilians were killed in the blitz as the capital was reduced to ruins. Within two weeks the Nazis were in control of all parts of the country. Yet it was to be a fatal fortnight for Hitler. The conquest of Yugoslavia, swift as it was, delayed the timetable for the planned Nazi attack on Russia. The postponed invasion then had to contend with the unendurable Russian winter which ultimately destroyed the German might. Hitler's generals later declared that the Yugoslavian action, ordered rashly in fury, was probably the most catastrophic decision of Hitler's career.* General Paulus testified at the Nuremberg trial that the foray into Yugoslavia nullified the carefully timed strategy of the Russian invasion.†

For the moment, however, Hitler's triumph in Yugoslavia was smooth and efficient. The country was divided up among the Germans, the Italians, and Balkan neighbors who rushed in to participate in the kill. On paper, Yugoslavia had been wiped out as a state. But only on paper. The resistance began at once and it took two forms. The first was official, under the direction of Draža Mihajlović, a Serbian officer who had served with distinction in World War I. He commanded what was left of the army—the bearded, sheep-capped Chetniks, loyal to the King, the church, and the social structure. They had the blessing of Winston Churchill and the support of the Allies. Their base of operations was in the mountain and forest hideouts. They were determined to move with caution, waiting to build up their strength in arms and manpower

---

* Shirer, *The Rise and Fall of the Third Reich,* pp. 824–5.
† Peter de Mendelssohn, *The Nuremberg Documents* (London: Allen & Unwin, Ltd., 1946), p. 273.

so that their attacks upon the invaders would not be hopeless and quixotic, triggering annihilative reprisal. Indeed, Mihajlović was warned by the Foreign Minister in exile *not* to commit his limited strength too early.

For Tito this was not only the sheerest kind of nonsense; it was an invitation to national suicide. As a long-time Communist he had little concern for the status quo—the monarchy, the church, and the established institutions. He insisted that the most effective way to fight the Nazis was to fight them, and he began organizing a resistance that would resist. His followers, at first pathetically limited in number, were steadily reinforced, and they relied on ambush and sabotage for effectiveness. They attacked in the dark of night—derailing trains, blowing up ammunition dumps, destroying communications, and soon the Germans knew that they had found a match in the native tenacity.

Some halfhearted attempts were made, through Allied intercession, to establish cooperation between the forces of Mihajlović and Tito. Several conferences were held to explore a coordinated military program. Surely the future of governance and structure in Yugoslavia could be left until liberation had been achieved. But could it? There was very little heart on either side for joint planning. Mihajlović had no intention of committing his forces to major sacrifice to achieve the dubious blessings of a Communist-dominated state. And it was furthest from Tito's thoughts to send his men into life-and-death combat to expel a brutal enemy, only to have the hated status quo become the legatee of his effort. By the end of 1943 there was savage open war between the Chetniks and the Partisans, a pitiless fratricide within the larger war. Mihajlović used his forces very little against the Italians and the Nazis, but increasingly to fight Tito and the Partisans. He hunted them down with a zeal that was not present against the invading enemies. He wrote to one of his commanders: "We must . . . mercilessly destroy those bloodthirsty men as they would destroy us. . . ."* Collaboration with the invaders, wherever they were locked in combat with the Partisans, was an almost inevitable development. Tito was constantly diverted by his resolve to liquidate the ideological foes who would certainly challenge his authority after the war.

At first the Allies were solidly behind Mihajlović; he represented the government-in-exile, the established order. Even Stalin, eager at

* Stephen Clissold, *Whirlwind* (New York: Philosophical Library, 1949), p. 88.

this stage to avoid offending the West by appearing to favor those whose objective was social revolution, played down the achievements of Tito and gave his endorsement to the Chetnik effort. As for Churchill, he had no wish to accomplish the liberation of Yugoslavia only to have it become a Communist stronghold. But the evidence kept mounting that the Chetniks were doing virtually nothing in the struggle against the Nazis. All the significant fighting was being done by Tito and his Partisans. By the beginning of 1943 he had recruited nearly 150,000 followers, thoroughly committed men, and brave, sturdy women, too. Indeed, 25 percent of his resistance squads were made up of women who fought gallantly at the side of the men.

In mid 1943, therefore, the Allies broke with Mihajlović and turned whatever support they could spare for Tito's resistance effort. The British dropped liaison officers by parachute into the Partisan camps to offer technical planning assistance. Churchill wired, "I wish I could come myself, but I am too old and heavy to jump out on a parachute." American planes, using newly acquired bases in Italy, coordinated their missions with the Partisans in their strikes against the German invaders.

Tito was now treating Mihajlović as an avowed enemy. Nazi and Chetnik became interchangeable as Tito laid out his battle strategy. By 1945 Mihajlović's forces had virtually disintegrated, and he was left with only a few diehards who starved with him. His own son and daughter were enrolled with Tito's Partisans. The British offered him asylum, but he proudly refused. He vowed to fight on to the end in his own country, even though all it had to offer him now was a grave, and not an honored one. Sick, half-blind, weary, and disillusioned, he was carried by litter from one hiding place to another. At last he was captured by the Partisans and brought to Belgrade, in filthy, ragged clothes and matted beard, to be placed on trial for treason.

He made no attempt to hide his hostility to the Partisan objectives, but he denied every imputation that he was traitorous to the long-range interests of his Fatherland. If Tito wished to punish him in a class war, he said, it was a penalty that was the expected price of defeat. But he would not accept the onus of betrayal. His relationships with the enemy, he insisted, as did Marshal Pétain in France, were dictated by his desire to save thousands of innocent civilians who would pay with torture and death if resistance came before it could be effective. "I never wanted the old Yugoslavia," he added, "but I had a difficult legacy. I was caught in a whirlpool of events. . . .

I wanted much, I began much, but the gale of the world carried me and my work away."* It was a poignant summary of the dilemma of many men of courage who were caught in the maelstrom of civil war. His final statement, therefore, was not an appeal for mercy; it was a testament for the judgment of history. The verdict was death and, though there were appeals for clemency from the Allied leaders, Tito turned them all aside and Mihajlović and his close collaborators were shot.

All of this tragic denouement came later when the Nazis had been routed and Yugoslavia liberated. Before this had been achieved, Hitler took full advantage of the many other internal animosities which fragmented the country and which he exploited with his usual skill. Besides the feuding Chetniks and the Partisans in every province, there were White Guards and Blue Guards and Yellow Guards in Slovenia, there were Whites and Greens in Montenegro, and quislings everywhere who could be easily manipulated.

Perhaps the most devastating manifestation of Hitler's cunning in disruption came in Croatia. Here he set up a puppet government under a terrorist leader, Ante Pavelić, a desperado who matched the most bigoted of the Nazis in his determination to destroy the minority elements in Croatia. He had been in training in Italy since 1939 for just such a role. He operated behind the façade of loyalty to the Catholic faith and commitment to a pure Croatian state from whence the Greek Orthodox and Serbian elements would be purged. He set up a dictatorship on the Nazi model and launched one of the great genocide massacres of the war. None was spared, women and children, old and infirm and wounded, as the orgy of killing, burning, raping, and looting went on, and the chief victims were the Serbians. In some areas whole populations were herded into their Greek Orthodox churches and burned alive. In one village, truck-loads of women and children were taken to the tops of mountains and hurled from precipices. In another, hundreds were flung alive into deep pits and done to death there. Some of Pavelić's henchmen collected the eyes of their victims and sent them to him to demonstrate how meticulously they fulfilled their role as defenders of the faith "against the Greek Orthodox barbarians." Sometimes the option of conversion to Catholicism was offered, and whole villages of panic-stricken inhabitants would crowd up to the baptismal font to be received into the loving arms of the church. But there were

* Maclean, *The Heretic,* p. 285.

technical obstacles, since church law called for long periods of preparatory indoctrination in cases of conversion, and there was no time here for such leisurely teaching. Hence there were learned discussions on what to do, while the massacres continued. Some of the Catholic priests, including the Archbishop Štepinac, pleaded with Pavelić to solve his political problems with more compassion. Pavelić taunted them as "snivelers" who did not understand the realities of life in Croatia. He was supported by other prelates who condoned his ruthlessness for its long-range benefits. One of them said, "Until now we have worked for the Catholic faith with missal and crucifix. Now the time has come for us to go to work with rifle and revolver."* Before the tide of war turned and the Nazis were driven out of Croatia, a million Serbians and people of other minority groups had been destroyed, more by far than the total Serbian casualties inflicted by the Nazis.

Updating this almost forgotten story, it should be noted that, when the terrorist regime fell, Pavelić made a brave last resistance speech to his distraught comrades. "It is better to live one day as a lion," he expostulated, "than a hundred years as a sheep. If we must die, let us fall as true heroes, not as cowards crying for mercy."† But when the commander of his bodyguard urged him to rally his men for a final stand, Pavelić stammered some excuses and was the first to flee. He took refuge with other quislings and Nazis in the Argentine. There the Croatian Hitler lived out his years until 1959, in peace and comfort. The books of justice and retribution do not always come out in balance.

Meantime, the guerrilla war against the occupying forces went on more ruthlessly than anywhere, but little known in the outside world, a struggle almost lost, Churchill said, in "the unestimated sum of human pain." Tito had ideal terrain in the woods and mountains of his homeland for his hit-and-run thrusts. It was his strategy to entrench himself in one area, master-mind devastating raids, and then, when the counterattacks came, to turn up in another part to continue the harassment. The Nazis had to divert sixteen battalions for Yugoslavia, supplemented by six Croatian and six Bulgarian battalions, a force of three hundred thousand that could have been used effectively, perhaps decisively, in Russia and on other hard-pressed fronts.

* Maclean, *The Heretic,* p. 130.
† *Ibid.,* p. 257.

Every form of terror was used to wear down the Partisan resistance. The Nazis executed at a ratio of 100 for every German casualty, concentrating on the intelligentsia—priests, doctors, lawyers. In central Serbia an entire high school, teachers and pupils, numbering seventy-five hundred, were taken out and shot to retaliate for a Partisan raid on the local Nazi headquarters. In one region the Nazis caught up with a mobile hospital and when the wounded crawled out into the fields, the Nazi tanks went back and forth over them until all of them had been crushed to death. In Belgrade, every day, hostages were strung up and their bodies left dangling in public places as a lesson to the disaffected. But the Nazi reprisals simply intensified the hatred and strengthened the resolve not to yield. The words of the national anthem became an irrevocable vow: "In vain the depths of Hell threaten."

Tito was everywhere, in the mountains of Serbia, in the caves of Bosnia, in cellar hideouts in the main cities. In May 1944, the Germans launched a parachute attack on his headquarters in Bosnia, and only the heroic defense of his bodyguard, which was completely annihilated, enabled him and his staff to escape. Since, until the end of the war, no one but his intimates had seen Tito, or even pictures of him, the legend of his exploits grew. Here he was a modern Robin Hood bringing in loot from the enemy to keep the starving villages alive; there he was a buoyant civil war chieftain leading his commandos against Mihajlović and the Chetniks. It was even rumored that he was really a woman, a modern Joan of Arc, beautiful, radiant, ever resourceful. When a British officer assigned to his staff asked Tito if this were so, he replied, "Well, if *you* were one, I could quickly prove that I am *not*." His tenacity, his ability to hold his hunted forces together, the undeviating confidence that he exuded, even won the grudging admiration of the Nazi chief, Heinrich Himmler, who held him up as an example of the man of good nerves. "I wish we had a dozen Titos in Germany," he said wistfully one day as the defeatism spread in the Nazi ranks.*

Himmler could have added that the resistance feat was all the more spectacular because Tito had to rely for weaponry, indeed for every military asset, almost exclusively on what he could appropriate from the enemy. Until near the end of the war he obtained no help from the Allies, and very little from the Russians. One of his ablest lieutenants noted later that his unit had started with two men who

* *Ibid.,* p. 240.

had fled with him to the woods, two men with two rifles and no ammunition. These grew to a battalion, mainly refugees who were armed with captured weapons. "All of our armaments," he wrote, "every screw of our equipment, we bought with our blood." Later, in the triumphal review of Tito's troops in Belgrade after the years of ceaseless fighting, the survivors who passed before him were a ragged throng, weary, footsore, bone lean, their weapons picked up on the battlefield, their uniforms stripped from the corpses of their enemies.

Tito had appealed continuously to Stalin for arms. The replies were invariably delayed and they took the form of vague phrases and soothing words but with no assurance of support. In March 1942, in one of his most tormented periods, Tito had sent an urgent request: "We are in a critical situation owing to the lack of ammunition. Tell us if we can expect anything, and when." The evasive reply suggested that there were many practical difficulties and that Tito had, therefore, better rely on the arms that he could capture from the enemy. The infuriating phrase was added: "And make the most economical use of what armaments you have." In 1943 there was a more desperate dispatch. Tito wrote, "Is it really impossible, after twenty months of heroic . . . fighting, to find some way of helping us?" Stalin's proffered aid was the advice to do nothing that would represent a complete break with the government-in-exile.*

It was not until the waning days of the war, when the Italians had been knocked out and the Germans had been in retreat on all fronts, that Russian help began to trickle in, just enough to complete the expulsion of the enemy from Belgrade. Tito never let the Russians forget that Yugoslavia was the one country that had won its liberation on its own, that the terrible toll of nearly 1,700,000 dead, and the destruction of whole regions, had been a sacrifice toward victory over the Nazis that had made the Partisan contribution one of the most decisive in the war.

The early hesitation of the British to provide help was understandable. In the first years of the war there was still faith in Mihajlović, and there was reluctance to build up the strength of Tito, who had made no secret of his determination to convert Yugoslavia into a Communist state. The opportunism of the Kremlin, in relation to the Partisan cause, was more bewildering. Apparently it went much deeper than the inability of the Russians to divert military

* *Ibid.,* pp. 144, 167.

resources from their own defense to buttress Yugoslavian resistance. Stalin's cooperation with Churchill to support the royal government-in-exile meant that, at least during the war period, he was using Yugoslavia as a bargaining pawn to promote purely Russian interests. He was even prepared to bring back the exiled King Peter and he urged Tito to accept this astute diplomatic gambit. When Tito refused, Stalin purred, "You need not restore him permanently. Take him back for the time being. Then you can slip a knife into his back at the appropriate moment." Tito passed no indignant moral judgment on such chicanery. It fitted well into Communist doctrine of means and ends. But he saw no reason why he had to put Russian interests ahead of those of his own country. He refused flatly to permit Russia to win concessions at the expense of Yugoslavia. "We demand that everyone shall be master in his own house," he declared. "We do not want to pay other people's bills." When Stalin tried to infiltrate the army and the police, through the advisers and technicians who were sent in, Tito denounced their inept intrigue and sent them packing.

All of this was incredible behavior from a disciplined Communist and it marked a decisive break with the tradition of subordination that Stalin had always counted upon in the satellite countries. He was livid with rage when Tito's intransigence was reported. "I will shake my little finger," he thundered, "and there will be no more Tito." He tried all the power plays that he had used on others—intimidation, internal subversion, conspiracies to assassinate the stubborn heretic, blockade, boycott—all to the accompaniment of tirades that Communists usually reserve for their class enemies. Tito was too solidly entrenched in the respect of his people, and he had too much confidence in his capacity to survive even the hostility of the Kremlin, for him to give ground. He rejected the insults and the slanders and asked how such language could be used against a people "who in thousands of battles had looked death in the eye." He reminded the Kremlin that he alone stayed to fight, "while all the other Balkan sycophants lived out the war years in Moscow and then were flown in by plane." He kept signing his letters "with comradely greetings," and this further infuriated Stalin, who exploded, "The puppy is feeling so good that he barks at the elephant." The quarrel did not become public until 1948; the astonished world learned how far it had gone only when Tito and his associates were expelled from the Cominform and the people of Yugoslavia were called upon by Stalin to rise and throw out the traitors.

Thus, a new force was launched, and the thrust had come from an insignificant Balkan state. Yugoslavia remained solidly Communist but it was no longer part of the Soviet empire. Tito saw the development as much more than a quarrel over specific issues. There was now a basic ideological difference that challenged the unquestioned Kremlin control. It was the difference between centralized power in a monolithic Communist world organization, and decentralized power which recognized the autonomy of various segments of the Communist world.

Here, for the time being, we leave Tito, in 1945, in vigorous, confident middle age, rounding out the role of liberator. There were to be tumultuous years ahead, dominated by the growing tension with Stalin, by whom he was soon denounced as an imperialist lackey, "a Fascist dog on his hind legs begging for American dollars." The tension was to lead to the reconstruction of the Yugoslavian state, with a nationalist type of communism that repudiated the dominance of the Kremlin. All of these developments were to be concentrated in the next quarter of a century. What lay behind were the revolutionary achievements of a career that ran the gamut from the days of a jailbird, a hunted guerrilla chieftain with virtually no resources, to the successful challenge of the great rival dictators, including Mussolini, Hitler, and Stalin. It was a career that established a defiant, independent Communist bastion in the Balkans; and that bore out the quip that contemporary Europe, like ancient Gaul, was now divided into three parts—the West, the East, and Tito.

21

THE MORALITY
OF COLLABORATION

NO STUDY OF THE WORLD WAR II PERIOD IS COMPLETE WITHOUT reference to the dilemma of the men and women who collaborated with the enemy against their own people and, depending on success or failure, were usually judged as heroes or as traitors. The old cynical gibe had it:

> Treason doth never prosper; what's the
> reason?
> Why, if it prosper, none dare call it
> treason.*

The study is much more than a drama of personal fate. The careers of Quisling of Norway or Amery of Britain, of Pétain and Laval of France, reveal a great deal about the nations themselves and the tenacity of their own commitment to their way of life. Because Norway was solidly grounded in its democratic heritage, a Quisling was just a freak, an excrescence, and inevitably his name evoked horror. An Amery who broadcast from Berlin against Britain all through the war could not move his people nor swerve them from their resolve, even in the darkest days of the blitz.

But the impact of the French collaborators was almost fatal, for they had a confused and fragmented people as their target. France had been disrupted for years. The thirties were a period of such convulsive disunity that when Léon Blum and the Popular Front

* Sir John Harington, "Alcilia."

came to power and initiated a program of social reform, the bitterness reached the level of virtual civil war. Whole segments of the population reacted as if they had more in common with Hitler and the Nazis than they had with their French political foes. During the Popular Front period, on thousands of placards the words appeared: *"Mieux vaut Hitler que Blum."*

In Norway, though the country was quickly overrun and every vestige of independence eliminated, submission was universally sullen, and the Nazi puppet, Vidkun Quisling, could recruit no influential following. The judgment on him was, therefore, quite uncomplicated: he was a monster. His defection to the Nazis was not the revolutionist's decision to eliminate what he believed was an oppressive government. Norway was a contented nation, with widely shared high living standards, and there were no yearnings for a Nazi utopia. Nor did Quisling's alienation have the excuse of a broken home, or corrosive poverty, or a loveless family background. He came of good stock. His father was a Lutheran minister; his mother a sensitive, wholesome lady who claimed kinship with Ibsen. "There was no dishwater in my veins," young Quisling boasted. His schooling was competent, and he performed creditably in the military academy that he attended.

But he was always on the make, always calculating angles. The main chance came for him, he thought, when he met Alfred Rosenberg, the pseudo-philosopher of Nazism, who had been preaching racism and Aryan superiority. Quisling decided that he could ride this vehicle to national prominence. But his warnings and appeals in a country where there were no disaffected minorities, no arrivistes, and no subversive cells, were dismissed as twaddle and he became a laughingstock. He was the only Nazi in the Parliament, a would-be Führer without a folk. He journeyed to Berlin several times on the eve of the war and, through Rosenberg, he twice met Hitler. He pleaded for the opportunity to serve Germany's forces when they were ready for the takeover in Norway.

The archives at the Oslo University Library, along with many records of this wretched period, would indicate that the Nazis, concerned about a British pre-emptive strike, made use of the data that Quisling provided and advanced their timetable of conquest. Quisling was assigned the puppet post of gauleiter, but only a handful of frightened notables, perhaps unwilling to lose their favored status, publicly supported the new order. These included Henry Johansen, the husband of Kirsten Flagstad; Knut Hamsun, the Nobel Prize winner in literature, considered in his old age senile, like Ezra Pound, the American collaborator; and a few hard-line conservative industrialists and shipping magnates.

Since no one of consequence was willing to join the Quisling government, he was not even a figurehead; he was simply a lackey. He held his phantom position for the years of the occupation and then, when the Nazi tyranny collapsed, he was trapped. His bravado did not desert him. He rode up to the Norwegian headquarters in the bullet-proof car that he had always used and announced that he expected to be treated with the dignity of a major prisoner of war. He was quite angry when he was consigned to an ordinary prison cell, and his suspenders taken from him to prevent suicide, which he had probably never contemplated. At the trial he claimed that he had followed two objectives: one was to save his country from the Communists; the other, based on the certainty of a Nazi victory, was the hope of winning better terms for his beloved people as their surrogate in defeat. His defense was treated with contempt and the verdict was almost automatic, that this was a gangster who was battening on his people's miseries. He was taken out and shot. Churchill's contemptuous reference to him as the classic traitor gave his name its odious connotation in the languages of the western world. Even the Nazis shared the contempt. A cartoon of the period depicts a meeting with Hitler where he introduces himself, "I am Quisling." "Yes," Hitler replied, "and what's your name?"

IN BRITAIN, TOO, TREASON FOUND NO SOIL. THE HARDSHIPS AND THE bleakness of the prospect in 1940–1 brought very little breakdown of morale. The deep disagreements on political and economic issues, while they stimulated vigorous party debate, never gave the slightest opening to fifth column attrition. No one raised the cry, "Better the Nazis than Labour," "Better Hitler than Attlee or Churchill." A tiny group followed Oswald Mosley into the British Fascist Union, but it made very little headway and was treated as a lunatic fringe. The few defectors who joined the Nazis and did their propaganda bidding were usually disoriented individuals with psychiatric problems, and they could make no impact on the British resistance spirit. The case of John Amery offers perhaps the best illustration.

John's father was Leopold Amery, one of the outstanding political leaders of Britain, a classmate of Winston Churchill at Harrow, a brilliant diplomat who became Secretary of State for India. He and his beautiful and popular wife were a model couple, but they suffered the misfortune of so many noted public families whose name is besmirched by an errant or disreputable son. John lived only thirty-three years, but beyond adolescence there was hardly a moment when he was not in trouble. He was a handsome boy with a persuasive manner, sharp, articulate, but already at fifteen he was organizing bogus projects, forever on the search for friends or acquaintances he could hoodwink, trading always on the family name. He was usually in the company of offbeat characters, charging bills, issuing false checks, and leaving it to his father to pick up after him. One of his affairs was with a Piccadilly Circus prostitute and he was constantly in the news for escapades with her that usually centered in fleabag hotels in desperate contrast to the fastidious moral standards of the parental home. Later he took up with another notorious trull much older than he was, and while his father used every legal means to prevent it, they were married, with sensational publicity, in a Greek Orthodox church in Athens. He organized a motion picture company for filming in Africa and then abruptly left its members stranded. At twenty-four, drained out and bankrupt, he joined the Franco forces in Spain as a gun runner. When war erupted in 1939, he was adventuring in the private army of the French Fascist leader, Doriot, knocking about the guerrilla camps with his women hangers-on.

It was in 1941, in Vichy France, that he was welcomed by the Nazis as the defecting son of the British Secretary of State for India. He began beaming a daily news and interpretative program to England, extolling the irresistible power of the Nazis and their historic mission to prevent the communization of Europe. All through the war years Amery's voice came through to the English, in the period of their deepest travail, reiterating the Nazi line—anti-Soviet, anti-Semitic, anti-Churchill. It was really the clumsiest kind of propaganda; it aroused deep sympathy for the Amery family and disgust with the Nazis. At the end of the war, with the Nazis finally routed and Germany in flames, Amery fled. He was captured by the Partisans in Italy and returned to England. He asked for a quick trial, pleaded guilty on all counts, and refused any attempts at intercession for clemency. He was convicted and, soon thereafter, hanged as a traitor. There was no more pathetic sight, even in the endless tragedy of war, than his broken father standing mutely outside the prison yard where the execution was scheduled, waiting for the death bell to toll.

The case of Amery, rare in Britain, offered no problem of judgment. Such men were casualties cast up by the distortions of life. No society is altogether free of such strays or castaways. From among them, festering in dark corners below reason and logic and love, come the assassins of noted public figures. And it was from this strange underworld that men like Amery emerged, representing individual pathology rather than any deeply rooted social alienation.

The charge of treason is much more complicated when one explores the motivations of the French leaders who yielded to the Nazis, collaborated with them, and then went on to destroy the Republic and to punish those who risked life and resources to remain loyal to it. The decision of May 1940, to yield to the Nazis, was never a moral issue. The defeat of the French forces was so complete that there was no alternative, and the surrender was not condemned as a crime. The recriminations that divided France and poisoned its politics in the postwar years were evoked by the despicable collaboration that was practiced during the Nazi conquest. They were directed against the leaders who lent themselves to the draft of hundreds of thousands of Frenchmen for enforced labor in Germany, and to the establishment of an ersatz corporative state with all too many of the Nazi embellishments.

The main target for what was denounced as treason was Marshal Henri Pétain, then in his mid-eighties. When the defeat of France seemed irretrievable, Pétain was invited to become the head of the state, apparently in the hope that his prestige would win some consideration from the Nazis. It is debatable what consideration he actually achieved, but it is not debatable that the liberal reforms of the past generation were abhorrent to him. Together with a considerable section of conservative France, he looked back with loathing on the French Third Republic, and hankered after *l'ancien régime*. He had always sided with Charles Maurras and the royalist fanatics in their aim, *"entangler la gueuse"* (to strangle the old hag—their contemptuous term for the democratic Republic). Hence he readily acquiesced in its destruction. It was this repudiation of the French democratic heritage, rather than the surrender, that brought the gibe from one of his own generals: "Pétain is our banner; but he is also our cross."

After the triumph of Allied arms and the establishment of the Fourth Republic, Pétain was placed on trial for his Vichy actions. He sought to justify the collaboration as an act of realism. The war had been lost; there was hardly a responsible leader who believed otherwise. Who could imagine that battered and beleaguered Britain had the power to reverse the verdict? Hence he felt it was his duty to remain at his post. He did indeed make occasional compromises, but these were sensible, practical actions to save his people from the horrors that befell Poland. After all, he was dealing with a relentless enemy, and every hour of the day had to be given to the parrying of threat and reprisal. As evidence that the interest of his country had been safeguarded, he noted that though he had refused to send the French fleet out of North Africa to ports in the West Indies, he had pledged that it would never be turned over to the Nazis. When there was danger that what remained of the fleet might be appropriated by them, he had ordered that it be scuttled. He had continuously resisted the Nazis when they attempted to violate the armistice terms. When he discovered that his Premier, Pierre Laval, was going too far in collusion with the Nazis, he had dismissed him. The Nazis must have recognized his underlying devotion to France, he said, because immediately after the Allied landings, he was dragged off to Germany by the Nazi command. Then, with a sarcastic gibe at De Gaulle, he reminded the court that his were the decisions of a man who remained in France to share the fate of his stricken people. Judgment on his actions came with poor grace from those who had fled to another land to preach bravery and resistance from the security of a radio station in London. "My honor," he declared, "consisted of staying at this post, facing dangers without an army, without a fleet, in the midst of an unhappy population." His defense was in the spirit of Byron's *Marino Faliero*:

> But would you know why I have done all this?
> Ask of the bleeding pelican why she
> Hath ripp'd her bosom? Had the bird a voice,
> She'd tell thee "twas for *all* her little ones."*

The old man, despite his years, was not bad in rebuttal.

But the psychological climate of the 1945 trial and the period that followed was not favorable to the defense of his motives. It was judged that he had gone far beyond mere compliance. The remembrance of the repressions he had ordered, under coercion or not, was too fresh in the minds of those who had suffered so long. The aping of Nazi judicial procedure, the relentless hunt for Resistance fighters, the anti-Jewish laws, the uprooting of hundreds of thousands of French families to labor in exile, how could such actions be condoned as ploys in a complicated scheme to win time? Who could forget

* Act 1, Scene ii.

Pétain's groveling message to Hitler when the British-Canadian forces, attempting an experimental liberation landing at Dieppe, were flung back with heavy losses? Then it was that Pétain wrote to the Führer, "I thank you for the prompt cleansing of French soil!" After Hitler had demanded that Laval be reinstated as head of the government, Pétain not only complied but said, "Laval and I are one." A commentator noted, "The country hid its head in shame, just as a family seeks to conceal a bastard." De Gaulle explained Pétain's policy as the action of a man who, always arbitrary, at last had the opportunity to exercise power. He wrote, "Too proud for intrigue, too forceful for mediocrity, too ambitious to be a time-server, he nourished in his solitude a passion for domination which had long been hardened by his consciousness of his own value, the setbacks he had encountered, and the contempt he had for others."*

Pétain was sentenced to death, as De Gaulle had been sentenced when he raised the flag of Resistance. However, in consideration of Pétain's age, now nearly ninety, De Gaulle approved the commutation of his sentence to imprisonment, and the unrepentant old man spent his remaining few years in the unrepentant captivity of a mountain fortress.

THE CASE OF PIERRE LAVAL POINTS UP EVEN MORE CLEARLY THE PAS-sion and the frenzy that were spun off by the political feuds in France. Laval had just the personality to attract the lightning to him. He was a wizard at intrigue, slippery, opportunistic; in his political career he boxed the compass in convictions or, rather, in lack of convictions. A modern psychiatrist pointed out that he seemed to have two faces, even as his name, Laval, which spelled the same backward and forward. From his first entry into politics he had fought with no holds barred, treating life as a battle and the world as a jungle. He earned little affection at play or in school, and he gave none. As a loner, he was most at home with animals and, to relax, he went to the zoo. It was he who connived with Samuel Hoare of Britain the so-called compromise deal by which Ethiopia was cut to pieces in order to placate Mussolini.†

In the crisis of the French defeat of 1940, Laval was in the fore-front of those who clamored for surrender and for the repudiation

---

* De Gaulle, *War Memoirs*, Vol. 1, p. 72.
† See Chapter 15.

of the Republic, "with all of its hogwash of liberty, equality, and fraternity, and its nonsense of the Popular Front." He urged the appointment of Pétain as head of state, certain that the Marshal, in the prime of his senility, could be easily manipulated by him so that he, Laval, would become the power behind the façade. When a deputy protested that Pétain was too old and frail for such a role, Laval snorted, "That doesn't matter; what will be asked of him? Just to be a statue on a pedestal!" He thrust Pétain forward to sue for the armistice, "in honor, as between soldiers." In fairness, it should be remembered that the 1940 vote for immediate surrender was 395 to 3 in the Chamber, and 229 to 1 in the Senate, and that the joint session vote that destroyed the Republic was 569 to 80. Later, when the Vichy nightmare was ended and the Free French returned, most of those who had voted in panic and despair were glad enough to find scapegoats in men like Laval.

But Laval actually invited the role of scapegoat. He was playing *Va Banque*, shoot the works, and almost every action was a defiant break with the past. He was the master patron for a new authoritarian France as a partner in Nazi Europe. When the French squadron at Mers-el-Kebir in Algiers refused to steam to a safer port in the French West Indies and was destroyed by Churchill, Laval urged a declaration of war against Britain. He flared, "Today we are at the bottom of the abyss where England has led us. I see only one way to restore France . . . and that is to ally ourselves resolutely with Germany and to confront England together."* He carried on secret negotiations with the German Ambassador to learn how best France could fit into the Nazi orbit. Even General Weygand, who had been a defeatist, was outraged. "Laval," he burst out, "you roll in defeat like a dog in filth!"

It was Laval who, in 1942, dreamed up the plan for a public trial of those who were allegedly responsible for the war against Germany and for the "fatal weakening" of France through the Popular Front. The two chief Popular Front premiers, Blum and Daladier, were taken from their prison cells to answer for their record. It was charged that France had been emasculated by the legislation of the Socialists—the forty-hour week, vacations with pay, the right to strike, the nationalization of the Bank of France and of the armaments industry. The prosecutor concentrated on what Blum, with deadly accuracy, described as "the venom argument," namely that Blum had

* Warner, *Laval,* p. 198.

injected into French society, and especially into its economy, the toxic element of class warfare, and that this had ruined French unity. Blum's defense of the Republic and the Popular Front won international headlines. He told the hostile court that the social welfare legislation sponsored by him was not disruptive, that it was the glory of his ministry. Indeed, the reforms had at last brought the workers into a meaningful relationship with their country. They had enabled the workers to sing the "*Marseillaise*" with a new pride, not the "*Marseillaise*" of the railroad station ceremonies, or of official functions, but the "*Marseillaise*" of Victor Hugo and of the men to whom the honor of France was sacred. He concluded, "We were not . . . some monstrous excrescence in the history of this country, because we were a people's government: we were in the tradition of this country, in the tradition of the French Revolution. We have not destroyed the chain, we have not broken it, we have fortified and strengthened it."* Blum was a master of oratory and he was at his best here, as he stood in the dock at Riom, with the verdict already announced in advance by Laval and Pétain. He succeeded in reversing the roles, placing the prosecutor on the defensive. Hitler was furious, and he ordered Laval to adjourn the trial. Blum and the other defendants were packed off to their cells and then consigned to a Nazi concentration camp. Blum was not executed. He was much too valuable as a prime hostage. He survived the horror of his confinement and lived to serve again later as a Premier of liberated France.

Meantime, in November 1942, with the Allied landings in North Africa and the beginning of their drive through France for the reconquest of Europe, the Nazis ended the farce of the Vichy Zone. They moved in their own troops, dragged Pétain off to Germany, and installed Laval as the puppet caretaker. As the Resistance movement gathered momentum, Laval's subservience to his Nazi masters redoubled. His attacks on the guerrillas became more relentless, the executions multiplied, and there were thousands of victims. Laval went all the way now in vindictiveness. He knew that if the Free French were to return, his life was over.

June 6, 1944, was D-Day, and the landings on the continent began in Normandy. The Vichy men, in panic, fled wherever asylum could open for them. Pétain was released from his German prison and sent to Switzerland. He refused sanctuary there, insisting upon a return

* Colton, *Léon Blum,* p. 421.

to France to stand trial and seek vindication. Laval fled to Barcelona, but he was unwelcome there, and was turned over to the Americans who surrendered him for judgment in France.

At the trial of Laval in July 1945, all the pent-up hatreds of his people exploded. It was not really a trial, for in a retributive reversal of fortune, he who had set up so many kangaroo courts faced one now. The scenes recalled bedlam. The jurors took turns shouting at him, vilifying him as a traitor, a swine, a scoundrel. Laval stopped answering questions. "I may be the victim of a judicial crime," he said, "and I do not wish to be an accomplice."* He wrote out his defense, in which he made the claim that he had always planned to outwit the Germans, and that he was responsible for the miracle that France had escaped the fate of other Nazi-conquered lands. He was condemned to death and, after a thwarted attempt at suicide, was carried half-conscious to the execution post and shot as a traitor.

The savagery of the trial, and the unwillingness to accord even a shred of dignity to the last anguished moments of a former Premier, came about perhaps because so many millions of Frenchmen were themselves implicated. In the last days of the Republic they had cheered the efforts to appease the Nazis. In the early days of Vichy they had shared the decision to accommodate to Hitler's new order and to destroy the Republic. What they hated in Laval may have been that he had successfully evoked their own most ignoble weakness. Rebecca West, commenting on the persuasive power of another wretched collaborator, wrote that "his discontents were fused into a powerful demon able to call to all like demons in other hearts and stir them into comradeship."†

Laval had flaunted his treason so flagrantly that the French had no qualms about his fate. But they did have an uneasy conscience about the punishment of Pétain. Too many of them subscribed to the premise on which the old Marshal had built his ill-fated decisions, no faith in the survival power of Britain, no hope that the Nazis could be defeated. Perhaps the guilt-ridden politics that corroded and brutalized the next decade in France came from this queasy conscience. Mauriac wrote,

The spirit of surrender and the spirit of resistance found themselves personified in two Frenchmen, Pétain and De Gaulle. Each represented far more than himself, and, since the humblest of us shares the glory of the

---

* Hubert Cole, *Laval* (New York: Putnam, 1963), p. 294.

† Rebecca West, *The Meaning of Treason* (New York: Viking Press, 1947), p. 20.

leader of the French Resistance, let us not forget that part of ourselves may at times have been guilty of complicity with that broken old man.

There was wisdom as well as compassion in Winston Churchill's judgment on all such tormented souls, damaged if not damned. "Let him rest in peace," he wrote, "and let all of us be thankful that we have never had to face the trials under which he broke."*

* Churchill, *Memoirs of the Second World War*, p. 663. In this judgment he was writing of Admiral Jean Darlan.

22

THE REACTION OF
THE WEST TO GENOCIDE

IT WAS LEFT TO THE CIVILIZED TWENTIETH CENTURY TO INVENT THE word "genocide" to identify the action that seeks systematically to destroy a whole people. The Turks, early in the century, were its first practitioners; the Nazis in mid-century gave it a horrible extension that eclipsed the earlier record. In the nightmare world of the mass killers all sanctions were turned upside down; atrocity became virtue to be praised, and murder became patriotism to be saluted.

The Turkish victims numbered more than a million and a half Armenians, a gentle, highly cultured, industrious people who, in 1915, behind the façade of war, were methodically done to death. It was the Sultan Abdul Hamid, known to history as Abdul the Damned, who formulated the solution to the dangerous presence of a contumacious minority: "The way to get rid of the Armenian problem is to get rid of the Armenians." The Turkish military was given a free hand, and when national hatred was released in unrestrained savagery, the commanders in charge offered no opposition. The rationale was stated simply by those who condoned the annihilation. Turkey was at war with Russia. The Armenians lived in critical strategic areas. They had always been a disaffected minority, prone to conspiracy and treachery that endangered the state. Turkey had to take security measures to protect itself. This rationale was repeated each time foreign diplomats or religious leaders made inquiries or entered protests. There was little attempt to conceal the slaughter in all of its revolting details. For that matter it would have been impossible to hide so vast a meshwork of murder. The blood of a million corpses somehow finds voice even from ravines and rivers and obscure trails in desert and mountain where most of the murders were carried out.

"Tiny Golgotha" was the name given to a mound of skulls in the desert of Dar el Zor, east of Aleppo, where nearly a million Armenians perished. The dispatches from the scene by the horrified American Ambassador, Henry Morgenthau, characterized the perpetrators of the massacres as a conscienceless breed of barbarians. "When the Turkish authorities gave the orders for these deportations," he reported, "they were merely giving the death warrant to a whole race; they understood this well, and in their conversations with me they made no particular attempt to conceal the fact."* There was a report from the head of the Protestant Mission, Dr. Johannes Lepsius, who wept as he described the heaped-up evidence of Turkish ferocity, which had been "as efficient as it was devilish, and without parallel in all history." Ambassador Morgenthau's dispatches were discounted as the usual exaggerated atrocity stories that are weapons in wartime. The Lepsius appeal for compassion became so embarrassing to Germany, Turkey's wartime ally, that he was transferred to The Netherlands in an attempt to stifle his influence. The sad truth must be recorded that it was well nigh impossible in 1915 to get worked up about mass tragedy, any kind of mass tragedy, in remote forgotten corners of the earth. The world was at war. Millions were being killed and maimed everywhere. So the special calamity of the Armenians was merged in the general tragedy of World War I.

The Armenians were an old people with a proud tradition that went back more than four thousand years. They referred to their land as the cradle of civilization, and a cherished site for them was Mount Ararat, where Noah's Ark rested at the dawn of history. They were the first nation to adopt Christianity. Living in a vulnerable buffer area, by the Black Sea and the Caspian, they contended throughout the centuries with successive marauding or invading master groups: the Persians in ancient times, the Saracens in the Middle Ages, the Turks in modern times. Yet, despite the unremitting confrontation of danger, the Armenians lived disciplined Christian lives as industrious farmers in the rural areas, and as the keen, ingenious com-

* Henry Morgenthau, *Ambassador Morgenthau's Story* (Garden City, N.Y.: Doubleday & Co., 1919), p. 309.

mercial class in the cities. In the mid-nineteenth century a resurgent nationalism emerged, centered around the Dashnaks who worked, mainly underground, to win more tolerable living conditions, and ultimately to gain autonomy, if not independence.

In the last part of the nineteenth century, the Armenians were trapped between the imperial ambitions of czarist Russia and the medieval despotism of Turkey. On the eve of World War I, there were about 1,850,000 Armenians in Ottoman Turkey. Russia tried to organize the Armenians from both sides of the fighting fronts, and made lavish promises of autonomy and freedom. Indeed, Sergei Sazanov, the Russian Foreign Minister, declared that one of Russia's most important war aims was the "complete liberation of Armenia from the Turkish yoke." The Turks, too, recognized the need to obtain cooperation from the minority groups, especially the Armenians. Hence they too pledged major concessions and reforms, after the war. The cynical double courtship carried life-and-death jeopardy, for cooperation with one side brought instant reprisal from the other. However circumspect and correct the Armenian national leadership tried to be, there were actions by individual groups and communities that could and did immediately set off the hostility of the opposing force. The Armenian dilemma paralleled the war dilemma of the Poles, where Germans and Russians vied with each other in promises which in effect aimed at setting Pole against Pole for the benefit of contending Germans and Russians. Many thousands of Armenians volunteered for the Turkish military. But there were thousands of others who looked to a Russian victory as the way out of the Turkish purgatory. It was an Armenian unit with Russian forces that helped to turn back the Turks at Sarikamish, and the effect on Turkey, in appraising Armenian loyalty, was catastrophic for the Armenians. Turkish leadership was certain that there was a powerful Trojan Horse inside Turkey and that the strategic areas bordering Russia were extremely vulnerable because of Armenian disaffection. It did not help to have Armenians in the Russian provinces make flaming forecasts of the day when Turkish defeat would at last bring peace and freedom for the Armenians.

About a quarter of a million, between the ages of twenty-one and forty-five, were conscripted when hostilities began, but there was no intention to have them serve with the military. The conscription was an efficient device to eliminate the able-bodied from the areas that were in the master plan for clearance, and to destroy the biological basis for any future Armenian national minority. The warrant for the death of a people was drawn up by a brutal, hard-nosed bureaucrat, Mehmed Talât, who had been Prime Minister, and two colleagues, Ahamed Cemal, and Enver Pasha, who were equally free from squeamishness where Armenian lives were involved. The conscripts were assigned to so-called labor battalions, and then they were systematically liquidated in small groups, after being transported to remote desert and mountain corners of the country. The butchery went on all through the early part of 1915. When Ambassador Morgenthau warned Talât that some day he would be brought to account, he replied, "It's no use for you to argue. We have already disposed of three-fourths of the Armenians."*

As the extermination reports became public there were desperate attempts at resistance. One such resistance point was in the Van Province. Here the Turks, reinforced by the undisciplined Kurdish tribesmen, had swooped down on villages whose young men had already been conscripted. They murdered about ten thousand of those who remained. Those who could fled for refuge to the city of Van, where a more organized defense was possible. There, for anguished weeks, an ill-prepared civilian populace held out against strongly organized Turkish military units. The Armenians dragged out some antiquated artillery; they manufactured other crude weapons—guns and bullets and grenades; they melted down their silver, their lead, their cutlery, their samovars. But even the bravest resistance could not withstand the military pressure, and ultimately the casualties went beyond fifty thousand. Then, miraculously, a Russian relief force broke through briefly and evacuated a remnant of the survivors. But it was not possible to transport the wounded, the aged, the crippled, and when the Turks occupied Van, these were all brutally dispatched.

Another last-stand defiance became an inspiring memory, the resistance of about four thousand survivors who took refuge on Musa Dagh, the Mountain of Moses, and held off vastly superior Turkish forces for more than six weeks until rescued by a passing French ship. The courageous saga was the central theme of a moving novel by Franz Werfel, *The Forty Days of Musa Dagh*, but it appeared twenty years after the Armenian martyrdom when it could serve only as a memorable epitaph.

Meantime, at midnight on April 26, 1915, as a prelude to the

* *Ibid.*, p. 338.

general massacre, the police of Constantinople rounded up 235 of the most prominent Armenian families, deported them, and then murdered them. This wiped out almost the entire Armenian leadership, and orphaned a whole nation. When the two Armenian members of Parliament who had been temporarily spared appealed to Talât not to go through with such a shocking, unprecedented purge, he blandly offered the usual rationale: the threat to security of an unreliable minority in a vulnerable area. Hard-line realists often thus justify relocation in the national interest. After Pearl Harbor, the United States uprooted thousands of Japanese families on the west coast—the Nisei—many second- and third-generation Americans, and sent them to camps in the interior. But the action was taken with deepest regret; the internees were treated with every consideration, and were later fully indemnified.

In Turkey, it was clear that the purpose of the deportations was not to ensure national security. It was to ensure total annihilation. The massacres were unsparing, and they were accompanied by the most degrading cruelty, province by province, city by city, village by village. Tens of thousands were sent, barefoot, almost without clothes, through defiles and pathless steppes, into the deserts and the mountains, most of them dying of fatigue, or starvation, or thirst, or from the cruelty of the accompanying guards. The survivors were shot or drowned or axed when they reached their wilderness of desolation. The staggering aspect of the whole inhuman process was its efficiency. The Turkish administration was not famous for competence. The Germans were accused of lending organizational aid, and while there was no proof of complicity, what was incomprehensible was the cynical reaction of the German Ambassador, Baron Hans von Wangenheim, who brusquely turned aside every appeal for intercession with Germany's ally. He, too, subscribed to the principle that the security of the state overrode all humane consideration. As he put it succinctly to the German naval attaché: "The weaker nation must succumb."* In Milton's *Paradise Lost*, Lucifer says to Evil, "Be thou my good." Thus, evil was no longer a relapse from good but was itself enthroned as good. Evil became the acknowledged ideal, and in this way the sovereignty of Satan was established. In

---

* A final macabre note: Talât asked Ambassador Morgenthau for a list of Armenians who had been insured by American firms. For both the holders and the beneficiaries had been killed, and thus, by Turkish law, the Turkish government was now the beneficiary! *Ibid.*, p. 339.

the tragedy of the Armenian massacre, it was not alone the mass murders that challenged civilized values. It was Talât's defense of atrocity as a national virtue, as a supreme act of patriotism.

To update the story, it should be added that, within a year, there was terrifying retribution. In 1916 the Russians succeeded in smashing many of the strong points on the Black Sea, and sent the Turkish forces reeling into the interior. The Armenian survivors in the devastated lands then rose up to settle old scores with their tormentors, and they responded to the remembrance of their sorrows with no more compunction than the Turks had shown to them.

There was special retribution for the "unholy three," Talât, Cemal, and Enver. After the war, the old corrupt feudal Turkish regime was overthrown and a new way of life began for Turkey under the leadership of Mustapha Kemal. The organizers of the Armenian massacres fled with the other remnants of the discredited Ottoman regime. They were tried in absentia and sentenced to death. Cemal, after hiding out in Berlin, ended up in Tiflis, in Russia, where he was assassinated by an unknown Armenian in 1922. Enver skulked about from one exile point to another, always persona non grata, until he was cut down during counterrevolutionary forays against the Soviet armies. The strong-arm, pudgy old blackmailer, Talât, lived a secluded life in Berlin, where he underwent plastic surgery to disguise his features. But he was tracked down by young Solomon Tehlirian, whose whole family in Armenia had been exterminated during the massacres. Tehlirian was arrested and charged with murder. His trial in a Berlin court was the opportunity for the Armenians to publicize their almost forgotten tragedy. Tehlirian was acquitted by the jury within an hour after it received the case. It had been his trial, but Talât and the callous masters whom he had served had been found guilty.

Retribution did not bring back the dead. Nor could they even be traditionally and reverently honored in their cemeteries. For most of the million and a half there were no cemeteries. Their bodies had been left to the jackals, the dogs, and the vultures, in the ravines and the deserts where they had been done to death. Their monuments were in the dusty volumes of the Lord Bryce report, in the Werfel novel, *The Forty Days of Musa Dagh,* and in the memorial documentaries of a few broken-hearted Armenian survivors. As for the rest of the world, it had its own problems of reconstruction and preparation for new wars. The Armenian massacres became a few paragraphs in history textbooks, with the passing tribute of an occasional sigh, and they were then forgotten.* Not altogether, however. When Hitler came to power, he found in the Armenian massacres a most useful precedent for the mass murder of a whole people.†

IN TRUTH, HITLER NEEDED NO PRECEDENTS TO SUSTAIN HIS LIFELONG resolve to annihilate the Jews. He made this program a priority part of his master plan for a new order, a *"Judenrein"* world, a world cleansed of Jews. At the peak of his power, with most of Europe prostrate before his legions, he left nothing undone to accomplish his mission.

By 1940, reports filtered out of occupied Europe that a gigantic murder operation was under way. They were at first discounted, as they had been with the Armenians, as the usual atrocity inventions of warring propagandists. But in August 1942, some Polish women were exchanged for German war prisoners, and they gave eyewitness accounts of the slaughterhouses of Poland and occupied Russia that were systematically gassing and burning millions of Jews and Czechs and Poles and Russians and other groups that Hitler had labeled as subhuman. Cables began to arrive at the State Department from its foreign representatives, noting, as one dispatch said: "There is no precedent for such wholesale dying in all history." Still, the officials refused to give credence to the reports. Even the testimony of escaped victims, with ineradicable marks in their flesh, could not convince the bureaucrats at the State Department desks or their superiors that there were men outside insane asylums who would go to such frenzied lengths to fulfill a mission of extermination. It was only when the invading Allied armies burst into Nazi-held territory and seized the concentration camps and the monstrous instruments of torture, and later, when the criminal war trials brought detailed confessions, that the world was made aware of the full implications of Nazi depravity.

Apparently as early as 1941 the orders had gone out to round up

---

* "While the Jews had their Nuremberg and the Asiatic nations had their Tokyo, where is the international tribunal that will hear, at long last, the Armenian complaint against Turkey for the 'mother' genocide of 1915–21?" J. H. Tashjian, *Genocide, the United Nations and the Armenians* (Boston: The American Committee for the Independence of Armenia, May, 1967), p. 11.

† After he ordered his Death Head units to kill without pity or mercy, he added, "Who still talks nowadays of the extermination of the Armenians?" Nuremberg Trial Records, Nov. 23, 1945.

the Jews wherever they lived, and to begin shipping them to specially prepared concentration camps. Only enough food was allocated to keep the inmates temporarily alive. They were beaten at the slightest provocation, or without any provocation at all. Since part of the purpose was to degrade the victims, they were worn down by humiliating duties, and by sadistic sports. In the war trials, medical men admitted the use of the Jews as experimental animals in every kind of pseudo-scientific experiment. They were tortured to test air pressure in planes, to determine the unendurable limits of starvation and thirst, to try out poisons. Their skin was taken for grafting operations on wounded German soldiers. The children were drained of blood to supply the blood banks. In these instances perhaps some remote military purpose was served. But apparently the objective was purely ornamental when human skin was peeled off to make ingeniously tattooed lampshades.

Meantime, giant gas ovens and crematoria had been built in which bodies could be disposed of in wholesale lots with assembly-line routine. There was lively bidding from German firms for this business. One major contract went to the C. N. Kori Company, and the enterprising manager added, when he gave the bargain price: "We guarantee the effectiveness of the crematoria ovens as well as their durability, the use of the best material, and of course, our faultless workmanship." Since the Nazis wished to avoid revolt, even the hopeless revolt of fists against machine guns, they devised the most ingenious stratagems to route the doomed millions to the gas chambers. Announcements were made that they were being selected for work opportunities in other parts of Europe, and these announcements and forged letters and cards from the deported lulled the suspicions of the survivors.

The deportations themselves were on the lowest animal level. Tens of thousands died in the sealed cattle cars for lack of food, water, and air. Those who reached the designated extermination points were usually held for only brief periods before consignment to the gas chambers. Children were torn from their mothers. One survivor noted: "Even a cat is led away before her kittens are taken."* The bodies, millions of them, were shoveled out of the gas ovens like so much garbage, and then burned in huge crematoria or buried in long common graves. The liberating armies later found piles of

---

* Marie Syrkin, *Blessed Is the Match* (New York: Alfred A. Knopf, 1947), p. 145.

baby shoes, toys, gold teeth, spectacles, all sorted out and catalogued meticulously. For the Nazis, even barbarism had to be methodical. Such was the sullenly given testimony that went into the record at the war trials, as the names of the infamous camps, Auschwitz, Buchenwald, Treblinka, Maidanek, and the others, entered the vocabulary of horror of the western world.*

When at last the Jews began to understand the scope of their tragedy, a determination to sell their lives dearly knit together some of the younger men in a few of the hell houses. Most had perished without a struggle. They had no alternative. They were unarmed, demoralized, completely surrounded by the Nazi military and by hostile populations. But there were a few who resolved, with full realization of its hopelessness, that there must be resistance, if only to exact some payment from the master race.

The Warsaw ghetto resistance was the most pathetically valiant of the resistance attempts. Here, half a million Jews had been herded together by October of 1940, most of them gathered up from the occupied countries of Europe. The Nazis worked out their extermination plans with cat-and-mouse malignancy, first destroying security, then human dignity, and then hope. For nearly two years the Jews languished in their Warsaw tomb, crowded, miserable, fighting epidemics without medication, winter's rigor without fuel, enduring the degradations of filth and lack of privacy, but trying pathetically to maintain a semblance of self-respect. They continued their schools, their religious services, their sports, their theatricals. A carefully trained choir sang. A symphony played. There was a children's library to keep open the sluices of remembrance of other happier worlds. There were vocational classes to train hands that death was soon to claim.

In July 1941, the consignments to the extermination camps began, six to ten thousand souls deported daily. For a year those who went simply disappeared, but the forged cards that came back to their kin brought a measure of assurance. By May 1943, when, out of the half million only about forty thousand remained, reports that had become common knowledge opened out the whole ghastly truth to those who were encysted in the ghetto. Resistance was organized, led by a few dauntless men and women, who demonstrated remarkable skill and

---

* "The spirit of 'classicism' was all-pervading. Goethe's favorite oak tree some miles outside of Weimar served as the central point round which Buchenwald concentration camp was constructed." Grunberger, *The Third Reich*, p. 26.

willpower in converting an unarmed handful of half-starved human derelicts into fighting units. In their wretched hovels, homemade hand grenades and incendiary bombs were prepared. The Partisans on the outside smuggled in other weapons and ammunition through the sewers, and through some Aryan-appearing Jews. The Nazis had hoped that there would be no cost to the liquidation. But the utter unexpectedness of the resistance and its fury did take a toll. The ghetto was not subdued for weeks, and then only when tanks and machine guns and flame throwers were rushed in. The battles went on house by house, room by room, and the men fought on until they had used up all but their last bullets, which they reserved for themselves and their families so as not to fall alive into Nazi hands. A few escaped through the sewers, to join with the Partisan underground.

In the ghetto of Terezin in Czechoslovakia, resistance took the form of a memorable moral defiance. To this ghetto had been dispatched some of the leading musicians of Europe, the core of many famous orchestras. Here Rafael Shecter, a brilliant conductor, used a cellar to rehearse the great Verdi *Requiem*. He kept losing his players and his singers daily to the vans of the condemned. But he steadily replaced them by starving and ragged newcomers, persisting until the triumphant performance of the Verdi classic, and then joining all of the others in the rendezvous with death.

Resistance that had more than token value took the form of underground fighting against the Nazis. But only small groups were able to pass through the fine Nazi sieve. Even after escape there was scarcely a moment of respite for the fortunate few. It was difficult enough for any European people to survive as guerrillas against as efficient an enemy as the Nazis. For the Jews it was a demand for daily miracles. They had to run the gauntlet of hostility of the native populations. Poles and Ukrainians and Slovaks may have hated their Nazi oppressors, but they also despised the Jews, and they would not think twice about betraying them.

There were honorable exceptions. In France, the Jewish guerrilla fighters achieved impressive results with the *maquis* forces; they all fought together as comrades against the Nazis and Vichy men. In occupied Czechoslovakia and in Yugoslavia the Jews were either assimilated into the guerrilla groups or organized their own. They were ideal emissaries in sure-death missions, because they had to get through or die. They felt too, that for them, this resistance was beyond war. Every blow struck by them was a shared act of vengeance on behalf of dear ones who had perished namelessly.

In the spring of 1945, the liberation troops poured into Germany and into the long-despoiled territories. The oppressed peoples, the Czechs, the Poles, the Greeks, the Yugoslavs, the Danes, the Norwegians, the Dutch, the Belgians, the French—all came out into the light again. Their inheritance, abused and drained by the Nazis, was damaged, deeply damaged. But the core remained. The land was there, and the people, and the basic resources that nature had provided.

For the Jews there was little rejoicing and less comfort. After the war, when the toll was assessed, in life, in human dignity, in material possessions, it was found that the reports that had strained credulity had been understatements. Six million men, women, and children had perished. And most of those who survived had no homes, no homeland, no means of livelihood, and they found very little compassion or concern. Of the six hundred thousand in Germany, not fifteen thousand were left. Of three million in Poland, a hundred thousand survived. France, Holland, Belgium, Lithuania, Greece, Hungary, Rumania—all once vigorous centers of Jewish life—had been rendered virtually *Judenrein*. This objective of the Nazis had been almost achieved.

Some of the Nazi criminals were tried and punished. Most of them, however, faded into the anonymity of the postwar climate of reconciliation, and these included men who had been an integral part of the extermination machine. For example, during the war, tens of thousands of slave laborers were used by the Krupp works, the huge armaments combine. After the war, the head of the firm was judged to be too ill to stand trial. The son, Alfred, was sentenced to twelve years in prison. In less than three years he was amnestied. The giant armaments corporation was returned to the family, as well as the personal fortune of ten million dollars. Albert Speer, Hitler's Minister of Armaments and War Production, who planned and supervised the slave labor battalions for the war machine, escaped hanging and was given a long prison sentence. When released he wrote a crocodile-tear *mea culpa* which became a best-seller, in which he confessed that he had fallen victim to the technological obsession of our times. He was extremely sorry that he had not investigated what was happening to the Jews, although he was warned that there were camps where the practices were "unfortunate."* But, as a special legal consultant at Nuremberg pointed

---

* "We had to create a new word after the war: *Schreibtischtater*, The Murderer at the Desk." Günter Grass, *Intellectual Digest* (April 1972).

out, Speer approved, on September 15, 1942, 13.7 million marks for building materials to construct three hundred barracks for 132,000 Auschwitz inmates, and there were other clear evidences of his continuous personal involvement in the agony of millions; yet these items were omitted from his volume. The foreword was written by a contemporary historian, Eugene Davidson, who was deeply moved by the "sincerity" of Speer's contrition.* The media tumbled over each other to arrange for interviews and articles, and Speer emerged as a much-sought-after celebrity. In a novel by Günter Grass, *Dog Years,* one of the characters comes up with an intriguing invention, a pair of magical spectacles which, when worn by the young, enables them to look back into the past and to note what their parents were doing during the "great days" of Hitler. The spectacles never got out of Grass's novel.

Imbedded in the tragedy of the unparalleled butchery was the awareness that tens of thousands of victims could have escaped if only some of the more fortunate lands had strongly voiced their protests or had opened their doors ever so slightly. The Scandinavian countries offered a model. When Hitler took over Denmark, the Jewish population numbered less than seven thousand, and they were, of course, on the Nazi extermination agenda. Danish leaders, working secretly with the underground of Norway, managed, through specially organized fleets of fishing boats, to smuggle out at night, into Sweden, virtually all of the Danish Jews before the apparatus of destruction had been set up. In France, throughout the Vichy period, thousands of Jewish children were hidden by Catholic and Protestant families at the risk of their own lives. Britain relaxed some of its immigration laws, and gave asylum to thousands of refugees who had escaped from Germany to Austria, from Austria to Czechoslovakia, then to Holland, fleeing successive Nazi engulfments.

The outstanding and most shocking disappointments were in the reaction of the Vatican and of the United States. Messages poured in on Pope Pius XII describing the inhuman slaughter. The minimum that was called for was a strong statement of Christian repudiation. There were no such statements, nor even milder ones, except for generalized references to "excesses" and these could refer also to the Allied bombing of German cities. The consistent rationale offered for the silence was that it was necessary first to corroborate

* Albert Speer, *Inside the Third Reich.*

the reports. Under pressure, there was an annoyed response that "in order to avoid the slightest appearance of partiality, His Holiness had imposed upon himself, in word and deed, the most delicate reserve." The "delicate reserve" was maintained even as Jews were being rounded up in Rome itself. Later, much later, a Papal spokesman indicated that the Pontiff had decided, after many tears and many prayers, that a denunciation of the Nazis from the Vatican might further rouse the ferocity of the Nazis and result in more, rather than fewer, deaths. There were, of course, not too many left to worry about after six million had been murdered. Monsignor Montini, later to become Pope Paul VI, added: "The time may come when, in spite of such a grievous prospect, the Holy Father will feel himself obliged to speak out." But that time never came. The duty to speak out was always counterbalanced by the fear of weakening Germany and opening the way to the triumph of atheist communism.

The largest opportunity to give reality to compassion rested with the United States. Every effort was made, once the magnitude of the Nazi annihilation program had been exposed, to persuade the State Department to ease the ironclad restrictions on immigration, at least transit immigration. There were expressions of sympathy, conferences with impressive agendas, greetings to conventions on the occasion of Jewish Holy Days, usually before elections, but very little emergency action. In the State Department most of the responsibility for decision lay with Breckenridge Long, the Assistant Secretary for Special Problems. He took it as a priority assignment to vitiate or delay any possible relief action, minimizing the reports of atrocities and emerging with resourceful stratagems to divert attention from the horror stories. We now know from his diaries that he was virtually paranoid on the subject of Jews and Palestine.

It was proposed by Senator Robert Wagner, Sr., of New York, before America entered the war, that ten thousand children be brought in from the war zone, as thousands of British children had come over during the blitz, with homes for them already assured. But the prestigious patriotic organizations, the American Legion, the Daughters of the American Revolution, and many others, at once went into action to keep the pitifully small immigration quotas intact. Politically, apparently, it was inexpedient to press for action. Roosevelt annotated the Wagner Bill: "File, no action, F.D.R.,"*

* Arthur D. Morse, *While Six Million Died* (New York: Random House, 1968), p. 268.

and the bill died in committee. And so did the hopes of ten thousand children.

In 1943, a possibility opened for the rescue of twenty thousand children when Sweden was prepared to request their release. They would be cared for in Sweden if Britain and the United States would share the cost of food and medicine, and place them, after the war, in Palestine or in some other haven. There was no problem of covering costs; private philanthropy was readily available, and Britain agreed. But the proposal was shunted from one office to another in the State Department for the whole of the year in which the crematoria operated. This was the period when thousands of Nazi prisoners of war were housed in comfortable American camps. It was suggested that similar camps might be opened for children, as enemy aliens, as a stopgap until the gas ovens stopped functioning. But the proposal roused no interest. One State Department official noted that any rescue concentrating on Jewish children might antagonize the Nazis, and prevent other possible cooperative acts. At the end of the year, when another million children had died in the crematoria, the proposal was dropped.

In 1940, a refugee ship carrying Jews who had escaped from Vichy France was turned away from Mexico and ordered back to Europe and certain doom. It stopped for coal at Norfolk, Virginia, and a Jewish delegation pleaded with Cordell Hull, the Secretary of State, to offer temporary asylum to the refugees. Hull pointed to the American flag and said that he had taken an oath to protect it and he would not break the law of his country. He was reminded by Dr. Nahum Goldmann that some anti-Nazi German sailors had leaped overboard from their ships, and that the Coast Guard had saved them and given them sanctuary at Ellis Island. Dr. Goldmann suggested that a message might be sent to the ship suggesting that the refugees jump overboard for they would surely be rescued by the Coast Guard. Hull sharply upbraided Goldmann as the most cynical man he had ever met. Dr. Goldmann replied, "I ask you, Mr. Secretary, who is the cynical one? I, who wish to save these people, or you, who are preparing to send them back to their death?"* In the end, through the personal intercession of Eleanor Roosevelt, this small group of refugees was saved.

Visas, of course, were almost impossible to come by anywhere during the war. Only suicides found a "land" easy of access. A con-

* Nahum Goldmann, *Autobiography* (New York: Holt, Rinehart & Winston, 1969), pp. 201–2.

temporary poet wrote of this land where suicides found no technical obstacles:

> This was the one country you could get a visa for,
> This country of the cold,
> The one unguarded frontier of them all;
> The only one that had an open door.
> The only one with quota still unfilled,
> Where race and credo mattered not at all.*

As one reviews the experiences of the civilized twentieth century—the massacre of a million and half Armenians, the holocaust that consumed six million Jews—there is incredulity that killers on such a mass scale could have been spawned among nations that were rooted in religious faith and commitment. But part of the tragic toll must be attributed to the bystanders, righteous bystanders, safe in the fellowship of virtuous platitudes that make the whole world kin, who so often fell back upon the absolving phrase: "We don't want to get involved."

* Reitza Dine Wirtschafter, "To a Dead Refugee," *Jewish Frontier* (May 1939), p. 20.

23

JAPAN AND
THE ATOMIC BOMB

WHILE THE GREAT POWERS OF THE EUROPEAN WORLD, BRITAIN, FRANCE, Germany, and Russia, were locked in their fratricidal struggle, virtually a white race civil war, the military leaders of Japan perfected their plans to penetrate and take over the weakly protected colonial dependencies of Southeast Asia and the Pacific. The justification for what was denounced as aggression was more than the quest for imperial glory. Japan was an island kingdom, smaller than California, only a fraction of its land productive and tillable, but its population, by 1941, had already gone beyond seventy million. Its assault on disunited and unstable China, and its victories there during the 1930's, had added substantially to its territory, but it would be decades before the full potentialities of its Manchurian spoils could be realized. The valuable colonial holdings of the western powers in the South Pacific offered much more alluring immediate benefits, and when the failure of nerve of the democracies and their military weakness were exposed in the easy victories of the Nazis, the time seemed ideal for the Japanese to strike. One of the militants contended, "This is the best opportunity in ten thousand years and it must be seized to win a place in the sun at last for the Fatherland."

In October 1941 Prince Konoye, who represented the moderates in the Japanese government, was ousted and leadership passed to General Hideki Tojo, who was committed to the policy of expansion that would make Japan self-sufficient. Tojo had little concern about

British or French or Dutch resistance. The deterrent factor was the opposition of the American government, which saw in Japanese control of the resources of East Asia a serious menace to the American military and economic position in the Pacific. During the Manchurian crisis, President Roosevelt warned that the Japanese were on a collision course that could lead to catastrophe. He followed the warning with embargoes that cut off oil and steel and other essential supplies for Japan's mechanized military operations. Tojo took the calculated risk that Roosevelt's warnings were rhetoric, that any American effort against the Japanese could be no more than token since Roosevelt was so completely involved in trying to save the broken and humbled Allies in Europe. He went on the assumption that a quick victory would lead to acceptance, however reluctant, of a fait accompli in Asia and the Pacific. It was apparently this reasoning that triggered the decisive action on December 7, 1941, when Japan launched the surprise attack on the American fleet at Pearl Harbor and simultaneously struck at the Philippines and the British and Dutch colonial holdings all through the South Pacific. It was astonishing that the attack at Pearl Harbor shattering the effective power of the American fleet should have caught the commanders completely off guard. The tension between the two countries had been building up steadily, and it required no prescience to realize that war was a distinct possibility.

The controversy has continued ever since over whether the attack could have been anticipated. The admirals whose reputations were destroyed by the disaster insisted that they were most inadequately briefed by Washington and by the intelligence units. One went so far as to charge that Roosevelt knew, from intercepted messages, that the attack was coming: he saw in it an opportunity to involve the country in a war that was inevitable anyway but for whose successful prosecution he needed the unity that the Japanese attack would instantly command. In later investigations these sensational charges were not sustained. A Japanese attack was always a possibility, but it was expected if it came that it would undoubtedly focus on the Philippines or somewhere in Southeast Asia and *not* on American territory. Of course, since the expansionist objectives of the Japanese militants were not secret, it was incumbent on the commanders at every American base to exercise the utmost vigilance and apparently the guard was down at Pearl Harbor.

For the Japanese the war had the most critical implications: it was victory or ruin. For the United States, the outcome would determine whether it would remain a Pacific power. Roosevelt declared, "We're in it all the way. Every single man, woman, and child is a partner in the most tremendous undertaking in our history." The motion for the declaration of war was passed in both Houses of Congress, with only one dissenting vote.

The initial success of the Japanese seemed to vindicate the confident daring of the militants. The American fleet in the Pacific had been virtually put out of action. The Japanese engulfed the Philippines and all the American bases in the far Pacific. They took over the Malay Peninsula and the Dutch, French, and British colonial possessions. Singapore, considered impregnable, fell; and on Christmas Day, 1941, the Japanese flag was raised in Hong Kong. Australia and India were threatened. In six months the Japanese conquered an empire with a hundred million people and priceless resources in minerals, rubber, tin, and other indispensable raw materials. The irresistible sweep was a duplication of the early successes of the Nazi blitz in Europe.

The United States gradually came out of shock and humiliation. It tooled up slowly but steadily, fighting for time to build its military forces and to meet the vastly increased production quotas. Roosevelt gave assurances that, though there was now a new challenge in the Pacific, the American commitment in Europe and North Africa would not be modified or weakened.

Roosevelt's war leadership was beyond every expectation. Within a year, American manpower had taken its battle places on all fronts, supported by the essential reserves of planes, tanks, ships, and submarines. The magnitude of the American effort was demonstrated in the production of aircraft carriers. In the fall of 1942, there were three. A year later there were fifty. By the end of the war, there were one hundred. The arsenal of weaponry was similarly reinforced for every military need.

The American counteroffensive demanded such mighty armadas and back-up support. The chain of islands from the Marianas to Japan stretched two thousand miles across the Pacific. They were defended in depth by squadrons of Japanese naval and air units, and the chain had to be broken in many places. A decisive turn in the war came with the American victories in the Coral Sea and in the Solomons. Saipan, Tinian, and Guam, Wake, Midway, and Guadalcanal became the names that were immortalized in American combat effort. The leapfrog offensive was sustained all through 1943 and 1944, and General MacArthur, who had vowed that he would return to the Philippines, kept his pledge when he led his men in the landing at Leyte and then hammered his way into Manila.

The punishment that the Japanese took during the counter-offensive would have shattered a less resolute foe. The losses at sea reduced their tonnage from five million to less than one and a half million, with disastrous effects on military strength and on the ability to maintain food and other imports to sustain life. The guerrillas in the occupied areas mounted ever more savage attacks on the Japanese invaders in every part of Asia and the Pacific, not only to clear them out but to win independence for themselves.

The decisive battle came in April 1942 with the crushing Japanese defeat at Midway. The reconquest of the Pacific proceeded steadily thereafter. When the Mariana and Caroline Islands were recaptured it became possible to launch full-scale air assaults on the Japanese cities themselves, assaults that brought devastation on a scale that even the German countryside had not experienced. In the series of raids on Tokyo, eighty-five thousand were killed, a quarter of a million dwellings were burned, and millions were made homeless. In succession, American firepower devastated Osaka, Yokohama, Kawasaki, Nagoya, Kobe, and scores of other heavily populated cities until much of Japan was one vast conflagration.

But the victories, however glorious, had to be paid for in heavy casualties that brought bereavement to every American community. Each Pacific island, even after the saturation bombing, had its Japanese Kamikaze squads, valiant fanatics who were resolved to die, but to take their enemies with them. Iwo Jima, 750 miles from Japan, cost twenty thousand American dead and wounded. It required eighty-two days to recapture Okinawa, 325 miles from Japan, and there were thirty-five thousand casualties. All was in readiness for Operations Olympia and Coronet, to begin the invasion of the mainland—thousands of ships, squadrons of planes, a million tough, battle-hardened men. But the nightmare that haunted the American planners was that there were seventy million Japanese who could be marshaled for the last-ditch resistance to invasion and conquest. If there were mile-by-mile suicide determination to die rather than to yield, the cost in American lives might go beyond half a million. Ambassador Joseph Grew, with long and authoritative experience in Japan, expressed the judgment that the Japanese would fight to the end in defense of their homeland. It was in this context that the atomic bomb played its role as the weapon that had to be employed to bring the Pacific war to an end.

Some of the world's most distinguished scientists had been at work for many years on the problems of nuclear chain reaction. In 1921, Walther Nernst, a Nobel Prize winner, had said, "We are living on an island of gun cotton. But thank God we have not yet found the match to ignite it."* By the 1930's considerable headway had been made, especially by the scientists in Germany, but their cooperative effort had been seriously impaired because Hitler had driven so many of them out—Einstein, Bohr, Frank, Teller, Oppenheimer, Meitner, Fermi, Szilard, and scores of others who, welcomed by Britain and the United States, gave their talents to the research centers. Yet no one could be sure where and when the incredible power of the atom would be harnessed, and by whom, and Hitler's Germany was still very much in the competition.

One of the German refugees, Leo Szilard, who had settled in the United States, was so concerned about the application of nuclear power to weaponry that he sought to warn the American government. He feared that if Hitler's scientists won the race, the Nazis would control the world. But Szilard was virtually unknown to the American government officials. He therefore sought the intercession of Albert Einstein who, in October 1939, wrote to President Roosevelt, "Through the work of Joliot in France as well as Fermi and Szilard in America, it may become possible to set up nuclear chain reactions in a large mass of uranium . . . extremely powerful bombs of a new type may thus be constructed."† He gave full credit to Szilard, noting later, "I really only acted as a mailboy. They brought me a finished letter and I signed it."

Roosevelt was impressed, and he initiated one of the most extensive research projects in all history. Since the work had to be conducted in utmost secrecy, Roosevelt took the gamble without approval from Congress. The Manhattan Project, as it was termed, was placed under the technical direction of General Leslie Groves and under the supervision of the Secretary of War, Henry Stimson, who was head of the National Security Council. Scientists were recruited from every area—the universities, the research centers, industry. The ablest brains were marshaled on a scale never before undertaken even for the war on cancer, heart disease, stroke, and other human killers. The management of men of such caliber was to

* Jungk, *Brighter Than a Thousand Suns* (London: V. Gollancz and R. Hart-Davis, Ltd., 1958), p. 8.

† Albert Einstein, *Einstein on Peace* (New York: Schocken Books, 1968), p. 295.

be a major task. Groves said to his staff at Los Alamos, "Your job won't be easy. At great expense we have gathered the largest collection of crackpots ever assembled." But they were remarkable crackpots, all concentrating on the one purpose, to perfect the bomb, with no higher priority, no expense to be spared. Ultimately, the project cost more than two billion dollars. Except for Groves and Stimson and an inner corps of distinguished scientists, the purpose of the research was not revealed. Roosevelt did not confide even in his Vice President, Harry Truman, nor in General Eisenhower, who was then the head of the Allied armies in the European war theater. He did indicate to Winston Churchill that the search was under way and that the results of the project, if successful, were to be shared by both countries.

The creation of the bomb was planned in what became three secret atom cities—at Los Alamos in New Mexico, at Oak Ridge in Tennessee, and under the stadium at the University of Chicago. More than 150,000 scientists and technicians participated, the assignments so distributed that only about a dozen at the summit level knew how one sector was related to another. Yet there were spies in the inner circles who broke through the secrecy and regularly reported their findings to the Soviet Union. There were heartbreaking fatalities when some of the research got out of control and infected the men in the laboratories. There were hair-breadth escapes when planes transporting classified cargo nearly crashed. There were scientists at work in German cities who were so horrified by the consequences of possible success that they deliberately slowed down the tempo of their research. There were a thousand other bizarre incidents, judgments, misjudgments, setbacks, betrayals, and all against the background of a relentless timetable.*

Then, just before the bomb was completed and tested, President Roosevelt suddenly died on April 13, 1945, two secret letters from Einstein and Szilard still lying unopened on his desk. The responsibility for the decision on the use of the bomb passed now to Harry Truman, who had not been informed of the existence of the Manhattan Project until after his first cabinet meeting. Henry Stimson then told him that "an immense program is under way, and if it is

---

* Though every precaution was taken, technological secrets were transmitted to the Russians by two of the British scientists, Klaus Fuchs and Alan Nunn May; the data included isotope separation, critical mass, and trigger mechanisms of the bomb, as well as many negative results which saved Russia considerable expense and experiment time.

successful, it will produce the most destructive bomb in all history."* The President did not ask for details, limiting himself at the moment to the hope that the program would indeed help to bring the war to a speedier end. But he soon realized that the power being harnessed would create "the most terrible weapon ever known in all human history." When he was confronted by reporters after the first cabinet session, he said to them, "Pray for me, boys. The sun and the moon and the stars have fallen on me."

On July 16 the test was completed when the bomb was detonated from a 100-foot tower at Alamogordo, creating a temperature four times that at the center of the sun. George Kistiakowsky, one of the designers of the bomb, equated this moment with "what would be seen by the last man in the last millisecond of the earth's existence." Oppenheimer wrote that when the blast came, he thought of the words of the Bhagavad-Gita describing the radiance of a thousand suns bursting into the sky: "I am become Death, the shatterer of worlds."†

President Truman, that weekend, was in conference with Churchill and Stalin in Potsdam to discuss the pressing problems of peace, and the plans to end the war in Japan. Word was relayed to him in code, "Babies satisfactorily born." Churchill was promptly informed that the bomb had been successfully tested, and was available for the strategy of the future. To Churchill, the cryptic message meant not only the end of the long agony in the Pacific, but relief from dependence on Russia to help in the defeat of Japan. Later he wrote of this exultant moment,

To quell the Japanese resistance man by man and conquer the country yard by yard might well require the loss of a million American lives and half that number of British—or more if we could get them there: for we were resolved to share the agony. Now all this nightmare picture had vanished. In its place was the vision—fair and bright indeed it seemed—of the end of the whole war in one or two violent shocks. I thought immediately myself of how the Japanese people, whose courage I had always admired, might find in the apparition of this almost supernatural weapon an excuse which would save their honour and release them from their obligation of being killed to the last fighting man.‡

Truman waited until the summit meeting was in its last session to break the news to Stalin. Then, without reference to the atomic

---

* Harry Truman, *Memoirs* (Garden City, N.Y.: Doubleday, 1955–6), Vol. 1, p. 10.

† Jungk, *Brighter Than a Thousand Suns,* p. 201.

‡ Churchill, *Memoirs of the Second World War,* pp. 980–1.

or nuclear ingredients of the bomb, he told Stalin that after long experimentation a new weapon had been perfected with far more destructive power than had ever been known before, and that it would be used on Japan unless it surrendered. The President and his staff were astonished at the casual response of Stalin, who expressed his satisfaction and hoped that the bomb would indeed be used. There have been various explanations for this impassiveness. One, which was hardly likely, was that Stalin did not appreciate the military importance of the achievement. Another came later, when the activity of the spies had been disclosed, that Stalin had been kept fully informed by them and the announcement was therefore no surprise to him.

But infinitely more important than the strategy of communication was the decision on whether and how to use the bomb. It was agreed by the President's advisers that an ultimatum should be presented to the Japanese government, couched in the strongest terms, calling for unconditional surrender and adding that the alternative for Japan would be "prompt and utter destruction." The ultimatum was rejected out of hand. The Japanese War Council declared that it could not accede to unconditional surrender or any jeopardy to the prerogatives of the Emperor. The defiant reply brought to a climax the debate on the use of the bomb. Szilard and some of his colleagues pleaded that it must not be dropped on the inhabitants of any Japanese city. Perhaps its potential for destruction could be demonstrated on an uninhabited island. Every populous city in Japan had already suffered indescribable misery, and the war was virtually won.

But the majority of the scientists disagreed. Arthur Compton wrote that he and his colleagues had spent agonizing hours without success trying to think of some way to demonstrate the lethal power of the bomb, without casualties, that would be influential with the militants who were in control of Japan. Oppenheimer, Conant, Fermi, Bohr, virtually all the others, sorrowfully conceded that the bomb had to be dropped to bring the warlords to their senses. The new Prime Minister, Admiral Suzuki Kantaro, had said, "Unconditional surrender will only mean that our national structure and our people will be destroyed. Against such boastful talk there is only one measure we must take, that is to fight to the last."*

In the light of such impassioned reactions, no persuasion, short of the awesome assault itself, could possibly be decisive. Robert Oppen-

* Cited in Michael Amrine, *The Great Decision* (New York: Putnam, 1959), p. 208.

heimer wondered how it was possible to expect that the Japanese government would be influenced by an enormous firecracker detonated at a great height that might be a dud and do little damage.*

General Groves and his staff argued that the bomb could not be dropped on an uninhabited island nor could even the nature of the intended attack be revealed, for then the Japanese would relocate the large number of American and British prisoners through the cities as hostages to deter the attack. They concluded that though the cost in human life for the dropping of the bomb would be heavy, it was the price that would have to be paid to end the bloodshed for the Americans, the British, and the Japanese themselves.

Truman gave the order to carry out the decision. The possible target cities were to include Hiroshima, Kyoto, Kokura, and Nagasaki. At the last moment, through the intercession of Edwin Reischauer, later Ambassador to Japan, Kyoto, with its sacred and precious monuments of the past, was removed from the list. The plane bearing the bomb was accompanied by only two others so as not to draw the anti-aircraft fire of a massive attack. They came in over Hiroshima and the bomb was released at 2,000 feet. In the log of Captain Lewis the entry read, "There will be a short intermission while we bomb our target," and then the next entry was, "My God."† The eerie light filled the sky, and more than seventy-five thousand men, women, and children were instantaneously immolated.

Once again the Japanese Imperial Council was requested to surrender. Millions of leaflets were dropped over Tokyo with the warning that the most destructive explosive ever devised would again be used, and then again. The immediate response of the warlords was another refusal, and the second bomb, which was dropped on Nagasaki, killed fifty thousand of its inhabitants. When General Groves was asked why the second bomb was exploded, he replied, "One bomb would show the Japanese what the bomb was like, and the second one would show them that we had more than one."‡ Even the second bomb did not end the Japanese irresolution. In the inner War Council the vote was 3 to 3. This time the Emperor took it upon himself to overrule the warlords, who preferred to die rather than to yield. Only then was the capitulation agreed upon, and the armistice was arranged.

---

* Len Giovannitti and Fred Freed, *The Decision to Drop the Bomb* (New York: Coward-McCann, 1965), p. 104.

† Amrine, *The Great Decision*, p. 202.

‡ Giovannitti and Freed, *The Decision to Drop the Bomb*, pp. 280–1.

The debate over the resort to the atomic bomb has gone on ever since and there has been increasing concern over the action and the consequences that have flowed from it. In recent years, many classified documents have been released, and a spate of memoirs by participants in the decision has thrown new light on the problems which confronted the policymakers. A school of revisionists has charged that the decision to drop the bomb was really meant as a power gambit in the developing struggle with the Soviet Union. Evidence has been offered from the statements by Truman and by those closest to him. The President was quoted as exulting when the bomb was successfully tested that he now had decisive power "to keep the Soviet in line." "I'll certainly have a hammer on those boys."* General Groves testified at the hearings where the loyalty of Robert Oppenheimer was challenged, "I think that it is important to state that there was never, from about two weeks from the time I took charge of this project, any illusion on my part, but that Russia was our enemy and that the project was conducted on that basis. I didn't go along with the attitude of the country as a whole that Russia was a gallant ally."† It was also pointed out that James Byrnes, who was special assistant to the President and soon became Secretary of State, had been hoping that the bomb would be ready for use as early as May, before Russia was obligated by treaty to enter the war against Japan, so as to keep Russia "more manageable." There were similar references which were cited to prove that the administration was prepared to snuff out tens of thousands of lives in a game of international power politics.

These were serious charges. Most of them were based on hindsight, on information as to Japanese intentions that was not available when the decision on the use of the bomb had to be made. They were based too on the second thoughts of many of the scientists, who were guilt-ridden because they had helped to bring into the world a terrifying power that had not been placed under responsible international discipline. When Churchill was later asked whether he regretted the bomb attacks on Hiroshima and Nagasaki he replied that, while we know the consequences of actions that are taken, we cannot possibly know the consequences of actions that are not taken.

* Gar Alperovitz, *Atomic Diplomacy* (New York: Vintage Books, 1967), p. 130.
† U.S. Atomic Energy Commission, *In the Matter of J. Robert Oppenheimer* (Washington, D.C.: U.S. Government Printing Office, 1954), p. 173.

The debate will continue, and since it centers on motivations, there can be no uncontroverted conclusion.

In the dread days of August 1945, when there was no clear knowledge of what the Japanese would do, virtually all the scientists shared the belief of the policymakers that the use of the bomb would save hundreds of thousands of American, British, and, ultimately, Japanese lives too. If the demonstration also helped to strengthen the American bargaining position *vis-à-vis* the Russians, then it was a factor, helpful in diplomacy, but not the dominating incentive in the decision to use the bomb. Stimson was as honorable a statesman as America had in this century, and his sincerity could not be impugned when he wrote, "I felt that to extract a genuine surrender from the Emperor and his military advisers, there must be administered a tremendous shock which would carry convincing proof of our power to destroy the Empire. Such an effective shock would save many times the number of lives, both American and Japanese, than it would cost."* Truman, in a television address to the country in 1965, summarized the situation that faced him when the Japanese continued in their intractable defiance: "The name given to our invasion was Olympia, but I saw nothing godly about the killing of all the people that would be necessary to make that invasion. The casualty estimates called for 750,000 Americans, a quarter of a million to be killed, and a half a million to be maimed for life. I could not worry about what history would say about my personal morality. I made the only decision that I knew how to make."†

One other footnote may be added. It relates to the mission of Leo Szilard. In the early days of Brandeis University, he served briefly as a visiting professor of physics. In an emotion-packed evening he told a student audience of his futile attempts to persuade the American policymakers not to drop the bomb. He could not reach President Truman, but he did get to James Byrnes, then the Assistant President. Byrnes said to Szilard that it would be political suicide to have spent two billion dollars on the bomb without authorization and then not to use it. Szilard commented bitterly that President Truman's decision was at least based on his Christian concern over the heavy cost of invasion; it was to save countless American lives.

* Henry L. Stimson, *On Active Service in Peace and War* (New York: Harper & Bros., 1948), p. 617.

† Truman's television series, *Decision: The Conflicts of Harry S Truman,* "Dialogue with the Future," Feb. 12, 1965.

Byrnes seemed to be more concerned with the political consequences of an immense expenditure for a weapon that was then not used.

There was heartbreak enough in the destruction that was wrought by the bombs. It was not assuaged after the war when there could be no agreement on a formula of control so that the power of the atom could be diverted for the uses of peace. Norman Cousins wrote that unless this were done, and done quickly, "then the birth certificate of the atomic age is in reality a *memento mori.*"* There were many opportunities to establish responsible regulation; first, when the United States was the sole possessor of the bomb, and later too, when Russia achieved nuclear power. The day would come when many other nations would acquire the capacity to manufacture the bombs, to deploy them not only from planes and ships and submarines, but from suitcases, by remote control. The day came with fearsome swiftness. The atom bomb was followed by the hydrogen bomb, and then by the cobalt bomb, and then by missiles with lightning techniques of delivery. A special computer was created to calculate the precision necessary for further escalation of nuclear power. It was called the Mathematical Analyzer Numerical Integrator Computer. It was known by its initials, and was therefore affectionately called MANIC. The world then began to learn about the genetic effect of the bomb where even those who survived would transmit fatal or degenerative defects to the generations of the remotest future. Perhaps the latent evil that lurked in the mushroom cloud over Hiroshima was best summarized by Jean Rostand, who said, "Science has made us gods before we are even worthy of being men."

* Norman Cousins, *Present Tense* (New York: McGraw-Hill, 1967), p. 123.

24

HITLER: ZENITH
AND RETRIBUTION

WHEN HITLER IN JUNE 1941 REPUDIATED THE NAZI-SOVIET PACT THAT
he had signed only two years before and sent his panzers and his
planes without warning into Russia, he told his generals, "We have
only to kick in the door, and the whole rotten structure will come
crashing down." He added that in this decisive confrontation with the
ancient enemy, there was to be no sniveling compassion, no concern
for rules or laws. Russia was to be finished forever as a competing
power. The objective, then, was much more than the repatriation of
German populations that were under foreign rule, which was the
rationale claimed in the assaults on Austria, Czechoslovakia, and
Poland. It was much more than a strategy to protect and secure
German frontiers or flanks. It was a plan to annex millions of square
miles of rich lands, twice the size of Germany, to make the Reich of
the future the most powerful nation on earth. Hitler coveted the
granaries of the Ukraine and the Crimea, the reserves of oil in the
Caucasus, the industrial resources of the Donets Basin. He was
determined to clear out tens of millions of peoples living there,
deporting, enslaving, exterminating, and then recolonizing the
conquered lands with his own Germans. The new frontiers of the
expanded Reich would be the Volga and the Vistula, and Russia
would be pushed back to become an exclusively Asian nation.
Göring told Mussolini's son-in-law, Ciano, at the outbreak of the war
that he expected twenty to thirty million Russians to starve to death
and said it "is well that this is so. Certain nations must be decimated."

[277]

It was because this objective had been proclaimed by Hitler ever since its formulation in his *Mein Kampf* that the resistance in Russia, despite every defeat, went on almost beyond human endurance, a resistance like few in all history. Hitler's early victories in Russia were so crushing that by every logic there should have been capitulation. Tens of millions had died in combat or by starvation, ill-treatment, and execution. The West had yielded Warsaw and Narvik and Brussels and Paris, and other vital points within days, when the outlook seemed hopeless. The Russians hung on in Moscow and Leningrad, in Sevastopol and Stalingrad and Kursk, until Hitler burst out in rage: "They don't fight like men. They fight like swamp animals!" The Russians knew that defeat would mean not only the destruction of the defending cities but the extermination of the Fatherland. For Hitler was no conquering warlord. He was the face of Death itself.

The Nazi offensive was labeled Operation Barbarossa. Hitler crowed, "When Barbarossa commences, the world will hold its breath." In its daring it stunned and frightened even the Nazi generals. Hitler planned to strike simultaneously on three fronts—at the Russian heartland itself, concentrating on Moscow; at the north, aiming at Leningrad; and at the south, through Kiev, for the Ukraine's granary and the oil reserves in the Caucasus.

The major objective was Moscow, and the initial victories there seemed to vindicate Hitler's gamble. The Nazi intelligence accurately pinpointed strategic locations, and the Luftwaffe established complete air control in the first few days. Most of the Soviet air force was destroyed on the ground. Within a fortnight tens of thousands of Russians had been killed and 150,000 taken prisoner. Despite poor roads and blasted bridges and death-defying resistance, the speed of the Nazi motorized forces was phenomenal, and soon they were within seventy miles of Moscow. Government officials fled 500 miles inland to Kuibyshev, although Stalin stayed behind hoping to sustain morale. The Russians then fell back on the scorched earth tactics that had ultimately defeated Napoleon. They kept retreating, fighting delaying actions, evacuating their villages and towns, transporting their peoples inland, leaving rubble and ruin for the conquerors. They held on grimly, counting off the days, waiting for the winter to block the Nazi advance and to disrupt it. Their determination never to surrender was clear when the Dnieper Dam, the industrial miracle of the new Russia, was blown up so that it could not serve the Nazis.

When the first snow fell on November 1, 1941, Hitler's generals pleaded with him to pull back, to consolidate his forces, and to resume his drive for Moscow in the spring. Hitler refused and upbraided them for their craven lack of confidence. On December 2 the invaders reached the suburbs of Moscow and the gilded towers of the Kremlin could be seen against the leaden sky. Goebbels, Nazi Minister of Propaganda, alerted all the newspapers to leave space for the headline story on the fall of the Russian capital. Then the full fury of the winter was loosed. The Nazis had flashed through hundreds of miles, obliterating resistance as if it were token; now these last miles to Moscow, through sleet and rain and fog, were a yard-by-yard agony. The thermometer fell to thirty-six below zero, and the machines could not move. The water froze inside the boilers of the locomotives, and the lubricants hardened in the artillery and rifles. It had not been expected that the campaign would go into the winter; hence the troops froze in their inadequate clothing, stumbling and staggering about, the icicles hanging from their noses.

The voice of a new Stalin now came through to his people. It was not the voice of the remote tyrant, nor of the incompetent whose aircraft had been caught and destroyed on the ground, whose stubborn smugness, despite continuous warning from reliable agents that the Nazis were getting ready for attack, had so badly used the years of grace during the Nazi-Soviet pact.* It was the voice of the symbol of Russia, appealing now, not on behalf of the party or its doctrine, but on behalf of holy Mother Russia. One day the voice would come up from the depths of the subway, the next day from the Red Square, and then from a bombed-out plaza. The refrain was constant: time was on the side of the Russians, if only the people would hold out, if only they would wait for the avenging deliverance of the winter. They waited, and they prepared frantically in the tormented interval. The women, the children, the old, the crippled, all gladly fulfilled assigned tasks inside the city, digging, blocking, piling up sandbags and earthwork barricades.

Then, at the end of December, when it seemed as if there were no strength left in the beleaguered city, the Russians counterattacked.

---

* Stalin's criminal ineptness in preparing his country for the inevitable attack has been validated by the release of documents that were impounded until after Khrushchev's denunciations in 1956. They are summarized in some detail in Roy A. Medvedev, *Let History Judge* (New York: Alfred A. Knopf, 1971), pp. 446–54.

General Georgi Zhukov and a crop of younger commanders who had been given leadership brought in their fresh reserves from the Far East, where they had been stationed as a precaution in case of a Japanese invasion. Stalin took the calculated risk that they could be transferred. They fell upon the exhausted German units stalled in ice and snow, bewildered by the Russian miracle of recuperation. Within a few days, Zhukov's relief forces had driven the invaders back a hundred miles and ended, at least for the winter, the threat to the Russian capital. They exacted a toll of a million German casualties, dead, wounded, and missing; but even more important, as Franz Halder, Chief of Staff, admitted, they erased the myth of German invincibility. Not long before, Colonel Charles Lindbergh, the American aviation oracle, had intimidated the West with his judgment that the Russians could never be counted on for military strength, for "they were rotten to the core." With the debacle of Moscow in mind, the Nazi general, Marshal von Rundstedt, noted grimly, "Soon after the attacks began, I realized how much that had been written about Russia was just pure nonsense."[*]

The Nazis, meantime, had been deep in the northern campaign aimed at Leningrad, whose capture was given a priority far beyond its strategic value. It was the cradle of the Russian Communist faith, and was named for the venerated founder of communism. Hence it was an emotional objective for the Führer, and he put his generals on warning that, even if surrender were offered, it was to be refused. He wanted Leningrad to be razed, wiped off the face of the earth.

The Nazis, having quickly won air mastery, blitzed their way through the Russian land area. They reached the environs of Leningrad by the end of August and then, in the next two months, almost completely encircled the city. For 880 days the most harrowing siege in history, to compel submission, continued to starve its three and a half million inhabitants. The Nazis bombed, strafed, and tightened the blockade until the toll of the victims could no longer be counted. The rations were steadily reduced; there was no fuel; water had to be carried up from the river, past the gauntlet of unremitting bombardment. Only one outlet to the outside world remained, a thin sliver of road across Lake Ladoga. Each night hundreds of those who were ringed in attempted the trip across the lake and back, to obtain supplies of food and war matériel. The

[*] Shirer, *The Rise and Fall of the Third Reich,* p. 855.

ice broke frequently; driver and vehicle would go down. Some of the children, lacking a sled, used frozen corpses on which to transport the precious cargo. It was hard in Leningrad to weep for the dead; the tears froze. When the Nazis broke into the city itself, the resistance went on more desperately, block by block, house by house, room by room. At the end of eighteen months more than a million civilians had died. A survivor wrote, "With each step the feet grew heavier. But better not pause for rest, perhaps Death sits beside the road, just resting too." "Today it is so simple to die," wrote another. "You just begin to lose interest, then you lie on the bed and never again get up." During the siege eight hundred thousand bodies, often so frozen that they gave off a metallic ring, went uncoffined to Piskarevsky Cemetery, to the largest mass grave in history.*

Hitler was so sure of victory that the conqueror's parade was planned to the last detail. Goebbels exulted, "We have smashed the Red Army to splinters. The Eastern continent lies like a limp virgin in the mighty arms of the German Mars." But the city had not yielded. The besieged had made a choice between dying in degradation as German vassals, or dying honorably in their own beloved city, and now they were rewarded by not having to die any more. For the day came when the siege could not be sustained. Under the heaviest pressure on the other fronts, the Nazis had to give way here. A Russian relief force broke through in January 1944, and the world of the living dead began again the slow painful way up from animal existence.

All this time Hitler was also engaged in a third simultaneous offensive, this one in the south—for the Ukraine, the Crimea, and the Caucasus. His generals were deeply worried. They believed that he was attempting too much at one time. General Halder said later that when the warning was sounded by one of his colleagues, "Hitler flew at the man . . . with clenched fists and foam in the corners of his mouth and forbade him to go on with such idiotic twaddle." At first this drive was more successful than either of the other two, and the conservatism of the generals seemed again to be repudiated. The Nazi tanks, with full Luftwaffe support, raced through the open country. Kiev, the capital of the Ukraine, fell in September, and the Germans rounded up more than 650,000 prisoners. But, as at Moscow and Leningrad, the momentum could not be maintained. Sevastopol and Rostov-on-Don became two rallying points where months of

* The siege of Leningrad is brilliantly described by Harrison E. Salisbury in *The 900 Days* (New York: Harper & Row, 1969).

siege could not force a surrender. Once again the Germans faced last-stand fighting in cellars, in quarries, in alleys. It was not until the summer of 1942 that Sevastopol and Rostov fell, but the surviving defenders destroyed everything that could be of value. The way was cleared for the oilfields farther east, but resistance seemed to feed on adversity. Every mile was contested. The objective was Grozny and Baku, where the chief oil reserves were, but the Germans could not make it. They were too thinly spread, very much overextended, and by now they were completely committed to the conquest of Stalingrad, far to the east.

Stalingrad was the key city of the lower Volga, the home of the giant tractor and armaments plants, a symbol of the new industrial Russia. If Hitler's forces could take it, they would retrieve all the temporary setbacks on the other fronts. They would outflank the strong points which protected a third of Russia's population and the basic industries that sustained them. If Stalingrad fell, it would be possible to isolate Moscow and Leningrad and cut off the vital oil supplies from the Caspian Sea regions. Then the Russian state itself would collapse.

For this critical objective Hitler assigned 330,000 of his best troops, under General Friedrich von Paulus. The armored and motorized units reached the west bank of Stalingrad at the end of August 1942. They had about two months of reliable weather in which to complete Hitler's dream. Paulus at once began the most concentrated bombing that had ever been undertaken, and it flattened three-fourths of the city in a single day. But when the Germans attempted to storm the city, they found that they had to fight for every street, every house, every wall, every pile of rubble; and when won, they had to be fought for all over again through September and October. Stalingrad became a graveyard of crumbling buildings, shattered utilities, rotting corpses. And time was running out for the invaders as the first dread signs of winter appeared.

Paulus appealed to Hitler for permission to retreat temporarily, to wait for the weather to turn, to regroup his forces. Otherwise, they would be trapped. Hitler raged against even a discussion of retreat. German honor was at stake. "Not a day to be given up, not a man to surrender." He was to rue these bold but fatuous words. November arrived and with it the worst winter in years. The blizzard was continuous. It grounded the Nazi air squadrons and it put the armored vehicles out of action.

This turn was what the ubiquitous General Zhukov had been patiently expecting. He began closing in around Paulus's crack army, all fourteen divisions. When he had recaptured the airfields, the supply lines were cut, the munitions dwindled, and the Germans starved and froze. General Kurt Zeitzler reported, "Hitler would not give way. In vain I described to him conditions inside the so-called fortress: the despair of the starving soldiers, their loss of confidence in the Supreme Command, the wounded expiring for lack of proper attention while thousands froze to death. He remained impervious to arguments of this sort as to those others which I had advanced."*

At the beginning of February, defying Hitler's orders to die at their posts, Paulus raised the white flag. The surrender comprised only a remnant of the great Sixth Army that had smashed through Holland and Belgium and France in the victorious summer of 1940. One hundred forty-six thousand German dead were picked up on the field and burned. It was the most devastating defeat of World War II, the graveyard of Hitler's ambitions. Churchill paid the supreme compliment to the Russian fortitude that turned the tide of war. "It was the Russians," he wrote, "who tore the guts out of the German army." The legend of Hitler's sure instinct in military affairs, a legend that had mesmerized his generals, had now been effectively and permanently destroyed.

Hitler had also lost the battle to destroy the Russian technological capacity that supported the military. He had expected that when the Nazis overran the Soviet industrial areas production would be crippled and the economy would grind to a halt. But Stalin transferred whole factories from the west to the inner recesses of Siberia and Central Asia. Far from the battle lines, the older men and women, and even the children, labored to build artillery and tank plants in Omsk and Sverdlovsk and Magnitogorsk, and in scores of other newly opened centers. The cold was bitter, life was primitive, with makeshift housing and inadequate food. But civilian morale was high and there was a stoic heroism among those who gladly toiled that linked them in kinship with the soldiers.

By the winter of 1942 the tide had definitely turned, and Russia took the offensive on all fronts. The sieges and the blockades were broken everywhere. Kursk fell to the Russians, then Rostov and Kharkov and the great cities of the Donets Basin that had held such promise for the Reich. Kiev was retrieved, and the whole of the

---

* Shirer, *The Rise and Fall of the Third Reich,* p. 927.

Ukraine and the Crimea was liberated. Though the Nazi retreat was disciplined and did not repeat the bloody rout of Napoleon's Grand Army, the losses were demoralizing, half a million lives in ninety days. There was a simultaneous counteroffensive in the north and it cleared the invaders out of the Baltic states and Poland; by 1944, Germany itself lay open to assault.

There was rejoicing in Russia over its narrow escape from Nazi conquest and all that this entailed, but the rejoicing was muted because there was hardly a family that had not paid heavily in blood and treasure for the miracle of survival. A summary of the toll was later referred to by President Kennedy in his appeal for a test ban. "No nation in the history of battle," he said, "ever suffered more than the Russians did in the course of the Second World War." The figures lose all meaning. Twelve million Russians died in combat, in executions, and as prisoners. More than twenty million civilians died of starvation and disease, mainly in the sieges when the Russians preferred death to submission. When seven hundred died in Coventry in the Nazi blitz on England, the tragedy roused the world. In the air attack on Stalingrad of August 23, 1942, forty thousand were killed in just one day. There were many battles in which fifty thousand casualties were routine.

These sacrifices for survival explain the ruthlessness with which the Russians treated soldiers and civilians alike when the counteroffensives began, and when Germany itself was invaded. They could not react in western sporting terms, "good fight, old boy, jolly well done." The remembrance was too fresh of the devastations of Leningrad, Moscow, Stalingrad, Rostov, Sevastopol, Kiev, and of the thousands of towns and villages that had been torn apart, of carnage so monstrous that for weeks the corpses lay unburied. When the Russians began slogging their way back to the home areas that had been occupied, virtually every region turned up mass graves. Their shoes kicked up the ashes of the dead in the crematoria and the concentration camps where millions had perished. Everywhere the air was heavy with the smell of death. One of the poets of Leningrad, who had survived the blockade, wrote:

Let no one forget; let nothing be forgotten.*

The ordeal of the Russians also accounted for their horrified reaction when the suggestion was advanced to restore Germany to full military power, or to sanction the reunion of the two segments, East

* Salisbury, *The 900 Days*, p. 583.

and West Germany. They remembered how quickly Germany recovered from the unconditional surrender of World War I. They were fearful that the day would come when Germany would be permitted, despite all the past, to share nuclear responsibility. Any discussion that opened the possibility of Germans near the nuclear button sent the Russians into a frenzy. When such reactions were berated as irrational and overvindictive, the Russians grimly recalled the long years of the Nazi occupation and its toll of thirty million dead.

Late in 1944 the long-deferred retribution overtook Germany itself. The preparations for invasion had been in progress all through 1943 and 1944. Major fronts were opened in the Mediterranean and in the west, and Germany was assaulted on all sides by the Americans, the Free French, and now by the Russians. On a single day in October 1944, more bombs were dropped on the city of Duisburg-Hamborn in the Ruhr Valley than on London during the great blitz. The Rhine was crossed at Remagen and the converging armies of the Allies, from the west and the south and the east, advanced in avenging triumph everywhere. The British raced to Bremen and Hamburg, the French to Munich. The Russians and the Americans met at the Elbe as Germany sank into chaos.

The military disasters and Hitler's arbitrary dismissal of leading generals, who were the scapegoats for the defeats, now encouraged some of the dissident army chiefs to try again to eliminate the Führer. They had always been concerned that he was dragging the country to ruin, but his uncanny success in browbeating the Allies and winning bloodless victories had immobilized them. They had been ready for a major coup before Munich, but they were thwarted when Chamberlain sold out and thus vindicated Hitler's bravado. There were dozens of abortive conspiracies during 1943, but Hitler miraculously escaped them all. Now, after the debacle in Russia, and especially after Stalingrad, the ouster of Hitler had the highest priority. It was clear to everyone except Hitler that Germany could no longer win, and a shortened war would surely be welcomed by the Allies who were also paying heavily. With Hitler out of the way, the Allies might be induced to negotiate.

A small group of highly placed military leaders, headed by a young aristocrat, Count Schenk von Stauffenberg, and including General Erwin Rommel and General Ludwig Beck, made the final despairing attempt. They were not motivated by the callousness of Hitler's life-and-death edicts, nor by revulsion to his political and racial policies. They were responding to the expectation of his military failure.

They reasoned that if he were destroyed, perhaps Germany could come off with less than unconditional surrender. It was planned, then, to assassinate the Führer, and to sue for an armistice. On July 20, 1944, Von Stauffenberg flew to the German Staff Headquarters for a strategy meeting. He had a time bomb in his briefcase which he slid beneath the table where Hitler sat. But when the bomb exploded, the heavy oak table blunted the force of the explosion and, though many of the military chiefs were killed and injured, Hitler escaped with recoverable wounds. The simultaneous plan to seize Berlin also went awry and, within a few hours, Hitler was again in control. Von Stauffenberg and the key conspirators were hunted down, and about five thousand others who were accused of complicity were either executed or sent to living death in the concentration camps. Rommel and Beck, in deference to their earlier military contributions, were permitted to commit suicide, and so were a few others whom Hitler excoriated as "the blueblooded swine." The personal vengeance brought little comfort to the badly shaken Führer; the shambles of the conference hall appropriately symbolized the wreckage of all his grandiose hopes.

There were still hundreds of thousands of German deaths ahead and the ruin of many more cities. For, though the situation had become hopeless, Hitler would not permit negotiation. To the end he was to remain the executor of evil in history. Sick and clearly insane, buoyed up by drugs from a quack doctor, ever more reliant on astrology, he ordered the destruction of all industrial installations in Germany, and called upon his people to die with him in a final pagan *Götterdämmerung*. "How," he asked, "could life be tolerable for any loyal German after defeat?" He and Goebbels and a few close collaborators had now taken refuge in the bunkers below the Chancellery. In his last hours he continued to command phantom armies, issuing wild orders into the void for nonexistent offensives, shouting that he was being betrayed by those who would not join him in the collective suicide of all Germans. "He sat there," an orderly wrote of these last hours, "apathetic and distractedly brooding, indifferent to everything going on around him, tormented, lifeless, a man dying slowly and with difficulty who was bound indissolubly to his destiny and was now being strangled by it. Then I knew that this was the end."* Then, when the Russian troops were almost in the Chancellery, Hitler administered poison to his mistress,

* Cited in J. Fest, *The Face of the Third Reich*, p. 61.

whom he had married a few hours earlier, and shot himself. The bodies were cremated in the Chancellery garden as the Russian guns boomed nearby.

In 1935 Hitler had vowed that the ambitious plans he had for Berlin would make it unrecognizable within ten years. On the predicted anniversary in 1945, the Russians mounted posters with photographs of the ruins that Berlin had become, and they captioned them with the quotation from Hitler. On May 7 and 8 the German armies on all the fronts surrendered, and the war came to an end five years and eight months after Hitler's planes had first roared out on their way to his Thousand Year Reich. Only after a measure of security and order had been re-established in the broken and devastated countries of Europe was it fully realized how close Hitler had come to victory and to the eclipse of all of western civilization.

25

GANDHI AND THE
POWER OF NONVIOLENCE

INDIA'S POPULATION AT THE OUTSET OF WORLD WAR I WAS MORE THAN 250 million, and it was growing at a rate that was to bring it to 400 million by the end of World War II. Its land mass was two-thirds that of the United States. Yet it was held in subjection by a country one-twentieth of its size, governed by twelve hundred civil servants, only half of them British, and patrolled by about sixty thousand British troops. The colonial forces, all too often a special breed, snobbish and haughty, led a self-contained life of privilege and authority, and they kept the native population, even the best educated, in Jim Crow exclusion. One of the Viceroys, Lord Mayo, averred that Britain was "enjoined in the magnificent work of governing an inferior race." This went beyond even Rudyard Kipling's arrogance in referring to the British responsibility as "the white man's burden."

The war transformed Britain's position in the world, and it stimulated the need to rethink and liberalize its imperial relationships. But an entrenched ruling class is always difficult to budge and every attempt at major reform in India collided with tradition-worn excuses for caution. The rationale had been endlessly repeated: India was sunk in ignorance and poverty; it was fragmented into many races and religions with scores of languages and dialects; it was further degraded by an ironclad caste system that perpetuated the divisions; above all, there were dangerous animosities between the Hindu majority and the highly belligerent Moslem minority. In this impasse between a reluctant government and a continent impatient for self-determination, inspired leadership was imperative. At the historic juncture, the leadership was provided by a wizened wisp of a man, Mohandas Gandhi, who made use of a new weapon, nonviolent resistance, which ultimately immobilized all the might that Britain could bring to bear to sustain its rule.

To his own people he was the Mahatma, the venerated saint, to be followed unreservedly. Millions throughout the world who were fascinated by him shared Albert Einstein's view, "In our age of moral decay, he was the only statesman who represented that higher conception of human relations in the political sphere."[*] To others he was a shrewd politician who knew how to apply the externals of humility and asceticism to sway the emotions of his people so as to win his objectives. Gandhi himself always insisted he was not a saint groping his way in politics, but a politician trying desperately to be a saint. But there was no disagreement that he belonged with the immortals, certainly the most influential Asian since the Buddha. For three decades, everything that he said, everything that he did, had to be taken into account: his demands, his defiances, his fasts, his very pulse beats, above all, his unique application of the techniques of civil disobedience. None could fail to grasp the dramatic contrast, a shriveled little gnome, clad in a homespun loincloth, confronting the redoubtable British Empire and bending it to his will. He did not live to witness the triumph of emancipation. Just after he had brought Britain to its decisive concession, he was cut down by a Hindu fanatic. But he had led his people through the wilderness, and had brought them to the threshold of fulfillment. Then his trusted disciple, Nehru, inherited the mantle of leadership.

Gandhi was born of the mercantile caste in 1869. His grandfather, his father, and his uncle all held positions as Prime Minister in their region, but this had little more significance than being the head of a clan. Nevertheless, the privileged family status gave young Gandhi advantages in education and in living standards that were not enjoyed by many others. In 1899, at nineteen, after his father's death, he was sent off to England to study law. The photographs of him at this stage show him to be not very prepossessing in his ill-fitting English clothes, his high stiff collar, the hair slicked back, a beaklike nose, large, batlike ears, a pendulous underlip. He was painfully shy and lonely, oversensitive, handicapped in social life by his vegetarian and

[*] Einstein, *Einstein on Peace,* p. 468.

teetotaler resolves. He tried hard to imitate the English gentleman, and he might have become the conventional English-trained Hindu, content to lead a comparatively privileged life among his own people. But soon after his return to India from his studies, his law firm offered him an assignment in Natal, in South Africa.

Here he was aroused by the disabilities imposed on the Indian immigrants, who numbered about 100,000. They had come as indentured workers on three- and five-year contracts and had stayed on. The dominant group were the fundamentalist Dutch Boers, hostile to the governing British, quite prejudiced against other races. The Indians were as shabbily treated by them as were the blacks. They were industrious and intelligent and offered serious competition for the poor whites who hated their diligence and ambition. One of the social workers told Gandhi that it was not the vices of the Indians that were feared; it was their virtues. Gandhi took up many of their cases, and then he learned how shamelessly discriminatory South African justice could be. He suffered personal humiliation when he tried to ride the trains or register in hotels. Once, when he refused, for reasons of Hindu tradition, to remove his turban in court, the magistrate had him thrown out as a "coolie barrister." When he realized what a long, uphill battle lay ahead of him to win rights for his countrymen, he returned to India to bring back the family he had left behind when he thought his assignment in South Africa was to be a limited one. But when his ship docked at Durban upon his return, since he had been pegged as a troublemaker, rowdies crowded around him and he was showered with stones, brickbats, and rotten eggs. Gandhi was saved from lynching only by the intercession of the wife of the superintendent of police. He refused to prosecute, saying that his assailants were the victims of a wicked system of education.

He began organizing the Indians for more effective political leverage, convinced that only through united action could they win stubbornly resisted concessions. He also labored among them, urging them to prepare themselves for the responsibilities that they sought by measuring up to the highest standards of citizenship. In the Boer War, which pitted the small Dutch-settled states against the British, Gandhi and the Indians fought loyally on the British side, an understandable decision in the light of the policy of discrimination and repression that had been followed by the Boers. Gandhi organized a medical corps; he served in hospital and nursing capacities, and he demonstrated exemplary courage under fire. After the Boer War, he renewed the effort to eliminate the restrictions that frustrated his people and other disenfranchised groups. He was frequently jailed and it was during these prison periods that the techniques of non-violence and civil disobedience were perfected. They were later to be successfully employed in the battles against Britain to win independence for India.

Gandhi was very much influenced by the work of western writers, above all by Henry Thoreau, whose volume on civil disobedience was virtually a textbook on the nonviolent defiance of governments and their institutions. Gandhi always kept before him Thoreau's injunction that "a minority is powerless while it conforms to the majority, but it is irresistible when it clogs by its own weight." Gandhi added features that came out of his own Hindu tradition, the positive emphasis on the power of spiritual love, and the discipline over the body—its passions, its appetites, and its fears. He emphasized nonresistance, but not as a passive gesture; rather, as a nonviolent defiance, potent because it was unyielding. He called it "Satyagraha," soul force, truth force. It did not mean helping the evildoer to continue his wrong or tolerating it by passive acquiescence. On the contrary, it required resistance to the wrongdoer by disassociating oneself from him.

Gandhi used the weapon of nonviolence resourcefully as he took up critical issues when they came into focus. There was a special registration of all Asians that included fingerprinting. There were discriminatory poll taxes. There was the practice of indentured labor which exploited thousands of immigrants. There were humiliating restrictions that confined Indians to ghettoes, closed public footpaths to them. Gandhi introduced the Indians to Satyagraha, demonstrating how noncooperation and civil disobedience, when practiced on a mass scale, could bend even the most determined government. In time there were twenty thousand violators in jail, including Gandhi. In the end the South African government was compelled to yield, and the restricted and humiliating acts were all revoked. Gandhi sent the sandals that he had woven in prison to General Jan Smuts, the sympathetic Governor who had most reluctantly administered the discriminatory laws. Years later, on Gandhi's seventieth birthday, Smuts returned the sandals to him, noting that he had used them but never felt that he could appropriately stand in the shoes of one of the noblest men he had ever known.

Gandhi, now forty-six, his temporary mission in South Africa having stretched to twenty years, yearned to go back to India. He returned in 1915, ready for the historic tasks for which all that had gone before was an apprenticeship. At this stage he was still a moderate, confident that there would be enough good sense in Britain to make changes that would keep India within the framework of the British Commonwealth. The world was at war, and once again Gandhi and most of his people loyally supported the Allied cause. Nearly nine hundred thousand volunteered for the fighting, and generous contributions were made for the war effort. Gandhi, as in South Africa, volunteered for work in the medical units. He organized an ambulance corps and, to fortify his self-discipline, insisted upon the most menial tasks.

He also used the war period to challenge some of the social evils that plagued his own people. Untouchability, for example, was a festering problem, condemning to hopeless degradation millions of families in a pariah caste so low that their touch, even their shadow, was defiling and required ritual purification. Gandhi renamed the untouchables the *"Harijans,"* the children of God, and set an example by bringing some of them into his own home and sharing their labors with them. He attacked the callousness of wealthy families who did all too little to improve the plight of the poverty-stricken, living in filth and disease and illiteracy. In 1916, in an address at the opening of a Hindu university in Benares, he berated the bejeweled in his audience for their addiction to luxury in the midst of wretchedness. He was pulled off the platform before he could finish his address, but the echoes of what he said and what he had done gave him increased moral stature in India and in England too, where he could count on the understanding and the goodwill of the liberal groups.

Because of the loyal cooperation of the Indians in the war effort, the British cabinet made the promise that, once the hostilities were over, there would be a re-evaluation of government procedures and that India would be dealt with justly. In 1919, the Government of India Act was passed, with the hope that it would open the road to conciliation. It called for a dyarchy, dual control, native legislatures to have jurisdiction over local affairs and the British to regulate defense and foreign policy. But the National Congress Party, under Gandhi's leadership, deeply disappointed that the act fell so far short of genuine dominion status, flatly rejected the overture. The spreading unrest, which took the form of nonviolent civil disobedience, brought punitive action from the imperial government. The Rowlett Act of 1920, aimed at the suppression of sedition, suspended free speech and press and assembly, and a major confrontation had been reached.

Then came the irretrievable tragedy of Amritsar, in April 1920; it proved to be the turning point in the struggle for Indian self-determination. The crowds that had made the pilgrimage to this holy city, the capital of the Punjab, reacted with passionate resentment when they learned that two of the Congress Party leaders had been ordered deported. In their protests, despite Gandhi's appeals, some of the demonstrators got out of hand; several English bankers were killed and a schoolteacher assaulted. The commanding general, Reginald Dyer, ordered the cancellation of all public meetings and, when one rally was held anyway, either in defiance or because the Dyer order had not reached the organizers in time, his soldiers, at his command, fired into the defenseless crowd of twenty thousand. More than 375 were killed, and 1,200 were wounded. Dyer did not permit any help to come to the injured, and he further ordered that all Indians who had to pass the street where the assault had taken place must crawl on all fours, and they were beaten on the way. His logic was that this would teach the recalcitrants, indeed all the inhabitants of the Punjab, a lesson that they would not forget. Dyer was relieved of his command, but the investigating committee condemned him only "for his grave error of judgment and his honest but mistaken conception of duty." He received a vote of confidence from the House of Lords, and he was congratulated for "the courage of his firmness." An appreciative tribute fund of £20,000 was raised to honor him and it was presented with the gift of a sword.

The mood of India was transformed by the episode. The Indian poet, Sir Rabindranath Tagore, who had won the Nobel Prize for literature and had been knighted by the King, turned back his British honor. "I, for my part," he wrote to the Viceroy, "wish to stand shorn of all special distinctions by the side of those of my countrymen who, for their so-called insignificance, are liable to suffer degradation not fit for human beings." He spoke for all of India, and for many in England, too, when he added: "For Europe this is a great moral defeat. Even though Asia is still physically weak, and unable to protect herself from aggression, nevertheless, she can afford to look down on Europe, where before she looked up."*

* K. R. Kripalani, *Gandhi, Tagore and Nehru* (Bombay: Hind Kitabs, 1947), p. 17.

Gandhi, denouncing the Amritsar massacre as satanic, now turned from moderation to repudiation, and he launched an all-out campaign for noncooperation and nonviolent protest. He had seen the ugly face of imperial barbarism, he said, and this led him to conclude: "I prefer Indian chaos to British order." He called for a total boycott of all western products. He urged his people to weave their own cotton, and he set the example by working daily at a spinning wheel to dramatize India's aspirations to win economic as well as political independence. The boycott of cotton was not merely a symbolic gesture. The cotton industry represented one-fifth of all British exports, an average of 140 million pounds; and a substantial portion of these exports was usually absorbed by India.

Gandhi's speeches and articles became increasingly defiant, and when he made the flat statement that "sedition was now the credo of the Congress," the government could not condone it. He was obviously courting arrest; in 1922 his wish was fulfilled, when a six-year prison term was imposed. In receiving the sentence he made clear that those who broke the law had the duty to accept the consequences, otherwise there was no sacrifice involved. He said to the court that noncooperation with evil implied voluntary submission to the punishment. "I am here, therefore, to invite, and submit cheerfully, to the highest penalty that can be inflicted upon me for what in law is a deliberate crime. . . ." He would have had little sympathy for those who later modeled themselves on his principle of disobedience but then cried out, "Foul," and demanded amnesty. The judge, in sentencing Gandhi, made public his bewildered admiration. "Even those who differ with you in politics," he said, "look upon you as a man of high ideals and of noble and even saintly life."* Behind the prison walls, Gandhi's influence was even more potent. He was out of reach of his jailors because he soared so far above them. Here was the most unpredictable rebel in British history, expressing love for his captors, joyously spinning at his wheel four hours a day, claiming to be happy as a bird, commanding the loyalty of millions, and directing their defiance.

No Colonel Blimp could cope with such frustrating paradoxes, but neither could a Lloyd George. Within two years, Gandhi was again released. But now he found that the divisions between Hindu and Moslem had become so threatening that he had to devote the next years to the task of healing the schisms within, softening suspicions

* Louis Fischer, *The Life of Mahatma Gandhi* (New York: Harper & Row, 1950), pp. 202–4.

and animosities. "It seems as if God had been dethroned," he wrote. "Let us reinstate him in our hearts." At one point he went on a fast for three weeks and, as fear for his life spread, millions of weeping Hindus and Moslems pledged themselves to seek solutions through peace.

In these years Gandhi was everywhere, visiting the provinces, teaching, praying, fasting, spinning. When he came to a village and found that the leaders had separated his audience by caste, he always sat with the untouchables. His likeness hung in peasant huts, even when there was nothing else there but a few pieces of decrepit furniture and some primitive cooking utensils. At the fairs, his picture was sold along with those that illustrated the legend of Krishna. His people hung on the words and actions of a spindly barebone who lived on fruit and nuts, who moved confidently and fearlessly through huge mobs, his thin, quavering voice more powerful than armies and imperial edicts.

Since Britain still could not come to a decision on the principle of autonomy, the Congress took the final step of defiance. On January 26, 1930, it proclaimed the Declaration of Independence. To signalize the break with Britain, Gandhi chose a method that could be instantly understood by even the simplest and most illiterate peasant. He planned to march to the sea to challenge the salt monopoly of the Empire. Salt, used by everybody, could only be manufactured and traded by the government. Gandhi centered his attack on the monopoly and on the tax, and he made it the prime example of imperial exploitation. On March 12, seventy-eight members of his entourage joined him in the march to the sea, 240 miles away, traveling about ten miles a day, and the world watched and listened during the twenty-four days of the march. There were stops at every village, talks with the peasants, patient lessons in the duties and responsibilities of self-government. There were gentle but firm admonitions to correct or to give up the abuses that shamed India—child marriage, untouchability, drugs. The roads were sprinkled by those who revered him so that no dust would trouble him as he walked. Flowers were strewn before him. There was a horse in the march for Gandhi's service if he grew weary but it was not used; Gandhi seemed to grow stronger with every passing mile. On April 5, the group reached the seaside, and there Gandhi filled a jug with sea water, heated it, and manufactured a pinch of salt. The action was to dramatize the repudiation of British control over the destinies of India.

At once the whole continent ignited. Every village, boldly and illegally manufacturing salt, became part of the fellowship of challenge. The British resorted to the usual routine of arrests, thousands of them, tens of thousands. Soon the jails were overflowing as more than a hundred thousand were interned. Still the defiance went on. Then came mass disruption. Hundreds of young and old lay before cars and buses to prevent them from passing and to paralyze traffic. They lay on railroad tracks to stop the operation of the trains. There were demonstrations, peaceful but demoralizing, in every city and hamlet. Goaded to violence, the police waded into the crowds, using their clubs and the butts of guns, but the masses responded impassively to the cudgeling, barely an arm raised even to ward off the blows. An eyewitness correspondent described a typical demonstration: "Those struck fell sprawling, unconscious or writhing with fractured skulls or broken shoulders . . . the survivors, without breaking ranks, silently and doggedly marching on, until struck down. . . . Hour after hour, stretcher bearers carrying back a stream of inert, bleeding bodies."* Almost literally a whole nation was following the Indian practice of *dharma*. It was traditional for a wronged person to take his place on the threshold of his oppressor and to stay there, often in a demonstrative fast, until there was redress. Gandhi was sitting *dharma* on the threshold of the British Empire, relying on shame and weariness to compel concession. And after months of sacrificial nonviolent disobedience, Gandhi and his people prevailed. A halt was called to the arrests, and Gandhi was invited to London to sit with the chiefs of the Empire to explore solutions for the impasse. "I always get my best bargains," he said with his toothless smile, "behind prison bars." Resistance by nonviolence could succeed against the British because they were basically a humane people. It could never have been effective against totalitarian governments that would ride over the protestors or permit them to fast to death. Gandhi admitted this. "I fasted to reform those who loved me. You cannot fast against a tyrant."

He decided to come several months in advance of the Round Table Conference to build up a sympathetic public opinion. He embarked in August 1931, with his own goat, which he milked for his abstemious meals. Upon arrival in London, he insisted on staying in the slums. He found a ready response to Indian independence among the common folk, who were disenchanted with British imperial practices. He was enthusiastically received at Oxford and at Cambridge, and then

* Fischer, *The Life of Mahatma Gandhi*, p. 273–4.

he was welcomed to the Round Table Conference by the King himself. Surrounded by all the pomp of imperial negotiations, Gandhi made the most of the historic occasion. He came in a simple loincloth and homespun shawl. When he was asked about the appropriateness of his dress, he remarked that the King would be wearing enough clothes for them both.

The Conservative opposition were aghast at such regal treatment for a rebel who threatened the integrity of the Empire. Winston Churchill was almost apoplectic in this period of frustrated imperialism. In an address, which he lived to regret, he denounced "the nauseating and humiliating spectacle of this one time Inner Temple lawyer, now a seditious fakir, striding half naked up the steps of the Viceroy's Palace, there to negotiate and to parley on equal terms, with the representatives of the King-Emperor."*

Despite the hearty reception and the cordial amenities, the Round Table was not productive. An Indian ascetic offered the advice to the British, "If you go, you will remain, but if you remain, you will go!" But the Establishment was not ready to yield independence without safeguards. There was still concern over security and over the protection of the British investments that had been poured into India for more than a century. It was Ireland all over again. Gandhi returned heartsick with disappointment to continue the dreary round of protest and demonstration.

Because of the rebuff in England, he now had to face formidable challenges to his own long-range policies. There was a growing opposition party inside India that had lost patience with the discipline of nonviolence, when all that could be dragged out of Britain was a series of postdated checks. To Gandhi, nonviolence was a sacred religious principle; to many of his colleagues and followers it was a tactic to be used, and if unsuccessful, to be discarded. They insisted upon a vigorous, militant approach, with violence where necessary. What else, they cried, would the imperialists understand and respect?

The next years were spent by the aging Mahatma in long, dangerous fasts to do penance for the intransigent groups. These included millions of Moslems who were fearful that a united India with a Hindu majority would threaten their welfare. They clamored for partition, and for their own independence. It was clear that problems so tangled in history and in racial and religious traditions could not be solved with simple formulae and spirited declarations.

* *Ibid.*, p. 277.

Fifteen years were to pass before independence came to India, and it was to be accompanied by the most destructive of civil wars. By then Gandhi had been martyred. The man of peace was to die by violence. In 1948 a Hindu firebrand, the editor of an extremist newspaper who had denounced Gandhi for his appeasement of the Moslems, burst through the crowd as Gandhi emerged from a prayer session and, after receiving his blessing, assassinated him.

Gandhi had not been able to resolve the centuries-old social and economic problems of the continent. He was not able to prevent the Hindu-Moslem civil war. But he did achieve an enduring dignity for his people. He had the capacity of eliciting nobility from the humblest of men, raising them often far beyond their commonplace routine. He forged a new technique to meet dispute and tension, the technique of dynamic nonviolence that proved potent enough to challenge the authority of King and Empire and all their military panoply. He had said: "They have weapons and we have not. Our only assurance of beating them is to keep it on the plane where we have the weapons and they have not." He became the inspiration in all parts of the world for the rebellion of the disadvantaged. He offered them all a model to help them overcome, not by force, which would be ineffectual, but by the power which came without weapons.

26

THE GENESIS
OF THE COLD WAR

IN MARCH 1946, AT WESTMINSTER COLLEGE IN FULTON, MISSOURI, IN
the presence of President Truman, Winston Churchill referred to
the Iron Curtain that now had fallen across the continent, from
Stettin in the Baltic to Trieste in the Adriatic, to divide the former
Allies, Russia, Britain, and the United States. It was a memorable
phrase: it emphasized more than separation, more than temporary
misunderstanding. The term was "Iron Curtain," solid, massive,
impenetrable, a precise symbol for the Cold War that was to dominate the diplomacy of the next generation, and that was to turn a
grand alliance into an international snake pit.

During the war Russia and the West had formed a mighty coalition, wielding the most awesome power in all history. Such power,
applied to a shattered world that had barely survived, could become
the guarantee for enduring peace and security. The peoples of the
coalition had responded to the fighting forces and their leaders with
confidence and admiration. In the mood of the period, American
hearts hung on Russia's gallant struggle to contain the Nazis. Moscow, Leningrad, Rostov, Kursk, Stalingrad, the defense bastions
behind which Russia held with a tenacity that defied death, were also
the defense lines of the West. The Russian missions that came to the
United States were feted with gratitude, despite popular misgivings
about communism. Timoshenko and Voroshilov and Zhukov were
American heroes, along with Eisenhower and Bradley and Marshall
and Patton. The American Ambassador to Russia, Joseph Davies,

[299]

wrote an extravagant tribute to Stalin and declared that it would be supreme folly to question his good faith.

But once the Axis powers had been defeated and their menace eliminated, the coalition fell apart. Cooperation turned to suspicion, partnership turned to hostility. In the controlled press of Russia, President Truman was denounced as the chained dog of the Wall Street monopolists, Walter Lippmann became a malicious warmonger, and the trade union leader, Walter Reuther, was vilified as a captive of the predatory imperialists. Churchill, as a spokesman for the West, wrote scathingly of the Allied aid that had gone to the Soviet Union and was now repaid with ingratitude and insult. He said: "The Soviet Government had the impression that they were conferring a great favor on us by fighting in their own country for their own lives. The more they fought, the heavier our debt became. This was not a balanced view. . . . Almost invariably I bore hectoring and reproaches with a patient shrug; for sufferance is the badge of all who have to deal with the Kremlin."

Where did the rupture originate? How could the rapport of an alliance, sealed with blood, become the alienation of the Cold War? In truth, there was no single point of break. For there never had been any genuine coalition built on mutual confidence. Ambassador George Kennan said that there had been "only simultaneous military effort," and often it was not so simultaneous. Even when the deepest crisis called urgently for common action, there was distrust and fear. Each side was almost as wary of the other as of the enemy. To the democratic statesmen of the West, communism was not an economic system that had purely internal impact. It was a conspiratorial apparatus whose overriding aim was to disrupt the social structures of all the other countries. It acted as a bacillus, potent in penetration, debilitating, corrosive.

The Russians distrusted the West with equal intensity, certain that it was determined to abort the revolution. The memory was ineradicable of the assaults on the Soviet Union in the years of its birth when Britain, France, Japan, and even the United States had encouraged counterrevolutionary forces and supported them with invasion. The Russians could not forget the humiliating years when the Soviet Union was treated as a pariah, excluded for long from the League of Nations. In their view, western diplomacy had consistently aimed at turning Hitler and the Nazis eastward against Russia.

These suspicions had festered for twenty-five years. Russia and the West, on the very eve of the war, had been in opposite camps, Russia actually in alliance with the Nazis through the pact that opened the way for Hitler to attempt the conquest of Europe. When Hitler became the common enemy, Churchill was frank to say that the newly forged entente was just an arrangement of mutual convenience. He confessed, "I would have made a pact with the Devil himself to defeat Hitler." It was significant that Allied pilots were given orders that, on their bombing missions, if there were forced landings on Russian soil, they were instantly to destroy all documents and any special technical devices. In his Memoirs Churchill noted, "We had always hated their wicked regime, and, till the German flail beat upon them, they would have watched us being swept out of existence with indifference and gleefully divided with Hitler our Empire in the East." Through an apocryphal story he illustrated how bizarre the alliance seemed to be after years of suspicion and hostility. He told of a Royal British Marine who was being shown the sights of Moscow by one of the Intourist guides. "This," said the Russian, "is the Eden Hotel, formerly the Ribbentrop Hotel. Here is Churchill Street, formerly Hitler Street. And here is Beaverbrook Station, formerly Göring Station. By the way, comrade, will you have a cigarette?" The Marine took the cigarette and then he replied, "Thank you, comrade, formerly bastard."*

With this underlying mistrust, one can better understand the maneuvering that went on as the strategy of counterattack was planned against the enemy. From the moment when Hitler hurled his legions against Russia in the summer of 1941, Stalin began to press for the opening of a second front in France, with a major thrust across the Channel. The second front would release the almost unendurable pressure in Russia by drawing off as many as forty Nazi divisions. The timely diversion would reduce the dangerous toll of Russian casualties; it could mean the difference between survival or collapse. But Churchill had no intention of immediately opening a second front in France, if at all. He knew that, unless there were thorough preparation, he would court disaster. He remembered the fiasco of 1939–40 when the British forces had been defeated in France. But quite apart from the long preparation time required, Churchill much preferred an assault against the enemy through the Balkans and Italy, the soft underbelly of Europe. To him this was the vulnerable area where the war could be quickly and decisively won. Undoubtedly too he wanted to be sure that, after the Nazi defeat, the

* *Memoirs of the Second World War,* p. 485.

Allied forces were in occupation of southern Europe to prevent a Communist takeover if the Russians were free to move into the vacuum. Churchill, however, did not categorically deny the Russian demand. He could never be sure of any Stalin commitment. A flat refusal by Churchill might again send Stalin into negotiations with Hitler for some kind of unilateral compromise. This mutual fear of desertion by each side plagued the coalition through the war and after.

Hence Churchill temporized, replying to Stalin with eloquent vagueness. He noted that a second front in France in 1942, too hastily prepared, would be costly to the point of suicide, and he reminded Stalin of Dunkirk. But he promised to relieve the pressure on Russia as quickly as the military operation had the assurance of success. Stalin refused to be sidetracked. He countered that wars could not be won without severe losses, that the Russians had paid in blood and land with sacrifice that had no precedent, with millions of casualties, tens of thousands of square miles. When the Allies gave such low priority to the attack on the Nazis in the West, they were encouraging Hitler to transfer the bulk of his military strength to the East. Implicit in Stalin's angry indictment was the suspicion that the long-range strategy of the West was aimed to prolong the bleeding of Russia to the point of exhaustion. Churchill maintained his diplomatic aplomb and couched his replies in courteous ambiguities. In his relations with the Russians he was determined to do unto others as others would do unto him.

By November 1942, the Nazis had been turned back at Stalingrad in one of the costliest battles in history. Stalin was eager to mount an offensive that would clear the enemy out of Russian territory. He kept up the pressure for a definite second front date, at least in 1943. When Churchill still remained evasive, Stalin made his wrath public even though he realized the comfort that the airing of disagreement would assuredly offer to the enemy. One of his addresses in November 1942 bristled and crackled with recrimination. His angry cables contained threats that were not too veiled. "I must give you a most emphatic warning, in the interest of our common cause, of the grave danger with which further delay in opening a second front in France is fraught." But Churchill continued to file the cables, to smoke his long cigars, and then he offered the same nebulous assurances.

The delays continued month by month, conference by conference, beyond 1942, then beyond 1943, into the spring and summer of 1944. D-Day did not actually come until June of 1944, when the Nazis had already been driven out of Russia and were in full retreat. By then the rupture was so complete that the Russian ambassadors had been recalled from London and Washington. Stalin never forgot that many hundreds of thousands of Russians had paid with their lives by what he considered unconscionable temporizing.

Meantime, Stalin too could play the exasperating game of diplomatic poker. He had power objectives to which he held with even more tenacity than Churchill. The ring of Baltic and Balkan states around Russia had to be in the Soviet orbit, or at least locked into guaranteed friendship. Russia had been victimized for ten centuries by invasions through neighboring states, especially Poland. Twice within living memory Russia had been nearly destroyed when Poland was used as the springboard for German aggression. Stalin vowed that the doors to Russia from the west and the south would never again become entrance points.

But Britain and the United States were committed to an independent Poland; Britain had gone to war to honor its pledge to defend Poland against Nazi aggression. In the United States, Roosevelt had millions of Polish Americans whose spokesmen flooded him with appeals for the reconstitution of their Motherland. Both Churchill and Roosevelt refused to accept Stalin's logic that Russian security could be achieved only by converting Poland into a Soviet satellite. The vocabulary of exchange became quite undiplomatic as they sought in vain to elicit a pledge of Polish restoration and independence.

Within the coalition each side had valid interests, rooted in national security, that transcended doctrinaire morality. At every summit conference there were protracted negotiations, but Stalin would never budge from his immovable position, that however Poland emerged from the war, and whatever its boundaries, it had to be a reliable neighbor, and the only certain way to achieve this was for the Soviet Union to control Polish national policy. How could Churchill and Roosevelt believe, he asked, that he would accept the return of the Polish government-in-exile, rabidly anti-Communist, whose policy would inevitably be hostile to every Russian interest? He therefore sponsored a rival provisional government, centered in Lublin, made up of Communists and their sympathizers. The impasse was complete and thus, while Churchill and Roosevelt fenced with Stalin over a second front, Stalin parried with Churchill and Roosevelt over the future of Poland.

Suddenly, in the midst of all the maneuvering, came a sensational disclosure by the Nazis that was to add new hostility to already tense relationships. In 1939, at the outbreak of the war, Russia had invaded eastern Poland and had captured 191,000 soldiers, and these included many thousands of Polish officers. They were sent off to several large prison camps and their families lost all communication with them. When Russia and the West became allies, the Polish government-in-exile in London demanded that the officers be released, on the assumption that they were still in Russian custody. Stalin turned all inquiries aside. In April 1943, Goebbels announced that the Wehrmacht, scouting the Smolensk area that was now in Nazi hands, had come upon a mass of graves in the nearby Katyn Forest and had discovered the corpses of thousands of Polish officers. He declared that they had all been murdered several years before by the Russians, and he called upon the international Red Cross to investigate. The London Polish government-in-exile already had its fill of Russian evasions about the fate of the deportees and the prisoners. When the announcement was made that the bodies of thousands of the captured officers had been found, the Polish leaders associated themselves with the demand for the Red Cross investigation. Stalin was outraged by the Nazi charge, but even more that the Poles should have given credence to it. He at once broke off all relations with the Polish government-in-exile in London, to which he had always contemptuously referred as "a handful of Polish emigrants in London."

Goebbels, eager now to exploit his propaganda victory and to widen the schism in the Allied ranks, called in a group, headed by a respected Swiss professor, to visit the grave sites and examine the exhumed bodies. They testified that the mass murder of forty-five hundred officers, all shot in the back of the head, had indeed been committed several years before by the Russians. Later in the year, in the Russian counteroffensive, the territory was recovered, and Stalin appointed his own commission. The bodies were again exhumed and, in January 1944, this commission reported that the officers had fallen into Nazi hands and had been massacred by them. Later still, in the autumn, in the testimony of anti-Stalin Russians, the crime was attributed to Stalin's secret police. So the controversy over the Katyn Forest massacre raged, further envenoming the resentments over the delays in opening the second front and over the guarantees for an independent Poland.

Friction and tension were fed by other disagreements. In the summer of 1944, the Russians in their triumphant resurgence pushed into Poland, crossed the Vistula, and were poised to take Warsaw. The Polish underground forces were thirty to forty thousand strong, with reserves of food and arms for about ten days. They had waited for the opportune moment to rise from within, for the attack on the Nazis who occupied their capital. At the end of July, the Russians had reached the outskirts of Warsaw and the air force had begun pounding the enemy strongpoints. Responding to the news of the advances that was coming from the Moscow radio, the Polish underground emerged and the great liberation action began. At once the Russian air activity stopped and the advancing ground forces came to a halt. The Polish resistance leaders realized to their horror that they had been trapped, for the occupying Nazi garrisons heavily outnumbered them and could easily pulverize them unless there was coordinated help from the Russians.

Churchill and Roosevelt appealed personally to Stalin to continue the attack on the Nazis or the underground would be annihilated. Stalin now borrowed some of Churchill's dilatory vocabulary and he blandly declared that the Nazi strength within the capital was much too powerful to challenge until the Russian forces had been consolidated. Of course, he added, this was likely to take a long time. Churchill volunteered to send over British planes, to parachute supplies to the beleaguered Poles. But since the aircraft could not make the round trip without refueling, it would be necessary to land within the Russian-held airstrips. Stalin flatly refused to permit this, noting that the Polish underground had only themselves to blame for rising prematurely and without coordinating their effort with the Russian forces.

The hopeless struggle against annihilation went on inside the city for two anguished months. Street by street the Poles were mopped up. They went down into the sewers and were systematically flushed out there. About two hundred thousand Polish civilians were killed along with the élite of the Polish resistance veterans. The last radio broadcast from dying Warsaw was picked up in London: "This is the stark truth. We were treated worse than the enemy, worse than Italy, Rumania, Finland. May God pass judgment on the terrible injustice suffered by the Polish nation." Only when the Nazis had completed their bloody liquidation did the Russians resume their attacks. They routed the Nazis out of Warsaw and immediately installed the Lublin group as the recognized government of Poland. There would now be no leadership left to challenge the complete Soviet dominance in Poland.

The anger that flared in Britain and the United States matched the anger of the Russians as the second front preparations moved at their frustrating tortoise pace. Churchill was at the point of recommending the end of Lend-Lease to Russia from the United States. But, of course, he thought better of it. How could he permit a wedge to be driven between the Allies when they were so close to victory?

As the war ground to an end in Europe in the spring of 1945, with the Nazis everywhere in retreat, there was a final summit conference at Yalta in the Crimea. Seven of the eight sessions were concerned with Poland and its future. The discussions were held in a climate that barely concealed the accumulated hostility. Russia was now in military control of nearly all the areas Stalin had coveted, and he could afford to remain firm on what was already a fait accompli. There were long days and nights of argument. Roosevelt applied all the charm that was still left to a dying gladiator. Churchill knew that charm would be wasted in dealing with the Russian bear and he relied on growl and barter. Stalin simply lived up to the steel in his name.

The agreements that finally emerged gave Russia all the Polish territory that had been taken in the Hitler-Stalin pact. But Poland was to be compensated through the absorption of German territory to the west. The nucleus of the provisional government of the new Poland would be the men of Lublin. But there was a pledge by Stalin of early elections, free, unfettered, with universal suffrage and secret ballot. When Stalin made the promises he knew very well that they would not be kept, and Churchill and Roosevelt were too realistic to believe that the old buccaneer would honor them.* Their hope was that, if the defensive expansion were permitted in eastern Europe, the farther advance of Soviet power westward and to the south would be contained.

The Yalta summit conference ended with many tongue-in-cheek protestations of understanding and friendship. Stalin offered the vodka toast to the "firmness of our three-power alliance. May it be strong and stable." Churchill reported to Parliament: "Somber indeed would be the fortunes of mankind if some awful schism arose between the Western democracies and the Russian Soviet Union." Roosevelt put on an impressive act of ebullience as he told Congress that Yalta "spells the end of the system of unilateral action, exclusive alliances and spheres of influence, and balances of power and all the

---

* "I want this election in Poland to be the first one beyond question," Roosevelt said to Stalin. "It should be like Caesar's wife. I did not know her but they say she was pure." "They said that about her," Stalin remarked, "but in fact she had her sins." Cited in Burns, *Roosevelt: The Soldier of Freedom*, p. 573.

other expedients which have been tried for centuries and have always failed."

How much the mutual assurances meant was quickly demonstrated when Stalin invited Polish delegates from the London-endorsed government-in-exile to journey to Moscow to discuss the procedures for his promised election. Sixteen delegates arrived under a guarantee of safe conduct. Not a single one ever returned. When inquiries were made Stalin kept postponing his reply. Later it was learned that the emissaries had been arrested and that they were to be tried for "treasonable" activities. On June 18, a whole series of abject confessions of guilt was made public, and all but three were sentenced to long prison terms. This was the judicial liquidation of the remaining Polish national leadership. The rank and file were already dead in the ruins of Warsaw.

These were but a few examples of the strains and conflicts that taxed the coalition from its very inception. There were others, many others, and they turned planning into nightmares and raised questions about who were the enemies and who the allies. The issues included the disposition of the Balkan and the Baltic states, the Greek and Yugoslavian civil wars, the fate of defeated Germany and Japan, reparations, Lend-Lease, the trials of the war criminals, and a hundred other explosive disputes, all with burning fuses attached.

Even the victorious end of the war brought its full cargo of fear and mistrust. The Nazi generals clung to the hope that they could surrender to the British and the Americans, and at all costs avoid falling into Russian hands. General Karl Wolff, in charge of a German sector in Italy, sent intermediaries to the American command, expressing his willingness to open negotiations in Switzerland. He was told that preliminary discussions could be arranged but that the only terms acceptable would be unconditional surrender, and that all three Allies, British, American, and French, would have to be involved. There was no reference to Soviet participation. The Russian intelligence reported the secret negotiations to the Kremlin. At once an acidly worded message came from Molotov, who wrote, "In Berne for two weeks, behind the backs of the Soviet Union which is bearing the brunt of the war against Germany, negotiations have been going on between representatives of the German military and representatives of the English and the American commands."* The imputation of bad faith was vigorously denied. The Allies explained

---

* Churchill, *Memoirs of the Second World War*, p. 943.

that these were preliminary explorations intended merely to test sincerity and authority, and that the substantive talks would of course include the Russians. Molotov was not mollified. He continued to rage and came close to labeling the Allied leaders and their generals liars and double-dealers. The tension between Russia and the West had reached such a point that Roosevelt sent one of the most bristling cables of the war to Stalin:

It is astonishing that a belief seems to have reached the Soviet Government that I have entered into an agreement with the enemy without first obtaining your full agreement. I would say this: It would be one of the great tragedies of history if at the very moment of the victory now within our grasp, such distrust, such lack of faith, should prejudice the entire undertaking, after our colossal losses of life, and material and treasure. Frankly, I cannot avoid a feeling of bitter resentment towards your informants, whoever they are, for such vile misrepresentations of my actions or those of my trusted subordinates.*

A week later Roosevelt was dead.

It was of course the hope of an irretrievable rupture in the Allied coalition that kept the Nazis fighting with such maniacal perversity, far beyond the slightest military prospects. I was a war commentator in those days for the Chicago outlet for CBS, and in the broadcast of April 21, 1945, a little more than a week after Roosevelt's death, I noted:

Increasingly, as the end has come in sight, men have wondered whether the Nazis are romantic lunatics for allowing their country to be burnt and seared and cut to pieces. Every opportunity for recovery when peace comes back to the land is thereby lost. But the Nazis are not romantic lunatics; they are realists. They know that coalitions do not have the consistency of a monolith; they have all the brittleness of a makeshift. With the passage of time, they hope circumstances will change, national interests will begin to clash, new leadership may not be able to cooperate effectively, and, above all, chaos and confusion and depression may bring different alignments. Since this is one of the few hopes left, they cling to it. They make ready for a long, fanatical, digging in, trading on a tenuous, flimsy conviction that time is on their side.

As the Russians and the Americans raced each other from East and West to pre-empt occupation, Göring gloated, "If this goes on, we'll get a telegram from the West in a few days!"

The final Nazi collapse came before all the pent-up animosities and frustrations actually smashed the coalition. The Nazi surrender

* *Ibid.,* pp. 943 ff.

was unconditional and only when this menace was out of the way did the erstwhile Allies launch their own vendettas against each other, without assistance from their defeated enemies. Then all the recriminations could be aired with no diplomatic restraint. And they were. Stalin excoriated Churchill as a warmonger and equated him with Hitler. Churchill's memos and speeches referred to the Russians as the Bolsheviks. Truman, having succeeded Roosevelt, canceled all Lend-Lease aid to Russia within hours of the Nazi surrender. Yesterday the West and the Soviet had toasted the fall of Berlin. Soon the Americans were to be defending the German people of the capital in a year-long airlift against a Soviet blockade. The national commander of the American Legion was advocating a preventive strike to knock out Russian power. "We ought to aim an atomic bomb right at Moscow and save one for Tito too."

So we come back to Churchill's address in Fulton, Missouri, in March 1946. "From Stettin in the Baltic," he said, "to Trieste in the Adriatic, an Iron Curtain has descended across the continent." The new age was to be lived in the bleak climate of the Cold War. The first battles had already been fought under the umbrella of the coalition.

27

TRUMAN AND THE
RECOVERY OF EUROPE

IN 1952, AT THE END OF HIS INCUMBENCY AS PRESIDENT OF THE UNITED States, Harry Truman said to a farewell crowd: "There are at least a million men who were better qualified as President than I was, but it was my job and I did the best that I knew how." Truman was unduly modest in describing his qualifications. The man who worked most closely with him, his Secretary of State, Dean Acheson, insisted that Truman was superbly qualified for the world's most powerful office. To be sure, the presidency came to him without the slightest warning, upon the sudden death of Franklin Roosevelt. He had virtually no briefing on many of the complex foreign and domestic problems that were now his to wrestle with. He had seen Roosevelt only twice, almost perfunctorily, since his nomination. Two days after the inauguration, Roosevelt had left for the summit conference at Yalta. Even as Vice President, Truman had not been taken into confidence about the project for the creation of the atomic bomb.

But, in Acheson's judgment, Truman had a rare grasp of political realities. In an interview that I had sought to fill out a televised interpretation of the Truman years, Acheson paid a glowing tribute to his old chief.* He disagreed emphatically with my opening statement, "it was a tribute to America's open-ended society that a man

* One of Dean Acheson's last interviews, in his Washington office, June 28, 1971.

who was so little prepared could rise to his responsibilities with such acumen and decisiveness." "Nonsense!" Acheson snorted.

Truman did not need formal schooling for his great decisions. He needed fact and judgment, and these he had in uncommon degree. He had read widely, going through virtually every volume on history and politics in the library of Independence. He had been toughened by experience in his political tasks at home and in the Senate. He demonstrated again and again, at global strategy meetings, that he had fully briefed himself to come to informed judgments. By temperament he avoided shilly-shallying. He had no need of the reminder on his desk, *The Buck Stops Here.*

Acheson's judgment may become the verdict of history. For already it is generally agreed that Truman has earned a place with the great American Presidents for the major decisions that were his: the Truman Doctrine, the Marshall Plan, Point Four, NATO, the Berlin airlift, the Atomic Energy Act, the recognition of Israel, the defense of Korea, and, with it all, the transition from a war to a peace economy without setting off a depression. In many day by day actions, and in some of his appointments, in his frontier habit of shooting from the hip, Truman could betray his small town courthouse background. Acheson used to say that the State Department had on hand, as a sort of first-aid kit, "a boxful of clarifications" for just such off-the-cuff judgments. But when the destiny of his country was at stake, Truman's sense of history was unerring. He was ever conscious that he had inherited the mantle of Presidents who had brought America to world leadership. He was no Lincoln, certainly no Wilson; he had little of the sophistication of Franklin Roosevelt. But, in his visceral reactions, he reminded one of the bluntness and the courage of Andrew Jackson or James Polk. There was no war in him, as in Hamlet, " 'twixt will and will not." When he took office the question was asked in every chancellery, "Who is Harry Truman?" When he left office, seven momentous years later, after standing up to the giants of his generation, even those who had downgraded him had to admit that America and the western alliance had been well served.

Harry Truman was born in 1884 on a Missouri farm. His formal education did not go beyond high school; his hopes for a West Point career were thwarted by poor eyesight. His early ventures in banking, railroad clerking, and farming were only moderately successful. He enlisted when the United States was involved in World War I, and he commanded an artillery unit as captain. When he returned to civilian life his poor luck followed him. The funds that he had inherited from an uncle were invested by him in a Kansas City haberdashery, in partnership with a comrade-in-arms, Eddie Jacobson, but the business went bankrupt in the postwar depression. At thirty-eight he turned to politics as a protégé of the Kansas City boss, Tom Pendergast, by whom he was named a county commissioner with the title of judge. He served several consecutive terms, an apprenticeship at the grass roots level, except for one defeat in 1924 primarily because of his vigorous resistance to the Ku Klux Klan.

In 1934, now fifty, he was hand-picked by Pendergast for the Missouri Senate seat, and was swept in by the Democratic landslide. Here he did his legislative homework as a back bencher, quietly, unobtrusively; but he left so little impression on the inside White House managers that the attempt was made in 1940 to substitute Missouri's Governor Lloyd Stark as the candidate for the next Senatorial term. Truman refused to be sidetracked. He told the President that he would run even if he got only one vote, his own, although he could surely count on his wife, and his sister, and his Aunt Sally. He fought hard for his seat and won without the blessing or the help of the White House.

Then the tide turned. Truman became chairman of a special committee to investigate the defense programs. Here, reviewing defense contracts, he became a national watchdog, ferreting out graft and winning national headlines. He deserved them, for undoubtedly he saved the country many billions of dollars. His chairmanship lifted him from obscurity and won him a reputation for integrity and good judgment. It won him also the respect of Roosevelt, who was about to stand for an unprecedented fourth term to wind up the war. Through the adroit management of his fellow Missourian, Democratic national chairman Robert Hannigan, Truman was urged upon Roosevelt as his Vice Presidential running mate. Roosevelt was ready to accept either William O. Douglas or Truman, but settled on Truman.* He was easily re-elected in 1944 and Truman came through the door with him. Then, on April 12, 1945, only a few months after his inauguration, Franklin Roosevelt died, and the small town courthouse Truman became the White House Truman, in the midst of unprecedented problems in a world that seemed to be coming apart. Eleanor Roosevelt broke the stunning news to him that the President was dead. He gently asked her what he could do for her, and she

---

* There is a widely current story that Hannigan obtained the President's permission to present both names to the National Convention, but reversing the order, listing Truman's first. Roosevelt's Pulitzer Prize-winning biographer, James McGregor Burns, does not credit the story. Burns, *Roosevelt: The Soldier of Freedom,* pp. 504–5.

replied, with her unfailing sensitivity, "What can we do for you, Harry? You are the one that's in trouble now."*

The need for decisions, especially in the final stages of the war, was immediate. Truman quite sensibly sought out the most reliable counsel. He was fortunate to have available Dean Acheson, Averell Harriman, and Paul Hoffman for foreign policy, and George Marshall, Omar Bradley, Dwight Eisenhower, and, until an unfortunate break, Douglas MacArthur for military strategy. Within a few weeks of assuming office, Truman was confident enough to journey to Potsdam for the final summit conference with the Allied leaders.

Truman had sent Harry Hopkins, one of Roosevelt's confidants, to Moscow to prepare for man-to-man working relationships with Stalin. It was a hopeful symbol to have the President of the United States play Paderewski's Minuet in G Major for Stalin and Churchill, after a state dinner at Potsdam. But he soon learned that the Russians were not to be diverted from their basic objectives. He noted with rising anger how blithely they repudiated their pledges on Germany, the Balkans, and especially Poland. When Truman inquired about the rights of the Catholics in Poland, Stalin had replied, "How many divisions has the Pope?" Truman wrote to his mother, "You never saw such pigheaded people. . . . I hope I never have to hold another conference with them." He upbraided Molotov sharply and the veteran Russian hatchet man flushed and said angrily that he had never been talked to in this way before. Truman replied grimly, "Carry out your agreements and you won't get talked to like that."†

Truman has been blamed by many historians and political figures of the West and the East for the sharp deterioration in relations between the West and the Russians. But, of course, the tensions were there long before he came to Potsdam. The coalition had been precariously held together by the danger from a common enemy, and not by any agreed concern to protect the peace in the postwar world. Only force could have diverted Stalin from his determination to take over Poland and the Balkans. His troops were already in control. Truman therefore based his policy on containment, on the need to prevent the Soviet from breaking through into new areas that seemed soft or vulnerable.

---

* It should be noted that Truman shared her sensitivity. On the day that Japan surrendered, his first thought was to telephone her and to say to her that, at this historic moment, he wished it were Franklin Roosevelt who could have given the message of national triumph to the American people.

† Truman, *Memoirs*, Vol. I, pp. 82, 402.

The first major test came in Turkey and in Greece, guarding the vital interests of the West in the Mediterranean. After the Nazis had been defeated, Stalin watched benevolently as Tito continued to support strong guerrilla forces in Greece who were committed to bringing the country into the Communist orbit. Early in 1947, Britain informed Truman that it had reached the limit of its resources; it could no longer join in the defense of the eastern Mediterranean. Truman knew that the withdrawal of the British would create a dangerous vacuum, virtually an invitation for massive Soviet penetration. In March he asked Congress for four hundred million dollars to shore up the defenses of Greece and Turkey and to provide them with advisers and technicians. The amount was comparatively modest, but he placed his request in the context of what became the Truman Doctrine, the pledge that the United States was bound to offer support "wherever free peoples resisted attempted subjugation by armed minorities or by outside pressures." Truman wanted no misunderstanding. He wrote later that a prepared first draft of his statement read, "I believe it *should* be the policy of the United States" . . . "So I scratched out *should* and wrote in *must.* . . . I wanted no hedging. . . . It had to be clear and free of hesitation or double talk."*

The Truman Doctrine represented a historic turning point; never in peacetime had the United States undertaken even limited responsibility for the protection of free peoples. In effect it made the United States the twentieth-century watchdog over what American leadership determined was the struggle to remain free and independent. It proclaimed a global guardianship. Yet, within two months, despite lingering isolationist misgivings and fears of overextension, Congress voted almost unanimously to support the Doctrine, and provided the requested funds to set it in operation. The strong undercurrent of anti-Communist sentiment in the United States, and the pressure from the ethnic groups that had originated in eastern and southern Europe, evidently made it politically feasible to advocate policies that considerably broadened the American commitment.

The Truman Doctrine became the immediate prologue to the Marshall Plan, perhaps the most far-reaching of all American actions. In the first postwar years the pattern of foreign aid by America had been piecemeal emergency subventions and loans to shore up shattered economies, to feed the starving, to give succor to the homeless.

* *Ibid.,* Vol. II, p. 105.

But it was clear from the chaotic conditions in most countries, the victorious, as well as the defeated, that this approach was homeopathic, that handouts would not stop the Communist exploitation of hunger and despair. What was needed was a long-range program of aid that would place national economies on a solid base so that their productive machinery could be in operation again.

The American offer of help to its Allies, but also to Russia and its satellites, was announced by General George Marshall, now Secretary of State, as a part of the 1947 Commencement exercises at Harvard. The plan was not accepted by some of the more conservative senators without protest. Robert Taft of Ohio argued that it was wrong to keep using the taxpayers' money for European internal needs. Senator Russell of Georgia jibed that America might as well add England, Scotland, and Wales as new states and let the King run for the Senate along with Churchill. Nor was the plan passively accepted by the more radical enclaves in the larger cities, who vociferously attacked it as another big business ploy. But the opposition was easily overcome. The Marshall Plan stirred the tired and discouraged European world that was described by Churchill as "a breeding ground of pestilential hate." The American offer of restoration and renewal at this providential moment, he said, was perhaps the most unsordid act in history.*

The foreign ministers of the European world convened in Paris on July 17, and the opposition of the Russians came boiling to the surface at once. Molotov denounced the plan as an insidious attempt by the United States to control the economies of Europe and to tighten its imperialist objectives. When Poland and Czechoslovakia, now in the Soviet orbit, expressed their gratification over the prospect of American aid for them, Molotov sternly upbraided them and, after several sessions, Russia and all the countries in its control withdrew. But sixteen nations became part of the Marshall Plan, and later West Germany was added. In the four years of operation

* A whole group of revisionist historians and New Left writers give no credit to Truman and his administration for concern over the parlous state of Europe. They interpret the Truman Doctrine and the Marshall Plan as devices to open the European markets to American business exploitation. In this interpretation, Truman deliberately mounted a huge scare campaign about the sinister schemes of the Soviet Union, and he united Democrats and Republicans in the Cold War phobia. The Soviet takeover of the Baltic and the Balkan states and the coup in Czechoslovakia are explained as defense measures by the beleaguered Soviet Union in the face of Truman's imperialism. See Richard M. Freeland, *The Truman Doctrine and the Origins of McCarthyism* (New York: Alfred A. Knopf, 1971).

it expended about twelve and a half billion dollars, creating a firm basis for European recovery. Italy might have fallen to the Communists, perhaps France too; both were on the brink of collapse when the war ended. It raised spectacularly the gross national product of the participants; many of the nations soon surpassed their prewar production. It led directly to the Common Market.

Meantime, with all of his involvements in foreign affairs, Truman had to protect the home front where every political problem was a virtual minefield. The end of the war brought insistent demands for quick demobilization. This was a repetition of the experience after World War I. The victory over the enemy then too was final and complete, but there was an immediate outcry to "get the boys home." Truman realized that a general demobilization would immensely weaken American leverage in negotiations with Stalin, who kept five million men under arms all through the postwar years. But he could not control a Congress that was avalanched with baby shoes whose attached cards read "I want my daddy back." Stalin marveled at the naïveté of the Americans, who could mount a full-scale sacrificial war and then proceed to dismantle the power to enforce the peace.

The overseas legions flooded back in their millions, all at once, tough, impatient men. They found serious housing shortages. They were in competition for jobs with a powerfully organized labor force that had become accustomed to high wages and heavily subsidized overtime. As war contracts were canceled, the pockets of unemployment created disaster areas. Truman applied brakes to prices and wages to curb runaway inflation. But such "interference" by government alienated both capital and labor, the one resisting limits on profits, the other unwilling to hear of a freeze on wages. The farmers and the cattlemen, in protest, withheld their dairy products and their meats from the market. The shortages in the cities turned the urban voters against the administration. There was a coal strike, and the threat of a rail strike ended only when Truman prepared to draft those who walked off their jobs. During a good neighbor visit in Mexico, Truman was asked by the Mexican President what he thought of the Paracutín volcano which was in eruption. "Frankly," Truman replied, "it's nothing compared to the one I'm sitting on in Washington." The accumulated discontent was reflected in the mid-term elections in 1946, when Truman's popularity touched its bottom level. The Republican campaign slogan was "Had

Enough?" and, for the first time in eighteen years, the Democrats lost both Houses of Congress.

Truman, always stimulated by opposition, took the offensive. As the heir to the New Deal, he chose this time to put forward a mass of progressive legislation. He urged the extension of Social Security with benefits for another ten million citizens; he pressed for national health insurance, for vastly expanded federal aid to education. Over the apoplectic opposition of the Southern leaders of his own party, he introduced a major program of civil rights for the blacks. Senator Olin Johnston of South Carolina called the program "integrated communism" and, at the Jackson Day Dinner, he bought a table of ten and then ostentatiously left it vacant, explaining that he was afraid that his wife might have to sit by a "Nigra." His colleague, Senator Strom Thurmond, was asked why he was so upset when, after all, political promises were a routine ploy before all elections. He exploded, "Yes, but Truman really *means* it."

Virtually none of the proposed legislation was enacted; it did not even get out of committee. But Truman gloried in the battle. He felt that time was on his side, that the country would have to come to the reforms that he proposed, and that the electorate would vindicate him. There were very few, however, who shared his confidence, even in his own inner group. As planning began for the 1948 national election, and the polls differed only in predicting the magnitude of Truman's defeat, the most influential Democratic politicians spoke soberly of trying to replace Truman as the candidate. James Farley, who had for long been a mentor for the Democrats, expressed the judgment in a radio interview that Truman had become dead political timber. "To err is Truman" was a popular Republican sneer. Even Truman's mother-in-law confided to friends that it was wasted effort for him to continue fighting for re-election.

Truman was never in higher spirits than when his back was to the wall. He remembered Woodrow Wilson's conception of the presidency—an office where one had always to wear his war paint. He crisscrossed the country by train, traveling 22,000 miles, making fifteen to twenty stops daily, whistle-stops he called them, appealing over the heads of the congressional leaders to the people themselves. "I'm going to fight," he cried, "I'm going to give 'em hell." He blasted the 80th Congress as "Do Nothing." "Don't vote for me," he told the workers, "vote for yourselves, vote for your interests. Go after the mossbacks, the gluttons of privilege. Don't let them make America an economic colony of Wall Street." "I can plow a straight furrow," he told the farmers. "A prejudiced witness said so—my mother." The ever-growing crowds loved it.

His Republican opponent, Thomas Dewey, exuded overconfidence. He did not make campaign speeches; he gave acceptance speeches, calm, unruffled, all the clichés sprinkled with holy water. On the eve of the election, the magazine *Newsweek* asked fifty leading political reporters for their prediction. They responded unanimously that Truman could not win. But he did, in one of the most surprising upsets in American political history. His chuckle was heard clear across the country as he read the early edition Chicago *Tribune* headline that conceded the victory to Dewey and hailed his election. When Truman returned in triumph to Washington, he was greeted by the sign on the Washington *Post* building—"Mr. President, we are ready to eat crow, whenever you are ready to serve it."

Truman had come to the White House on the coattails of Roosevelt. Now he had won a personal mandate, and he squared away for new major battles on the domestic front and for new departures in foreign policy. In his inaugural address he summarized the major contributions to peace and stability that flowed from American support. Then he revealed still another program that became known, from the order of his recital, as Point Four. It was a plan for technical assistance to expand opportunities for the developing countries, the United States to supply the know-how, the experts in engineering, health, education, and agriculture.

Point Four was humanitarian in its objectives, but it was bound to have major diplomatic implications since it would create strong bulwarks against the blandishments of communism that fed on despair and frustration. The program was not enacted until June 1950, and it was launched with a modest sum; but it brought to the participating countries industrial, agricultural, and scientific equipment, and training in the skills to use them, to move from the past into the technology of the twentieth century. Point Four became the inspiration for other foreign aid programs that followed later, including the Peace Corps. Truman made the proud entry in his Memoirs that "it was an adventurous idea such as had never before been proposed by any country...."*

In March 1948, there was a Communist coup in Czechoslovakia,

---

* Truman, *Memoirs*, Vol. II, p. 230.

and, next month, the Soviets made an unsuccessful attempt to drive the Allies out of West Berlin by blockading all ground access to it and to its two and a half million inhabitants. The continued Russian infiltration and expansion was met by a far-ranging North Atlantic Treaty Organization, that pooled the military strength of the North Atlantic nations, with the later addition of West Germany, Greece, and Turkey. NATO was placed under the command of General Eisenhower, and his staff was drawn from the most important military figures of the participating states. There was a specific obligation for each signatory to come to the aid of any member that was threatened by an armed attack. The Senate gave Truman an impressive 6 to 1 endorsement for this collective security commitment; it extended the American frontier to the Elbe in Europe and all the way to the Dardanelles in Asia Minor.

But the deterrent effect of all these long-range actions—the Truman Doctrine, the Marshall Plan, Point Four, NATO, all of them—could be quickly nullified, if Russia were armed with nuclear power. To be sure, at the moment the United States had the monopoly. But it was inevitable that this monopoly would soon be broken. Russian scientists were frantically at work to produce the first Russian bomb. Truman and his advisers, therefore, gave highest priority to the development of a formula that would establish recognized international control of nuclear power and in June 1946 a proposal was brought officially to the United Nations. It included the proviso that there must be international inspection and the establishment of safeguards to prevent the hazards of violation and evasion. It also denied the right of the Security Council of the United Nations, in this area, to exercise its veto power. Obviously, if the veto were retained, it would be impossible to control and punish violations. Such safeguards and restrictions Stalin flatly refused to accept. He also insisted, although he had none of the bombs, that all existing stockpiles must be destroyed, so that Russia and the United States would be on an equal footing. Truman replied bluntly, "We should not under any circumstances throw away our gun until we are sure that the rest of the world can't arm against us." The impasse on inspection, and on the prior destruction of all stockpiles, killed all further negotiations. The suspicions and mistrust, from which neither side could free itself, defeated all efforts to contain the nuclear threat to civilized life.

Meantime the Russian scientists were giving every priority to the task of producing the bomb and, within three years, in 1949, they astonished the world by their first successful tests. Simultaneously several major spy rings were uncovered in Britain, Canada, and the United States, and angry cries were raised that the lax administration and sloppy surveillance of the security systems in the democracies had played into Russian hands. The spies were not responsible for the Soviet success; it was to be expected that the Russians would master the secret of the bomb. But, undoubtedly, the stolen data speeded up the achievement. A congressional investigation committee concluded in 1951 that the operations of the spy rings had "advanced the Soviet atomic energy program by eighteen months at a minimum." It was inevitable that the issue of national security and the disloyalty of trusted officials within the government should become highly combustible political issues. They were eagerly played upon by the freshman Republican senator from Wisconsin, Joseph McCarthy, and he quickly attained the national visibility that he had long been seeking in the "soft on communism" attack.

McCarthy charged that the State Department and many other sensitive areas of administration were riddled with Communists and fellow travelers. He included Dean Acheson and General Marshall in his accusation that the Communists had been coddled, and that there had been criminal negligence in permitting dangerous infiltration. He labeled the Democratic Party the "party of treason." He found support that went beyond unreasoning bigotry in the anxieties that troubled large pockets of American life—conservatives, especially among Catholics, who had never adjusted to the American-Soviet alliance of World War II, and the not too clearly articulated class hostility to the Ivy League composition of the State Department.

Though McCarthy never produced any evidence, his innuendos, heavy with irresponsibility and malice, helped to poison the diplomatic, educational, political, and economic life of the country. McCarthy's charges frightened institutions that catered to the public, and many a reputation was destroyed by what became known as "McCarthyism." The senator from Wisconsin took his place with Judge Lynch and Captain Boycott as another malevolent word was added to the vocabulary of threat and defamation.

Truman's second term was a very rough period, where dogmas were fought with stigmas, where smear and name-calling turned politics into swamp and jungle, in what the correspondent William S. White called "the blood-in-the-nostrils approach." Ultimately, McCarthy overreached himself and when he included the Protestant clergy and the United States army in his unrestrained attacks, he became a serious nuisance to the Republicans too. In 1954, halfway through Eisenhower's first term, he was censured by his senatorial colleagues, and his demagogic career collapsed as quickly as it had been inflated. But the mischief had been done. It took many years to restore morale in the departments of government and in the foreign service from where McCarthy's calumnies had driven some of the ablest public servants.

Truman had still another major crisis to face as the Cold War took on ever more serious proportions in his final years as President. Near the end of June 1950, a force of more than sixty thousand North Koreans, trained by the Soviet and heavily supported by Soviet-made planes and tanks, suddenly invaded South Korea, in defiance of the World War II settlement that had divided the country at the 38th parallel. Korea, like several other unfortunate buffer nations, had been temporarily partitioned to reflect the spheres of interest of the Communist and non-Communist powers. It had been agreed at the Cairo summit conference that there would be nationwide elections, supervised by the United Nations. But Russia refused to cooperate in the election and the two halves of Korea were frozen at the partition lines. There had been many border incidents since the agreements at Cairo, but now the North Koreans, undoubtedly encouraged by Russia and possibly by China, made the unilateral attempt to reunite the country as a Communist bastion.

The attack was another of the many challenges of the Cold War, and Truman acted promptly. He believed that if the conquest of South Korea were permitted, many of the weaker nations of the Far East would be in jeopardy. For it would put the Communists on the Strait of Tsushima, ten minutes by jet to Japan, and it would be a signal to the world that the United States was no longer concerned with its announced policy of collective security. He obtained approval in the Security Council of the United Nations to counter the aggression.*

Most of the nations that voted the authority for the military resistance to the North Koreans made no contribution to give it meaning. The United States was obliged to carry more than 90 percent of the burden. The war seesawed, the North Koreans, at the outset, almost driving the unprepared South Korean and the United Nations forces into the sea. But General MacArthur, who had been

---

* The delegate of the Soviet Union had been boycotting the sessions of the Security Council. The Russian veto was therefore not applied and Truman could get the vote that he needed for the action in Korea.

assigned the command, demonstrated brilliant initiative. His forces landed behind the enemy lines, routed the invaders, and turned initial disaster into near victory. However, flushed with overconfidence, he refused to stop at the 38th parallel and, despite Chinese warnings, advanced the United Nations forces to the borders of Chinese Manchuria. This brought China into the war, although its forces were disguised as volunteers.

The campaigns then bogged down into a long and frustrating stalemate and precipitated an irritating quarrel between MacArthur, who wished to strike at the Chinese supply bases which he denounced as "privileged sanctuaries," and President Truman, who, with the unanimous backing of the Joint Chiefs of Staff, was wary of widening the conflict into World War III. General Omar Bradley said that "it would be the wrong war, at the wrong place, at the wrong time, and with the wrong enemy." Truman also feared that the Korean invasion might have been a diversionary tactic by the Soviet Union to make possible a successful assault upon vulnerable areas in Europe. The defiance of the President by his general became so serious that Truman, citing the American tradition of civilian leadership, relieved him of his command, and the ensuing uproar in the United States, where there was strong support for MacArthur's position, further divided the country. The war dragged on and as the casualties mounted turned increasingly unpopular, contributing to the defeat of the Democrats in the presidential election of 1952. But Truman never deviated in his conviction that the defense of South Korea put the Communists on notice that aggression would not be condoned.

Truman's final year ended with the frustrations of the Korean War, and with the partisan din over his relations with General MacArthur. But his presidency, so suddenly and unexpectedly thrust upon him, had included seven of the most turbulent years in modern history. It called for decisions that profoundly affected the future. It had to be judged as a whole and not by segments. And judged as a whole, it was a memorable incumbency. Truman could be extravagantly partisan on the political platform. He was often guilty of overzealous loyalty to men who did not deserve such devotion. But when the destiny of his country was the issue, he stood out in courageous integrity.

The capacity for decision was the key to the stature he attained. The great foreign policy judgments in a world that was going down the drain required more than briefing from department heads and brain trusters. They required sweep and imagination and daring. Truman had little patience with wordy doctrinaires, what the philosopher Francis Bradley called "the ballet of bloodless categories." His eloquence was action. Most of his resolute actions were fraught with peril. But after he listened to all the alternatives, he acted with vigor and despatch and, in Milton's phrase, "with native honor clad." The little man who came up the hard way to the Senate, to the vice presidency, and to the presidency itself, with every temptation to place career above country, made his decisions *amor patriae.*

This instinctive patriotism came naturally because, in personal life, Truman valued loyalty above all other virtues. He went to the funeral of Tom Pendergast, the old party boss of Kansas City, who had ended his career in disgrace. He went, the President of the United States, because he could not forget that he was given his start by Pendergast. Truman stood by his men in fair weather and foul. They loved him for it; it welded them into a loyal fighting team. Dean Acheson often quoted Shakespeare's *Henry V* and the tribute there to another Harry:

> Beholding him, plucks comfort from his looks.
> A largess universal like the sun
> His liberal eye doth give to every one,
> . . . .
> A little touch of Harry in the night.*

America had this "little touch of Harry" when it needed it most, suddenly bereft of leadership, in the dark night of the expanding Cold War.

* Act IV, Prologue.

28

ADENAUER
AND THE REDEMPTION
OF GERMANY

WHEN WORLD WAR II ENDED IN NAZI DEFEAT, GERMANY LAY IN RUINS.
For the first time in modern history the country itself had suffered
total invasion and the Allied air assaults had left virtually all of the
cities as wastelands of twisted girders, jumbled masonry, and huge
piles of rubble. Hitler had ordered defiance unto death, even if the
Fatherland vanished in flame and desolation. Four million men were
killed and maimed, and boys too, as young as fourteen, who had
been thrown into the decimated lines in the oversized uniforms of
their dead fathers. Seven and a half million were homeless and many
now lived in cellars like animals in burrows. German currency had
become valueless and cigarettes and food items were virtually the
only acceptable tender. Walking along even the most famous streets
was like coming upon the ruins of defunct civilizations. The most
beautiful cathedrals were eerie, ghostly skeletons, in Willa Cather's
phrase, "as if God Himself had fled and abandoned them." Hitler
had threatened, "When we slam the door, the whole world will be
shaken." The world was shaken, badly shaken, but Germany itself
had crumbled and was close to death, leaving behind a hatred so
passionate that it seemed ineradicable.

Yet, within three years after such disaster, the Americans and the
British were carrying out the greatest airlift in history to save West
Berlin from the Russians. Within ten years, West Germany was
again a sovereign state, with the strongest economy in Europe, a full
rearmament schedule, and membership in NATO, the North

Atlantic alliance that had been created to counter possible Soviet aggression.

This was a diplomatic revolution which changed the course of history in our time. It came about because, with the collapse of the Allied coalition, both Russia and the West put aside their hostility to Germany and began courting it as a possible useful ally. It came about also because of the astute statesmanship of Dr. Konrad Adenauer, whose late-in-life career as Chancellor of the new Germany made him the architect of its revived commercial and industrial life. The story of the death and resurrection of Germany is a fascinating commentary on the mercurial character of international coalitions, and the impermanence of national enmities and friendships.

Hitler's Nero legacy of havoc and chaos is what the Allies first saw when they took charge of the surrendered areas. In the face of so much human misery there might have been a measure of compassion to temper anger and vengeance. But then the concentration camps and the crematoria were uncovered, and the full horror was revealed of what the Nazis had done to their victims. Earlier reports of mass torture and death had filtered out, but they were so incredible that they were dismissed as comparable to the atrocity propaganda of World War I. Now there was eyewitness confirmation of the treatment of the conquered and the doomed. The Allied troops came upon the ingenious paraphernalia of torment—the gas chambers, the whipping blocks, the vivisection rooms, the huge piles of baby shoes, the meathooks, the bodies still unburned, piled like cordwood. Allied soldiers used gas masks as they buried the dead in Buchenwald, Dachau, Auschwitz, and the other death camps. General Eisenhower brought in groups of American legislators and journalists so that they could see for themselves how technology and barbarism could function in tandem. He also brought in German leaders to confront them with the depravity that the Nazis represented. The mayor of Munich afterwards committed suicide.

The confirmed bestiality of the Nazis not only eliminated compassion; it also reinforced the Allied determination to proceed vigorously with German demilitarization, with the punishment of the war criminals, and with plans for a long period of occupation. Hence the first postwar directives were unqualified in their rigor. Germany was to be treated as a defeated nation. There was to be no fraternization with Germans; living standards were to be set so as to ensure only physical survival. Above all, every precaution was to be taken to prevent rearmament. There was to be no military research camouflaged as pure science, no paramilitary societies masquerading as social clubs. The mistakes of the years that followed World War I were not to be repeated. Roosevelt said: "The German people are not going to be enslaved, because the United Nations does not traffic in human slavery. But it will be necessary for them to earn their way back into the fellowship of the peace loving and law abiding nations. And in their climb up that steep road, we shall certainly see to it that they are not encumbered by having to carry guns. They will be delivered of that burden we hope forever."

The quarrels of the Allies, at this stage, did not divert them from the determination to place on trial and to punish the main war criminals. Hundreds had already committed suicide when it appeared that they might fall into enemy hands. Thousands who had held positions of responsibility had fled, and they lived out obscure lives in fairly safe refuge, shielded especially in Spain, in the Argentine, and in the Arab lands. Other thousands, however, who had stayed behind or were captured alive, were now arrested. In the years that followed there were trials in every zone, at first conducted by the occupying powers, and then by the German courts themselves. But the trials quickly became unmanageable. Large sections of the German adult population had been associated with Nazi activity, voluntarily or involuntarily. How could hundreds of thousands be brought to trial? What would be the guidelines for judgment? Hence, after some fruitless attempts to fasten on activities that might be considered chargeable (the Americans actually scheduled 170,000 trials), it was decided to proclaim a general amnesty for most former members of Nazi and affiliated organizations. Only those who had committed war crimes were sentenced by the Allies and, later, by the German courts. The Allied courts condemned 668 war criminals to death. After jurisdiction over these cases was transferred to German courts in January 1950, approximately eight thousand more war criminals were sentenced.

The mass trial at Nuremberg, of twenty-one captured high Nazi officials, became the showcase effort to punish the ringleaders and establish the principle that wars of aggression and war crimes would no longer be condoned. There were protests in many lands that the trials could establish no such principle because they took on the character of the vengeance of victors against the vanquished. And it did seem like a travesty to have Russian judges sitting in the court when, just before the war had been launched, Stalin had entered into a pact with Hitler, had invaded Poland, and had seized the Baltic states. Besides, the Nazi hierarchy was being tried for "crimes against humanity," and there had been no such category in international law.

These inconsistencies were not permitted to interfere with the carefully prepared trial. The *ex post facto* character of the indictments was countered by the reminder that international law is not governed by legislation, it is governed by treaties. And there had been a whole series of treaties, adhered to by successive German governments, which had outlawed wars of aggression and crimes against humanity.

The Nuremberg court was presided over by one of Britain's most distinguished jurists, Sir Geoffrey Lawrence. The American representative was Justice Robert Jackson of the United States Supreme Court. The defendants were given every opportunity to defend their case. Much of the testimony emerged from captured documents that had been kept with German precision. It came also from the guards at the concentration camps, underlings who could now speak up without fear of reprisals. It was the Germans themselves who validated the stories of horror.

Most of the inner Nazi cabal had already committed suicide, including Hitler, Goebbels, and Himmler, but eleven of those who were tried at Nuremberg were hanged.* Several against whom there seemed to be insufficient evidence of personal complicity were freed, among them bankers and industrialists who, though visibly enriched by Nazi slave labor, claimed that they had been victims of compulsion. When historic post-mortems became the order, hardly anybody had been a Nazi. There was a grim jest that when Hitler's body was found in his bunker, there was a note in his clenched hand that read, "I was not a Nazi."

After Nuremberg, most of the trials ended in either acquittal or minor sentences. From time to time a prominent official of the Nazi period was flushed out and brought back from hiding. This happened in the case of Himmler's main deputy, Adolf Eichmann, who was tracked down in the Argentine where he had been in hiding for twenty-five years. He was kidnapped by Israeli agents and was hanged in Israel after a long and internationally publicized trial, not so much because any punishment could sufficiently fit his crimes, but so that the lesson of the Nazi terror would be renewed for a

---

* Göring committed suicide after he was sentenced to death by the Nuremberg court.

generation to whom it had become quite remote. But the passing of time dampened the flaming enormity of the Nazi terror, and those who were born and came to maturity after Hitler's day did not wish to be reminded of a past that was so full of shame and guilt. There was almost no interest in the commutation of the sentence of Alfred Krupp, whose mammoth arms combine had plundered the conquered lands and conscripted 100,000 slave laborers, *Untermenschen*, who were beaten and starved and frozen as they fed the war machine. Krupp had been tried and sentenced when his father, Gustav Krupp von Bohlen, could not stand trial due to his deteriorating health. The younger Krupp was given a twelve-year sentence but he served only three, and when he was released, the entire empire was restored to him and his family.

By now the Allies were no longer allies. The Iron Curtain had fallen, and East and West were following collision-course policies. Nowhere were their divergent interests more in opposition than in their revised objectives for Germany. All plans to dismember it, to postpone sovereignty, to prevent any possibility of rearmament, were no longer relevant. Instead, as the Cold War heated up, the West and the East began to vie with each other to add the German potential strength to their own. Two new Germanies rose out of the ashes of the Third Reich. Russia converted its eastern German zone into a full-fledged satellite, and the West combined its assigned areas to create West Germany and to concentrate on a major program of assistance for its reconstruction. A visiting Michigan senator, Arthur Vandenberg, remarked, "It would truly appear that the Germans have divided the Allies into four zones. . . . The Big Four would soon have little control over the fate of Germany; it would be Germany that, in the long run, would decide the fate of the former Allies!"

How far the situation had changed was pointed up in a memorable speech by the new Secretary of State, James Byrnes. In September of 1946, he addressed a group of fifteen hundred American military and government personnel in Stuttgart. One hundred and fifty Germans, working in the American administration, were in the audience. Byrnes made an electrifying statement. He said, "The German people, throughout Germany, under proper safeguards, should now be given the primary responsibility for running their own affairs. . . . The American people want to help the German people to win their way back to an honorable place among the free and peace loving peoples of the world. All that the Allied government can and should do is to lay down the rules under which German democracy can govern itself."* No wonder the Germans in the audience wept in relief. Here was an outstretched hand, a promise of understanding and friendship that not even the most optimistic could have imagined so soon after the horrors of the Nazi regime. The Russians were outraged by this extraordinary courtship, suspecting that the Allies would soon begin rebuilding Germany, strengthening it, perhaps even rearming it, so soon after the assaults on Russia, the millions of dead there, the ruined cities, the uprooted populations, the concentration camps. But the western Allies insisted that the Kremlin had only itself to blame, after its brazen subversion in eastern Europe and its incessant calls for revolution in Europe and Asia.

By the summer of 1947, acting upon the revised policy of rapprochement, the Allies announced that most of the restrictions which had been in force in German economic and political life would be abolished. To blunt the threat of inflation, a new mark was issued which became the foundation for one of the firmest currencies in all Europe. The Marshall Plan, which was to subsidize the recovery of the European countries, was extended to West Germany, whose leaders could say with confidence, "We are now allies." In March of 1948, the representatives of the United States, Britain, and France met in London to consider plans for the establishment of a West German state. Ten days later, when the Four Power Council convened in Berlin, the Soviet general demanded to know what the Allied intentions were for German unification. When General Lucius Clay, the American representative, refused to divulge details, the Soviet representative walked out and the quadripartite administration of Germany blew up amidst angry charges and counter-charges.

The Russians now began to harass the western routes across the Soviet zone into West Berlin. They blocked all ground access to the city and to its two and a half million inhabitants. They cut off all transportation and utility services, expecting to starve and freeze the city into yielding. Under the leadership of President Truman, the West accepted the challenge. Truman announced: "We shall stay, period!" There began an unprecedented airlift to bring in the food and clothing, the fuel and the medical supplies, and the other necessities. The huge planes loaded at Frankfurt and Wiesbaden and landed at the American airport in Berlin every three minutes, around the clock, around the calendar, building up to 16,000 tons

* James F. Byrnes, *Speaking Frankly* (New York: Harper & Row, 1947), pp. 188–91.

daily. The airlift, known as Operation Vittles, went on for 320 days, and more than 1,600,000 tons were transported. By May 1949, Russia concluded that it could not wear down the Allied determination, and it gave up and lifted the blockade. Less than three years after Hitler, the West had risked war with Russia to defend Berlin and the airlift had forged a new alliance.

The man who dominated this period of reconciliation and did most to bring his country back into the West European concert was Dr. Konrad Adenauer. The impressiveness of his achievement was highlighted because his service as Chancellor began at the age of seventy-three, and it lasted fourteen years, the most extended incumbency since Bismarck's. In his Memoirs he notes that when he was sent to a Gestapo prison near Cologne, after an unsuccessful escape from a concentration camp, the commandant asked him not to make extra trouble by attempting suicide. When Adenauer asked him why he thought he might, the commandant replied that, after all, the prisoner was already past seventy, and he had nothing more to expect from life.*

Adenauer was born in 1876. His father was a secretary in the law courts, and his mother had strong political connections through her family. His tradition was Roman Catholic and basically conservative. An oft-repeated story noted that when he took the train to Berlin and crossed the Elbe he glowered as he murmured to himself, "Now we enter Asia." He studied law and followed his father into the civil service. In 1917 he became the lord mayor of Cologne and he held his office until the eve of the Nazi takeover in 1933, when he was removed by Göring. He had ordered Nazi flags taken down on a bridge that was on the route of Hitler's triumphal entry to address a party rally. When Hitler came to power, Adenauer took refuge in a monastery. In the years that followed there were hair-breadth escapes, arrests, and imprisonments, solitary confinement, and exile —all in consequence of his anti-Nazi convictions and reputation. He was not overt enough in his activity to be executed, but he was considered sufficiently unreliable by the Nazis for him to go underground. At one point his name was on the list for transport to the gas chambers of Buchenwald, but at the last moment a prison doctor arranged a simulated heart attack, and he was assigned to the prison hospital.

When the war came to an end, and the American forces poured into his village in March 1945, Adenauer headed the list of accepta-

* Konrad Adenauer, *Memoirs* (Chicago: H. Regnery Co., 1966), p. 17.

bles, and he was released and called upon once again to take over the administration of Cologne. He was thus in an ideal position for leadership in national politics. He helped to organize and to guide the Christian Democratic Party, a centrist coalition, where Catholic influence was strong. As the Cold War was exacerbated, the western Allies authorized the consolidation of their three zones and called for a free election. Adenauer's party polled 31 percent of the vote and in September 1949 he became the first Chancellor of the newly established Federal Republic.

He was seventy-three, but in the circumstances, his age was a prime advantage. He was a welcome representative of pre-Hitler Germany, pre-Weimar Germany, too. He symbolized the golden early century days when Germany was in the forefront of science and the civilized arts, admired and respected. Adenauer, patrician in personal bearing, unblemished in experience, fulfilled a nostalgic role, the link with the good days of the other Germany, the Germany of Goethe and Schiller, of Lessing and Heine and Beethoven.

Adenauer worked deliberately, soberly, scarcely raising his voice, with just a touch of skepticism to discipline any temptation for an emotional outburst. To be sure, he did not suffer fools gladly; he used to say that God Almighty made a great mistake in limiting the intelligence of man but not his stupidity. He could be sharp with colleagues who did not bend easily to his views. During a long, stubborn session, one of his cabinet members complained that Adenauer had no right to expect him simply to say "Yes" and "Amen." Adenauer suggested wryly that it was not necessary to say "Amen," "Yes" would be quite sufficient. When some fatheads in Austria pressed demands for reparations, Adenauer's response was devastating; he offered to send them Hitler's remains.

But in his essential diplomatic missions, he never forgot that the vanquished must be patient. He had his feelings so much under control that some of his adversaries wondered whether he wore a mask. Adenauer needed this diplomatic equipment, for his task called for acrobatic statesmanship. His overriding aim was to retain the confidence of the West that Germany's commitment was unreserved and unshakable. Yet he had to reassure his own people that he was not simply the flunky of the West. He never forgot the insulting barb of his chief political rival, Dr. Kurt Schumacher, who labeled him "The Chancellor of the Allies." Again, he could not surrender the hope, with eighteen million Germans in the Soviet zone, for the reunification of Germany. Yet he could not move toward any collaboration with the Soviet, for fear of reawakening lingering suspicions in the West that he was playing off the power rivals until Germany was strong enough to begin again on a reactionary nationalist binge.

So Adenauer, now affectionately termed *"Der Alte,"* the old one, zigged and zagged for fifteen years, through all this complicated web. When the posture of firmness was called for, he could be inflexible. When concessions were advantageous, he was a model of conciliation. Every three weeks, imperturbable behind his inevitable starched collar, his face resembling a Chinese Mandarin, with his three aides carrying brief cases, *Der Alte* would be driven up to the Petersberg Hof in Bonn, there to be received by the Allied Commission. He would go through the routine of explaining his views, and defending his acts, and presenting his requests. Then he would listen with resignation to instructions and to complaints, or to both. He probably exhausted them by so patiently listening to them. After each report ordeal, he would find comfort in his Rhine wines and his medieval paintings, and in his meticulous cultivation of roses. Inevitably, a day came when the Commission relaxed its reserve and brought Adenauer into its inner councils as a reliable ally.

One of Adenauer's master strokes was the reconciliation that he established with the ancient enemy, France. He was determined that the centuries-old feud, with its legacy of distrust and hostility, must end. He found a kindred spirit in General de Gaulle who, despite a lusty nationalism, was convinced that a new powerful Europe could emerge from a Franco-German entente.

In 1952 West Germany joined with France, Italy, and the Benelux nations in an international union that combined their steel and coal resources, a union that was to lead, in 1958, to the Common Market. During the negotiations Adenauer made his first official trip to Paris and he was a model of discretion at the ceremonies. When asked to speak he said quietly, "No, we Germans had too much to say, and were heard from much too often from 1933 onwards. If I have anything to say, I'll wait till last." De Gaulle paid a return visit to West Germany in 1962 and, in excellent German, pledged to the thousands in the main square in Bonn his friendship for *das grosse deutsche Volk,* the great German people. Next year the pact of friendship was sealed in a German-French treaty.

Meantime, Adenauer went forward with another dramatic act of reconciliation, an offer of atonement to the Jews. He publicly expressed his nation's responsibility for the Jewish tragedy during the Nazi holocaust, and promised reparations to Israel and to the surviving victims in other lands, wherever they might be, as a symbol of national remorse. For a year and a half, German officials sat with representatives of Israel and of twenty-two world Jewish organizations to work out the formulae of reparations. The Jews of the world were seriously divided over the issue. Many whose kin had been wiped out wanted no part of what they called "blood money." They insisted that no reparations could atone for the evil that had destroyed millions of families. Adenauer did not regard the offer as compensation. He treated it as a pledge of contrition that would have material importance at a time when Israel was on the verge of bankruptcy, after its war of liberation and its crushing defense burdens. In March 1953, the reparations agreement was signed by which about nine hundred million dollars in goods and credits was pledged to Israel, and further compensation was authorized, through special courts, to families, wherever they now lived, who proved confiscation or damage during the Nazi regime. When the agreement was voted, the Bundestag stood in silence, in memory of the martyred.* It was another caprice of fate that in the crises of Israel and the Arabs, West Germany proved to be Israel's most reliable European ally.

Adenauer broke with many other long-established precedents in his pursuit of enduring friendships, a unified Europe, and a democratic Germany within it. Of course his policies were not universally applauded, even by his inner family. British and American critics chafed when he followed too deferentially the rigid anti-Communist obsession of John Foster Dulles; perhaps he should be called John Foster Adenauer, they said. Those who could not abide De Gaulle's prima donna tantrums were worried when Adenauer seemed to be too much under the Frenchman's mesmeric spell.

But the issue that caused the greatest concern, especially outside Germany, was Adenauer's apparently tepid attitude in the ongoing political battle against latent Nazism in Germany. From time to time there were upsurges, as splinter parties defiantly proclaimed their allegiance to many of the old Nazi objectives. Every year there was renewed conflict over the reaction to the men who had participated in the July 20, 1944, assassination attempt against Hitler and who had been brutally executed when the plot failed. Were they

* Nahum Goldmann, *The Autobiography of Nahum Goldmann* (New York: Holt, Rinehart & Winston, 1969), p. 256. Dr. Goldmann conducted the negotiations on behalf of the major Jewish organizations.

patriots who had tried to save the country from a madman, or were they traitors who had betrayed the Fatherland in a time of war? Adenauer consistently refused to be drawn into the dispute. What sense was there, he asked, in weakening the vitality of a recuperating Germany by quarrels that were doctrinaire? He believed that, with the passing of time, the Nazi blight would be eroded and fade, and that it was politically unwise to reopen old wounds when no practical issues were at stake.

No one accused Adenauer of the slightest sympathy with Nazism. He had suffered too much, and had too often proved his commitment to Christian decency. But his reply seemed irrelevant and was unacceptable when former Nazis were permitted to serve in high federal positions. The case of Dr. Hans Globke verged on scandal, for he had been given the key position of State Secretary in the Chancery even though he was the author of a semi-official commentary on the Nazi racial laws. Adenauer refused to dispense with him, arguing that Globke had simply followed orders as a loyal civil servant, and he retained him as a trusted adviser until he retired at the age limit of sixty-five, a few months before Adenauer himself stepped down.

Adenauer was not insensitive to the criticisms that were aimed at his incumbency. His Memoirs reveal how seriously he took them, and how much they made him bleed. He often had great difficulty in reconciling compromise with conscience. But, in looking back on a long chancellorship, he was satisfied that, in the perspective of history, he would come off well. For his diplomacy not only brought his country back into the mainstream of European life; it also served the cause of European integration and recovery.

Yet Adenauer never deceived himself about the motivations of the Allies in speeding German rehabilitation. They were primarily concerned with the dangers of the Cold War and the need for strength to cope with them. When Russia and Red China stepped up their threats in Asia, there was every expectation that Europe would soon feel the thrust too. Then the military potential of Germany would be a most welcome reinforcement. In 1952 some of the French leaders proposed a special European Defense Force, under NATO, to include substantial German manpower and weapons. The United States, which was now deep in the Korean War, enthusiastically endorsed the plan. To the chagrin of the American sponsors, there was considerable opposition in Germany, especially among the younger generation, who were pacifist to the core, and they demonstrated with passion, often with violence, against rearmament. They were the *"Ohne Mich,"* the "Without Me" generation. Basically, Adenauer shared their disenchantment with any military posture, but he was ready to cooperate with the Allies because German inclusion in an overall European army would be another step in the readmission of Germany to the concert of Europe.

Ironically, the European army proposal, which had been fathered by the French, was defeated in the French Chamber of Deputies. There were still too many veterans who could not forget the Nazi invasion that had nearly destroyed France and its people. But a compromise was quickly worked out through the initiative of Anthony Eden of Britain. His proposal brought the German contingents into the military system of NATO with ingenious restrictions that gave Germany no national command authority over these forces. The rearmament proceeded with dispatch and, when Adenauer relinquished his post in 1963, West Germany had 420,000 men under arms, the largest military establishment in Europe outside the Soviet Union. Once Germany was part of NATO it was inevitable that complete sovereignty would follow. And it did, on May 5, 1955, when the last limitations were lifted for what was now the sovereign Federal Republic of Germany. It was an exultant day for Germany and the climactic personal triumph for Adenauer.

With the last restrictions of the occupation rescinded, all the tireless capacity of the people could be released to set Germany on its way to becoming the most powerful nation in western Europe. The country quickly reached the highest level of production in its history. It was able to assimilate more than twelve million Germans who had been expelled or had fled from countries which had been taken over by the Soviet Union. The absorption created no labor crisis. On the contrary, it provided an indispensable reservoir to maintain the tempo of Germany's surging economy. Foreign trade boomed as German enterprise sent its technicians and its investors to the far corners of the earth—to build steel mills for India, and bridges over the Nile for Egypt, and factories to process oil for the Sudan and for Iran. The old days were back when the trademark— "Made in Germany"—was known in every land, and was eagerly sought as a guarantee of good quality and reasonable pricing. Adenauer was deservedly as proud of the *Wirtschaftswunder,* the economic miracle, as of any of his diplomatic triumphs, although the credit for the spectacular recovery rightly belonged to his Minister of Economics, Dr. Ludwig Erhard.

Yet the crucial achievement, certainly Adenauer's most coveted hope, was still only in the emergent stage. It had to do, not with governmental structure nor with economic growth nor even with international acceptance. It had to do with the spirit of the New Germany. What was it to be? For nearly a generation, in the Nazi bondage, this spirit had been mauled and assaulted and manipulated, and had expressed itself sometimes in vile servility and sometimes in raucous belligerency. In a moment of remarkable candor, Adenauer had referred to the people whose destiny was in his keep as "carnivorous sheep." Adenauer had steadily transformed the spirit that dominated Germany when he became Chancellor. He had brought the world's most hated people to respect and admiration. He had saved the land from Balkanization and had anchored it in constitutional government. Most of the conservative unrepentants who still clung to the brutal glories of the Third Reich were either gone or careful to conceal their yearnings. But had the long years of Adenauer's chancellorship left a sufficient mark on the next generation, the post-Hitler young people, to assure an enduring commitment to the democratic faith? As Adenauer neared retirement, he wanted very much to believe that the commitment was safe, and that it would be the crowning achievement of his incumbency.

29

ATTLEE'S BRITAIN

IN JULY OF 1945 WINSTON CHURCHILL SAT WITH STALIN AND TRUMAN at Potsdam to plan the reorganization of Europe after the surrender of the Nazis. Japan was still in its last-ditch resistance in the Far East, but it was clear that there too the war would soon be over. For nearly fifteen years Britain had been governed by a Coalition of the Conservative and the Labour parties, with Churchill as the wartime Prime Minister. He had led his people with incomparable courage and resourcefulness and he urged that the Coalition be continued for the tasks that lay ahead. But Labour, remembering the Liberal debacle of 1918, insisted that it was time now for a new national mandate, with a return to normal party interest, and the election was under way.

Churchill confidently expected, with the victory over the Fascists now complete, that his Conservative Party would fare well at the polls and that the responsibility for the next crucial years in Britain would again be assigned to his safe and tried leadership. The election posters played up a fighting pose of Churchill, bulldog face, and the caption read, "Vote Nationalist. Help Him Finish The Job." To the astonishment of the world and to his own chagrin, Labour swept into power with a gain of two hundred seats, in one of the major political upsets in British history. For the Conservatives it was not simply a defeat, it was an eviction. Conforming to the British tradition of immediate transfer of authority, Churchill resigned. His place at the Potsdam summit conference was taken by the Labour chief, Clement Attlee, the deputy Prime Minister in the Coalition. Churchill had been a very tenacious negotiator, a formidable match for Stalin, whom he had constantly frustrated and kept at bay. Now Churchill was out. For two days Stalin was unavailable, and rumor had it that he was uproariously drunk from the ruddy cup with which he celebrated Churchill's defeat and elimination. The depth of Churchill's disappointment was revealed in his later Memoirs where he noted that he had exercised power for five years and three months of world war, at the end of which time, "all our enemies having surrendered unconditionally, or being about to do so, I was immediately dismissed by the British electorate of all further conduct of their affairs." When it was suggested that he accept the honor of a Knight of the Garter, he asked wryly, "Why should I accept the Garter from His Majesty after I've been given the boot?" But these were statements for much later Memoirs. On the night of the election his disciplined sportsmanship was the only outward show that he permitted. He yielded with his usual eloquent grace and he pledged his cooperation to the new government.

What happened to topple the national idol at the very moment of fulfillment? Most students of the period, even when they disagree over details, conclude that the verdict was not the response of fickleness or ingratitude. Rather, it reflected the determination of the British public, after the hardships of a long and agonizing war, to make the future more meaningful, to assure opportunities that had been too long postponed. Apparently they preferred to place their trust in the party that had prepared most carefully to give reality to these expectations. They had no wish to repudiate Churchill himself. They knew what they owed to him. But while he was undoubtedly indispensable for the war effort as an inspirational force, they no longer demanded a personality, they demanded a program. Rebecca West summarized the paradox of dismissal as the epilogue for victory. She wrote, "We asked Winston Churchill to do the work of six men in our time of trial, and he did the work of five of them excellently, but of the sixth not so well . . . unfortunately, it was the sixth man that we wanted in our time of peace."*

The quality of leadership for "this time of peace" had indeed to be quite exceptional. For the country, despite victory, was at the brink of bankruptcy. It needed billions in imports to feed and

* *Harper's* (November 1945).

clothe, to house and defend, its forty-eight million people. Where were these huge sums to come from? The years of resistance to Hitler had eaten up all the reserves, and the world's proud creditor was now staggering under an unmanageable debt. Hundreds of thousands of homes had been demolished, more than four million had been damaged. The major business establishments and factories in London, and the other industrial cities, had been bombed and burned. Even without such devastation, the economic structure, committed to the needs of national survival, forfeited its competitive advantage. As equipment wore out it had not been replaced; it had been patched. To maintain its worldwide trade required an adequate merchant marine and a fleet to protect it. But half the merchant marine had been destroyed and the fleet that was its defense arm had been decimated. Britain had won a global war; it was listed with the great powers. But its strength was façade, screened by worn-out traditions and fading dreams of glory.

Churchill, with overriding concern for the problems of war and diplomacy, could give only peripheral attention to the economic disintegration of his homeland and the stirrings and expectations that lay beneath its patriotic exterior. The Labour strategists had served loyally in the War Coalition but they had not neglected their plans for a new Britain in a new world. For years their task forces and their commissions had analyzed proposals for housing and transport, for health and social security, for land reform and steady employment. Their charts and their graphs and their statistics could not compete in drama with Churchill's majestic oratory, but they were more relevant now in the task of upgrading the key industries or providing living standards for returning veterans.* When the war was over and the electorate were given their choice, they decided to entrust the tasks of reconstruction to the men who had created the blueprints for tomorrow. They bypassed Churchill and the Tories and they voted in the first independent Socialist government in Britain.†

Labour came in on an evangelical tide. There were no limits to their hopes. Their contingent in the House of Commons included

---

* And yet the pens of some of their intellectuals were like razor blades and they could draw blood. Beatrice Webb had a style that gave devastating force to any Fabian attack. "My aunt embraced us all unaffectionately, with a politician's kiss: a greeting with rather less than met the eye."

† The governments of Ramsay MacDonald had only minority mandates and functioned on the sufferance of cooperating parties.

thirty-five ex-miners, and sixty-six former railroad workers, and these sat side by side with professors and writers and social workers; impatient men, and women too, eager to apply the plans that had been hibernating in pamphlets and reports. As they convened they sang William Blake's moving hymn:

> I shall not cease from mental fight,
> Nor shall my sword sleep in my hand
> Till we have built Jerusalem,
> In England's green and pleasant land.

In Britain, revolution is usually low-keyed, restrained, conducted with concern for those who may be unfairly hurt. The nationalization that had been spoken of so fervently during the election was to be confined to selected public services, with considerable leeway for the participation of private enterprise and with fair compensation to those whose property and interest were to be nationalized. The government was headed by the perfect symbol of the "revolution by consent," Clement Attlee, who was tapped by destiny to pioneer the new Jerusalem.

He was born in 1883 in a suburb of London of upper-middle-class parents. He had the privileged tutelage of the affluent—Northaw, Haileybury, then Oxford, where he read history and where his record was outstanding. He followed his father's profession into the law and could have enjoyed an exceptionally lucrative practice. Then, as he notes in his Memoirs, the artificial Victorian world was suddenly revealed to him in all its hideous callousness when a friend took him to visit the East End of London. He saw its slums and its sweatshops, its verminous tenements and its primitive living conditions, and the scenes did not leave his mind. In one of the poems that he wrote he referred with angry grief to "the streets that have no pity, the streets where men decay."* To the dismay of his family he gave up his law practice and became a social worker, centering at Toynbee Hall, one of the settlement houses in the notorious Limehouse District. He immersed himself in the literature of protest—William Morris, John Ruskin, the reports of the Fabian Socialists, the Webbs, Bernard Shaw, and the others who were intent upon reconstructing old England without violence, by "the inevitability of gradualness."

* ". . . a little barefoot girl came and joined me. She said, 'Where are you going, Mr. Attlee?' I said, 'I'm going home for tea,' 'Oh,' she said, 'I'm going home to see if there *is* any tea.' This seemed to me to put very neatly the difference between the comfortable and the insecure classes." Clement Richard Attlee, *As It Happened* (New York: Viking Press, 1954), p. 45.

At the outbreak of World War I, Attlee promptly enlisted, and he served in the fighting fronts in Gallipoli and Mesopotamia and France. He was severely wounded and was invalided as a major with the Distinguished Service Cross. He resumed his duties in the settlement house and, in 1922, stood for Parliament from the Limehouse District. "Sometimes I carried the soapbox," Attlee recalled, "sometimes I stood on it, and sometimes I got knocked off it." He was elected and he never thereafter lost his hold on an extraordinarily devoted constituency. An ardent supporter said, "If yer wants to get yer face bashed in, just run 'im dahn, that's all."

He was now part of the very small parliamentary Labour contingent that was struggling for respectability in Britain's most exclusive club. The apprenticeship was an arduous one, through the years of Conservative dominance, the locust years of Fascist aggression in Europe, the frustrating years of Baldwin and Chamberlain and the appeasement of Hitler. The rise of Attlee was due in part to the absence of other leadership, after the split in Labour ranks in 1931. But his steadiness and his thoroughness of application won the esteem of all his colleagues. He represented Labour in the War Coalition, serving as Deputy Prime Minister at Churchill's side, with responsibility for the domestic front. Now, with the upset Labour victory of 1945, he was named Prime Minister to shepherd the country through simultaneous revolutions in the social structure at home and in the Empire on the Seven Seas.

A more unlikely leader for a Labour revolution would have been hard to imagine. He was slight of build, bald, meek-mannered, soft-spoken, almost mousey. All the adjectives that described him said "unimpressive," in different ways. His garb was drab, his style calm and subdued. The wags had a field day and Churchill joined in the not-so-innocent banter. "Attlee," he said, "is a very modest man, and he has a great deal to be modest about." He added, "Attlee is a sheep in sheep's clothing." Attlee himself staked no claim to oratory or to showmanship. "My speaking is laconic," he said candidly, and he made no attempt to embellish it for rhetorical effect. It was inevitable that the style of the new Prime Minister should be constantly compared with the Rabelaisian gusto and buoyancy of Churchill, always the Thespian, ever conscious of being on front stage.

Yet there was perhaps even greater impact in the matter-of-fact way in which Attlee managed drama. When he was called by the King to become Prime Minister and to form a government, his wife drove him to the Palace in the old family car. In his **Memoirs he** notes simply that he went in and she "waited outside for me."* The episode fitted the national mood. The people now wanted less of Churchill's flamboyance and his coruscating brilliance. They wanted reliability and Attlee provided it. The integrity and the decency of the man showed through his lackluster exterior. In a field of rough, hard-hitting Labour men, Attlee cut through emotional tirades and unionist exaggeration, identifying what he believed was needed, and then charting practical ways by which to fulfill the need. Typical was his response to a civil servant who suggested that the working classes in London could make their income go further if they bought coal in larger quantities and stored it. Attlee explained that this was not feasible since the sacks would be too large to get under the beds. He knew from his years in Toynbee Hall that their cramped little world would not be reformed by theory.

Attlee brought in with him a gifted group of strong-willed colleagues, representing the combination of trade union stalwarts and upper-class intellectuals. He had worked with them, trusted them, and he readily shared responsibility. "If you have a good dog," he said, "don't bark yourself."

There was Herbert Morrison, the new leader of the House, who had been a long-time member of the London County Council and was credited with preserving London as a Labour stronghold. He was the son of a policeman and a housemaid, Cockney to the manner born in dress and accent, with only an elementary schooling, but superbly self-educated. As a youngster he welcomed the job of a switchboard operator because it gave him off moments to read the Socialist classics. London knew him well—a one-eyed, tireless public servant—and affectionately referred to him as "Quint," since he did the work of five. When he was chided for inveterate untidiness, he chuckled that it was more important to tidy up London. In the blitz period it had been his resourcefulness and efficiency that had kept London alive and thriving despite bomb and fire.

Then there was Ernest Bevin, whom Attlee chose as Foreign Secretary, a 250-pound burly, irascible trade union leader who had risen from the most abject poverty. His father, an agricultural laborer, had died when Ernie was only eight. The boy went to work then and he never stopped—a flunky in a restaurant, a train conductor, and then a beer cart driver. He virtually lived on the

---

* Attlee, *As It Happened,* p. 207.

London docks, and when he became the secretary of the Dock Workers Union, he used the post as the base for building the powerful Trade Union Council where he was the undisputed boss. He directed the general strike of 1926 which paralyzed the life of Britain, and he blithely upset the meticulous routine of the coronation of King George VI by calling out a taxi strike at the height of the ceremonial season. He worked such long hours that his wife chided him for not remembering that he was supposed to be the advocate of shorter working hours for Labour. This dockside brawler, comfortable only in his workman's cap and cheap mackintosh, was given the portfolio for foreign affairs, and the immaculately dressed diplomats of Europe must have found him as truculent and difficult as his own people did. He was particularly contemptuous of the Communists, whom he despised with all his proletarian soul.

The most radical of the group was the breezy, eloquent Aneurin Bevan, who came up out of the coal pits where he had begun working as a boy. He never forgot the coal dust runneled into sweaty faces. He could not abide the aristocratic élite, "the vermin in their ermine." He had the oratorical charm of an earlier Welsh Prime Minister, David Lloyd George, combining the bard and the gutfighter with a lyrical ferocity that left his adversaries in confused helplessness. Nye Bevan was slated for the Ministry of Health, and he was to ram through the most far-reaching health service act in modern times, against the opposition of most of the medical profession.

These were the cabinet roughnecks—Morrison, Bevin, and Bevan. Representing the other component, the upper-class intellectuals, was Sir Stafford Cripps. Like Attlee he came from a wealthy background. His father was Lord Parmoor, and he had all the privileges that came with the old tie, the élite schools, and the proper social connections. His identification with Labour was part of his flight from what he denounced as the abuses of his own inheritance. He was a genius in economics and the strategic post of Chancellor of the Exchequer went to him when the times called for sacrificial austerity. His blunt integrity was unfortunately clothed in arrogance, and he was never really at home, as Attlee was, with his easygoing corduroy-clad Labour colleagues. Churchill, repelled by his hauteur, used to say of him, "There, but for the grace of God, goes God." But the quip carried a truth that Churchill had not intended; it emphasized an overriding sense of mission that was essential when taxes and special levies had to be imposed and when unions had to be persuaded to live on frozen wages.

In the first session of the new Parliament, Attlee and his mavericks rushed through eighty-four major bills, the most astonishing mass of social legislation in parliamentary history, comparable to the great days of Roosevelt's New Deal. The 261-year-old Bank of England was nationalized. Coal had been a sick industry with intolerable living conditions for the miners that bred long and rancorous strikes. Now two thousand mines were taken over by a National Coal Board, and the owners were compensated with long-term bonds. The means of transportation—the railroads, the buses, the canal services—were nationalized. Throughout Attlee emphasized that he was not advocating a soak-the-rich program nor Santa Claus legislation for handout bonuses to the poor. Each reform carried a price tag to be paid by every stratum of society.

There was no letup in the second session of Parliament, which went on into 1947. The anomalous power of the House of Lords was cut so drastically that it became an ornamental body and could no longer do more than briefly delay legislation. There was nationalization of the remaining public utilities—electricity and gas. In 1947 came the epoch-making Health Services Act that socialized medicine. The comprehensive proposal had been advocated in the war period when Sir William Beveridge had published his report on social insurance, outlining individual and family insurance protection "from the cradle to the grave." The Coalition government had approved it in principle, but the enabling legislation had been continuously postponed. Nye Bevan now took the Beveridge plan out of limbo, updated it, and gave it legislative priority. As presented, it was to apply to all British people, regardless of ability to pay, with no humiliating means test. It was to cost billions but it would at last give every family access to health and security, with dignity.

The act was so all-encompassing that it could not operate at once with complete effectiveness. It was to take several years before its major imperfections—waste, duplication, cheating, graft, bureaucratic red tape, and the other inevitable pioneering obstacles—could be overcome. Churchill labeled the program a fool's purgatory and sneered at a Socialist government that paid for its prodigality by calling on capitalist America for Marshall Plan support. Bevan brushed off all criticism and when the expenditures ran 500 percent beyond estimates, he coolly pointed to the deficit as proving how urgently Britain had needed such reform. By 1950, 95 percent of the population was eligible for the benefits of the act, and 90 percent of the doctors and the dentists had registered for participation. Later, when the Conservatives took over the government, they could no more jettison the program than the Republicans could turn the clock back on the social legislation of the American New Deal.

The Labour government proceeded with a second revolution that was to transform the character and structure of the British Commonwealth. Attlee had always been identified as a "Little Englander," ideologically opposed to colonial control. To him the Empire was not an asset, it was a burden. He did not believe that good trade relations depended on keeping far-off areas and peoples in subjection. Hence, after the war, when the colonies pressed for autonomy or independence, Attlee was eager to cooperate. Churchill had always resisted, announcing grimly when he was Prime Minister that he had not undertaken the responsibility in order to preside over the liquidation of the Empire. Attlee and Labour had no such inhibitions.

The decisions on the imperial structure did not, of course, rest exclusively on abstract doctrine. The factor of cost had to be faced. To hold on in the teeth of native resistance would call for annual billions in military outlay. Britain could not possibly afford such a drain on dwindling resources, especially when it had pledged major social welfare benefits for its own people.

Hence the pace of devolvement was accelerated in what became, within two or three years, a major colonial revolution—India-Pakistan, Malaysia, Burma and Ceylon in Asia, Ireland in Europe, Egypt and Palestine in the eastern Mediterranean, the black empire in Africa. Each emerging state was given the right to secede altogether, or to stay on, free and sovereign, within the framework of a redefined Commonwealth. Burma, Ireland, Egypt, and several others opted for complete secession. The rest negotiated ingenious ways of reconciling republican institutions with a continuing relationship to Britain. The Conservatives fought a halfhearted rearguard action, but they knew that the day of Empire and colonies, for good or ill, was over. The Labour leaders carried through the revolution on a high note of righteousness, as if they were paying off a long-postponed moral obligation. They were really pursuing missionary enterprise in reverse.

Yet the transition was not an altogether peaceful one. In India there were long and sanguinary internal wars between Hindus and

Moslems that took a toll of more than a million lives. In Palestine the departure of the British precipitated renewed conflicts between Arabs and Jews that kept the Middle East in continuous turmoil. Some of the smallest countries interpreted the speedy withdrawals to mean that anyone could now twist the British lion's tail. Guatemala cast eyes on British Honduras, the Argentine began to make noises about the Falkland Islands off its coast, Spain revived its claims on Gibraltar, Iran nationalized all the foreign oil interests, Iraq overthrew a British-supported government and confiscated the British holdings in the country. Labour could take pride in the ethics of its program, but the practical problems of readjustment in the interregnum period were as painful as in any major surgery.

Despite the inevitable dislocations of change, two revolutions had been telescoped into the six-year incumbency of Clement Attlee's government—the social reconstruction at home and the reordering of Commonwealth relationships abroad. The cost of the welfare state was now so far beyond expectations that the rapture period for Labour had little impetus left, and Bevan's cheery Welsh epigrams no longer buoyed up the dispirited. Every British family had to contend with the mounting bills, not only the rich and the well-placed. Indeed, this group was virtually eliminated. By 1950 only a small proportion of British families had gross annual incomes beyond $25,000.* The minimum income tax had been set at 45 percent and it climbed to almost confiscatory levels. The new housing units that were planned with so much confidence in 1945 could not be built because of the shortage of materials. Since imports had to be severely curtailed, rationing was introduced, with restrictions on meat, tobacco, and fuel, and the quality of the workingman's beer. The long queues of shoppers for minimum necessities became a common sight. Churchill needled the Socialist doctrinaires for their queue-topia.

All over Britain now there were second thoughts about Labour's "New Jerusalem," especially when the loans which had been advanced by the United States and Canada were exhausted long before the five-year period that had been planned for the transition to self-support. The dissatisfaction was keenest, of course, among the affluent. But the disenchanted middle-class families that had been exposed to the most galling irritations now deserted Labour in droves. They were just fed up with being fed up. Labour began

* *The Economist*, May 23, 1965. Based on income tax returns.

losing the by-elections as vacancies occurred, an emphatic warning that there was danger ahead. In the general election of 1950, the substantial majority of the 1945 victory was almost totally whittled away. When the proposal for the nationalization of the steel industry came before the new House of Commons, it was passed by a razor-thin margin, 306 to 300, much too slim a majority for Labour to dare to put it into effect. Soon the margin fell to three, and Attlee could remain in office, when votes of confidence were proposed, only by rounding up every supporter, even on stretchers and in wheel-chairs.

The Labour team itself began to fall apart. Cripps was too exhausted to continue. The indestructible Ernie Bevin fell ill, and he was obliged to retire. The more radical left wing of the party turned on the more moderate right wing, and there was a raging internecine war, Nye Bevan leading the extremists. Attlee put as good a face on the inner war as he could, explaining that the Tories settled their differences at the Carlton Club, but the Socialists fought out the battles in public. It was a gallant try, but the time was out of joint.

Six momentous years in office, with the responsibility to carry through a highly controversial mandate, had taken their toll. One is reminded of Disraeli's summary when, in his day, he surveyed the front government bench of tired Liberals and termed them "a range of exhausted volcanoes with not a single flame on a pallid crest."

Attlee faced the inevitable and called for another general election in 1951. Labour was now the victim of its own re-districting. It garnered more votes but the results were translated into a smaller number of seats. It was definitely a reversal of the verdict of 1945. Old Winston Churchill, now a ripe seventy-five, was called back to begin a new long span of Conservative control in Britain.

Attlee and his party had been given six brief years to apply their program to a nation in flux. There were many disappointments, many hopes that were not fulfilled. Yet the achievements, when evaluated in perspective, beyond the din of electioneering and recrimination, were impressive. Despite all the gloomy forebodings, the little man with the quiet voice, who could sit calmly and work geometric doodles while the debates raged about him, had laid the foundations for a modern welfare state. The disappearance of the Empire could be interpreted as the conversion of an anachronism into "a Commonwealth by consent." Perhaps the greatest tribute to Attlee and to Labour came in the admission of their Conservative opponents that none of the social welfare legislation would be repealed. All that they could promise was that they would administer the reforms with more efficiency. It is the fate of trailblazers to have stones thrown at them for their heresies, and then to have the stones later gathered for appreciative monuments.

30

THE FRENCH
FOURTH REPUBLIC

PARIS WAS LIBERATED BY THE ALLIES ON AUGUST 19, 1944. GENERAL de Gaulle's triumphant entry into the redeemed city, his march down the Champs Élysées, the Thanksgiving *Te Deum* in Notre Dame, were experiences shared by millions of delirious Frenchmen to whom they represented the end of the shame and deprivations of the Nazi nightmare. De Gaulle, the inspiration for the Resistance, who had not wavered during the darkest days of the war, was hailed as the unifying force and was unanimously named Premier.

His prestige was so commanding that he did not hesitate to use it to overcome the instability of the multi-party system which had disastrously fragmented political life in the three earlier Republics. He had in mind a strong presidency, with clear executive authority that would not be endlessly dependent on the vagaries of party maneuvering in the Chamber of Deputies. France, he warned, could no longer afford the luxury of political infighting. "Let us try to silence the noise of our absurd quarrels," he said, "because the tasks of reconstruction now are infinitely more difficult than they were in 1919 after World War I."

These were disquieting statements to Frenchmen. Certainly the Socialists and the Communists refused to regard their differences with the Conservatives as merely "absurd quarrels." The Communists, who polled about a third of the electorate, were realistic enough to know that a strong De Gaulle presidency would drastically weaken their position. The other parties could not shake off the foreboding that there was a strong streak of Bonapartism in De

Gaulle, and that it would be dangerous to turn over unchallenged executive authority to him. They were fearful of potential dictatorship, even when tempered by epigrams. They quoted from the Roman senator, Cato: "The hero saves us. Praise the hero. Now who will save us from the hero?" Even De Gaulle's glamorous war record and his towering position could not overcome the misgivings of the majority of the party leaders.

Thus even before the debris of the Nazi occupation had been cleared the political battles flared. Many of the sessions with the party leaders turned into stormy disputes and De Gaulle grew ever more impatient. He had been an ideal war leader. His manifestoes, his eloquent defiance, his unshakable optimism, had kept flagging spirits from defeatism. But apparently he was not prepared by temperament or by circumstance for niggling party negotiation. He had often said that nothing great is ever done "in the midst of chatter." His boiling point was always low. Then, on a day in January 1946, in office as Premier only a few months, De Gaulle suddenly appeared in full uniform before a special cabinet meeting and announced his resignation, adding that he was leaving politics irrevocably. Perhaps, with judgment worn thin by frustration, it was no idle threat. Or perhaps with confidence that he was the indispensable man, he expected to be called back on his own terms. As it turned out, he was to wait in the wings for twelve years before the summons came.

With De Gaulle sulking in his tent, a new constitution was approved in a referendum that anchored final authority in the National Assembly. The major parties remained so evenly divided that it always required precariously balanced coalitions to command a majority. From the liberation in 1945 until 1958, when the French Fourth Republic expired, there were twenty-one governments.

Yet the Fourth Republic did survive for more than twelve years, and despite its cliff-hanging instability, it achieved some enduring reforms. Under the leadership of the nonpolitical Jean Monnet, the economic genius of the period, a thirty-billion-dollar five-year plan and a major program of social welfare were launched. The wrecked ports were restored, the roads were rebuilt and, with timely Marshall Plan aid, the main industrial plants were modernized. The automobile industry was considerably expanded and French cars again became popular for export. The franc was stabilized, and the public began to take their savings from under the mattresses to put them to productive work. Tourist trade boomed again, and Paris in the spring gave the world a rosy hue. The Fourth Republic clearly had surprising recuperative power.

What ultimately brought it down was not the ramshackle political structure; it was wrecked by the costly struggle to retain the French colonial empire in Indochina and in North Africa. By 1954 the casualties in Vietnam had risen to 150,000, and hundreds of thousands of French troops were bogged down in Tunisia, Morocco, and Algeria. The steady attrition of men and resources drained the vitality of the faltering economy, which was already paying out heavily for the wars of yesterday with pensions and annuities to the wounded and the widows. The country would have bled to death except for the courage of one of the Premiers, Pierre Mendès-France, who decided, in 1954, to forego pride, cut losses, and withdraw.

INDOCHINA, MANY TIMES LARGER THAN FRANCE ITSELF, HAD ALMOST inexhaustible resources. One-fourth of the world's exports of rice came from there, and one-third of the world's natural rubber. It was not only a rich source of food and raw materials; it was a market for French goods and investment capital. At the beginning of World War II, it had been overrun by the Japanese, who turned it into a satellite state. The native populations resisted Japanese control, even as they had resisted their earlier French masters. When the war ended in Japanese defeat and expulsion, the French attempted to move back. They offered a measure of reform to placate the nationalists, but they were adamant about the retention of basic control. The French concessions were completely unacceptable to the nationalists. They wanted independence and they were prepared to continue all-out war to achieve it. It might have been possible to work out a compromise within the framework of a French federation, but the nationalist leader was Ho Chi Minh, a resolute, never-wearied rebel with a long record of Communist collaboration. There was the gravest risk that to yield autonomy, with Ho in control, would mean a Communist takeover with far-reaching effects on the East-West balance of power in Asia. Here was the impasse.

The French had a detailed dossier on Ho Chi Minh. He was born in 1890 or 1892 in central Vietnam, the son of a poor prefect. In 1911 he left home and shipped off to France as a cabin boy and he kept traveling around the world as a cook's helper. At one time he washed dishes and served as baker for the peerless French chef, Escoffier, at the Carlton Hotel in London. He read widely in the

Marxian classics, and he acquired remarkable facility in languages, mastering perhaps six or seven. His middle years were spent in France, where he earned a meager living by painting designs on Chinese "antiquities" manufactured for tourists. He was now a Communist and gave most of his time and energy to the organization of cells among the sixty thousand Vietnamese who lived and worked there. Often in Moscow and its training school for Communist agents, he was an apt pupil and won the favor of key Russian functionaries, who counted on him for their future Communist strategy in Southeast Asia.

When he returned to his home in Vietnam, the French listed him as a dangerous revolutionary, and he went underground. For a while he was presumed to be dead, a presumption that was frequently publicized whenever he melted into the jungle. When the Japanese took control of his homeland, the French made peace with him, and the Allies supplied him with weapons for his resistance to the Japanese. But Ho never ceased organizing underground partisan groups, united by the commitment ultimately to clear Indochina of all foreign control. When the Japanese surrendered in August 1945, Ho at once established headquarters in Hanoi and announced the independence of Indochina.

In his inaugural address he took as his model the American Declaration, and he began his manifesto with an almost verbatim prologue: "We hold these truths to be self-evident, that all men are created equal, that they are endowed by their Creator with certain unalienable rights, and that among them are Life, Liberty, and the Pursuit of Happiness." He concluded, "Vietnam has the right to be free and independent and, in fact, has become free and independent." As he spoke, two American planes flew in salute over Hanoi, their stars clearly visible, and they were cheered by the huge crowd.*

The French were furious with the Americans. They would not accept Ho Chi Minh's fait accompli. De Gaulle, now at the beginning of his brief incumbency as Premier, was ready to negotiate possible concessions, but he would not relinquish control of one of France's most prized colonial possessions. When Ho Chi Minh refused to retreat from the demand for independence and sovereignty, General Jean Leclerc, a French military hero, was sent out for the reconquest. Leclerc entered Saigon on October 5, 1945, and by the end of the year he had retaken all of South Vietnam up to

---

* Ellen J. Hammer, *The Struggle for Indochina* (Stanford: Stanford University Press, 1954), p. 105.

the 15th parallel. Already the de facto division of the country was emerging: the French in control of the south, and Ho Chi Minh and the Communists in control of the north.

A last effort was now made to reach some kind of compromise, and Ho Chi Minh was asked to come to France for a summit conference at Fontainebleau. His appearance and personality astonished the West. The fiery revolutionist, the tough guerrilla, turned out to be a frail, spindling little man, deceptively gentle, humble, witty, quite a charmer. He was wined and dined, especially by the Americans, who hailed him as a great Asian. He counseled the French to be sensible, to stop thinking in obsolete colonial terms, and to make substantial enough concessions so as not to play into the hands of those whom he called "the extremists." "Do not let me leave like this!" he urged as he left the conference. "Support me against those who are trying to go further than I. You will never regret it!"* But the French negotiators were adamant. They interpreted Ho Chi Minh's appeal as a cunning propaganda maneuver. How could they place reliance in a man with Ho's long revolutionary background, orating as a nationalist but acting as a Communist, and maintaining closest ties to Russia and China? How could they trust such a man to keep his country out of the Communist orbit? The French were supported in their inflexibility by the American negotiators. John Foster Dulles saw Ho merely as a tool of the Chinese Maoists. He did not contribute to any relaxation in tensions when he deliberately refused to shake hands with the Chinese Foreign Minister, Chou En-lai.† Ho Chi Minh then made a prophetic threat. To an American correspondent he said, "It will be a war between an elephant and a tiger. If the tiger ever stands still the elephant will crush him. . . . But the tiger does not stand still. He lurks in the jungle by day and emerges by night. He will leap upon the back of the elephant . . . and then he will leap back into the dark jungle. And slowly the elephant will bleed to death. That will be the war of Indochina."‡

In December 1946, the war exploded in all of its ferocity, and it was to continue for eight years. Ho Chi Minh had at his side General

---

* Guy de Carmoy, *The Foreign Policies of France* (Chicago: University of Chicago Press, 1970), p. 136.

† Two decades later, when President Nixon made his historic visit to Red China, Chou En-lai still remembered the studied insult and referred to it.

‡ David Schoenbrun, *As France Goes* (New York: Harper & Bros., 1957), pp. 234–5.

Giap, one of the most resourceful guerrilla leaders of modern times. Giap had been a brilliant lawyer and teacher. He moved into a military role during the latter years of the war against the Japanese invaders, and was then receiving indispensable help from the American Office of Strategic Services which was masterminding the common effort against the Japanese. But once the Japanese had been expelled, the French again became the enemy. The guerrillas concentrated on a war of attrition, carefully avoiding any open confrontation. They ambushed unwary units and burned warehouses and supply depots. They threw hand grenades in strategic places, in markets, in theaters; they blew up bridges; they spread terror and confusion. The French could not tell deadly enemy from peaceful peasant. By day the man who waited on table, who drove the taxi, who cleaned the streets, who sold the food, seemed harmless enough. But by night he could mine the roads, and raid the barracks, and could cut down bands of soldiers. Ho Chi Minh had vowed, "We will make Indochina uninhabitable for the French." This threat became terrifying reality.

By 1949 the tempo of the war was again accelerated. The government of Chiang Kai-shek had collapsed and China had passed into Communist control. The North Koreans, armed and abetted by Russia and Red China, had attacked and invaded South Korea. The Communists had apparently launched a coordinated offensive to drive the United States and the West out of Asia. Inevitably the American position *vis-à-vis* Indochina radically altered. Ho Chi Minh was no longer a nationalist patriot seeking freedom from colonial control for his people. He was a Communist ally in the global struggle between East and West. Hence, the United States began stepping up its aid to the French, a thin trickle at first, then more and more, billions more. Within a few years it was bearing 80 percent of the cost of the war in French Indochina.

The agony for France went on into 1954. Tens of thousands of French colonial troops were dispatched to Vietnam and Cambodia and Laos, and the return ships and planes brought back full loads of the dead and wounded. The guerrilla forces of Ho Chi Minh and General Giap suffered much greater casualties, their men decimated, their women and children burned out and mowed down, their villages reduced to ashes. But Ho's forecast was fulfilled. The French killed ten, the guerrillas killed one, but the toll for the French became increasingly difficult to accept.

In March 1954, after eight frustrating years, the French High

Command made a bold effort to maneuver the guerrillas into open battle. They flew fifteen thousand of their choice troops into Dien Bien Phu, a valley pocket about 200 miles beyond the guerrilla lines, a challenge to General Giap to emerge in force to prevent being out-flanked. It was a calamitous gamble. The Chinese had built up powerful reserves for General Giap, and he turned the tables on the French, locking them into an almost hopeless siege. Dien Bien Phu took on the tragic significance of the Alamo. The French now appealed to the western Allies for a massive air strike to relieve the beleaguered fortress. They warned that if it were permitted to fall, all of Indochina would be abandoned to the Communists, bringing repercussions in Asia too terrifying to contemplate.

There was increased diplomatic activity in London and in Washington. Anthony Eden, backed by Churchill, expressed certainty that direct western intervention would inevitably lead to a general land war in Asia and perhaps to a third world war. In Washington, President Eisenhower took counsel with his closest advisers for one of his most far-reaching decisions. Dulles, his Secretary of State, Richard Nixon, his Vice President, and Admiral Radford, his Chief of Staff, all strongly urged intervention, even if it meant bringing Russia and China into a full-scale war. Dulles went so far as to include among the options the use of nuclear weapons for the relief of the French. Eisenhower weighed the various alternatives carefully and then determined that, having just extricated the country from the Korean experience, it would be catastrophic to become involved in a jungle war without the collaboration of any other Allies.* The relief was not sent. Dien Bien Phu fell.

The French Premier, Laniel, knew then that an era had ended for France. Laniel was in the lion's den, but there was no providential miracle this time for escape. The French government collapsed, and this brought to the head of affairs Pierre Mendès-France, who had been urging for years that independence for Indochina was inevitable and that French withdrawal could no longer be postponed.

Pierre Mendès-France was born in 1907 of a Jewish family that had originated in Portugal but had been living in France for more than six hundred years. He had studied for the law, and was admitted to the bar at twenty-three as the youngest lawyer in France. Two years later he was elected to the Chamber of Deputies, again as its

---

* Dwight D. Eisenhower, *The White House Years* (Garden City, N.Y.: Doubleday, 1963–5), Vol. I, pp. 343–56.

youngest member. He was a specialist in the economic problems of the country, a clear-headed realist who could not abide the myths and fantasies that fatally tempted France to live beyond its capacity. When France fell to the Nazis in 1940, Mendès-France had fled with other Resistance leaders to North Africa, where he was captured and imprisoned by the Vichy leadership there. He managed a dramatic hacksaw-bedsheet escape and made his way to England, where he joined De Gaulle and flew bombing missions in the Free French air force until the Nazis were driven out of France. He was a member of De Gaulle's first liberation government and there he continued to press for sound budgeting policies, sacrificial taxes, unsparing anti-inflation measures, so that France could return to solvency and responsible administration. Tinkering and patching, he said, would not serve now. "You cannot cauterize a wooden leg." When he could not persuade the Assembly or his colleagues, he resigned, continuing from the sidelines to offer advice and dissent.

As France bogged down in the colonial wars in Asia and North Africa, Mendès-France became the main spokesman for a realistic cutting of losses so that France could turn its energies and resources to the insistent needs for social welfare at home. When Dien Bien Phu fell and the bankruptcy of the colonial policies of the past was exposed, Mendès-France was called to crisis leadership.

In his first statement as the new Premier he pledged that he would negotiate a cease-fire agreement in Indochina within thirty days, or he would resign. The deadline period was a frenetic one, and Mendès-France had to steer through the most treacherous shoals. In a summit conference at Geneva he ran into hard bargaining sessions with the delegates from Indochina, Molotov of Russia, and Chou En-lai of Red China. Dulles too tried to keep him in line. Mendès-France, in firm rapport with Anthony Eden and Britain, would not be deterred. He came away with an agreement that called for the temporary partition of Vietnam at the 17th parallel, the north to remain under the control of the Ho Chi Minh government, the south to remain under non-Communist control. Laos and Cambodia were to be neutralized, all foreign forces were to be withdrawn and, within two years, there were to be free elections in all Vietnam under United Nations supervision to determine the future government of a united country. Dulles was so furious with what he termed the surrender of Mendès-France and Eden that, though he did not repudiate the settlement, he would not place the American signature on the agreement. When the treaties came before the Chamber of

Deputies, many harsh words were spoken—"betrayal," "scuttling," "appeasement." But Mendès-France easily carried the day. The French casualties had gone on for too long and they were to be stopped at last.

Yet the wars in the Indochina provinces were not destined to end quickly. As France relinquished its jurisdiction, the United States took over the responsibility for keeping the area out of the Communist camp. At first there was only nominal participation, but gradually the commitment drew the United States into one of the most ruinous wars in its history.*

Meantime Mendès-France was already wrestling with nationalist uprisings in the North African protectorates of France. Here the stakes were even higher. In Southeast Asia a small enclave of Frenchmen had been holding down a huge native population. But for decades, hundreds of thousands of Frenchmen had migrated to Algeria, Morocco, and Tunisia, and these provinces had become their home. Their plantations and factories, their clubs and schools and churches were extensions of France itself. In the defeat of France by the Nazis in 1940, most of the North African French leaders had sided with the Nazi collaborators. But toward the end of the war the Free French and the western Allies had ousted the Vichy men and North Africa became the launching pad for the reconquest of France.

Now, as everywhere in the colonial world, there were vigorous demands by the native populations for independence or at least autonomy. But none of the French coalition postwar governments had been able to act with resolution. The wealthy ruling group in North Africa invariably aborted any attempts at compromise which would challenge their authority. The native extremists were equally adamant. They were pledged to cut ties with France. Their alternative for the French was the suitcase or the coffin; pack up and get out, or expect death. Soon the sorry round began, already so tragically familiar in Indochina—terrorism, repression, assassination, reprisal. The ultras among the Arabs killed not only the French landowners but the moderates of their own people who advocated any compromise proposals. The colonials, backed by the tough army contingents, responded in kind. By 1954, North Africa was torn apart by the contending forces.

It was at this juncture that Mendès-France was named Premier,

* See Chapter 48.

committed to a revaluation of colonial policy. He flew to Tunis to negotiate directly with the Sultan, and he reached agreements that were to lead, in two years, to independence within a French federation. He also worked out a formula for Morocco which promised the end of bloodshed there. It was not easy during the violently partisan debates to listen to the insults, nor to bear the abuse, of the colonials and the deputies in the Chamber.* But Mendès-France had never shrunk from painful solutions: "To govern is to choose" had always been his working credo. He was to have the satisfaction, before too long, of watching the nationalist leader of Tunisia, Habib Bourguiba, as the first President, become a valuable liaison between his emancipated country and his French foster land.

But when Mendès-France turned to Algeria and proposed solutions there on the models of Indochina, Tunisia, and Morocco, all the bitterness that had accumulated from previous compromises burst out into the open. The denouement came when De Gaulle, from his suburban cloister, counseled his followers to reject what he termed a disgraceful retreat. Mendès-France was voted down in a humiliating scene in the Chamber and was booed off the rostrum.†

In the context of later developments, the incumbency of Pierre Mendès-France stood out as perhaps the most effective in the history of the French Republic. Even the failure in Algeria was a failure only for the moment. The final settlement there was complete independence. Ironically, it was yielded by General de Gaulle, who went very much further in concessions than Mendès-France had proposed. Indeed, De Gaulle went so far that he precipitated a revolt against himself by the outraged colonials and the military leaders who had brought him back to power to preserve French control in Algeria.‡

---

* One of the Deputies offered an explanation for the popularity that Mendès-France was enjoying in the country and the highly charged partisan climate that he was encountering in the Chamber. "Mendès is having a wonderful love affair with the country, but the country isn't an institution, the Assembly is, and the dullest marriages last better than the most passionate affairs." Reported by Sir Denis Brogan, *The New York Times*, April 20, 1958.

† Some years later, on a visit to Brandeis University to receive its honorary degree, Mendès-France told me of a poignant conversation with one of his close friends in the Chamber. "It was fortunate for France," his friend said to the man whose family had lived in France for six centuries, "that you were the Premier when the amputation of French territory had to be done. A *real* Frenchman could never have gone through with it." Apparently the comment was meant kindly. Mendès-France was not of peasant, Gallic, Catholic stock and hence, however far back his ancestry went in France, the mark of alienism was still upon him.

‡ See Chapter 39.

By then, however, in May 1958, the whole issue was no longer any man's decision, nor the decision of any party. Every form of colonialism had become indefensible. What in 1954 had been, in De Gaulle's words, "shameful retreat," had, four years later, become "statesman-like realism." The old general was obliged to be more Mendès-France than Mendès-France himself. But by 1958 De Gaulle did not have to worry about his consistency. He had been voted complete authority and the mandate that he had always sought was his. The parliamentary system had committed suicide on his doorstep, and the Fourth Republic had gone into another of history's dustbins.

31

STALIN: THE CULT OF PERSONALITY*

AT ONE OF THE SUMMIT MEETINGS DURING WORLD WAR II STALIN confided to Anthony Eden of Britain that he admired the intuitive genius of Hitler. His fatal failing, he added, had been that he just did not know when to stop. Eden smiled quizzically and Stalin went on, "You smile because you believe that I, too, don't know when to stop. But you're wrong. I shall not make the same mistake." There were few even among those closest to Stalin who would agree. In his last years he seemed to be a driven man, completely obsessed by fear that enemies, without and within, continuously threatened national and personal security. He trusted no one, and he functioned as if Death was poised to take advantage of any lowering of the guard.

He used every artifice of power and deceit to build a ring of satellites around Russia, even when this meant the subversion of independent states and the most ruthless suppression of the elementary rights of their peoples. By infiltration, by coup, by conquest, he took control of all the neighboring states in the Baltic and the Balkans to make certain that the Russian heartland could not be penetrated.

Stalin's concern for security was understandable. Russia's losses in World War II were so enormous that the figures defied meaning: tens of millions in lives, tens of billions in material damage, many times the toll in World War I. Twenty-two million men had been

* This was the term applied at the Twenty-second Party Congress when Stalin was assailed for corrupting the true aims of Lenin's October revolution.

[360]

mobilized for war and had been withdrawn from family life for more than four years. Seventy thousand villages, two thousand cities —including Leningrad, Moscow, Rostov, Stalingrad—had been leveled or devastated, first by the Nazis, and then by the Russians themselves in their sacrificial scorched earth strategy. It was as if all the land in the United States east of the Mississippi had been blasted and denuded. The invasion entry points, as so often before, had been through Germany, Poland, and the Balkan states, and these entry points Stalin vowed must never again be areas of vulnerability.

He had no faith in the power of international entities such as the United Nations, nor in treaties, even with alleged allies, to protect the future. During the war the Nazis had been the enemy; but in Stalin's mind, the Nazis had been only the *foremost* enemy. There were others, and there would be still others, and they included the present Allies too. Churchill reported that in 1942, when Molotov visited London, he kept a gun under his pillow, and he brought his own security police and even his own cleaning women. Considerable Lend-Lease aid was assigned to Russia by the United States, but American planes were not permitted to fly it in. Russian crews were sent to Alaska to receive the supplies and personally transport them to Russia. During the summit conferences at Teheran and Yalta and Potsdam there were ceremonial toasts and banquets, but Stalin never relaxed his vigilance.

The unceasing quest for security was the motive that Stalin always emphasized for the expansion of control far beyond Russian frontiers. Even before the war had ended, there were outright annexations. Stalin made Estonia, Latvia, and Lithuania part of the Soviet empire. Only in this way, he insisted, could the vulnerable Baltic flank be protected. Security was also the rationale for retaining the provinces of eastern Poland that had been seized after the Hitler-Stalin pact of 1938. Russia acquired 70,000 square miles of Polish territory, cleared out millions of Poles, and repeopled the land with Russian peasants. When Russia and the West became Allies, Stalin would not yield even a mile of what had been taken. He proposed instead that Poland should seek compensation at the expense of their common enemy, Germany. The trade was made, and 40,000 square miles of German territory on the western frontier were resettled with six million Poles.

All this was prelude to the installation of a subservient Polish government that would faithfully represent the Russian overlord.

Stalin had pledged Roosevelt and Churchill a free election in Poland, but he knew better than to risk an unsupervised referendum. The Polish Peasant Party was still too powerful, and its hostility to communism would require years of indoctrination to soften. Stalin took the short-cut. The promised elections of January 1945 were conducted on the well-established Communist model. Every form of intimidation and terrorism was applied. Peasant Party candidates were beaten, scores were imprisoned, many were murdered. Thousands of known anti-Communists were arrested or deported. In ten of the provinces the Peasant Party was peremptorily disqualified. There were only thirty-two witnesses for 5,200 polling places, and the ballots were counted by Communist Party functionaries who claimed a landslide victory of 327 to 24. The wonder was that even twenty-four hardy souls got through the sieve. Poland had gone Communist, and it was now safely berthed. One of the election officials drew on the special double-tongued Communist vocabulary to announce the people's victory: "We took over, not by force, but by revolutionary methods."

The pattern for Poland was followed in determining the fate of East Germany. Poland had been the gateway for the invasions of Russia, but the Germans had been the invaders. Stalin vowed that they would never again be given a favorable opportunity for aggression. Strategic areas on the Baltic, the heart of old Junker Prussia, were therefore annexed outright and millions of Germans who lived there fled. Their lands and their possessions were confiscated and redistributed. Then the eastern zone of Germany, whose administration had been assigned to Russia in the Allied summit conferences, was set up as a puppet state with its seventeen million inhabitants. Even before the war had ended, planeloads of Communist functionaries landed at Berlin Airport, ready to carry through the prepared blueprints for consolidation. The primary responsibility for this task was given to a German party regular, Walter Ulbricht, who for years had been carefully prepared in the Soviet Union for this assignment.

Ulbricht, the son of a tailor, was a Leipzig carpenter who had turned Communist after World War I. He directed the minuscule party through the Weimar period, editing the fly-by-night party papers and propaganda organs. He fled to Russia when Hitler came to power, became a Russian citizen, and won the favor of the major party *apparatchiks*. When he landed in Berlin in 1945 with the contingent of Stalinist collaborators, he was prepared to become the carpenter for the planned Communist regime. Ulbricht had none of the qualities of a popular leader. He was a dull, plodding administrator, as servile as a lapdog. But he needed neither color nor personality. He had the Soviet power behind him, usually some twenty Russian divisions. Stalin gave him as much confidence as he ever gave to anyone, and Ulbricht repaid his master with undeviating submissiveness. He liquidated open opposition, dispossessed the recalcitrants, and integrated the East German resources with the Soviet economy.

For the first few years emigration to West Germany was still permitted, and several million of the youngest and the most daring fled. When the sustained exodus began to threaten the vitality of the state, further emigration was forbidden. But even the most strenuous precautions failed to staunch the refugee flow, especially through Berlin, and Stalin ordered a barbed wire wall to be built.* To the West it was a most appropriate symbol of the prison that East Germany had become. Stalin did not worry about symbols; Russia now not only had buffer protection on its western front; by maintaining the dismemberment of Germany, it had effectively minimized the recuperative military power of its ancient enemy.

Meantime, Stalin had turned his attention to the Balkans. Bulgaria was the most vulnerable for a quick takeover; historically the Bulgarians were the little Slav brothers, allied to Russia in race and faith and culture. Bulgaria was a peasant state, whose politics had been dominated by the Socialist Agrarian Party under the leadership of Nikola Petkov, one of the most courageous patriots in Balkan history. His father had served his country as reform Prime Minister in the years that followed World War I, and Nikola carried his father's mantle with pride, battling totalitarianism wherever it threatened. During the hegemony of Hitler, the Socialists and the Communists had worked together, in a Fatherland Front, to resist the Nazi occupation.

Petkov was ready to continue the coalition after the war, to face the problems of reconstruction together. But Stalin would have none of this now. Even before the Nazis had been expelled, cadres of Soviet-trained Communists arrived and, supported by Red Army units, took over the key administrative posts. They arrested those whom they identified as enemies of the state and conducted showcase trials on the Stalinist kangaroo court model. There was no distinc-

* See Chapter 40.

tion between those who had collaborated with the Nazis and those who would not now pledge Communist allegiance. When the dissenters had been purged, the Communists were ready for an election. It was held in 1946, and there was little effort made to hide the intimidation and repression that were employed. It was a tribute to the stubborn independence of the peasantry that Petkov's party still was able to win a third of the total vote. Petkov refused to remain silent as he watched the Soviet juggernaut roll over democratic safeguards. One plague of predatory locusts had only just been eliminated and now the independent life of the Fatherland was threatened by another. "You are ruling the country by sheer terror," he cried out in Parliament at the end of 1946. "The concentration camps are full again as you, the Communists, eliminate your allies, in spite of the promises to work within the frame of our Fatherland Front." Petkov was arrested at his seat in Parliament. His trial, where all the judges were Communists, was a propaganda spectacular. He was sentenced to death as a traitor, and in September 1947, he was hanged. Later a government document was issued containing Petkov's signed "confession," filled with gibberish about his betrayal of the revolution, concluding that he deserved whatever fate had been decreed for him. The United States was so outraged by the crudeness of the coup and the cynicism of the trial that diplomatic relations with Bulgaria were broken off, and they were not restored until there was a temporary diplomatic thaw in 1959.*

Another prize that Stalin coveted to reinforce his Balkan cordon was Hungary. He knew that to gain his objective here it would be necessary to destroy the Magyar Catholic leadership which held the country to its long tradition of anti-communism. There had been hatred for the Nazis who occupied and ravaged the country during the war period but there was equal hatred for the Russians who, after sweeping out the Nazis, kept their troops in the country and ruled it as if it were a conquered province. The first election in 1945, despite extensive rigging, gave the Communists only 17 percent of the total vote. It was deemed politic, therefore, to go on with the charade of coalition government for the time being. Stalin bided his time, relying on the Communist representation in the cabinet to undermine the government and to prepare for the later absorption.

* The correspondent for *The New York Herald Tribune* wrote that soon after the execution of Petkov, he told one of the Bulgarian officials that he was leaving the country to take up a new assignment in Yugoslavia. The official expressed surprise. "Oh, not to Yugoslavia! Why, that place is a dictatorship!"

The responsibility for the termite task was entrusted to the secretary of the party, Matyas Rákosi, who was to dominate the scene in Hungary for the next decade.

Rákosi had been a lifelong Communist with a revolutionary record that went back to World War I, after which he participated in the abortive attempt to establish Communist control in Hungary. He rotted in prison for the best years of his early manhood, often in solitary confinement. It must have been this exhausting purgatory that drained out the last vestiges of any human compassion. He spent many years in Russia, training in its school of revolution. During World War II he was back in Hungary and was part of the underground resistance to the Nazis. He surfaced after the war and was named by the party to the first cabinet of 1945, with the mission to destroy the coalition. A shrewd manipulator, he began to place his agents in each of the most sensitive leverage points—the police, the army, the unions, the government service, the communications media. One by one they were sliced away in what he labeled a salami strategy.

In May 1947, he was ready for the coup. Prime Minister Nagy was in Switzerland for a medical checkup. Rákosi called him by telephone to suggest that he had better not return. He had uncovered a plot, he said, by the non-Communist parties to restore the old reactionary gang. If Nagy returned, he would, of course, have to stand trial for treason. Besides, Nagy's five-year-old son was now in custody, and surely his father wanted no harm to come to him. Nagy yielded to the blackmail and announced his resignation. Rákosi, with the Russian forces standing guard, carried out a wave of new arrests and the coup was almost bloodless.

There followed the usual Communist reorganization. Since Hungary was virtually feudal in its economic and social fabric, many of the reforms were long overdue. But it was unfortunate that there was so much indiscriminate violence in the takeover. The Communist technique of brainwashing was held up to scorn and condemned in the outside world when the primate of Hungary, Cardinal Mindzenty, was kept in prison for several months, then dragged into court to confess that he had conspired to restore the Hapsburg monarchy and had been a spy for the American Legation in Budapest. He was sentenced to life imprisonment. Stalin paid no attention to the resolutions of indignation meetings, nor to the representations of diplomacy. Rákosi kept slicing the salami and another key Balkan state had been successfully infiltrated according to the prepared timetable. It should be added that since internal power upheavals in a dictatorship are as frequent as they are unpredictable, Rákosi fell out of favor in a few years and was summarily purged. He learned, along with most of his colleagues, how much heartburn the salami could produce.

Stalin was already busy setting another buffer block into place. Rumania not only had primary strategic importance, commanding the entrance to the Ukraine and the Black Sea, but its abundant oil reserves were among the most valuable in the world. Here, too, it was evident that only force, without squeamishness, would be required to convert it into a Communist satellite. The old Rumanian government had fully collaborated with Hitler during World War II. Its regiments had fought by the side of the Nazis in Stalingrad and had helped to take Sevastopol. Stalin never forgot that the marauding Rumanian troops had treated the Russian invasion as Operation Plunder, and had even marched off with all the seats in the Odessa Opera House. The Soviet forces that drove the Nazis out of Rumania therefore stayed on.

The abrasive, no-nonsense Andrei Vyshinskii was sent in as Stalin's hatchet man. He confronted young King Michael as the Russian troops stood guard outside the palace, and he dictated the composition of the new government, all Communists. In leaving the King, Vyshinskii slammed the door to accentuate the point that the orders were now being given by the Russians. Then, to formalize the seizure, an election was arranged for early 1946. Arranged is the precise word. Explicit promises had been given to the Allied leaders at Yalta that the election would be free. But Stalin had no scruples about repudiating such pledges. When, he sneered, had corrupt Rumania ever had a free election? The voting followed the routine Communist procedure—the arrest of many of the non-Communist candidates, the intimidation of those who ventured to come to the polls, the fake ballot counting. Soon afterwards the King himself was ousted and Rumania was officially declared a Communist state. The political takeover was quickly followed by economic reorganization in a technique that the Russians had perfected to control foreign industries. Companies were set up where the Russians and the Rumanians were each assigned 50 percent of the stock. But, since the Rumanian representatives were all loyal Communists, the industries were as riveted to the Soviet economy as any native Russian enterprise. Within a few years the face of the old Rumania was unrecognizable.

The dominant Communist figure during this transition, and almost to the day of Stalin's death in 1953, was the chunky Ana Pauker, who must have been hewn from the same tough texture as Stalin himself. She was built like a tank, and she rode over the opposition as if she were one. She had been an early revolutionist, with a long record of jail terms and exile. She had spent many years in Russia, had become a Russian citizen, and had served as an officer in the Red Army. She had lived for the party even when the leadership liquidated her husband for deviation from the accepted party line. When Rumania was dragooned into the Soviet bloc, Ana Pauker became the Foreign Minister and was the power behind the functionaries who bore higher titles, including the succession of Prime Ministers. Her approach to government was demonstrated when she eliminated the entire staff of the Foreign Office, until only the doormen remained. Stalin could count on her unreservedly, and she served him well as the disciplines of Communist reorganization were swiftly enacted. She was repaid for her devotion with the gratitude that she herself had encouraged. She was purged in 1952 with the cooked-up charge that she was living on "the slopes of aristocracy." But in the years when Stalin was reorganizing the power base of the Balkan states, Ana Pauker, in her bullet-proof Cadillac, was at the center of every major decision.

The climax of Stalin's plan to achieve buffer state control was reached in the usurpation of 1948 in Czechoslovakia. The treachery and the foul play that was practiced to destroy independence there probably did most to discredit the hope that a coalition including Communists could ever escape corrosion and ultimate engulfment. Czechoslovakia had already been through the purgatory of the Nazi occupation. About 360,000 civilians had perished through judicial murder or liquidation. As the war ground to an end, the Russian and the American forces raced from east and west to pre-empt the key points. General Patton could easily have captured Prague, but at the summit conference it had been agreed that the Russians would be given precedence there upon the pledge to conduct free elections after the war. General Eisenhower, therefore, ordered Patton to slow down the American drive, and the Russians completed the liberation of Czechoslovakia.

In the elections that followed, the Communists polled 38 percent, a tribute to their vital role in the resistance to the Nazis. The government that emerged was a working coalition of Social Democrats and Communists. The presidency was assumed by Dr. Eduard Beneš, one of the founders of the democratic Czechoslovak republic after World War I;* Klement Gottwald, an old-line Communist, was named Prime Minister. There were optimists who presumed that, at least in Czechoslovakia, there would be cooperation, that the country would be the bridge between East and West. Others, less sanguine, had the gravest misgivings. They remembered that a bridge is usually trodden upon. They had little expectation that the West would resist the inevitable encroachments of the Communists, any more than it had resisted the bullying of the Nazis at Munich.

All too soon their foreboding was fulfilled. The familiar Communist provocations reappeared that were intended to subvert the coalition. In February 1948, the Communist Minister of Interior began to pack the police force, replacing the unreliables with loyal Communists. The twelve moderate members of the coalition cabinet, disappointed by this exhibition of Communist behavior, submitted their resignations in the expectation that Dr. Beneš would call for a general election. The Communists were delighted and they seized on the inanity of the moderates to accelerate their planned objective. Dr. Beneš was threatened with the direst consequences unless he immediately accepted the resignations and, foregoing any new elections, filled the vacant cabinet places with Communists. Two hundred thousand demonstrators were marshaled in the great square in Prague, and Russian military reserves were deployed further to emphasize the point that the days of collaboration were over.

Dr. Beneš yielded to the inevitable, even as he had yielded in 1938, after Munich. A few months later, physically ill and heartbroken, he resigned. In the next week the body of the Foreign Minister, Jan Masaryk, son of the first President, was found in the courtyard of his apartment. The government announced that he had committed suicide, but there was substantial evidence that he had been pushed out of an open upper-story window by "Beria's gorillas," Stalin's strong-arm executioners.†

With the opposition parties out of the way, Czechoslovakia joined the countries that had passed under complete Soviet control. Since there remained a dangerous popular veneration of Thomas Masaryk and Eduard Beneš, who had originally won the independence and the sovereignty of the country, the Communist purge spilled back into the past, to include the dead as well as the living. An intensive

---

* See Chapter 10.

† He could have fled, but he refused. He told his friend, the correspondent Ed Murrow, "Maybe a corpse, never a refugee."

campaign of distortion was launched to rewrite the history of the years since World War I. Masaryk was identified as a Wall Street tool, the creature of American imperialist designs, and his democratic colleagues were labeled with adjectives of denigration that made them out to be worse than the Nazis. On the majestic hill on the outskirts of Prague a monumental statue of Stalin was mounted to look down upon his handiwork.

Thus, within a few years of the end of the war, Stalin had created a formidable phalanx of subservient states, guarding the west and the south of Russia. He had failed to command docility only in Yugoslavia where Tito, though a dedicated Communist, had firmly resisted Soviet dictation.* But the Baltic states and the Balkans were all firmly locked into the Soviet empire.

Yet, though the Russian forces were poised with massive strength to deal with disaffection or heresy, Stalin still worried about security. He would take no chances even with the lackeys who had engineered the Communist coups with complete servility. Whenever any of them dared the faintest expression of independent judgment, or seemed to show the slightest nationalist loyalty, Stalin had no scruples about their liquidation. Many of the original leaders of the Communist revolutions in the Balkans and in Central Europe were placed on trial, on trumped-up charges—treason, Fascist collaboration, Zionist imperialism, C.I.A. spying. They included Slansky of Czechoslovakia, Rejk of Hungary, Ana Pauker of Rumania, and Kostov of Bulgaria. They were usually held long enough to persuade them, not too gently, to see the error of their ways, as they had so often manipulated others. They were then brought to court where they publicly made their abject confessions before they were executed by firing squads or hangmen, or were disgraced and demoted.

It should be added that the obsession with security that so deeply influenced Stalin's foreign policy dominated his actions within Russia itself. The elimination of the Fascist menace, the burgeoning strength of the economy, the expansion of the Soviet empire, brought Stalin no peace of mind in his last years. Perhaps his suspicions were justified. The rigor of his dictatorship spawned opposition that became ever more desperate. Or perhaps Stalin was now paranoid and saw threats in every movement and enemies in every shadow. The purges of the thirties were now revived on an expanding scale. The men in government and industry, in the agricultural collectives,

* See Chapter 20.

in the military and the secret police, were cut down in their tens of thousands, then in their hundreds of thousands. Past loyalty through the darkest days of Russia's mortal danger counted for little. Even survivors of the heroic siege of Leningrad were liquidated in 1949. The concentration camps filled up again. In the largest of them, Vorkuta, in the subzero arctic region of the Urals, a million deportees were worked and starved to death, as if Stalin were envious of Buchenwald and Auschwitz. Khrushchev revealed at the Congress of 1956 that when the highest officials of the Politburo left Stalin's presence, they were never sure that they would survive to see the morning.

On a March day in 1953 the news was released that the old dictator had died. There is still no certainty whether he suffered a stroke or was murdered before the ongoing purge would include the Politburo officials around him who felt threatened. The moment of death was described by his daughter, Svetlana: "He suddenly lifted his left hand as though he were pointing to something above and bringing down a curse upon us all."* We come back then to Stalin's judgment on Hitler. Stalin said that he would not make the same mistake. But he did. For it is the fatal vulnerability of the dictator that he does not know when to stop.

---

* Svetlana Alliluyeva, *Twenty Letters to a Friend* (New York: Harper & Row, 1967), p. 10.

32

THE RISE OF
ISRAEL

THE ARAB-ISRAELI CONFLICT IS SO INTERTWINED WITH EMOTIONAL reactions that only the unconcerned can even pretend to be objective. As in most controversies each side has a case. But the problem is vastly complicated because, for the advocates, the evidence keeps stretching back, filtered always through the prism of memory, and inevitably the realities of the present get lost in the mists of ancient claims and grievances.

The Jewish claim comes from the continuity of a folk linkage with the land, stretching over more than sixty generations. There had never been a severance of the living connection between the Jews, in their worldwide dispersion, and the land of their biblical ancestors; nor was there ever a time without a Jewish community in Palestine. The age-old prayer read: "If I forget thee, O Jerusalem, may my right hand lose its skill." The intense longing for a return was further nurtured by an almost unrelieved history of persecution. In the late nineteenth century Zionism was born, the movement whose purpose it was to convert prayer and hope into practical attempts to re-establish a homeland in Palestine for those Jews who wished to find new lives there. There were modest immigration movements; those who settled in the land never referred to their immigration as coming or traveling or going *to* Palestine. They referred to their return. But since the Turkish overlord of the Near East never favored outside immigration, the early settlements were minor and always precarious.

When World War I erupted, it was clear that an Allied victory would mean the dismemberment of the Turkish Empire and the redistribution of those lands that were not inhabited by the Turks themselves. Many pledges were made by the Allies, some to the Jews, some to the Arabs. The pledges were often conflicting because they were made primarily to help win the war or to safeguard future national interests. When one Prime Minister was later accused of breaking the word of Britain, he replied, "It was not a *word* we inherited. We inherited *words*, and they were not always consistent."*

One of these commitments by Britain, in the darkest days of the war, was the Balfour Declaration of 1917, a pledge that Palestine would be established as a national homeland for the Jewish people, the mandate to be held by the British under the League of Nations. After the war, in April 1920, when the special treaties were signed with Turkey, the Balfour Declaration was incorporated in the Turkish treaty, and it was validated by all of the Allied governments. The Jewish leader who was primarily responsible for this successful negotiation was Dr. Chaim Weizmann. Russian born, trained as a chemist, he had migrated to England in the 1890's and had become a research scientist at the University of Manchester. He came to know Lloyd George well during the war period when he perfected chemical formulae that were crucial for Britain in the war effort. The way was further opened for him to leading figures in the government through the friendship of C. P. Scott, the influential editor of the *Manchester Guardian*. These included James Arthur Balfour, the author of the Declaration, a former Prime Minister and Foreign Secretary during World War I. Weizmann's skill in diplomacy later elicited the judgment from Lloyd George that, at the Versailles Peace Conference, the two most adroit statesmen represented the two smallest states, Venizelos of the Greeks and Weizmann of the Jews. The Emir Feisal, who was a representative of the Arab world at the Peace Conference, was also impressed by Weizmann and there was a brief period of friendly cooperation. It led to a memorandum that was signed by both men in which Feisal agreed to immigration of the Jews into Palestine "on a large scale" and Weizmann agreed that the Zionist organization would use "its best efforts to promote the natural resources and the economic possibilities of the Arab State." But Feisal was careful to add that the agreement was posited

* Cited in Christopher Sykes, *Crossroads to Israel* (Cleveland & New York: The World Publishing Company, 1965), p. 118.

on the assumption that the Allied powers would fulfill their promise to unite the Arab world under his leadership.

None of the other spokesmen in the Arab world agreed with Feisal. They strenuously opposed the establishment of the Jewish homeland under any circumstances and the immigration that it attracted. They insisted that Palestine was an Arab land, that it had been Arab in population for centuries, and that it was not for any of the great powers, even after a victorious war, to allocate any part of it. If the British wished to counter French influence in Syria by garrisoning Palestine, this strategic consideration must not be fulfilled at the expense of inalienable Arab rights. They referred to the explicit pledge by Sir Henry McMahon, the British High Commissioner in Egypt, that the whole Arab world would be given national independence.

At this stage, the Allied governments did not take the objections too seriously. Arab nationalism in Palestine was dormant and its significance was underrated. Palestine itself was not thought of as a country "but only a patchwork of sub-provinces ruled from Damascus and Constantinople."* Moreover, the British reminded the Arab critics that Allied arms had eliminated the corrupt and repressive rule of the Turks and had given the Arabs independence for the first time in centuries over areas a thousand times the size of minuscule Palestine. Britain was therefore certain that the Arab opposition to the minor concession that had been made by the Balfour Declaration would fade. In the first decade after the war, Jewish immigration was encouraged and it grew steadily.

Then in the 1930's came Hitler and for tens of thousands of Jews Palestine became much more than an emotional fulfillment; it was a sanctuary from degradation and death. They flooded into the country and the steadily mounting immigration increased the friction with the Arabs. The British mandatory power felt that it was trapped between irreconcilable forces. Already sorely beset by colonial problems in other parts of the world, exasperated by the unexpected difficulties in Palestine, it had second thoughts about the wisdom of the Balfour Declaration. Hoping to mollify the Arabs, it began to whittle down the quota of the Jews who would be permitted to settle in Palestine. The Arabs were adamant. The restriction on Jewish immigration was unacceptable. They wanted no Jewish immigration at all and a government in Palestine that represented

* *Ibid.,* p. 13.

the current population proportions. When Britain temporized, the Arab leaders entered into an alliance with Nazi Germany. The Jews, on their part, exerted their pressure in the opposite direction. They employed every stratagem to circumvent the British immigration restrictions. They came in legally, within the drastically diminished quotas, and illegally, by land and by sea, suffering every hardship, twisting through mazes of red tape, but somehow getting in. By 1939, the Jewish population had increased from sixty thousand to half a million.

The quest for a haven and the passion for redemption became, for the Jewish immigrants, the driving power to create a new civilization in Palestine. Tel Aviv had been founded in 1909 on the dunes of the Mediterranean just beyond the limits of stagnant three-thousand-year-old Jaffa. Thirty-five years later it was a thriving all-Jewish city of 250,000, with advanced schools, smart shops, trim boulevards, modernistic homes, a brilliant literary and artistic life. Jerusalem had been the shrine of three world religions but, until 1920, it was left primarily to the pilgrims, the tourists, and the beggars. By 1945 the Jewish population of sixty-five thousand outnumbered all other groups. To the Old City, the symbol of the romantic and revered past, were added many new sections, beautiful garden suburbs, soon to become the heart of the aesthetic and scientific achievements of renascent Israel. Equally spectacular was the development of Haifa, the country's chief port, the oil terminus from Iraq, and the aerial hub of the Near East. By 1945 it was a booming city whose seventy-five thousand Jews comprised more than three-fourths of the population.

A chain of communes studded the countryside from the borders of Syria in the north to the edge of the desert in the south. The typical commune consisted of fifty or sixty families who found a new way of life close to the soil. Many of the large agricultural settlements were almost urban in their social diversity. Petach Tikva, with its population of twenty-five thousand, its busy streets and schools and recreation centers, could easily pass for a fair-sized town. Rehovoth was the seat of what was to become the world-renowned Weizmann Institute of Science. Rishon le Zion was famous for its prosperous citrus culture and for its wine cellars.

The agricultural developments of Palestine did not come easily. They demanded unflagging cultivation of a niggardly, grudging soil. The country had been neglected for centuries by Turkish maladministration. It was parched, disease-ridden, a menace to the pioneer who dared to challenge its alleged sterility. The new Jewish settlers were not discouraged. The pioneering spirit had been eloquently expressed by Joseph Trumpeldor, one of the early settlers who died defending the northern frontier. "Is there a wheel lacking? I am that wheel. Nails, screws, a block? Take me. Must the land be dug? I will dig it. Is there shooting to be done, soldiers needed? I will enlist. Policemen, doctors, lawyers, teachers, water-carriers? If you please, I am ready to do all. I am not a person. I am the pure embodiment of service, prepared for everything. I have no ties. I know only one command: Build."*

Such pioneers brought in water by modern boring methods. They harnessed the Jordan to supply electrical power. The Dead Sea was tapped for its mineral resources, especially potash and bromide. The groves, luxuriant with oranges, lemons, and grapefruit, the almond plantations, the wheat fields, were all redeemed from areas that had been abandoned as barren. In their reintegration they testified to the tenacity and the resourcefulness of the Jewish pioneers. Dr. Weizmann set the pattern. When asked why, with all his political activity, he worked so hard in his chemistry laboratories, he replied that he was creating "absorptive capacity" for the country.

Before the mandate it had been necessary to import nearly every manufactured product; now Jewish Palestine planned to supply its own materials for buildings, furnishings, clothing, and all the arts of life. The country was knit together through a modern bus system. Harbor facilities were also expanded to meet growing shipping and passenger needs. A maritime training school was established, and a new generation of young people emerged to join their ancestors in the tradition of Jews "who go down to the sea in ships."

Yet, though the miracle of renewal raised living standards for the Arabs as for the Jews, the Arabs remained unreconciled. The postwar younger generation, stimulated by the independence movements of surrounding Arab countries and by the fervent nationalism that swept every part of Europe and Asia, were no longer the docile fellahin who had meekly submitted to Turkish despotism. They were a proud, highly charged, militant group who saw danger in every new immigrant, a threat in every land sale, and no guarantee that their rights would be protected could soften their opposition. There were serious outbreaks against the Jewish settlements in 1929, more serious ones in 1936.

* Cited in Vladimir Jabotinsky, *The Story of the Jewish Legion* (New York: B. Ackerman, Inc., 1945), p. 100.

In the fall of 1938, Hitler and Mussolini burst through the status quo. The Chamberlain government had been retreating from obligations that threatened the peace and it was determined to avoid a dangerous confrontation with the Arabs. In May 1939, Chamberlain released a White Paper that, in essence, scrapped the Balfour Declaration. It decreed that, after a ten-year period of transition, during which immigration would be severely restricted, Palestine would become an independent state with the population frozen permanently in a ratio of 2 Arabs to 1 Jew.* Churchill and the anti-appeasement Conservatives joined with the Labour Party in denouncing the White Paper, labeling the action as a betrayal of pledges and a blemish on British honor. But the debate was soon academic. Appeasement did not stop the Axis powers, and Britain found itself drawn into the war for survival that it had tried so hard to avert. David Ben-Gurion, the Jewish leader in Palestine, immediately pledged the support of his people to the Allied war effort. He declared, "We shall fight the war as if there were no White Paper and we shall fight the White Paper as if there were no war." Thirty thousand men and three thousand women, an extraordinary proportion in relation to the total number of eligibles in Palestine, enlisted in British fighting units.

Throughout, the Arab leaders remained hostile. General John Glubb, who was in command of the British-trained Arab Legion in Transjordan, said later that with the exception of his own unit, "every Arab force previously organized mutinied and refused to fight for the Allies or faded away in desertions." The Grand Mufti, who headed the Arab League, took up residence in Nazi Germany as Hitler's personal guest, and from there, as a rabid partisan of the Nazis, he continued to direct Arab opposition to the Allied war effort. The British vowed, as they had during World War I, that they would never forget who had been friend and who had been foe when survival itself was at stake.

The war, and what Hitler termed the Final Solution, practically destroyed Jewish life in Europe. Most Jews who survived the crematoria and the concentration camps now had no homes, no means of

---

* Dr. Weizmann made an unavailing appeal to Chamberlain to dissuade him. Chamberlain tried to reassure him. "I will guarantee the Jewish minority rights," he said. "Perhaps," Weizmann responded icily, "but who will guarantee the guarantor?" "It is not politic to be so bitter," Chamberlain warned. "I am a friend of the Jews." "You were also a friend of the Czechs," Weizmann quickly retorted. Cited in Sachar, *Sufferance Is the Badge,* p. 465.

livelihood, no native land to welcome them back. In liberated Poland pogroms erupted to complete the unfinished work of Hitler. The one Jewish hope to sustain morale was that after a few months in what were called Displaced Persons camps, emigration to Palestine would be reinstated. After all, there was now a Labour government in Britain whose leaders had denounced the White Paper as a shameful betrayal.

But the Labour government completely reversed itself once it had the responsibility for British foreign policy. What had seemed morally right and diplomatically advantageous in 1939 had become morally confused and diplomatically ruinous in the changed world conditions of 1945. The Iron Curtain had fallen in Europe and the cabinet was very much perturbed by the threat of Russian expansion and infiltration. It seemed of supreme importance to the British international position to preserve the goodwill of the Arab world. The problem of the Jews could not be considered any longer except in the context of its impact on Arab hostility. Unfortunately the Labour Foreign Secretary, Ernest Bevin, a blunt trade union leader, self-educated, with little knowledge of history, not at home with problems of such emotional depth, treated the issue as if it were a wage dispute. He refused to modify the White Paper, then exacerbated the shock for the Jews by enforcing it with unprecedented severity. To a people living in the shadow of the holocaust it was gratuitously brutal to chide them for "pushing their way to the head of the queue."*

It was a devastating setback for the Jews of Palestine. While the war was in progress, the cause of Britain had been their cause. They had been, in the life-and-death struggle, undeviating allies. They had been assured not only by Labour and by the arbiters of British policy but even by Chamberlain that their loyalty would not be forgotten. Now, confronted by Bevin's decision to keep the doors of Palestine closed to Jewish refugees, they had to oppose the British decision and to fight them as if they had joined the enemy.

They organized an ingenious worldwide program of illegal immigration. The base was in Palestine where the Hagana, the Jewish militia, took over in a coordinated clandestine operation. There were agents in every part of Europe and the United States who purchased or leased the ships, selected the immigrants, shepherded them with their children across the frontiers, and then, often with the

---

* Cited in Sykes, *Crossroads to Israel*, p. 284.

cooperation of resistance forces in France and Italy and Yugoslavia, tried to smuggle them past the rigid British blockade. Only a few of the ships got through. Most were intercepted and the British then transferred the disappointed but undaunted human cargo to specially built detention camps on the island of Cyprus. The heavy odds against success were well understood in the Displaced Persons camps. Yet the frantic attempt to get on the favored lists never slackened. Those who could not be immediately chosen formed into small bands and walked across Europe to remote ports whose advantages had been puffed up by the flimsiest rumors. There they negotiated for any available boat, however unseaworthy; and from there, with understandable foolhardiness, they sailed. Men and women who had brushed with death so often could not be deterred because their plans were reckless. To them, if there was the thousandth chance of reaching and entering Palestine, it was worth it.

The ships hardly deserved their name. They were usually leaking little tubs, always loaded far beyond their safe capacity. They stole out at night or in fog from Constanza or Athens or Bari or from other obscurer ports. If they were not apprehended en route they delivered their passengers to fishing boats close to unpatrolled Palestine shore points. Those who finally landed, after surmounting these hazards, were then whisked by truck to the villages and quickly absorbed into the general population. The newspapers and the radio of free Europe and the United States gave extensive coverage to the plight of the refugee ships. Hardly a week passed without its tale of heroism and despair.

The most publicized episode involved the *Exodus,* a tragic example of bureaucratic insensitivity. In 1947, forty-five hundred derelicts tried to get into Palestine through Haifa. Their ship, appropriately enough named the *Exodus,* was intercepted. All the passengers were herded onto British ships, whose captains, under orders, then shuttled them from one port to another when they could not be compelled to disembark. They were finally sent, of all places, to Hamburg. The refugees refused to be interned in the land where mass graves with Jewish bodies were still fresh. The Union Jack with swastikas attached was hung out by them from the portholes. Many of those who resisted the debarkation were beaten by the overwrought British in the presence of German civilians who stood by and watched the unbelievable lunacy. It was only two years after the death of Hitler.

It was inevitable that such experiences should turn many of the moderates of Palestine into extremists. The Hagana, the regular militia, could no longer control the groups that refused to accept the discipline of nonretaliation. Their loved ones had nearly all been exterminated by the Nazis. A few remnants here and there had managed to reach Palestine, a last brother, a lone surviving son. The guerrilla bands—Irgunists, Sternists—emotionally exhausted by frustration, harried by the desperation of those who came up to the very shores of freedom only to be transported to internment camps, flailed out at the perverted and ill-timed appeal to fair play. The bizarre turn of events paralleled the pattern of modern Irish history where Sinn Feiners and Republicans fought savagely over the limits of resistance and reprisal in the struggle for Irish independence. The details of the guerrilla and British encounters dominated the headlines of 1946 and 1947. There were continuous bombings of oil pipe lines and railway stations and trains, assaults on the police and the military personnel. The British imposed martial law on nearly half the settlement in Palestine. But neither martial law, nor deportations, nor even executions could end the violence and the reprisals. Bevin was livid with frustration. He exploded angrily to Richard Crossman, a member of the Anglo-American Commission that had been appointed to recommend a solution to the problem of Palestine. Crossman, after an interview with Bevin, reported his statement that: "He would not be surprised if the Germans had learned their worst atrocities from the Jews." From this tirade Crossman deduced that Mr. Bevin was insane on the issue of the Jews.*

Early in 1947, frustrated and exhausted by the military complications in many parts of the globe, the British Labour government decided that Palestine had become too great a liability and announced that it preferred to relinquish the mandate. A special United Nations Commission was authorized to prepare recommendations for final disposition by the General Assembly. The Commission was made up of representatives of smaller states, not directly involved. It explored all the alternatives of accommodation that would take into account the historic claims of the Jewish people, the fate of the dispossessed Jews of Europe, the welfare of the Arabs and their relationship to the area. It then proposed radical surgery, the partition of the country into Arab and Jewish states, with complete independence for each. The territory allocated to the Jewish

---

* Letter from Richard Crossman to David K. Niles, assistant to President Truman. From the unpublished papers of Niles, in my custody—ALS.

state was a shred of the area that had been reserved by the Balfour Declaration. It was fragmented, vulnerable to attack on every frontier, its waist only ten miles wide, hardly a viable entity. But within this area there would be a sovereign Jewish state. It would have the authority to receive unrestricted immigration and thus end the reliance on Britain for the passports to a new life. The Jews, therefore, joyously acclaimed the recommendations. They prayed that they would not again dissolve into the sterility of empty words.

The Arabs passionately denounced the Commission report. However small the size of the proposed Jewish state, it was not a concession, it was still a betrayal. The recognition of an alien entity thrust into the Arab heartland could not be accepted and it would be fought every step of the way.

The first objective was to prevent the adoption of the report by the United Nations Assembly. The diplomatic activity was intense, with both sides bringing every influence to bear that they could command. The American representatives, with prodding from President Truman, favored partition, and worked zealously to line up other delegations. Partition also received staunch support from the Russian representatives, a rare instance when the United States and the Soviet Union were in agreement on a controversial international issue. Andrei Gromyko, speaking for the Soviet Union, declared: "The representatives of the Arab states claim that the partition of Palestine would be an historical injustice. But this view of the case is unacceptable if only because, after all, the Jewish people has been closely linked with Palestine for a considerable period of history."* The support by the Russians was not based on any special concern for the Jews. The Soviet Union was eager to get the British out of Palestine and the Near East. Abdication of responsibility there would create the power vacuum to facilitate easier Russian penetration in the time ahead. But whatever the motive, with Russia and the United States in concert, the affirmative decision was assured. Late Saturday afternoon, November 29, the momentous action was taken and independent Arab and Jewish states in partitioned Palestine received international validation.

There was to be a six-month interregnum for the British to wind up their thirty-year mandate. This period, which should have provided the transition for an orderly withdrawal, initiated new friction and near warfare. The Arabs girded for the battle to pre-

* Cited in Maurice Samuel, *Light on Israel* (New York: Alfred A. Knopf, 1968), p. 98.

vent the establishment of the Jewish state. The British watched with complacency the Arab preparations for the showdown. When the Jews demanded that they be given the right to defend themselves, the British refused to recognize the Hagana as a militia and attempted to disarm its members. The bitterness of the Jewish population was now so intense that the terrorist groups, which had long been held in check by public opinion, achieved respectability.

It was a pathetic end to thirty years of mandatory administration by the British. To be sure, the colonial officials had always been an unfriendly élite. They had never hidden their hostility to the aspirations of the Jews in Palestine. But taken in historical perspective, Britain had offered thousands of uprooted Jews of eastern and central Europe their first opportunity, however qualified, for a new freedom. It had set standards of modern administration and legal procedure in a part of the world which had been misgoverned for centuries. To have all of this repudiated by what Winston Churchill called "Bevin's sulky boycott" was a tragic valedictory.

At midnight on May 14, 1948, the British High Commissioner and his staff, and the last soldiers of the British colonial power, sailed away from Haifa. Even as the British colors were hauled down, a provisional government proclaimed the independent state of Israel and vowed "to defend it forever with life and with honor." The Arab states struck at once, on every frontier, in full-scale war, confident that the weight of numbers and superior armament would quickly overwhelm the severely limited islands of Israeli resistance. Neither the United Nations nor any single state within it made any military effort to sustain its own resolution. It was left to Israel alone to fight for its right to survive as an independent state.

All the Arab states were involved in the attack—Syria, Lebanon, Egypt, Iraq, Yemen, Saudi Arabia. There was a crack Transjordan Legion that was financed and officered by the British. Additional volunteers came from the Sudan and from the North African states. The Arabs drew their support from a population of more than thirty million; the total Israeli population was about 650,000, and their settlements were dispersed among hundreds of thousands of Arabs.

But the Israelis had a special kind of strength. Their army was small but its nucleus had been superbly trained and disciplined while fighting with the British and the Allies in World War II. They had young, resourceful commanders. There were volunteers from the United States and the western democracies, and these were especially helpful in preparing the diminutive Israeli air force and in coping with the problems of organization and supply. Above all, the Israelis knew in their hearts that the land they defended was the last stop. If it were lost, there would be no alternative, no second chance, either for them or for the millions who were still trapped in the transit camps and in the waiting points of Europe and Asia and Africa.

The war was fought in a series of short, intense efforts, punctuated by truces. The Israelis, outnumbered thirty to one, relied on holding actions as they waited for indispensable armament, for reinforcements in manpower, and for effective consolidation. Egypt won early victories in the Negev; Transjordan took over the Old City of Jerusalem. But after the initial defeats, the Israelis rallied, and each new thrust cleared the Arabs not only out of the areas that the United Nations had assigned to Israel, but out of strategic sectors that the Arabs were compelled to relinquish. By August 1948, all the warring Arab states were ready for a truce, and this was arranged under United Nations auspices.

Meantime, within a few hours after the Israeli Declaration of Independence in May 1948, President Truman announced the de facto recognition of the new state. "The old doctor [Weizmann] will believe me now," he chuckled. It was not full de jure recognition but it was a decisive act of friendship in a moment when the outlook for Israeli's survival seemed bleak. Russia, which had spearheaded the resolution for partition, was not to be outdone. Three days after Truman's announcement, the Kremlin extended de jure recognition and, because it was the first to make this gesture, the Soviet minister became the dean of the diplomatic corps in Israel. The United States promptly raised its mission to an Embassy and the American Ambassador took precedence over the Soviet minister. In the light of future developments, it was almost comic to read of the vying that went on between Russia and the United States for the friendship of the new state.*

In the years ahead there were to be a multitude of problems for the new state—the healing of the much-abused land, the development of its untapped resources, the assimilation of immigrants from the

---

* Later Dr. Weizmann, as first President of Israel, called on President Truman and, in the Rose Garden of the White House, presented him with a Torah, the scroll of the law. Truman was a little flustered but he managed to reply: "O, I've always wanted one." From the unpublished papers of David K. Niles.

ends of the earth, the creation of a common language, above all, the defense of the land against the implacable hostility of the Arabs. None of the problems weakened the confidence of the new nation. For the kaleidoscope of shreds and patches which had been pieced together in the earlier United Nations proposals had been scrapped by the decisions of the war. There was now a sovereign state of Israel, its territory small but homogeneous. For the first time in two thousand years the fate of Jews would not hang on the sufferance of outsiders. It would be largely determined by the will and the stamina of the Jews themselves.

33

DE GASPERI'S ITALY

MIDWAY THROUGH WORLD WAR II, IN JULY 1943, THE DICTATORSHIP of Mussolini was abruptly ended. As noted earlier he had, for more than twenty years, debased the democratic traditions of Italy, had misled its people and then, in 1940, had joined the Nazis to plunge the country into a disastrous war. As he attacked his French neighbor without provocation, he remarked cynically that Italy needed a few hundred deaths to be able to sit at the peace table. He was sure that he was taking no risk because it was his judgment that the Allies were already at the edge of defeat. He expected quick rewards in territorial concessions, control of the Mediterranean, colonies in Africa, the glory of a modern Caesar. But all his hopes were thwarted. His "seven million bayonets" were a bluff, and his people had no will for his squalid adventures. The Italian military could not overcome even little Greece until reinforcements had been rushed in by the Nazis. The western Allies were not the easy victims that he had presumed them to be and, when they turned the tide, Italy became the entry point for the counteroffensive into Europe. In May 1943, all the Italian forces in North Africa surrendered. In July, the Allies landed in Sicily, and then Rome itself was bombed to demonstrate how vulnerable the country had become.

The Fascist leaders, like gangsters on the run, were already worrying about their personal safety. They appealed to the King, himself no model of loyalty or courage, to repudiate Mussolini. They urged that he open negotiations with the Allies to seek some way by which Italy could extricate itself from the unholy mess in which it was mired. On July 25 the Grand Council, whose members had battened on Mussolini's predatory rule, turned on him and voted no confidence. When the King who had cowered before Mussolini for twenty years dismissed him, the dictatorship collapsed. The philosopher Benedetto Croce declared that the entire Fascist era would be only a parenthesis in Italian history. But Italy was not to get off so easily, simply by eliminating Mussolini. There was costly expiation ahead for two decades of fascism.

To begin with, the Nazis did not withdraw. They were well aware of the double-dealing of the opportunists in the government and they moved at once to protect their flanks. They trebled their forces in Italy to hold the northern points. In a dramatic maneuver in September 1944, their parachutists snatched Mussolini from his captors and brought him to their own camp. There they converted him into the servile head of a puppet regime which they set up in northern Italy. The one-time swaggering bully of Europe made statements written for him and signed documents put under his nose. He lived by the sufferance of the Nazis, sunk in self-pity, seeking comfort in the embraces of his mistress. He kept hoping for the discovery of some secret weapon, perhaps a science fiction death ray, that would reverse his bad fortune. He became obsessed with the power of magic and the stars, relying on the obscurantist nonsense of Nostradamus, a sixteenth-century astrologer. But the stars gave him no warning that the Italian partisans were near and they caught up with him on a road north of Como when he fled his Lake Garda retreat, and they hanged him by his heels in a public square in Milan along with his Claretta. Italy had absorbed and survived many barbarians. Mussolini and the greedy tramp who went to death with him were among the worst. There was unlikely to be any nostalgic Napoleonic legend to confuse future generations. Mussolini ended in the gutter as a thug, and not with dignity as a martyr.

Meantime the Allies kept fighting their way up the peninsula, and the Italians found themselves caught between the Nazis, who were living off the country, and the Allies, who sought to shorten the war by blasting through Italy into the bastions of Germany. For two more years the war raged over the body of Italy. The Allied landing at Anzio, southeast of the capital, came in 1944. Rome itself was liberated in June, Florence in August. But the retreating Nazis, destroying whatever they were compelled to abandon, were not finally driven out until mid-1945. Since Italy had quit the war, and its resistance forces had cooperated with the Allies in the last stages, it was not treated as a conquered nation. Yet the penalty for its earlier partnership with the Nazis was severe. It lost the territory that had been in dispute with Yugoslavia. Its protectorates in Africa were all forfeit.

The country itself was reeling with shock, the ports bombed out, roads, bridges, canals, the means of communication, all in ruins. The industrial capacity of the country, never adequate except in the north, had been reduced by more than a third. The giant Fiat automotive complex that had a schedule of five thousand cars monthly could now produce only twenty-five. More than 80 percent of the merchant marine had been sunk. Yet the drastically weakened economy had to absorb the demobilized armed forces and hundreds of thousands of refugees from the former Italian colonies. The lira lost virtually all its value, and inflation devoured the hard-earned savings of the already impoverished people.

This was the background for the struggle for political advantage by the major parties. The Communists had captured the powerful trade unions and were firmly entrenched in many of the largest cities. The threat of a takeover of the government itself was so near that it impelled the moderates to close ranks to prevent the destruction of the traditional values that were sacred to them.

The protagonists in the Cold War watched the struggle for the soul of Italy with more than spectators' interest. Italy was a master chess piece in their own diplomatic game. A victory for the Communists in Italy would extend their power up to the Alps and deep into the Mediterranean. The political bifurcation of Italian life was dramatized in the rivalry of the contending leaders, Alcide de Gasperi and Palmiro Togliatti. De Gasperi, one of the founders of the Christian Democrat Party, carried the hopes of the conservatives and the moderates; Togliatti, a party tactician who approached the stature of Lenin himself, was looked upon as one of the giants of the European Communist movement.

De Gasperi, the son of a petty administrative official, was born in 1881 in the Italian-speaking portion of the Tyrol, when it was still part of the old Austria. He trained for the law, but turned to politics and represented his district briefly in the pre-World War I Austrian Parliament. After the war, he joined the newly formed Christian Democrat Party which had been organized by the fiery Sicilian priest, Don Luigi Sturzo, who interpreted his Christianity in social welfare terms and offered a political haven for millions of Italians who were loyal Catholics but were anti-clerical. De Gasperi became Sturzo's most trusted lieutenant, working primarily with labor, and he succeeded his mentor as head of the party.

When Mussolini came to power in 1922, De Gasperi was one of his most tenacious opponents, and he called upon the King in person to urge him to curb Mussolini's tyranny before the Fascist adventurer destroyed the country. Mussolini had him jailed, and the hardships of the prison experience undermined his health. In 1929, after eighteen months of confinement, he was released through the intercession of the Pope and found refuge in the Vatican. He spent the Mussolini years working in the library, supplementing his meager monthly salary by ghost-writing for foreign correspondents, at five cents a page, and tutoring in foreign languages. When the Fascist dictatorship collapsed, De Gasperi joined in the guerrilla warfare against the occupying Nazis. In 1944, when the first coalition government was formed, De Gasperi became Foreign Minister and soon afterwards, at sixty-five, Prime Minister, committed to the Catholic religious spirit but not to clerical dominance. "To get on one's knees," he wrote, "is all very well. But religious education should teach one how to stand on one's feet."

He was a new kind of leader in Italian politics, with none of the purple oratory and flamboyance of Mussolini and his imitators. De Gasperi was restrained, unemotional, mainly at ease in conference, where he was matchless as a negotiator. He had to be, for he was destined to head up shifting party alliances through a dizzying succession of governments. He had to demonstrate there the sure-footedness and the tenacity that he had achieved in his favorite sport of mountain climbing. Many times he had hung at the end of his rope over precipices, ideal training for postwar Italian politics.

His rival for the control of Italy was Palmiro Togliatti, the son of a poor bookkeeper, who was also prepared for the law but early turned to journalism. As he witnessed the disintegration of the free institutions of Italy after World War I, he took the path of communism. In 1923 he was caught by the Fascist police and sentenced to be shot. He was actually against the wall, but apparently the executioner was none too sympathetic with his Fascist masters, and he cooperated in Togliatti's escape. He spent long years abroad, mainly in Russia, where he was tagged by Stalin as a resourceful agent who could be trusted to carry through Communist assignments.

In 1944, after eighteen years of exile, he was back in Italy, ready for his revolutionary missions. Always immaculately groomed, well spoken, courteous, disciplined, he could be taken for a middle-class business executive. But he gave his days, and his nights also, to organizing Communist cells at the grass roots level, especially in the labor unions. His influence lay in his power to paralyze the industrial and social life of Italy by calling the unions out on national strikes. His life was a harried one, with constant assassination attempts; the one in 1948 almost brought him down.

In the first postwar years of Italian renewal and reconstruction, the anti-Fascist parties agreed to try coalition government, with De Gasperi as Prime Minister and Togliatti as Deputy. Within the coalition both sides sparred, aiming to win the support of the swing middle group of Socialists and center moderates. Togliatti played the political game low-key, respecting Catholic educational demands and promising to make no attempt to sponsor radical reform. De Gasperi was even more determined to press for reconciliation, to forget the past, to seek no reprisals, even against the former Fascists. "We did not fight against the barrack state," he said, "in order to substitute for it the executioner state." The early legislative recommendations of the coalition avoided the controversial social issues that might bring disruption. A great to-do was made over the future of the monarchy, and after considerable public debate and a referendum, the royal house of Savoy was sent into exile. The average family, concerned with peace and security, cared very little about an issue that had become trivial and irrelevant. But it was sporting diversion until the political battle lines had firmed.

By 1947 De Gasperi was ready. In a reshuffle of the cabinet, he excluded the Communists and waited confidently for the repercussions. Togliatti called for strikes and slowdowns, but his timing was off. The country was too tired and exhausted for the renewal of civil war. De Gasperi had shrewdly calculated that a platform of law and order, and the pledge of steady, disciplined reform, would be endorsed. When the strikes threatened to sabotage the unloading of Marshall Plan supplies, De Gasperi called out the military and the danger of economic paralysis quickly passed. De Gasperi then arranged for a national election in April 1948, and appealed for a mandate to build the new Italy on solid Christian Democratic principles. Both sides went into the campaign with the knowledge that it was a decisive test of strength that would affect the future of

Italy. If the Communists won, it would be the first time that they had taken over a state through a free popular referendum instead of through coup or conquest. It would plant the red flag in the Catholic heartland.

For months the shrill of campaign oratory and the flood of campaign literature reached into the remotest villages. There was every expectation that the verdict would be close and there was a battle for every qualified voter. The moderates were staggered and dismayed when the left-wing Socialists threw their support to the Communists, strengthening the odds for their triumph. The fear of such a victory precipitated a flight of capital and the offices of foreign consulates were deluged with requests for visas. A headline in a New York newspaper summarized the significance of the Cold War in the election. "Italy chooses Uncle today. Will it be Sam or Joe?"

It turned out to be an unprecedented victory for De Gasperi and the Christian Democrats, who won 307 seats of the 574 in Parliament. At no time in modern Italian history had there been a clear-cut majority for one party. The vote for the Christian Democrats had risen from eight to twelve and a half million, a 55 percent increase in two years. The mandate that De Gasperi had requested was unmistakable.

The victory had been earned by intensive, unremitting preparation. All the anti-Communist forces had sublimated their differences, and they united against what De Gasperi had dramatized, perhaps overdramatized, as a fatal common danger. The Communists had just engulfed Czechoslovakia, and the Italian liberals and the moderates were determined that this fate must be avoided in Italy. The Vatican too knew how much of its own destiny was at stake. Cardinal Shuster of Milan publicly announced that absolution would be denied to anyone who voted Communist; the Pope himself moved into the election with undisguised partisanship. Eighteen thousand Catholic Action volunteers canvassed every city, every village, every hamlet, interpreting, persuading, detailing the consequences in daily life if there were a Communist takeover. On election day they transported thousands of voters to the polling places, if need be by bicycle, or wheelchair, or even by wheelbarrow.

Officials in the United States entered the lists with all the fervor of an American election. President Truman chose the timing carefully to transfer twenty-nine merchant ships to Italy to help the sagging economy. The Italian gold reserves that had been looted by the Nazis, and recovered by the Americans, were now hurried back to replenish the depleted exchequer. A steady line of Marshall Plan ships came steaming into Italian harbors loaded with supplies, and each arrival was widely publicized. Families of Italian ancestry in the United States, millions of them, were encouraged to write to their relatives, urging them to support the democratic cause. Special tape recordings by Frank Sinatra and other well-known personalities of Italian origin were rushed to the campaign headquarters. The Soviet Union, fresh from its violent coups in the Baltic and the Balkans and, of course, in Czechoslovakia, was indignant about such unethical interference in the domestic affairs of an independent nation.

Above all, in accounting for the Christian Democratic victory, there was De Gasperi himself. In the three years since Italy had repudiated the Fascists and had repelled the Nazis, this quiet, sober-tongued statesman had won the confidence not only of his people but of the Allied statesmen as well, upon whom so much of the assistance to Italy depended. It was an explicit personal compliment to him, as a confessing Catholic, that he was given this decisive vote of confidence. While Italy was almost entirely Catholic, it was also militantly anticlerical. The clergy was respected for its religious ministrations, but it usually aroused deep suspicion and often hostility when it expressed itself on social issues. Since 1870, when Italy became a sovereign nation, there had been Prime Ministers who were agnostics and atheists and Protestants, and even a Jew. A practicing Catholic had never been named to the post. De Gasperi was the first one to break the tradition. Apparently the Italian people, worn out by the cynicism of fascism and the callous paganism of the Nazis, were ready to turn for leadership to the simple, ascetic De Gasperi, whose bedroom had as its only adornment a crucifix and a painting of the Madonna.

After the election, several attempts were made by the Communist leadership to reverse the tide. In July an enraged student tried to assassinate Togliatti, who was pumped with bullets and left for dead. The outrage was seized upon by the Communists to call for a general strike, to register their indignant protest but, more urgently, to demonstrate their power. For two days the country was under the severest tension. There were revolutionary barricades in many of the northern cities. But the military acted promptly to put down the disturbances and the riots and the general strike petered out.

De Gasperi, freed at last of Communist harassment in the cabinet and with a comfortable majority in Parliament, turned to effect the long-postponed reforms. His mandate took him through the interim period of reconstruction during which he survived the challenge and the changes of eight successive governments. He worked adroitly, without the emotional appeals so dear to Italian hearts, conceding here, persuading there, remembering always that not only his own tenure but the program of the Christian Democrats depended on his ability to hold a moderate center group together— Catholic, traditionalist, progressive, republican.

The tasks he faced called for the highest statesmanship. Italy was only half the size of France but it was much more populous. Its land was poor; agriculture, the base of the country's economy, was still primitive. A beginning had been made after the war to mitigate the peasants' distress by a modest redistribution, but it had been only the barest beginning. Now De Gasperi accelerated the pace, especially in the south, where landlessness and poverty were most serious. He organized what was called the *"Cassa del Mezzogiorno,"* the Fund for the South, and, through this medium, estates beyond 750 acres were parceled out in units of 10 acres per peasant household.

There was encouraging progress too in reviving and expanding industry. Here, De Gasperi was assisted by Enrico Mattei, the son of a *carabiniere,* and a wartime partisan, one of Europe's most resourceful engineers, who triggered a new industrial revolution by tapping valuable undeveloped sources of power. Through the borings of his geologists he opened out the natural gas and oil reserves of the Po Valley, and then he created refining factories and tanker fleets for processing and transportation. He thus made available to Italian industry the cheapest fuel in Europe. He hoped ultimately to release Italy from dependence on "the Seven Sisters," the giant Anglo-American companies that controlled most of the oil products of the Middle East. He established a new petro-chemical industry, a complex at Ravenna, one of the most impressive in Europe. A nuclear power station was imported from Britain and installed about thirty miles from Rome. Major support to fulfill Mattei's ambitious plans was provided through Marshall Plan funds, international loans, and through local capital investment.

Tourism was encouraged and Italy was once again a favorite vacation attraction, drawing more than eleven million visitors annually. Rome became one of the world's fashion centers. A new film industry grew up under Italian skies, and precedent-breaking directors, De Sica, Visconti, and others set exemplary standards in realism without the extravagant props of Hollywood. Ingenious designing for automobiles and in ship construction brought new respect for Italian functional imagination. De Gasperi gave Mattei full leeway and the slim, wiry, human dynamo used his authority, until his death in a plane crash in 1962, to bring about a major industrial and commercial revolution. It was a matter of pride when the statisticians noted that the industrial index had risen by 71 percent in the few years since the collapse of fascism. The scourge of the centuries, malaria, was now vigorously attacked with insecticides that were provided by American and British science teams. Though such a program produced no headlines, in its impact on health and daily living, and dying too, it was undoubtedly the single most important development in modern Italian history.

In conducting foreign affairs, De Gasperi was of course influenced by the exigencies of the Cold War and the overriding necessity for a firm commitment to the West. He was vigilant in promoting Italian interests, but he was also a fervent European, in the forefront of the movements for European economic, scientific, and political cooperation. He belonged with Schumann and Monnet, with Adenauer and Spaak, as a spokesman and an advocate for European integration. It was his dream some day to be the first President of a United States of Europe. Italy was a founding member therefore of the coal and steel condominium that brought together France, West Germany, and the Benelux countries. Italy became part of the Euratom Authority that supervised the peaceful uses of atomic power. It was a pioneer in the development of the Common Market, and its undeviating commitment to the West brought with it membership in NATO.

Yet, with all of De Gasperi's international stature and with the progressive legislation of a memorable incumbency as Prime Minister, the problems of his country were too serious for him to be shielded from political attack. He was also handicapped because his reliance on conservative support made it impolitic to attempt the more fundamental agricultural and social reforms that the new era demanded. Togliatti and the left-wing Socialist leaders carefully cultivated the frustrated peasantry of the south, who grew ever more impatient with the slow pace of improvement in living standards. The Communists built strength also in the pockets of hard-core unemployment that remained despite all the projects that were launched to cope with them. De Gasperi was not spared the inevitable complaint of all the disenchanted. "We were better off when we were worse off."

With the passing of years, even the austere personal integrity of De Gasperi could not prevent the infiltration of graft and inefficiency, the inveterate enemies of public service in southern Europe. This was an ideal climate for the continued power of the Mafia which flourished in Sicily and in the south. In the elections of 1953, De Gasperi, who had survived the crises of eight successive governments, was now too worn out to prove a match for his tenacious political foes, and his government fell. Italy was apparently ready to move into a new era, much to the left of the coalition that had been piloted through the dangerous postwar shoals by De Gasperi and the Christian Democrats. A year later, in the winter of 1954, he died in a little mountain hamlet where his family usually spent stolen holidays.

His body was brought back reverently to Rome and the train stopped at stations all along the way for the mourning thousands to pay their last respects. He had earned their homage. His legacy was the stabilization of the shattered country. He had applied modern technology, the massive American aid, and membership in the European Common Market, to break with the sluggish, obsolete past. Above all, he had brought the land out of the guilt and shame of Mussolini's histrionic fakery and had set it firmly again in the democratic tradition of Mazzini, Cavour, and Garibaldi.

34

MAO TSE-TUNG
AND THE COMMUNIST
CONQUEST OF CHINA

LATE IN 1949 THE NATIONALIST LEADER, CHIANG KAI-SHEK, DECISIVELY defeated in the Chinese civil war, fled from the mainland to set up a rump regime in Taiwan. The Communist victor, Mao Tse-tung, took control of a nation of over five hundred million and all the fabulous resources of half a continent. For the United States it was perhaps the most serious diplomatic disaster in its history; it converted the firmest ally in Asia and the Pacific into a dangerous and implacable enemy. The development was also to have continuous divisive effect in American domestic politics. Through the next generation the question was in the forefront: Who lost China? Many hard-line Republicans took the view that the nation fell to the Communists, not through popular revolution, but through conspiracy, and they excoriated President Truman and the Democrats as "soft on communism" and criminally naïve in dealing with it. Each year when the admission of Red China into the United Nations had to be considered, the response became a litmus test of loyalty. Those who urged that China ought to be brought in on the ground that one-fifth of the world's population could not be diplomatically ignored were denounced as subversive or as Communist dupes.

The fall of Chiang Kai-shek was totally unexpected. He had led his Nationalist forces through a long and devastating war with Japan, a war that tempered China's national consciousness. In 1945, after victory, China was ready to take its place as a reliable Asian ally of the democratic West. Yet within four years, the world-renowned leader who had participated in the summit conferences with the movers and shakers of our times was driven to an island refuge, and mainland China had succumbed to an inner-Communist assault. How could this have come about? How could such a stunning reversal take place, one that wrought the most significant changes in the modern world since the Russian revolution of 1917?

There are no simple explanations, of course, but any analysis must begin with the fact that the hold of the western world on China was at most a tenuous one. The revolution of 1911 which overthrew the corrupt obscurantist Manchu dynasty, and which was hailed by the West as creating a renascent China, proved to be superficial and ineffective. The party of reform, the Kuomintang, was influenced by western-educated leaders who followed the usual pattern of doctrinaires: much more impressed with flashy theories than with stubborn realities. They orated in western terms with well-worn quotations from Jefferson and Lincoln, and they invited learned intellectuals to offer counsel in the transformation of feudal China into a modern democratic state. But their words often had very little relevance for the intractable social problems of China. The western powers gave lip service to idealistic objectives but none was willing to relinquish the economic privileges that had been dictated in the earlier period of unrestrained colonialism.

Soon the unity of the 1911 revolutionaries was disrupted. Whole provinces broke away; the warlords re-established themselves in their bailiwicks, primarily concerned with personal power and the opportunities it offered for looting and extortion. When the Russians, sensing Communist advantage in the drift and confusion of the 1920's, despatched their agents into the country and began the cultivation of the more radical notables of the Kuomintang, the conservative wing of the party—the merchants, the bankers, the landowners—took alarm, and they turned for leadership to General Chiang Kai-shek to meet the threat to their own vested interests.

Chiang was born in 1887, one of five children, the son of a salt merchant in a family of rather modest means. It was the tenacity of his widowed mother that sent him to the best military schools in China and Japan. He returned to Shanghai in 1911 and was quickly drawn into the revolution that overthrew the Manchu dynasty. He shared the resentment of the new breed of patriots who saw their country garrisoned by foreign troops, their rivers patrolled by foreign gunboats, their frontiers and their cities exploited by foreign customs and tax officials. When the father of the revolution,

Dr. Sun Yat-sen, welcomed Russian help, Chiang was at his side as a favorite protégé and in 1923 he was assigned to Moscow for further military and political training. Stalin thought that he saw in Chiang a very promising Communist agent. Chiang returned from Russia to establish and to command the Whampoa Military Academy, sponsored by the Soviet Union. Ostensibly it was to be the training center for Nationalist objectives, but Stalin hoped that it would become an outpost for Communist penetration that would ultimately bring China into the Soviet camp.

Chiang, however, was already moving into more conservative circles. He was attracted to one of the three Soong sisters, whose mandarin family was among the wealthiest and most powerful in China. Ching-ling had married Dr. Sun Yat-sen, Ai-ling had married the country's most prominent international banker, H. H. Kung. Chiang was captivated by Mei-ling, the most beautiful and accomplished of the sisters, Wellesley-trained, highly intelligent, a most charming hostess, and a persuasive diplomat in her own right. Chiang already had a wife but he put her aside, accepted Mei-ling's Methodist faith, and became part of her social coterie. It was not the marriage into the Soong family that transformed Chiang into a conservative. He had already been alienated by Communist machinations that outraged his Nationalist loyalty. He had little need of Mei-ling's wealth since he had parlayed his own savings into a fortune in the stock market. But his marriage to a Soong fortified the confidence of the old-line conservatives that they could trust Chiang's leadership.

Even before his marriage in 1926 Chiang, now the Nationalist generalissimo, had begun excluding the Communists from high office. He suspected that government bodies had been thoroughly infiltrated with Communist agents who were assiduously working, behind the facade of Nationalist unification, to deliver the country to the Soviet Union. Apparently Chiang got word of a Communist plot, or he said he had, to seize power. When his men raided the Communist headquarters, he claimed that they found incontrovertible evidence of a plan to eliminate the Kuomintang "like so many squeezed lemons" and to convert the country into a Soviet satellite. Chiang had no intention of playing Kerensky to a Chinese Lenin and he acted quickly to beat the Reds to the act.

In March 1927 he struck suddenly in Shanghai and, using carefully prepared lists, his squadrons hunted down and summarily executed thousands of Communists, many of them students. In April he spread the net to other major cities. The widow of Sun Yat-sen fled to Moscow with the proscribed Russian leaders, denouncing her sister and Chiang for what she termed the betrayal of the revolution. It was estimated that by the end of the year Chiang had liquidated about forty thousand Communists and fellow travelers, and had eliminated Stalin's Russian agents. But one core Communist group remained, still small in 1927, disunited, fuzzy in objectives, but led by one of the most extraordinary personalities in modern history, Mao Tse-tung, who was to rank with Lenin in the power of his decisive role.

Mao was born in 1893, the son of a peasant rice farmer. He grew up in the humiliation of foreign control of China and he joined his fellow students in the repudiation of the age-old Confucian passivity which they all blamed for Chinese nonresistance and abasement. Mao hated the western image of China as a picturesque dreamland with its blue porcelain bowls, its exquisite silk scrolls, and its quiet submissive people living by Confucian maxims. He noted the helplessness of China as it was cannibalized by the imperial powers, unable to stand up even against the smallest. He lived through the rice riots as the peasants starved, and he bled with them as the rebels were rounded up and executed. He was an early disciple of Dr. Sun Yat-sen and was swept into the revolutionary ferment that Dr. Sun created. But he was quickly disenchanted when the Nationalist objectives turned out to be only surface changes and left the clamorous problems of the peasantry virtually unheeded. In 1918, he was on the staff of a teachers' training college and later he held a junior-level librarian's post at the University of Peking. Personal tragedies which would have broken a less resolute character now followed one on another. He married one of the women of the staff who was killed during the civil wars. He married again and his wife, who was a Communist, was purged. His sister was tortured and beheaded; his brother was strangled. They were all the victims of their political activities. His most searing youthful memories were of emaciated corpses on the roadside and the heads of decapitated rebels on bamboo poles.

Mao was twenty-six when he began editing a Marxist journal, and in 1921 he helped to organize the Communist Party in Shanghai. But he had little patience with the dogmas and the dialectics of the Russians. "There are people," he said bluntly, "who think that Marxism is a kind of magic truth with which we can cure our disease. We should tell them that dogmas are not as useful as cow dung; at least dung can be used as fertilizer." He broke sharply with the principle that communism, to succeed, must build on the foundation of an urban proletariat. Perhaps this was true, he said, in the already industrialized countries, but China's strength was in the countryside. "Whoever has the support of the peasants will win China, and whoever solves the land question will win the peasants." He concentrated on the plight of the peasantry, their poverty, their landlessness, their desperation, and to them he became the Saving Star. When Chiang eliminated the Russian agents who had swarmed into the country, Mao was left as virtually the sole survivor for leadership.

At this stage Mao was an ascetic figure—tall, gaunt, at one with his soldiers, living as they did in crude cabins or in the open, eating their food, wearing their crumpled uniform, sharing their hardships and their dangers. In his merciless revolt against the established order, he condoned and encouraged the terror that was loosed against it by infuriated peasants and city workers. He said ". . . a revolution is not a dinner party, or writing an essay or painting a picture or doing embroidery . . ." The landlords had brought retribution on themselves for their crimes of exploitation and gouging, for their reprisals by torture and lynching. These views, nurtured by his experiences as well as by the plight of the peasantry, explained his purge of five million class enemies when he later came to supreme power.

In the years between 1927 and 1931, Mao was hunted by Chiang with a price on his head. He was safe only when he could fade into the anonymity of the trackless jungles. When he realized that he could not survive in the areas of the south and east of China that Chiang and the Nationalists controlled, he undertook an astonishing mass relocation in what became legendary as the "Long March," a trek of 6,000 miles to the great northwest, mainly on foot, a Communist republic-on-the-move. The trek took 368 days, through twelve provinces; it involved whole villages and towns en route, men, women, and children. They forded the rivers, climbed the mountains, crossed the deserts, hacked through the forests, everywhere pursued and attacked. They manufactured arms on the way, cut and sewed their clothing, grew their food, built their temporary shelters. During the scaling of the great Snow Mountain, 16,000 feet high, Mao was dangerously ill, and he had to be borne by litter under constant fire. But he never lost his will to victory. Indeed, he wrote poetry, good poetry, to signalize each triumph over danger and catastrophe. There were dreadful losses all along the way, until only 20,000 of the original 150,000 survived. They settled in North Shensi, with Yenan as the base from which to expand. Within a few years the whole area south of the Yellow River had been taken over by Mao to become a rural Communist bastion of perhaps thirty million people, supported by one of the largest land armies in the world.

Meanwhile, as Mao and the Communists bided their time in the fastnesses of Shensi, Chiang labored to consolidate the provinces under his control. The decade from 1927 to 1937 offered new hope and opportunity. The western powers, finally realizing that China could no longer remain an exploitation resource, gave up many of their privileges and extended cooperation through loans and military support. They supplied technicians to improve the silk and cotton crop and to modernize agriculture and industry. Chiang seemed to vindicate the confidence of his patrons and of the liberal moderates who believed that China could fulfill its historic destiny without revolutionary violence.

But all too soon plans and reforms had to be thrust into the background. Japan was again on the rampage. The war party there had warned that the sleeping Chinese giant was awakening, and surely Japan could not risk the emergence of a strong, unified China. The pre-emptive Japanese strike began in July 1937, soon to be merged into World War II, and destined to continue until 1945. In the early stages, though Chiang's forces fought back with great courage and tenacity, the Japanese assault could not be contained. In the eight years of warfare against the Japanese, twenty million Chinese soldiers and civilians perished, and fifty million of the population fled into the hinterland in one of the great mass migrations in history. Chiang moved his forces a thousand miles inland, deliberately destroying en route whatever could be of value to the invaders. He chose as the temporary capital Chungking, from where, with Allied aid, he carried on a gallant and tenacious defense. In this period his name was linked with the heroes of the western world who were rallying their people to resist the Fascist bid for supreme power. Chiang was included in the summit conference in Cairo in 1943, and the promise was made there that when the war ended, China would be assigned a master role in reordering the world.

Through the war period, it was hoped that the common danger from the Japanese would have the effect of suspending the intensity of the civil war between the Nationalists and the Communists. Arrangements were made by American intermediaries for Chiang and Mao to meet so that their plans to eliminate the Japanese could be coordinated. But none of the agreements lasted long beyond the promised word. Mao had no intention of contributing to a Nationalist victory that would release Chiang for his expressed determination to crush the Communists. Chiang was even more unwilling to see Allied aid flown to the Communists for undoubted later use against his own forces. He said grimly to the American intermediaries when Japan was at the peak of its strength: "You think it is important that I have kept the Japanese from expanding during these years. . . . I tell you it is more important that I have kept the Communists from expanding. The Japanese are a disease of the skin. The Communists are a disease of the heart."

Roosevelt persisted. He called upon General Stilwell, "Vinegar Joe," a tough-minded soldier-diplomat who commanded the American forces in the Chinese sector, to try his skill in achieving an accommodation. Stilwell and Chiang disliked each other intensely from their first meeting. To Stilwell, Chiang, whom he contemptuously called the "Peanut," was pigheaded and ignorant and concerned only with personal prestige. "He's a vacillating, tricky, undependable old scoundrel who never keeps his word," he wrote to Roosevelt. He was appalled that the United States had been maneuvered into supporting his "rotten regime" for, he noted in his diary, he "is the head of a one-party government supported by a Gestapo and a party secret service. He is now organizing an SS of 100,000 members."* Chiang heartily reciprocated the antipathy for a man whom he found impulsive and contemptuous of Chinese values and to whom he referred as the "Dummy."

Even if Stilwell had been more personally acceptable, he could not have made the slightest headway. Mao refused to merge his fighting units, numbering more than a million, with the Nationalist forces, and he demanded complete autonomy in the areas that were now under his control. In essence, he was laying claim to the whole of northwest China as an independent Communist state. Chiang scoffed at the arrogance of such demands. All his life had been dedicated to the ideal of a united China; he would never consent to its partition. Stilwell was recalled and other troubleshooters were

---

* Barbara Tuchman, *Stilwell and the American Experience in China* (New York: The Macmillan Company, 1971), pp. 340, 371.

despatched as the efforts continued to create some working coalition. But even General George Marshall, Chief of Staff and the architect of the Allied victory in Europe, with all his prestige, had no effect. Marshall had to report to the President that he too had failed, that the animosities were now too fundamental to budge. He blamed the dominant reactionary group around Chiang, and the unyielding Communists around Mao, and he added with sadness that a heavy price for such extremism would have to be paid by the long-suffering people of China.

After the defeat of the Japanese in 1945 there was no longer a common danger to serve as a restraining force and the civil war erupted with renewed fury. The province of Manchuria, with its rich mineral resources and its excellent ports, was one of the prizes that both sides were determined to have and to hold. In the last days of the war the Russians, ostensibly as part of their bargain to help fight the Japanese, had invaded the province. They had pledged at Yalta that they would remain only long enough to expel the Japanese and then, in return for special trade concessions, would evacuate the territory. But they were very leisurely in fulfilling the pledge, and they first stripped the country of supplies and equipment worth nearly eight hundred million dollars. They encouraged the steady infiltration of the Chinese Communists until a Red Army of 130,000 men had been entrenched, and they turned over to these forces the military equipment that was surrendered by the retreating Japanese.

Chiang was urged by his American advisers to bypass Manchuria for the time being, and to concentrate on reorganizing his forces in southern China. He already had critical problems in attempting to shore up the shattered economy, to stem the galloping inflation, and to get millions of refugees relocated. But Chiang insisted upon giving priority to Manchuria before the Communists were too firmly entrenched there. He committed his élite forces to this precarious venture, far from his home base. The decision was a fatal blunder. Mao's forces won shattering victories everywhere they struck. The one remaining hope for Chiang was to obtain massive American help and he pelted the White House with cables. But President Truman refused to get bogged down in the Chinese civil war when there was already a national outcry for a quick return of American forces from Europe and Asia. Besides, Truman now had little hope that Chiang could retrieve the situation, even with major American reinforcements.

By the end of 1948, Mao had all of Manchuria. The Nationalists lost a million men, and about half a million American rifles. One by one, the main centers in China fell, and whole Nationalist armies surrendered or defected. At the end of 1949, recognizing the futility of further resistance, Chiang fled the mainland to Taiwan, 100 miles off the China coast. All of China fell to Mao and the Communists, who proclaimed the People's Republic.

The Nationalist debacle became a burning political issue in the United States. Many Republicans not only challenged the military and diplomatic judgment of President Truman, Secretary of State Acheson, and their advisers, but labeled the entire Democratic Party "the party of treason." Senator McCarthy of Wisconsin included General Marshall in his denunciation of men who had betrayed America by their "softness on communism." But as the passing years provided better perspective, it became evident that there were reasons for the Nationalist defeat that had little to do with American advice or support. To begin with, the Nationalist regime was hopelessly inefficient. The early idealism generated by Dr. Sun Yat-sen had evaporated completely. The Kuomintang was shot through with bureaucratic graft. Huge sums for assistance, hundreds of millions annually, had been poured in by the United States and by U.N.R.R.A., but they were wasted and often misappropriated. Chiang Kai-shek himself was probably incorruptible. He had little reason for temptation and he shared the privations of his people. But he had no firmness in administration and many of the men around him used their high position shamelessly for personal advantage.

Even more telling was the inability of the Nationalist leadership to respond to the needs of the peasant base of Chinese life. The challenge that was often raised in the United States "Who lost China?" was a non sequitur; the West never had China to lose. The government that it supported had no roots in the lives of the people. Chiang was warned by General Stilwell that he could never get his people to fight until he gave them something tangible to fight for. This counsel had been even more urgently advocated by General Marshall. The strength of the revolution could be retrieved, he said, only if Chiang gave precedence to the problems of land reform. Chiang had other priorities, and he paid for his obtuseness by losing the loyalty of his people.

What Chiang failed to do, Mao did earnestly and with fervor. He developed a unique form of guerrilla warfare especially adapted for the climate and terrain of China. The Shensi Province to which he transferred his forces in the Long March became the launching center for a war of endurance, skirmishing, sniping, pecking away at the stamina and the resources of halfhearted antagonists. Everywhere the guerrilla warriors penetrated, Mao took over the holdings of the large landowners and distributed them to the peasants, and with the land went purpose and hope. He took every opportunity to glorify the peasant's humble cotton-clad figure as the heart of China's liberation. He made him feel that it was his courage and his will that had shaken off the hold of the foreigner and the exploiter. In return for the restoration of pride and dignity, Mao received unyielding loyalty.

By 1949 Mao had driven out the most powerful leader of modern China and had himself taken control of nearly half a billion people. In the vast main square of Peking, in September 1949, he announced to the sea of exultant upturned faces, "The Chinese who comprise one-fourth of humanity have from now on stood up. . . . We have united ourselves. Our nation will never again be an insulted nation. We have stood up."*

* Cited in George Paloczi-Horvath, *Mao Tse-tung* (London: Secker & Warburg, 1962), pp. 240–1.

35

JAPAN: THE AMERICAN INTERLUDE*

AFTER THE ATOMIC BOMBS HAD EXPLODED OVER HIROSHIMA AND NAGA-saki in August 1945, Japan surrendered unconditionally to the United States. A Red Cross worker referred to the doomed city of Hiroshima as a necropolis, and then added, "In what remained of the station facade, the hands of the clock had stopped at 8:15. It was perhaps the first time in the history of humanity that the birth of a new era was recorded on the face of a clock."

There was the gravest anxiety on both sides over what was to follow. The American authorities, planning many years of occupation, expected determined obstruction to the fulfillment of the surrender terms. There was concern that bands of guerrilla diehards would harass the invaders from the moment of landing. Some might continue the resistance in the Kamikaze tradition that the Americans had already encountered as they fought their way from island to island in the Pacific. Some might respond with pillage and terror to the years of propaganda that had led them to expect the most horrendous vengeance when the American devils came. Japan was a wounded beast, but it could still use claws and teeth to rip and tear.

Yet when the occupation began, both sides were astonished at the resigned reaction. A few fanatics attempted to thwart the landings and the occupation, but they were quickly subdued by the Japanese themselves. The Americans turned out to be understanding and compassionate. They proclaimed that they had come to protect the future from aggression, and that they would assist the Japanese in their recovery if the American objectives were loyally accepted.

* This is the phrase used by the late Kazuo Kawai and the title of his fine work on post-war Japan.

[404]

Many explanations have been offered for this unexpected response. There was the fatalism of the Japanese people. The divine wind had brought defeat instead of victory; so be it. There was the national inclination to imitate what was practical and successful. There was the tradition of obedience to the commands of the Emperor, who had announced that his people must now endure the unendurable. These factors were undoubtedly all present, but they did not clash with what was perhaps the simplest explanation.

The Japanese submitted as quietly and as peacefully as they did because this was the most realistic way to salvage their own role in the future. They would bend to the will of the conqueror for the time being. He would thresh about with his edicts and his theories and his reforms, and then, inevitably, he would tire of the tedious responsibilities of occupation. There would be the usual outcry from the American home front to bring back the troops. The Japanese would then have their country back.

There was nothing devious about such reckoning, no need for conspiracy to circumvent American objectives. For after their decisive defeat the Japanese had no wish to return to the old discredited imperial policies. They persuaded the Americans that they were cured of the belief that they could solve their survival problems by conquest or aggression. It was expected therefore that the Americans would leave, not when they were worn out, but when they had accomplished their mission of converting Japan into a peaceful ally. This was what actually happened in the years 1945 to 1952. The occupation was an interlude in the long Japanese history, but it was an interlude in which the transformation of Japanese life was accomplished with the willing, indeed, the enthusiastic, cooperation of the Japanese themselves.

The tasks of reconstruction were sufficiently awesome to test the capacity and the statesmanship of both the conqueror and conquered. The land was a shambles. The atomic apocalypse had wiped out two key cities instantaneously, but much more extensive damage had been inflicted throughout the country by the fire bombs in the continuous air attacks through the months that preceded the surrender. Tokyo had been a main target and the raids had desolated the capital. In one night, a hundred thousand of the population had been killed. Virtually every other major city had been stricken, Osaka, Nagoya, Kobe. There were 1,850,000 deaths, a third of them civilians, each week's casualties surpassing the horror that went before.

[405]

The physical destruction had been only part of the national ordeal. The economic life of the country had been wrecked. Production had been paralyzed and was reduced to a minor fraction of the prewar output. Japan as a trading nation depended on its merchant marine and its shipping to preserve its tenuous lifeline. But 80 percent of the merchant marine had been sunk. In the cities there was little food, and what there was could be obtained only on the black market, at prices that were out of reach for the average family. The inflation had reduced the yen to but 1 percent of its prewar value. The Japanese had been a proud and sensitive people, meticulous in dress, in cleanliness, in courtesy, in civil amenities. Such standards disappeared as the population scrabbled for food and shelter, as a new breed of racketeers shamed the honored traditions of the past. Out of such social spasm it was the task of the American authorities to bring back security and discipline and concern for human values. The formidable responsibility was assigned to General Douglas MacArthur, who was named as pro-consul and whose genius in administration converted the disastrously defeated nation into one of America's staunchest allies. His gold glittering garrison cap and tilted corncob pipe were to become as familiar as Churchill's oversized cigar and his V for Victory sign.

MacArthur, born in 1880 in Wisconsin, was reared in a military environment. His father had fought gallantly in the Civil War as a Union officer and had later been appointed the first Governor of the newly acquired Philippines. He had served as commandant at West Point and then as Chief of Staff. His son, Douglas, surpassing the father, garnered an impressive record of firsts. He headed his class at West Point; he was the youngest division commander in World War I, where he was several times wounded, and where one of the men under him was Captain Harry Truman. When, at fifty, MacArthur was named Chief of Staff by Franklin Roosevelt, he was the youngest officer ever to attain this distinction.

Unfortunately for his popularity, there was a wide streak of exhibitionism in his make-up. Virtually every personality study emphasizes his flamboyance, and his continuous posturing, his Pomp and Circumstance style. He was a tower of inaccessibility, a mystique that he carefully cultivated, insisting, as Charles de Gaulle did, that the charisma of leadership demanded aloofness. He spoke always as if he were dispensing the law from a mountaintop, and it may have been frustrating for him that Sinai was at the other end of Asia. At every turn in his career he left a train of phrases and flourishes that were obviously meant to impress Clio. He thought he was being modest when he confided to a reporter, "Though I am a Caesar, I rendered unto God what was His." When he waded ashore at Leyte in the Philippines, under camera, as the first step on the way to the conquest of Japan, his broadcast prose was clothed in regal purple. "I have returned. . . . The hour of your redemption is here. . . . Rally to me. . . . Let no heart be faint. Let every arm be steeled. The guidance of Divine God points the way. Follow in His name to the Holy Grail of righteous victory."* It was after this trumpet call that some of his men called him God's cousin.

When he set a course for himself, he was prepared to fight for it even with a President of the United States. During his tenure as Chief of Staff he had a remarkable confrontation with President Roosevelt. The army budget had been cut and he insisted upon seeing the President personally to urge him that the full amount had to be restored. The account in his Memoirs pointed up his combative enterprise. "The President turned the full vials of his sarcasm upon me. He was a scorcher when aroused. . . . I spoke recklessly . . . to the general effect that when we lost the next war, and an American boy, lying in the mud with an enemy bayonet through his belly and an enemy foot on his dying throat, spat out his last curse, I wanted the name not to be MacArthur, but Roosevelt. The President grew livid. 'You must not talk that way to the President.' "† MacArthur shot through the door and vomited on the White House steps. But then Roosevelt gave in and restored the full budget. This was the man, in Gunther's phrase, "with the plumage of a flamingo," indefatigable in work and purpose, who, having conducted the bloody but triumphant war in the Pacific, was called upon by President Truman to administer the occupation of Japan.‡

* Douglas MacArthur, *Reminiscences* (New York: McGraw-Hill, 1964), p. 217.

† *Ibid.*, p. 101.

‡ Apparently the two men, poles apart in style and outlook, had genuine regard for each other's grit. Later, after MacArthur had been relieved of command by Truman because of serious disagreement on policy in the Korean War, the general noted, "You know, he is a man of raw courage and guts. The little bastard honestly believes he is a patriot." After MacArthur's death, when I asked President Truman for an evaluation of MacArthur, he responded, "He was one of the two or three most gifted American military men, and he thoroughly deserved the highest place in our history. But let me tell you why I fired the bastard!" Then he proceeded to explain, with a scrupulous competence that would have gratified any authority in constitutional history, the principle of civilian control that was basic in American government.

One of MacArthur's first tasks, though a negative one, was to fulfill the pledge that the brutalities of the war would be punished. As in Nazi Germany, twenty-five officials, mainly high political and military personnel, were brought to trial as war criminals before an international tribunal in Tokyo. Significantly enough, the Japanese took little interest in the trials and, as they dragged on, there was no drama in the courtroom and only boredom outside. The war belonged to the past and the trials and punishments were regarded as the expected penalty of defeat. Indeed, there was a measure of scorn for the wartime Premier Tojo, who had so badly led his nation, and then had botched up his attempt at suicide before he was led to the gallows. General Yamashita was hanged because he had executed British and Australian officials. General Homma was shot for his responsibility in the Bataan death march. In all, seven defendants were executed, and all but two of the others received sentences of life imprisonment.

But a major decision had to be reached with reference to the fate of Emperor Hirohito. There had been an implied concession after the Potsdam ultimatum that if the Japanese surrendered promptly they could, if they wished, continue the royal tradition in some modified form. But there was strong residual feeling in the Allied lands that the Emperor should be tried as a war criminal, or, at least, be deposed. Otherwise, even as a powerless symbol, he might become a rallying point for the jingoism that had brought on the war in the first place. Hirohito came to MacArthur to make clear that, if anyone deserved punishment, it was he. For his was the final responsibility for the acts of his subjects. The unsentimental old warrior was genuinely moved. He wrote, "He was an Emperor by inherent birth, but in that instant I knew I faced the First Gentleman of Japan in his own right."* All discussion to include the Emperor's name in the war criminal list was terminated. The more sober counsel was followed that a discredited god would be more useful to the Allies than a martyred god. Instead of suffering punishment the Emperor became the conduit to his people for the fulfillment of the occupation mandate and its far-reaching social and political changes.

Another priority for MacArthur at the outset of his incumbency was the elimination of the men and the organizations that had been, in the words of the directive, "the active exponents of military nationalism and aggression." Thirteen hundred such organizations

---

* MacArthur, *Reminiscences*, p. 288.

were placed on the proscribed list, and two hundred thousand former military officers and influential business leaders who had been identified with the discredited expansion policies were banned from future public office. There was little attempt made, however, to purge the lower echelons—civil servants, teachers, the rank and file of workers, professional men. After all, the entire nation had been compulsorily involved in the war effort. Besides, it would be impossible to maintain the functions of government, education, and the economy, if the guidelines for guaranteed trustworthiness were too rigidly enforced. Within three years the winnowing process came to an end. But since most of the older leaders had been eliminated, the new order was set in motion with fresh direction and with more sanguine outlook.

The most ambitious undertaking but, as it soon turned out, the most ephemeral, was the attempt to fulfill the constitutional prohibition by which Japan renounced forever the right of belligerency, even for self-defense. It forbade the maintenance of land, sea, and air forces, and even scientific research that had any relationship to military effort. There was no difficulty in obtaining acceptance for this basic law. The ghastly experience of the war years had turned most of the Japanese people into ardent pacifists. The Allies were relieved of any of the fears that followed World War I, where every artifice was attempted by the defeated Germans to contravene the prohibitions against rearmament, and where camouflaged social clubs proliferated that were really recruiting entities.

There was pressure for Japanese rearmament within a few years, but it came from the United States and the western Allies, when the Cold War transformed the international scene. Renewed Communist expansion, climaxed by the demands of the Korean War, reversed American policy, and Japan was now built into defense planning as an indispensable ally. There was no overt rearmament, but the forces for inner domestic defense were vastly expanded, with MacArthur's blessing, so that they could be quickly converted for military service if it became necessary. Significantly, these new policies were passionately resisted by students and the younger generation of Japanese to whom the disarmament pledges of the constitution, enjoined by the Americans themselves, had become an inviolate article of faith. One of them summed up the irony of the policy somersault, "I had to report to the police once a month because I didn't surrender my family's samurai sword. Now you want us to build jet fighters!"

But the overriding task of the occupation was to help democratize the country, to modify its feudal institutions. This major reform was not undertaken because it was considered the God-given responsibility of the United States to dictate the character of government in a foreign country, even a conquered country. It was undertaken because a long, costly war had been fought that had been initiated by the fiat of a tightly contained oligarchy. It was hoped that a more responsible government which represented the will of a free electorate would reduce the dangers of dictatorial aggression.

Several years were assigned to the drafting of a new constitution. It was ostensibly worked out by Japanese representatives but with supervisory cooperation from American task forces, drawn mainly from government and the universities. The language in the proposed constitution reflected this influence faithfully. The American inspiration was so obvious that a news magazine parodied the opening words of the preamble, "We, the Japanese people . . . ," and they read "We, the mimics . . ." But rhetoric aside, most of the reforms were welcomed. Provision was made for a Parliament, the Diet, to be elected by universal suffrage, and for a Prime Minister and cabinet responsible to this Diet. There was to be an independent judiciary, capped by a Supreme Court, that would have the authority to pass finally on the constitutionality of any law. The national police, formerly directed by a thoroughly loathed Home Ministry, were stripped of their authoritarian procedures. These reforms were extended into every area of local government, where elected assemblies were to share responsibility with executive and judicial bodies.

The most dramatic showcase change was, of course, in the function of the Emperor. Hirohito had been a remote figure, invested with divinity, his unchallenged word used by the ruling coterie as the sanction for their actions. He was a shy, quiet, almost mousey little man, with a toothbrush mustache and very thick glasses, who had always seemed incongruous in the role of a deity. He was primarily interested in marine biology, and, if Fate had not decreed royalty for him, he would have been happiest in a laboratory or on a marine research cruise in Sagami Bay fishing for specimens. He cooperated fully in the constitutional transformation that restricted him to purely ceremonial duties, and he surrendered the aura of divinity without regret. Some irreverent staff members in the Embassy suggested that MacArthur gladly assumed this status.

Hirohito now began to appear in public and he was a familiar figure at dedications and civic functions, at concerts and art exhibitions, and at the baseball games which had become the national sport. His rejoinder, when he wished to note approval, was "Ah so, Ah so," and he was soon affectionately referred to as Ah So-San. In 1954 nearly four hundred thousand people crowded on the multispan bridge that led to the Palace to pay their New Year's respects. Annually, thousands of women came out to sweep the Palace grounds as their tribute of love and respect.

Perhaps the most far-reaching of the occupation reforms came through an extensive program of land redistribution. MacArthur was no agrarian reformer, but he was realistic enough to know that democratic institutions could hold no attraction for a hungry and insecure people. The problem of landlessness, to be sure, was not as serious in Japan as it was in most of the underdeveloped countries. There were five and a half million farmers, so that one could not say here that the land was in the hands of a small feudal aristocracy. But the great majority of the farmers owned less than two and a half acres, and there were millions who owned nothing at all.

The reform of the land system was given the highest priority by MacArthur. He announced that he wanted action and he wanted it quickly. The landlords had not yet tested his mettle and they resisted, calling upon their supporters in the Diet to remember their class obligations. The initial so-called Reform Bill that emerged would have exempted about 70 percent of the tenant lands from any change. MacArthur reacted promptly. He expressed his dissatisfaction and, with military bluntness, threatened unilateral confiscation. The legislators got the point at once, and the result was a revised bill that compelled the sale to the government of large estates, a total of about five million acres. These were then made available through twenty-year loans at minimal interest to peasants who wished to undertake ownership. "I am convinced," said MacArthur, "that these measures . . . will finally and surely tear from the soils of the Japanese countryside the blight of feudal landlordism which has fed on the unrewarded toil of millions of Japanese farmers."* MacArthur succeeded in raising the ownership tillage from 54 to 89 percent in four years. The land reform was ridiculed by the Soviet representatives as merely token and, conversely, the right-wing critics, including some American legislators, threw catfits as they denounced the measure for its "Socialist attack on the rights of

---

* Russell Brines, *MacArthur's Japan* (Philadelphia and New York: J. B. Lippincott Company, 1948), p. 222.

ownership." The magisterial MacArthur never imagined that the day would come when he would be identified with the Socialists. But none of the criticism deterred him. He had made the decision not to repeat the mistakes of the Chinese Nationalists. He argued that his program would effectively undercut the chief propaganda appeal of the native Communists.

There were still many obstacles to be cleared before the redistribution had decisive impact on the social structure. Stubborn landlords kept filing suits to slow down action, and many of the peasants did not sufficiently understand their rights under the new laws. One old farmer said, "Japan is being baptized at a very old age." But the reform took the peasantry a long way toward at least minimum security, and it redeemed the American pledge to make the interest of the Japanese people the overriding objective of the occupation. It was the measured judgment of Dr. Edwin Reischauer, later Ambassador to Japan, that MacArthur's land reforms were "almost as sweeping as those of the Chinese Communists which originally won them the support of the peasant masses, but they were accomplished far more smoothly and without any violence."*

MacArthur had still another responsibility on his agenda of reform. It related to the Zaibatsu, the family combinations and trusts that had been an integral part of Japanese life for centuries. It was estimated that 60 percent of the entire economy had been concentrated in eight families. Through a maze of affiliates and interlocking companies and subsidiaries, they had a virtual monopoly of banking and insurance, shipping and mining, communications and the export trade. Two of these combines, the Mitsui and the Mitsubishi, produced more than 40 percent of all Japanese goods and they had played the largest role in the financing and fueling of the war. MacArthur had studied the causes of Japanese military aggressiveness and he considered it essential, if any of the reforms in Japan were to have substantive meaning, that the holding company pyramids be dismantled. He pressed for enabling legislation that flabbergasted those who had regarded him as a hard-bitten reactionary. He endorsed virtually confiscatory taxation and capital levies to reduce the Zaibatsu financial power. The securities of the élite families were placed in trust so that they could be offered for sale to the general public.

* Edwin O. Reischauer, *The United States and Japan* (Cambridge: Harvard University Press, 1950), p. 280.

As it happened, and to MacArthur's deep disappointment, the prime intent of the reforms could not be fulfilled. By 1947 a resurgent Russia was stoking the Cold War as vigorously in Asia as in Europe. Mao Tse-tung had taken the offensive in China and he was well on his way toward turning it into a Communist bastion. In 1950 the Korean War placed the Communist danger on the doorstep of Japan. MacArthur reluctantly agreed that it was more important for the moment to utilize Zaibatsu experience and efficiency than to promote social democracy. The Zaibatsu trust-busting was slowed down and the planned reorganization suspended. Thus, within a few years, while the unhealthy prewar control of the Zaibatsu families had been modified, they had regained considerable influence and prestige in Japanese economic and political life.

In all of his administrative activity MacArthur worked closely with the Prime Minister, Shigeru Yoshida, who had been a moderate in the prewar days and had unsuccessfully tried to restrain the militants. Yoshida was a consummate politician and an effective Japanese representative for the occupation period of transition. He was conciliatory without being obsequious, and his realism did not go to the extreme of cynicism. He advised the Crown Prince not to get too involved in constitutional matters, and suggested riding and hunting rather than the study of documents. "Reading is the beginning of worry!" He had to answer to the Diet where there was ill-concealed opposition from the more radical elements. Simultaneously he had to cooperate with the occupation authorities but to slow them down when, in his judgment, they lost themselves in western preconceptions. He won the confidence of MacArthur, who often defended him against the irate complaints of his own staff. Yoshida, in turn, grew to respect MacArthur as a soldier-statesman who was sincerely devoted to the long-range interests of Japan. In his Memoirs, Yoshida expressed admiration for MacArthur's perceptiveness in dealing with a defeated nation and contrasted his policies with the heavy-handed Japanese rule over conquered peoples in Asia that evoked so much loathing and resistance.

As MacArthur's administrative career in Japan drew to a close, he had the right to look back with satisfaction on what a Japanese historian called "the induced revolution." MacArthur said in his Memoirs, "I had to be an economist, a political scientist, an engineer, a manufacturing executive, a teacher, even a theologian of sorts."* He

* MacArthur, *Reminiscences,* pp. 281–2.

had some failures, major failures—keeping to the promise of a disarmed Japan, and liberalizing the economy. But he had enduring triumphs too—the peaceful transformation of a shattered and despairing people into a nation with new confidence and pride; a constitutional government where power had shifted from an ingrown oligarchy to a popularly elected legislature, buttressed by an independent judiciary; a stable economy with a solvent currency; a strengthened labor movement with a union membership that had grown from little more than a hundred thousand to six and a half million; a historic land redistribution that brought dignity and hope to millions of peasants. The style of the man, his rhetorical peacockry, continued to irritate. But in five transition years MacArthur earned a deserved reputation among the Japanese people to whom he came as a fearsome conqueror and whom he left with their undisguised respect. Ambassador Reischauer judged him to be one of the towering figures of the postwar world. "As a great military hero in his own land, and a still greater peace-time hero in the land he helped to conquer, his place among the great names of history is doubly secure."*

It was not surprising that the appreciation of the Japanese for the American achievements should take the paradoxical form of growing restiveness. The very democratic sentiments preached with such evangelical fervor by the Americans brought impatience with the paternalism of the occupying power. Japan was emboldened to urge return of full sovereignty, insisting that it was time to become master again in its own house. The United States did not resist. It had not undertaken the occupation either in vengeance or in altruism. It had undertaken it to reorient a dangerous enemy and to transform it into an ally. This job had now been done. The diplomatic task for the future, as new winds blew out of Asia, was to make sure that the job stayed done. It was a day of thanksgiving for Japan when the occupation was officially ended in 1952. It was a day of satisfaction, too, for the United States.

* Reischauer, *The United States and Japan,* p. 227.

36

NEHRU, JINNAH, AND THE PARTITION OF INDIA

EARLY IN 1947, THE NEW LABOUR GOVERNMENT OF BRITAIN MADE THE historic decision to end 182 years of colonial rule in India and to grant independence to the subcontinent. The action climaxed decades of incessant agitation. Every attempt, until after World War I, to win even limited autonomy had been thwarted by British opposition. Such attempts had also been weakened because there was little unity in a land where four hundred million people were fragmentized by divergent faiths, castes, and languages, and were dominated by feudal rulers in hundreds of principalities.

After World War I, the situation changed drastically. The incomparable Mahatma Gandhi emerged to give meaning and direction to the dream of freedom.* He brought the country to the threshold of independence in the new era, but his protest technique of nonviolence was apparently no longer effectual for the battle to final victory. This responsibility was assumed by a beloved disciple, Jawaharlal Nehru, who was to dominate the life of India for the next two decades.

Nehru was a complex man, charming and outgoing in one mood, morose and withdrawn in another. F. R. Moraes, his countryman, found him completely unpredictable because he was so often inclined "to draw down the blinds of his mind and enclose himself in a shuttered world." He held himself to be above petty parochialism and he preached a Himalayan internationalism—"The idea of

* See Chapter 25.

[415]

nationalism is a myth," he said in a 1928 address. "The world has become internationalized; production is international, markets are international, transport is international. Only men's ideas continue to be governed by a dogma which has no real meaning today."* But he often irritated his fellow statesmen beyond endurance as a kind of Brahmin Polonius, who lectured them on the ethics of international conduct which he then belied by his own inconsistencies. He refused arbitration in the border disputes with China and in the problems of Kashmir that poisoned Indian relations with Pakistan.

Nehru was born in Allahabad in 1889, a high-caste Brahmin, the eldest son of a brilliant, influential lawyer. He was brought up like a British nobleman, surrounded by a doting family, with retinues of servants and all the luxuries of an aristocratic home that included two swimming pools, tennis courts, a stable of horses, and the first imported motorcar in India. The mansion was always filled with guests from the political and artistic world. There were three kitchens to cater to the dietary tastes and restrictions of Hindus, Moslems, and British. Nehru was repelled by the patronizing airs of the colonial officials, the signs in the railway cars, "For Europeans Only," the discrimination in public places. He hated the arrogance of the colonial set to whom all men were brothers so long as they were British.

Nehru, however, rarely suffered any of these humiliations. At fifteen he was sent to England for his education, several years at Harrow and at Trinity College in Cambridge, and then the Inns of Court in London for the law. Here he was introduced to the Fabian socialism of the leading literary lights, Bernard Shaw, H. G. Wells, Bertrand Russell, the Webbs; the democratic socialism that had its beginnings here became a basic part of his economic and social policy when the destiny of India was later his to guide. He married the lovely Kamala, a scion of another high-caste family, but he lost her early and the hostess of his later long public career was his only daughter, Indira, whose training under her father prepared her for the post of Prime Minister.

When Nehru returned to India he was not yet a confirmed nationalist; too much of England still clung to him. He confessed, "I was a bit of a prig with nothing much to commend me." What

---

* Cited in Michael Brecher, *Nehru* (London and New York: Oxford University Press, 1959), p. 125.

transformed him, in April 1919, was the traumatic experience of the Amritsar Massacre which had exposed the ugliest side of British imperialism.* Resistance to the continued British presence in India had been mounting and had at last found voice and a program in Gandhi. Nehru was drawn to the Mahatma, "whose irresistible power," he said, "could make heroes out of clay." He wrote later, "This little man of poor physique had something of steel in him, something rocklike which did not yield to physical powers however great they might be."

Under Gandhi's spell Nehru joined the Congress movement that had been organized to battle for India's independence. Gandhi grew to love and trust young Nehru, whom he called "his favorite son," even though they were poles apart in temperament and in the techniques they believed in to fulfill their common objectives. Gandhi, with his homespun shawl and dhoti, his oversized clumsy glasses, his wide toothless smile, in his hut of mud and bamboo, was the symbol of the old mystical India. Nehru, in his immaculate knee-length cream-colored jacket, with the daily red rose in his buttonhole, was the finished product of the modern world—suave, sophisticated, somewhat skeptical, science-oriented. Gandhi relied on the spiritual power of nonviolence. Nehru would not cross his mentor in his technique but he was to move ever further away from it and, when he assumed leadership, he virtually repudiated it. Nehru rose steadily and quickly in the Congress movement. In 1929, at the age of forty, he reached the presidency.

The years that followed were filled with protests and defiances and Nehru served ten prison terms. During World War II the agitation for Indian autonomy kept growing. Even Churchill, who had vowed that he would never consent to the liquidation of the Empire, was now ready to concede that, after the war, there would have to be a radical reappraisal of relationships. But the Congress was already fed up with promises and half-measures. Gandhi was scornful about accepting "a post-dated check on a failing bank." He and Nehru insisted that a firm pledge of at least Dominion status be made at once. When there was further hesitation and delay, civil disobedience flared in the very heart of the war effort. There were riots in 1942 with four thousand casualties and the imprisonment of a hundred thousand nationalists, including Gandhi, Nehru, and the most notable Congress dissenters. The breakdown

* See Chapter 25.

[417]

in administration was so complete that when famine struck in Bengal in 1943, millions starved to death. Little wonder then that there was no enthusiasm for participation in the war by the population, even when the Japanese in 1942 were at the gates of India. But once the Labour government assumed office in 1945, Britain ended all hesitation and moved to settle the dangerous uncertainty.

Already the problem had gone beyond the status of India in the Commonwealth. The issue that now loomed was the relationship of the Hindu and the Moslem populations. The projected new state would have a controlling Hindu majority and this terrified the Moslems; there were tens of millions of them in the Punjab of the northwest, tens of millions more in the provinces of Bengal in the northeast, and many more millions again in solid pockets of central India. There was equal apprehension among the Hindus, for there were tens of millions of them in the areas of Moslem concentration. If the issues of security and welfare were not adequately enforced, what would become of these considerable minorities? There had been long negotiations to produce a formula that would keep India united, with protection for the rights of both groups. But as independence approached, it was clear that no formula short of partition and the establishment of a sovereign Pakistan would be acceptable to the Moslems. Yet how would even partition protect the minorities in alien jurisdictions? Gandhi expressed the dilemma that partition represented for the Congress. "They have been handed a wooden loaf in this new plan. If they eat it, they die of colic. If they leave it, they starve!" Nehru hoped that his influence would quiet fears and allay panic. But would the Pakistani protagonist, Mohammed Ali Jinnah, have equal powers of reassurance? What the times demanded was a conciliatory force. But Jinnah was as deeply feared and distrusted by the Hindus as Nehru was by the Moslems.

Jinnah was born in Karachi, in 1876, the son of a wealthy dealer in hides. Like Nehru he was sent off to England in his teens to study law. When he returned he found that his family had suffered serious financial reverses, but he built up his own fortune in Bombay through a successful law practice there. He was almost without peer in India in forensic eloquence and incisive logic. He helped to organize the Moslem League to protect Moslem interests and, at this stage, committed to Hindu-Moslem cooperation, he worked closely with the Congress Party and was a respected member of its inner circle. But he became increasingly concerned that Hindu leadership, including even Gandhi, was not providing sufficient guarantees for Moslem political and cultural autonomy, and he began moving away from a solution through integration. Nehru always felt that Jinnah's conversion to the stance of a separate Moslem state, even at the expense of Indian unity, was a direct result of his frustrated ambition to lead the Congress forces. In any case, by the late 1930's Jinnah had turned his back on the Congress, and was unreservedly committed to an independent Pakistan.

Jinnah was now at the peak of his influence and India united or divided would depend upon the way he used it. Six feet tall, bone lean, less than 120 pounds, with sunken cheeks in a face almost cadaverous, he had none of the warmth or the outgoing quality of Nehru. He was often tart, especially biting in repartee, undeviatingly formal to the point of imperiousness even with those who were closest to him. He inspired respect, even admiration, but rarely love. Perhaps his personality was conditioned by the early death of his beautiful Parsee wife, and by the shattering experience of disowning his only daughter when she married a Christian. He never let down the guard even when the overtures to him were friendliest. The last British Viceroy, Lord Mountbatten, after negotiations with him cried out, "My God, he was cold. It took most of the interview to unfreeze him."*

This was the mountain of obstinacy upon whom Gandhi and Nehru concentrated at the threshold of independence, to try for a unified India. Jinnah would not budge. He insisted that the Moslem had nothing in common with the Hindu except "his slavery to the British." He reiterated that he had little confidence in Hindu forbearance once the state passed under Hindu control.

The British leadership made a final attempt to avoid partition. They feared that it would mean the Balkanization of the whole continent and would condemn it to the sorry fate of Africa. If religion became the basis for statehood, they warned, then the Sikhs would call for independence too, and so would many other groups, and the atomization of India would make it an easy victim for the ambitions of Soviet Russia.

In March 1946, Prime Minister Attlee announced that he was sending a mission, headed by Sir Stafford Cripps, for a final effort to achieve an amicable settlement. To almost everyone's astonishment, the mission succeeded in effecting compromise. It called for a

---

* Alan Campbell-Johnson, *Mission with Mountbatten* (New York: Dutton, 1953), p. 56.

united Indian government with jurisdiction over defense and foreign affairs and communications, but it gave an autonomous Pakistan complete control in all domestic concerns. For a glorious moment it appeared that Indian unity was to be salvaged.

Unfortunately, as so often in history when a sudden personal decision, a petulant move, or an unexpected turn of fate changes the course of events, the caprice of Nehru's mood that day doomed the compromise. Nehru chose this historic juncture, bright with promise, for what his biographer confessed was "one of the most fiery and provocative statements in his forty years of public life."* After the painfully hammered-out agreements of the mission, Nehru declared in a press conference that he still intended to seek modification of the compromise so that the national government would have wider jurisdiction. Jinnah took this to mean that Nehru's concessions had been made just to get the British out of India, and that then his dominant Hindu majority would ride roughshod over all protective guarantees to the Moslems. He said bitterly, "The trouble with the Hindus is that they always try to get seventeen annas for their rupee!" He assailed what he called Nehru's duplicity and at once withdrew his assent. He set August 16 as Direct Action Day, calling for mass rallies to demonstrate the force and strength of the uncompromising Moslem commitment to independence.

Nehru now tried to make amends. He drove out to Jinnah's home in Bombay to appeal personally to Jinnah's sense of history. He reminded him that they both had labored for a lifetime to reach this supreme moment when freedom was at hand, that they both had made endless personal sacrifices for this blessed fulfillment. But even as they talked the ghosts of the past haunted the room. Each apparently remembered too well the repeated insults of the other in the long years of their rivalry. Nehru had been quoted as saying that "Jinnah was a narrow-minded racialist with no real education, a mediocre lawyer with a passion for Pakistan." Jinnah had been quoted as saying that "Nehru was an arrogant Brahmin who covers his Hindu trickiness with a veneer of western education." The encounter, and it was an encounter, lasted eighty minutes and it ended in disaster for India and the western world. As Nehru drove away he saw the black flags of mourning outside Moslem homes and the shuttered shops that Jinnah had ordered in proclaiming Direct Action Day.

All the volcanic fury that boiled within the age-old conflict then

* Brecher, *Nehru,* p. 316.

erupted. The riots began in crowded, poverty-stricken Calcutta where, between dawn of August 16 and dusk of August 19, six thousand people were hacked and battered to death and more than twenty thousand maimed. Even the Moslem religious leaders applied no restraint. One of them cried out, "Bloodshed and disorder are not necessarily evils in themselves, if resorted to for a noble cause." The noble cause was to kill, to torture, to pillage. After the first assaults by the Moslems, the Sikhs came out for their reprisals, and then the Hindus, until the city was heavy with death. There were some Hindus who risked their lives to save the Moslems; there were some Moslems who risked their lives to save the Hindus. There were groups of young people, Moslem and Hindu, who locked arms and marched through the streets appealing for brotherhood and peace. But their actions were mocked by the piles of corpses in the dirty little alleys and in the bloodstained streets where the vultures picked them clean. The riots of Calcutta then spread to other cities and provinces, and raged on for months. Of course there had been worse tragedies in this brutal period. In the famine of 1943 in Bengal, about three million men, women, and children had starved to death. But the horror of Calcutta and the civil war that it loosed was man's doing. It was religious fanaticism gone berserk. It was, therefore, as much a turning point in the history of the continent as was the massacre of Amritsar.

The British now gave up all hope of preserving the unity of India and they hurried to complete the arrangements for independence. In February 1947, Prime Minister Attlee announced the appointment of Lord Mountbatten as the last British Viceroy, whose responsibility it would be to transfer sovereignty to the authorized native officials. When Mountbatten arrived the situation was *in extremis*. In addition to the task of mediating the main issues of partition, he had to negotiate agreements on specific boundaries and on the allocation of national assets. In the Punjab, the heart of West Pakistan, there were twelve million Hindus, Sikhs, and others who would now be placed under the jurisdiction of a state with sixteen million Moslems. In Bengal, the heart of East Pakistan, there were twenty-seven million Hindus who would be living among thirty-five million Moslems, under a Moslem government. In the length and breadth of India that would be under Hindu control, there were sixty million Moslems. Where would all these beleaguered minorities find protection for lives and livelihoods when passions were already running so high?

Yielding to the demands of the determined nationalists, the organic economic units that had been created by history were arbitrarily severed. Raw materials remained in one country, the factories and the plants to process them in another. The principal product of East Pakistan was jute, but the mills to process it were in Calcutta. Riverbeds rose in one jurisdiction, the lands they watered were in another. The British arbiters attempted to create a Punjab Water System to be managed by an authority that would be responsible to both countries. Jinnah insisted that he would rather have deserts than fertile lands that were watered by the courtesy of the Hindus. Nehru responded by vowing that there would be no trifling by any Pakistani officials with the rivers of India.* Each proposal for common advantage ran headlong into the pent-up animosities and suspicions that had been nurtured by years of hostility. And time was running out. Armies were already on the move on the borders of the Punjab and Bengal, and the fears of millions of affected families approached hysteria.

On the night of August 13, 1947, the Union Jack came down in New Delhi and Karachi. It should have been an occasion for thanksgiving and rejoicing. Nehru and Jinnah tried to make it so. Nehru saluted the new flag, with the charkha, the spinning wheel, and he spoke of "the tryst with destiny," when an age ended and when the soul of the nation, long suppressed, at last found utterance. Jinnah saluted the flag of his newly born nation, the fertile crescent of Islam. "History," he declared, "seems sometimes to move with the infinite slowness of a glacier, and sometimes to rush forward in a torrent. Just now our united efforts have melted the ice and moved the impediments in the stream, and we are carried onwards in the full flood."

But the exultant speeches were soon forgotten in the violence which dwarfed everything that had gone before. When the partition boundaries were announced after the ceremonies, millions who feared they were to be trapped in lands governed by their enemies went into panic. They fought their way onto the overcrowded trains with whatever pitiful belongings they could carry. As the cars passed through hostile territory there were robberies and assaults and wholesale slaughter. Those who fled on foot or by bullock cart or boat went through the gauntlet of hate and death. Trains came into the Lahore station in Pakistan on which the passengers had

* Sanity prevailed later when a river water agreement was signed in 1960.

all been murdered and the painted message on the car read "A present from India." The Moslems sent back trainloads of slain Hindus and Sikhs with the identical message on the cars: "A present from Pakistan." Christians pinned cloth crosses on their coats to court protection. "Freedom must not stink," a journalist exhorted in a widely distributed pamphlet. But freedom did stink as the bodies piled up in hundreds of villages and towns and cities.

In the nine months that followed the emotional salute to freedom and independence, as many as six hundred thousand unfortunates perished in their frantic exodus. In the next ten years fifteen million Moslems, Hindus, Sikhs, and other refugees abandoned their homes, their livelihoods, their communities, their ancestral graves. India received nine million refugees; Pakistan six million. When the derelicts arrived in territory where they sought protection there were all too few opportunities for them to fit into the economic structure. Hopelessly, they settled in demoralizing, unhygienic relocation centers, an easy prey to disease and epidemic. This was the land where Gandhi had taught the discipline of nonviolence. But the fate of Gandhi himself was its most tragic defiance. He was cut down in 1948 by the bullets of a fanatic Hindu who believed that the Mahatma had been too generous to the hated Moslems.

In time the paralysis of panic eased. Fifty million Moslems remained in India and Nehru labored to make them feel that they belonged and that their welfare would be safeguarded. Millions of Hindus stayed on in the Pakistan provinces and Jinnah offered every assurance that they would not be hostages. Both governments, though militantly opposed, now turned from the carnage and the pillage in which their freedom had been born to face the problems of national survival. But the scars of the partition never healed, nor did the manner of its achievement.

For Nehru the overriding concern was to hold his nation together. Even with the secession of Pakistan there were more than three hundred and fifty million people in the land and the population was to grow at a phenomenal rate, more than seven or eight million annually. There were 562 states within the country, with a hundred million people, ruled over by their rajahs and their maharajahs, their Nizams and their Jegadirs, all holding fast to special rights that had been assured by treaty with Britain, and all with assured incomes and powers beyond the law. Nehru knew that unless this proliferation of petty sovereignties was quickly ended India would become an administrative bedlam.

The first years of independence were therefore taken up with the most sensitive negotiations to bring the separate units into the Indian state. Nehru was at his best in this kind of diplomacy, and one by one the princes accepted the carrots that were offered—the guarantee of a life pension, or the validation of a title, or the promise of a coveted honor. A few held out and created emergencies where Nehru quickly forgot the teachings of Gandhi. Hyderabad, a kingdom with a population of more than sixteen million, mainly Moslem, refused to yield. Nehru sent in the army and put a forceful end to the sovereignty of the state although the Nizam was kept on as a figurehead.

Meantime Nehru launched a five-year plan to develop industry, to modernize agriculture, and to stimulate commerce. With the help of teams of international experts, dams and hydroelectric plants were built, atomic power was applied for peaceful projects, programs were introduced to safeguard health and to expand education.

More frustrating was the alarming growth of population that thwarted every attempt to raise living standards. The situation of Calcutta, a city of two and a half million, was only the most critical among scores of others. In a 1961 survey, more than a decade after independence less than 20 percent of the population lived in minimum comfort. Seventeen percent still had no housing and slept in the streets and alleys the year round; 33 percent had one room in which three families existed; another 33 percent had one room to serve an entire family; and the facilities for the most elementary human functions were so primitive that the great majority of the population survived on little above an animal level. Nehru remarked sadly, "India must run very hard just to stand still."

It was inevitable that with so much human misery there would be powerful Communist pressure in the state. In one election in 1957 a whole province, Kerala, temporarily went Communist. But Nehru, while maintaining meticulously correct relations with his Communist neighbors, always fought against the native Communists. He once commented that India had more Communists in prison than any other country. Wedged between the two Communist giants, Soviet Russia and Red China, he clung to neutralism and nonalignment in foreign policy. But his commitment to a democratic socialism for India itself was never in doubt. Long before, he had written that he had too much of the West in his blood ever to be really alien. Gandhi used to tease him that when he talked in his sleep he talked in English.

[424]

The democratic world therefore remained hopeful that, despite the avuncular scolding and the sanctimonious lecturing that it received all too frequently, India under Nehru could be relied upon to remain a democratic bastion. And when he died in 1965, his successors, first one of his trusted disciples, Lal Shastri, and then his own daughter, Indira, though as meticulous as Nehru had been in adhering to nonalignment, sustained the confidence that one of the world's most populous nations would not fall before the blandishments of the Communist neighbors.

AS PAKISTAN STRUGGLED WITH THE TASKS OF RECONSTRUCTION IT seemed to be pursued by a malevolent fate. The pioneering drive of Jinnah was soon unavailable; he died of lung cancer within a year of independence. Three years later his successor, Liaquat, fell before the bullets of an assassin. The country was wretchedly poor and the economy was shattered by the dislocations of partition. It was primitive in agriculture and it had little industry. Its rate of population increase was among the highest in the world. Above all, its energies and slender resources were continuously sapped by the disputes with India and, even more, by its inability to bring contented unity to the widely separated segments of its territory.

The controversy with India centered on the disposition of Kashmir, a contiguous province rich in resources and especially important to a country as poor as Pakistan. Its Moslem population far outnumbered the Hindus. Jinnah and his successors demanded a plebiscite, Nehru's own favorite solution for the disputes of other nations. But in the issue of Kashmir, Nehru peremptorily refused all overtures. He was already profoundly shaken by the partition of India and he would not risk further political or economic fragmentation, however plausible the theoretical arguments for ethnic or religious self-determination. Within a few months of partition the angry threats and recriminations flared into open warfare and the troops of each country moved in to pre-empt what they could— Pakistan the fertile north, and India the southern valley with most of Kashmir's four million population. The United Nations frequently called for a plebiscite and several times there were near agreements. But at the last moment Nehru would find some rationale to compel delay. Warfare again erupted in 1965 and an uneasy truce, the Tashkent Declaration, was achieved only through the mediation of the Soviet Union. Kashmir remained an open wound to infect the relations between the two countries.

Even more serious, indeed threatening the very survival of Pakistan, was the bizarre geopolitical structure that the partition agreement had created. Two populous regions, separated by nearly 1,000 miles of Indian Hindu territory, were haltered to form the independent state. The physical disjunction was further aggravated because the peoples of each area had little in common except their Islamic faith and their grinding poverty. The West Pakistanis were usually tall, light-skinned, martial, aggressive. The East Pakistanis were smaller physically, dark, placid, much more concerned with the arts of peace. The physical differences would not normally be a divisive factor; most nations are a congeries of heterogeneous groupings. But for centuries the western peoples had looked upon the easterners with contempt as inferiors. Though the population of the eastern province, Bengal, was seventy-eight million, and of the west fifty-eight million, it was the west that commandeered most of the economic and social advantages. Seventy percent of the civil service was in the hands of the west and the military was entirely under its control. Ninety percent of the officers' group was drawn from the west; virtually no Bengali held a rank above colonel. In the five-year plans, heavily subsidized by outside loans and grants, the bulk of the funds for investment and modernization went to the west. The east provided more than half of the exports but most of the revenues were spent in the west for the bureaucracy, the schools, and the social welfare programs.

For a decade and more the sense of outrage of the East Pakistanis expressed itself in sullen complaint; there was little organization for resistance and no leadership. But after twenty years of what was considered ever more brazen exploitation, the resentment exploded and blew the state apart. The spark was supplied by Sheikh Mujibar Rahman, whom his countrymen called Mujib. Personal courage that ran often to recklessness, and a unique talent for mass oratory, combined in him to give voice and thrust to the long-suppressed aspirations of his people. Mujib was born in 1921 in a hamlet near Dacca, the son of a middle-class village family. His early progress was seriously retarded by an attack of beriberi which left him with permanently impaired eyesight and he did not complete his high-school education until he was twenty-two. His university training was in the Islamic College in Calcutta and he then went to the law school in Dacca. But like most of his contemporaries he was a rebel against British rule, constantly in trouble with the authorities and frequently jailed. When he became involved in the strike of menial workers in the law school he was expelled. He gave up his ambition for a professional career and turned his energies to political agitation. After the partition and the establishment of a sovereign Pakistan, the main target for his opposition became the West Pakistani government. Mujib was jailed, this time by Jinnah's government, when he resisted the decree that aimed to establish Urdu as the official language of Pakistan. On release he helped to found the Awami League, the nationalist organization that was committed to the achievement of autonomy for East Pakistan.

In the next fifteen years, during which governments came and went, Mujib continued his defiance. He was a major torment for Ayub Khan, who had come to power in 1958, for he now combined defiance of the dominance of West Pakistan with resistance to the social and economic policies of the government that kept the whole country in bondage. Twenty families controlled two-thirds of the national industry, four-fifths of the banking. Corruption and nepotism flourished more openly than ever. In 1966 Mujib became so much of a menace that Ayub arrested him and the chief Awami leaders. For three years, while Mujib was imprisoned, the agitation mounted. The riots and strikes came with such frequency, in the western provinces as well as in the east, that the country was threatened with chaos. In April 1969, Ayub announced that it was impossible for him to continue and he called in the army commander, General Yahya Khan, to take over.

Yahya was a tough professional soldier with a record of brilliant military competence in World War II. To cope with the paralysis of unrest, he immediately placed the country under martial law. But he was ready to try for a new deal under constitutional guarantees, with a radical revision of the relationship of East Pakistan in the national union. He freed Mujib and announced that there would be new elections in December 1970, with universal suffrage. How much the nationalism of the east had intensified was made clear when Mujib returned to Dacca and was jubilantly welcomed by more than a million Bengalis in the Race Track stadium. Mujib's first announcement was his determination to go beyond autonomy for East Pakistan: now the demand was for *"purbodesh,"* a kind of associate statehood, virtual independence, with the most tenuous ties to the national government. It was on this platform that Mujib fought the election. The returns in the east brought a sensational victory for the Awami League, which carried all but two seats; indeed, the sweep was so complete that in the National Assembly of 313 seats, the Awami, with 169, would command a majority. This would make Mujib the Prime Minister and the government would be dominated by East Pakistan.

The new Assembly was to meet in March 1971. Yahya proceeded to cancel the election, to outlaw the Awami Party, and to drag Mujib off to a West Pakistan prison, there to be court-martialed for treason. The Awami leaders who had not been apprehended then repudiated all ties of the east with the national government, declared the sovereignty of Bangladesh (the Bengali homeland), and raised the flag of independence. The civil war was now in the open.

Within a month Yahya had despatched eighty thousand crack troops to the east. He was determined not only to suppress the rebellion, but to wipe out the cadres of East Pakistan leadership so that the authority of the national government would never again be threatened. Thousands of the best educated and trained were rounded up, butchered, and dumped into mass graves. The invading forces were merciless and more than a million Bengalis lost their lives in the holocaust of repression. There was justifiable panic and nearly ten million terrified men, women, and children fled, mainly into Bengal, the northeast province of India, where the shelter afforded was at best no more than primitive.*

The repression may very well have succeeded even though Bangladesh guerrilla activity would undoubtedly have prolonged the disturbances far into the future. But the civil war was not left exclusively to the Pakistanis. India, for a variety of reasons, now intervened to save the Bangladesh cause. The human problem was the most immediate. The care of ten million refugees, huddled into the already impossibly crowded area of the northeast province, could not be borne by India for more than the briefest period and, until East Pakistan was safe for them, they could not be sent back. Equally compelling, the long-standing border quarrels could now perhaps be permanently resolved if Pakistan disintegrated and a friendly state became the neighbor on the northeast frontier and the buffer between India and China.

---

* "Where are you going, Abba?" asked five-year-old Akbar of his father. "I am going to the mosque to pray." "Pray to whom, Abba?" "To Allah, of course!" "Allah! Haven't the Pakistani soldiers killed him?" Abou Ahmed, *The Longest Night.* Cited in *The New York Times,* Jan. 30, 1972.

From the outset, therefore, Indira Gandhi, now Prime Minister of India, encouraged the Bangladesh movement. She supplied arms to the Awami guerrillas and, within a few months, a hundred thousand of them were harassing the occupying forces of Yahya. In December, Indira decided upon actual intervention, despite the sternest warning from the United States that she was precipitating a serious international confrontation. The danger was genuine; the Soviet Union supported the Indian action, and Red China stood with West Pakistan. It was ironic that Indira, the daughter of Nehru and the disciple of Gandhi, would take the calculated risk that had given pause to the most bellicose nationalist statesmen.

Indira's gamble paid off. Though the West Pakistan military units were strongly entrenched in the rebel territory, they could not be easily supplied over the thousand miles that separated them from the national base. Red China was apparently too deeply involved with its own problems to risk war at this stage and contented itself with vituperative rhetoric. President Nixon repeatedly appealed to the United Nations to order a cease fire, but the veto of the Soviet Union thwarted all American efforts. The West Pakistan forces were quickly immobilized and, within two weeks, a triumphant Indian commander received their surrender. The independent state of Bangladesh became a reality.

The catastrophic defeat brought down Yahya, who resigned in favor of the foreign minister, Zulfikar Ali Bhutto. Bhutto knew there was no hope of persuading Bangladesh to accept some form of federation that would preserve even a tenuous union. Time would be needed to heal the hatreds that had been spawned by the horrors of the repression. But he hoped for at least a restoration of economic relationships, since both parts of the former state would need to supplement each other's resources. One of Bhutto's first acts therefore was to release Mujib and he personally escorted him to the plane that was to send him on the way to freedom and the leadership of his people. Mujib's reception in Dacca by the hysterical crowds of hundreds of thousands all the way from the airport strip to the heart of the city—the massed humanity along the roads, hanging from the balconies and housetops, the flowers strewn along the route, the prayers and the tears—was part of the fervent hope that the long nightmare was over at last. Mujib assumed the post of Prime Minister and announced at once that the new state would be based on socialist principles and would take its place in the nonaligned camp in international affairs.

The nightmare of brutal warfare was over, but not the ordeal of reconstruction. Every family mourned its dead, its maimed, and its dishonored. The farmers had lost their homes, their tools, and their livestock. The famed tea gardens of the country and the jute factories, the core of the export trade, the ports for shipping, the roads for transportation, communications, all had been shattered and would need hundreds of millions in foreign loans to bring them back to operation and production. Ten million refugees would have to be resettled in homes destroyed and lands despoiled. There was an ugly spirit of vengeance abroad that sought atonement for the three million who had died during the months of horror.

These were all terrifying problems; Mujib's statesmanship had thus far been tested only by agitation and not yet by responsibility. But the country was free from the yoke that had so long burdened it, India was a concerned and cooperative neighbor, and there were overtures from West Pakistan to build a more reliable friendship upon the foundation of the common Moslem faith. Even the goodwill of the United States was not an irretrievable loss, for the Nixon foreign policy that had resisted Bangladesh and India had been widely denounced by strong blocs of American liberals who pressed for early reconciliation. There was hope that if the economic viability of the battered nation could be protected with major international assistance, Bangladesh could vindicate its passionate battle for independence.

37

THE DECOLONIZATION
OF BLACK AFRICA

THE CONTINENT OF AFRICA OCCUPIES ABOUT A FOURTH OF THE EARTH'S surface. It is larger than the United States, China, and India combined, and, while 40 percent of its surface is inhospitable desert, it has rich resources for agriculture and immense mineral wealth. During the nineteenth century, there was a scramble by European powers to carve out empires there, and the choicest spoils went to Britain, France, Belgium, and Portugal. The Mediterranean littoral in the north, and the areas in the extreme south, with favored climate for Europeans, beckoned large numbers of white settlers, and they imported western traditions in education, health, and social institutions. But the millions of square miles in between, tropical Africa, were only sparsely colonized. Until the war period the white men who came to govern or to exploit the resources could overcome resistance with no great effort, since the blacks were too fragmented by tribe and language, with no access to modern weaponry, to challenge the intruders and escape subjugation. When the exploitation became too oppressive it was easy to conclude that the major contributions of the whites were the bottle, the bullet, and the Bible.

The two world wars that loosened political and economic relationships in every sphere of life had comparable impact in the colonial systems. As the wars drained the contending nations to the point of exhaustion, they lost their aura of invulnerability. One Berber chieftain scornfully summed up the exposed fragility of the

[431]

European facade. "The French," he said, "will stay in Africa as long as France exists, but does France exist?" The demand for change was raised boldly and defiantly by the African leaders, especially those educated in Europe and the United States. They came back from studies abroad with the resentful conviction that colonialism meant not only physical exploitation but psychological debasement. One of the most perceptive, Alex Quaison-Sackey, formulated it as the deliberate castration of Africa in *esse* and *posse*. The reaction was reminiscent of the response to Lord John Russell in 1854 when he advised the Italians to subside since they would be treated with more humaneness by the Austrians. The liberator of Venice, Daniele Manin, flared back, "We do not ask that Austria be humane and liberal in Italy—which, after all, would be impossible for her even if she desired; *we ask her to get out*. We have no concern with her humanity and her liberalism; we wish to be masters in our own house."*

Within twenty years after World War II, more than thirty-five tropical African states had achieved independence and sovereignty, seventeen in 1960 alone. The pace was set by Britain which, after decades of reluctance and resistance, moved rapidly to transfer authority to the Africans themselves. Its program of devolvement was felicitously termed "creative abdication." This meant that Britain, realizing that the days of imperial exploitation were over, proposed voluntarily to offer freedom to its dependencies; then, perhaps, amicable relations could be sustained within the framework of the British Commonwealth itself. The Labour Foreign Minister, Ernest Bevin, expressed the policy with his usual blunt realism, "Give—and keep." The experiment was initiated in the Gold Coast in West Africa, and in Kenya in East Africa, and it established a pattern that was eagerly sought in most of the dependencies of the continent.

The story of independence for the Gold Coast, which later became Ghana, is centered in the career of Kwame Nkrumah who, with all his exhibitionism and his lust for power, embodied the age-long strivings of his people and gave them direction and fulfillment. He was born in 1909 in a remote village of the Gold Coast. His father was a low-income goldsmith who sold trinkets. In 1925, when Nkrumah was sixteen, an uncle staked the youngster to passage

* Rupert Emerson, *From Empire to Nation* (Cambridge, Mass.: Harvard University Press, 1962), p. 43.

money to the United States so that he could attend Lincoln University in Pennsylvania, a Negro college that had attracted many Africans and prepared them for careers in their homelands. Nkrumah earned his schooling as a librarian's assistant and, when he achieved his degree in philosophy, he taught briefly as an instructor. But the next years of search for a livelihood in eastern seaboard cities were an ordeal of degradation. Racial restrictions kept him in menial jobs—a fish hawker, a waiter, a bellhop. He was often penniless and hungry and, without lodgings, he would ride the Brooklyn subway all night long, eating charity meals at the mission of Father Divine. He never forgot the humiliation of an experience in the segregated bus station in Baltimore; he asked a clerk where he could get a drink of water and the clerk pointed to a spittoon.

In May 1945, after ten years in the United States, he moved to England where he resumed his studies at the London School of Economics. Here, too, he scrounged around in odd jobs, living in the shabbiest sections of the East End, a lonely, embittered black in a hostile or indifferent white community. He met kindred spirits who sought comfort in Communist fellowship, and apparently he flirted for a while with their objectives. Together with other young Africans he helped to organize the Pan-African Congress in Manchester. All through these frustrating years, the fury in him burning away in his belly, he remained in communication with his home country. The leader of the nationalist movement there, J. B. Danquah, had for years been vainly pressing for some modest measures of local autonomy. In late 1947, impressed with Nkrumah's activities in England, Danquah invited him to return to become secretary for the nationalist party, the United Gold Coast Convention. Nkrumah, who had now been away for twelve years, accepted the bid, though he was quite contemptuous of the low-keyed techniques of the party.

He initiated a much more aggressive program and, within the first year, he had organized five hundred branches throughout the country. His first major defiance came in February 1949, when he called for a boycott of stores that were selling European goods. Some of the black war veterans marched to the Government House in an unauthorized demonstration. Their dispersal by the police set off a major riot, with many deaths and injuries. Nkrumah was arrested, and investigation revealed that he had been actively organizing an inner revolutionary group, with aims that went far

[433]

beyond the more modest objectives of Danquah. He was given a minor two-month prison sentence, but the confrontation that he had maneuvered compelled the appointment of a Royal Commission, and it endorsed the first grants of limited autonomy in any British African state.

When Nkrumah's two-month sentence expired, he dramatized his release by publicly denouncing Danquah's whole approach as submissive and therefore self-defeating. He organized a party of his own, the C.P.P.—the Convention People's Party—committed to press for independence for the Gold Coast and for the other colonies. He dreamed of a united Black Africa that would rise above tribes and states, that would play a decisive role in a world too long dominated and manipulated by white power blocs. His program was outlined in a widely circulated volume, *Toward Colonial Freedom*. When he followed his manifesto with the call for a general strike to paralyze the life of the Gold Coast, he was quickly re-arrested and, this time, he was sent off to prison for three years. The punishment as well as the provocation for it made him an international hero among the blacks, a kind of African Nehru, and his voice from inside the prison walls wielded greater influence than when he was free.

The Labour government in Britain, having already pledged independence for India and other parts of the Empire, was now ready to negotiate for an autonomous government in the Gold Coast. A constitution was drafted that went a long way toward the "creative abdication" that the Labour government had sponsored, and a general election was set for February 1951. The imprisoned Nkrumah was the candidate for Accra, the capital. With twenty-three thousand ballots cast, he received virtually unanimous support, and his party carried thirty-four of the thirty-eight official constituencies. The British Governor could not bypass such an emphatic mandate and Nkrumah was released. One hundred thousand of his followers waited to welcome him as he emerged from the prison gate. When he stepped barefooted, seven times, into the blood of a sacrificial sheep, to cleanse himself of the stain of foreign captivity, the crowd cheered itself into a frenzy.

Nkrumah went directly from prison to head up the new government, with the temporary title of Leader of Government Business; a year later, in 1952, this was changed to Prime Minister. Nkrumah believed in the power of symbols, and among the first that he dramatized was the selection of the ancient African name, Ghana, for the newly emancipated state. The initials P.G. were always displayed on the colorful regal costume that he adopted, to remind his people that he was a Prison Graduate and that he had endured many hardships on the road to national freedom.

Symbols, however, could not solve the clamorous problems which faced Nkrumah. Even as he took office, the economy was threatened by a virulent disease that invaded the cocoa crop of the country. Ghana had five hundred million cocoa trees that supplied a third of the world's cocoa needs. They represented 70 percent of all the exports of the country. But the swollen shoot disease had infected millions of the trees and the British had ordered their destruction in order to save the economy. Nkrumah had joined the distressed farmers in strident resistance. But now that the responsibility for the welfare of the country was his, he abandoned his demagoguery and sanctioned the elimination of the affected trees. However, with technical experts, he arranged for compensation to the farmers whose livelihoods were jeopardized. The industry, with expert scientific counsel, retrieved its losses, and out of later reserves came the funds for the improvement of roads, and for a network of scholarships and fellowships for gifted young Africans to complete their education at home and abroad. Nkrumah also muted his extravagant attacks on "foreign imperialism," and he welcomed outside capital to help in the building of factories and railroads, and for the development of the gold, bauxite, and timber resources of the country.

Nkrumah's most ambitious undertaking was the Volta Dam project, a miniature Ghana TVA that would make available the hydroelectric power to serve the country's new industries. The undertaking required substantial investment, and several European countries offered help. Nkrumah returned to the United States to solicit American participation; he was greeted warmly by President Eisenhower and assured of major support. Unfortunately for Nkrumah's reputation, the completion of the Volta project in 1966 came only after he had been overthrown by disenchanted followers.

They had grown weary of Nkrumah's growing authoritarian actions and of the shocking graft and wastefulness that emptied the national coffers. Nkrumah had built an oversized palace to house the Organization of African Unity with special sections for every African nation. The palace was never used and, empty and incongruous, was referred to sarcastically as Job 600, a monument of ostentatious squandering. Nkrumah laid no claims to modesty, and the squalor of his earlier experiences did not chasten the extravagance of personal life now. He was easily satisfied with the best of everything. He lorded in splendor in the old Government House by the sea, with retinues of servants, a personal bodyguard of hundreds, and a 525-ton yacht. He ordered his image on the Ghana coinage. The postage stamps carried his likeness along with that of Abraham Lincoln. He had streets and schools and clinics named for him, and he declared his birthday to be a national holiday. He climaxed the self-rendered honors by authorizing a towering 40-foot statue of himself, giving the freedom salute, outside the National Assembly Building.

But these were personal vanities and, by themselves, would probably have been indulgently condoned. However, Nkrumah's authoritarianism was compounded by his close relationship with the Communist bloc. Nkrumah opened the country to agents, spies, intelligence officers, and instructors in guerrilla warfare and commando tactics from many of the Communist countries. Through the Kwame Nkrumah Ideological Institute and the African Affairs Bureau, Ghana became a center for dissident movements in the other African states. Nkrumah justified the activity as nationalist-oriented, the fulfillment of his dream of a Union of independent African states. But the men who were trained in Ghana were all drawn from the Soviet Union, Red China, and East Germany. It was significant that two of Nkrumah's books were dedicated respectively to George Padmore, his West Indian ex-Communist mentor, and to Patrice Lumumba, the Congolese nationalist leader who had been identified by the western Allies as a Soviet bloc collaborator. Nkrumah's cabinet was in accord that Ghana should follow a nonaligned foreign policy, accepting aid wherever it could be negotiated and remaining on good terms with East and West. But Nkrumah's clear preference for the extreme left was unacceptable.

The opportunity for action was seized by the police and army leadership in February 1966. Nkrumah was a guest of Mao Tse-tung in Red China and, during his absence from Accra, there was a bloodless coup. Immediately afterwards, the Chinese and the Russian officials in Ghana were expelled or fled. A Ghana Blue Book, obviously biased, ridiculed the agents who ran "like animals in front of a forest fire, 1,100 Russians, 430 Chinese and scores of other Communists." The long-demeaned and abused colleagues, who had been reduced by Nkrumah to the status of flunkies, salved their injured pride by toppling the statue of the father of the Republic.

They released hundreds of political prisoners who had been rounded up by order of the ex-prisoner who was proud of the P.G. on his garb. When the men emerged from confinement, the emotional greeting that they received carried as much hatred for Nkrumah as relief and gratitude for their freedom.

Nkrumah took refuge in the neighboring state of Guinea, where he was welcomed by Sekou Touré, the nationalist leader who had cut all ties with France. Nkrumah used the Guinea base to wait out a hoped-for return to Ghana, when, as he confidently expected, the political climate would change. He died in exile in 1972.

The personal career had ended abruptly, in disgrace, in early middle age. But an enduring contribution remained through the inspiration that Nkrumah evoked, not the man with feet of clay, but the liberative force, the founder of the first black state in tropical Africa that had won independence. The time had been propitious since the Labour government in Britain was an ally and was eager to cooperate in the achievement of independence for its African wards. But Nkrumah had resisted half-measures, and his tenacity, crowned with triumph, hastened the fulfillment of black nationalist hopes in every other part of Africa.

Ghana itself did not recover quickly, however, from Nkrumah's squandermania. The army turned over control to a civilian government but it could not cope with the serious economic problems that it had inherited. For more than five years the struggle went on, with deficits, falling foreign trade, internal crises, and a currency devaluation of nearly 45 percent. In January 1972 while Kofi Busia, the civilian head of the government, was in London seeking aid, the army again intervened and Ghana succumbed to a military dictatorship.

ON THE EASTERN SIDE OF THE CONTINENT WAS THE COLONY OF KENYA, with its population of eight million blacks, long dominated by seventy thousand British, who had settled in the White Highlands and controlled eighteen million acres of the country's prize land. Here the thrust for freedom was spearheaded by a high-spirited, militant tribe, the Kikuyu, numbering about three-quarters of a million. Their hostility could not be mollified by negotiation or compromise; they had owned the rich, fertile highlands, and had been evicted. Whenever they raised their eyes to the beautifully cultivated plateau, they contrasted the squalor of their lives with the opulence of the overlords, who exacerbated the subjugation by imposing gratuitous humiliations on the dispossessed—the galling color restrictions in living and mobility, the taxes that made the Africans pay heavily for their own subjugation, the contemptuous references to Kikuyus as "Kuks," the signs in public accommodations, "For European Gentlemen," "For Asian Gentlemen," with no provision at all for Africans.

The resentment exploded in 1952 in violent outbreaks by an extremist Kikuyu group, the Mau Mau. They regarded themselves as freedom fighters, but they perpetrated acts of such fanatical brutality that their very name struck terror. Since they were intent upon driving the British out of the lands that had been theirs, and out of Kenya itself, this was exactly the purpose of their terrorist technique. Countermeasures against them simply deepened their ferocity. Only a small number of their victims were British, less than one hundred, but they were usually highly placed officials, and each episode was a sensation. Even worse fate was in store for Africans who refused to collaborate with them, or who continued to maintain normal relations with the British. The number of victims went beyond fifteen hundred and the killings were always widely publicized in all their grisly detail.

The British did not look upon the Mau Mau as militant patriots. They regarded them as thugs gone berserk, and they hunted them and their confederates down without mercy through four years of the grimmest guerrilla warfare, during which fourteen thousand Africans were killed and seventy-seven thousand were rounded up and imprisoned.

The head and front of the rebellion, though perhaps not part of the Mau Mau assaults, was the Kikuyu leader Jomo Kenyatta, who emerged as another of the dramatic symbols of African freedom. He was born about 1893 in a primitive Kenya village to a family of witch doctors. He was orphaned early, and was taken into a Scottish mission school. He lived by odd jobs—houseboy for a European settler, carpenter, farmer's aide—but he missed no opportunity for continued self-education. In 1929 he left Kenya for England, an absence that was to stretch to seventeen years. In England, he studied with one of the most influential anthropologists, Bronislaw Malinowski, and he wrote a well-received volume on Kikuyu tribal customs. He was always deep in African nationalist agitation, and he collaborated with Nkrumah in the organization of the Pan-African Congress in Manchester in 1945.

Next year he returned to Kenya, all afire with the mission to hasten the pace of British withdrawal. He made a striking appearance, powerful in physique, militant, impatient with Fabian tactics. He took a post as principal in one of the newly founded teachers' colleges, and used the school system as a medium for nationalist agitation. The Mau Mau terrorist raids began in 1952, and Kenyatta was arrested by the British, who accused him of master-minding the attacks. After a five-month, widely reported trial, he was sentenced to seven years' imprisonment and then to exile in a village near the Sudan border. But from his exile point, he continued to command the devotion not only of the Kikuyu families, but of all the nationalist groups in tropical Africa, to whom he became a legend of resistance.

While Kenyatta remained in confinement, active management of the freedom movement passed to a young lieutenant, Tom Mboya, a brilliant, eloquent labor leader.

Mboya was born in 1931, the son of a poor Luo tribal workman. He received his elementary training in one of the Roman Catholic schools, and he did well enough to earn a two-year scholarship to Oxford. But studies seemed quite remote in a world where action was paramount, and Mboya did not take full advantage of the Oxford opportunity. He became a sanitary inspector in Nairobi, and it did not quiet his bitterness against the colonial system when he knew that his salary was one-fifth of what white co-workers received for similar tasks. He became active in the trade union movement and very quickly rose to the treasurer's post. He was then all of twenty-three. He could not avoid the resentment of much older colleagues, especially those to whom he was an upstart from the rival Luo tribe, and their hostility was probably responsible for his murder before his fortieth year. But, at this stage, he had the full confidence of Kenyatta, and when the chief was imprisoned, Mboya became his political surrogate. He traveled widely, especially to the international labor conferences, where he earned the friendship and enthusiastic support of American labor leaders—Walter Reuther, George Meany, David Dubinsky—men who could offer influential counsel and could conduit necessary propaganda funds for the cause of African independence.

By 1960, the policy of decolonization had transformed the face of Africa and Kenya had achieved complete autonomy. Inevitably, Kenyatta was called from confinement to become the first Prime Minister. Three years later, Kenya opted to become a Republic, although it retained membership in the British Commonwealth.

At midnight on December 11, 1963, the picturesque ceremonies to inaugurate sovereignty were held. Kenyatta demonstrated a sensitivity that seemed to indicate that the brutality of the guerrilla war period had been a conscious strategy. He was enough concerned about British feelings to have all the lights dimmed as the Union Jack came down. Then the lights blazed on as the Kenya flag was raised, and the new Republic came into being. The poor farm apprentice, the houseboy, the hunted rebel, the convicted terrorist, now took the oath as head of state, in the presence of dignitaries from around the world and of the Duchess of Kent, who represented the Queen and the British Commonwealth.

The technical achievement of sovereignty for Kenya was a gratifying climax after the long ordeal of rebellion. But there were tasks ahead that would test the capacity of the most experienced statesman. Agriculture, in a rapidly rising population, was pathetically primitive. Foreign experts were indispensable for progress in education, for the modernization of the economy, for population control. There were seven hundred and fifty doctors in the entire country, virtually none of them African, and a minimum of nine thousand was needed.

There were frustrating tensions in the relationship to neighboring states. Kenyatta had labored with consummate diplomacy to create a federated union with Uganda and Tanganyika, and with the offshore spice island of Zanzibar. Such a union seemed to provide a natural melding of common interests that would stimulate trade and education. But tribal and nationalist feeling could not be quickly overcome, and the Cold War now penetrated the remotest areas of Africa, as it had everywhere else in the world. Zanzibar, after uniting with Tanganyika to form the state of Tanzania, fell under the influence of Chinese Maoist sympathizers. The Prime Minister of Tanganyika, Julius Nyerere, a committed democratic Socialist, clung to nonalignment and resisted Communist penetration. But for the present at least, common planning and action became impractical. Even the cooperative effort of the struggling universities had eventually to be abandoned.

The nationalist leaders of Kenya were learning that the arts of rebellion could be mastered more easily than the skills to adjust an underdeveloped land to the complexities of the mid-twentieth century. In 1964, Kenyatta, hailed now as the first President, was already past seventy. Who could succeed him and apply his prestige to the tasks that lay ahead? It was one of history's strange reversals that the rebel whose name struck terror a decade earlier was now considered the anchor of discipline and cooperation. He was affectionately referred to by the British themselves as "Mzee," the Grand Old Man, and there were frequent expressions of anxiety over what would happen if he were no longer there.

GHANA CARRIED THROUGH SMOOTHLY THE HISTORIC TRANSITION FROM colonial dependence to sovereignty. Kenya accomplished it with more travail. As noted earlier, within two decades after World War II thirty-five new African states had emerged, and virtually all of them had to go through agonizing years of civil wars and tribal vendettas and foreign intervention. Perhaps the most heartbreaking were the developments in the Belgian Congo.

The chaos that followed independence there was fed by many causes. There were historic tribal animosities, dangerously accentuated because the normal outlet for differences did not exist; political parties had been proscribed by the colonial masters. Further, Belgian policy had withheld any kind of training in government for the natives, so that when Belgium moved out with precipitous irresponsibility, there was a vacuum in mature and experienced leadership. The outreach of the Cold War nations, and their determination to protect their investments and their strategic advantages, did not help when they goaded and armed the warring elements. In any case, the achievement of Congolese independence in June 1960 immediately plunged the nation into the bedlam "politics of fragmentation,"* and produced years of bloodshed and terror on a scale that threatened the whole of central Africa.

The stakes were worth fighting for. The Congo offered almost limitless opportunities for economic exploitation. It was as big as all of western Europe, 900,000 square miles, seventy-seven times the size of the mother country, Belgium. Yet it had been the last part of Africa to be explored by the Europeans. Joseph Conrad called his novel of the Congo, *Heart of Darkness*. It was first opened out to the western world in 1874 by the audacious explorations of a young adventurer, Henry Stanley, who had been sponsored by a New York newspaper to seek the missionary Dr. David Livingstone. Stanley

* The phrase is René Lemarchand's in *Political Awakening in the Belgian Congo* (Berkeley: University of California Press, 1964).

found him deep in the jungle ("Dr. Livingstone, I presume"), and then he entered the employ of the King of Belgium to chart out the hidden riches of the vast empire. An international conference in Berlin in 1885 partitioned the central belt of Africa and, in an astonishing move, the whole of the Congo basin was assigned to King Leopold II of Belgium as his personal fief, giving him the largest personal domain in history.

The exploitation that followed, long hidden from the world, was carried on with an obscene callousness that gave the lie to the pretensions of the psalm-singing missionaries. The profits in copper and diamonds, in cobalt and uranium, came not only from the bowels of the earth but from the hides and the guts of slave labor. The population in the basin, which had been fourteen million before the Europeans arrived, was steadily decimated until it reached less than twelve million at the beginning of the twentieth century. Leopold blandly claimed that his government was a blessing for the benighted natives. "Our only programme," he said piously, "is that of the moral and material regeneration of the country."* In 1904 Roger Casement, an Irishman who was serving as a British Consul, revealed the scandalous abuses, which included unbearable flogging and the mutilation and amputation of limbs. These so shocked the world that in 1908 Leopold reluctantly agreed to relinquish personal control of the Congo.† Its administration was transferred to the Belgian government itself, although Leopold and his concessionaires retained the economic rights that they had acquired.‡

For the next two generations, until after World War II, the Congo was ruled as a Belgian crown colony. The policy of the governors became a model of paternalism. The workers were carefully protected, with every consideration for their material welfare. There was an end to indentured labor and to the use of the *chicotte*, the hippo hide, to exact the fulfillment of production quotas. The wages were good, the housing adequate, and there were

* J. A. Hobson, *Imperialism* (London: George Allen & Unwin, Ltd., 1938), p. 198.

† Casement was knighted for his achievement. Later he joined in the Irish nationalist uprising of 1916 and was hanged by the British as a traitor.

‡ Vachel Lindsay's poem *The Congo* referred to Leopold's cruelty:

> Listen to the yell of Leopold's ghost
> Burning in Hell for his hand-maimed host.
> Hear how the demons chuckle and yell
> Cutting his hands off down in Hell.

frequent holidays and protective pensions. In 1950, a ten-year plan was added through a billion-dollar allocation for expanded social welfare benefits. But every precaution was taken to keep the workers from any participation in government or from attaining executive responsibility. They could enter the civil service but could rise no higher than modest clerkships. The political restrictions applied not only to the blacks. The white population of eighty thousand was similarly disfranchised and there was no attempt to stimulate European immigration. The Home Office wanted no problems of white settler friction. The children were encouraged to enroll in the Catholic mission schools but these provided no education beyond the elementary level. On the eve of independence there were not twenty men in the whole country who had college degrees. The Congo, then, was a monopolist's paradise, no political parties, no unions, no strikes, no protests, no demonstrations. The colonial motto was *"Dominer pour servir,"* Rule in order to serve. The rule was firmly absolutist; only enough service was rendered to keep the natives in docile contentment.

Then the great nationalist movements whipped through the continent and it was not possible, even with the most alluring cumshaw benefits, to keep the Congo insulated from the winds of change. All through the 1950's Britain was accelerating its decolonization programs in its African empire, and especially in neighboring Ghana. In 1958, De Gaulle visited Brazzaville in the French Congo, across the river, and he made a dramatic *"Oui ou non"* announcement: its people could remain part of a worldwide French federation or could leave the French jurisdiction if they opted for independence. The ensuing excitement caught up every black community, and leadership emerged to give voice and striking power to long-deferred hope.

Joseph Kasavubu, of the Bakongo tribe, began rousing the province of Kasai to the advantages of independence even if this meant less material advantages at the outset. Patrice Lumumba, of the Batatela tribe, whose base was in Stanleyville,* returned from an all-African conference in Ghana determined to set in motion a national movement that would purge out "the rapacious white intruders" who had so long dominated his people. The manifestoes came in a period of falling commodity prices and growing unemployment.

---

* Very soon such names as Stanleyville, Leopoldville, and others that bore humiliating reminders of the past were substituted by others that were linked with native pride. The Congo itself took the name of Zaire.

In December 1958, thirty thousand displaced blacks marched through the streets of Leopoldville with menacing signs, shouting defiant slogans, and the contagion of unrest and riot spread. The Belgian government took fright. It began exploring ways to extricate itself from the galling problems of native turbulence without jeopardizing its economic investments. In January 1960, at a Round Table Conference in Brussels, it blandly announced that, within six months, the government of the country would be turned over to the blacks. The decision created astonishment since, until then, there had been virtually no preparation for even shared government. In effect Belgium was proposing not an orderly devolution but an irresponsible abdication, and there were to be frightening consequences.

June 30, 1960, was Independence Day and the colorful exercises, centered in Leopoldville, were attended by representatives from every part of the world. President Eisenhower's emissary brought a bust of Abraham Lincoln and announced that three hundred scholarships would be set up in American colleges for competitively selected young Congolese to begin their training for future service to their homeland. The King of Belgium spoke eloquently of his hope for a future of full cooperation. But when Patrice Lumumba was called upon he eschewed the amenities, and denounced the exploitation of the past and "the atrocious suffering" that his people had endured. From this day, he exploded, "we are no longer your monkeys," and he pledged that the new era would be built "by the Congo's own children." The King sat pale and furious and it was clear that there were to be troubled times ahead.

Preceding the day of independence, there had been an election for the first Parliament, but neither Kasavubu nor Lumumba garnered enough seats to claim a clear mandate. They formed a coalition, with Kasavubu as President and Lumumba as Prime Minister. But it was an uneasy alliance, strained with mistrust and incompatible personal ambition. Within a few days all discipline broke down. The army was made up of mercenaries who had little loyalty to the newly established ramshackle government. They mutinied, expelled their white officers, and were soon out of control, looting and killing with anarchic abandon. Simultaneously the rich province of Katanga announced its secession and its determination to form an independent state with continuing ties to Belgium. The dizzy pace of disintegration hastened the actions of the Cold War protagonists—the Russians, the Chinese, the British, the French, and the Americans—to safeguard or to advance their interests.

The Congolese leaders, unable to hold the country together, flailed about in confusion. They distrusted each other as much as they distrusted the foreign overlords. Lumumba had many natural talents for leadership but they were distorted and misdirected by continuous impetuousness and by hatreds that submerged judgment. His early years had been full of angry frustration, menial service in a post office, salesmanship for a brewery, and, after conviction for embezzlement, a stretch in prison. It was when he turned to politics and began expressing the nationalist strivings of his people that he seemed to find himself and was able to get his habitual drunkenness and his addiction to dope under some control. His participation in the all-African conference in Ghana in 1958 made him an ardent disciple of Nkrumah and he returned as an uncompromising advocate of an independent, unified Congo.

Kasavubu was much more moderate. He had attended a mission school and his parents had expected that he would enter the priesthood. He early abandoned such plans and filled a succession of odd jobs in a timber firm and in the civil service until he was drawn into the politics of nationalism, rising rapidly to prominence. His Bakongo tribe numbered more than a million, but they had been arbitrarily divided up among the Belgian, French, and Portuguese colonial empires, and it was Kasavubu's dream that someday they could be reunited. Such aspirations, expressed with eloquence, identified him as a dangerous radical and, in 1959, he was deported. Next year, when independence was promised, he was recalled and he now shared with Lumumba the responsibility of trying to keep the state alive.

The task seemed impossible. The rumor had spread that the white population was being butchered and the panic that ensued sent thousands of families into flight. They flooded into the French Congo and into the northern towns of Angola. Those who did not cross the frontiers camped in the embassies or in the public buildings of the better protected cities. The casualties would very likely have been heavy, but Belgium rushed back five thousand soldiers and paratroopers to protect the beleaguered whites. Lumumba accused the Belgians of overplaying the danger and of using the inevitable dislocation of an interregnum experience as an excuse to re-establish their colonial control. When their forces refused to leave, Lumumba broke relations with Belgium and called upon Khrushchev and the Soviet Union to intercede. He also appealed to the United Nations to send in its own forces, not only to cope with the disturbances, but to eliminate the pretext for the continuation of the Belgian occupation.

The United Nations, at this critical juncture, was under the direction of a remarkable Swedish diplomat, Dag Hammarskjöld, whose talents were to be tested to the full by the complexities of the Congo problem. He came from an old aristocratic family; his father had been the Swedish Prime Minister during World War I. He had a solid training in international economics and he taught advanced courses at the University of Stockholm. He was equally at home in literature and art and had mastered a number of European languages. It was a measure of his versatility that he could become president of the Swedish National Bank at thirty-six, and be writing critically acclaimed essays in the philosophy of mysticism. In temperament he was urbane, unruffled, even in the most difficult confrontations. He had succeeded the more flamboyant Trygve Lie in 1953 as Secretary General of the United Nations. He had proved his diplomatic skill in 1956 when he prevailed upon the British and the French to withdraw from Egypt in the dangerous Suez crisis, and earlier, in 1955, when he successfully negotiated the release of fifteen pilots who had been captured and held by Red China.

In turning to the Congo crisis, Hammarskjöld knew from earlier experience that there was little chance for United Nations success unless he could persuade the two international giants, the Soviet Union and the United States, to cooperate. He got them to agree that only the "sister African nations" were to provide the security troops to restore order, although the assignment to ferry them in and to evacuate the refugees was given to the Americans, who could quickly supply the necessary air equipment. Since virtually all of the Belgian doctors and medical officers had fled, Hammarskjöld assigned a task force from the World Health Organization to save the bereft communities from plague and epidemic.

Much more complicated were the negotiations to obtain the withdrawal of troops. They agreed to make way for the United Nations contingents, but they insisted upon remaining in copper-rich Katanga until satisfactory accords had been reached to ensure the safety of their nationals and to protect the investments of their cartels. They had a powerful ally in Moise Tshombe, one of the most influential blacks in the country. He was the leader of the Lunda tribe and had the leverage of wealth, inherited from a remarkable father who had risen above all obstacles of race and station to build a national empire of general stores and plantations. Tshombe, encouraged by the Belgians and buttressed by an army of white mercenaries, refused to bring Katanga back into the Congo jurisdiction. Hammarskjöld, caught in the violent recriminations between the Leopoldville government and the secessionists in Katanga, and in the cross fire between the Soviet Union and the Belgians and Americans, could not give orders to Tshombe without appearing to intervene in domestic affairs.

Soon the drama of irreconcilable Congo rivalries turned into travesty, names and events and motives tumbling over each other in almost hopeless confusion. Kasavubu fired Lumumba and Lumumba in turn fired Kasavubu, while Tshombe applauded the actions of both. Kasavubu outwitted Lumumba and succeeded in placing him under house arrest. Lumumba eluded his guards and tried to reach his base in Stanleyville. He was captured by one of Kasavubu's units and shipped off to Katanga to be handed over to his mortal enemy, Tshombe. No one was surprised when the announcement came, on January 17, 1961, that Lumumba had been killed "while trying to escape." There was little doubt that the Tshombe captors had murdered him. He became a martyr figure to the African nationalists and to guerrilla patriots around the world. There were demonstrations and riots in every continent. Even in far-off Southeast Asia there were repercussions.

Hammarskjöld's patience had now been exhausted. He asked for and received authorization from the Security Council for the United Nations troops to expel the mercenaries. But it took nearly two years of fierce warfare before the mercenaries were driven from their last holdout in the Union Minière buildings and the resistance was crushed. In December 1962, Tshombe agreed to place Katanga under the national government.

The most desolating casualty of the civil war period was the untimely death of Dag Hammarskjöld. He was on a special mission to arrange the truce between the United Nations forces and the Katanga secessionists when his plane crashed mysteriously near Ndola, northern Rhodesia, on September 18, 1961, and he was one of the victims of the tragedy. He did not live to negotiate the end of the conflict, but it was his tenacious resourcefulness that had not only prevented the disintegration of the newly created state but also revived the prestige of the UN. In the following year, Hammarskjöld was posthumously awarded the Nobel Peace Prize.

Meantime there were serious problems beyond the pacification of Katanga. New disorders erupted in the spring of 1964 which again threatened to get out of hand. Kasavubu found it increasingly difficult to cope with the many warring factions and finally, in July 1964, in an unexpected gambit, he called in, as the new Prime Minister, his old adversary Tshombe. Only yesterday Tshombe had led Katanga in secession; he had enlisted white mercenaries to defy the Congo government; he had been denounced by the other African states as a Black Judas. Now he was recalled as Prime Minister of the Congo to put down other secessionist groups. His uncanny ability to bounce back after every adversity earned him the title of "the rubber man."

But Tshombe had little more success than Kasavubu himself. In December 1964, Stanleyville was recaptured by rebels who were supplied with guns and ammunition by the Soviet Union, Egypt, and Algeria. Once more the Congo was convulsed by civil war. At one point the rebels seized hundreds of white hostages, and sixty of them were massacred, including missionary priests and nuns.

The Belgian government again flew in a rescue force to protect its nationals, and they were reinforced with troops supplied by NATO. The outraged protests against the Belgian action from the Soviet Union and many of the left-oriented African states, charging aggression and intervention, pointed up how completely the Congo was a pawn in the East-West hostilities that divided the world. One of Adlai Stevenson's most acidulous speeches was given at a United Nations session in the waning days of 1964 as he excoriated the Russians for playing with the lives of hostages to advance their Cold War objectives. "If every internal rivalry," he warned, "is to become a Spanish Civil War, with each faction drawing in other Africans and great powers from other continents, the history of independent Africa in this century will be bloody and shameful."

It was not until the end of 1965 that the new rebellion was suppressed. But by then Kasavubu and Tshombe had again fallen out and each was undermining the prestige and the effectiveness of the other. There had now been five years of civil wars, tribal vendettas, secessions, looting, massacre, and international manipulation. The attendant confusion and despair were taken as the warrant for a military coup which brought to leadership the commander of the army, Joseph Mobutu. In December 1965, he abruptly dismissed both Kasavubu and Tshombe and declared that there would have to be an interregnum of strong personal rule to end the agony of internecine turmoil and to permit the country to recover its depleted strength.*

Mobutu demanded undeviating obedience, and when some of the old political stalwarts proved intransigent, he gave the country an exhibition of summary punishment. Four of them, including a former Prime Minister, were hanged in the public square of the capital. There had been twelve provinces with a tradition of considerable autonomy. Mobutu now reduced them to eight. He called their governors together, paid them extravagant compliments and distributed flashy medals, but he stripped them of executive authority. He reorganized the provincial police and incorporated them into the national security force.

He then proceeded with the overriding task of restoring national stability. Though he ruled through the army, he was not really a military man. He had come up out of small town journalism and had been brought into the Force Publique by Lumumba as a political commissar, monitoring the loyalty of the commanding officers. He had won his way steadily into the highest ranks of the hierarchy, surviving all of the political changes that had convulsed the country. Now, at forty, all power gathered in his hands, he pledged that he would heal the wounds of his people and fulfill the promise of their central position in renascent Africa. He was the officer who had hunted down Lumumba and had turned him over to the Katanga executioners. Now he appropriated the legend of Lumumba's martyrdom and proclaimed him as a national hero. At the first rally, when the public proclamation of his command was made, Mobutu appeared with sleeves rolled up. He ordered his staff to follow his lead to symbolize to the people that the time of slogans and manifestoes was over.

Mobutu now turned to the obsessive problem of the economy, determined to free it finally of foreign domination. Despite the changes that had occurred since independence, the power of the cartels had remained virtually unshaken. As late as 1965, the Union Minière had shown a profit of 774 million dollars and, while sub-

---

* Kasavubu retired to his home at Boma where he lived quietly until his death in March 1969. Tshombe, forced into exile, took up residence in Spain. He was condemned to death in absentia in 1967 by a Congo court for having thrown white mercenaries against his own people. A few months later, through a ruse that he was to be shown some real estate possibilities in Majorca, he was lured onto a plane which was hijacked. He was taken to Algeria and, while extradition to the Congo was denied, he was kept in prison until his death was announced in mid-July 1969. He was only forty-nine.

stantial taxes were channeled into the Congo treasury, most of the profit went to the foreign investors. Mobutu began the transfer of control with the order that at least 60 percent of the stock of all corporations must be owned by the government. Each enterprise was carefully evaluated and reorganized to conform to Mobutu's mandate. The foreign investors, through their government officials, threatened severe economic reprisals, but Mobutu persevered, declaring that after decades of exploitation the Congolese people preferred "poverty in freedom to wealth in servitude." As he appropriated the billion-dollar empire that foreigners had built, he jubilantly announced the end of paternalism, the end of *"Le Congo de Papa."* He claimed that he was following the salutary lead of President Nasser when the Egyptian leader defied the French and British and nationalized the Suez Canal.

By 1967 the recriminations, the threats, and the counterthreats stopped. The cartels determined to negotiate the best bargain that was still available. An exchange of official visits was planned. Mobutu journeyed to Brussels and announced that no good purpose would be served by continuing to live with memories of the past. He explained that the violence of the transition had been due primarily to the lack of experience of a people too long deprived of opportunity. The Belgians responded in a similar spirit of conciliation and a treaty of friendship was signed. In July 1970, to celebrate the tenth anniversary of Congo independence, the King of Belgium visited Leopoldville, which had now assumed the name of Kinshasa, and there were effusive expressions of goodwill.

THE JOURNEY OF THE CONGOLESE AND OF SCORES OF OTHER BLACK peoples from dependence to sovereignty had been made after years of travail. Ghana went through the expulsion of its liberator, Kenya suffered the agony of Mau Mau extremism. Nigeria almost bled to death in the war with Biafra, Rwanda was racked by continuous civil strife and massacre. The Congo was several times on the brink of chaos. All through the 1960's, as the defiances and the disorders were not promptly contained, there were critics quick to conclude that the Africans were still too immature to assume responsibility. Conversely, there were native extremists who raged that all whites must go, echoing the Algerian xenophobia, "Pack your grip, or we will fill your coffin."

The critics should have remembered that a decade was an

insufficient testing span for nations to pass from servitude to independence, from the torpor of bondage to the discipline of self-government. Europe endured centuries of warfare as it moved painfully from its feudal economy to the Industrial Revolution. The American colonies when they repudiated British control had advantages that were not enjoyed by any of the underdeveloped nations. Yet ninety years after they wrote the Declaration of Independence, the bloodiest fratricidal war of modern times had to be fought to validate the pledges that had been written in such sanguine spirit at the beginning of independence. The blacks had a right to ask why so much more was expected, within a decade, from the long-exploited millions of the Dark Continent. Centuries of deprivation were imbedded in the first years of self-government. Their influence could not be eliminated by the stroke of a pen or by a dramatic ceremony. Hence the bloodshed that stained these early years of independence did not represent the pangs of death; they represented the pains of birth. From these beginnings, the blacks promised, there would follow, slowly, agonizingly, but surely, what they called *"Uhuru,"* the dignity and the grace of secure freedom.

38

THE SINO-SOVIET RUPTURE

DURING WORLD WAR II THE ALLIES OF THE UNITED STATES WERE Russia and China. The enemies were Germany, Japan, and Italy. Within a few years, the interests of all the involved powers changed radically and Germany, Japan, and Italy became the firm American allies and Russia and China the most dangerous enemies. The 1960's brought other basic shifts in national interest; France was more often in opposition to American foreign policy than in agreement. Once again, dogmatic assumptions about the permanence of friendships and enmities were invalidated. The most sensational case in point was the rupture that shattered the Communist monolith and set Soviet Russia and Red China against each other.

In the first years after World War II, the two Communist giants appeared to be in solid embrace. The Soviet poured out more than seven and a half billion dollars in aid and loans to China; trade between the two empires increased each year. Russia sent in thousands of technicians to tutor the Chinese as they hurdled over age-old impediments to adapt to the mid-twentieth century. Russia welcomed Chinese scientists and students to its universities and its research laboratories. In 1957 Khrushchev, who had succeeded to the leadership of the Soviet Union, offered secretly to share atomic data with Mao Tse-tung and to assist China in acquiring nuclear capacity. The Soviet Foreign Minister, Shepilov, hailed "the fraternal alliance between the two great Communist powers that will always be united, garrisoned by nine hundred million people, headed by the Chinese and the Russians, brother nations."

[452]

Suddenly, after 1958, the leadership of Russia and China began upbraiding each other, at first in private, then openly, in language that had been reserved for their common enemies of the West. The recriminations often took the form of personal insult, Khrushchev assailing Mao as an irresponsible incendiary who was eager to plunge the world into nuclear war, and Mao tagging Khrushchev as a traitor to the revered principles of Lenin. The Soviet canceled its aid programs and its loans, and cut back substantially on its shipments of machinery and equipment. It recalled its technicians, who took home with them the unfinished blueprints of long-planned master projects. In turn, China severely restricted its trade with Russia, diverting its purchases of essentials to such citadels of capitalism as Canada and the Argentine. At an international conference in Tanganyika, China went so far as to contend that Russia had no business in a continent that had been too long exploited by the white people. This drew the angry Russian rejoinder that it was reprehensible for China to interject racism into its harangues.

The Communist inner-strategy group were realistic men of the world and they must have known that alliances drift and shift and even turn somersaults. But it was difficult for their following, to whom the movement was virtually messianic, to believe that the law of change applied to communism. It had been postulated for them that communism superseded national interests always, that it could not be affected by the ebb and flow of political activity, that Communist nations would surely stand together in the face of a hostile world. Hence when Communist solidarity was shattered as Russia and China belabored each other, the shock was dumbfounding. It was also bewildering to the western world, which had based its foreign policies on the polarization of East and West. In its Cold War strategy it had assumed that Russia and China and their satellites would invariably respond to a common gravitational pull. The eruption of 1963, with its farrago of name-calling, threats, reprisals, the massing of Red forces against each other, and the actual border incidents, meant a major shift in the balance of power, and called for a drastic reappraisal of strategy.

How could such a revolution have taken place? What transpired to turn an apparently impregnable alliance into an enmity that impelled hard-nosed politicians to throw all caution to the winds and, in the earshot of dangerous foes, to denounce each other with such rancor?

In truth the Sino-Soviet alliance was never really as firm as the doctrinaires imagined it to be. There were immutable physical factors that always carried potential friction. By the late 1950's China had a population of six hundred million, with growth at a phenomenal rate. It was estimated that by the year 2000 there would be a billion and a half people in China, and the year 2000 was almost as close as the year of Lenin's death in 1924. If its compelling land hunger were to be satisfied, it would have to be by expansion into the virgin territories of the north and west that the Chinese claimed had been stolen by Russia under the Czars. Later when the quarrels had destroyed all hope of rapprochement, the Chinese published maps that marked out the provinces that had been taken from China when it was too weak to resist. "Thank God," a Polish Communist diplomat exclaimed, "we have a buffer state between my country and China."

Apparently the danger from the East was always in the mind of Stalin. He never allowed the doctrines of Lenin, to whom he paid lip service, or any other consideration, to divert him from the long-range interest of the Soviet Union or of his master drive for power. He hailed the victories of Mao Tse-tung because they seriously weakened the strength of the West in Asia and the Pacific, but he was never anxious for China to become a too strongly unified state nor independent of the Soviet Union for economic and military support. There is evidence that Stalin regretted the magnitude of Mao's victory over Chiang Kai-shek. During the civil war it was Stalin who tried to discourage Mao from driving for a Communist takeover for all of China instead of seeking some accommodation with Chiang. Mao did not follow his advice and he did not let the Russians forget that the Chinese victory came without any significant help from the Soviet Union. As early as 1951, when an agreement was reached dealing with Amur River water rights, the meticulous spelling out of restrictions in crossing the river made it clear there was mutual suspicion in the very act of signing the treaty. There were western Kremlinologists who wondered whether the emergence of Communist China, and its inevitable rivalry with the Soviet Union, might not create a more effective counterpoise to protect the independence of the smaller Asian states than could be achieved by the surveillance and often costly intervention of the western powers.

However, so long as Stalin was alive there were no signs that the military alliance signed in 1949 was in jeopardy. The Korean War brought Russia and China closer in the common effort to drive the

West out of South Korea. The Chinese supplied substantial military manpower; the Russians shipped the arms and equipment. At the funeral of Stalin in 1953 the Chinese Foreign Minister, Chou En-lai, marched with the front rank of mourners. Malenkov, who had become the head of the Soviet Union, eager to demonstrate his favored place in the hierarchy, faked a photograph that showed him and Stalin and Mao standing together; the photograph was published in *Pravda*, and was widely circulated.

The first indications of trouble between the Communist allies appeared in 1956 after Khrushchev had clawed his way to control in Russia. There was immediate personal friction when the old Chinese veteran of revolution and civil war found that the less-seasoned Khrushchev expected to inherit Stalin's place in the international Communist power structure. Mao was quite ready to acknowledge the historic debt of communism to the fathers of the revolution, but what were Khrushchev's credentials for him to expect that he could call the tune?

Khrushchev had come out of the Ukrainian countryside, the son of a coal miner, bred in poverty and in the roughest of menial labor. He was in his early twenties when he committed himself to the Bolshevik revolution and he moved up steadily in the local party councils. In 1937, when Stalin met dangerous resistance from the Ukrainian peasantry who defied his agricultural collectivization, he assigned to Khrushchev the responsibility of crushing the opposition. Khrushchev proved to be an ideal hatchet man. He mixed with the peasants most convivially, trading earthy pleasantries with them, brawling with them, getting drunk with them, but behind his peasant camaraderie there was a ruthlessness that matched Stalin's own. Khrushchev systematically purged all the dissentients, beginning with the old guard.

In 1939 Khrushchev was called upon for an even more extensive "pacification" program in Poland. Stalin and Hitler had concluded the pact whose terms called for the partition of Poland between the Soviet Union and Nazi Germany. Both knew that the alliance was a temporary one but they were each fighting for time. Stalin was determined, whatever the ultimate duration of the pact, to retain the territorial loot in Poland. It was necessary, therefore, quickly to liquidate the Polish national leadership and whole communities of Poles, to minimize the later problems of complete assimilation. Here too Khrushchev was Stalin's man, and the task in Poland, which involved the execution of tens of thousands of Poles and the deportation of more than a million others, was fulfilled by him to Stalin's complete satisfaction.

Khrushchev continued to serve the old tyrant to the very end. But when he was safely dead and out of the way, Khrushchev denounced him for mass murders in which he had himself collaborated, and threw him out of the tomb that had been shared with Lenin. Khrushchev had the opportunism that usually goes with men on the make. He was servile to those above him who had power and oppressive to those below him over whom he had power. Stalin enjoyed baiting him. Once, at a banquet, he ordered him to dance before the assembled guests as if he were a trained monkey, and the burly, hard-breathing master of the Ukraine performed the fast-paced whirligig gopak until he was on the verge of collapse. But to those below him Khrushchev could be equally cruel and insulting. After he replaced Malenkov, the demoted head of state was frequently humiliated by him, even in the presence of foreign embassy officials. He lived and acted by hunches, trusting them more than logic. He believed ardently in the old Russian proverb, "If you're born lucky, even your rooster will lay eggs." When it served Khrushchev's purpose to eliminate comrades who had helped him reach the eminence of supreme power, he allowed neither friendship nor gratitude to deter him. He could hug like a bear, but he had the sharp teeth of the barracuda.

This was the character who was to be acknowledged by Mao as the heir of Lenin and the interpreter of Communist doctrine. Mao, who combined brilliant guerrilla leadership with rare intellectual depth, had accepted the supremacy of Stalin with good grace, for Stalin held the Soviet Union together in the difficult years after Lenin. Mao was not repelled by Stalin's ruthlessness. He could match this quality when he was convinced that it served the purposes of the Communist revolution. His record of political extermination was not far behind Stalin's. But when Stalin was gone, Mao had become the senior statesman in the Communist world and he thought of himself as the heir of Lenin. To him the pygmies in Moscow who fought each other for power and authority were not on his level, and as he received reports of Khrushchev's tours of Europe and the United States, he had nothing but contempt for the way in which the interests of communism were represented. Banging his shoe on a desk in the Assembly Hall of the United Nations, posing with Hollywood starlets, pulling up his coattails and going into a parody of a cancan at a San Francisco reception—these antics of

Khrushchev's were condemned by Mao as the insufferable gaucherie of a buffoon.

As it happened, Khrushchev was to belie all of Mao's impressions of his clownishness. He remained a boor—coarse, gauche, often in his cups, speaking out of turn. But as he moved into the nuclear age, and the welfare of tens of millions of his people were his responsibility, he became a force for restraint. It was this very policy of restraint that provided another source of dissension in the relations with Mao and Red China. At the Twentieth Congress in Moscow in 1956, Khrushchev delivered two crucial addresses, one in secret session and one in public. The off-the-record address, in which he denounced Stalin as a paranoid murderer, was the more sensational when it was leaked to the outside world. The second, which advanced the theme of competitive co-existence with the West, proved to be more important, for it challenged the Chinese view of unremitting warfare until the evils of capitalist imperialism had been destroyed. In this address Khrushchev denied that it was necessary to wage the battle exclusively through war. This approach had been an original tenet of communism, but Khrushchev argued that circumstances had now drastically changed and strategy had to be revised to conform. War now meant total nuclear destruction. It was therefore not only wiser but a matter of self-preservation to seek ways to victory that would not incinerate most of mankind, capitalists and Communists together. Communist strength had now grown sufficiently to ensure ultimate victory through competitive co-existence and war was therefore not "fatalistically inevitable." Later, in an address to Hungarian Communists, Khrushchev elaborated on this theme. He noted that a higher standard of living should be the primary goal for communism. "It was more important to eat good goulash than it was to prate doctrinaire slogans. It was better to fight a revolution on a full belly than on an empty one."

Mao Tse-tung was outraged by Khrushchev's public denunciation of Stalin. He had no love for the old buccaneer, but for Khrushchev to take it upon himself to flail out against the symbol of Communist unity was arrogantly assuming that he had the right to speak for the whole Communist world. His assault was stupidly playing into the hands of the imperialists, who would welcome the evidence of Communist infighting. He disagreed also with Khrushchev's overtures to the West for co-existence. It was all very well for Khrushchev to speak as he did, from the vantage point of a Russia that had become self-sufficient. But China was only just emerging as a modern state. It still had a long way to go to bring its population to security, and so did the underdeveloped nations of Asia and Africa and Latin America, exploited and ravished by imperialism. Neither they nor China could hope to achieve their goal without unceasing war, for no possessing groups ever yield their power voluntarily. Khrushchev's bleating pacifism, Mao said, was a logic of slaves; it would paralyze the will of the people and bind them in submission to the curse of imperialism.

These verbal exchanges were fascinating exercises in oratorical flim-flam. They were conducted in veiled language, with substitute names and subjects, with analogies and parables that gave them the allegorized format of Aesop's Fables. Mao was not referred to by name. He was "a certain Chinese person." Khrushchev was not directly denounced. He was "a certain Soviet high official." More often the targets were proxies. When Mao meant Khrushchev he assailed Tito, who had led Yugoslavia into nationalist deviation. When Khrushchev meant Mao he lashed out at the obscure Enver Hoxha, whose Albania had become a center of faithful Maoist propaganda in the heart of the Balkans. After one tempestuous session of a Communist Congress, where the Albanian delegate actually named names and leveled his attack on the Russian leader himself, Khrushchev denounced the Chinese for teaching the Albanians to deliver the insults that they hesitated to deliver themselves. "Someone has taught them to pronounce foul words, and they walk under windows and shout hooligan curses at the Communist Party of the Soviet Union. . . . For their swearing they get the promised three kopecks. And when they begin to swear more violently and colorfully, they get another five kopecks and are praised."*

Each of the protagonists had no trouble finding texts in the Lenin canon to prove his orthodoxy. The ritual recalled a comment by Khrushchev when he was asked how the body of Lenin, lying in state for more than forty years in his crypt in the Red Square, could look so fresh. Khrushchev responded, "Oh that's easy; we take it out every little while and we re-embalm it." Both Khrushchev and Mao took out Lenin's texts every little while and re-embalmed them to bolster their opposing arguments to give them contemporary validity.

The conflicts of course were not limited to academic interpretations of Marx and Lenin, to the dialectics of orthodoxy and heresy. The arguments, the hair-splitting, the insults, were usually the ration-

* Harry Schwartz, *Tsars, Mandarins and Commissars* (Philadelphia and New York: J. B. Lippincott Co., 1964), p. 191.

ale for policy decisions and actions where national interests clashed. For example in 1960 the Soviet Union courted influence in the Middle East by offering credits, loans, and military assistance to Egypt and to Iraq. Mao denounced the gestures as the coddling of bourgeois governments that were imprisoning their local Communists. Again in 1962 serious tensions between China and India, with frequent border incidents, led to full-scale war. Chinese troops invaded India and won so decisively that they could have gone forward into Calcutta. Khrushchev announced the neutrality of the Soviet Union during the dispute and the war itself. He regretted that the issues had not been arbitrated. He reminded Mao that China and Russia had better synchronize their watches. Mao replied with fury that there were two watches and it was not for Khrushchev to assume that the master watch was his. He was appalled that a Communist ally should remain neutral when the enemy was a state that had invariably leaned to the West.

There was an even more serious conflict in September 1962, when Khrushchev yielded to President Kennedy's ultimatum and withdrew the missiles he had installed in Cuba.* Mao was furious. He upbraided Khrushchev as an adventurer for moving in with the missiles, and as a coward for moving out when Kennedy made his threats. He insisted that Khrushchev should have stood up to the imperialists. Kennedy then would assuredly have backed down because, after all, the western nations were paper tigers with neither the will nor the courage to fight. Khrushchev answered sharply that he had placed the missiles in Cuba to protect Castro from American invasion in the future and, when he elicited the Kennedy promise that the United States would not seek to overthrow the Castro government by invasion, his mission had been successfully fulfilled and he could withdraw. As for Mao's easy dismissal of American power, he warned the Chinese armchair strategists that the paper tiger had nuclear teeth. He virtually accused Mao of wishing to prod Russia into a war with the United States so that China could emerge from the holocaust to inherit the ruins. His intimation was strongly reinforced when a grim boast of Mao was repeated that, after the next war, there would be only five million British survivors, twenty million Americans, fifty million Russians, but three hundred million Chinese. Khrushchev was no model of pacific statesmanship, but he labeled this kind of reckless goading as warmongering megalomania.

* See Chapter 41.

There were many other embroilments and the schism became a chasm. Hardly a month passed without angry recriminations. They were exacerbated by Mao's continuous attempts to infiltrate the world's Communist parties in order to undermine and subvert Soviet influence or control. Then in midsummer of 1963 the world learned through public statements how serious the breach between the Soviet and Red China had become. All the quarrels since 1958 had taken place behind the scenes or had been fought with proxy targets. Now the entire catalogue of hostility was recounted in detail by both sides. On August 15 came the revelation that, as far back as June 1959, Khrushchev had canceled the agreement to provide China with atomic data so that it could become a nuclear power. All the fury and the frustration of language and action of the past few years were now better understood in the light of the Soviet decision to deny atomic access to the Chinese.

The United States took full advantage of the discord that tore the Communist camp apart. On June 10 President Kennedy delivered an address at American University in Washington that offered the hand of friendship to the Soviet Union with a cordiality that had not been present since the days when the two countries were firm allies against Hitler. He noted that Russia and the United States had never fought a war against each other. After paying tribute to Russian gallantry and sacrifice in World War II, Kennedy referred to the crushing military burden that was borne by the great powers in their quest for protection and security. He repeated the prayer of all men of goodwill that such sterile expenditures could be better applied in the war against poverty and ignorance and disease. The address was not distinguished by any profound originality but it summarized negotiations that had been conducted for many years in private. The timing for a detente, after the sobering lessons of the Cuban missile crisis, was especially appropriate. The address was immediately reprinted in full in *Pravda*. Within a month, the United States and the Soviet Union signed a treaty that banned all nuclear testing except for what could be conducted underground. The treaty further aggravated the already deteriorated relations between the Soviet Union and Red China. Mao denounced it as a fraud and an attempt by the United States and the Soviet Union to retain their nuclear monopoly.

In the fall of 1964, while Khrushchev was away from Moscow, he was abruptly ousted by his colleagues in the kind of coup that he had himself perfected. There was a reawakening of hope among the Chinese that the shift in Soviet leadership might involve a shift in policy and bring a rapprochement. Chou En-lai at once paid an official visit to Moscow and he was cordially received by Khrushchev's successors. But the truce was short-lived. The schism went deeper than Khrushchev's personality; it went deeper than Mao Tse-tung's personal hostility. The divergent national interests could not be reconciled by the substitution of one set of functionaries for another. By May 1965 the *Red Flag*, the Chinese government's official organ, was again fulminating against the new Soviet leaders as collaborators with the "bandit chiefs of American imperialism."

Thus, within a decade after Stalin's death, the solid Red front had been shattered and, in the phrase of the Italian Communist leader, Palmiro Togliatti, a "polycentric world" had emerged. There was now an orthodox communism anchored in Peking; there was a revisionist communism anchored in Moscow; and they were related only through the mystique of Lenin's name.

These developments compelled thoroughgoing reappraisals in the posture of defense for the western world. In every foreign office and state department there were sharp divisions in the planning councils. Of course no one believed that Russia was as conciliatory as the Chinese had charged, nor that China was as bloodthirsty as Khrushchev had warned. But some of the policymakers insisted that the strategy of containment, devised during the period when there was a strong united Communist front, was now obsolete, and that it must be altered to fit the conditions created by the rift in the Communist world. If aggression were threatened in Asia surely it was no longer necessary for the United States and its allies to be the world's policemen. The vigilant rivalry of China and the Soviet Union could now provide a very effective balance in the foreseeable future.

There were others who believed that China was now clearly following national rather than class interests. They agreed with De Gaulle, who put it with his usual epigrammatic bluntness: "The banner of ideology in reality covers only ambitions." Hence it might be profitable for the United States and the West to explore the possibility of a détente with China. At the end of 1971 this logic was acted upon when President Nixon, who had been blasting Red China's policies for most of his political career, took leadership in bringing China into the United Nations and announced that he would journey to Peking to explore a more cooperative relationship.

Yet there were very serious reservations by others about placing too much reliance on the struggles within the Communist family. After all, though Khrushchev spoke of co-existence, he *did* put missiles into Cuba and he edged to the very brink of nuclear war in testing President Kennedy's intentions. Mao had often declared that tens of millions of lives were expendable to achieve a national purpose. It was also to be remembered that just as Communist allies could become enemies, it was conceivable that changes in the national interest could again convert enemies into allies.

These debates dominated the diplomatic planning of the western world and especially of the United States. They were conducted with the sober realization that now more than ever the decisions carried the most awesome consequences. In the new world saber rattling had become nuclear threat and the future was not what it used to be.

39

DE GAULLE AND
THE FRENCH FIFTH
REPUBLIC

THE FRENCH FOURTH REPUBLIC THAT EMERGED FROM THE WRECKAGE
of World War II and the Nazi occupation lasted until 1958, fourteen
tempestuous years during which twenty-one ministries followed each
other.* It is quite accurate to say of this period that France was not
governed; it was administered. It could survive from month to
month when the problems were routine. But when the Republic was
confronted with a virtual civil war in Algeria, its existence was challenged and the national hero, Charles de Gaulle, was called out of
his sulky retirement once again to ward off disaster.

De Gaulle had hoped that France, after enduring the afflictions of
war and the Nazi occupation, would rise above the petty politics
that had crippled the Third Republic. When the Nazis were expelled
in 1944, he had stepped naturally into the premiership, eager to
restore French honor and respect. But he had been quickly discouraged when the politicians went back to their charades, and he
had quit "irrevocably" in January 1946, vowing that he was
through with the hacks who seemed to worry only about their own
little soup pots, on their own little fire, in their own little corner. His
friend André Malraux complained, "He took us full speed to the
Rubicon and then told us to get out our fishing rods." When De
Gaulle was asked what would happen to France after his resignation,
his contempt for parliamentary gamesmanship blazed out in his

* See Chapter 30.

angry reply, "They will return to their vomit." He believed that the French were so constituted that there had to be periods of abandon and irresponsibility. "Would monarchy be a solution?" he was asked. "Not really, not really," he replied. "The French would need two kings, one to admire and one to revile." Now, in 1958, with the uprising in Algeria out of control, the parachute troops poised to take over Paris, he accepted the Assembly's bid to leadership and pledged to put the house in order.

Algeria proved to be the testing point. The province, four times the size of France itself, was no ordinary colonial possession. Though the native Arab population numbered ten million, there were about a million Europeans, most of them French citizens, and they had been an integral part of the country for generations. They had built its industry, its commerce, its mechanized agriculture, its comfortable western standards. They were not absentee landlords, or bureaucrats who came only to govern. They counted themselves as much French as did the Parisians or the Normans or the Gascons. In the postwar years, as the colonies of France were turned back to the natives, one by one—Indo-China, Black Africa, Tunis, Morocco—the colons became ever more concerned that they too, as they put it, would be "sold out." They resisted every attempt to restrict their authority, fearful that concessions would lead inevitably to the loss of their painfully created patrimony. When one of the Prime Ministers, Guy Mollet, came to Algeria to explore the situation, he was greeted by the French with catcalls and rotten fruit, and he returned sobered by the irreconcilable position into which the contending interests had hardened.

By November 1954, the Arabs, encouraged by the eclipse of colonial domination in every corner of the world and especially in other parts of Africa, began organizing on a major scale to eliminate the Europeans. At first they were dismissed by the home government as "bandits." But their guerrilla tactics became ever more effective and deadly—Europeans gunned down, convoys ambushed, palatial suburban homes blown up, moderates among their own people assassinated, terror everywhere. So the three-cornered conflict moved in 1958 to its fiery climax, the old settlers more fiercely committed to hold on, the Arab nationalists determined to drive them out, the French government wavering, floundering, muddling along. The climacteric came on May 13. There was a military coup in Algeria, led by a French Committee of Public Safety, guided by defiant Old Settlers and some of the army officers. It was an almost bloodless coup, all resistance quickly crushed by the cooperating army units. An officer commented, "No casualties, fortunately, except the Republic, and that's not serious." From Algeria the military moved swiftly to take over Corsica and was poised for the parachute attack on Paris and the establishment of a military dictatorship. It was then that the thoroughly intimidated government yielded, and De Gaulle was called upon by the President, René Coty, to take charge. There were some technical procedures to be executed, but in essence the Fourth Republic was dead. One of the deputies pronounced the epitaph: "You are not abandoning power. Power has abandoned you."

De Gaulle himself was not yet sure how the crisis could be resolved except that Algeria must remain in French control. He knew that his prestige as a national hero was a powerful asset, especially in the agony of impending civil war, and that he could count upon it as he played for time. He spoke and wrote in the vaguest terms, offering something to pacify each of the contending factions. He led the French settlers to believe that he would fully protect their interests;* the military that he would not tolerate further damage to French prestige; and the French electorate that he had no intention of governing as a man on horseback. He insisted that all changes in the structure of government must be accomplished through legal means. He would, of course, need exceptional powers for an exceptional task at an exceptional time. But these powers, authorized by a revised constitution, must be submitted to a popular referendum. All of his demands were quickly granted.

The proposed new constitution provided for a President with strong executive authority. Further, the electoral law was reformed to check the capacity of splinter parties to create continuous parliamentary crises. The constitution was submitted to referendum and it was approved in a 4-to-1 landslide. In November elections were held for the new Assembly and all but the Communists climbed on the Gaullist bandwagon. Now sixty-seven, De Gaulle was elected and installed as President with a mandate for virtual personal government.

It was a tribute to De Gaulle's political subtlety that he was able to reverse himself completely on Algeria and still come off with the reputation of statesmanship. When he faced the Old Settlers in Algeria in 1958 he said, with the guile of a Delphic oracle, *"Je vous*

---

* At Mostaganem on July 4, 1958, he drew frantic applause from the Old Settlers when he shouted: *"Vive l'Algérie française!"* Cited in Anthony Hartley, *Gaullism* (New York: Outerbridge and Dienstfrey, 1971), p. 168.

ai compris" (I have understood you), and since they thought that this was a pledge to fulfill their aspirations to have Algeria remain French, they cheered themselves hoarse.* De Gaulle knew that he was playing on their hopes. In his final Memoirs, completed just before his death in 1971, he wrote ". . . I tossed them the words, seemingly spontaneous but in reality carefully calculated, which I hoped would fire them with enthusiasm, without committing me further than I was willing to go."† Meantime De Gaulle continued to fight the Arab nationalists to compel them to accept a compromise that would safeguard the welfare of the million Frenchmen in Algeria. As late as March 1960, in his tour of the Algerian officers' messes, he kept up his reassurances that there would be no capitulation to the nationalists. "There will be no Dien Bien Phu in Algeria. France must not depart."‡ But despite the most drastic military measures the National Liberation Front would not retreat from their demand for complete independence. They had no formidable organized strength in the key cities, Algiers and Oran, but they dominated the rest of the country, where fifteen thousand well-trained guerrillas harassed the colonial establishment. They administered the daily life of the areas that they controlled, and their government-in-exile, based in Tunis, was recognized by thirty-one countries.

After nearly four years, during which about half a million French troops were tied down in the frustrations of guerrilla warfare, De Gaulle recognized the futility of further attempts to retain any kind of French control. He agreed to a cease-fire in 1962 and, in the negotiations that followed, the Arab nationalists won every demand that they had prescribed. The settlement went far beyond the cooperative program that had been formulated by Pierre Mendès-France some years earlier and then been blasted by De Gaulle as virtual treason.

As the French tricolor came down, De Gaulle was vilified by the French in Algeria for betraying the men who had brought him to power. But those who were most bitter should have known that De Gaulle always had a personal code that justified his priorities. "If one walks through mud," he said, "one cannot help being stained." This flexible code was implicit in his reply when he was asked later

---

* Alexander Werth, *The De Gaulle Revolution* (London: R. Hale, 1960), p. 184.

† Charles de Gaulle, *Memoirs of Hope: Renewal and Endeavor* (New York: Simon & Schuster, 1971), p. 47.

‡ Hartley, *Gaullism,* p. 173.

about the use of torture by the French army in Algeria. "It's unpardonable," he admitted, "unpardonable, but it is also secondary."

The French settlers did not give up without a struggle. They organized the OAS, secret military cadres that fought a double front war, against Arab nationalists, but even more furiously now against De Gaulle's forces—Frenchmen against Frenchmen. In 1962, as Independence Day approached for Algeria, the OAS took to the barricades again, hoping, as in 1958, to overthrow the Establishment. But 1962 was not 1958; De Gaulle was now solidly entrenched. The French were weary of war, especially civil war, and they supported De Gaulle's independence proposal and the rigorous suppression of the French in Algeria who opposed it. Some of the irreconcilables were captured and brought to trial for treason. They were condemned to death and, though their sentences were afterwards commuted, they embarrassed De Gaulle by quoting the pledges that he had made to them when he was on the way to power.

Perhaps if the settlement had been reached without the protracted bloodshed, there might have been an orderly transition in Algeria as there had been in the British colonies. But after so much rancor and terror, the peace that followed brought all the dislocation that the French settlers had feared. Arab control compelled steady liquidation of most of what the Europeans had created in their century-long sojourn. Virtually all of them fled in the next few years to attempt reconstructed lives in mainland France. De Gaulle salvaged no friendship in Algeria by his capitulation. Instead of remaining in the western orbit, Algeria became one of the most extreme of left-oriented states, following closely the Soviet line in the East-West confrontations.

Algeria had dominated the first years of De Gaulle's incumbency. But he did not neglect the major task—restoring the health of the domestic economy. Here, although he was considered a pillar of conservative tradition, he astonished supporters and opponents alike by the dynamism of his approach. He encouraged investment in heavy industry, in steel, in chemicals. He exploited the newly discovered oil resources of the Sahara. When he had launched the Fourth Republic in 1945, he nationalized the railroads and most of the automobile plants. Now he carried the nationalization program very much further. He encouraged long-range economic planning and took leadership in Common Market negotiations.

Throughout, he operated with little interference from the party maneuvering that had haunted the past. Politics was not eliminated. How could it be, in France? But it played little role in basic decisions. Since the French were now enjoying unusual affluence, with employment at a peak, so high indeed that foreign workers had to be imported, then why trouble over whether France was or was not a genuine democracy? Papa De Gaulle's wife, Yvonne, was fussy, puritanical, not very French in moral tolerance; Tante Yvonne, they called her. But since all was right with the world, let the critics hiss, or even bite, so long as they did not subvert.

But De Gaulle's main interest was not in domestic affairs. He was much more concerned with the image of France, with its return to first rank. He never tired of reiterating, "France could not be France without greatness." Yet he was in an impossible dilemma. France no longer had a base for pre-eminence. It had been debilitated by two costly wars, and had been shorn of its dominions. It could not possibly compete with the super powers, the United States and Russia, nor even, in the foreseeable future, with West Germany and China.

De Gaulle was not deterred by the disparity between pretension and power. He could command leverage in defiance, he could veto, he could spring the unexpected. To say "Yes" might be interpreted as "Me-too"; to say "No" usually compelled courtship. Perhaps it was this compulsion to appear important that drove De Gaulle to insist upon squandering the thrifty taxpayers' money on nuclear power for France. The expense was prohibitive, but the research was doggedly pursued until the bomb was successfully exploded in the Sahara Desert at the end of 1961. It was to cost a billion dollars a year, and even by 1975 it would have very little sophisticated delivery capacity. But to De Gaulle it was "a diplomatic argument." Belonging to the nuclear club would mean that France could not thereafter be treated as just another Belgium or Sweden. In a radio broadcast in January 1963, he said, " . . . for a great people to have the free disposition of itself and the means to struggle to preserve it is an absolute imperative, for alliances have no absolute virtues."*

Much more to the point was De Gaulle's determination to carve out a special place for France, as head of a Third Force, a loose but influential alliance of the western European states, that could be the arbiter between the super-hegemonies, the United States and Russia. This ambition was not all personal vanity or French chauvinism. De Gaulle believed that the polarization brought on by the Cold War

---

* Cited in Roy Macridis, *The De Gaulle Republic* (Homewood, Ill.: Dorsey Press, 1960), p. 143.

had been a stupid blunder, the product of the myopic diplomacy of Roosevelt and Churchill and their successors. Besides, he had little faith in any sustained American commitment to Europe. He was on guard against America's oscillations in national mood, now cooperative, now isolationist. His attitude was undoubtedly also influenced by the searing rebuffs that he had endured from Churchill and Roosevelt, who found his pretensions insufferable. Roosevelt had appraised him as a very able man, but suffering from a messianic complex. He told Churchill that De Gaulle thought of himself as Joan of Arc. It was reported to De Gaulle that Churchill had chuckled, "Well, that may be so, but I can't get my bloody bishops to let me burn him." These were quips but they were elicited by a hearty dislike of De Gaulle's style, his hauteur, above all his overreach, when the situation of France called for lower-keyed diplomacy.

In any case, De Gaulle seemed to Britain and the United States to lose no opportunity to play the prima donna. He appalled them by continually decreasing the French participation in NATO. In 1958 he served notice that he planned to quit NATO unless there were a tripartite directorate that included France along with the United States and Britain. When his condition was not accepted, he withdrew the French forces from the NATO command, and in 1965 he canceled all commitments to the Asian alliance, SEATO. He seemed to go out of his way to belittle attempts to settle disputes through international efforts. He refused to pay the French assessment for the United Nations peacekeeping mission in the Belgian Congo. He often referred scornfully to the "so-called" United Nations.

De Gaulle's veto of British membership in the Common Market in 1963 might conceivably be explained as a clash in national interests. But the cavalier method of announcing the veto, at a televised press conference meticulously rehearsed for hours before a mirror, bespoke undisguised hostility. The nations of western Europe had counted on the inclusion of Britain in the pooling of economic and trade resources. De Gaulle's peremptory action stunned the other members. Chancellor Erhard of West Germany said in dismay, "This is a European funeral." For there had been steady progress in promoting agreements that coordinated the processing of coal and steel, that stimulated the peaceful uses of atomic power; and the Common Market, quite apart from trade advantages, was a key factor in the advancement of European integration.

The American representatives in the European international bodies were bewildered by De Gaulle's continuous manifestations of ill-will. In 1959, they knew how serious the rift had become when De Gaulle refused to permit the Americans to continue storing nuclear weapons on French soil unless they were brought under French control. They were too realistic to expect gratitude for the billions that the United States had provided through the Marshall Plan when France was at the edge of disaster. But the unremitting suspicion and hostility were shocking and bred counter-resentment that affected trade relations. At one point there was even a tourist boycott.

As De Gaulle grew older and as the status that he coveted for France did not materialize, he became even more overbearing and contrary. He spoke more often with spleen than with heart, and he abandoned altogether the discipline of consistency. He accepted American aid and then taunted the United States as the greatest menace to peace since Hitler. He courted the black African states but he kept selling military jets to South Africa which were used to buttress the policy of *apartheid*. Even as he reached out for better relations with Mao Tse-tung, he could lose his temper and berate "the wretched yellow multitudes of China." He outraged most Canadians when he accepted official hospitality and then hailed the militant separatists in Quebec, encouraging them in their defiance.

There came a day, in 1968, when the histrionics, even of a national hero, no longer held the old charismatic appeal. In his pursuit of grandeur De Gaulle had neglected too many urgent priorities. Housing was woefully inadequate, the roads were archaic, the social welfare plans were far behind the reforms of other countries, and the educational system was a hodgepodge of petrified tradition. In the summer, while De Gaulle was off in Rumania on one of his prestige missions, the long-simmering resentment exploded. Riots began in the universities with student dissenters, to whom the heroic exploits of the Resistance and the liberation were just pages in history books. Their posters read: "Ten Years: It's Enough." The barricades went up in Paris and, within hours, they signaled their defiance to all the major cities. Then the unions called out their men and women, and ten million workers responded. De Gaulle's lieutenant, Georges Pompidou, tackled the crisis in the absence of his chief, and he offered enough concessions to the rioters to send the students back to their books and the workers back to their plants. But the spell was broken, the halo askew, and the deglamorization was well under way. Don Quixote was no longer indispensable; Sancho Panza would do.

Early in 1969, De Gaulle insisted on a number of administrative reforms, including an overhaul of the Senate, and he astounded supporters and opponents alike by ordering a national referendum on the issue, converting it into a plebiscite on his own continued incumbency as President. Perhaps after the humiliating experiences of the previous year, he needed personal reassurance. Perhaps he felt that he had only to place his prestige on the line and his countrymen would immediately respond. Ironically, in converting the presidency, in the constitution of 1958, into a strong decisive post, he had eliminated his own indispensability. In any case, he completely miscalculated. When the returns were in, De Gaulle had been decisively defeated. He had bullied once too often.

True to his pledge, he immediately resigned, and went back to his country retreat to complete his Memoirs. "Old man," he wrote, "exhausted by ordeal, detached from human deeds, feeling the approach of the eternal cold, but always watching in the shadows for the gleam of hope."* In little more than another year, in the winter of 1970, the tired gladiator was dead. He was fortunate in the manner of his departure. In his lifetime he was fearless, except for one terror, the decline, through aging, of physical power. "Old age," he used to say, citing Chateaubriand, "is a shipwreck." He was spared the indignity of failing mental power and his last days were as vital as any in his prime.

In evaluating the career of De Gaulle what comes through clearly, first of all, is his reflex identification with his mission, the mission to restore the grandeur of France and to protect it. In an extraordinarily self-revealing speech, he said that during the war he discovered " . . . that there was a person named de Gaulle who existed in other people's minds and was really a separate personality from myself . . . From that day on I knew I would have to reckon with this man . . ."† In his final memoirs he magisterially saluted his double roles as liberator and savior, writing of himself in the third person, "On June 18, 1940, answering the call of the eternal fatherland bereft of any other alternative to save its honor and its soul, de Gaulle, alone and almost unknown, had to assume the burden of France. In May 1958, on the eve of a disastrous tearing-apart of the nation and faced with the annihilation of the system which was allegedly in control, de Gaulle, now well-known, but with no other weapon save his legiti-

---

* Charles de Gaulle, *War Memoirs: Salvation* (New York: Simon & Schuster, 1960), p. 330.

† David Schoenbrun, *The Three Lives of Charles de Gaulle* (New York: Atheneum, 1960), p. 105.

macy, must take destiny in his hands."* He often referred to France as if he were its lover, using the terminology of romance. He wrote, "The emotional side of me tends to imagine France like the princess in the fairy stories, or the Madonna in the frescoes, as dedicated to an exalted and exceptional destiny."† To men like Franklin Roosevelt and Churchill and to many of his own countrymen, De Gaulle's identification with France in this way, usually declaimed in the accents of the *"Marseillaise,"* was pompous and absurd. But it was better understood by those who remembered how beaten and humiliated France had been during the war, who remembered the occupation by the Nazis, the degradation from which De Gaulle had rescued the land and its people. For De Gaulle to identify himself with France at such a time was not much of an honor. He demanded recognition from the great powers with such irritating tenacity exactly because he had no weapons to match theirs. "I was too poor to beg, too weak to yield." Britain and the United States noted that whenever his bargaining power was insubstantial, his imagery became more fustian and pretentious, and his intransigence increased. He was the creation of his own imagination, but he was always astute enough to know it.

Of course, De Gaulle's impact went far beyond the renewal of national pride. He was proudest of his achievement in ending "the ferments of disintegration inherent in the French people." He brought order and discipline into government after nearly a century of such confusion that democratic procedure became a caricature. De Gaulle always had before him the sorry fate of the Third and Fourth Republics, with their endless succession of ministries that swiveled and wheeled, as if politics were a pirouette. His expressed contempt might have gone too far; he sometimes, in temper, referred to the French people as *"cette canaille,"* this rabble. One critic wrote that "he looked upon his own ministers with boredom, like a god looking on the imperfections of his own creation." His constitutional solutions might have placed too much reliance on the integrity of the men who would be invested with authority. But De Gaulle did moderate the capriciousness of the old political system, without destroying the spirit of democracy. It was a major achievement to accomplish change without mutation.

In substantive statesmanship, De Gaulle prided himself most on the reconciliation of France and Germany that ended centuries of

---

* De Gaulle, *Memoirs of Hope: Renewal and Endeavor,* p. 18.

† Charles de Gaulle, *War Memoirs, Vol. I* (New York: Simon & Schuster, 1955), p. 3.

unremitting hostility. Chancellor Adenauer cooperated in the spectacular achievement, but De Gaulle appropriately deserved the largest share of credit because France had most often been the victim and had paid dearly in blood and treasure and territorial desolation. De Gaulle had to overcome an almost congenital hatred. Earlier in his career he had said, "Germany is a menace. I've been saying it for the last thousand years!" This was a far cry from his addresses, interspersed with German, in the major German cities, which paid the highest tribute to *"ein grosses Volk."*

De Gaulle was undoubtedly influenced by the need to develop a counterpoise to the leverage of Britain and to the political power of the United States. But he was realistic enough to know that France could no longer cope with revived German economic strength; hence, assured Franco-German solidarity would solve at last the problem of security that had haunted every generation since the Middle Ages. When De Gaulle and Adenauer exchanged visits, their emotional declarations augured a new and happier era in the diplomacy of their homelands.

These were enduring historic contributions. They were marred by the abrasive personality and the temperament of the man, and the extravagant humbug which he himself had listed as essential in the quiver of a leader if he is to succeed in a modern democracy. There was arrogance in his claim, "Every Frenchman has been, is, or will be, a Gaullist!" But the contributions would assuredly survive the inflated *amour propre* which De Gaulle so often confused with protective armor.

One failure however could hardly be condoned—the default of his opportunity to create an integrated Europe. De Gaulle's obsession with the grandeur of France and with himself as its incarnation kept him from staking his unparalleled prestige to build the supranational Third Force that was the dream of the enlightened Europeans. NATO and other military alliances were perhaps not reliable vehicles toward that objective, and De Gaulle may have been wise to minimize their relevance. But the cooperative ventures that were advocated by the statesmen who thought in European terms—Spaak, Monnet, Schumann, De Gasperi, Adenauer—desperately needed the blessing of De Gaulle for wider acceptance. He could have been at the side of these men. The spirit of history, which he so often evoked, beckoned him. But he preferred to go off on his own, the eternal maverick. In the long perspective of history, the giants must be judged not only by what they do, but by what they fail to do.

40

WEST GERMANY AND THE DÉTENTE WITH THE EAST

IN 1961 THE APPARENTLY INDESTRUCTIBLE CHANCELLOR OF WEST Germany, Dr. Konrad Adenauer, could celebrate two anniversaries with immense satisfaction. He was now eighty-five, the oldest of the world's active statesmen. And he was in the thirteenth year of his chancellorship, with an incumbency already longer than that of the nineteenth-century Bismarck. His achievement had been memorable. When he was released in 1945 from a Nazi prison camp, the country was desolated, the economy in ruins, the people in shock and despair. After the horrors that had been perpetrated by Hitler and the Nazis, Germans were universal pariahs, as passionately hated as any nation in all history. Dr. Adenauer, who was sixty-nine when he again became mayor of Cologne, won the confidence of the western Allies and soon achieved sovereign status for the new Federal Republic. He took fullest advantage of the Cold War and offered the recuperative strength of his country to Britain and France and the United States as they struggled to prevent Russia from dominating the continent. Germany, yesterday's arch enemy, became the valued ally of the West, welcomed into the family of nations, into NATO and the Common Market, and authorized to begin rearmament. Aided by ingenious lieutenants, Adenauer wrought an economic miracle and so substantially expanded the country's productive strength that it surpassed its conquerors in western Europe.

It would have been an ideal time for Adenauer to retire at the peak of prestige as the architect of the phoenix German Republic, if not loved at least revered. But since he was only eighty-five, he would not step down, or even up, to the honorary presidency that was waiting for him. When a *New York Times* correspondent asked him at eighty whether he had thought of a successor, as Churchill had done with Anthony Eden, he chuckled, "Why, Churchill is an old man!" He turned aside the counsel of a wise deputy who said, "Better to leave a few years early, than one day too late!"

Inevitably the attrition of reputation and support set in, accelerated by embarrassing errors in judgment that multiplied with advancing age. There were indiscreet references to the allied nations that kindled indignation. It seemed like sheer ingratitude for the Chancellor, who was created by the Allies, to refer to the British as "half friends." He was furious with the United States for selling wheat to the Soviet Union, holding to his unyielding conviction that no concessions, no détentes, could ever mellow the autocrats of the Kremlin. "Lenin was right," was his choleric comment, "the capitalists will sell the rope to the hangman in preparation for their own execution." In conferences he displayed mounting impatience even with loyal colleagues, and high-handedness replaced finesse and resiliency. And these personal acerbities were compounded by his unwillingness to recognize that there was anyone capable enough to replace him. "My God," he used to say, "what will happen to Germany after I am gone?"

But it was not merely the desire for more flexible leadership that created the impatience with the old Chancellor. There were now deep reservations about policies that might have been wise, that might even have been unavoidable when the fledgling Republic was fighting to establish itself, but that needed reappraisal to fit into the transformed world of the 1960's. Could nothing more be done to bring an accommodation with East Germany so as to open access to the millions of Germans trapped behind the Iron Curtain? Was it not self-defeating to stand by the Hallstein Doctrine through which Adenauer had threatened the severance of diplomatic relations with any country that gave diplomatic recognition to East Germany? Was there not some point to the admonition of the Russians that he who lives on an island must make friends with the ocean?

The Social Democrats, the main opposition party, had been asking these questions for years. Now millions outside the Social Democrats were asking the same questions. In the earlier years of the Federal Republic, Adenauer was too powerful to be challenged openly. But when he turned eighty without giving a sign of retiring gracefully, the murmuring became louder than the protestations of gratitude. The Social Democrats meantime had been making inroads politically, and they now had vigorous young leadership in Willy Brandt, whose more adventurous views on foreign policy were winning ever wider acceptance.

Willy Brandt was born Herbert Frahm, in Lübeck, a Baltic seaport, the illegitimate son of a shopgirl who had been deserted by her lover. He had an agonizing boyhood but was befriended by a Socialist leader, Julius Leber. Brandt wrote later in gratitude, when he learned that Leber had been executed for complicity in the 1944 plot against Hitler, "I grew up without a father. There was an emptiness in my life. Leber filled it." When the Nazis took over Germany, he changed his name to Willy Brandt, his writing pseudonym, and, hunted by the Gestapo, he escaped to Norway. There he acquired Norwegian citizenship, married a Norwegian girl, and lived out the Hitler period. It was there, too, that he saw a popular constructive socialism in operation, and it was to have a permanent impact on his political and economic philosophy.

After World War II he came to Berlin as a press attaché in the Norwegian mission that was to help administer the divided city. He settled in Berlin, reassumed German citizenship, and became the trusted aide of the courageous postwar Berlin mayor, Ernst Reuter. Together they battled to preserve the independence of the sturdy enclave with its two million people who were marooned deep in Communist territory, precariously linked to West Germany and the outside world by specially assigned road and air channels. In 1948 the Soviets attempted to compel the capitulation of West Berlin by preventing land and water access, cutting off food and fuel and other necessities. It was then that President Truman made the decision to sustain the beleaguered city by an around-the-clock airlift. American and British planes poured in millions of tons of food and other supplies for nearly a year. Reuter and Brandt led the West Berliners in their valiant resistance. The Berliners froze and hungered, but they held on and, at last, the Russians lifted the blockade.

In 1957, Brandt was chosen as mayor of West Berlin and kept up the unremitting fight to keep the city from being engulfed by the Soviet Union as East Germany had been. There were frequent challenges, enforced slowdowns at checkpoints, ingenious nuisance devices to harass and to frustrate. But none of them succeeded and the life of the city went on. Indeed, with subsidies from West Germany, it thrived and became a showplace of free enterprise and high living standards. The contrast with the dull, gray, depressed way of life in East Germany induced millions to leave, and they included the youngest, the most ambitious, the best trained. In the first nine months of 1961, 160,000 fled the country. In that one year, 700 doctors abandoned their practices, leaving their communities dangerously below minimum medical coverage. In many districts there were alarming defections even of the police and armed forces. The drain on East Germany became so serious that the economy was threatened with collapse. But every attempt to stop the flight, by multiplying the difficulties of migration, failed. Khrushchev said candidly that the open access of West Berlin was a "bone in the throat."*

Suddenly, beginning on the night of August 13, 1961, the access points from the east were closed, and construction began on an eight-foot wall that was to wind its crooked, jagged way through twenty-seven miles of the city, cutting through roads and streets and gardens and parks and homes, and even through graveyards. Houses by the wall were boarded up and their tenants transferred. Pillboxes went onto the wall, every few yards, with armed sentinels always on the ready, and the ground behind the wall was plowed up, indented with barricades, interlaced with barbed wire and explosives. The order on attempted infiltration was "Shoot to kill." The construction of the wall was in clear violation of the treaties that governed the administration of the city, and the succeeding days were among the tensest of the postwar period.

Khrushchev at once announced that if there was any interference by the West with an action that he claimed the East Germans had every right to take, the Soviets would respond with force. He threatened Britain directly with a rain of nuclear bombs. There were hurried consultations among the western Allies. De Gaulle played down the seriousness of the challenge. Macmillan, the British Prime Minister, lodged a protest, and went off to shoot grouse in Scotland. President Kennedy decided that, since the wall had technically been constructed on the eastern side, there was not a sufficiently provocative issue to risk a nuclear war. He waited forty-eight hours before even lodging an ineffectual protest. Khrushchev's bluff, if it was a bluff, was not called.

The reaction of West Berlin was one of fury mixed with despair. Mayor Willy Brandt said dejectedly, "Kennedy has cooked our goose."

---

* East Berliners enjoyed telling the story, *sotto voce,* of a visit by Ulbricht to a medium for advice on how to cope with the unendurable housing and food shortages. "Easy," said the medium. "Just open the western borders."

He labeled his retreat as another Munich, though he must have realized how ironic it was for a German to refer to Munich in an appeal for courageous action against appeasement. Morale was so low in Berlin that President Kennedy despatched his Vice President, Lyndon Johnson, and the former military governor of the American Zone, General Lucius Clay, to renew the American pledge to prevent any encroachment on the freedom and independence of the city.

As the months passed, the wall cast ever longer and darker shadows. The Communists extended it to close in all the borders of East Germany up to the Baltic, down to Czechoslovakia, 830 miles of barbed wire. There were grisly stories of almost daily deaths in attempted flight. On the anniversary of the construction of the wall, in August 1962, as thousands of West Berliners massed just under its towers and pillboxes to shout their protests, a twenty-year-old East German boy raced across the potted field and was felled by a fusillade of bullets just as he reached the wall by the American exit point, but no one was permitted to attend to his wounds. He lay there writhing in agony until he bled to death in the full view of the horrified West Berliners and Americans. His dying plea, *"Hilfe, Hilfe,"* voiced the tragedy of seventeen million Germans, locked in behind the wall.

For Chancellor Adenauer the development was a political disaster. There was nothing that he could have done. He had no expectation that the Allies could risk war by intervention. Nevertheless, he was blamed for having relied too supinely upon the West and their pledges, always to defend the long-range interest of the beleaguered city. Would there not be a more reliable defense, his critics asked, if the friendship of the West were supplemented with more adequate German power? In the September 1961 elections, a few weeks later, the Christian Democrats lost their absolute majority, and the continuance of the Adenauer government for the first time was in jeopardy. To stay on in office, Adenauer had to bring into coalition one of the smaller splinter parties.

In the next year Adenauer lost further ground when a major scandal discredited his judgment and nearly brought down the government. A widely read news magazine, *Der Spiegel*, published a cover story in October 1962 that attacked the military competence of West Germany and exposed the vulnerability of the country if there should be a nuclear war. It was obvious that the classified material in the article could not have been obtained without security leaks. Adenauer and his Defense Minister, stung by the revelations, ordered the publisher and the editors arrested on charges of treason and bribery. Some of them were routed out of bed in the middle of the night. Little effort was made to follow the procedures of due process. One of the editors who was vacationing in Spain with his wife was arrested and jailed by the Spanish police at the request of the Adenauer government. Another was on holiday in Communist Yugoslavia, and Tito must have chuckled as he blandly offered asylum to him. There were stormy sessions of protest in the Bundestag and names were bandied about in debate—*"Fascist,"* *"Gestapo"*—names that it would have been inconceivable to pronounce a few years earlier. Students took to the streets, appearing with copies of *Der Spiegel* in their hands and with their mouths taped. The protests grew. A Frankfurt paper noted that when there was a knock at the door in the middle of the night, it was not a drunken neighbor wandering into the wrong house, but probably a government agent aping the procedures of the Nazi Gestapo.

For the editors of *Der Spiegel* the turmoil was a bonanza. They had ordered three hundred thousand extra copies of the exposé issue that were sold out within a few hours, and the black market copies were hawked at handsome bonuses. The circulation of the paper, with the editor holding court in jail where he was confined for fourteen weeks, zoomed by several hundred thousand.

The whole episode burgeoned into a humiliating disaster for the now aged Chancellor. The Free Democrats, whose votes were needed to preserve the government majority, refused to go on unless there were an explicit renewal of a pledge that Adenauer had made in 1961 that he would resign as Chancellor before the end of 1963. It was a promise that he honored, though with the deepest chagrin that a political career placing him with the contemporary immortals should close with so little dignity.

Yet the ugly *Der Spiegel* affair had value. The storm of protest at the high-handed methods used by the government to punish criticism carried the message that the democratic system was not simply imposed on Germany by the western powers. It now had roots, its meaning was understood and prized. A powerful government had been shaken to its foundations when it trifled with the rights of free speech. There was reassurance here also to the western world that the outbursts, ultranationalist or neo-Nazi, that came occasionally from the offscourings of society need not send worried neighbors into a tailspin of panic. Even an Adenauer, with his "Chancellor democracy," could not now ride roughshod over democratic practice. Such reassurance to the western world was almost worth the whole tempest.

There was a brief epilogue to the era that carried Adenauer's name when *Der Alte* was succeeded by his Economic Minister, Ludwig Erhard, who, though continually downgraded by Adenauer, had managed the nation's economy for fifteen years. He was really responsible for the miracle that had lifted Germany out of ruin and debris to the astonishing strength it now commanded. The transfer of leadership represented very little change in policy; it was only a shift in style. The rotund, cheerful, rumpled little man, affectionately known as *"Der Dicke,"* Fatty, was softer in manner, more easygoing, more patient than his dour, stiff, peremptory chief. He was perhaps more friendly to Britain, strongly favoring its membership in the Common Market. He was not as well disposed toward De Gaulle as Adenauer had been. But, like Adenauer, he insisted upon firm and undeviating relationships with the West, and continued reliance upon the free enterprise system that was the fulcrum of German prosperity. His three-year incumbency until 1966 was really part of the Adenauer period. Indeed, for most of his regime, he had the old Chancellor close by, still watching, not so paternally, over his shoulder.

Adenauer died in April 1967, at the age of ninety-one. He had outlived virtually all of his contemporaries. The new generation could see him only as an embittered old man, watching in frustration the construction of the wall that partitioned Berlin, an exasperated patriarch defying the sanctions of due process in an undignified battle with recalcitrant editors. But there were more representative memories that the passing of time would surely place in proper focus. There was the concerned father, who had brought home twelve million refugees and absorbed them as self-supporting nationals, who had pioneered fifteen years of extraordinary economic progress including six and a half million housing units, who had increased the foreign trade of a bankrupt land until it reached nearly thirteen billion dollars annually. There was the remembrance of the astute diplomat who had transformed ancient enemies into firm allies. Who could have imagined at the Hitler *Götterdämmerung* that only a few years later the German Chancellor would be standing in the Arlington cemetery at the grave of the Unknown Soldier after a cordial welcome to the United States, the American band playing the German national anthem; or at the side of General de Gaulle, listening to the French leader repudiate centuries of national hatred, hailing the German people as *"Das grosse deutsche Volk"*?

[480]

The body of the old Chancellor went up the Rhine to his birthplace. The flag that draped the coffin symbolized the more significant memories which most likely would embody history's ultimate verdict.

In the election of 1966 that followed the fall of the Erhard cabinet neither major party could command a clear majority and, after intensive negotiations, a surprising modus vivendi was arranged. The old opponents who had fought each other from the founding of the Federal Republic now combined forces in a coalition, with a Christian Democrat, Kurt Kiesinger, as Chancellor, and a Social Democrat, Willy Brandt, as Deputy Chancellor and Foreign Minister, the other cabinet posts divided between the two parties. For the Social Democrats, who had steadily penetrated the ranks of the middle class and the younger voters, it was at last an opportunity to demonstrate to the electorate that they had the capacity to govern constructively. For Willy Brandt, who had suffered the taunts of detractors, it was an emotional fulfillment after the long frustrating years in the wilderness.

The collaboration of the two rival parties was a political anomaly. The leadership in the coalition by Kurt Kiesinger roused considerable uneasiness. Kiesinger, a handsome, well-educated, law-trained protégé of Adenauer, had enrolled in the Nazi Party when Hitler took over Germany in 1933. Like so many others he had joined opportunistically, without genuine commitment. But what troubled many of his countrymen and the outside democratic world was the revelation that he had retained his party identification until the defeat of the Nazis, and that he had served all through the Hitler period, under Ribbentrop, in the propaganda division of the Foreign Office. He faithfully pursued the Nazi line in the same studios where William Shirer of the Columbia Broadcasting Company worked as a correspondent and he always wore the swastika in his lapel.* The question was inevitably asked, "How could one with Kiesinger's background be chosen as the *symbol* of the new Germany?" Kiesinger, a resourceful lawyer, politically adept, pointed to the choice as an example of German maturity. He bracketed Brandt's record with his own. Yes, he had indeed been tainted with his youthful identification, just as Willy Brandt had been blemished by his surrender of German citizenship. The fact that the country turned to leadership of this regenerated kind, Kiesinger claimed, was a happy

* William Shirer, "From Jesse Owens to the Summer of '72," *Saturday Review* (March 25, 1972), p. 40.

augury, for it indicated that German politics had now entered a climate of reconciliation. He said blandly, "We simply cannot and must not forget the terrible things that happened in our history. Yet this memory must not paralyze our energies."

For three years, until 1969, the incongruous coalition administered the country, avoiding major decisions. There were troublesome problems for both parties in the challenge of nationalist reactionaries who were making headway in the old Nazi centers of Lower Saxony, Franconia, and Hesse, creating anxiety as they polled between 5 and 10 percent of the vote in local elections. One of Brecht's characters warned that, though the Hitler days were over, the bitch that bore him was in heat again. There were dangers too from extremists among the younger generation, sunk in what was called "*Kultur pessimissmus*," an anarchic repudiation of middle-class values. Overall there was fear that the economic stability, a constant since the beginning of the Federal Republic, might disappear as the old economic approaches seemed to be losing their effectiveness. The coalition was held together for three years, not by any common objective, but by resistance to common dangers.

In these years, Brandt grew in stature and in reputation. Already at the party conference of 1959, in Godesberg, the rigorous Socialist doctrines of the past had been considerably modified. The mood of the country was changing and Brandt's unorthodox views were less disquieting now. Two-thirds of the men, more than half of the women, were under forty. They were a post-Hitler generation and they had no personal guilt about the past. They were ready to approach more boldly the impasse with the neighbors on the east. The older attitude had been one of hopelessness. Willy Brandt refused to accept the immobilism as inevitable; succumbing to it he called "complacent impotence." He was convinced that it was much more important to strive for technological, scientific, and cultural reunification than for the political reunification of East and West Germany which was pure chimera. "In the affairs of the world," he said, "we are economic giants but political dwarfs. We must break through." This did not mean, he hastened to add, that the commitments to the West would be repudiated. Very few questioned the necessity of the alliance with the United States. But Brandt wished to free himself from the relationship that Adenauer had with Dulles, where the two old men always turned flinty faces to the east, and were resigned to the Cold War.

The coalition broke up in 1969. It had not been a partnership; it had been a liaison. It had plodded along with increasing strain. Cabinet decisions usually came only after acrimonious debate. There was a widening split on foreign policy, although the appearance of unity was publicly maintained. Kiesinger and his party thought that Brandt's *Ostpolitik* was dangerously naïve. It would leave Germany without adequate safeguards. Brandt was certain he could achieve a breakthrough that would fully protect the welfare and the security of West Germany.

The campaign of 1969 was hard-fought. Early in the election evening it seemed as if Kiesinger had triumphed, and President Nixon actually used the hot line to convey his congratulations. But when the final votes were tabulated, neither the Christian Democrats nor the Social Democrats could form a government by themselves.* The balance was held by the Free Democrats, who this time agreed to assign their crucial votes to the Social Democrats, and their adherence brought Willy Brandt in as Chancellor. The Christian Democrats, in power from the founding of the Republic, were stunned. When Brandt came forward to take the office of Chancellor not a single Christian Democrat applauded, nor would more than a few stay on to shake hands and wish him well.

Brandt announced at once that the postwar era was definitely over, and that a new orientation was to be charted for Germany. Much more extended programs were begun to broaden the concept of social welfare. While the new government continued to encourage private capital investment, restrictive measures were established to ensure that such free enterprise would no longer dominate the economy.

But Brandt's major innovations came in foreign policy. He took the initiative in exploring with his eastern neighbors—Russia and Poland, Rumania and the other Balkan states—the possibility of better communication and improved trade relations. Brandt hoped, by what he called "the policy of small steps," to create an initial confidence that would gradually broaden the areas of mutual concern. Suspicious Communist critics scorned the small steps as "aggression in carpet slippers," but Brandt persevered.

By the end of his first year in office, West German trade with the Iron Curtain countries, while still only 4 percent of the total foreign trade of the Federal Republic, had grown to two billion dollars. Full-

---

* Actually the Christian Democrats won 242 seats and the Social Democrats 224. The Free Democrats had the 30 swing votes.

scale diplomatic relations were established with Yugoslavia. In his Polish round, Brandt let it be known that he favored the withdrawal of all claims to the 40,000 square miles of German territory that had been taken over by Poland after World War II. His dramatic announcement in effect ended the fractious boundary controversy with Poland that had haunted a whole generation. He said wryly to critics who excoriated him for a craven renunciation that one cannot renounce what one does not have anyway.

Above all, he appealed to his people to stop thinking of West Germany as a "half state," truncated by the loss of East Germany, subordinating all practical considerations to the ephemeral hope of reunification. He urged the view that there were two German states, each free, each the friendly neighbor of the other, separate political entities but part of one German people. He hoped that such a formula could initiate a new era of reconciliation between East and West.*

All of this was audacious statesmanship. One could never know how the Kremlin would react if too many windows were opened in the satellite states. The first year of the new Chancellor was filled with crises and alarms. But Brandt never lost patience and he was helped by the mellowing of relationships with the Soviet that all the western powers were enjoying. By the end of 1971, Russia and the West had so modified their bristling guardianship of interests in West and East Germany that it was possible to negotiate an agreement to offer easier access from West Berlin to East Berlin, despite the forbidding presence of the dividing wall.

Yet Willy Brandt's major task was more difficult than his quest to facilitate communication between the East and West. Even as with Konrad Adenauer, he had to shepherd his generation to adjust to a new identity. Every great nation builds on its past with pride and self-esteem and confidence, drawing inspiration from its ancestral legacy. But in Germany the future could not flow naturally from the immediate past. Indeed, the initial obligation to safeguard the future had to be the repudiation of the matrix from which the present Germany had emerged. The new Germany dated from 1945 and, significantly, this was often referred to as "Year Zero." To adjust to an *ex nihilo* background was especially difficult for the younger generation, born or come to maturity since Hitler. They had to repudiate

---

* Brandt's initiative in seeking a détente in the relations of West Germany and the Iron Curtain countries was recognized in October 1971, when he won the Nobel Peace Prize.

the parent generation, often the parents themselves. They had to seek their identity either in a long-ago historic Germany, or else in a new Europeanism that would supersede all nationalism, especially their own, so that they could be absorbed in it, or by it. Willy Brandt, whose whole background, personal and national, was a mélange of rejection and renewal, was perhaps the best symbol of the forces powerfully at play within the tormented genius of one of history's most gifted peoples.

41

THE EISENHOWER
AND KENNEDY YEARS

IN THE DECADE AFTER THE ADMINISTRATION OF PRESIDENT TRUMAN, national leadership was successively exercised by Dwight D. Eisenhower and John F. Kennedy, two men of such utterly contrasting types that inevitably the country was governed in radically different ways. Eisenhower was just plain "Ike"—genial, benevolent, well-meaning, outwardly unruffled, with a Main Street conception of civic virtue and cultural values. He was uncomfortable with doctrinaires. He read little and amused himself, even when President, with Westerns and pulp writing. Kennedy was urbane, restless, perceptive; Robert Frost caught his complexity—"Part Harvard, part Irish." He was thoroughly at home with politicians, and socially at ease with writers, scientists, and musicians. Eisenhower came out of poverty. He lived through the ordeal of his father's rural business failures. He spent his boyhood working at menial odd jobs, selling surplus vegetables, stoking furnaces, tending to chores in a creamery, all to round out the precarious family income. "Our pleasures were simple," Eisenhower wrote in his Memoirs; "they included survival." Kennedy was born to wealth. His father had parlayed his investments into a major fortune, and multimillion-dollar trust funds were set up for each of his many children.

When they came to the presidency, both Eisenhower and Kennedy had to cope with social revolution that called for emergency action—the plight of the blacks, the agony of the disinherited, the riots in the cities, the national budget that defied control, the terror of nuclear power in enemy hands. Eisenhower approached these problems dispassionately, emotionally uncommitted. His Secretary of the Treasury, George Humphrey, meant it as a compliment when he said, "The President is always quick to jump in with a suggestion. He almost never jumps in with a decision." Eisenhower relied on familiar military staff procedures, devolving responsibility, venturing no further than he had to. Kennedy was an activist. He was always thoroughly involved. He welcomed ideas but they were sterile for him unless they were applied to decisions. He was irritated by effusive liberals. He said that his glands did not operate as Hubert Humphrey's did. Perhaps the most revealing appraisal of the man came from Adlai Stevenson, after Kennedy had won the Democratic nomination for President in 1960. In a remarkable demonstration of self-analysis, Stevenson compared himself and Kennedy by citing the difference between Cicero and Demosthenes. When Cicero finished an address the crowd responded, "How eloquent, how felicitous." When Demosthenes finished an address the crowd roared, "Let's march." Kennedy was no mean orator and he too was a master of the telling phrase. But he gave significance to it through action, and Stevenson, in defeat, chivalrously saluted the electorate for recognizing this.

Eisenhower was born in 1890 in Denison, Texas, but he was brought to Abilene, Kansas, as an infant when his father, a mechanic, was unable to support the family in Texas. Kansas at the time was Wild Bill Hickok country, rough and primitive, and young Ike received the usual toughening of the frontier. Nothing in his early career indicated any special promise. He entered West Point and was commissioned in 1915, but barely in the upper half of the class, just another shavetail. His assignments for many years were all within the country, the routine army barracks life, and promotion was frustratingly slow. It was during a stint in Washington that Eisenhower attracted the attention of Douglas MacArthur, who was Chief of Staff, and in February 1933, he accompanied the general to the Philippines where a national army was to be created on the way to promised Filipino independence. The two men did not like each other. Later, MacArthur, deeply chagrined over the rise of Eisenhower above him, labeled him "the apotheosis of mediocrity." Eisenhower in turn commented, when asked if he knew MacArthur, "Oh, yes. I studied dramatics under him in the Philippines for four years."

Eisenhower returned for new duties in the United States. The turning point for him, as for so many others, came in 1941 with

Pearl Harbor. General George Marshall, now Chief of Staff, was seeking a commander for the American forces in Europe. Impressed with the dependable way in which Eisenhower managed his assignments, and especially his uncanny talent for friendship with the political powers in Congress, Marshall tapped him for the historic assignment, advancing him ahead of 366 men who were senior to him.

Eisenhower more than met his chief's expectations. First as head of the American forces and then as Supreme Commander for all the Allied armies, he demonstrated a rare capacity for coordination.* He had to deal with unusually exasperating prima donnas, brilliant but stubborn—De Gaulle, Montgomery, and Patton, Churchill and Roosevelt, to say nothing of the incredibly fussy Queen Wilhelmina of Holland. Eisenhower's strategy in defeating the Axis powers was little more resourceful than the strategy that he had to improvise to keep these rugged characters in tandem. By the end of 1943 the Allies were ready for the decisive assault across the Channel into France, and thence onward into Germany itself. Churchill and Roosevelt agreed that for this historic assignment, so full of peril, the choice ought to be General Marshall, who had been the strategic brains of the American effort. But after urgent appeals from Admiral King and others in the top echelons of the military that Marshall could not be spared, Roosevelt agreed, in his words, not "to monkey with a winning team." Eisenhower was then chosen as Supreme Commander and Marshall gallantly accepted the verdict. The Allied armies stormed the beaches successfully and broke up and overwhelmed the Nazi forces. If political considerations had not compelled them to halt their onrush so that the Russians could garner their share of victories in eastern Europe, they would have swept into Prague, Vienna, and Berlin. But there was triumph enough for Eisenhower in achieving the unconditional surrender of the Axis powers. He was hailed as the architect of the Allied victory and deservedly became the undisputed hero of the western world.

In the years that followed, while he served as Chief of Staff, then as President of Columbia, and finally as the head of the newly created NATO, it was inevitable that he should have prime consideration as

---

* His primary task was to weld differences and to produce unity in action. During his planning an American colonel turned on his British counterpart and called him a "British sonovabitch." Eisenhower had the colonel cashiered at once. He said, "You can call anyone you like a sonovabitch. But you cannot call him a British sonovabitch."

a presidential possibility. At first he protested vigorously. "I furiously object to the word candidate," he exclaimed. "I ain't and I won't." He noted that he had reached the highest assignments in the military, where he belonged, and that there were no honors he sought beyond. But the more he protested, the more the clamor grew, and from both parties. He seemed to be the answer to America's need for a shining knight, after the miserable stalemate in Korea, the backbiting of the political vendettas, the stain of corruption in the highest levels of government, the exposure of spy rings that had purportedly penetrated the inner recesses of national security. He was the father figure, the warrior who had directed the greatest coalition in history. Who better could be entrusted with the country's welfare? The Secretary of Defense, James V. Forrestal, put it to him bluntly. "Ike," he said, "with that puss, you just can't miss being President." Eisenhower yielded at last and, in the spring of 1952, he announced that, as a Republican, he would be available for the presidential nomination. He was pitted against Adlai Stevenson, a brilliant and appealing interpreter of the country's priorities, whose speeches sparkled with wit, his barbs particularly effective against the ponderous and banal clichés of routine politics. Eisenhower's campaign performance, in contrast, was depressing. "He runs like a dry creek," one of the supporting newspapers complained.* The correspondents who traveled with him were appalled by his platform ineptness. One woke up on the campaign train and asked where he was. "We are crossing the 38th platitude."

But the electorate was not concerned at this stage with brilliance or wit. It yearned for calm and restraint. It demanded an end to the mess in Korea. Eisenhower's disarming grin, exuding benevolence, his homely assurances, even his hopelessly tangled syntax, inspired confidence and bespoke protection from the overclever eggheads surrounding and advising Truman, who had led the country into a morass.† He was elected with one of the largest majorities in American history.

---

* Cited in Marquis Childs, *Eisenhower, Captive Hero* (New York: Harcourt, Brace, 1958), p. 149. The famous editorial—"Ike Is Running like a Dry Creek"—appeared on the front pages of Scripps-Howard papers across the country in September 1952.

† It may be that some of his foggy dingdong prose was quite calculated. He assured his press secretary, James Hagerty, when the Formosa crisis heated up in the first years of his presidency, "Don't worry, Jim. If that question comes up, I'll just confuse them." Eisenhower, *The White House Years*, Vol. I, p. 478.

During his low-keyed campaign, Eisenhower's image of courageous loyalty was blemished by an unfortunate surrender to the appeal of his political advisers. All through the Truman administration, Senator Joseph McCarthy of Wisconsin had been on a ferocious witch hunt, where every liberal nuance was assailed as "soft on communism." He had carried his attacks right up to the White House and had included General Marshall as a "dupe of traitors." It was a shocking accusation against perhaps the most wholesome exemplar of loyalty and decency in American public life. As Eisenhower passed through Wisconsin on the campaign trail, he had prepared a paragraph in his address that was a tribute to Marshall, who had been his mentor and to whom he owed so much of what he had become. The politicians around the candidate urged him not to antagonize the senator from Wisconsin and to omit the reference to Marshall. In a sorry moment Eisenhower yielded. It was a lamentable action, all the more disappointing because it was not even dictated by political necessity. Eisenhower did not need the Wisconsin votes. No one questioned an impending victory by a landslide.

Perhaps not since George Washington did any President come into office with greater goodwill at home and abroad. Even Democratic opponents were resigned, after twenty years of continuous national dominance, to give the two-party system the opportunity to function less monopolistically. It was hoped that domestic and international problems would now be faced with greater prospect of solution exactly because Eisenhower could enforce decisions that no one else would dare to attempt.

At first it seemed as if he was ready for just such a role. He was able to negotiate a truce in the unpopular, wearying Korean War and he brought back the American troops who were mired there.* The terms were such that, had they been accepted by Truman, they would have hopelessly divided the country. Truman said later that if he had ended the war as Eisenhower had, he would have been impeached or lynched. Only Eisenhower, with his unassailable military prestige, representing the conservative tradition in American

---

* He wrote in his Memoirs that he compelled the acceptance of the armistice by the threat that the alternative would be unrestricted war, including the use of atomic weapons against China. "The Joint Chiefs of Staff were pessimistic about the feasibility of using tactical atomic weapons on front-line positions . . . but such weapons would obviously be effective for strategic targets in North Korea, Manchuria and on the China coast." Eisenhower, *The White House Years*, Vol. I, p. 180.

politics, could bring off the settlement and get it accepted.* But, having eliminated one of the major sources of bitterness that had worn out the country, would Eisenhower now get on with the priorities which excessive factionalism had blocked?

The testing point came quickly. The status of the huge black community called for sensitive and courageous statesmanship. A hundred years after Lincoln and the Civil War, the blacks were now in mounting revolt over the frustrating gradualism of reform. In 1954, Earl Warren, Eisenhower's own appointee as Chief Justice, led the Supreme Court to the unanimous decision which outlawed segregation and called for its elimination "with all deliberate speed." There was passionate resistance in the Southern states and among the diehard segregationists in the Northern cities where schooling, housing, and employment would be vitally affected. Undoubtedly, there would have been resistance no matter what Eisenhower had done. But he set no example of concern. He said that for him to comment on the Supreme Court decision "could tend to lower the dignity of government." The segregationists were reinforced in their obstruction because they knew that "all deliberate speed" was interpreted by the President to mean more stress on "deliberate" and less stress on "speed."† Publicly he kept repeating that legislation could not change men's hearts. Yet exactly because this was true, the court had ruled that the compulsion of legal action was essential to achieve meaningful reform. One wonders how much of the violence and the bitterness of the period might have been avoided if the President had used his invulnerable prestige for the conciliatory leadership that he gave in Europe when he dealt with its passionate national rivalries.

Eisenhower also had great difficulty in coping with Senator Joseph McCarthy, who continued to spread the charges of disloyalty and treason that had dominated the headlines in the immediate postwar period. Truman was no longer there to serve as the target for the senator and his gumshoe boys, David Schine and Roy Cohn. But

---

* There was a historic parallel in the case of the Algerian uprising, where Pierre Mendès-France could not accomplish a moderate settlement but Charles de Gaulle, the army's hero and France's saviour, could concede complete independence, precipitate the flight of half a million Frenchmen, and be hailed as a conciliatory statesman.

† I was present at a dinner party at the White House for a group of college presidents when Eisenhower bristled as he referred to the unreasoning black demands for speed and to the imprudence of the Supreme Court in moving too fast in the school integration decision.

[491]

McCarthy was shrewd enough to know when he had a political bonanza, and he continued his attacks with malevolent abandon. The appeal was made to Eisenhower to put a damper on McCarthy's irresponsibility. He was in the best position to challenge the Senator. He admitted that "no one was safe from charges recklessly made from inside the walls of Congressional immunity." But he said that he would not "get down into the gutter with that fellow." So the raucous voice of McCarthy spread its terror for two more years until he overreached himself by attacking the highest officials in the army itself. This was too much for a small band of courageous senators, who took leadership in bringing McCarthy down with a stinging vote of censure. He died soon after, a deflated windbag. But in the long period in which the strategy of timid patience was applied to him, he had succeeded in wrecking hundreds of reputations in government, in industry, in the universities, and above all, in the foreign service. It took years to recover from the poisonous miasma that he spread. Here, too, the Eisenhower passivity avoided a noisy showdown, but it permitted the destruction of promising careers that America could ill afford to waste.

In one area, however, it was easy to waken enthusiasm and even dynamism in the President. He responded promptly when his advisers urged him to relax federal controls over trade and industry, to permit a return to the freer laissez-faire policies of his boyhood days. He cooperated eagerly in the attempt to compel the TVA to share its operations with private utilities. But the outcry was so emphatic that he quickly drew back. His Secretary of the Treasury, George Humphrey, encouraged him to take a stand for a balanced budget. But this put the economy in a painful straitjacket and brought on the most serious slump since 1932. The President's reluctance to broaden governmental responsibility for social welfare affected his outlook on federal support for education and health. In opposing a modest federal allocation for research, he said, "The cure for cancer will probably be found by some little guy working in an attic without a federal grant." It was a surprising reaction from a man who had lived his life fully protected by the largesse of public taxation.

It seemed for a time that Eisenhower would be spared a decision about a second term. He was stricken with a severe heart attack midway through his incumbency and even the most ardent Republicans who needed his name and prestige for the party ticket were certain that they could not persuade him to run again. But his remarkable constitution saw him through not only the heart attack but also a severe bout with ileitis that required drastic surgery. Again pitted against Adlai Stevenson, he was re-elected in 1956 by an even larger majority than in 1952.* By now the national urge for quiescence had subsided, and it was expected that Eisenhower would turn from passivity to action. But a series of catastrophes crowded upon each other to bedevil the second term and to leave his political reputation in shreds. As his Pennsylvania Dutch family would say, the forwarder it went, the behinder it got. Sam Rayburn, Speaker of the House, summarized the Eisenhower phenomenon: "Good man, but wrong business."†

It was mainly in foreign affairs that the setbacks occurred. In his dealing with foreign nations Eisenhower relied almost exclusively on John Foster Dulles, a haughty, strait-laced moralist. One of the President's speech writers was appalled by the Dulles rigidity and "the icy breath of his self-esteem." Dulles himself defined his policy as "brinkmanship": this meant, in his words, "having the courage to go right to the brink of war in the confrontation with adversaries, but making sure not to become involved." Hence there were bristling threats about "liberation" and "rollback" in eastern Europe and of "unleashing" Chiang Kai-shek to help him dislodge the Chinese Communists. The retreat was swift when the bluff was called. Dulles encouraged Britain and France to go to the brink in the Suez dispute with Nasser, and then, at the last moment, repudiated the Allies who had taken his assurances seriously. He used strong words that emboldened the Hungarians to defy their Communist masters, but when they rose in revolt Eisenhower limited himself to florid praise of a people "so gallant and brave." The Russian tanks quickly crushed the revolt and executed the Hungarian Prime Minister. Near the end of Eisenhower's administration Dulles arranged for a summit conference in the summer of 1960, where the President and Khrushchev could meet face to face to calm the tensions of the Cold War. But just before the conference convened, an American U-2 spy plane, flying over the heart of Russia, was shot down and the pilot captured. The ill-timed episode was handled with astonishing ineptness—first a denial that it was a spy plane, and then a confession from Eisenhower that he had been fully aware of the flight and its timing. The President of the United

---

* After his second defeat, Stevenson said ruefully, "I think I missed my calling. In fact, I think I missed it twice."

† Truman, *Memoirs,* Vol. II, p. 187.

States was publicly humiliated when Khrushchev canceled the summit meeting and rescinded the invitation for him to visit Russia. As the foreign crises exploded like Chinese firecrackers, Eisenhower became more and more bewildered. He put his perplexity wryly: "It is terribly difficult to promote unity among the nations when they love their hates so much!"

Long before the end of 1960, Eisenhower had become exhausted by the strains of the presidential office. He had been ill several times again. His stamina had clearly been affected. He withdrew more and more from functional responsibility. He still retained the grateful, uncritical affection of his people. Undoubtedly if the constitutional restriction on a third term were not in effect, and he had wished it, he could again have been elected. It was significant that, after he had left the White House, he reverted to the title of "General," used military stationery, and preferred the military pension rather than the one reserved for an ex-President. It was as if he, too, were content to let his reputation be judged by his shining record as a Soldier for Peace rather than as President of the United States.

THE EISENHOWER ADMINISTRATION WAS REALLY ONLY A BRIEF REPUBlican interlude. It was not even securely Republican. For most of Eisenhower's eight years he had Democratic Congresses. In the 1960 election, Eisenhower was no longer a candidate, and, under the leadership of John F. Kennedy, the Democrats recaptured the White House. The youngest elected President in American history, born after World War I had begun, succeeded the oldest, who remembered carrying a coal rag torch in the McKinley campaign of 1896.

Kennedy was prepared from his earliest years for important political responsibility. He came of an Irish family that had settled in Boston in the mid-nineteenth century. His maternal grandfather was a colorful mayor of Boston. His father had become enormously wealthy through liquor, real estate, and the stock market; he had been involved in regional and national politics, and had been given high office by Franklin Roosevelt. During World War II he served as American Ambassador to Britain. He was determined that his sons were to have major roles in national life, and his eye was on the presidency itself. After the wartime death of his eldest son, Joseph, Jr., everything was lavished on John—wealth, political and diplomatic experience, all pointed at the presidential goal.

For John it was Choate, Harvard, The London School of Economics, worldwide travel, and then, in 1946, at twenty-nine, the successful try for Congress from an east Boston district. He entered politics on the same day as Richard Nixon of California. Scarcely in his thirties, Kennedy aimed for the Senate and in 1952 defeated the Boston Brahmin, Henry Cabot Lodge, even though Massachusetts went heavily for Eisenhower and elected a Republican governor. Young Kennedy was definitely on the way.

His record in the Senate was not particularly impressive. Like Eisenhower, he was initially blemished by the McCarthy touch. In his Pulitzer Prize-winning *Profiles in Courage*, Kennedy had written eloquent tributes to a group of men who placed their integrity above political advantage. His would have been a profile in courage, too, if he had followed their example in the heyday of McCarthy. But if he had joined in the vote to censure the Wisconsin demagogue he would have alienated large numbers of his Boston constituents to whom McCarthy was a patriot. Kennedy lived down this early act of political opportunism by steadily supporting advanced social welfare legislation. He was enthusiastically endorsed by the liberal Democratic wing in 1956, when he unsuccessfully sought the vice-presidential nomination on the ticket with Adlai Stevenson.

Immediately after the Eisenhower landslide, Kennedy began planning for the election of 1960, four years later. His campaign organization was a model of political effectiveness. He overcame the opposition of former President Harry Truman and Eleanor Roosevelt, who believed he was still too young and unseasoned and had not earned a presidential nomination. His Republican opponent was Richard Nixon, and the hard-fought campaign had all the inevitable issues plus the added one of Kennedy's Catholicism. No Catholic had ever been elected to the presidency. Kennedy brought the issue into the open and expressed his confidence that the nation had at last reached the maturity not to permit forty million Americans to lose their chance of being President on the day of their baptism. His victory was so narrow that less than one-tenth of 1 percent of the vote swung the balance. But it ended, hopefully for always, the disqualification of a candidate by virtue of his religious affiliation.*

---

* When the Vatican expressed displeasure because it believed that Kennedy had leaned over backward to prove his freedom from Papal influence, he bantered: "Now I understand why Henry VIII set up his own church."

Kennedy had scarcely taken office when he had to deal with a crisis that was a legacy from his predecessor. Cuba had become a formidable menace to American security. The guerrilla hero, Fidel Castro, who had driven out a hated tyrant, Batista, and who was at first hailed as a democratic emancipator, turned out to be a committed Soviet client. In 1960, Eisenhower had encouraged the C.I.A. to give military assistance to bands of Cuban refugees who were prepared to cooperate with the Cuban underground to overthrow Castro.* Kennedy was briefed by those who had mapped out the original plans. He was assured by Dr. Miró Cardona, the head of El Frente, that once the invading force had landed, there would be a popular uprising in Cuba itself where, he reported, the disaffection had become almost universal.

The expedition was a model of perfect failure. Everything went wrong. The secrecy had long before been penetrated. The existence of the training camps had been in the news stories as early as October 1960, in the final months of the Eisenhower administration. By mid-April of 1961 when the invasion was ready, Castro had rounded up thirty thousand suspects and these included most of the leaders of the underground. Kennedy raged, "Castro doesn't need agents over here. All he has to do is to read our papers!"

The expedition consisted of fourteen hundred men. When they landed at the designated Bay of Pigs sector, they were met by a thoroughly alerted and prepared superior force, supported by jets and tanks. With thousands of the dissidents imprisoned, the C.I.A. hopes for a coordinated uprising went glimmering. Kennedy, appalled by the faulty intelligence, refused to commit an air cover for the invaders, with all the consequences that such direct American intervention would involve. This refusal, of course, ended any lingering hope for the expedition and it was easily repulsed. About ninety men were killed, about two hundred fled to the hills, and all the rest were captured. Castro had a propaganda circus. He found a few former police of Batista's day among the prisoners and they were identified before the TV cameras. Castro scoffed that these were typical of the "gallant patriots" who had come to bring freedom to the island. All the captured men were held as prisoners

---

* In his Memoirs, Eisenhower denied that he had planned military assistance to the refugees. He wrote that he had authorized their training only because "my successor might want some day to assist the refugee forces to move into Cuba." Eisenhower, *The White House Years*, Vol. II, p. 614.

until, more than a year later, they were exchanged for fifty-six million dollars in food and medical supplies.

It was a wretched foreign policy beginning for the new Kennedy administration. It called into question the young President's judgment as well as his competence. What was difficult to fathom was the willingness of the President to undertake the invasion, but not to go through with it; the flimsy pretense that America had no part in it, when all the world knew that the planning and the training had been under American auspices.* Privately Kennedy exploded in anger for having been so misled by the experts. "The advice of every member of the executive branch brought in to advise was unanimous, and the advice was wrong." But he did not shrink from accepting responsibility for the disaster. He quoted an old Chinese proverb: "A victory has a hundred fathers, but a defeat is an orphan."

Since Kennedy had so ineptly managed a crucial international responsibility, Khrushchev continued to press his advantage. In the summer of 1962, when he badly needed some new prestige to shore up a deteriorating political position, he took the calculated risk of secretly establishing missile sites in Cuba, whose middle-range shots would menace any target within an arc from northern Canada to Peru. The Russian technicians worked frantically round the clock to install the missiles before they could be discovered. When completed, with many major American cities in the nuclear range, Khrushchev would have acquired new bargaining leverage.

On October 14, with several weeks of the installation work still needed, American U-2 surveillance planes brought back clear photographic proof of the Russian missile activity. When inquiries were made, the Russian Foreign Minister, Gromyko, blandly assured the State Department and the President himself that only defensive weapons would be released to Castro. While Gromyko spoke, Kennedy had the U-2 photographs on his desk. He made no reference to them and did not give the lie to Gromyko; he had thoroughly learned the lesson of the Bay of Pigs. His strategy for the showdown called for the most detailed preparation to take every contingency into account, including the likelihood of Russian diver-

---

* One participant told the correspondent, Stewart Alsop, scornfully: "The trouble was that we were acting like an old whore, and trying to pretend that we were just the sweet young girl we used to be." Haynes Johnson, *The Bay of Pigs* (New York: W. W. Norton, 1964), p. 225.

sionary aggression elsewhere. "This time," the President remarked with satisfaction, "it was the best kept secret in government history."

When all military and diplomatic preparations in every part of the world had been completed, word went to Khrushchev that a quarantine of the island had been established, and that no ships bearing missile equipment would be permitted to cross the line. Kennedy also demanded that whatever had already been installed would have to be dismantled or else the task would be performed by the American military. The explanatory TV broadcast on October 22 contained the ominous warning: "Any nuclear missile launched from Cuba, against any nation in the western hemisphere, will be regarded as an attack by the Soviet Union on the United States, requiring a full retaliatory response upon the Soviet Union." Then he added, "We will not prematurely or unnecessarily risk the costs of world-wide nuclear war in which even the fruits of victory would be ashes in our mouth, but neither will we shrink from that risk at any time it must be faced." The issue was sharply drawn in what Dean Rusk called "an eyeball to eyeball confrontation," and the fate of the world hung on Khrushchev's next step. Kennedy said grimly to his aides, "It can go either way."

The crisis kept the world on tenterhooks for five days. The apocalyptic mood of those agonizing days was pointed up by the grim comments of those who carried responsibility. Undersecretary George Ball, coming into a final crisis meeting from the glorious sunshine of the Washington autumn, said, "It reminds me of the Georgia O'Keefe painting that has a rose growing out of an ox skull."*

At length, when Khrushchev had persuaded himself that Kennedy's nerve would hold and that he would actually carry out the commitment of his warning, he decided to back down, without even the courtesy of consulting Castro. He made it appear that all he had sought was to protect Cuba from future invasion. In his conciliatory message to the President, he used a peasant analogy. "The crisis was like a rope with a knot in the middle. The more each side pulled, the more the knot would tighten until it could be severed only with a sword. But, if each side slackened, the knot could be untied." He therefore agreed to withdraw, if there were an explicit pledge from Kennedy that no attempt would thereafter be made to oust Castro by force. When this was assured by Kennedy, the Russian

* Élie Abel, *The Missile Crisis* (New York: J. B. Lippincott Company, 1966), p. 203.

ships were ordered to return.* As they wheeled about, they seemed to symbolize that a change of course had been achieved in the relations of the superpowers. Both leaders knew that such a confrontation, where the slightest inadvertence could have meant the destruction of mankind, must never again happen. It was significant that not too long after the travail of the missile crisis, the agreement for the test ban treaty was signed. It became Kennedy's proudest foreign policy achievement.

In domestic legislation, Kennedy was continuously stymied by the coalition of the minority Republicans and a solid phalanx of conservative Democrats. His New Frontier agenda called for major breakthroughs in civil rights, in health and education and, above all, in social welfare legislation for a vigorous attack on poverty and unemployment. He said, "If a free society cannot help the many who are poor, it cannot save the few who are rich." But the legislation that he sponsored was either bottled up in committee or, if it reached the Congress, it was usually emasculated. He was fond of quoting Hotspur on summoning spirits from a vasty deep. Any man can summon, but will the spirits come? Kennedy knew after several futile attempts to "call up the spirits from the vasty deep" that he would have to wait for a more decisive mandate from the voters. He looked to the 1964 elections to gain this mandate. It was not to be.

There had been an ominously prophetic note in Kennedy's inaugural address. "All this," he said, referring to his high hopes, "will not be finished in the first one hundred days. Nor will it be finished in the first one thousand days, nor in the life of this administration. . . . But let us begin." There was endless promise on that snow-tossed inaugural day, when the poet Robert Frost hailed the possibility of a new "Augustan Age." But it was destined that Kennedy could only begin. An assassin's bullets in November 1963 destroyed the glowing promise.

But Kennedy was not to be evaluated by his record of legislation, which was meager, nor by his negotiations with foreign powers, where setbacks were more numerous than achievements. He was to be evaluated by the animating spirit that he brought into the White House, by the youth and the courageous confidence that he exemplified. His style, never artificial, always casual, was incandes-

---

* The exchanges of letters between Premier Khrushchev and President Kennedy are included in Henry M. Pachter, *Collision Course* (New York: Frederick A. Praeger, 1963), pp. 217–28.

cent. It was demonstrated in the choice of guests who were invited to the White House functions at Kennedy's call. His invitation list was, of course, not drawn up exclusively to honor intellectual and aesthetic distinction. Kennedy never lost sight of political advantage in his bids to White House soirees. He understood Napoleon's dictum: "With enough ribbon I could conquer the world." But his tributes to the life of the mind were no less genuine because they brought dividends. Throughout his brief presidency he functioned, in Hemingway's phrase, "with grace under pressure."

The grief over Kennedy's violent death was not limited to his countrymen. Thousands of Japanese trudged for miles to Tokyo to stand reverently before the American Embassy. Students bore memorial torches in Berlin. There were mourning crowds in Tel Aviv and Karachi, in Athens and Istanbul. For years afterwards, streets and parks and schools were named for him around the world. A special area was set apart in his memory at Runnymede. The tributes were evoked not only by his martyrdom, but because every family could identify with a tragedy where potentialities are suddenly and capriciously snuffed out. Abba Eban, in his memorial address in Israel, said, "Rarely has a statesman had a more universal sepulchre in distant lands."

Symbols do not pass legislation. They do not resolve crises. But symbols do inspire emulation. And because Kennedy opened the windows of the White House for the brisk refreshing air to enter, windows were opened at least for a brief flashing moment for all the young and the adventurous everywhere.

42

THE DEVALUATION
OF BRITAIN

IN 1951 THE VIGOR AND THE REFORM ZEAL OF THE BRITISH LABOUR
government had burned out, the Attlee cabinet fell, and Winston
Churchill, now seventy-seven, was back at the head of affairs. His
defeat, immediately after the war, had seemed to him the sheerest
ingratitude and, because it had rankled so, the return to office,
though inevitably for a very limited period, had all the sweet savor
of vindication.

The epilogue years were quiet ones; the main concern seemed
to be to lift restrictions for the worker and the burdened housewife,
and to keep the ship of state on an even keel. Now that Churchill
had his coveted vote of confidence, he held on only to fulfill a sentimental responsibility. He had been active politically during five
reigns, reaching back to Queen Victoria. The death of George VI
in 1952 had brought the King's young daughter, Elizabeth, to the
throne. Churchill hoped to preside at the Coronation of the new
sovereign. He had his wish and he saluted "the fair and lovely
Princess," wakening nostalgic remembrances of the first Elizabethan
era and stimulating the hope that her own reign, likely to reach
into the twenty-first century, might preserve the exalted tradition
of British pre-eminence.

By 1955 Churchill was ready for retirement. His health had been
visibly failing and the burdens of office were now wearisome. Lady
Churchill tried to console him by reminding him how Mussolini
must have felt, nearing the end not in triumph but in disaster. The

[501]

mischievous sparkle could not be snuffed. Churchill chuckled, "Ah, but at least Mussolini has had the satisfaction of murdering his son-in-law."*

Churchill's chosen heir, Anthony Eden, had been waiting in the wings all too long. He came to the Prime Minister's post on the crest of great popularity. He was stunningly handsome, the matinee-idol type, setting fashion with his immaculate grooming. His lineage was impeccable, representing one of the oldest families in Britain. He served in World War I with gallantry, a captain before he was twenty, several times wounded, winning the Military Cross. He was meticulously educated for statesmanship—Eton and Christ Church, Oxford, reading for honors in Arabic, Persian, and the politics of the Middle East. He entered Parliament at twenty-six and devoted himself at once to the problems of diplomacy. He was named Foreign Secretary in 1935 when he was barely thirty-eight, the youngest to hold the office in a century. A loyal disciple of Churchill, he tried valiantly to block the bullying rampage of Hitler and Mussolini, but there was no support for this stance of resistance from his Prime Minister, Chamberlain, and soon Eden was virtually isolated in the appeasement cabinet. After the rape of Ethiopia and the betrayal of Austria had elicited no more than halfhearted protests, Eden resigned. At the time it seemed as if he were wrecking a promising career. Chamberlain was in full control, and placating the dictators was considered the best road to peace. Churchill, who at this time was also in the political wilderness, later described his frustration that, with Eden's resignation, nothing barred the British road to craven retreat: "There seemed one strong young figure standing up against long, dismal, drawling tides of drift and surrender, of wrong measurements and feeble impulses . . . he seemed to me at this moment to embody the life-hope of the British nation. . . . Now he was gone. . . ."†

But after Hitler repudiated all his pledges to Chamberlain and plunged the world into war, Churchill was recalled to leadership. He brought Eden in with him, first as War Minister and then again as Foreign Secretary. Eden shared with his chief the long years of wartime diplomacy and then carried most of the party's opposition tasks during Attlee's Labour incumbency. When the Tories

---

* Harold Macmillan, *The Blast of War* (New York: Harper & Row, 1968), p. 419.

† Churchill, *The Gathering Storm*, pp. 257–8.

were back in 1951, Eden was at Churchill's side and at long last his day came in 1955.

As it turned out, it was a short incumbency, a bare eighteen months. The high expectations of Eden did not materialize. It was, of course, very difficult to succeed one of the titans in British history. Perhaps Eden had been compelled to wait too long, the perpetual second in command, with little opportunity for decisions that were final. As Harold Macmillan later noted: "Churchill had been a beech tree, overshadowing the saplings all around, not an oak that allowed other trees to grow too." By now, Eden's health had become precarious, undermined by an intestinal ailment that required periodic operations at the Lahey Clinic in Boston. He had the bad luck, within a few days after he moved into 10 Downing Street, to be confronted with the most serious railroad strike in nearly thirty years, a strike that all but paralyzed the country. Then, as world problems multiplied that affected all national economies, the crisis in Britain had to be met with emergency budgets and ever higher taxes.

Eden was much more at home in the complexities of foreign policy and, though he had an experienced old hand close by in Harold Macmillan, he did most of the directing. He stood up to John Foster Dulles, despite pressure that often reached the point of threat. He would not permit Britain to become involved in the Indochina war, and he remained adamant when Dulles was ready to go to the extreme of using nuclear bombing if he could persuade the British to join in the all-out assault. Eden also supported the creation of a coordinated European defense force that would include West Germany. When the effort was defeated by the French, it was Eden who worked out the compromise that brought Germany into NATO, but imposed specific controls over the military forces that Germany would contribute to the common pool.

Ironically, Eden was less successful in coping with the problems of the Middle East—in Iraq and Jordan and in the areas where he was perhaps the best informed and best prepared of all the British statesmen. The breaking point came in 1956, in a disastrous conflict with Egypt over the Suez Canal. It was a sorry development that not only ruined a brilliant career and exposed the vulnerability of Britain, but shifted the balance of power in the Mediterranean and the Middle East.

Egypt had been a British dependency, and one of President Nasser's first historic triumphs had been to negotiate its independence and the agreement that all British forces would be removed within a few years. Nasser also had the promise of Britain and the United States for massive financial help to build a gigantic dam at Aswan that would revitalize millions of acres of arid land. But Nasser had ambitions that went far beyond the resurrection of Egypt. In a volume that detailed his aspirations he dreamed of a United Arab Empire from Baghdad to Casablanca. One of his priorities was to avenge the defeats of the 1947–8 wars which had resulted in the creation of a sovereign Israeli state in the heart of his projected Arab Empire. He initiated negotiations with the Soviets to acquire arms for this purpose. The United States and Britain were deeply disturbed, because Nasser's entente with the Kremlin opened the way for the Soviet Union to move into the Mediterranean, the Persian Gulf, and Africa itself.

Nasser's connivance with Russia, while courting aid from the western Allies, called for the most sensitive kind of diplomacy. At the crucial moment Dulles was at his peremptory worst, and Eden was in one of his periodic depressive tantrums. Both played into Russian hands by abruptly canceling the promised aid for the Aswan Dam. Nasser immediately nationalized the Suez Canal and took over its operation and income. Eden faced a major dilemma. He was undoubtedly influenced by the memory of Munich. He saw in Nasser another of the dictators who, in the thirties, had been encouraged by the success of blackmail to venture ever-widening aggression. Eden was convinced that Nasser must be stopped if the Munich pattern were not to be repeated. The crucial problem was to develop a defensible strategy of resistance to Nasser. The plan to bring him down by an overt military attack was loaded with danger, for even if the assault succeeded, what was to follow? Who would supplant Nasser and how would the national resentment be controlled? Unfortunately, Eden was egged on by the avowals of Dulles, upon whom he counted for full support even in a military adventure. It was this implicit reliance on a prickly moralist which probably became the decisive influence in the disastrous action that Eden initiated.

We now know that the three states that had a stake in resisting Nasser's actions entered into a secret arrangement to overthrow the Egyptian leader. Israel was determined to open the guaranteed international waterways which had been closed by Egypt to its shipping, and to secure more defensible frontiers to protect it from the Arab hit-and-run raids which menaced its existence. The French who

[504]

had built the Canal and had the heaviest investment in it were eager to be rid of Nasser, who had also become a major source of military supplies and recruits for the Algerian insurgent forces. To the British, the Canal was a lifeline to the Middle East and Asia, indispensable for the unrestricted flow of oil from the Persian Gulf, and for its naval security. Eden insisted that he could not permit Nasser to have his thumb on Britain's windpipe.

The Israelis carried through their mission with despatch and efficiency. They attacked on October 29, 1956, and within a few days they had completely destroyed the Egyptian resistance in the Sinai Peninsula, and had reopened access to the Red Sea and the Indian Ocean. They had so demoralized the Egyptian forces that they could have moved on to the Canal itself.

But everything seemed to go wrong with the British-French military operation. There was a delay of more than a week after the Israeli attack. The parachutists did not come down on Port Said and Suez until November 5. By then irresistible pressure had been built up from within and without, to abort the invasion and to compel withdrawal. Nye Bevan, speaking for Labour, had a field day. "The Government," he scoffed, "resorted to epic weapons for squalid and trivial ends." Khrushchev notified Eden that unless the aggression was immediately terminated there would be a nuclear attack on Britain. By trans-Atlantic telephone, Dulles let Eden know that the run on the banks in Britain was only a prologue for worse disaster unless the expedition was recalled.

The threat that came from the Soviet Union could be dismissed as typical Khrushchev bluff; it came at the very time that Russian tanks were pouring into Budapest to crush the nationalist Hungarian rebellion. The protests from the Labour benches in Britain could be bypassed as routine political maneuvering. But what dumbfounded Eden was the reaction of Dulles and his indignant homilies on ethics in international relations. He remembered that it was Dulles who had exploded in wrath when Nasser arranged with the Soviet Union for rearming. It was Dulles who had canceled the promised aid for the Aswan Dam; his brusqueness had triggered Nasser's seizure of the Canal. He had then said to Eden that it was "intolerable" to permit the Canal to be dominated by Egypt and that "a way *had* to be found," even if force had to be used, "to make Nasser disgorge what he was attempting to swallow." Eden had worked patiently with Dulles for months to find such a way. There had been several fruitless meetings with the representatives of countries that made use of the Canal to devise a formula of cooperation.* There had been an appeal to the United Nations which was promptly vetoed by the Soviet. All efforts at negotiations or compromise with Nasser had been contemptuously dismissed. Somewhere during the critical weeks that led up to the British and French strike, Dulles must have changed his mind. But he changed it with so much tortuous winding and turning that Eden wrote later with ill-concealed resentment, "I had the greatest difficulty to determine what Dulles really meant and, in consequence, the significance to be attached to his word and his actions."

But Eden could not fight back against Dulles's ultimatum, especially when it was clear that the unexpectedly swollen expenditures of the Suez reprisal would require considerable American financial support. It was heartbreaking for him to have American delegates in the United Nations join with the Soviet delegates in the censure of the entire action. There was no similar judgment as the Russians crushed the Hungarian national rebellion. Eden had no alternative but to yield, and then France and Israel followed in withdrawal. Dulles admitted afterwards to the French Foreign Minister that if he had to do it again, he would respond differently. Eisenhower, too, intimated when Nasser turned swiftly into a major threat to American interests in the Middle East that the American action in repudiating and humiliating the oldest of its Allies had been a mistake. He noted, in a rare flash of sheepish humor, that it was unfortunate the British behaved so badly, and that they were so inefficient about it. But by then it was too late; Nasser had triumphed over two world powers. He had become a hero to the Arab masses. Khrushchev had taken the credit for defeating the invasion by his threat of nuclear reprisals against Britain and France. Russia had now leapfrogged over all logistic obstacles and, through Egypt, was solidly established in the Middle East.

Eden's party loyally supported him but he could not survive the Suez disaster. He was tired, emotionally exhausted, disillusioned, and then the old illness flared again, more threateningly than ever. A vacation in Jamaica did not restore his spirits, and, with less than two years in office, he asked the Queen to name a successor. He left the political arena after forty years, his great days almost forgotten— his gallant fight against the blackmail aggression of the dictators, his diplomatic skill as Churchill's Foreign Minister. He had lived

---

* Anthony Eden, *Full Circle* (Boston: Houghton Mifflin, 1960), pp. 486–8.

for his national service, subordinating all other interests, including his family. His first marriage ended in divorce when his wife could not adjust to the situation where political and diplomatic responsibilities crowded out all personal life. Yet Eden was certain that when the diplomacy of the Suez period became public, and when the full impact of appeasing Nasser and the Russians was felt in the Middle East, history would restore perspective and vindicate his judgment.

After some intricate political maneuvering, one of the most experienced of the Tory leaders, Harold Macmillan, was named as the new Prime Minister. He was a cartoonist's dream, with his Edwardian mustache and grenadier's bearing—suave, immaculate, a model of the British aristocrat. He was the exact opposite of Eden in temperament—casual, self-possessed, "unflappable" in his approach to the most exasperating problems. He was wounded three times as an officer during World War I; when he was pinned down with a broken pelvis in a shell hole in Flanders, surrounded by corpses, he quietly and serenely read through Aeschylus in the original Greek. He could turn a neat phrase and devastate an opponent with an acid epigram. He was at his best in raillery, tongue-in-cheek, often self-deprecatory. Churchill jibed affectionately that he spoke with "calculated improvisation." When he became Foreign Minister he warned that he would probably satisfy very few, "since a Foreign Minister is always poised between a cliché and an indiscretion." He had his doubts about the idealism and the nobility of motivation in the United Nations. He described its headquarters as "a vast glass edifice filled with people throwing stones at each other." His sharp business ability he attributed to his uncanny wisdom in choosing his ancestry. His grandfather had been a thrifty Scots tenant farmer who had walked to London to seek new opportunities, and there founded a modest publishing firm which his son expanded into the world-famous Macmillan's, Ltd. Macmillan's mother was an American girl from Indiana, and he took delight, as did Churchill, in referring to a half-American ancestry. He married the daughter of the Duke of Devonshire and was thereby also related to many of Britain's traditional élite families.

He entered Parliament as a Tory in 1924 and was early identified with its extreme left wing. During the depression years of the 1930's, having studied the problems of the ghost towns and seen the misery of the unemployed, he wrote a volume, *The Middle Way,* in which he advocated many of the welfare projects of a planned society, "that should be neither jungle nor bee hive." He matched his liberalism in domestic affairs with vigorous opposition to the appeasement of the dictators. When Chamberlain advocated that sanctions be lifted against Mussolini's Italy, Macmillan, like Eden, refused to answer the call of the party whip.

In 1940, Churchill brought him into his war cabinet for a succession of diplomatic missions which he fulfilled most impressively. He was sent to North Africa in 1942 as the British political representative at the headquarters of General Eisenhower and formed there the personal friendship that was to serve both countries well in later years. He was fluent in French and tactful in negotiation and he was able to pick his way through the feuds of De Gaulle and Giraud in the critical months of their rivalry. Two years later he was commissioned to Italy and he negotiated the surrender of Badoglio and the turnabout of Italy that brought the country over to the Allied side. He had to deal with suddenly contrite Fascists and he wrote sternly that they must be removed. But he worked with them and the comment in his Memoirs perhaps best summed up his first-things-first procedure: "Directives are more useful in protecting the writer than instructing the recipient." He managed several difficult assignments in the Balkans, which included stormy confrontations with the Communists who almost took control of Greece.

His impressive diplomatic record gave him highest rating with Churchill and the party when the Tories had another turn at office beginning in 1951. Macmillan was named Minister of Housing, and though it seemed foolhardy to project the creation of three hundred thousand units annually, Macmillan surpassed the goal. In 1954 he was shifted to the Ministry of Defense and carried through the complicated task of converting Britain to the responsibilities of the atomic age.

When Eden became Prime Minister, Macmillan took over the Foreign Ministry and then the Exchequer. Inflation now loomed as the most serious national problem and Macmillan's fiscal surgery cut to the bone. Since *The Threepenny Opera* was the vogue, it was inevitable that he should soon be known as "Mac the Knife." Then, in 1956, came the unfortunate Suez venture. It ruined Eden, and Macmillan, now sixty-three, took his place. He proved to be one of Britain's most durable political figures. His incumbency lasted until 1963, the longest uninterrupted tenure of any Prime Minister since the pre-World War I days of Asquith. He served notice on his cabinet that he expected clear heads and no dudgeon when he posted a quotation from *The Gondoliers.* "Quiet, calm deliberation disentangles every knot."

Macmillan's first task was to restore the impaired relationships with the United States. He had thoroughly agreed with Eden on Suez; he had deeply regretted what he too considered the shortsightedness of the American action. But, to him, diplomatic defeats were not emotional problems. He wrote off the Egyptian failure and he sought to emphasize common interests in the dangerous world where the Russian bear and the Chinese dragon had to be confronted together. He renewed the warm personal friendship with Eisenhower that had been established in the days of their military service in North Africa. Eisenhower, who already felt that the rupture had gone too far, was more than eager to respond to Macmillan's overtures. The two men met informally in Bermuda and the relaxed conferences were extremely cordial. There was steady cooperation henceforth between the United States and Britain, and it reached into the Kennedy administration even to the point of sharing America's H-Bomb data. Britain could not really afford membership in the nuclear club but Macmillan, like De Gaulle, probably thought it important to sustain the romantic notion that Britain was still a great power.*

Macmillan had been intrigued by the concept of European integration. He had been appalled by the disastrous effects of national rivalries and the wars that had followed, when even the victors had barely survived. The misery that was spawned by World War II, and the murky economic climate in which each nation lived, reinforced his conviction that the only salvation for Europe lay in its cooperative effort to transcend national barriers in trade and defense. He was, therefore, in the forefront of every effort to promote European integration. He was strongly committed to British membership in the Common Market when it was viewed with misgiving by most of his colleagues, by the Commonwealth statesmen, and by his Labour opponents. Macmillan persevered and took personal charge of the negotiations to clear the obstacles for Common Market membership and he revolutionized the traditional Tory position in international economic policy. It was perhaps his deepest personal disappointment when, at the threshold of success, all the

---

* "The long trail back from Suez continued, as it were, under the smokescreen of a mushroom cloud." Anthony Sampson, *Macmillan* (London: Allen Lane the Penguin Press, 1967), p. 125.

carefully developed negotiations were voided by De Gaulle's sudden veto.

Meantime Macmillan would not give up the hope that by personal conference he could help establish better relationships between East and West. He was warned by the career diplomats that climbing summits was a dangerous sport; Khrushchev was not Eisenhower. He alarmed the West Germans, who were almost paranoid on the possibilities of disastrous concessions by the over-eager democracies. Macmillan insisted that it was the height of folly to be afraid of negotiation. "Are we to live forever," he asked, "in this sort of twilight between peace and war?"*

The angel rushed in where the foolish feared to tread. In February 1959, he journeyed to Moscow to advocate a summit meeting that might open the way to a general détente. Khrushchev blew hot and cold and, ultimately, the negotiations collapsed. Another later summit attempt at Geneva also failed, when an ill-timed American U-2 spy plane, shot down over Russia, sent Khrushchev into another of his angry tirades. Macmillan was quite philosophical. "It's no use crying over spilt summits," he said.† He consoled himself that he had at least helped to achieve a test ban treaty that restricted the effects of the escalating nuclear competition.

The peripatetic, undiscouraged Prime Minister had greater success in protecting the Commonwealth from the accelerated pace of decolonization in Africa. The day was long past for any Churchillian approach to Empire: the very word had become anathema. Macmillan was now mainly concerned that the former colonies should retain a family relationship, within the Commonwealth, after independence. He undertook long interpretive trips, visiting parts of Africa that no previous Prime Minister had penetrated. Everywhere he assured the native leaders that Britain recognized "the wind of change" that was blowing through the continent, and that his goal was a multiracial Commonwealth. In the heart of *apartheid* South Africa he outraged the white ruling groups by his "wind of change" avowal. Before he had relinquished the seals of office virtually every African colony, having achieved its independence, opted, as Macmillan had hoped, to remain a part of the British Commonwealth.

But it was Macmillan's skillful management of the ailing domestic economy he inherited that won him the broadest support. The till

* *Ibid.*, p. 134.
† *Ibid.*, p. 145.

was virtually empty when he became Prime Minister. There were serious pockets of unemployment. Macmillan turned back boldly to his earlier social liberalism. He scolded the reluctant Tories: "We have lived too long on old port and over-ripe pheasant." The welfare program of the Labour pioneers was expanded and it was paid for by levies upon the wealthier groups, even as taxes were cut substantially for those in the lower-income levels. Aided by general improvement in world conditions, the economy came out of its doldrums. Foreign trade improved spectacularly. Average British families began to enjoy the comforts of cars and television and refrigerators and washing machines. The popular cartoonist, Vicky, referred to the Prime Minister as "Super Mac" and the name became part of the image. Macmillan was able to go to the country in the election campaign of 1959 on the platform, "You never had it so good." He was returned with the largest majority of any of the Tory governments since the early Baldwin days.*

But the pace could not be sustained. Early in the 1960's, the economy once again turned wobbly. There was a severe sterling crisis as rumors spread that the pound was to be devalued. The winter of 1962 was the coldest in nearly two centuries. Unemployment again climbed steadily and the old magician was now unable to cope with it. The Labour opposition grew more formidable and the criticism of individual ministers shifted to Super Mac himself. Nye Bevan asked: "Why do we attack the monkey, when the organ grinder is here?" Perhaps the quip of another opponent was really a compliment: "God created Harold Macmillan in order to confirm the ordinary Englishman in his distrust of intelligence." Nevertheless, the feeling grew that it was time to turn to a much younger man, as the Americans had done when Kennedy succeeded Eisenhower.

Then, ironically, came a silly scandal that deeply embarrassed the government and hastened Macmillan's resignation. The scandal rose out of the clumsily handled indiscretions of John Profumo, the War Minister, whose dalliance with a London call girl, Christine Keeler, might have passed off quietly if Profumo had not lied about his involvement when he made his explanations in the House of Commons. Inasmuch as Christine had also been offering her favors to a Russian diplomat who was trying to find out if Britain planned

* The magnitude of the victory was doubtless influenced also by the serious rift in the Labour Party, where Bevan, and later Harold Wilson, waged uncompromising war on Hugh Gaitskell and the parliamentary leadership.

to share H-bomb data with West Germany, the charge was raised by the Labour opposition that Profumo's indiscretions could have led to serious security leaks. Britain was reeling at the moment with other spy ring disclosures. No one profited from the scandal, except perhaps Christine, who was delighted to find that "vice indeed hath golden cheeks." She sold her kiss-and-tell stories to the tabloid press for large sums, and then accepted nightclub appearances with earnings that were twenty-five times as large as those of the Prime Minister.

Britain, in the throes of one of its periodic outraged-virtue binges, reveled in the puffed-up disclosures. It would not be accurate to conclude that a saucy tart had brought down a powerful British minister.* But, since there were now many other problems that plagued the government, Macmillan decided that he had served long enough. He was not too well and, when his physician warned him that, in the face of a difficult operation, he could no longer carry aggravating responsibilities, he asked the Queen to relieve him and his Foreign Minister, Sir Alex Douglas-Home, took over. He told a party conference that, now seventy, and having carried the Prime Minister's awesome burdens longer than any predecessor in nearly fifty years, he had earned relief. With his usual grace, Macmillan quoted Shakespeare:

> "Let me not live," quoth he,
> "After my flame lacks oil, to be the snuff
> Of younger spirits . . ."†

Preferring to remain the Scots crofter's grandson, he refused the earldom that was the traditional honor for retiring Prime Ministers. He was more honored by his election as Chancellor of Oxford.

It was a pity that Macmillan's exit had to take place in the climate of an embarrassing scandal. He had given Britain seven years of level-headed leadership. When he succeeded Anthony Eden the country was sharply divided by the Suez failure, its Middle East

---

* A popular limerick was read and repeated gleefully:

> What on earth have you done, said Christine,
> You have wrecked the whole party machine.
> To lie in the nude
> Is not at all rude,
> To lie in the House is obscene.

† *All's Well That Ends Well,* Act I, Scene ii.

policy in bankruptcy, its prestige low. Macmillan had re-established a line of confidence with the United States; he had rationalized the welfare state; he had guided decolonization in a way that retained the goodwill and the loyalty of the former African dependencies. Above all, he had softened the asperities in politics after the frenetic pace of Labour reform. Santayana was one of his favorite authors and he often turned to his philosophic serenity as an exemplary conservative guideline: "The Englishman carries his weather in his heart wherever he goes, and it becomes a cool spot in the desert and a steady and sane oracle amongst all the deliriums of mankind."

Macmillan did not succeed in solving the British postwar dilemma —the hope of remaining a great power without the leverage of great power resources. But, unlike De Gaulle, who was frustrated by a similar dilemma for France, Macmillan was convinced that Britain could protect its status by promoting the policy of "interdependence," strengthening the alliances with the United States and the democracies of Europe. In one of the Common Market debates he said: "I believe that our right place is in the vanguard of the movement towards greater unity of the free world, and that we can lead from *within*, rather than outside." De Gaulle's sudden veto of Britain's entry in the Common Market in 1963 was a blow, although not altogether unexpected. But Macmillan was certain that through interdependence leadership, Britain would retain its great power status.

SIR ALEX KNEW FROM THE OUTSET THAT HIS WAS A CARETAKER GOVernment and he prepared to obtain a new popular mandate by setting a general election for October 1964 after a year in office. The campaign was hard-fought, both sides often reaching below the belt, perhaps because their positive records were so difficult to defend. Labour blasted away at the bumbling of the Tories, the burdensome taxes, the unfavorable balance of trade, the unfulfilled social welfare pledges and, above all, the reduced role of Britain in the councils of the major powers. The Tories reminded the voters how skillfully they had managed decolonization and steered a bruised and battered economy through thirteen years of unremitting danger. They did not too seriously reject the demagoguery of one of their firebrands, Enoch Powell, who had made himself the spokesman for the attack on continued immigration from India, Pakistan, and the Black African dominions, and the million nonwhites who

[513]

were already concentrated in the major city ghettoes of England. Powell's posters were everywhere: "If you want a nigger neighbour, vote Labour."

When the returns were in, Labour had the slimmest majority of the century, a bare four votes, having polled 44.1 percent as against the Tory total of 43.4 percent. Indeed, the incoming Prime Minister, Harold Wilson, on his way down to London on the train from the Midlands, did not know for certain whether his destination that day would actually be 10 Downing Street. But four votes still meant a Labour victory and the long thirteen-year incumbency of the Tories had come to an end.

Wilson represented a major break with tradition. He was born in 1916 of Yorkshire family background, the son of an industrial chemist, and he was the first Prime Minister in British history who did not attend a select private school as a preliminary to his university education. But he was a brilliant student and won a scholarship to Oxford, where his record in economics was so outstanding that he was made a don at twenty-one. He served in World War II as a civil service economist and then decided on politics as a career.* His first try for Parliament was successful; he was swept in on the Labour landslide of 1945. When he was named to the cabinet as president of the Board of Trade at thirty-one, he was the youngest cabinet member since the days of William Pitt. He took his place in the ranks of the left-wing contingent of Labour, so close to Bevan that he was referred to as "Nye's little dog." As the older leadership of the party withdrew or were eliminated, Wilson moved up rapidly, and upon the sudden death of Hugh Gaitskell, who had succeeded Clement Attlee, Wilson took command. In the election of 1964 in which television played a crucial role, Wilson was the consummate master, witty, sharp, ebullient, more than a match for his rival, the patrician, slow-moving, irritatingly disdainful and ponderous Douglas-Home.

At forty-six Wilson was the youngest Prime Minister of the century. He could not command the exultant evangelism that marked the advent of Labour when it ousted the redoubtable Churchill in 1945; his margin of victory was too tenuous. Indeed, there were

---

* "I think I was born with politics in me," he told an interviewer after he became Prime Minister. "I think the influence of friendly teachers and others has been considerable, but merely in guiding me in the direction I wanted to go anyway." Anthony Howard and Richard West, *The Road to Number 10* (New York: The Macmillan Company, 1965), p. 300.

uneasy remembrances of Attlee's 1950 government with its majority of six and the consequent marshaling of members in wheelchairs, on crutches, and in bandages for decisive divisions. One of Wilson's colleagues semi-jokingly wondered whether it would not be a wise precaution to have all the Labour members promptly inoculated against influenza. Any illness that would prevent attendance could precipitate a parliamentary crisis. With his flimsy majority, how could Wilson venture any daring legislation? There was a sinking feeling in the country, somberly alluded to by the press, that Britain was again destined to undergo a period of drift and stagnation because of the virtual paralysis of a stalemate.

Yet Wilson was not to be diverted. At his very first Cabinet session he said emphatically that Labour was not only prepared to govern; it was prepared to stay. He would pay no attention to the size of Labour's majority, whether four or forty or four hundred. If there were rocks in their path, they would navigate around them. If there were storms ahead, they would drive through them full tilt.* He took his cue from a young contemporary whom he greatly admired, the late President Kennedy, who had also assumed responsibility in the heart of crisis with a mandate so precarious that a few thousand votes differently distributed would have brought in his rival. Wilson's opening appeal to his people was an echo of Kennedy's inaugural, "We have got to think less about what we can get out of the economy and a great deal more of what we can put into it."† He announced that his government would sponsor the expansion of social welfare services, the nationalization of steel and other basic industries, the acceleration of reform in education to open wider opportunities for thousands of working families. He promised also that the pound would not be devalued and that there would be immediate action to stem the rise of living costs. These were all bold pledges and the country reserved its verdict to give him a sporting opportunity to fulfill them.

By 1966 Wilson felt confident enough to ask for a new mandate. His party was returned with a strong working majority of ninety-six; thereafter, his promises were no longer inhibited by the dangers of a sudden parliamentary upset. Yet it was clear all too soon that the fate of Britain did not rest on which party held the levers of authority. British resources were too narrow, the competition too

* Anthony Shrimsley, *The First Hundred Days of Harold Wilson* (New York: Frederick A. Praeger, Inc., 1965), p. 20.

† *Ibid.*, p. 66.

formidable, for the country to maintain major power status. Even if Wilson had more dynamism and more political sagacity than he demonstrated, and he had considerable, these talents could not substitute for power. Wilson's dilemma, indeed the dilemma of any postwar British statesman, was well summarized by *The Times* at the moment when the new government accepted its almost hopeless challenge. England was really only an island "still detached from continental Europe, preserved from the necessity of too much thought by the nuclear diplomacy of the United States, scattering her armed forces by handfuls to fight in the last remaining and least rewarding fragments of a once incomparable empire. . . ."*

Wilson had defiantly announced that come what may the pound would not again be devalued. But with all the credit support that was rushed in, especially from the United States, to shore up the banking institutions in their crisis, the level could not be maintained. In November 1967, the inevitable action was taken and another 18 percent of value cut out of the once impregnable sterling coinage. It had been fully expected that a Labour government would have the required leverage to keep the discontented workers in line. But a seamen's strike that had been inherited from the earlier regime dragged on with mounting bitterness that sapped the vitality of the economy and created deeper fissures in the quarreling ranks of the Labour Party itself. All the bravado about the quick nationalization of steel had to be muted; the government could not command the support to see through any major reorganization of industry. Wilson found that he could keep his fractious party membership together only by grimly holding to middle positions. When he visited Moscow on one of his missions he smiled painfully at Kosygin's jibe: "Sometimes I think you joined the Labour Party to save it from socialism."

In foreign policy too, Wilson found that goodwill and eloquence were no substitute for political clout. Britain was faced with the threat of secession from Rhodesia when the stubborn quarrel over the rights of blacks reached an impasse. Wilson's most threatening admonitions, sanctions, and boycotts were defied by the Rhodesian Prime Minister and in the end it was Britain which had to retreat in humiliation. Wilson attempted to mediate the war that broke out between Pakistan and India in 1965, a war between two nations within the British Commonwealth, but he could not exert sufficiently effective authority, and it was the Soviet Union that brought about

* Cited in *The Reporter,* Nov. 5, 1964, p. 18.

the truce. In the Vietnam crisis, Wilson faced open revolt from the left wing of his party when he supported the American position. At a White House dinner the band committed the *faux pas* of playing "London Bridge Is Falling Down" and "I've Got Plenty of Nuthin'." The choice of numbers was inadvertent but it carried all too much truth.

By the end of 1969 many members of the party were calling for Wilson to step down. He found it difficult to appear in public without provoking hostile demonstrations. Yet there was not much more visible enthusiasm for the Tory leadership, and as the election of 1970 approached, the mood of the country seemed to be "a plague on both your houses." The polls indicated that, since there was little to choose between the two parties, Labour would probably be returned. The election brought out the smallest proportion of voters in forty years, and this factor, compounding the unpopularity of Labour, created the upset victory of the Tories. Edward Heath took office in 1970, and within a few weeks he was so engulfed in problems, old and new, that he must have wondered what an easygoing bachelor with a yen for a quiet life was doing in the eye of the hurricane.

43

THE SATELLITES
CHALLENGE THE
SOVIET UNION

THE DEATH OF STALIN, IN MARCH 1953, ENDED A THIRTY-YEAR RULE during which the old tyrant had pursued his terror with such malevolence that a popular book in Italy referred to the "planet" Russia, as if it were indeed another world. Near the end, he had become completely paranoid, seeing plots against him everywhere, suspicious of everyone, especially those who had served him longest. "I trust no one," he told Khrushchev, "not even myself."* Apparently, in his last months he was making ready for another all-inclusive purge to liquidate the leaders closest to him. It was of this hopeless period that Orwell had written, "If you want a picture of the future, imagine a boot stamping on a human face, forever." Then Stalin died, perhaps helped along to his death by those who felt the threat of his mania terribly near.

There were two views as to the policy that ought now to be followed. One urged the retention of the rigid dictatorship. Of course the most obnoxious forms of tyranny could be eliminated—the capricious executions, the mindless cruelty; these were really part of Stalin's illness. But to Molotov, Kaganovich, Voroshilov, and other unyielding hard-liners bred in the Stalinist tradition, it was deemed essential to keep intact the massive apparatus of intimidation to ensure stability at home and in the satellite states.

* Nikita Khrushchev, *Khrushchev Remembers* (Boston: Little, Brown, 1970), p. 307.

The other view insisted that it was an ideal moment to take advantage of Stalin's death to modify the tight dictatorship. The essential features of the Communist dogma would remain, the one-party monopoly, the censorship of press and speech, the Marxian economic structure. But the plug in the spout could be, must be, removed, to permit freer discussion, less inhibited literary and artistic expression. It was especially important to loosen the constraints on nationalist feeling in the satellite states, where the restlessness was building up to dangerous tension levels. This was the view of Malenkov, who had become the titular head of the government in the period immediately following the death of Stalin. It was also the view of Nikita Khrushchev who, though still in the background, was rising fast in the hierarchy.

At the outset, the revisionist view prevailed. The cabal in charge moved quickly to make sure that there would be no return to the Stalinist cult of personality. Malenkov was to be an equal among equals, a kind of chairman of the board. In this new climate people breathed easier. For years, even the most highly placed had operated in sullen silence in what was called *"Perestrovkofka,"* super-insurance, where none dared to risk open dissent, where safety demanded servility and the avoidance of any involvement. Now the incubus was partially lifted. Ilya Ehrenburg caught this spirit of release in his novel, *The Thaw,* and the title became the name for this interregnum period. Ehrenburg had his characters speak with unaccustomed frankness of the poverty of life under Stalin, its intellectual and emotional sterility, the risks of the slightest dissent. One said: "We have taken a lot of trouble over one-half of the human being, but the other half is neglected . . . and, in essence, men live in emotional slums." It was not a very good novel. One critic wrote: "It was Piltdown prose, primitive and phony." But the very fact that it could appear and could criticize the established order was significant.

It was not, however, until February 1956 at the historic 20th Congress of the Communist Party in Moscow that the lid was blown off. Nikita Khrushchev, inching his way to leadership, now felt secure enough to go all the way in the denunciation of the excesses of the Stalinist dictatorship. In a closed session that went on for hours, in twenty thousand words of withering recrimination, he detailed how much Stalin had besmirched the ideals of communism by his senseless murders, his criminal barbarism, his fantastic errors of judgment. He was careful to pay tribute to Stalin's earlier contributions, in the days when the Soviet Union was fighting to survive, and he reiterated his faith in the validity of the Communist program. But, he noted, the abuses of Stalin's capricious despotism had made *him* the chief enemy of the Communist cause.

The tirade stunned the veteran Stalinists. To them, no matter how reprehensible Stalin's conduct had become, such an attack before the assembled delegates, who could not possibly keep it secret, was suicidal. It was bound to undermine party discipline in Russia and to create dissension in the rank and file of the Communist parties around the world. But Khrushchev had accurately gauged the mood of the assembly. Virtually every delegate had, in some way, been victimized by Stalin's evil eye. None had ever felt safe, especially in the last years when Stalin was in the final throes of his dementia. They cheered Khrushchev, and the attack established him as one of the dominant forces in the Soviet Union.

The dismal predictions of the old guard were quickly fulfilled. De-Stalinization may have cleared the air for the routines of government in the Soviet Union, but it released long-pent-up forces in the satellite countries that were already churning with repressed alienation. Among the faithful there was confusion. If so much horror could be practiced by the revered symbol of communism, how reliable could anything be in the Communist gospel? If yesterday's gods become today's villains, if yesterday's executed could become today's martyred victims, then it was quite possible that today's truths could become tomorrow's lies. Here was a dilemma to trouble deeply the loyal Communists. As for those to whom communism was an imposed terror, they were quick to seize upon de-Stalinization as a golden opportunity to burst through the restraints. Nowhere was the effect of Khrushchev's Congress assault more immediately challenging than in Poland and Hungary. The impasse there was so serious that Soviet control was never again to be the same.

The Soviet domination of Poland had been established in the last days of World War II. Stalin had then made sure that the government was not only in the hands of Communists, but that they were Communists who would do the Russian bidding. In the decade that followed, there were frequent purges that flushed out both the surviving nationalist leaders and the Communists who might place their Polish loyalty above their subservience to the Soviet Union. But neither the purges nor the litmus tests of loyalty could eliminate all the intransigents and, now that de-Stalinization had become official Soviet policy, many of them decided to surface. They found a tenacious spokesman for nationalist communism in Wladislaw Gomulka, and he was to become the key to Polish history in the next fifteen years.

Gomulka was born in 1905, the son of an oil worker who had migrated to the United States but had returned with the family to his native Poland after disillusionment with early-twentieth-century America. Young Gomulka, who began working at fourteen as a blacksmith's apprentice, was equally repelled by the semi-feudal order of Poland and was an early convert to communism. His view of life and opportunity was perhaps influenced by recurrent illness, a frail constitution, a debilitating lung ailment, the nagging pain of a knee that carried a bullet. He was often jailed during the Polish independence period between the two world wars. When the Nazis invaded Poland in 1939 and established their dominance, Gomulka became part of the resistance. After the abortive uprising in 1944 that decimated so many of his comrades, he managed to escape to Russia and remained there until Stalin set up the Soviet-controlled government for Poland. Gomulka was named Deputy Prime Minister and he was assigned responsibility for anchoring communism in the annexed western provinces that had been taken over from Germany.

Gomulka proved at this stage to be a very unreliable Soviet surrogate. Though a loyal Communist, he would not cooperate in treating his native Poland as a milch cow for Russian exploitation. "The struggle for social emancipation," he declared, "cannot be separated from the struggle for national emancipation . . . I fought the Nazis. I will not allow Poland to become the 17th Soviet Republic." With such convictions, openly expressed, Gomulka was soon serving a long prison sentence on charges of Titoism. No amount of brainwashing could break him, and he was slated for execution when Stalin died in 1953. He was released soon after and, to his astonishment, he found himself to be something of a national hero, the symbol of opposition to Soviet domination. He became the rallying point for those who insisted that the national interest must be the primary objective of government.

In the years of the Thaw, the Polish Communists bided their time and made only minor attempts to obtain more flexibility in fulfilling the national interest. After Khrushchev's sensational attack on Stalinism in 1956, and the timely death, two weeks later, of the Stalinist hack who had ruled Poland, party discipline was severely strained. There were workers' riots in June in Poznań. They were quickly squelched but the growing restlessness became alarming to the Kremlin. In October the Polish party leaders insisted that Gomulka be brought in as the new Premier, and Khrushchev knew that he had a major crisis on his hands. It was one thing to permit the loosening of tyranny; it was quite another to permit outright defiance of the Soviet regulation of a satellite state.

The challenge was serious enough for Khrushchev to fly to Warsaw, with a battery of Soviet officials, to compel submission. The Polish party headmen met the Soviet delegation at the airport. When Khrushchev spotted Gomulka among them, he turned purple with rage. He bellowed his insults without restraint, calling Gomulka a traitor, accusing him of complicity with the Fascist gangsters and threatening the direst consequences if there was any further challenge to the Soviet Union's position. "We have shed our blood," he raged, "to liberate this country, and now you wish to hand it over to the Americans." The confrontation went on for four days. Yet, though a contingent of the Soviet fleet was anchored just off Gdynia, and though Soviet army units had encircled all of Warsaw, neither Gomulka nor his colleagues were intimidated. They insisted that the Soviet troops must be withdrawn from Poland, that General Rokosovsky, who had been sent in from Russia to head up the Polish Defense Ministry, would have to resign. They demanded the authority to modify the economy of the country, especially the highly unpopular collectivization program in agriculture. Gomulka made it clear that if the Soviet Union attempted a military coup he would arm the workers of Warsaw for resistance. Khrushchev stormed and threatened further. But when he had convinced himself that repression would precipitate a Communist civil war and that, though the Russians would undoubtedly win out in a showdown, it would be a Pyrrhic victory, he made the best of the situation. Gomulka was recognized as the head of the Polish state and the national party demands were virtually all granted. A special concordat was negotiated with Cardinal Wyszynski which protected the Catholic educational system.

Gomulka had faced down the successor of Stalin in what was thereafter referred to jubilantly as the Polish October. Poland was still a satellite, but its orbit was no longer determined exclusively by the Soviet Union. Next day, when word of the triumph became known, the great Warsaw Square filled up with a quarter million cheering and weeping people who hailed Gomulka's settlement as the restoration of national pride.

It was more of a compromise than an outright victory. Gomulka's defiance was not anti-Communist: it was pro-Polish. It did not go as far as Tito's defiances of the Soviet Union which, while confirming Communist identification, repudiated any Soviet jurisdiction in Yugoslavia. Gomulka gave explicit assurances to Khrushchev that Poland was a loyal part of the Communist bloc. When he faced the cheering masses in the great square, he announced that Soviet troops would, after all, stay on in Poland, and that they were indispensable to protect the country against possible German resurgence. The cheers died quickly when he made the announcement. But sober second thought must have brought the realization that, while the confrontation with Khrushchev had won a measure of autonomy for Poland, this autonomy had been achieved only because Poland remained an integral part of the Soviet family. From the point of view of the Soviet Union, it was also a realistic compromise because, as the years passed, though Poland followed its own interpretation of communism, Gomulka strenuously supported and protected the Soviet tie.

A simultaneous rebellion in Hungary meantime proved to be a much more serious menace to the entire Soviet satellite structure. Communist control in Hungary had been precarious from the beginning of the Soviet takeover in 1945. It had been imposed in the teeth of the bitterest opposition. The Russian-trained Communists who were used by the Soviets to maintain their control were the most hated men in the country. They could function only because they sat on Russian bayonets. The de-Stalinization process was therefore welcomed by the Hungarian people as providing an opening wedge for much more than a few superficial reforms.

On October 23, 1956, word came through of the Polish October, and of the successful defiance of the Russians by an unarmed, virtually defenseless nation, that stood its ground and won a large measure of autonomy. The effect was galvanic. Hundreds of students marched to the Polish Embassy to express their solidarity with the Poles. Circulars appeared, denouncing the Russian occupation and reminding the nation of its heritage of freedom. The Communist Council hurriedly issued a ban on further mass protests, but the ban was ignored and the historic Parliament Square was quickly filled beyond capacity with defiant demonstrators. The secret police, the AVH, panicked and the crowd was fired upon. Hundreds were killed and injured, and "The Massacre," as it was termed, converted the protest into a rebellion. In the square stood the 25-foot-high statue of Stalin that had, through the years of repression, been the symbol of the national humiliation. It was now toppled and smashed, the massive head, with a traffic signal protruding through it, lying in the street, spat upon by the passers-by. The remnants of the statue were steadily chipped away as if the outraged Hungarians wished to leave no trace of their degradation. When Hungarian flags were hoisted, and it was noted that the Russian hammer and sickle had been cut out of the design, the crowd went into a frenzy. A young actor appeared on a balcony and began reciting the ancestral poem: "Up on your feet, Hungarians, the country calls,"* and the crowd roared in refrain: "We swear, we swear by the God of the Hungarians that we shall no longer be slaves." Many of the members of the AVH were hunted down and lynched. The long-imprisoned primate of the Catholic church, Cardinal Mindszenty, made a triumphant entry into Budapest, as the bells of all the churches pealed out their welcome for him. The "peace priests," who had collaborated with the regime and the secret police, were ousted. When demonstrations spread through other parts of the country, the Communist Council called out the army units. But by now most of the troops had also been caught up in the mass contagion and they refused to fight the demonstrators. Instead, they distributed their weapons to them and fraternized with them. Completely rattled, the Council called upon the Russians to hurry reinforcements. But Khrushchev was not yet sure that invasion was the wisest course and he temporized and stretched the negotiations.

As in Poland, a more acceptable Communist leader, Imre Nagy, was recalled from prison to take over responsibility. Nagy had been a lifelong Communist, trained in the Moscow School, part of the Communist apparatus that had come into power at the end of World War II. Like Gomulka, he had fallen out of favor because he would not go all the way in subordinating the national Hungarian interest to the Soviet. He had therefore been expelled from the party and had remained in prison until the death of Stalin. He had then been rehabilitated and he was now drafted, on October 24, to come into a new coalition government as Prime Minister. The Russians hoped that his popularity would damp down the revolutionary zeal and make it unnecessary to resort to more strenuous efforts to contain it.

Nagy was not a strong character, and he had little enthusiasm for the more extreme position in which he found himself. He was eager to eliminate the worst features of the dictatorship in Hungary,

* Pitof's "Arise Hungarians!"

but not to undermine and repudiate Soviet authority. Yet he was pushed steadily into ever more radical action that he had never originally intended. When he was rushed to the balcony in Parliament Square on the night when the resistance had been ignited, he began his address with the conventional salutation, "Comrades." He was bewildered as hundreds of those massed below him angrily shouted back: "No—we are *not* Comrades!"

Yet, since Nagy was now the national spokesman, he dutifully presented the demands as they were formulated by his new cabinet and, since the Russians were anxious to restrict the controversy to inner Communist reforms, they made a number of surprising concessions. The Soviet Foreign Minister went so far as to admit that there had been "unfortunate bureaucratic errors," and that they would be corrected. It was agreed that the hated AVH would be disbanded, that the occupying Russian forces would be gradually recalled, that reforms would be instituted to eliminate the major discontent. The concessions simply accelerated the momentum of a revolution that could no longer be braked. The demands now reached into dangerous forbidden areas. On November 1, Nagy, still spurred by his colleagues, denounced the Warsaw Pact and indicated that Hungary must be given the neutral status that had been granted to Austria.

The new demands meant that Hungary planned to secede from the Communist bloc. If this were permitted there would undoubtedly be pressure from other satellite states, and the power structure throughout eastern Europe would be catastrophically transformed. In Poland the requests had all fitted into the framework of a loyal Communist state, allied to the Soviet. Here what was contemplated was clear defection. Khrushchev made ready for the kill. Some ameliorative promises were offered to gain time; simultaneously a quarter million army troops were moved to the borders of Hungary, backed up by hundreds of paratroops and forty-five hundred tanks.

On November 4 the Russians invaded in full force. The Hungarians fought back—students, workers, women, children—taking the full brunt of Soviet massed strength. There were teen-agers lugging rifles almost bigger than themselves, who helped to man the barricades. Children threw themselves on the Russian tanks and were mowed down. The slaughter went on for nearly a week, leaving thirty-five thousand casualties, and few prisoners were taken. Every public place soon had its hanged victims to warn the populace of the punishments to come.

[525]

For years Dulles had been using brave phrases, "Roll back," "Liberation." For months Radio Free Europe had been urging the Hungarians to rise up against their oppressors. The Freedom Fighters, hemmed in on all sides, waited in anguish for the Americans to back up their eloquent exhortations. They hardly expected actual intervention, but they hoped that the kind of pressure that had been applied by the American government against the British, the French, and the Israelis in the Suez attack of the previous week, and that had compelled withdrawal, would be applied here. But all that came out of the White House, on the eve of the national election, was a message from Eisenhower praising the Freedom Fighters for their bravery and their gallantry. Nagy, who had been ousted in the rebellion, appealed to the United Nations to intervene. In the session that was hastily convened, the vote to request Russian withdrawal was 50 to 8, but no action could follow since the Russian veto prevented it. There had also been a considerable number of abstentions, notably from the Indian delegation, which was instructed by Nehru to remember that the Hungarian suppression was "a domestic matter." Inevitably the rebellion of the poorly armed, unorganized, unaided people was drowned out in blood. Khrushchev had vowed that Communist control would not be relinquished in the areas that were crucial to Russian security. He had added grimly that those who expected a different policy might better wait "until a shrimp learns to whistle." In disposing of the rebellion in Hungary, he was no longer the Khrushchev of the Thaw nor the apostle of coexistence. He was once again the hangman of the Ukraine. Thousands of Freedom Fighters died under his guns and his tanks and on his gallows. Two hundred thousand fled the country, most of them to neutral Austria; many of them later migrated to the United States.

Some of the rebel leaders who remained behind sought asylum in the Yugoslavian Embassy. The new Prime Minister, Janos Kadar, who had cooperated with Nagy until the Soviet invasion, offered a safe-conduct to Nagy and his colleagues. He sent his written word that his government had no intention of taking any punitive action, and that therefore his former comrades could go freely to their homes. They took Kadar at his word and emerged from the sanctuary of the Embassy. But as they attempted to enter a waiting car they were abducted by Kadar's agents and shipped off to Rumania. Later they were returned to Hungary, where, after a long prison wait of two years, there was a secret trial for treason; months afterwards, the world learned that they had all been executed.

The dangerous crises had been successfully contained in both Poland and Hungary. Yet the rebellions left their mark on the position of the Soviet Union. The clear warning had been sounded for the Kremlin that its foreign military contingents could not be trusted. There were one and a half million of them that policed the satellite countries of the Baltic and the Balkans. In the crunch, if there were war, these troops might as easily fight against the Russians as with them. Certainly it would not be wise to place sophisticated weapons in their hands. Khrushchev would not soon forget the experience in which Hungarian soldiers turned over their guns to the demonstrators.

The Russians also learned that though concentrated Communist indoctrination had been applied for more than a decade in the satellite countries—in their schools, their clubs, their press, their rallies, their party conclaves—the subject peoples had not been won over. The uprisings in Poland and in Hungary were triggered by the youth, the industrial workers, the intellectuals, the very groups that had been most persistently exposed to the benefits of Russian paternalism.

Again, the world, and especially the nonaligned peoples of Asia and Africa, had been shown the ugly vindictiveness of the Soviet state. The punitive action was not taken against the reviled capitalists, nor against the bourgeoisie. It was the workers and their families who were shot down or ground under tanks. The propaganda that had been most common during the period of decolonization had painted the democracies as the heartless imperialists. Now the goodwill painfully established in the former colonial areas was in jeopardy. Albert Camus wrote that this kind of Marxism, the Kremlin brand, brought on nausea. "It was a dish with really too much blood in the sauce."

Above all, the myth of the Communist monolith, which had withstood the defiance of Tito, could not withstand the eruptions in Poland and Hungary. In a few years it would be irretrievably repudiated by the hostility of Red China. The Soviet Union would be compelled hereafter to live with many varieties of communism, in which the peoples, even in the Soviet orbit, would inevitably place their national interest above their Communist affiliation.

All these were the ultimate consequences of the revolutionary defiance. For the moment, however, it created no lasting problem for the chameleon temperament of Khrushchev. In the book entitled *Khrushchev Remembers*, which may or not have been wholly written by him, but which surely represented his thought processes, he described the Hungarian episode as the repayment of a debt that Russia owed to Hungary. He remembered that, in 1848, Hungarians had sought to win their freedom, but the Czarist legions had crushed the rebellion. In 1956 the Fascist saboteurs had sought to rob the Hungarians of their Communist freedom. The Russians had then come to the aid of the loyal, endangered Hungarians. He added: "Our country owed a historic debt to the people of Hungary. In 1956, we finally paid it off. Now we're even."*

* Khrushchev, *Khrushchev Remembers,* p. 429.

44

THE ORDEAL OF
GREECE

BY OCTOBER 1944, AS WORLD WAR II WAS BEGINNING TO WIND DOWN, with little doubt that the Allied victory was near, Winston Churchill journeyed to Moscow to discuss the outstanding problems of peace with Stalin. In his Memoirs Churchill described with frankness how he proposed a realistic settlement for the Balkans. "Don't let us get at cross-purposes in small ways," he said. He then passed a sheet of paper to Stalin with figures scribbled on it, noting that the Soviet Union should have 90 percent predominance in Rumania, 75 percent in Bulgaria, 50 percent in Yugoslavia and Hungary, and that Britain should have 90 percent predominance in Greece. After Stalin had heard the translation he took a blue pencil and placed a check mark by the figures. Churchill added, "It was all settled in no more time than it takes to set down."*

Stalin must have had tongue in cheek when he so casually used the blue pencil. Even before the Axis powers had surrendered the Soviet Union had 100 percent of Rumania and Hungary and, until the break with Tito in 1948, Yugoslavia too was very much in tow. Stalin could afford to pass up Greece for the time being, relying on the strongly organized Communist Party and its guerrilla units there to win control of the country when circumstances were favorable. The poor bloodied land, already worn to despair by the war and the Nazi occupation, was to be further devastated by years of civil strife.

* Churchill, *Memoirs of the Second World War*, pp. 885 ff.

Greece had been one of the early victims of World War II. At first Hitler had no intention of committing Nazi troops for its forcible occupation. But his Axis partner, Mussolini, had dreams of imperial glory, and Greece seemed to be an easy prey. Without informing Hitler of his plans, Mussolini launched an invasion through Albania, in October 1940, and, with superior numbers and matériel, he expected that the conquest would be completed before the rigors of winter set in.

The Greeks resisted with a valor that astonished the world. They routed the Italians, drove them back, and then went on the offensive, while the British bombed the Italian navy and immobilized it. Mussolini's shabby adventure in Greece turned into an irretrievable disaster, from which neither he nor his Fascist regime recovered. The threat from the southern flank became so serious that Hitler, who was learning fast that it was safer to have Mussolini as an enemy than as an ally, was obliged to send in substantial Nazi forces which he had planned to use elsewhere. Once the Nazi war machine moved into Greece, neither the courage and will of the Greeks nor the British reinforcements were sufficient to cope with the Luftwaffe and the panzers. By the beginning of 1941, the swastika went up on the Acropolis.

The Nazi occupation lasted about three years and they comprised perhaps the darkest period in the modern history of Greece. Hitler requisitioned resources and supplies with no concern for the fate of the population in a country that, even in normal times, was obliged to import most of its food. Famine and disease decimated virtually every family. When the Underground fought back with sabotage and ambush and tied down 120,000 troops, whole villages were razed, and there were fifty executions of Greek hostages for every Nazi casualty.

The war turned against the Nazis in 1944, and it was then that Churchill and Stalin struck their bargain for the future of the Balkans. But the agony for Greece was destined to be prolonged. Stalin's blue pencil had ratified Churchill's plan for spheres of influence, but the Communists in Greece were unwilling to submit to the old order. They had carried the brunt of the resistance during the war and the occupation years. Their forces were the strongest and the best organized. They drew little distinction between Hitler or Mussolini and Churchill or King George. For them, liberation was still to be achieved; their battle was only a continuation of the struggle against the Germans and the Italians.

They were commanded by one of the most resourceful of the postwar guerrilla leaders, General Markos, who was able to sustain the resistance through four years. Markos drew his main manpower support from the party faithful. But he had indispensable collaboration from the neighboring Communist states—Bulgaria, Yugoslavia, Albania. From them came arms and equipment, and there the guerrillas established training bases and found sanctuary when they were flushed out of their mountain redoubts. The Communists might have won out. Few realized how close they were to victory even as late as 1949. Greece as a western bastion was saved only because the British were determined that the peninsula, with its strategic control of the eastern Mediterranean, must not fall to the Communists.

But in February 1947, having spent a quarter of a billion dollars to shore up the defense of the Greek loyalists, and now deep in their own economic problems, the British announced to the American government that they could no longer continue the support that held the Communists at bay. President Truman then agreed to take over the responsibility, and in March he received the enthusiastic endorsement of Congress for what became known as the Truman Doctrine, a pledge that the United States would offer help wherever the life of a free nation was threatened by aggression. The United States contributed about three-quarters of a billion dollars for the final three years of guerrilla combat. But it was listed as an investment and it proved decisive. The resistance of the Communists tapered off and, as earlier noted, when the break between Tito and Stalin came in 1948 and Tito closed the frontier to the shipment of arms to the guerrillas, the civil war came to an end.* Its cost to Greece was as great as in the tormented years of World War II and the Nazi occupation. Both sides had fought without mercy. When the Communists retreated, they usually took hostages with them. They kidnapped twenty-five thousand children who were brought for indoctrination to camps in Bulgaria and Albania and most of them were never heard of again. In the next generation it was a common sight, in every city and town of Greece, to encounter the legless, the armless, the blind. A million Greeks had been uprooted and when American and U.N.R.R.A. relief officials began their tasks of reconstruction, they found tens of thousands of bewildered families on the edge of their burned and wrecked villages, aimless, distraught, mourning their dead or their missing. The UN reported that the

* See Chapter 20.

Communists had inflicted forty-seven thousand casualties in the first two years after World War II ended, then another fifty thousand up to 1949; their own losses must have reached half a million. Virtually all the casualties were Greeks, killed by Greeks. After the civil war, the purges and the bloodletting did not stop, for the executions were planned equally as reprisals and punishments for the past and as a warning for the future.

After the liberation, even though a civil war was brewing, the first popular elections were held in March 1946. The center groups and the conservatives won a two-thirds majority in the Parliament. The Establishment, though, could not yet congratulate itself as vindicated since the Communists had called for a boycott, and they and their secret sympathizers had stayed away from the polls. But a special plebiscite was held in September on the future of the monarchy and King Paul, who had headed the government-in-exile in London, received 69 percent of the vote, and was recalled.

It was inevitable that the first few years of comparative peace should be influenced by the passions of the civil war period. The Prime Ministers and the cabinets were all drawn from the old order. Their overriding objective was to make sure that there would be no revival of Communist power. Basic reforms were critically needed after the dislocations and the deprivations of the past decade. Such reforms might have been an effective antidote to weaken the Communist appeal. But the successive governments decided it was safer to rely on repression, and hence there was a moratorium on reform.

Equally disheartening to the liberal rank and file was the return of the old-style politicians who came trooping back. There was a tradition of sacrificial patriotism among the common people. They had resisted fascism when Mussolini invaded; they had resisted Hitler until they were pulverized by his powerful war machine. But they could not defend themselves against the hacks who treated government as a reservoir for jobs and nepotism and profiteering. Thucydides had written of them two thousand years earlier and had laid many of the ills of classical Greece at their barter counter. The breed had not changed very much through the centuries. It was because of them that the maxim was current: "After shaking hands with a Greek, count your fingers."

The most pressing problem was the care of more than seven hundred thousand refugees, most of whom had flooded into the cities when their homes had been destroyed. There was need also to rebuild almost completely the transportation system of the country

—the railroads, the airports, the canals, the highways, the bridges—all blasted by the invaders and by the Greeks themselves during the years of conflict. The underwriting for the tasks of reconstruction came primarily from the American aid funds. When the emergency programs had been completed, the ruling officials turned to the modernization of agriculture, the erection of new factories, and the revival of the merchant marine. Once the wheels of commerce and industry began turning, the exports of tobacco, currants, and olives reached their prewar levels.

But the revival would have come more quickly, and the impact would have been more far-reaching, if there had not been so much waste and graft. The bureaucracy and the political bagmen all had their sticky fingers in Uncle Sam's largesse. One of the American supervisors said grimly, "Never have so few asked for so much, and done so little with it." But, at least, Greece was on the way to recovery, and it was a happy augury that tourism again flourished and the visitors again crowded the historic and artistic points of interest.

Then, in 1959, Greece was convulsed by one of the perennial problems that had tormented the Mediterranean world and that now clamored for resolution—the fate and freedom of Cyprus. It was a remote little island nestling under the mainland of Turkey, part of the British Commonwealth, with about half a million population, 80 percent Greek and 20 percent Turkish. There in legend the lovely goddess Aphrodite rose from the sea, but the history of the island told of little save friction between the two peoples, whose hamlets and villages were so intermingled that even partition was not a practical solution. To the Greek Cypriots, the objective was *enosis*, union with Greece, integration with the Motherland whose language, religion, and cultural traditions were a common heritage. The Turkish Cypriots, with memories of humiliating minority experiences, vowed that they would resist to the end any such union with Greece. They were sure that despite any protective pledges made, *enosis* would drive them deeper into minority dependence. Turkey, of course, sided with its compatriots, not only as their guardian but because of the fear that Greece, erratic in its politics, might some day be taken over by its Communists. The threat had been barely escaped after World War II. Turkey could not permit a Communist base on its southern flank when it was already menaced on the north by the Soviet Union itself. It remembered the old Turkish proverb: "An open door invites callers." As for Britain,

Cyprus was a strategic fortress to protect its east Mediterranean interests.

After World War II, the Greek-Cypriot agitation focused first on getting the British out and leadership in this thrust for independence was taken by the Greek Orthodox primate of Cyprus, Archbishop Makarios. He was an ordained priest, but he could be a very worldly figure too, as the canniest diplomats soon discovered in negotiations with him. He was a consummate politician—wary, stubborn, quite adroit in using the clerical office to win advantage. He could preach with the fervor of an evangelist, but he could manage affairs with the shrewdness of a tycoon. Indeed, he conducted a thriving wine business for the church with substantial profit.

Makarios (Mikhail Christedoulos Mouskos) was born in Athens in 1913. His family had planned from the outset for him to become a priest. He was enrolled in a monastery school at thirteen, and then studied theology at the University of Athens. He received a fellowship to Boston University and filled a Greek Orthodox pulpit in Lowell, Massachusetts. In 1950 he was called back to Cyprus as archbishop, and he was at once involved in the struggle to eliminate the British control of the island. He cooperated fully with the guerrilla bands, which proved as ruthless and intractable as any of the rebel groups that the British were then fighting in many other parts of the world. The British denounced him, the man of God, whose name meant blessing, for condoning terror that included murder and reprisal. Makarios became such an affliction to the British that they deported him to the Seychelles Islands in the Indian Ocean.

The rebel leadership was then assumed by another Cypriot firebrand, General George Grivas, who had fought bravely against the Nazis and had been invaluable to the British in their struggle to prevent a Communist takeover in Greece. Grivas, now charged to drive the British out of Cyprus, returned the honors they had bestowed on him and fought them with a fury that took an ever-mounting toll. Living in caves and under cellar floors, escaping capture and death miraculously, he became a folk hero. He attacked with no compunction, cruel when he felt that he had to be, drawing the British into bloody ambush, killing, executing, counting on attrition to compel them to yield. He said, "To shoot down your enemies in the street may be unprecedented, but I am looking for results, and not precedents." By 1959 the British reluctantly concluded that the struggle was jeopardizing larger interests. It involved pledged NATO allies—Britain, Greece, and Turkey—and the effectiveness of the eastern anchor point of NATO was being challenged. Prime Minister Macmillan therefore called for negotiations and the historic conference was held in London in March 1959 with representatives from Turkey, Greece, and the Cypriot rivals. Makarios was recalled from exile and joined the deliberations as an honored negotiator.

The conference, almost as a portent, began with tragedy. In a thick London fog the plane bringing in the premier of Turkey, Adnan Menderes, and his key cabinet colleagues crashed at the airport. Many of the passengers were killed and Menderes himself was severely injured. But the issues were too pressing for further delay. The conference went forward and Menderes signed for his country in his hospital room.

The agreement that emerged gave independence to Cyprus, with membership in the British Commonwealth. It called for a Greek Cypriot as President, a Turkish Cypriot as Vice President, and a Parliament that would reflect the 80–20 population proportion on the island. To protect the 20 percent minority, it was stipulated that the Vice President would always have veto power over any legislation that vitally affected the interest of the Turkish population. The British were to retain two bases on the island but were to have no executive authority. The large troop contingents of Greece and Turkey were to be reduced to token forces of a few hundred.

The emotional stake of Greece in Cyprus was demonstrated by the hysterical salute in Athens that Makarios and Grivas received. A quarter of a million people cheered Grivas; many must have marveled that the gaunt haggard figure of Grivas could have been the scourge that had brought capitulation from the British Commonwealth. The Archbishop of Athens presented Grivas with the traditional silver laurel. "Your name," he said, "is a Doric column in the Parthenon of the great heroes of our glorious nation." Grivas, weeping unabashedly, offered the mayor of Athens a bag of earth from his mountain retreat. "This bit of soil," he said, "soaked with the blood of Cypriot fighters, will be the link between Cyprus and Greece." The welcome to Makarios was even more tumultuous. The modern Greeks had savored all too few occasions of national triumph and they made the most of an opportunity that salved pride and honor. Makarios pledged that, though technical *enosis* had not been fulfilled, Cyprus, so precious to Greece, "was united with it in spirit and always would be." He referred to the settlement as a historic fulfillment and "the resurrection of our country."

Makarios became President of Cyprus and his actions very quickly reduced the agreement to an uneasy truce. The Turkish population fretted and fumed over what they considered his continuous discrimination in the use of tax funds, allocations for education, employment, public construction. In 1963 violence flared, and Turkey actually strafed Greek-Cypriot positions. The resentments simmered, then boiled, and in 1967, when Makarios attempted to eliminate the Turkish veto, full-scale war was threatened. The climate of forbearance was not improved when Grivas was sent by Makarios into Turkish villages to restore order. Schooled in guerrilla warfare, sensitive diplomacy was not Grivas's forte. One of the rebellious villages had changed its name from Greek to Turkish, and there were acts, mainly symbolic, that Grivas interpreted as provocation and defiance. During a punitive assignment, twenty-four Turkish Cypriots were killed.

Turkey, outraged by what it termed a "massacre," now decided that Greek provocation had gone as far as could any longer be tolerated. It authorized mobilization and prepared to attack. President Lyndon Johnson, alarmed over the disruptive conflict within the NATO alliance, knew that the time had passed for half-measures. He sent over Cyrus Vance, a Defense Department executive, and after several plain-spoken sessions, with the Turkish forces poised for bombardment, the Greek government yielded.

The pledge was given that there would be an end even to indirect activity to achieve *enosis*. The last military and political ties to Greece were cut. Many of the Greek nationalists, led by Grivas, protested that this was an abject surrender, that Greece had been humiliated. But the free world breathed easier as at least this potentiality for disaster was defused. No one could penetrate the inner feelings of Makarios, but there were strong suspicions that he too was very much relieved. He had paid lip service to the objective of *enosis* but, in the decade since Cyprus had won its freedom from Britain, he often showed how much he preferred that the Cypriot tie with politically turbulent Greece remain symbolic. That he had become militantly Cypriot and resented the slightest Greek intrusion became clear by 1972 when Athens ordered that a shipment of arms from Czechoslovakia be turned over to the Greek command. And Grivas was in hiding once more on the island, but this time in the interest of *enosis*. Keeping up with the convolutions of Balkan politics required all five senses for alertness and several more for intuition.

Meantime there were new problems for Greece that threatened its survival as a democracy. All through the 1960's, the liberal and radical forces had been growing increasingly restive because few of the reforms in government tended to go beyond superficial tinkering. The leader of the opposition was George Papandreou, one of the oldest and most durable of the liberals, who hoped now to climax a stormy political career with a crusade for a new deal for Greece. In the election of 1963 he achieved a very narrow plurality, but in the following year he was returned with the largest popular vote of any election since World War II. He counted the victory as a mandate for the reforms that he had advocated, but he had to move carefully. The old King died soon after the election and the views of his successor, twenty-three-year-old Constantine, were unknown. The military and the security forces had always been linked with the extreme right wing. Greece was the only country in Europe where no attempt had been made, after the Germans had been defeated, to clear the pro-Nazis and the collaborationists out of the ranks and officers' corps. Papandreou was convinced that neither the military nor the security forces could be counted upon to protect constitutional procedures. He therefore began to shake up the senior ranks, retiring or transferring those whom he considered unreliable. The army officers knew full well what the old fox was up to. They planned their counterattack with precision, and by 1967 they were ready.

Their brilliantly executed coup used a blueprint that had been held in secret reserve by NATO in case of a threatened Communist bid for power. The tanks that rolled into prepared positions had all been part of the NATO arsenal. The "spring cleaning," so called, that followed, was thorough. Hundreds of the liberal and radical leaders who were unable to flee were rounded up and jailed. Since Papandreou's son, Andrea, was in the United States, his name was placed on the prosecution list in absentia. Freedom of press and assembly was severely restricted. The judiciary was ordered to follow the dictated political line. Strikes were outlawed. The Junta announced that parliamentary institutions would be suspended until stability had been restored. There was to be stern screening of art exhibitions and plays and music "that transgressed the canons of good taste and classical Greek dignity." Melina Mercouri, the popular and beloved actress who was touring the United States, denounced the dictatorship and was stripped of her citizenship for having "lost her soul and her conscience." When old George Papandreou died and there was a demonstration at the funeral, forty of the demonstrators were arrested and given long prison terms.

King Constantine found himself caught in a vice. He had opposed the projected reforms of Papandreou because they went too far. But he was equally opposed to the Junta that bludgeoned its way to dictatorial power. For a few months he bided his time, working secretly, or so he thought, with conservative ministers whom he believed that he could trust. Then he too tried a coup, using the techniques of the Junta.

But military coups are not for amateurs. Everything that Constantine planned and everything that he did seemed to go wrong. His preparations to win over loyal sectors of the army leaked out or were betrayed so that the Junta was thoroughly prepared. His radio broadcast to the Greek people, excoriating the Junta and announcing that he had assumed leadership, was jammed and failed to reach his expected audience. To escape capture the King and his family flew to Rome and, from there, he appealed again for popular support. The Junta managed the crisis with low-keyed professional calm. They expressed sympathy for the King for having been "misled" by bad advice, and invited him and his "well-loved little family" to come home. Then they added, deadpan, that he would be welcomed if he remembered the restricted role of a constitutional monarch. They continued to act in his royal name and although after a few months they named a Regent, they continued to send him his regular royal allowance.

The Junta took in stride the strictures and the cancellation of a multimillion-dollar loan by the European Economic Council. The United States at first refused to extend recognition, but the Junta's reaction was that just as soon as there was another Communist threat to NATO, the Americans would come begging the Junta to accept aid. Its intuition was sound. When the Soviet Union built up its strength in the eastern Mediterranean, though President Nixon still embargoed the shipment to Greece of jets and tanks, he permitted the flow of rifles, trucks, and spare parts—what the policy circles called the "rinky dink." When public protest in the United States mounted and Congress refused to appropriate the regularly assigned funds for military aid to Greece, the Junta resorted to nuisance and scaremongering byplays to fight back. In September 1971 General Grivas was seen in Cyprus again and the implication was clear—no money from the United States, then no peace in Cyprus and new problems for NATO.

The dilemma for the American policymakers was acute. The Truman Doctrine had pledged military protection where freedom was in jeopardy. The Greek Junta was indeed a dictatorship that was ruthless in suppression of Greek democracy. But the security of the eastern Mediterranean depended upon the NATO alliance and the Junta was pledged to cooperate in the surveillance. It was therefore considered safest by the Nixon administration to play for time.

There in 1972 Greece waited at the crossroads. The thirty-odd years since the Fascist invasion of 1940 had been a long nightmare— war with the Axis powers, occupation by the Nazis, civil strife when the Communists made their bid to control the future, the Cyprus crisis, and the dangerous confrontation with Turkey. Now came the overthrow of democratic institutions and the entrenchment of a dictatorship of the right, only two decades after Truman had rushed aid to Greece to save it from a dictatorship of the left. The fate of Greece was a concern that went far beyond the peninsula. Homer had described it with sadness but with pride as "a poor soil, but a mother of men." Those who breathed free had a stake in its destiny. Classical antiquity was part of their heritage: its art, its literature, its philosophy, its traditions of free government. When these were wounded, the whole free world bled.

45

CÁRDENAS AND CASTRO: TWO ROADS TO REVOLUTION

UNTIL EARLY IN THE TWENTIETH CENTURY THE LATIN AMERICAN continent was very little known to the European world, or even to the United States. History texts rarely included its story in the marshaling of significant developments. Will Rogers chuckled that the continent exported wheat and gigolos, and that America received the gigolos but could do better with the wheat. Most of the countries were in the grip of home-bred dictators who traded off the rights of their people to foreign interests that drew exorbitant profits from the abundant mineral, oil, and cattle resources. In rare instances, as in the Argentine or Uruguay, living standards, according to some economists, were higher than in Italy and even France. But in most countries, the plight of the workers and peasants was wretched. The Catholic church was powerfully entrenched but, far from protecting its charges from exploitation, it was usually allied with the foreign cartels or with the grandees who had acquired vast estates. The church leaders offered the cold comfort that there would ultimately be rewards in Heaven for long-suffering obedience on earth.*

The upheavals that transformed Africa and Asia inevitably also stimulated defiance of foreign economic control in the Latin American countries. But at first, the revolutionary zeal brought little relief

---

* From the Archbishop of Guadalajara: "Poor, love your humble state and your work; turn your gaze towards Heaven; there is the true wealth." Cited in Clarence Ollson Senior, *Land Reform and Democracy* (Gainesville, Fla.: University of Florida Press, 1958), p. 19.

to the disinherited and the dispossessed; only the pattern of exploitation changed. The men who rode to power on the *argumentum baculinum* and moved into the abandoned palaces were, in most instances, little more than gangsters. Juan Vicente Gómez, the Tyrant of the Andes, and Pérez Jiménez, who disguised his absolutism as the New National Ideal, had no concern for the plight of the people of Venezuela, and their decades of military rule were a nightmare of graft supported by assassination. The domination of Getulio Vargas of Brazil lasted a quarter of a century until the high-handed martinet committed suicide. Somoza of Nicaragua, Trujillo of the Dominican Republic, "Papa" Duvalier of Haiti, and the bizarre characters who were contemporaries, treated place and position as unparalleled opportunities to mulct a personal fief. They usually reserved secret Swiss bank accounts for the virtually unlimited plunder that was there for the taking. There were honorable exceptions, Batlle in Uruguay and Alessandri in Chile, but they could not do more than leave a temporary personal mark on the social landscape; Alessandri himself turned heavily reactionary at the end of his incumbency. Even a nation as sophisticated as the Argentine had to endure for more than a decade the charlatan team of Juan Perón and his Evita, and when he fled, he left behind a thoroughly exhausted and bankrupt state.

In two countries, however, Mexico and Cuba, a revolutionary leadership emerged that was genuinely dedicated to the transformation of the social order. The techniques of change that they instituted were markedly different in each, but they became the lenses through which the nations of Latin America could watch and learn.

Mexico was a very poor country, with little land that was cultivable, but its precious metals—gold, silver, copper, and iron—and its oil reserves gave it a trade potential that could have had significant impact on the national standard of living. Yet Mexico was identified as a "beggar sitting on a bag of gold," for most of its natural wealth was in mortgage to foreign concessionaires. Father Hidalgo led the struggle that won independence from Spain, Benito Juárez expelled the French who hoped to build a new empire in Mexico. But though both tried valiantly to include major social change in their revolutions, their people remained fixed in the "culture of poverty."* In mid-nineteenth century the United States invaded and annexed California, Texas, and other large sections of

---

* The phrase is Oscar Lewis's, and is the title of one of his books.

the Mexican heartland; in what remained, American and British investors obtained control of land and resources that ensured fabulous profits at the expense of the people. The jibe had it that Mexico was mother to the foreign interests, but stepmother to the Mexicans.

Many of the deals were negotiated with Porfirio Díaz, whose iron-fisted rule extended, with one brief four-year interlude, from 1876 to 1911. He was the loyal surrogate for the small group of *hacendados* who had title to most of the land. One family in Chihuahua owned twelve million acres; three brothers in Hidalgo owned the entire state. For the exploitation of the subsoil resources, Díaz authorized transactions with foreign cartels that conveyed millions of acres to them. The compensating bribes to Díaz were skillfully managed through the purchase by the cartels of his wife's holdings at inflated prices. When the expropriated peasants resisted they were butchered by his private police. But the reputation of Díaz for reliability and efficiency was respected in the capitals of the United States and Britain. He built the railroad system, made a start in the modernization of agriculture, and regularly paid off international accounts.

Mexican credit stood high too in the foreign exchanges. After all, "banditry" had been reduced, the land was quiet, business went forward peacefully, and the investment returns on American holdings of a billion and a half dollars were phenomenally rewarding. President Taft, whose brother was a director of one of the oil companies, visited Mexico City to offer a personal salute for the long Porfirian peace, and when Díaz was ousted he wrote him a cordial letter to praise his achievements and to express appreciation and goodwill.

A day of reckoning came in 1910, when Díaz, passing his eightieth year, still insisted on the retention of office and chose as his running mate a notorious slave trader, one of the most execrated men in Mexico. At the celebration of the centennial of independence from Spain, the revelry was interrupted by the news that revolts had broken out in various parts of the country. Clearly these were no minor local defiances; even the federal forces joined the revolutionists. The dictatorship collapsed and Díaz fled. As he boarded the German ship that was to take him into European exile, he offered the ominous forecast: "The rebels have unleashed a tiger; let us see if they can control him."

Diaz needed no prescience for his warning. He was well aware how much lava had been boiling beneath the deceptively placid surface. The next decade was a period of almost continuous civil war. The insurrections flared in widely separated provinces and none of the men who seized control could command national respect or authority. There were vendettas, murders, reprisals, as Madero, Huerta, Zapata, Villa, and Carranza followed each other in bloody succession. Quite apart from the vacuum in responsible leadership which the long dictatorship of Díaz had ensured, many of the insurgents came out of poverty and indignity. They had lived in hovels, harried and insecure, hardly ever knowing where their next meal could come from.* Then they found themselves at the levers of power, in the haciendas of the aristocrats, and the sudden ascent to glory and its perquisites was dizzying. Many of the rebel chieftains also had personal grievances to avenge. Villa had taken to the hills after killing a *hacendado* who had raped his sister. Zapata never forgot how his meager plot of land was expropriated without due process. The foreign governments did not contribute to stability as they took turns in encouraging and arming various factions. The American ambassador, Henry Lane Wilson, whose relatives were part of the Rockefeller and Guggenheim interests in Mexico, was an outright partisan. Madero, whom he helped to overthrow and whose assassination he did nothing to prevent, cried out to one of the American correspondents: "Why does your government persecute me? Why does it put its heel upon me and grind me down like a worm?"† Wilson's shabby manipulations were not forgotten in later relations with the Colossus of the North.

Despite the turmoil of the decade, the revolution became the proudest part of the Mexican heritage. It was the most pervasive presence in Mexican life, the rallying symbol for every patriotic effort, supplanting religion itself as a cohesive national force. One of the ablest students of Latin America wrote: "The word Revolucion has taken the place of the blessed Virgin upon the national altar."‡ Its clearest expression was to be found in the constitution that was promulgated in 1917. This set limits on the power of the great landowners, the clergy, and the employers; it was especially emphatic on the subordination of foreign interests. Article 123, referred to as the Magna Carta for labor, guaranteed the workers' right to organize, to strike, to bargain collectively, and it pledged

---

* Madero, however, was the scion of a well-to-do family.

† Anita Brenner, *The Wind That Swept Mexico* (Austin, Tex.: University of Texas Press, 1971), p. 33.

‡ Hubert C. Herring, *Good Neighbors* (London: Oxford University Press, 1941), p. 311.

[543]

support for benefits which, if achieved, would mean the minimum security of a welfare state. Unfortunately, it was very nearly lost in the pandemonium of the period. Carranza, in whose regime it had been drafted, was assassinated in 1917, and the civil wars continued to plague the land.

A measure of stability finally came in 1920 with the emergence of two strong personalities, the brilliant one-armed General Álvaro Obregón, and the once poor, shoeless schoolteacher Plutarco Calles. During the fifteen years of their presidencies they not only restored order, broken only occasionally by provincial insurgency, but they were able to advance the revolutionary objectives in the economic and social life of the country. The redistribution of land, frequently promised, received new impetus and, under the guidance of a dedicated educator, Vasconcellos, a significant beginning was made in combatting the illiteracy of the villages. Every encouragement was given to a new school of artists who applied their talents to glorify revolutionary ideals. Diego Rivera and David Siqueiros became national idols and their murals were given full play on the most important public buildings of the chief cities. As they stood in stained overalls on the splintered scaffolding, they carried pistols in their holsters to demonstrate their identification with proletarian concerns.

There was no armistice in the continuing struggle with the Catholic church. Both Obregón and Calles carried their anticlerical antagonism to the point of confiscating the church lands and outlawing the religious orders. The church fought back by canceling religious services and rites, and the archbishop placed the government under an interdict. Loyal Catholics were urged to withdraw their deposits in Mexican banks and a heavy propaganda barrage was mounted in foreign countries, especially in the United States, where intercession was demanded to end "Catholic persecution by the Mexican Communists." Calles retaliated by expelling the foreign priests and liquidating the religious orders. Fortunately, the quarrel did not get out of hand. In 1927 President Coolidge named as Ambassador his Amherst classmate, Dwight Morrow, a Wall Street banker, the father-in-law of Charles Lindbergh, and Morrow astonished his critics by conciliatory diplomacy which helped to reduce the tension and to bring the disputes to the negotiation table.

The benefits of the revolution were substantially advanced by one of Calles's protégés, Lázaro Cárdenas, whose incumbency as President, from 1934 to 1940, left an enduring mark upon the life of the country. In temperament and personality he was unique, a man of the people who, reaching the highest office, remained of the people. He needed no speech writers, no protocol, no statisticians, no planners of the gross national product. He was Papa, and his heart listened. He seemed to be just right for this stage of the revolution, which had cooled considerably in the final years of Calles. After inauguration, he promptly cut his salary in half and, refusing to live in the Chapultepec Palace, converted it into a museum. He preferred the modest lodge where he could more easily receive the humblest of the petitioners who sought him out. He was forever on the go, day and night, by bus and train, on horseback, on foot, moving into the remotest parts of the country, chatting with the villagers, listening to their grievances, acting upon them promptly as if they were the gravest matters of state.* The telegraph system was opened for an hour each day in which anyone could send his complaint or request directly to the President. No one called him Cárdenas; he was always Lázaro. In a land of frequent political assassination he wanted no security guards and he dismissed them whenever he mingled with the crowds in the public square and the market place, or when he sat with them on the hard floors of humble cabins. "It is important," he explained, "that the people know I come among them without fear." He had two children but his home was filled with others whom he brought back with him from his trips into the countryside. He was a *mestizo*, proud of his Indian blood, and he named his son Cuauhtémoc for the last Aztec emperor. He gloried in the reference to him as the first President of the Indians. He defended his people with compassion against detractors who derided their lack of ambition: "How can you expect a watch to keep good time if you use it as a hammer, or an Indian to function as a modern man if you use him as a beast of burden?" Waldo Frank, who compared him with Gandhi, wrote that he governed as the sculptor modeled—"by intimate touch."

---

* A man and wife biographical team described a visit with him: "General Cárdenas was eating bread and boiled beans by the light of an oil lamp in the telegrapher's room of the rickety railroad station. His great ten-gallon hat pushed back on his head, his short goat-skin coat buttoned up around his neck, and his brown leather riding boots covered with prairie dust, he got up from his seat and politely welcomed his unexpected guests, at the same time apologizing for his personal appearance as well as that of his camp. 'We just stopped here for a few hours rest,' he explained. 'It is our intention to push on at three o'clock in the morning. I am sorry that I cannot offer you much in the way of comfort, but what I have is yours!'" Nathaniel and Sylvia Weyl, *The Reconquest of Mexico* (London and New York: Oxford University Press, 1939), p. 92.

Cárdenas was born in 1895, in the province of Michoacán, one of eight children. His father died early and Lázaro went to work at fourteen to help support the orphaned family. He filled odd jobs as a printer's apprentice, a clerk in the tax collector's office, and a jail warden. He was sixteen when Díaz was overthrown and, taking along with him his sole prisoner, Lázaro joined up with the revolutionary forces and fought under Zapata, Obregón, and Calles. He was an excellent soldier, respected by his men for his *madrugar* skill, his lightning quickness on the draw. At one point he was captured and was about to be executed but he made a dramatic escape hidden in a burlap sack. He rose steadily in the impromptu armies of the various rebel bands, and at twenty-five he was already a Mexican general, although the rank carried no more prestige than that of a Kentucky colonel. But he caught the eye of Plutarco Calles, one of the country's kingmakers, who entrusted him with important assignments, including the governorship of his native province. He refused to follow the practice of accepting bribes and he even returned the "loans" that came from merchants upon whom assessments had been imposed in return for protection. Calles sponsored him as his successor in the presidency and, though such support was a virtual guarantee of election, Cárdenas campaigned as vigorously as if the issue were in doubt. When he was elected and took office, he was no longer an unknown who was expected to serve in the shadow of a political mentor. Within a few months this became clear when disagreements emerged over the tempo of the revolution and Cárdenas felt strong enough to break with Calles and place him on a plane for exile across the border.

In the six years of his presidency, Cárdenas still had to contend with disaffection and with minor uprisings. But he forbade any reprisals, and there were no political executions during his incumbency. He maintained the traditional restricted electoral system whereby the nominations were presented by the only official party that was recognized. But he gave full play to criticism even when it touched the rawest nerves. And it often did. For despite his reforms and his personal example, the regime remained vulnerable to charges of inefficiency and graft, especially the *mordida,* the bite, the payoff. Cárdenas knew that this endemic problem could not be quickly solved. He said ruefully, "Whenever I put my hand in a basket, I pull out a thief." Uncensored criticism, he therefore hoped, might help in the process of re-education.

With his blessing, Mexico now became a refuge point for political exiles who fled their homelands. Leon Trotsky was offered asylum despite the protests of Stalin, which became threatening enough to lead to a rupture of diplomatic relations between the Soviet Union and Mexico. The defeated Republicans who escaped from Franco's Spain were welcomed in their thousands, along with the rebels whose lives were in jeopardy in the many Latin American dictatorships. Cárdenas even invited back the political refugees who had opposed him. But there was no hospitality for the Fascist groups. Cárdenas took Mexico out of the 1936 Olympics which were scheduled for Hitler's Germany, and when the Gold Shirts, the home-bred Nazis, began organizing in Mexico, he suppressed them. He could operate with confidence not only because of the rapturous popularity he commanded from the peasants and the workers, but because he thoroughly reorganized the army, bringing in younger officers, loyal to him and to the regime, to take the place of older revolutionaries who had begun to live in the past.

Among all the tasks that crowded in on Cárdenas, the most compelling was the liquidation of the great estates and the redistribution of the land. Every past rebel leader had made the promise that the peasants would soon enjoy secure lives on their own patrimony, but the results had usually been token. Cárdenas was determined not to fail. He cut through reams of bureaucratic red tape and the ingenious strategems of obstruction by the *hacendado* families. He eschewed the Communist technique of confiscation and, instead, authorized purchase and compensation to the owners of record. There was a measure of retributive justice in setting the purchase price. The owners had always listed their holdings at a fraction of actual value so as to evade appropriate taxation. Now they were to be paid off on the evaluation that they had themselves contrived. In the first three years twenty-four million acres were made available to the peasants, more than all that had been done for them since the constitution of 1917 had included the pledge of peasant security.

Cárdenas linked redistribution with a return to the *ejido* system of collective farming, the dream of the democratic socialists, which gave the peasants access to communal equipment and resources but retained and protected their private ownership. By 1938 Cárdenas had increased the number of *ejidos* from four thousand to twenty thousand, and he exulted that more than 45 percent of the peasants had opted for such *ejido* living. To complete the program, Cárdenas authorized government support for road building, dams, the installation of electrical power, sanitation, and other improvements to bring the peasants into the twentieth century. He welcomed the help of the United States and friendly foreign governments in providing advanced modern equipment and the credit to make its purchase possible.

It was inevitable that there would be a decline in efficiency as the inexperienced peons wrestled with their sudden responsibility and as the native engineers and the other technicians could not rise quickly to the emergency pace of an expanded national program. There was sabotage from the *hacendados* and from many of the outraged clerical leaders whose lands had been taken over. Pressing foreign claims for agrarian indemnity drained off funds that were urgently needed at home. Production fell off and there was widespread distress. But Cárdenas remained firm and the nation supported him fully as he carried through the most far-reaching revolution in Mexican history.

Meantime, in the continuing battle with the Catholic church Cárdenas turned out to be a conciliator. To be sure, he fully shared the hostility of his predecessors to the reactionary mischief of the clerical hierarchy. Soon after he took office, he spoke bluntly of the provocations of the church that had compelled the state to take defensive measures. "In Mexico," he said grimly, "the Roman clergy has been the instigator and sustainer of most of our bloody internal warfare, and is still guilty of treachery to the Fatherland." But he concluded that much more could be achieved by social change than by punitive actions that gave the clergy the aura of martyrdom and alienated millions of devout families whose Catholic worship was sincere, and who had joined in a *cristero* resistance. "It is an error," Cárdenas argued, "to fight against religious fanaticism with antireligious fanaticism." He was convinced that the economic reforms he had instituted would, in the long run, deprive the church of its manipulative power. He had faith too that the educational reforms would dissipate the ignorance of the population which had made it an easy prey to the machinations of a politically motivated clergy.

He therefore ended the attacks on priests and nuns and the desecration of religious symbols which had blemished the regimes of Obregón and Calles. He no longer enforced the law that limited the number of churches to 1 in 100,000 population, and he offered full protection for worship. He authorized the return of the religious orders that had been expelled, but warned them that they must stay out of politics. He then mounted a vigorous campaign for the erection of new schools and recruited thousands of teachers who were persuaded that it was an act of patriotism to go into the remotest villages. When Cárdenas took office, virtually all of the rural schools were one-room shanties, and, of two and a half million rural children, less than a third had been enrolled. Before he retired from the presidency, in 1940, the number of schools had tripled and so had the enrollments. "Despite the difficulties of the task and the meager financial resources available," wrote the Weyls, summarizing the Cárdenas program of education, "the rural teachers are transforming the illiterate peasant mass into a self-reliant citizenry able to play its part in the public life of the nation."*

The severest test of statesmanship for Cárdenas came in the battles against the foreign investors to compel them to relinquish their hold upon the oil and mineral resources of the country. In the decisive confrontation, all the forces of the revolution converged: the intense nationalism of a reawakened people, its well-nigh fanatic anti-imperialism, and its determination to retrieve the country's resources for the common good. The constitution of 1917 had long before established the principle that the subsoil of Mexico belonged inalienably to the state. But the principle had not been honored; the cartels, mainly British and American, had little trouble in buying the cooperation of the dictators and their venal political machines. Edward Doheny of the Sinclair Oil Company, who had already earned an unsavory reputation in the United States in the Teapot Dome scandals, had acquired cheaply more than 600,000 acres of oil-rich land. A single lease that had produced tens of millions in profits had been swindled from a Mexican widow for a fee of two hundred pesos annually. Cárdenas, exposing other examples of chicanery, now determined to end the racket. When the labor unions insisted upon a revaluation of wages and working conditions, he gave them every encouragement. The oil combines apparently did not realize that the party was over and brusquely refused to meet the union demands. The dispute was referred to the Supreme Court of Mexico, which found in favor of the unions. The oil companies still resisted, and it was then that Cárdenas intervened. On March 18, 1938, he announced the expropriation of the 450-million-dollar empire of Sinclair, Shell, and Standard Oil.

The cartels fought back with their own formidable weapons. Labeling the product as "stolen goods," they prevailed on their

* N. and S. Weyl, *The Reconquest of Mexico,* p. 329.

worldwide affiliates to refuse to purchase Mexican oil and to with-hold the tankers in which the oil had to be transported. They cut off the sale of tetraethyl lead for the production and refining operations. They initiated complicated legal action in each country to delay and harass business relationships with Mexico. Above all, they appealed to their governments for protection against the "Communist theft" of their rightful possessions. Britain broke diplomatic relations with Mexico, and the United States seemed to be preparing for similar drastic reprisal.

Cárdenas refused to be intimidated. He told the American Ambassador, Josephus Daniels, that "if the richest oil fields in the world stood in the way of maintaining our national dignity . . . we would burn the oil fields rather than sacrifice our honor."* He reminded the Ambassador that Mexico was not without recourse; it could sell its oil to the Nazi and Fascist countries which were only too eager to receive it in exchange for heavy machinery and equipment. Cárdenas said bluntly, "We prefer to trade with the United States but we cannot pay too great a price for this preference."

At this juncture President Roosevelt concluded that the situation had become too dangerous to permit its further deterioration. The war clouds were ominous everywhere and it was no time to give the Axis powers a major diplomatic victory in the western hemisphere by throwing Mexico into their willing arms. Besides, Roosevelt was eager to change the image of the United States as the Yankee Colossus that was always interfering in the affairs of its southern neighbors. He therefore ordered Daniels to seek a conciliatory way out of the impasse. The Ambassador had little sympathy for the oil barons anyway; he was unwilling, as he put it, to be their collection sheriff. So he urged the oil companies to take what they could get in compensation, and then to establish more equitable formulae for future business relationships. The oil companies had learned their lesson, and they reluctantly agreed. The United States offered generous credits to enable the Mexican government to fulfill its obligations and all claims were amicably adjusted by 1941. The crisis that had threatened to explode into war was averted, and "the good neighbors" actually became comrades-in-arms in World War II.

It was a striking victory for Cárdenas and for Mexico. There were still major foreign investments in the mines and the wells. But the government was now in control and could make sure that the

* Jamie H. Plenn, *Mexico Marches* (Indianapolis: Bobbs-Merrill Co., 1939), p. 19.

profits of the oil fields were shared by the Mexican people. Cárdenas did not escape the charge of the old-line conservatives that he was a Communist and that he had adopted the strong-arm techniques that had been perfected in the Kremlin. But, as in all of his other battles, he paid little attention to the irreconcilable critics. The revolution was safe and the return of the land and its resources to the Mexican people, so long promised, was now at last fulfilled. March 18 became a national holiday to signalize the achievement of economic independence.

As Cárdenas's term approached its end in 1940 there was persistent pressure upon him, especially from the labor groups, to devise some way of remaining in office. It was urged that Mexico could not relinquish decisive leadership if the objectives of the revolution were to be permanently anchored. Though Cárdenas was still only forty-five, and in the prime of his vigor and influence, he firmly refused. The constitution had denied the right of any President to seek re-election and, having advocated respect for the law, he insisted that he must set an example of honor and fidelity to principle. He had no patience with the rationalizations of men in power that they were indispensable. There were indeed many unfulfilled goals that would tax the broadest statesmanship, but he had faith that there were other men to take the nation along the road to these goals.

There were other men, some nominated by Cárdenas, some emerging from the challenges of new issues and new needs. They did not all see eye to eye with Cárdenas, nor with his interpretation of the revolution. Some of them downgraded his efforts as the naïveté of "the eternal rustic," who never really understood the problems of a technological age. In the 1950's and 1960's most of them turned more conservative. There were grave inadequacies in the economy and in educational and health programs. Shady politicians and bureaucrats were able to steal back into positions where they could traffic at the expense of the public welfare. They rode in their Mercedes cars and had lush parties in their ostentatious homes. Cárdenas himself, though scrupulously remaining aloof from political activity, voiced concern over the trends in government and in foreign policy. Had the revolution run out of fervor and was it moving to its Thermidor?

He need not have been downcast. Perhaps the highest tribute to his historic achievement came in the influence that Mexico commanded in the Latin American world. The core of its revolution had survived all attacks upon it. Its representatives were listened to with respect in the Inter-American conferences. Relations with the United States remained friendly, executives often exchanging visits; the chief disputes that arose were amicably settled. Many of the countries south of the Rio Grande tried other ways of solving their social and economic problems, often through dictatorship of the left or of the right. The Mexican way offered an alternative for the peaceful transformation of a feudal society into a welfare state.

IF MEXICO OFFERED ONE ROAD TO SOCIAL REVOLUTION, CUBA OFFERED another. Its plight since it had won a shadowy independence from Spain at the turn of the century was not a very happy one. Its rulers usually held office by force and were quite shameless in their exploitation. One of the worst of the lot was Fulgencio Batista, a brazen martinet who surpassed all his predecessors in corruption and terror. Kickbacks, embezzlement, blackmail were taken for granted and, since the military and the trade union leaders shared fully in the graft, Batista felt quite secure. One Chief of Staff stole the entire army retirement fund of forty million dollars. When students from the University of Havana rioted, he suppressed their demonstrations, dismissed the faculty who sympathized with them, and finally padlocked the university. Others who continued to express dissent were rounded up, tortured, and fed to the sharks. In 1957, in retaliation for the slaying of a brutal army officer, twenty-seven hostages, all youngsters, were hanged on trees along the main plaza of Havana.

The American interest in Cuba came from the considerable investments of its corporations and from the strategic location of the island, only ninety miles from the American mainland. The reports of the outrages in Cuba created concern in liberal circles, but the administration in Washington seemed to go out of its way to pay honors to men whose conduct was reprehensible by the most minimum political standards. Vice President Nixon, visiting Batista in Havana, was lavish in his praise of him in the very period when the dictator had become most malodorous.

It was out of this climate of institutionalized gangsterism that, in 1953, a young firebrand emerged, Fidel Castro, who was to transform the life of his country even as he kept revolutionizing his objectives. Castro was a volatile man, burning with resentments, moody at times, euphoric at other times, generous but arbitrary, kind and compassionate in many situations, in others possessed by spasms of such passionate cruelty that he frightened his closest associates. One of his biographers called him a dormant volcano, ready to erupt at any moment. He was never very clear about his long-range objectives. He seemed, to use a Shakespearean phrase, to have "quicksilver in his clay."

Fidel was born in 1926. His father was a Spanish immigrant who had come up from penniless pick-and-shovel days with the United Fruit Company to affluence as a sugar planter. Fidel was one of the sons of his father's liaison with the household cook, later legitimatized, in a menage that was full of sound and fury, and where there was little love either for parents or among the many brawling children. Fidel was close only to one brother, Raul, who later shared many of his experiences. He attended Catholic boarding schools and a Jesuit College in Havana, where he was involved in student politics that were so frenzied that he was several times arrested, once on a murder charge. The knavery and chicanery that flourished in Cuba and the neighboring Latin American countries stoked the rebellious fires that were never low heat anyway.

In the next few years, Fidel participated in a number of quixotic expeditions against the Cuban and the Caribbean dictators. The one that was aimed at Trujillo of San Domingo was really harebrained. The pathetic little rebel boat was intercepted and Fidel escaped only by swimming three miles with his rifle on his back. Another expedition was planned to take the Moncada Barracks at Santiago de Cuba with one hundred and fifty men and a few old guns. The date in 1953 became the rallying name, "July 26," for the whole revolutionary movement. The attack was easily repulsed and Fidel was captured. He used the ensuing trial to air his defiance. "Condemn me," he cried, after listing the inequities of the dictator. "It does not matter. History will absolve me." Only seven months of the long-term prison sentences for Fidel and Raul were served. For in one of his expansive moods, Batista issued a general amnesty and the Castros went on to Mexico. In November 1956, no better prepared or equipped, they were ready to try again. They set sail in an old yacht and disembarked on the southern shore of Oriente Province, where the rebel band was quickly decimated by Batista's waiting forces. The few survivors, who included the Castros, marched for twenty days, holing up in the Sierra Maestra wilderness, and there they began to build the guerrilla cadres that were to wear down the Batista tyranny.

Now Fidel was no longer a lone fighter for an apparently hopeless cause. His fame had spread through the island and he had excited the admiration of many influential American liberals. Funds and arms began to flow to him. Legions of youngsters were attracted to the cause, and they became part of a formidable underground that wreaked havoc in the cities and the towns. They were relentlessly hunted by Batista's highly professional army, and reports of Fidel's death circulated frequently. But his guerrilla bands grew in numbers and experience and, taking fullest advantage of the almost impenetrable terrain, they exacted heavy casualties in each of Batista's counterattacks.

Batista's generals had no reason, other than pelf and power, to remain loyal to him and, when they sensed his vulnerability, they began to grow jittery. Some of them opened secret negotiations with Castro. Batista caught the message and apparently decided that he could enjoy life more fully in a safe exile point, luxuriously supported by the millions he had accumulated. On New Year's Day, 1959, he suddenly fled. Castro's men triumphantly entered Santiago de Cuba, and took the surrender of the Moncada Barracks where, less than six years before, the first assaults had been attempted. A few days later the jubilant *"barbudos,"* the bearded ones, marched into Havana to the cheers of the hundreds of thousands who crowded streets, windows, and rooftops to welcome him.

There followed an explosion of vengeance as the long-suppressed victims of despotism sought out their suspected tormentors. Their hatreds were apparently too deep for civilized restraint. Castro had been trained in the law; he was proud of his doctorate. But he permitted charges to be made, judgments to be rendered, executions to be held, all within a few hours. There was no pretense of due process, and hundreds died by the firing squad and were tumbled into mass graves. Sympathizers in many lands who had cheered him on were saddened that he should now take on the habiliments of the men whose lawlessness had driven him to the revolution.

Soon there were other misgivings. Castro had come to power as the shining knight of democratic socialism. He proclaimed that "he was opposed to Capitalism because it killed people with hunger, and he was equally opposed to Communism because it suppressed the liberties which were so dear to men." He promised to bring liberty with bread and without terror. His first pledge was "for a government based on free elections." He planned a major redistribution of land and resources to open wider opportunities to the common people, but this would be done with fair compensation to the expropriated owners. When he visited the United States in 1959, he was enthusiastically welcomed, especially by university audiences.

Castro's actions soon belied his fervid oratory. The promised free elections were continuously postponed and then altogether canceled. The courts were purged of democratic liberals and their places taken by committed Marxists. The nationalization of the sugar plantations, industries, banks, utilities, was all done by fiat, and there was no compensation. Foreign holdings in Cuba, totaling more than a billion dollars, were sequestered. Castro justified his strong-arm methods by the need to rescue the depressed masses of the population from the peonage in which they lived.

One of Castro's first objectives was to broaden the base of the economy. Cuba's historic misfortune, he said, was its almost complete dependence on sugar and its control by American imperialists.* He sharply reduced the acreage that was given over to the crop and channeled a major part of the national effort into industry —steel, cement, tractors, textiles, shoes. Diversification, he promised, would free Cuba from its dependence on the outside world and raise the standard of living for the workers. But he soon discovered that it was easier to demolish than to create. The transformation of an economy could not be accomplished with oratory even when the speeches were five or six hours long. The industrial developments could not be quickly brought about without capital, and his methods had alienated investment support. Soon there were serious shortages. To bolster the economy of the island, Castro had to concentrate again on the sugar crop, the reliable staple for which the climate was ideal. It was embarrassing for Castro to have to admit that rationing, even for bread, was necessary.

Castro turned increasingly for support to the Soviet Union. In 1960, the Soviet trade chieftain, Anastas Mikoyan, came to Cuba for a state visit and pledged that Russia would buy the entire five-million-ton sugar crop; and he offered a hundred million dollars in low-interest credit. Next year he was followed by a Russian military mission, which arranged for the training of complete com-

---

* In fact, sugar was not dominated by American corporations, whose interest had been declining steadily since 1928; by 1958 it involved about 35 percent. Sugar production then represented 16 percent of the Cuban economy. American companies employed seventy thousand Cubans out of a working population of two million and they received the highest wages on the island and were protected by the strongest unions. Cited in Theodore Draper, *Castroism: Theory and Practice* (New York: Praeger, 1965), pp. 102, 109.

bat units of mechanized troops and for the installation of anti-aircraft batteries with the most sophisticated ground-to-air rockets.* Castro's speeches became more and more sarcastic about the degenerate democratic system, petit bourgeois hypocrisy, American imperialism.

Within a year of his assumption of power, Castro announced that he was a Marxist-Leninist. "I will be one until the last day of my life," he added.† Most of the wealthy had already fled. Now the exodus was joined by tens, then hundreds of thousands of moderates who had hailed Castro as a liberator. They included many who had fought at his side in the July 26 movement—the first President of the new Cuba, the first Prime Minister, two-thirds of the first cabinet, the head of the Supreme Court. They were convinced that Castro was now substituting a totalitarianism of the left for the repudiated totalitarianism of the right.

Castro's pendulum politics raised many fundamental questions. Had he come to power as a democratic liberator and then been forced into the arms of the Soviet Union by the hostility of aggrieved business interests and the American government? Had he been a Communist right from the beginning, at first dissembling his intentions, winning control of Cuba in a general appeal to oust a hated dictator, and then coming out into the open for objectives that were always primary? Or had he been skillfully used by the Soviet leaders, who had perfected the technique in underdeveloped lands of enthusiastically supporting nationalist revolutions, and then, through the medium of local Communist parties, throwing out the Kerenskys and taking over the control of the government?

Those who held the view that Castro was forced by American hostility to solicit Soviet collaboration had plausible supporting evidence. American businessmen assuredly could not be happy with the confiscatory reforms that Castro instituted. They fought back and their reprisals cut deep into the Cuban economy—the reduction in the sugar purchase quotas, the severe curtailment of credit. To survive, Castro had to rely upon the Soviet agreement to provide credit and loans for military hardware and technicians. Khrushchev chuckled over what he interpreted as American obtuseness. He is alleged to have remarked to President Kennedy, "Castro is not a Communist, but you Americans are making him one."

* The East Germans trained Castro's secret police, even as they had trained Nasser's force; for such a program they had no peer anywhere.
† Cited in Johnson, *The Bay of Pigs,* p. 260.

There were others who believed that Castro had always been a committed Communist. They could not agree that it was American hostility that had goaded him into the Soviet camp. They insisted that the American actions were not initiatory, they were reflexive, taken as reprisal after provocation. Washington had watched with growing concern the economic and military collaboration that brought the Soviet Union into the Caribbean. Every action of Castro since assuming power could only mean that he was determined to eliminate what he called "the American imperialist interest."

But whether Castro was a crypto-Communist from the outset or had been edged into Communist policy by American hostility, there was little doubt that he was a bonanza for long-range Soviet objectives. He could be used most effectively by Khrushchev as a wedge for the Soviet penetration into the Latin American area. A base in Cuba, so close to the American mainland, would provide ideal blackmail leverage. Hence Khrushchev welcomed Castro's nationalist revolution, but remained discreetly in the background until Batista and the old guard had been eliminated. Then came the negotiations for the economic and military aid that locked Castro securely into dependence on the Soviet Union.

Meantime President Eisenhower, as detailed in his Memoirs, took a dim view of the way the Cuban revolution was now conducted. Early in 1959 he had authorized a study in depth to learn whether Castro was a Communist or just a naïve amateur. The report concluded that, however Castro may have begun, he was now well on his way to a Communist commitment. Vice President Nixon, having studied the report, concluded that Castro was a captive of the Kremlin, and he favored the training of guerrilla forces to effect his overthrow. Eisenhower agreed and the C.I.A. was given the hazardous assignment, with the understanding that the United States itself was not to be directly involved. Any invasion would have to operate through the refugee groups and the Revolutionary Democratic Front, El Frente, which was the coordinating body for many of the exile organizations. There were thousands of uprooted Cubans in the Miami area and in smaller enclaves in the United States and Central America from whence volunteers could be drawn. Training centers for them were set up in a number of neighboring countries—in Guatemala, Nicaragua, and also in Puerto Rico.

By the time the actual invasion was to take place, in 1961, there was a new administration in Washington, and President Kennedy had to review and judge its validity. He was briefed by those who had mapped out the original plans and by the C.I.A. As was noted earlier, Kennedy gave his consent to the Bay of Pigs expedition.* It was wretchedly planned and was executed with diaphanous secrecy. When Kennedy realized what a trap the entire expedition had become and stopped short of air support for it, it ended in disaster and humiliation.

By the fall of 1962 Castro's Cuba had quite clearly become a Communist beachhead in the Caribbean and the ties with the Soviet Union were military as well as economic. Khrushchev, having sized up Kennedy as a bungler surrounded by rhetoricians, now sought to solidify the Cuban base by surreptitiously placing missiles on the island. This time the United States was better prepared. Kennedy made it clear that he would not hesitate to go to the limit of nuclear war unless the missiles were immediately removed. After a tense period of confrontation which brought the world to the brink of war, Khrushchev backed down, eliciting a pledge, however, that no further attempt would be made by the United States to overturn Castro by force.†

Though Castro's international importance was considerably deflated by the missile experience, he did not subside into an isolated phenomenon in Cuba. He continued thinking of himself as a twentieth-century Bolívar, with the mission to help all the nations of Latin America, from the Rio Grande to Tierra del Fuego, to free themselves of Yankee exploitation. A picturesque Argentine-born lieutenant, Che Guevara, who had given up his profession as a surgeon, was placed in charge of Operation America, with plans to establish schools for secret agents, workshops for propaganda, and training centers for guerrillas. His highly theatrical adventures as he plotted revolutionary activity in many parts of Latin America and the Caribbean gave him a Robin Hood aura until he was killed in October 1967 in one of the underground campaigns in the highlands of Bolivia. He became a hero-martyr for the New Left in the United States and in many parts of the world. His Basque beret, his beard, his swagger, his mystical language, were widely imitated and he was linked with Ho Chi Minh and Mao Tse-tung as one of the gurus of the revolutionary cult.

Yet these conspiratorial operations were now largely peripheral. Castro remained as an inspirational symbol for the nationalists of

* See Chapter 41.
† See Chapter 41.

the underdeveloped countries, but he was no longer a major menace to the United States. He became a noisy irritant, a nuisance to live with, but no longer able to exert intimidation.

One consequence in the American relationship to the western hemisphere was not ephemeral, however: a drastically altered application of the Monroe Doctrine emerged. Distinction was now drawn between the threat to American corporate enterprise when there were revolutionary political changes in a Latin American country, and the threat to American security when a Latin American country collaborated with a foreign power to set up a military challenge. In the Bay of Pigs intervention, the United States had planned to overturn a government that was deemed to be Communist. This was in fulfillment of the policy enunciated as late as 1954 by John Foster Dulles. He had then declared that "if the international Communist movement should come to dominate the political institutions of any American state, that would be a threat to the sovereignty and political independence of us all, endangering the peace of America and calling for appropriate action."* Kennedy, in effect, repudiated this Dulles policy when he agreed that all attempts to bring down the Castro government by force would be ended.

On the other hand, Kennedy had now emphatically reaffirmed the principle that any threat to the military security of the United States would be resisted, even to the point of resort to nuclear war. In September 1970, there were reports that the Soviet Union was secretly building a nuclear submarine base near Cienfuegos, and Washington reacted promptly. It needed only the inquiry from the State Department to elicit a hasty denial that any such provocation was under way or planned.

Of course, the basic issue remained: What was a threat to American economic investment, and what was a threat to American security, and where did they merge? There would undoubtedly be a continuing problem of interpretation. But it was unlikely that anything but a challenge such as Khrushchev had offered would henceforth be considered a serious security threat. It was significant that the hard-line Nixon administration reacted calmly in 1970 when Chile elected the Marxian, Salvador Allende, as its President. When Allende was asked how he would pay for the quart of milk promised for every Chilean child, he replied, on his way to the

* John Foster Dulles in a statement of March 8, 1954, at the Tenth Inter-American Conference in Caracas, Venezuela. *Intervention* (pamphlet, Washington, D.C.: Department of State, 1954), p. 1.

nationalization of the American copper interests, "If we run out of four-legged beasts we can always start milking the two-legged ones." But even this baiting provoked no angry response from those who only a few years before would have insisted upon the intervention of the marines. The United States offered no resistance, and it quickly extended diplomatic recognition.

For the world had moved into a new era since 1963 and its brush with the Angel of Death. Every responsible statesman now knew that the nuclear threat could not, must not, be used for economic or political bargaining. The nuclear warheads were not simply bigger or more sophisticated weaponry; nuclear warheads carried total annihilation, with no winners, no losers, only victims.

46

NASSER AND THE DREAM OF AN ARAB EMPIRE

LATE IN JULY 1953 A MILITARY COUP TOOK PLACE IN EGYPT AND KING Farouk was packed off into exile. There was universal rejoicing that he was out at last for he had brought little but degradation and defeat during his dissolute and inept reign. Egypt hailed the vigorous leadership that promised happier days and new opportunities for its long-suffering people. The head and front of the revolt, Gamal Nasser, only thirty-five, had been dreaming of this moment of liberation and planning for it since he was commissioned as an officer in his early twenties.

He was a totally new phenomenon for a people cocooned for centuries in sullen resignation to the miseries of poverty, disease, and ignorance. He stood tall and proud, rallying his countrymen to the vision of the twelfth-century Saladin who had united the Arabs in a victorious Golden Age. At the threshold of the revolution that routed the old order, Nasser had said: "Within the Arab world there is a role wandering aimlessly in search of a hero." He never doubted that it was to be his destiny to fulfill that role.

Nasser was born in Alexandria in 1918, the eldest of eleven children. His father was a post office employee, lost in the subservient faceless masses that hoped for little and got less. He was never a good student but his failures were the result of alienation and not of incapacity. He rebelled against the government that ruled with cynical disregard for Egypt's needs and against the politicians who kept the people in superstitious inertia. But when he enrolled in the Royal Military Academy his natural talent flowered and he developed into an impressive, resourceful officer. He underwent a valuable apprenticeship in World War II, but he had no loyalty to the British whose occupation of Egypt he bitterly resented. He and a comrade-in-arms, Anwar-al-Sadat, were in frequent communication with the Nazi command and they hoped for an Axis victory.

The British were well aware of the conspiratorial activity that threatened their lifeline. There was no time to be lost nor was there leeway for squeamishness. Rommel was on the outskirts of Alexandria; the Italians were on the march; there had just been a coup in Iraq that had installed an anti-British government. On February 4, 1942, a column of British troops broke down the gates of the Abdin Palace and compelled Farouk to name Nahas Pasha, friendly to the British interest, as Prime Minister. The high-handed action was apparently a crowning insult for many of the young Egyptian officers. Nasser often referred to the episode as decisive in his objectives. He held no brief for the King whom he despised; later he joined in the revolt against him. But the spectacle of the British marching into the Palace and dictating who should be the head of state was a humiliation that no self-respecting Egyptian could endure. Nasser dated his active determination to be rid of the British from the Abdin Palace insult. He wrote to his brother, "I am glad for this incident. This cut of the knife has given life back to our young officers."

When World War II ended in complete Allied victory there were new disappointments to feed the scarcely contained rebellion of the Egyptian nationalists. We have seen how the United Nations in 1947, after long and acrimonious negotiations, decided upon the partition of Palestine and the creation of independent Arab and Jewish states; further, how Arab countries refused to accept such a solution and at once invaded the areas that had been assigned to Israel.* They were routed by the Israelis on the crucial fronts and Nasser, fighting with the Egyptian forces, was trapped with several regiments in a completely surrounded pocket. He noted with contempt how thoroughly the servility and corruption of the Egyptian government agencies had infected the military itself. The Jewish leader Dr. Chaim Weizmann summarized the Egyptian predicament: "The officers were too fat and the men were too lean."

When the Palestine wars ended in a truce and he was repatriated,

* See Chapter 33.

he was further appalled by shocking revelations that implicated the top echelons of government, including the King. Typical was the overpricing of obsolete Spanish rifles and the fobbing off of defective Italian grenades with little concern for the welfare of the fighting men.

Nasser now gave priority to the task of organizing a Free Officers Corps that would become the nucleus for the revolution he felt was inevitable. He succeeded in winning the cooperation of Colonel Muhammud Naguib, one of the few officers who had emerged from the Palestine fiasco with prestige. By July 1952, they agreed the time had come to strike. The ruling clique put up surprisingly little resistance. The revolution was swift and bloodless, and the successors of the ancient Pharaohs went into their unlamented exile. Farouk was quite philosophical. "Kings are on the way out anyway," he said. "Soon there will be only five left—The Kings of spades, hearts, diamonds, clubs, and England."

For two years Naguib and Nasser worked as a team, Naguib as head of state, Nasser behind the scenes. Their major achievement, and a spectacular one, was the agreement by Britain to end its seventy-two-year occupation of Egypt. But Nasser, a loner, was restless in any shared responsibility. He steadily undermined Naguib's position and, by 1954, was strong enough to dismiss him and place him under perpetual house arrest. Then, the role having found the hero, Nasser was ready for the problems of consolidation and reconstruction.

He did not underestimate the magnitude of the task. The poverty of the population of twenty-two million was without a parallel outside the world of aborigines. The birth rate was the highest in the world, a hopeless challenge to even the most disciplined reform. And the existence of this exploding population hung precariously, as it had done from time immemorial, on the Nile River, which wound its way through endless desert stretches. Poverty usually went together with disease; the plague of bilharzia, carried by parasites in the drinking water, worked its way into three-quarters of the population, debilitating them and rendering them sluggish and listless. Trachoma, malaria, tuberculosis were not occasional family episodes; they were community epidemics.

All this Nasser saw but he was not discouraged. He was a dynamo of energy, extraordinarily resourceful, avid for technical advice, quick to learn, and fired by a sense of historic mission. He had the goodwill of the democratic world, where the hope was expressed that he could accomplish for Egypt what Ataturk had done for Turkey and what Nehru was undertaking for India. His first years were marked by wide-ranging reforms. He decreed the nationalization of the lands confiscated from the royal family and its numerous freeloaders, and he allocated individual holdings to some of the landless peasantry whose situation had become unendurable. He outlawed the Moslem Brotherhood, who were the main obstacle to change. He brought in experts to cope with disease and illiteracy. Above all, he negotiated successfully for international assistance to build the high dam at Aswan that was to bring life to more than a million acres and power the economy for ambitious industrialization projects.

How far Nasser might have gone in the modernization of Egypt if he had concentrated on the welfare of his people, none can say. Perhaps even all of his energy and his incomparable prestige would still have been insufficient to affect seriously the staggering load of inherited problems.* But he did not concentrate on a strong, solid economic and social base at home. Almost from the outset he was diverted by visions of a revived Arab empire, a union of the Arab people over whom he would preside as a twentieth-century Saladin. Since the Arab world was corrosively fragmented, seething with ancestral vendettas and dynastic rivalries, Nasser's dream called for complete immersion in the savage politics of a dozen neighboring states. A great part of the talents and resources that were indispensable for Egypt's welfare were thus diverted to fratricidal warfare. Dean Acheson sized him up as a male Cleopatra, with a genius for playing off the super-powers against each other as he clawed his way to supreme Arab leadership. Nasser confessed, "I have been a conspirator for so long that I mistrust everyone around me."

One of his first objectives was a union with Syria. In 1958, after intense personal diplomacy, there was a jubilant joint announcement from Cairo and Damascus that the two nations had agreed to merge, with coordination of the economy, the political structure, and military organization and deployment. The new flag for the United Arab Republic took its eagle from the coat of arms of Saladin. "This generation of the Egyptian nation," Nasser exclaimed, "is one

---

* The desert reclamation plan ultimately involved 900,000 acres and by the time of Nasser's death in 1970, cost Egypt more than a billion dollars. The inept planning, the paper shuffling of the swollen bureaucracy, brought deep disappointment with the results. When Sadat succeeded Nasser he had to reorganize the effort from top to bottom. Cited in *The New York Times*, Sept. 26, 1971.

of those generations ordained to live great moments of transition, moments that are like pageants of sunrise."* Some of his counsellors warned Nasser that he was treading a minefield. The two countries were separated by hundreds of miles, with Israel in between. They had different traditions and economic objectives. The Syrian President said, only half-jestingly, "Fifty percent of my people consider themselves leaders, twenty-five percent think they are prophets, and ten percent imagine they are Gods!"

Nasser hardly listened. With scant concern for Syrian national pride he took over completely. He appointed not only the Egyptian delegates to the newly launched Assembly but the Syrian delegates as well. The economy of Syria, whose per capita income was many times larger than Egypt's, was geared to Nasser's poverty-ridden state. The Syrian army was infiltrated with Egyptian spies. The political parties that flourished in Syria were disbanded and replaced by a National Union such as Nasser had imposed on Egypt. As resistance grew, Syria, already a police state, was turned into a garrison, and all the security positions passed into the keeping of Nasser's own intelligence officers. This was not a partnership, it was an absorption.

The Union lasted for about three years until Syrian resentment boiled over. In October 1961, while the puppet Prime Minister was in Moscow, there was a military coup in Syria and the Union was abruptly dissolved. The Prime Minister cabled that he was on his way back. He was assured that he would be eagerly received and promptly hanged upon arrival. The repudiation was an embarrassment for the Kremlin in its complicated game of infiltration in the politics and economy of the Middle East. But for Nasser it was a serious setback and he continued to give major effort to the task of restoring cooperative relationships. In July 1963, a counter coup was attempted, but it failed and twenty-seven Nasserite officers were executed. Optimistically, Nasser still retained the name of the United Arab Republic, but his "pageant of the sunrise" had turned into a dreary twilight.†

The attempt to infiltrate Iraq was a much bloodier tale. Iraq was a British creation and was the nucleus of the Baghdad Pact, an

---

* Cited in Keith Wheelock, *Nasser's New Egypt* (New York: Frederick A. Praeger, 1960), p. 259.

† Nasser's successor, Sadat, tried again in 1971 and a new Federation that added Libya to Syria and Egypt came into being. This time, Sadat was determined to learn from Nasser's mistakes.

anti-Communist alliance that included Turkey, Pakistan, and some of the Middle Eastern states. It had been sedulously built by Dulles and Eden. The Russians used Nasser's personal popularity to discredit the Baghdad Pact and to undermine the position of the West. In July 1958, a carefully laid conspiracy was successful, and it brought a major revolution in the Middle East. The military commander, General Kassim, led the coup. The twenty-three-year-old Iraq King, Feisal II, was butchered along with members of his family. The pro-British Prime Minister Nuri, a durable, wily old politician, who had held office all through the turbulent years, attempted flight disguised as a woman. But he was apprehended and torn to pieces by the mob that tracked him down.

Nasser was in Moscow when news of the coup reached him. He had been waiting for these tidings, and he hurried back to Cairo to take fullest advantage of the diplomatic somersault. For Iraq was now blasted out of the British and the western orbit, and the Baghdad Pact was in ruins. There was such fear that Jordan and Lebanon might also be engulfed that Prime Minister Macmillan and President Eisenhower rushed troops to both countries at the urgent request of their endangered governments.

For a little more than two years, until 1960, Kassim cooperated in the Khrushchev-Nasser game. But the unreliability of alliances in the Middle East was again demonstrated as Kassim turned on Nasser and the masters in the Kremlin. Soon he was jailing and executing Soviet and Egyptian agents whom he now regarded as the prime national menace. His revisionist line inevitably set him up as a Moscow-Cairo target. Thirty-eight attempts were made on his life, but he kept escaping with miraculous consistency and he boasted that no assassin's weapon could ever reach him. In 1963 the spell was broken and he was cut down by one of his own protégés. His body was displayed on Iraqi TV for all the country to ruminate how yesterday's heroes could become today's villains.

In the next four years conspiracy and thievery flourished on such a scale that though Iraq was an oil-rich country it was brought to the brink of bankruptcy. One successor of Kassim died with the leading members of his staff in a mysterious plane crash. Another was so brazen in his peculations that he was called the Thief of Baghdad. The inevitable reaction came in 1968 when angry students were joined by outraged business leaders, religious heads, and then by sections of the military itself, and a revolutionary junta came in on an anti-Nasser, anti-Communist wave. They had to remain vigilant because Nasser, still undiscouraged by the oscillations of fate, waited in the wings for any promising cue that would bring his supporters back into the performing cast.

The kingdom of Jordan, elevated from its emirate status by the British after World War II, was a special magnet for Nasser's most persistent diplomatic effort to make it a part of his Arab Union. The young King Hussein, British-educated, physically dauntless, completely reliant on British military support and on substantial American financial aid, was clearly in the western camp, and he had to be to survive. But he was an Arab nationalist and, though it required the rarest acrobatic skill, he tried to remain on good terms with Cairo. Nasser, however, regarded him as a pliant tool of the West. He sent agents into Jordan to cooperate with guerrilla groups who sought Hussein's overthrow. The main square of Amman was so often filled with demonstrators that the British named it Riot Plaza. Hussein several times broke off diplomatic relations with Egypt. In August 1960, after ambassadors had again been exchanged, the Jordanian Prime Minister was murdered by a bomb that exploded in his office, and Hussein condemned Egypt at the UN General Assembly. In a bitter broadcast from Jordan, he castigated Nasser as an agent of the Kremlin, a petty Farouk, a bloodthirsty madman. In 1962 he demanded that the headquarters of the Arab League be moved from Cairo. The mid-century years were studded with plots against Hussein's throne and his life, with occasional insincere reconciliations. When there were state visits to Cairo and cousinly embraces, Hussein was never sure whether he would return alive. His autobiography was most appropriately entitled *Uneasy Lies the Head*.

Nasser was kept busy with his plots and counterplots in most of the other Arab states—in the Sudan, in Saudi Arabia, in Lebanon, in Tunisia and Algeria. His military intervention in Yemen bogged down sixty thousand Egyptian troops, and a dreary war in which he resorted to poison gas dragged on with such wasteful futility that it was labeled Nasser's Vietnam.

After more than a decade Nasser could look back upon his imperial adventures with little but disappointment. He spoke of one God, one faith, one destiny, but every attempt at even modest coordination ended with recrimination and suspicion. One objective, however, could always be counted on to transcend differences and to bring agreement for common Arab action: the defeat and destruction of Israel. Nasser was the acknowledged leader in this fulfillment and he relied upon it, not only for the wars against Israel, but as a political catalyst when so much else seemed to fail. Of course his implacability to Israel was not simply an expedient used to rally Arab unity. He was appealing to a hostility which had been present from the days of the Balfour Declaration in 1917 and had continued with intensified force right through the partition resolution of the United Nations of 1947 and the unsuccessful war that followed. But loosing the passions against Israel could always be counted on to drown out other frustrations and disappointments.

From the moment he became President of Egypt Nasser gave the highest priority to a return round against Israel. By 1955 he could rely upon solid Soviet support. Khrushchev, hoping to use Egypt as a base for the penetration of the Mediterranean, poured in arms, supplied technicians, and encouraged the guerrilla attacks on Israeli outposts and borders.

Early in October 1956, Nasser announced that Egypt, Syria, and Jordan, bridging their differences, had united their military command "in the event of war with Israel." When Nasser ran afoul of the British and the French by unilaterally nationalizing the Suez Canal, Israel joined in a pre-emptive strike, and astonished the world by a quick and decisive victory. Under the leadership of Moshe Dayan, the brilliant one-eyed Chief of Staff, the Israeli forces outflanked all the enemy bases. It was significant that, despite elaborate assurances and demonstrations of solidarity, not a single Arab state felt constrained to come to Egypt's assistance. Nasser managed to survive only because the UN insisted that the French, British, and Israeli forces withdraw from the positions that had been captured. Indeed, he capitalized on the Suez affair to ameliorate some of his economic problems. Egypt had been facing bankruptcy and it was a windfall to nationalize the foreign investments as reprisal for the attacks.

Nasser waited eleven years, until the summer of 1967, before his next major strike. This time he was certain he could not fail. The Soviet Union had allocated more than two billion dollars in military aid. His forces now included 288,000 completely equipped men and hundreds of the most modern jets and tanks, and their deployment represented years of training by Russian technicians. Nasser massed his full strength on Israel's borders, and Syria, Jordan, Lebanon, and Iran were poised for a coordinated attack on all the other fronts. Nasser demanded from U Thant, Secretary of the UN, that the international peace force withdraw from the demilitarized areas it had been patrolling ever since the Sinai war had ended. U Thant complied at once and as the UN units moved out, the Egyptian forces promptly moved in. Nasser, holding Sharm-el-Sheikh, then closed the Gulf of Aqaba, whose freedom of navigation had been guaranteed when Israel withdrew after its victories in 1956. The closure of the international waterway cut off Israel's only access to the Red Sea and the Indian Ocean.

Once again, Israel forestalled attack. Winston Churchill, Jr., wrote: "Israel like a cowboy of the old Wild West, did not wait for the enemy to draw—she had seen the glint in Nasser's eye."* In a few hours of precision air strafing Israel eliminated virtually the entire Egyptian air force before it got off the ground and proceeded to smash the tank armada in the Sinai Peninsula. In succeeding days the Israelis immobilized the armies and the bases of Jordan, Syria, and Iraq. In ninety-six hours they were at the Suez Canal and the Soviet Union's two billion dollar investment had been wasted. Once again Nasser's ambition to eliminate Israel had been thwarted.

The defeat was the worst of Nasser's career, and it was all the more humiliating since, in this war, he had not only the cooperation of all the Arab states, but also major military assistance from the Soviet Union. He was still unwilling to concede on any of his objectives but he knew that he would need a validating mandate if his leadership were to be respected. In an emotional address he resigned his post as President, and then waited for the response. It came, overwhelmingly. A million men, women, and children poured into Cairo, shouted their confidence in him, and pleaded with him to go on. "Don't leave us, Nasser," they kept repeating in virtual hysteria—"Don't leave us." Nasser announced that he would bow to the will of his people and resumed his post. As if his had been the decisive victories, he then demanded that Israel must withdraw from all occupied territories or the massed might of the Arab states would again be loosed.

In the years that followed, the familiar pattern of guerrilla warfare was resumed to support his threats of annihilation. It was clear that as long as he lived and held control there could be no peaceful settlement with Israel, nor would the grandiose dreams of Arab Union under his supervision be relinquished. Fate now intervened in late 1970. Though he was still in middle age, he died suddenly of a coronary attack.

* Randolph S. and Winston S. Churchill, *The Six Day War* (Boston: Houghton Mifflin Co., 1967), p. 75.

It had been a tempestuous career, and the evaluation was inevitably a mixed one. Nasser was an authentic liberator; he brought not only freedom out of exploitation, but self-esteem out of servility. He inherited a country sunk in poverty and disease, degraded for centuries by foreign occupation. The nationalism that he wakened restored pride to a people that already had a leadership mission at the dawn of history. He began reforms that took advantage of modern technology and would, in time, revitalize large sections of the misused soil. He launched these reforms against the most formidable obstacles—the cynicism of government and the fanaticism of religious vested interests. Even his dream of Arab Union was positive. It carried the potential for giving the Arab world, with more than a hundred million people, a restored position of influence and dignity.

His failure came because he did not prepare an adequate base on which to build. He relied on balcony oratory and manipulatory skill rather than on substantive strength. He was really a sheep in wolf's clothing. For his dreams of grandeur could find no reality when his own nation offered so little example of fulfillment.

It should be added that his obsession with personal power, when he had to deal with proud and sensitive national leaders, was a fatal obstacle. In his negotiations with other Arab states, he rarely made place for their dignity or their aspirations. His cavalier treatment of Syria, when he created the United Arab Republic, was typical of his abrasive egocentrism.

Above all, he frittered away the resources of his country in the reckless wars with Israel. Of course it was too much to expect collaboration with Israel in the utilization of science and technology to free the resources of what was once the Fertile Crescent. Years of co-existence, perhaps decades, would be required before there could be the mature realization that there were common benefits in Arab-Israeli cooperation. But Nasser refused to accept the reality of Israel's existence, the compelling fact that it was there and that it could not be eliminated. His was the failure of the extraordinarily endowed popular leader who probably himself never knew what was statesmanship and what was hallucination. As a young officer Nasser had said that in Egypt there was a role wandering aimlessly in search of a hero. All his life he tried to prove that he was the answer to the search. But he converted the drama in which he found that role into a tragedy with an ignominious ending.

47

ISRAEL AND
THE ARAB WORLD

ONE OF THE MOST SPECTACULAR DEVELOPMENTS OF THE EARLY POST-
war period was the emergence in 1948 of the state of Israel. As was
noted earlier, Britain relinquished its thirty-year mandate for what
had been Palestine, and the United Nations, after long and acrimonious debate, voted to partition the land that was fiercely disputed
between the Arabs and the Jews, and to create two independent
states. The neighboring Arab nations refused to accept the United
Nations decision and, as soon as the British colors were hauled
down, they attacked on all fronts. In the wars that followed, the
decisiveness of the Israeli victories signified the emergence of a new
power in the Middle East. The outstanding figure in its survival
was David Ben-Gurion, one of the master builders of the twentieth
century.

Ben-Gurion was a strange blend of statesman and prophet—practical in negotiation, visionary in objective. He was a stocky little
man, blunt, truculent, determined, whose corona of white hair
rising in unruly disarray and deceptively cherubic face and pixie
expression offered exceptional opportunity to the caricaturists. He
was broadly educated, immersed in the Bible, the Greek classics,
and the Buddhist wisdom of the East. His interpretation of Jewish
history was audaciously simple. His people had been defeated by the
Roman legions nineteen hundred years before and had been driven
from *"Eretz Yisroel,"* the land of Israel. He bypassed the nineteen
succeeding centuries as merely a deplorable episode. In an audacious
act of faith he leaped a hundred generations and linked the present

exultant moment of regeneration with the courageous but unavailing resistance when the Second Temple fell; the intervening period represented sterile chronology. His contemporaries were the intrepid spirits who had created the Bible, the Maccabees who had defied the Syrians, and the zealots who had defended Masada to the last man against the might of Rome. Ben-Gurion made this quantum jump across the flux of time without the resort to fantasy. Every mile that he walked, every hill that he climbed, every corner that he turned, validated the reality of his vision. Here was the Jordan that flowed through all the stirring episodes the Bible had immortalized. Here Gideon confounded the Midianites. Here Deborah inspired Barak in his victory over the Canaanites and the chariots of Sisera. Here Joshua challenged the Walls of Jericho. And here another diminutive David fought the mighty Goliath. To Ben-Gurion and his comrades it was all the resumption of action in a drama where the People of the Book had temporarily been offstage during an intermission. With such a view, they responded with confidence to the challenge of forty million enemies who were determined that there was to be no such continuity.

Ben-Gurion was born in Poland in 1886 when it was part of czarist Russia. Periodically the news would come through of the government-encouraged pogroms that made every Jewish family potential victims. Ben-Gurion was caught up early in the dream of a new life in Zion although, since the Turkish Empire dominated all the Near and Middle East, it seemed to be a vague Messianic dream. In 1906, as a young man of twenty, he managed to fulfill his hope. In all his judgments Ben-Gurion was soberly prosaic, but he would lapse into the lyrical when he thought of Palestine as a homeland. Galilee, where he first made his way, was a wilderness that promised little more than privation and death. But upon settlement there he wrote, "We had left behind our books and our theorizing, the hair-splitting and the arguments, and come to the Land to redeem it by our labor. We were all still fresh; the dew of dreams was still moist in our hearts. . . ."*

He labored to drain the marshes, to plant the trees, and to prepare the foundations for self-supporting communities of immigrants, most of whom perished in the reclamation struggle. His attempt to organize the first immigrants for their own protection was interpreted by the Turkish authorities as political agitation, and he was

* David Ben-Gurion, *Israel: Years of Challenge* (New York, Chicago, and San Francisco: Holt, Rinehart & Winston, 1963), p. 7.

arrested and deported. His papers were stamped *"Never to Return."* He was in the United States at the outbreak of World War I and shipped out to join the Jewish Legion, which fought with distinction under British auspices. After World War I he rose to leadership in the Palestine Labor Movement. He created *Histadrut,* the all-encompassing labor federation that was later to dominate the economic and political life of Israel. He was part of the Jewish Agency, an unofficial shadow government within the mandate, and he planned the resistance to the British attempts to curtail Jewish immigration. The partition resolution of the United Nations created a sovereign Jewish state and it was Ben-Gurion who read the historic Declaration of Independence on May 14, 1948. When the neighboring Arab states struck, vowing to nullify the UN mandate, Ben-Gurion served as the civilian commander in chief, and he was the rallying point for the Israeli victory. The state having achieved its sovereignty on the battlefield, the white-maned soldier-prophet was called upon to serve as the first Prime Minister.

The pledge had been made in the Declaration of Independence that any Jew who wished to come to Israel from any part of the world would be welcomed and would immediately receive citizenship. The centers for Displaced Persons that had been established in Europe were crowded with hope-deferred refugees, the remnants of the holocaust and the concentration camps, and Israel took it as a prime obligation to empty these as quickly as transportation could be provided. Within three years, by 1951, a total of 638,000 immigrants had arrived, virtually doubling the original population of Israel; and by the end of the first decade the population had again almost doubled. The immigrants poured in from the lands that had been ravaged and despoiled by the Nazis, and from the Arab lands where the reprisal assaults on historic Jewish settlements ended security and threatened life. Those who left could take nothing with them and the international migration agencies were compelled to pay per capita ransom. The entire community of Yemen was evacuated, fifty thousand Jews whose roots in the country went back to biblical days. They were flown to Israel in Operation Magic Carpet, 150 to the plane, and as they emerged from the C-54 Skymasters into the freedom of the new Israel, their rabbis recited the passage from Exodus that "ascent would be on the wings of eagles."* The ancient settlement of 120,000 Iraqi Jews abandoned their

* Exodus 19:4.

possessions and were transported in Operation Ali Baba. When Morocco obtained its independence from France and the ominous cry was raised, "Morocco for the Moroccans," when Algeria identified itself with the Moscow-Cairo axis, when Nasser tightened his hold on Egypt and proclaimed his dream of Pan Arab Union, the Jewish settlements, centuries old, knew that their day had come. They fled, dispossessed of everything except their dreams for renewal in Israel. These waves of immigration and those that followed disruptive crises in the other lands brought the Jewish population to 2,600,000 by 1971.

The immediate need was housing. Where were these heterogeneous masses to be accommodated, even temporarily? The old British military camps were pressed into service, then the homes and primitive huts that the Arabs had abandoned. The special transit centers that were established were quickly filled. The privations of overcrowding, and the absence of purposive activity until absorption into the economy could be accomplished, sorely tried the immigrants. The authorities wrestled with what they called "the ingathering of the exiles." The Israelis had a wry expression for the ordeal of those first years of adjustment: "It was hopeless but not serious."

Of even more concern than physical readjustment was the problem of social and cultural assimilation. Many of those who fled from Asia and North Africa had virtually nothing in common with those who came out of the European environment. They had to learn everything from the mastery of the alphabet to the most elementary precautions for health and sanitation. They had to cope with the effects of centuries of malnutrition, of trachoma and tuberculosis and all the ailments of the depressed societies from which they emerged. Those who came out of the western tradition often brought with them polarized political and religious loyalties that were inflexible. There were passionate, corrosive debates in the Israeli Parliament, the Knesseth, and in press and forum, on the structure of the state and on theocratic conformity. Dr. Weizmann, the founding President, had to warn the more fanatical partisans: "The walls of Jericho fell to the sound of shouts. But I never heard of the walls being raised by those means!" Winston Churchill jibed that wherever there were three Jews, there were two Prime Ministers and a leader of the Opposition.

Integration was achieved primarily by three factors—the educational system, universal military service, and the prod of common danger. Schooling in Israel reached from the kindergarten, which enrolled 95 percent of the children, to a network of universities; the national budget for education was second only to that of the defense needs. Teaching was a highly respected profession, and the youngsters, through every stage, had expert as well as compassionate guidance. In the school the behavior and outlook of the ghetto were transformed. The Babel of eighty languages was muted since Hebrew very quickly became the national tongue.

Equally effective in the integration process was the military draft. Service was universal, the men inducted for thirty months, the women for twenty-four, and the reserves on call up to the fiftieth year. The military therefore became a sturdy anvil on which the differences imported from countries of origin were hammered out and the unique nationalism of Israel tempered and hardened. Within a decade the proportion in the armed forces of the native born, the Sabras,* became predominant. The women especially were a new breed, self-reliant, graceful, contributing their share to what was proudly counted as perhaps the most effective military organization in the Middle East.

The dominant influence for integration, however, was the sense of common danger. It was referred to as *"Ain B'reira,"* No Alternative, and it served as a defense in depth that in any emergency quickly fused the nation so that it could act as a unit. Everyone lived in the knowledge that Israel was the last stop. The enemy could be thrice beaten, or ten times, or a hundred times; it could suffer casualties, or some miles of territory, or the loss of face. Yet its existence would not be threatened. Defeat would not carry with it the penalty of annihilation. But the Israelis knew that if they lost once, that was the end. There could be no second chance for retrieval, no reliance on time as after Dunkirk or Pearl Harbor. The Arab leadership had made it clear that in victory it would erase every vestige of the Israeli presence. It was this grim realization of No Alternative that gave the Israelis the will to face the never absent crises.

It should be added that this sense of ever-present danger contributed to the eager welcome that all immigrants received. Those who came to start afresh were redeemed, of course, in their own lives. But they also promoted the security of Israel. Tens of thousands preferred to settle in established cities or in the agricultural communities that years of pioneering had already created. But others

---

* Sabra is the cactus plant and the name was meant to imply a tough, prickly surface but a gentle, tender interior.

moved into, or were channeled into, the undeveloped stretches, the areas of extreme vulnerability. They were assigned to the hills that had to be cleared, the sand dunes and the marshes that centuries of neglect had condemned, and, above all, the frontiers that had to be guarded. Within a few months of arrival they were an integral part of the defense bastion.

Ben-Gurion gave primary attention to the Negev Desert. It had been regarded as a vast nothingness, politically a sop thrown to Israel by the diplomats who negotiated the partition. But Ben-Gurion believed that the desert, larger than the rest of Israel, bore within it major potentialities for the future. Modern science and technology, directed by the brainpower of Israel, could surely bring it to vibrant life and productivity. It could ultimately absorb many millions in the migration tides of tomorrow. Ben-Gurion authorized a whole series of pumping stations to bring in water. He encouraged research in desalinization, in capturing solar rays for power. He successfully negotiated with the American government for a special reactor in the desert in the hope that atomic power could be applied for intensive irrigation. He personally supervised the establishment of scores of agricultural cooperatives. He had six- and twelve-inch pipelines laid down from the Red Sea to Haifa, carrying millions of barrels of oil from Asia to the Mediterranean. When the Suez Canal was blocked and closed in 1967, the pipelines became an invaluable asset. At the northern entrance to the desert Beersheba, once a minor religious shrine, became a thriving community. It even boasted a university that concentrated on desert ecology. At the southern Red Sea outlet the obscure hamlet of Elath received thousands of refugees from the abortive 1956 Hungarian revolution and from the African states, and it became the port for the traffic to Asia and Africa. Ben-Gurion never tired of extolling the significance of the desert. He set up a modest three-room prefabricated home in S'de Boker when he retired as Prime Minister, and he moved into it with his Paula to dramatize his confidence in the desert. His farewell speech consisted of one word: "Follow!"

Meantime the economic life of the country expanded, despite wars and war scares and the unremitting boycotts of the neighboring Arab states. Every week licenses were granted for the opening of new factories whose local manufacture helped to stem the flight of hard currency, even as it provided increasing employment. The merchant marine grew, and there was more than ordinary pride in the scheduling of regular service between Lydda and the large cities around the world through the Israeli-owned El Al airlines.

Israel's assistance to the emerging African and Asian countries, her cooperation in solving technical and educational problems, was gratefully received. Israeli scientists, educators, and technicians were welcomed as they converted blueprints for industrial plants, irrigation projects, public health programs, and school systems into realities. Israel cooperated with Ghana in organizing the Black Star Line, with joint stock control in a merchant marine. Friendly trade and cultural relations brought Israelis to Guinea and Ethiopia and far-off Burma.

Yet with all the exultation of freedom and economic security, one persistent danger remained to haunt every aspect of national life: Israel was an enclave, completely surrounded by Arab states, all fanatically committed to its destruction. By 1952 there was a new vigorous revolutionary government in Egypt, led by Gamal Nasser, and he was a far cry from the inept King Farouk who had bungled the war of 1948. Nasser had dreams of an all-encompassing Arab Union, with himself as head.* The Arab states were rent by divergent interests so that Nasser made little headway, but they were united in their determination to avenge the defeats of 1948. It was in the shadow of this hostility that a beleaguered Israel sought survival.

In the next decade the Israelis fought two wars against the Arabs and each time they had to depend upon a pre-emptive strike. In 1956 the Soviet Union had built up the Egyptian armaments to the point that Nasser was certain of easy conquest. The Israelis did not wait. Anthony Eden said, "The marked victim of the strangler is not to be condemned if he strikes out before the noose is around his neck." The victory of the Israelis under the effective leadership of Ben-Gurion's protégé and his hoped-for heir, General Moshe Dayan, was swifter and more crushing than in 1948. General Dayan pushed down to the tip of Sinai to take Aqaba, which commanded access to the Red Sea. He moved into the Gaza Strip, which had been the main base for the guerrilla incursions.

Virtually the entire membership of the United Nations demanded that Israel must withdraw. Ben-Gurion held out for months, insisting that his nation must not again be exposed to the strangulation that Nasser had threatened. He finally yielded in February 1957, when he received assurances from President Eisenhower and his Secretary of State, John Foster Dulles, that the United States would

* See Chapter 46.

protect the right of innocent passage of Israel in the Gulf of Aqaba, and that it would support any UN action that would prevent the Gaza Strip from being used as a base for guerrilla operations.* But even as Ben-Gurion yielded he knew in his heart that, though such pledges were offered in good faith, they would be as quicksand under shifting national interests.

His forebodings were quickly borne out. The years that followed until 1967 were an agonizing period of undeclared war. The raids and the reprisals did not stop. Nasser would not give up on his determination to liquidate the state of Israel. He fell back constantly on the analogy of the Moslem struggle against the Crusaders. It took two centuries and more to dislodge the Christian intruders, but the Moslems confidently fought their wars of attrition and at length they won out. Nasser declared that however long it took, the Arab states too would win this war of time.†

In 1967 Nasser was again ready. His voice came over the radio assuring the Arab world that now, at last, all scores with the Israelis would be settled. On May 28, in his broadcast beamed to Israel, he vowed that he would put an end to Israeli aggression and he added, "Israeli existence is itself an aggression." On June 4 he announced, "We are facing you in battle and we are burning with desire for it to start."

The Israeli government reminded Washington of the written pledges of 1957 to protect the lifelines on which depended access to the Indian Ocean and Africa. The response was evasive enough to bring home the lesson that realists had noted earlier: whatever had to be done for Israel, even for survival, had to be done by Israelis. They therefore prepared for the pre-emptive blow and let Nasser have the "burning wish" of his radio clarion. They knew that there could be no errors when they moved. Every man and woman had to fulfill the assigned mission perfectly; every weapon had to gain its total objective. Air Force General Hod said that eighteen years of training had to be telescoped into the eighty minutes which the Israelis had to immobilize the entire Egyptian air force and its tank armada.

In six days the war was over. The Israelis took the Sinai Peninsula down to the Red Sea. They captured the Golan heights. They occu-

---

* Dwight Eisenhower, *The White House Years,* Vol. II, p. 184.

† Nasser's analogy never perturbed the Israelis. They remembered that the Crusaders had come as conquerors, bent on loot, and set down no roots. To the Israelis the soil they guarded was homeland to be defended to the last man.

pied the west bank of the Jordan and the Gaza Strip. They reunited Jerusalem, whose Old City portion with its sacred shrines had been held by Jordan and forbidden to the Israelis since 1948. With the chastening experience of the previous rounds they declared that, this time, the fruits of victory would not be dissipated. The cost to the Arabs was staggering, more than fifty thousand dead, another quarter million refugees. Later, there was an exchange of prisoners and 11,500 Arabs were returned, including nine generals, for sixteen Israelis.

Still there was no peace. And in any realistic appraisal it was not possible until two issues were resolved by mutual consent. The first was the right of Israel to exist as a sovereign state; the other was the necessity to end the degradation of more than a million Arab refugees who lived by the reluctant charity of the United States and a few of the western powers. So long as the Arab states would not recognize that Israel was a reality, and so long as the Arab refugees continued to exist as pariahs, victories and defeats were only truces.

After each round of war the stalemate on these interrelated issues remained. The Arabs were adamant. The defiance of the political leaders could be discounted as the traditional Arab rhetorical flamboyance. But the pronouncements of the Arab summit conference in Khartoum in 1968 could not be so dismissed. There, three "No's" were unanimously adopted: No recognition of Israel; no negotiation with Israel; no peace with Israel. Conversely, the Israelis consistently refused to accept more than token responsibility for the Arab refugees. They claimed that the original refugee problem was created in 1948 when the Arabs repudiated the mandate of the UN and launched the war. They further claimed that the problem could have been solved long before if the recommendations of the UN Relief Commission had been accepted—that the Arab states absorb the refugees in their own thinly populated lands, the resettlement to be underwritten by Israel.

But this diplomatic line infuriated the Arabs. For the Jews had not entered an unpopulated territory when they settled in Israel, and the Arab families that had been panicked into flight, or had been dispossessed, were the innocent victims of what Dr. Weizmann himself had called "the conflict between two rights." Thus the charges and the recriminations continued, bloodied by the incursions of the guerrillas and by the punishing reprisals of the Israelis. The tragic buildup of arms continued and the preparations for renewed war never ceased.

In the summer of 1970 there appeared to be a break in the weary reiteration of defiant negatives. Nasser began making conciliatory statements, at first to journalists, then to officials of friendly foreign governments, and finally, through diplomatic channels, to the Russians, the United States, and the UN. They all included his readiness to consider the recognition of Israel, under certain circumstances. Golda Meir, the rugged old lady who had become the Israeli Prime Minister, pledged that there would be appropriate withdrawal from occupied territory to secure borders, once the sovereignty of Israel was recognized. The disposition of the Arab refugees and compensation for their losses would be subject to negotiation.

There was still a long way to go to bring both sides together, and the United Nations and American intermediaries labored to narrow the areas of disagreement. After Nasser's sudden death in the fall of 1970 his successor, Anwar-al-Sadat, reaffirmed his wish for a détente, and Golda Meir replied that Israel sought a secure peace, not territory. There was clearly eagerness at last, on both sides, for the conflict to be resolved. Even the venerable Ben-Gurion who had been the tough hard-liner of the Suez war negotiations agreed that, after so much bloodshed, the time had come to be less suspicious of the internationally supported pledges of peace.

Thus, as Israel moved into the decade of the 1970's, there was a cautious spirit of optimism. It was no longer the Messianic exultation that had pervaded the climate when the state was proclaimed. It was rather a sober realization that, even with peace, there were no easy answers. Dr. Weizmann used to say, "Some problems do not get solved, they only get older." When Ben-Gurion resisted the introduction of television into Israel as frivolous, he said wryly, "A nation surrounded by Arabs has no need of stories of cowboys and Indians."

But faith in the capacity of the state to survive was still the most reliable source of national strength, and it transcended the immediacies of logic. There was considerable truth in the quip that Israel was a future-oriented society, a land of unlimited impossibilities. Its dogged confidence was as vital in sustaining the national will as the gratifying statistics of actual physical progress. This is what Ben-Gurion, the old prophet of the desert, must have meant when he reiterated his lifelong credo: "Whoever does not believe in miracles is not a realist!"

48

LYNDON JOHNSON:
THE GOOD ROAD AND
THE WRONG TURN

LYNDON JOHNSON'S INCUMBENCY AS PRESIDENT OF THE UNITED STATES was trapped between two tragedies: the assassination of John F. Kennedy, which enshrined the young gladiator as the martyr of Camelot, and the war in Vietnam, whose cost in blood and treasure and whose moral validity were passionately questioned. With all of his unusual political skill, Johnson could not extricate himself from either. He could never shake off the feeling that he was surrounded. Even his intimates referred to his Alamo complex. He had to contend with the comparison between the Kennedy image as the paradigm of grace, charm, and wit and the image which his critics and opponents portrayed of him as a party wheeler-dealer—plebeian, earthy, often gauche and crass. Even after he was elected on his own record with the largest plurality of the century, the Kennedy entourage, who could not forgive him for the caprice of Fate that displaced them, missed no opportunity to identify him as a devious corn-pone politician. "I never accept a report as true," said one of his detractors, "until it is denied by Johnson." The Vietnam incubus was, of course, an even heavier burden. The initial American commitment in Vietnam had been made by Eisenhower and was substantially broadened by Kennedy. But Johnson turned it into a full-scale war and, as the casualties mounted, it left his reputation in shreds. A sniper's bullet cut down Kennedy at the threshold of his brightest promise. A tragic decision to expand the commitments of his predecessors cut down Johnson at the flood tide of one of the most productive legislative achievements in American history.

It was ironic that the Kennedy personality and reputation should have been a haunting problem for Johnson. In fact, Johnson stood closer to the American hero-syndrome, the just-folks leader who came up the hard way from the open plains, determined not to be fenced in. It had always been an advantage politically to boast of log cabin origins and frontier breeding. The typical American was enthralled by the covered-wagon saga, the cowboy, the tall, gaunt roughrider, quick with his gun, who did not try to make his way with fancy words. It had been no advantage to Adlai Stevenson when, campaigning against the soldier from Abilene, Kansas, he used polished epigrams and scintillating rhetoric. The term "egghead" was not meant to compliment him.

It remains a mystery why Johnson, emerging from the Texas frontier land, regarded his origins as a political liability rather than an asset. His father served in the state legislature. His mother was the daughter of the secretary of state for Texas. She was a plain-spoken, independent-minded, God-fearing schoolteacher. It was a lineage that could compare fairly well with the heraldry of the second-generation near-patricians. Perhaps part of Johnson's problem came from the flood of university intellectuals who had been brought to Washington by Kennedy. They were sparkling and highly quotable in their judgments and they found kindred spirits among the pundits of the media. What had been sophisticated with Kennedy was philistine with Johnson, "that awful accent," "those boorish manners." As one of the Washington correspondents reported, "They were sure that Texas blood and Ivy ink did not mix."* In the heyday of Senator Joseph McCarthy, they had been vilified for their liberal views, their patriotism had been called into question, and their academic independence had been jeopardized by intimidation. The searing experience of those locust years should have taught them that it is wise for power to walk with humility. But when they came into the counsels of government they shed their academic scrupulousness and sat in the seats of the scornful. Most of them were asked to stay on by the new President but it was almost impossible to assimilate the Kennedy men and the Johnson men. An aide growled, "I don't know whom to turn to. It's like Noah's Ark. There's two of everybody!" When they lost their hold on the levers of power they departed with a massive Camelot hangover, and were brutal in their appraisal of actions which many of

* Max Frankel, *The New York Times*, Feb. 9, 1969.

them had helped to initiate. One of the liberal critics called his volume: *Our Hero LBJ, And Other Dirty Stories.* John Roche of Brandeis University, commenting on such gallantry, noted that the difference between a self-righteous liberal and a cannibal is that a cannibal eats only his enemies.

Johnson was born in 1908 in ranch country, in the hills of southwest Texas, bleak, hardscrabble land that yielded only to backbreaking cultivation. He borrowed seventy-five dollars to stake himself for enrollment at Southwest State Teachers' College, where he worked as a part-time janitor before he became one of the president's secretaries. He earned his degree in three years, one of which was spent teaching in a school for Mexican children, and he never lost his devotion to the underprivileged Latinos. He demonstrated his concern later when he was a first-term senator and learned that one of the Mexican-Americans who had been killed in Korea was denied burial in the regular white cemetery. He had the Pentagon send a plane to bring the boy back for burial in the Arlington National Cemetery. The Latinos called him, in affection, *"Muy Hombre,"* very much the Man.

He was all of twenty-three when a multimillionaire ranch owner, Richard Kleberg, was elected to Congress in 1931 and took Lyndon with him as one of his assistants. Roosevelt came to Washington two years later to launch the New Deal and Johnson had his lifetime hero for emulation. In 1937 there was a vacancy in Congress from Texas and ten men competed. Johnson was the only committed Roosevelt New Dealer among the candidates and he won the seat, launching his long congressional career when not yet thirty. Sam Rayburn, one of the most influential congressmen in Washington, was a friend of the family, and his recommendation brought Johnson onto the powerful Naval Affairs Committee where he was a stalwart supporter of Roosevelt's rearmament program for the inevitable showdown with Hitler.

When Pearl Harbor catapulted the United States into the war Johnson was the first man from Congress to volunteer, and he rose to the rank of lieutenant commander. He won a coveted decoration after a bombing mission, and he served until the President ordered back all congressmen who were in the service. After Roosevelt's death, Truman could count fully on Johnson's party loyalty. In 1948 he tried for the Senate, pitting himself against the well-entrenched Governor Coke Stevenson, and he won, after a recount, by 87 votes out of 900,000. He took considerable joshing as "Landslide Johnson." But within four years, he had been named the Democratic minority leader in the Senate, and two years later, in 1954, when the Democrats regained control of both Houses of Congress, he became the majority leader. He shared governance power with President Eisenhower, who was now largely dependent on Johnson to maneuver major bills through the sensitive legislative minefields. Such constructive cooperation was especially important in foreign policy proposals. The Republican Senate leader was William Knowland of California, who did not agree with his chief on liberal financial aid for other nations. Johnson also united the Democrats in the decision to prick the bubble of Senator Joseph McCarthy's reputation. He supported the Senate Investigation Committee in the censure battle, when half of the Republicans deserted Eisenhower as the crucial decision was reached which deflated the McCarthy threat.

Suddenly Johnson's career almost came to an abrupt end. In July 1955 he suffered a massive heart attack and there seemed little hope that he could continue with his unusually exacting leadership responsibilities. But his durable constitution saw him through and he recovered fully. Though he thereafter followed a more sensible discipline, the routine of intensive effort and long hours never stopped. His wife, Ladybird, later said resignedly, "Lyndon always works as if there were never going to be a tomorrow."

When Eisenhower was re-elected in 1956, the gathering drive of the blacks for equality could no longer be ignored. The Supreme Court had already rendered its unanimous verdict that integration in education had to be achieved with "all deliberate speed." The opposition of the Southerners was sullenly defiant. The senators from the old confederate states signed a Southern Manifesto that protested the Supreme Court decision and the signators included William Fulbright and John Sparkman, Adlai Stevenson's running mate in 1952. Only Lyndon Johnson laid his political life on the line, both in Texas and in the Senate, by refusing to place his name on the manifesto.

As the election of 1960 approached, Johnson's stature had grown sufficiently for him to be considered as a presidential possibility. Kennedy was the front runner and there was very little chance for a Southerner to receive the nomination. When Kennedy won, he tapped Johnson as his running mate, for he needed all the influence that Johnson could command. Texas had been twice lost in the Eisenhower sweep and some of the other Southern states were by no means safe for the Democrats. The strategy was vindicated. Kennedy was very narrowly elected, the margin of victory clearly supplied by the Vice President.

Johnson was given many task force assignments by his young chief—national commissions, international representation—and he clocked more than 110,000 miles around the world. But for a man of his quicksilver personality and abundant energy the vice presidency was frustrating. After the activities that fell to a Senate majority leader, his present duties seemed to be merely ceremonial trivia. Then in November 1963 the caprice of some human driftwood in Dallas changed the course of history. Johnson suddenly found himself in the air force plane that was to bring Kennedy's body back to Washington, and he was taking the oath of office as President of the United States.

The Johnson record of domestic legislation was spectacular. There was a formidable backlog of Kennedy proposals that had been pigeonholed in committee by the coalition of Republicans and die-hard Southerners. Johnson read the riot act to the recalcitrants of his party. He used all the arm-twisting methods of his days in the Senate when he was majority leader. He knew each man's vulnerable concession point. He demanded what his staff called "the two shift day" and himself set the example. He spent long hours in man-to-man conferences; he was endlessly on the telephone, persuading, cajoling, trading. As the bills tumbled in and out of the legislative hopper, one congressman grumbled, "He has so many irons in the fire, he damn near puts the fire out." Another who had just been nose-ringed into acquiescence said wearily, "How do you say 'no' to a man who refuses to hear the word?"

Johnson demonstrated his overpowering persuasiveness only a few days after he had succeeded to the presidency. He knew how crucial it was to probe the Kennedy assassination and to quiet rumors, many of them hysterical, that dazed the American people. It was essential that the composition of the investigation commission be of such unimpeachable character and quality that the findings would carry decisive credence. He turned at once to persuade Chief Justice Warren to head the commission, and Richard Russell, the dean of the Democrats in the Senate, to be a member. Warren resisted, in the conviction that a Justice of the Supreme Court should not be thus involved. Johnson would not accept the declination. He declared that just as Warren had loyally served his country in wartime, he had a similar duty now, in a national crisis, when he was summoned by his commander in chief. Warren resignedly yielded. Russell was unwilling to serve on a commission with Warren, an old political enemy. Besides, he was suffering from a chronic lung disorder and his physician had warned him against fatiguing extra duties. Here too Johnson's tenacity proved stronger than Russell's aversion and the new President had his way.

In 1964 Johnson was re-elected with the largest popular majority in American history, a compelling mandate that negated the resistance of the coalition which had so long blocked earlier reform efforts. Johnson hammered through educational aid bills that released billions to schools and colleges for scholarships, loans, and research projects, and for long-deferred facilities. Medicare had been the dream of advanced reformers since World War II. Johnson rode roughshod over the opposition of the conservatives in the medical profession, and a broad program of medical aid became a reality. He wheedled hundreds of millions from Congress as rent subsidies for the poor. He liberalized the oppressive immigration laws. His immense energy seemed inexhaustible, and he involved himself in every detail. One of his aides said, with understandable awe, "Not a sparrow falls that he doesn't know about." The enabling legislation rolled on and on, and a social revolution was in the making that was to transform the lives of tens of millions of his countrymen.

All this time the most critical of America's domestic problems had to be faced squarely—the raging impatience of the black population, aggravated by the superficiality of what had previously passed for reform. The 1957 law had established the procedures to protect the blacks who were determined to exercise the right to vote. There had been a stronger act in 1960 that put teeth into the protective measure. But there was still little change in the routines of daily living, employment in more than menial positions, housing beyond the stinking, festering ghettoes, educational opportunities to equip the disinherited to live with security and dignity.

Voice was given to the impatience by an inspiring young leader, Martin Luther King, Jr., who was looked upon by his people as almost the last hope if the country was to avoid a ruinous war between the races. Dr. King, a Baptist minister, had come to national prominence in 1956 when he led a successful boycott in Montgomery, Alabama, that broke the Jim Crow practice of the bus system. In the next few years he had organized and personally participated in freedom rides, sit-ins, demonstrations, marches, teaching his people to make their mass protests effective and, in the spirit of

[586]

Gandhi, to accept the jailings and the beatings that would serve to rouse the dormant conscience of the country. In 1963 he had led a march to Washington and spoke to more than three hundred thousand people in the great open mall in the shadow of the Lincoln Memorial. His address—"I Have a Dream"—spelled out his objectives with rare spiritual power for his nationwide television audience.

By 1964, Johnson, now firmly established in the presidency and cooperating with Dr. King, was ready for the next giant step toward racial justice. An omnibus civil rights bill, emerging from strenuous planning sessions, covered voting, schooling, employment, and housing. Johnson's lieutenants were marshaled for the long legislative ordeal as if they were planning an all-out war. And it was a war. It went on for 142 days, during which Johnson did not for a moment ease the pressure. He managed the strategy for the bill every step of the way, maneuvering among the many crippling amendments, fighting back the filibusters, keeping the nation informed with frequent addresses and press conferences. Precisely 104 years to the day after Lincoln had proclaimed the emancipation of the slaves, Johnson signed into law the most far-reaching civil rights bill since Reconstruction.

But though the law was on the books, it had to be validated against determined opposition in hundreds of recalcitrant communities, in the North as in the South. When ingenious technicalities slowed down or nullified fulfillment, leadership was seized by more militant groups who now refused to be restrained by King's nonviolent forebearance. The year 1967 was especially heartbreaking. Riots erupted in Boston, where black welfare recipients chained themselves inside a municipal building. They spread to Cincinnati and Tampa, Newark and Detroit, Plainfield and Atlanta. They burned out whole blocks of the residential and business sections in many other cities. There were scores of fatalities and injuries and incalculable damage to property.

Johnson was neither discouraged nor disillusioned. He was realistic enough to know that whatever he had done was still only a beginning in relation to the urgent tasks that remained. He reminded those who reacted with outrage that "when great accomplishments are undertaken they are soon overshadowed by rising expectations." Then, as if to accentuate the irreconcilable nature of the problems that now beset the land, Dr. King was assassinated on April 4, 1968, by a white sniper in Memphis. He had come to participate in a strike of the garbage workers and he was cut down as he talked with his aides. He was thirty-nine. This time the renewed rioting went out of control. Burning, looting, sniping, fed by despair and mass hysteria, spread to communities that had hitherto escaped the ordeals of racial violence. Washington itself looked like a blitzed city as the smoke from whole sections that had been put to the torch billowed over the Potomac.

Calm was restored by the end of the long hot summer. Even the extreme segregationists were now on notice that they were in a new era, and that the point of no return had been passed. King had left a dying pledge: "We will match your capacity to inflict suffering with our capacity to endure it."

All the problems of the administration, however, were dwarfed by the deadly guerrilla war that kept widening the area of disaster in Vietnam. The hapless land had suffered through occupation by the Japanese and the agony had continued during an eight-year struggle for independence from the French. Since 1954, by international action in Geneva, Vietnam had been partitioned; the north under a Communist government supported by the Soviet Union and Red China, and the south under an anti-Communist regime supported by the United States. Since then there had been continuous conflict and the civilian population had been the chief victims. American policy was confused and highly controversial but this was because the meaning of the conflict was subject to diametrically opposite interpretations. Was this a civil war and should it therefore be left to the Vietnamese? Was it aggression from the north abetted by the Communist powers to whom Vietnam was a major international chess piece? Was it a combination of both? Even if the conflict was a product of Communist aggression, was it in the American interest to concentrate men and resources to hold the line in Vietnam? Eisenhower had decided that the issue was indeed flagrant Communist aggression, and he had promised the regime in South Vietnam that the United States would not permit the land to fall into Communist hands. It was at a press conference in 1954 that he used the analogy, in his quaint English, which became a stock defense for intervention in Indochina. He said, "You have a row of dominoes set up, you knock over the first one, and what will happen to the last one is a certainty that it will go over very quickly." In January 1961, he solemnly warned his newly elected successor that Laos was the key to Southeast Asia and that it had to be held even if there was no support elsewhere.* He saw the defense of South Vietnam as assurance to the beleaguered nations of Asia that the United States was prepared to resist any further Communist encroachment. Kennedy had confirmed the Eisenhower pledge and the men whom he had inherited, especially McGeorge Bundy, kept pressing him at this stage to prosecute the war with full strength so as to wind it up victoriously. By 1963 there were more than ten thousand technicians in South Vietnam to assist in the war effort, and financial support totaled many hundreds of millions.

Johnson authorized a complete reappraisal. When the report established that the Communist strategy now concentrated on infiltration as a means of achieving control, his Security Council urged unlimited American resistance. Johnson always had before him the experience of Munich and the cost to the world of the craven buckling before Hitler. The lesson to him was that small wars sometimes had to be fought to prevent big ones. On the basis of the report, and the recommendation of the Security Council, Johnson ordered the all-out effort to win the war in Vietnam. When he made his decision he added the grim words, "No more Munichs."†

In the late summer of 1964 it was reported that torpedo boats from North Vietnam had attacked American naval units in the Gulf of Tonkin, off the shores of Vietnam. Johnson at once asked for general authority to defend American interest in any manner that he judged necessary. The Tonkin Gulf resolution, which became the constitutional basis for all the escalation that was to follow, passed the House by 414 to 0. The Senate approved it with only two dissenting votes. It gave Johnson virtually unquestioned power to manage the war as he saw fit.

---

* Arthur M. Schlesinger, Jr., *A Thousand Days* (Boston: Houghton Mifflin, 1965), p. 163. In a later interview, Eisenhower credited the American stand in Vietnam as the determining factor in saving Indonesian independence and keeping the world's fifth largest nation out of the Communist orbit. "Well," he said, "I could tell you one thing. The presence of 450,000 American troops in South Vietnam . . . had a hell of a lot to do with it."

† One of Johnson's most infuriating disappointments was the unwillingness of Britain to join with the United States in holding the line in Asia, even as the United States had so often come to the aid of Britain. A British correspondent recalled the bitter reproach of Secretary of State Dean Rusk: "All we needed was one regiment. The Black Watch would have done. Just one regiment, but you wouldn't. Well, don't expect us to save you again. They can invade Sussex, and we wouldn't do a damn thing about it." Louis Heren, *No Hails, No Farewells* (New York: Harper & Row, 1970), p. 230.

Up to this point Johnson undoubtedly had the mass support of the American people. He was still opposed to any major widening of the war that might precipitate Chinese or Russian intervention. But the American commitment to prevent a Communist victory in South Vietnam had been made clear in his campaign and he was re-elected in a landslide. The endorsement undoubtedly assumed that the victory in Vietnam would come quickly and would not require a major commitment of men and resources. But the Communists continued to rely on the strategy of attrition. Johnson was persuaded that the assignment of enough troops and the intensive bombing of North Vietnam would bring the enemy to capitulation. In what turned out to be his gravest miscalculation he decided on full-scale war, the manpower to be mainly provided by conscription. Soon there were 100,000 men in Vietnam, then the number doubled, and doubled again, and by mid-1968, a peak was reached at 548,000. By then American deaths had gone beyond forty thousand. The wounded brought the casualties to a quarter million. The loss of planes and equipment, whose total was not always revealed, along with the enormous outlays that were necessary to sustain the military effort at the other end of the world, reached thirty billion dollars each year, and there was no windup in sight. The columnist Art Buchwald wrote that he had a terrible nightmare that "Barry Goldwater had been elected and we were bombing North Vietnam." Johnson had been certain that the military effort would not affect the blueprint for reform which he had pledged—the support for social welfare, for health and education, for the blacks, and for the families who existed below the poverty level. But even a land as affluent as the United States could not absorb both the astronomical costs of the war and the outlays that were necessary to reach the goals of the Great Society.

Gradually the mood of the American people changed. The majority did not question the cynical motives of the Russian and Chinese suppliers and sustainers of the North Vietnamese Communists who had captured the nationalist revolution. They did question the wisdom of such heavy sacrifice to accomplish a limited purpose in a remote corner of the world that did not seem to be indispensable for American security. Later, Dean Rusk admitted two substantial errors of judgment: "I underestimated the persistence and the tenacity of the North Vietnamese, and I overestimated the ability of the American people to accept a protracted conflict." As television brought the misery and cruelty of the war into the homes of millions of families, as their young people were siphoned out and shipped off, the opposition became more strident. There had been understanding and loyal service when the United States fought Japan, Nazi Germany, and North Korea. But when Hanoi held on tenaciously despite all the punishment that it absorbed, when South Vietnamese villages and towns were temporarily retrieved by napalm and death and then quickly slipped back to Viet Cong control, when the government in Saigon was exposed as venal and oppressive, the disaffection became disruptive. Congressional support for the war effort steadily crumbled. The Kennedys and their inner circle now reinterpreted the intentions of the slain President and joined the protesters. The Senate leadership began to have second thoughts. There were anti-war demonstrations on college campuses and they spread to the streets of every city. The defenders of the war objectives could scarcely get a hearing.

Johnson used all of his skills to stem the anti-war tide. He noted that this was a new kind of war. It could not be won quickly or cheaply. It called for a special kind of strength, tensile strength, and a special kind of courage, the courage of confident patience. But his appeals were ridiculed, his facts were challenged, and he was subjected to tirades of personal abuse. In 1965 the Gallup Poll had asked for judgment on the war policy and 25 percent had responded that it was mistaken. In 1968 the negative reaction had risen to 47 percent. Only three years before, the salutes that greeted Johnson on his tours around the country were "All the way with LBJ!" Now he did not dare to appear at open rallies and the cry had changed to the taunting chant: "Hey, hey, LBJ, how many kids did you kill today?" "I'm like a jack rabbit hunkered up in a storm," Johnson said ruefully.*

By March 1968 the master of consensus concluded that he had personally become too divisive an influence to risk continued leadership. He realized what many men before him had been obliged to remember, that Americans will support any war, immoral or moral—the Mexican and the Spanish-American as well as the war against the Nazis and the Japanese—so long as they are winning and have confidence in their chief. When he attempted to defend his policies on Vietnam he found that he had lost his credibility. He said perhaps more sadly than bitterly, "Jack Kennedy was

* Eric F. Goldman, *The Tragedy of Lyndon Johnson* (New York: Alfred A. Knopf, 1969), p. 415.

assassinated. I'm being assassinated, too, and the only difference is that I am still alive." In a nationwide broadcast, he announced that he would not be a candidate for another term as President and that he would bend all of his efforts until the end of his incumbency to seek an honorable political compromise that would bring the war to an end.

Johnson sought consolation in the precedents of the Lincoln period, when the war President suffered from more sustained attack than any of his predecessors in American history. Lincoln knew that it always took the healing therapy of time to provide the perspective which contemporaries could not possibly have. Johnson was certain that he too would ultimately be vindicated for his judgment that the war in Vietnam was part of the Communist master plan to take over Asia, and that his decision to resist, at whatever cost, was in the best long-range interest of his country.

The soundness of his analogies with the appeasement of Munich and with the validity of the American stake in a remote corner of Asia would have to wait for the more objective judgments of another generation. Meantime the special kind of courage for which he had pleaded so long, the courage of patience, would have to be practiced by him, too, until the future determined what the verdict of history was to be.

49

INDONESIA: THE
SUKARNO AND SUHARTO
YEARS

IN THE MID-TWENTIETH-CENTURY COLONIAL WORLD THAT WAS DOM-
inated by the European powers, Indonesia represented one of the
most precious assets. It consisted of over three thousand islands,
some of them larger than European countries. It stretched 3,400
miles across the Pacific, skirting the Philippines and Malaysia and
Vietnam and Australia. It was the fifth most populous nation in the
world. It had immense resources in rubber, palm oil, timber, sugar,
tin, bauxite; it had a proven potential of eight billion barrels of
oil, and its production of 20 million tons annually made it Southeast
Asia's most valuable oil reserve. The soil could yield two crops
annually in many of its lush provinces. There was an aphorism that
acclaimed the land's fertility: "Stick a piece of wood into the earth
and you have a tree the next day." This fabled empire had been
acquired by the Dutch in the seventeenth century. They followed
the usual pattern of the colonial masters, draining out what they
could from their possessions and returning just enough compensation and welfare services for the native population to keep them
quiet and reasonably efficient.

Inevitably the freedom movements of the twentieth century
influenced Indonesia too, and the schools to which the most promising young people were sent for training became centers of revolutionary ferment. World War II, loosing uncontrollable forces on
every continent, provided the opportunities for which the impatient
Indonesian Nationalists had been waiting. Their rebellion was ig-

nited by young Sukarno, born Kuono Sosro, who flashed across the landscape of his times like a flaming meteor and burned out as quickly.

Sukarno was an amalgam of contrasts. He was a genuine emancipator, sincere in his passionate nationalism. But he was so flamboyant in manner and expression, and he used symbols in his highly charged emotional appeals with such extravagance, that ultimately he fell victim to his own high-decibel oratory. "Oh my brothers, you must keep the flames high. You must be the logs on the fires of revolution!" It was easier for him to dissemble a problem by a torrent of mesmeric words than it was to face up to the stern realities of budgets and exports. He was an undoubted revolutionary genius, but he had little practical talent to support it. Dryden's judgment on Buckingham fitted Sukarno admirably:

> Stiff in opinions, always in the wrong,
> Was everything by starts, and nothing long.*

He regarded himself as the fusion of Indonesian heroes, historic and legendary, and in his speeches he constantly alluded to them. The Indonesian audiences invariably responded, for they knew the names that he evoked and the nostalgic references. To impress and to baffle foreign diplomatic observers, he played the modern and the "world-knowledgeable" by identifying himself sometimes as a Lenin and at other times as a Jefferson. He was precise and orderly in devising strategy to win back his country from the Dutch and from the Japanese. But he had faith in magic and astrology, and he could be as mystical and superstitious as the courtiers of the ancient sultanates of Java. In his Autobiography he noted that among the symbols heralding his birth was the eruption of Mount Kelud, a nearby volcano.† His natal date was June 6, the sixth day of the sixth month, and he was born under the sign of Gemini, the twins. He therefore usually hid on his birthday, fearing the bewitching powers of the double six.

Sukarno thrived on crises; they deepened the dependence on him, and when they did not come he created them, expanding trivia into threat or triumph. It was perhaps the same compulsion that drove him to bring endless processions of women into his private life—wives and mistresses, and affairs of the moment. They fed his vora-

---

* John Dryden, *Absalom and Achitophel*, I.
† Cindy Adams, *Sukarno* (Indianapolis, Kansas City, and New York: Bobbs-Merrill, 1965), p. 18.

cious inner ego, even as the crises fed the exhibitionism of his public life. Psychoanalysts would assuredly find significance in his penchant for yellow-haired white women and his obsession to make love to Dutch girls. "It was the only way I knew to exert some form of superiority over the white race and make them bend to my will."* Perhaps the most perceptive judgment on the dualism that possessed him, and that both exalted and destroyed him, was offered by Adam Malik, one of the men who overthrew him and tried to retrieve his earlier idealism from the chaos of his later years. Malik said of Sukarno: "The climate came closer and closer to madness, and yet, to quote Hamlet, 'how much order there was in this madness.' "

Sukarno was born in Java in 1901; his father was a schoolmaster, his mother a beautiful Balinese. He was orphaned as a child and was sent at fourteen to live as a foster son in the home of a nationalist patriot whose anti-Dutch dogmas were among Sukarno's earliest memories. He was a student of engineering at Bandung University and he practiced for a while as an architect. But he was drawn irresistibly into revolutionary activity and, at twenty-seven, he helped to organize the Indonesian Nationalist Party which became the nucleus for the movement that later won independence for the country. He was identified by the Dutch authorities as a dangerous troublemaker and spent many years, until World War II, in and out of jail.

In the spring of 1942 the Japanese, in their great Pacific sweep, conquered the East Indies, and they courted the young rebel for the common effort against the western powers. Sukarno, the restrictions on his movements lifted, was treated with exceptional deference; he was even granted an audience with the Emperor in Tokyo, where he received a royal decoration. Because of this episode he was later accused of opportunist collaboration with the Japanese. But he insisted that he fitted into the Japanese effort so that he could hasten the emancipation of his country from colonial bondage. In 1945, when the Japanese surrendered and withdrew, he saluted the red and white flag of liberated Indonesia as its acknowledged founder.

At this point however, independence was still little more than a proclamation. When the Japanese were driven out, the Dutch fully expected to resume "their interrupted mission of civilizing the

---

* *Ibid.*, p. 45.

natives." Indeed, they acted as if there had been no war and no nationalist resurgence. Sukarno led the resistance and the Dutch, already exhausted by the long Nazi occupation of Holland, now faced further attrition of manpower and resources. Grudgingly they began to offer concessions that would open to the Indonesians broader participation in the government and the economic life of the country. Sukarno would settle for nothing less than complete independence. The war dragged on until 1949 when the Dutch decided that they could no longer hope for an accommodation that would save any part of the empire. The decision was hastened by the threat from the United States that Marshall Plan aid would be suspended unless the Dutch yielded.

Sukarno was elected President of the Republic of Indonesia; when he was formally installed in December 1949, three and a half centuries of colonial rule came to an end. Three more years of warfare were needed to bring several dissident provinces into the Union. There were rebellions in the Celebes, in the Moluccas, in Java itself. But by 1952 the last major resistance had been eliminated and the tasks of peace and reconstruction could at last begin.

Sukarno the liberator had to become Sukarno the statesman and the consolidator, and here he was completely out of character. There had been a steady exodus of the Dutch technicians who had efficiently managed commerce and industry and the mechanics of administration. But few of the native Indonesians had the experience to take their place. The country now had well over eighty million people and the birth rate was adding two and a half million more each year. The per capita annual income was seventy dollars. Sukarno, to be sure, had no effective control of Indonesia until the middle 1950's but he used none of the influence that he did command to cope with the problems of the expanding population and its living standards. Instead, he spent tens of millions on grandiose building programs that were meant for display and prestige. He loaded the bureaucracy with hangers-on until it was swollen beyond control. There had been considerable initial interest in Indonesia by the western powers and the United States, and they extended aid in grants and loans. Sukarno squandered what was sent in as if he were a little boy let loose in a toy shop full of gimmicks. When he turned to the printing presses to meet budgetary needs the currency collapsed; the cost of printing was greater than the value of the money. His oratory became more florid and more fervent. In one address, on the anniversary of independence, he called for "an expanding wave of heave-ho, and pulling together." But he offered no personal example of heave-ho and there was very little pulling together.

Perhaps it was to divert attention from approaching bankruptcy that Sukarno promoted military adventures against the neighboring Malaysian states. The British policy of decolonization had brought independence to North Borneo, which was renamed Sabah, to Sarawak, and Singapore, and in 1963 these states organized into the Malaysian Federation, which opted to remain part of the British Commonwealth. Sukarno denounced the Federation as a British plot to encircle his country, and to "endanger the Indonesian revolution." Relations with the Federation deteriorated steadily and by 1964 there was open warfare. Sukarno boasted that he would win quickly, "by the time the first cock crows on January 1, 1965." It was stupid bravado; the Malaysians were fighting on their own soil, and they had the support of British and Gurkha forces and well-trained Sarawak-Chinese auxiliaries. The conflict raged on in several jungle areas and the expense ate into the dwindling national resources of Indonesia.

The United States cautioned Sukarno that his continued belligerent opposition to the peaceful life of Malaysia was an obstacle to American-Indonesian relations. He replied angrily: "To hell with your aid, we can do without it." When the United Nations elected the Malaysian Federation to a seat in the Security Council, Sukarno became so furious that, in January 1965, he took his country out of the United Nations, the first to resign membership in the international body. With characteristic melodrama he compared the move with the Prophet Mohammed's hegira from Mecca, pointing to the parallel between the Prophet's ordeal in the face of implacable enemies and his own battle against those who had turned their faces from him. He stepped up the anti-American tirades and launched punitive measures against American business interests. Street mobs were encouraged to stage noisy demonstrations, and the unions harassed American enterprise by refusing to keep the utilities in operation. Propaganda posters yelled their hatred at every passer-by. The Peace Corps had already been expelled.

By now Sukarno had abandoned any pretense of constitutional government. He ridiculed "50 percent plus one democracy." He dissolved Parliament, announcing that he would govern through "Guided Democracy," and he had himself elected as President-for-life. If these actions had meant government that was efficient and realistic, they might have been accepted as temporarily useful in the emergencies that confronted the fast-sinking state. But as applied by Sukarno, "Guided Democracy" meant personal caprice and further extravagance. While his was not a jackboot dictatorship, it was irresponsible, easygoing, with more emphasis on display and parties than on the problems of state and the plight of his people.

The two strongest forces in the imperiled state were the Communists and the military, and each now reached for control. The Communists had developed formidable strength during and immediately after World War II; they had been the most active element in the resistance to the Japanese and the Dutch. They were fortunate to have an organizing genius in Dipa Nusantara Aidit, who in 1951 took over the leadership of the party, the PKI, and built its membership to three million, the largest in the non-Communist world, ranking with its only peers, the parties in the Soviet Union and in Red China. In addition, the network of labor and youth organizations had been thoroughly infiltrated, and Aidit claimed that he could count upon the loyalty of perhaps another twelve or fifteen million adherents. As relations with the West and the UN deteriorated, Aidit maneuvered for a firm alliance with the other international outcast, Red China, and by 1965 he had achieved a virtual Djakarta-Peking axis. He became a confidant of Chou En-lai, who encouraged him to develop a people's militia that could counteract the regular army when the inevitable confrontation occurred.

The military, despite setbacks in the Malaysian wars, also had impressive strength. Its force of three hundred thousand had been toughened and disciplined by the years of conflict to eliminate the Dutch and to consolidate the diverse territorial segments that made up the Republic. Its commanders had little stomach for Sukarno's adventures and they watched with concern the cunning with which Aidit flattered and seduced his way into his confidence. They could not imagine that Sukarno would actually succumb to the allurements of communism. They took seriously his disclaimer: "How can I bow to Moscow? I would have too much ego to be anyone's slave." But they did believe that with his alienation from the West and the United Nations he would increasingly favor the Communists, if only for counterpoise and for blackmail advantage. Though he would not bow to Moscow he was in a dangerous embrace with Peking. Thus, by late 1965, the fifth largest nation in the world, strategically centered in the heart of Southeast Asia, in the hands of an erratic playboy dictator, was an alluring prize in the impending showdown between the Communists and the military.

Sukarno became quite ill in 1965. He consulted Chinese medical specialists and their diagnosis of his serious kidney ailment revealed he was in mortal danger. They passed the word to Aidit, who was fearful that, if Sukarno were to die, the army rivals might move in at once. They would then undoubtedly undo the patient work of infiltration Aidit had accomplished and the strategic position he had achieved in promoting Sukarno's cordial relationship with Red China. He decided to take no chances and to arrange for a purge of the top army leadership. It is possible that he confided his plans to Sukarno, who was now so furious with the obstructionist army command that he was ready to welcome their elimination. The night of September 30, 1965, was to be a watershed point in the history of Southeast Asia. The Communists sent their execution squads out after the eight ranking generals, six of whom were trapped and murdered. However, the Minister of Defense, General Nasution, was able to escape through a back window, although he broke his leg as he climbed the wall of his lawn and his five-year-old daughter was killed. His deputy, General Suharto, was not on the proscribed list for reasons that were only tangentially political, and he too escaped the assassination net. The failure to eliminate these key figures circumvented the conspiracy. Suharto was in charge of the Army Strategic Command, the élite of the military forces, and when he reached the army headquarters he quickly and effectively organized the counterattack. He pinpointed the coup leaders in the army and the air force, talked them out of continued resistance, and took the rebel base with hardly a shot. It was said that the single casualty was a water buffalo.

The leadership of the People's Militia and of the PKI were vigorously hunted and most of them captured. Aidit fled to Central Java and several weeks later was trapped in the home of a confederate. When all information had been wrung out of him, he was put to death.

There followed one of the great mass killings of modern times. The most conservative estimate listed 150,000 victims; *The Times* (London) investigators raised the figure to nearly a million. The army took the assignment to despatch the PKI following and it was carried out with military precision. The conservative Moslems were given freest rein to settle scores with those whom they regarded as the atheistic corrupters of the country's youth. They went about their gruesome tasks as if they were participating in a jihad, or holy war, fulfilling the wishes of Allah. Personal animosities that had simmered and boiled through the years could now also be avenged behind the facade of ideological principle.

The killings were concentrated in North Sumatra, Central and East Java, and Bali. The victims were lined up and decapitated, or shot or thrown from windows, then flung into mass graves or into the rivers that were soon too polluted for their fish to be used as food. A British observer told of a football match where a Communist head was used for the ball. The Pulitzer Prize-winning journalist Horace Sutton explained the cruelty of a traditionally gentle people: "The Javanese is like a Caribou [water buffalo], slow to get started and once started, impossible to stop."*

The phrase "to run amok" has a Malaysian origin, and it was literally fulfilled in these horrendous months. Some 200,000 persons were confined to prisons and concentration camps, and late in 1971 there were still 50,000 who had not been released. The military was sure, after the decimations and the imprisonments, that the PKI would no longer menace the future.

Inevitably the question was asked how it was possible for the Communists to suffer a defeat that was so decisive. The Indonesian party had three million members and the allegiance of perhaps another twelve to fifteen million in the unions and the many front organizations. It had the protection of Sukarno and the goodwill of Red China. Yet when some details of its carefully prepared coup had been bungled, all resistance collapsed and even the slaughter brought no last-stand reaction.

Perhaps the actual capacity of the Communists had always been overestimated. Membership in the party or ideological identification was no substitute for organized power, and the military, with its main leadership intact and unharmed after the abortive coup, could quickly overcome the managers and the dialecticians. One of the Communist major-domos said scornfully, "The PKI resembled a goatherd more than a group of truly conscientious revolutionary fighters. When the organization at the top broke down, the bottom scattered."

The role of Sukarno in the thwarted Communist coup was not clearly known until later. It was thought at first that he was the intended chief victim and that the army intervention had saved

---

* Horace Sutton, "Indonesia's Night of Terror," *Saturday Review,* Vol. 50 (Feb. 4, 1967), p. 28.

him. But as the story emerged at the trials and the interrogation sessions of the main participants, and as its pieces were put together, it was clear that Sukarno had been kept informed and was eager to be freed of the army recalcitrants. Aidit's farewell statement just before his execution confirmed the surmise: "If you shoot me, you must also shoot the President." The cry was soon raised from the Moslem leadership and from the infuriated student groups that Sukarno too must be punished and eliminated.

The new government was now headed by General Suharto, an experienced and cautious commander. He was almost the antithesis of Sukarno—cool, unhurried, well balanced, a devout patriot, with no wish to become involved in dramatic adventures. Confronted with the decision on Sukarno's fate, he judged that it would be prudent to avoid martyring the legendary liberator. Instead, if Sukarno's position were discreetly reduced to purely symbolic status, he could do no harm and the risk of new disruptions would be reduced. He summarized this view in a report to Parliament. "Do not let the present generation be blamed by the coming generation," he said, "for the improper treatment of the patriotic leader of the people."

Sukarno was therefore permitted to keep one of his palaces, to entertain his retinue of women, and to emerge on special ceremonial occasions with all of his flashy decorations. When he sometimes forgot his powerlessness and demanded too much, Suharto called for the intercession of Sukarno's sixth wife, Dewi, a beautiful Japanese former nightclub hostess who was a model of shrewdness in manipulating her consort, and in protecting her own always precarious position. Sukarno lived out his life in a kind of petulant peace under modified house arrest, shielded from any temptation to impede the national recuperation. Gradually he faded from view and when he died in 1970 he was not buried in the Heroes' Cemetery in Djakarta, but in the remote small town of Blitar in East Java.

Meantime, General Suharto had turned to the task of bringing the country out of the devastation of the long wars and the lavish projects and commitments of his predecessor. He was now forty-eight, at the peak of his effectiveness. Sukarno had never traveled without a preceding cavalcade escort, sirens blaring; Suharto went about his duties with quiet dignity, his mind and effort on the job to be done. As a professional soldier he knew that he could cope with the problems of defense and security. He added two colleagues for the competence and sophistication that they could apply to the areas where he did not trust his own experience. Adam Malik, also forty-eight, was named Deputy Prime Minister for Foreign Affairs. He was a former newspaperman, as practical as Sukarno had been profligate. The Sultan of Jogjakarta, Hamengku Buwono, became Deputy Prime Minister for Finance and Development. His royal lineage had been no handicap for thorough training in the intricacies of modern economics in the best schools of Holland. The three men comprised a compatible team for the problems of a bankrupt economy and disrupted foreign relationships.

Highest priority was given to the need to bring Indonesia back into the family of nations. Malik wound up the war with Malaysia and obtained the readmission of the country to the United Nations.* The Soviet Union and Red China declared that Indonesia was now in the grip of Fascist thugs and terrorists, and recalled their technicians and canceled their aid programs. Suharto and his colleagues were not intimidated. They insisted upon scrupulous nonalignment, but they sought the best possible relationships with the United States and the West. By 1968, Malik had procured loans of six hundred million dollars from a consortium of nine nations, headed by Japan and the United States, and he had succeeded also in refunding the staggering two-and-a-half-billion-dollar debt that had been accumulated by Sukarno. Negotiations were also opened for a Common Market arrangement that would include Malaysia, the Philippines, and Burma. Within two years Indonesia was well out of the economic dangers that the jag of irresponsible demagoguery had threatened.

The major unresolved question, however, remained. Indonesia had been buffeted by twenty-five years of almost continuous warfare, foreign and internal; it was part of the most contested area in Asia, a tempting prize as it straddled the vital sea lanes between the Pacific and the Indian oceans. The policymakers of the Soviet Union, Red China, and the United States were well aware that whoever controlled the archipelago, with its population beyond 110 million, and with immense proved and potential resources, would profoundly influence the fate of Southeast Asia and the Pacific.

* Malik served as President of the United Nations in 1971.

50

SOUTH AFRICA,
RHODESIA, AND
APARTHEID

IN THE QUARTER-CENTURY THAT FOLLOWED WORLD WAR II, A RESUR-
gent black nationalism triumphed in virtually every part of the
African continent, and scores of new sovereign states emerged.
There were two exceptions where the most strenuous attempts of
the solid black majorities to challenge white supremacy were consistently thwarted. The control of Portugal could not be broken in
the colonies of Angola and Mozambique, and the white populations
of South Africa and Rhodesia created fortress states to prevent what
they forecast would otherwise condemn them to engulfment. They
developed a special relationship, or perhaps one should say a non-
relationship, that was termed *"apartheid,"* literally, separation.
South Africa enforced it with a perverse tenacity, and Rhodesia
only slightly less oppressively, in the face of the protests of the
United Nations and of countries around the world. In South Africa
as each succeeding government applied more rigor to *apartheid,*
every Prime Minister became a moderate in retrospect, since his
record seemed so much milder than the actions of those who followed.

The first migration of the whites to South Africa was undertaken
in the seventeenth century. In 1657, a few intrepid Dutch pioneers
set up facilities at the tip of the continent to provide food and
refreshment for the ships of the Dutch East Indies as they made
their way into the waters that led to the legendary riches of Cathay.
They stayed on, and they urged their countrymen to join them, for

they had found what they called "the fairest Cape in all the world," a luxuriant land, a hospitable climate, the cheap labor of aborigines who, at the outset, were friendly and submissive. For two centuries a new thriving Dutch world offered easy income to the mother country and high living standards to the Dutch families who developed the land. In 1806, during the Napoleonic wars, the Dutch had to yield control to the British, whose settlers introduced their brand of colonialism, paternalistic and snobbish but basically humane. The commercial society they built did not depend on native labor, so they could accept the forms of egalitarian legislation that came from the British homeland. Their statesmen were certain that the imperial structure was the fulfillment of God's long-range purposes. "How marvellous it all is!" declared the Liberal Prime Minister Lord Rosebery as he addressed an audience at Glasgow University. "Built not by saints and angels, but the work of men's hands; cemented with men's honest blood and with a world of tears, welded by the best brains of centuries past; not without the taint and reproach incidental to all human work, but constructed on the whole with pure and splendid purpose. Human, and yet not wholly human—for the most heedless and the most cynical must see the finger of the Divine. . . ."*

The Dutch farmers, *"Bauer,"* or Boers, as the British called them, found their new status intolerable. They could not abide the British and most of them gave up the homes that they had established and undertook the difficult trek inland to open out new settlements for an independent future. They clashed often with the Bantu natives who were moving down from the interior. Over the succeeding decades, the Boers cleared two large provinces, the Transvaal and the Orange Free State. They were a hardy folk, living by the literal precepts of the Bible, the gun, and the whip, grimly guarding their borders and their patrimony, grateful to be away from the British, keeping a tight hand on the native labor to make sure that their own way of life would not be disturbed. In Olive Schreiner's earliest novel, which is set in the 1870's, she notes that when family prayers were held on the farm the Kaffir workers were not present "because Tant' Sannie held they were descended from apes and needed no salvation."†

---

* Cited in William Langer, *The Diplomacy of Imperialism* (New York: Alfred A. Knopf, 1951), p. 94.

† Olive Schreiner, *Story of an African Farm* (London: Collins, 1959).

In the late nineteenth century, diamond and gold mines were discovered in Kimberley and in Witwatersrand. The stories circulated of gold in profusion, diamonds as large as almonds, to be obtained with very little labor or investment. They precipitated a gold and diamond rush and the territories that had been redeemed and regenerated by the Boers were overrun by the hordes of new prospectors. The British, scenting the extraordinary value of the territory, claimed it as part of the original cession and went to war to enforce the claim. The resistance of the outnumbered and outgunned Boers roused the sympathy of the world and of liberal groups in Britain, who denounced the war as imperialist and immoral. "It is well enough to speak of Empire," said John Morley, a spokesman for the liberals, "but we do not want a pirate Empire." The protests were unavailing and, when the Boers surrendered, the entire territory came under the jurisdiction of the British. When the Liberal Party took office in 1905, Prime Minister Sir Henry Campbell-Bannerman tried to conciliate the Boers by offering the fullest measure of self-government. The action was strenuously opposed by the leading Conservatives, who wished to postpone such concessions until extended immigration had built up a British majority. They expressed grave misgivings as to what the race-conscious Boers would do with autonomy. Young Winston Churchill warned his colleagues that they were throwing the reins on the horse's neck.

In 1910, despite the angry protests, all four provinces—the original Cape and Natal, and the predominantly Boer territory of the Transvaal and the Orange Free State—were federated to become the Union of South Africa. No attempt was made to place political restrictions in the way of the more numerous Boers. The route was thus opened to retrieve what had been lost on the battlefield, though it took nearly four decades for the politically inept Boers to attain their objective. Then their day came. After World War II, under the leadership of Daniel Malan and the power of his Nationalist Party, the Boers won the country back by ballot and avenged the compulsory trek and the defeats of their fathers.

Malan was born in 1874 of Huguenot stock. Dour, paunchy, bald, he was not an attractive figure, but he had the driving power of the fanatic to compensate for a lackluster personality. He was reared in the Calvinist tradition and studied in Holland for a career in the ministry. When he returned to South Africa in 1905, he accepted a pastorate in the Transvaal, and for ten years his Hell-and-damnation preaching followed the strictest fundamentalist line. He then turned to political journalism and his Bible-saturated editorials thumped away at twin objectives: to create an independent Boer Republic and a social structure that would preserve white supremacy. His endlessly repeated thesis was that all men are created unequal, that the blacks are a congenitally inferior people, destined by God to remain in their menial status.

In the 1930's Malan founded the Nationalist Party, not at all discouraged that it began with only seven adherents. After all, he reminded his detractors, Hitler's Nazis had also begun with only seven. During World War II, as an avowed Nazi sympathizer, he resisted any cooperation with the British in the expectation that Hitler's victory would assure emancipation from the British Commonwealth.

The election of 1948, in which no blacks voted, was fought with no holds barred. Malan campaigned on the platform of *"Baasskap,"* rigid white supremacy, warning the electorate that the rest of Africa had gone wild under the misguided liberalism of the frightened colonial powers. Therefore, if the Nationalists lost in South Africa, white girls would be compelled to marry "coons," and he pronounced "coons" with all the hatred and contempt that he could pour into his squeaky voice. The election went to the Nationalists. Malan became Prime Minister and he formed an all-Afrikaaner government for the first time since the creation of the Union of South Africa.

For the English, it was a setback but not a disaster. Their dominance in trade and banking and the basic professions was very little threatened. But for the ten million blacks, the triumph of the Nationalists was to pinion them to a new level of degradation. South Africa, of course, was not the only land where discrimination against the blacks was oppressive. Everywhere in the white world their opportunities were severely limited in education and employment and in the exercise of the franchise. But now, under the bigoted guidance of Malan, discrimination was congealed into a government-supported and enforced system, *apartheid,* uncompromising, holding out no hope of gradual moderation.

If it had been possible, Malan would have preferred to uproot all the blacks and ship them off to segregated areas, cut off permanently by the highest walls of law, to prevent any association with the whites. The disruption of the lives of millions of human beings seemed to trouble him very little. "A black," he said, "doesn't need a home. He can sleep under a tree." But the economy of the country

[606]

made geographical *apartheid* impossible. Agriculture needed the collaboration of the blacks. Commerce and industry would grind to a standstill without their labor. Every white household depended upon their domestic service.

Malan, declaring that resistance to *apartheid* was treason, hurried through legislation that provided the most practical substitute. The Minister of Labor was given unlimited discretion to determine what occupations the members of any race could pursue, and all skilled jobs were reserved for whites. The Minister of Education cut back severely the grants for feeding black schoolchildren. Segregation was ordered for the shanty towns on the outskirts of the urban centers. In Durban 100,000 blacks were moved so that when they traveled from their homes to their places of work they would not pollute white residential neighborhoods by passing through them. If a black servant received permission to live on white premises, there were meticulous regulations about the location and the size of the occupied room, which was to be shielded as if it were a prison. As indeed it was. Passes had to be carried by the blacks, with every personal detail noted, and no move could be made without express permission. Invariably about fifty thousand blacks were jailed each year for infractions of the Pass Laws.

The disabilities of the mulattos, who were referred to as the "colored," had been slightly less severe than for the pure blacks. Some could even vote for a few white candidates who were to represent them. But in 1951, fifty thousand of these "coloreds" lost their limited franchise. When the action was declared unconstitutional by the highest court, still dominated by English judges, Malan defied the court, adding six of his own followers to its membership to destroy its independent status. The brutal routine of repression was climaxed in 1953 by a law that was intended to destroy the hope for change. It was made a crime for blacks "to support any campaign for the repeal or modification of any law." Inevitably there was a sharp upturn in violence and crime, in drunkenness and drug addiction. Malan's response was to keep building jails and detention centers until South Africa, with one-quarter the population of Britain, had four times as many prisons.

In 1954, Malan, past eighty, retired full of years and with smug satisfaction over the fulfillment of his "Christian trusteeship." His heir, Johannes Strijdom, was an interregnum figure. His incumbency was limited to four years and since he faithfully modeled himself on his mentor, they were shadow years that prepared the way for his successor, Dr. Hendrik Verwoerd, to build even greater rigidity into the practice of *apartheid*.

One recalls the biblical confrontation of King Rehoboam and his rebellious people. Rehoboam warned them: "My father flogged you with whips. I shall flog you with scorpions." Verwoerd, like Malan, grounded his actions in biblical authority and he could have spoken to the blacks in Rehoboam's threatening words. He was the classical bigot, his mind a steel trap, obsessive, uncompromising, certain of his divine mission. He calmly told a reporter, "I don't have the problem of wondering whether I'm ever wrong."

Verwoerd was born in Holland in 1901 and brought to South Africa at the age of two by his missionary father. He received his training at Stellenbosch University, a font of Afrikaaner nationalism, and he pursued his post-graduate studies in Germany during the period when Hitler was riveting the country to Nazi doctrine. Verwoerd was completely fascinated by the Nazi racial philosophy, and he brought it back with him when, at twenty-six, he became a member of the faculty at Stellenbosch and headed its department of sociology. Like Malan, he was drawn to political journalism, and for many years he edited *The Transvaaler*, the major party organ of the Nationalists, which was notorious during World War II for its explicit Nazi identification. When a rival editor wrote that his spiritual home was nearer to Hitler's Berchtesgaden than to South Africa, Malan sued for libel. He lost the suit, the judgment noting that he had faithfully followed the Nazi line and that he knew it. He continued his diatribes against "the dangerous liberal doctrine of the equality of races, regardless of color or smell." He joined the secret Broederbond, a select group of eight thousand that included most of the Boer extremists. Soon after Malan's victory of 1948, Verwoerd was tapped for high office and, as Minister of Native Affairs, he helped to ram through the legislation that guaranteed white supremacy.

Thoroughly schooled by Hitler and by Malan, and with an impressive record of barbed wire racist legislation, Verwoerd became Prime Minister in September 1958. He turned at once to the old dream of geographical *apartheid* which had been considered unpractical by his predecesssors. Many of the barracks for the black workers housed only men. In the Cape Province, 68 percent of them were married, but they were forbidden to have their wives with them, except with passes and on special occasions. He announced a plan to create, over a period of years, more than two hundred and fifty large-scale reserves for the blacks, self-governing *Bantustans*, as he called them, into which ultimately all the blacks would be gathered. Some of them would be located on the outskirts of the major urban centers so that they could continue to work among the whites, but they would live isolated social and political lives in their sharply separated *Bantustans*. The government would provide support for their schools and recreation centers and there would be subsidies to help create industries within their own settlements. But the separation of the races, except for the unavoidable proximity at work, would have to be, he said, as final and complete "as the separation of elephants from lions."

During all these unilateral decisions, where the lives of millions of human beings were manipulated and arranged and disposed of as if they were pounds of inanimate meat, the blacks suffered in sullen silence. They were helpless to offer tangible resistance, for they were unorganized and their tormentors were armed with the most formidable weaponry. Jets roared daily over the black encampments, in military formation, not to impress foreign nations but quite obviously to drive home the threat of instant and terrifying reprisal if there were the slightest contumacy.

In March 1960, the point of unendurance was reached. Under the leadership of a few daring blacks giant demonstrations were planned to protest the humiliations and the hardships of the Pass Laws, which had become identified as the most galling symbol of black degradation. Having deliberately left their passes behind, thousands of blacks converged on the police headquarters in scores of cities and towns, courting arrest. The demonstration at Sharpeville, twenty-nine miles from Johannesburg, got out of hand as the police, armed with tanks and machine guns, fired into the crowds, killing sixty-nine and wounding about two hundred. The massacre brought worldwide reactions of horror. But the Prime Minister was as unruffled as he was contemptuous. He ordered the rounding up of the "troublemakers," increased and strengthened the army and police contingents, and encouraged pistol-shooting classes and the drilling of vigilantes. He justified the repression as the response of provocation. "If they want to bait us and to test us," he said, "they'll have to learn their lesson." By an unhappy coincidence, Sharpeville fell on the fiftieth anniversary of the creation of the Union of South Africa, giving further validity to Philip Guedalla's reference to "the ghastly ineptitude of anniversaries."

Later in the year, when the Prime Ministers of all the Commonwealth countries met in London, Verwoerd was upbraided for the unabashed racism of his government. He took the occasion to announce that his people really wanted no part of Commonwealth membership and that South Africa would withdraw, as of the end of May 1961.

He kept his word to the day. It must have been a special satisfaction for the Boers, when the Union Jack was hauled down and fealty to the Queen was forsworn, that another of their objectives had been fulfilled. Since all ties with the British Commonwealth had now been severed, no technical restrictions remained to countercheck the most extreme repressive legislation. In 1963, a special ruling was enacted which authorized detention without warrant, if there were any suspicion of disturbing intent. On being sentenced to life imprisonment, one of the defiant blacks, Nelson Mandela, made a statement that was so moving that it echoed around the world and became part of the literature of political dissent. But Mandela continued to languish in prison.

For the next two years, the committees of the United Nations passed resolutions of censure. Several countries announced boycotts. There was a nervous flight of capital, and hundreds of scholars and students and professional men migrated. But the votes of censure were shrugged off. When had they ever been taken seriously? The boycotts and the sanctions were very little respected, even by the countries that proclaimed them; there were many American banks that continued their policy of business as usual. Hence the South African economy suffered no setback, and the stock market quickly righted itself. By 1963, there was such a decided upturn that Verwoerd could boast of unprecedented prosperity.

In September 1966, as Verwoerd was getting ready to address the House of Assembly, a parliamentary messenger who had been employed only a few months before came up behind him and stabbed him to death. In the summary trial that followed it was quickly established that the assassin, a white immigrant of Portuguese origin, was acting on his own. But it was ironic that his dementia took the form of protest that Verwoerd was doing too much for the blacks and too little for poor whites like himself.

The new Prime Minister, Balthazar Vorster, had been Verwoerd's irascible police chief, in temperament and outlook a chip off the old block. He had been a small town lawyer who had studied at Stellenbosch under Verwoerd. In World War II he masterminded a Nazi underground organization and had been imprisoned as a subversive. His views were so far to the right of even the Nationalists that Malan at first would not accept him as a candidate for the Assembly. But by 1953 the racist bigotry of the party had gone far enough toward Vorster's views so that he could be considered respectable. He was soon assigned cabinet rank, with responsibility for the repressive measures that became the mortar of the Nationalist regimes. He supervised the house arrests and the detention orders and the Pass Laws. He was in charge of the surveillance cadres that patrolled the most dangerous demonstration areas.

As Prime Minister, Vorster was the target of the international protests and the virtually unanimous condemnations of each session of the UN and its commissions. His widely reported replies were always the same:

Our actions are rooted in self-preservation. . . . Our people have poured centuries of labor into the creation of a land that was carved out of the jungle. . . . We are more than ever isolated now in a vast hostile black majority. . . . We shall never repudiate the sacrifice of our ancestors in deference to the fuzzy idealism of those who preach ethics from the security of their sanctuaries where they do not have to face our *swart qevaer* [black peril].

Vorster was especially sarcastic about American protests. He reminded his critics that when the pioneers came to American shores and were faced with the hostility of the Indians, they solved the problem by clearing the land and annihilating the Indians.

Vorster therefore continued his "flogging with scorpions." He tightened the laws, redoubled the vigilance, and defiantly accepted the boycotts and sanctions as part of the price of survival. "Just as God stood by the Voortrekkers in their time of adversity," he said grimly, "so He would stand by us in our time of greatest need." It was futile to react to such self-righteous determination with resolutions and prayers and fasts.

THE FEAR OF BLACK ENGULFMENT THAT WAS THE RATIONALE FOR uncompromising *apartheid* was not limited to the Boers. The experiences in neighboring Rhodesia were clear proof that, when English settlers faced similar problems, they reacted with almost equal inflexibility. In this richly endowed land lived 220,000 white settlers, mostly from Britain, set down in the heart of four million blacks, thus outnumbered by more than eighteen to one. Rhodesia was an integral part of the British Commonwealth but, as the pressure for native enfranchisement and independence grew, the white settlers closed ranks. They did not go to the lengths of cruelty and indignity that became the practice in the Nationalist citadel of South Africa, but they doggedly refused to risk the fate of the white minorities of every other land in Africa when the blacks achieved dominance.

The Rhodesian spokesman was a rugged character, Ian Smith, straight out of a frontier adventure novel. His father had migrated from Scotland, drawn by the mining discoveries of the period, and Ian grew up in the climate of gold prospecting and farming. He joined the RAF during World War II, flew many dangerous missions, and was shot down in one of the North African aerial battles. His face had to be almost completely rebuilt and, though the plastic surgery was skillful, the right side remained paralyzed. After recovery he rejoined the RAF to fight the Italian Fascists. He was again brought down, was rescued by the partisans, fought at their side in the underground for many months, and was finally smuggled out of Italy to Britain.

After the war he returned to Rhodesia and to farming but, deeply upset by what he considered the irresponsible liberalism of the dominant United Party, he organized the Rhodesian Front in 1961 to fight against concessions to the blacks. A Federation of white-dominated provinces had broken up in 1966 when a number of sovereign black republics had been established. Malawi had been carved out of Nyasaland, Zambia out of North Rhodesia. Smith was determined that what was left must never be yielded to the blacks. By 1964 he had routed the United Party and he became Prime Minister on a platform of rigorous white supremacy, even if this meant secession from the British Commonwealth.

Britain now had a Labour government and the Prime Minister, Harold Wilson, was seriously embarrassed by the confrontation with Rhodesia. Quite apart from the moral position of Labour on the issue of racial equality and majority rule, there was concerted pressure from the many black-governed countries within the Commonwealth. They threatened that unless an unequivocal stand was taken by Wilson to repudiate the white dictatorship that Smith defended, they would all secede and the Commonwealth would disintegrate. Wilson attempted negotiation in the hope of achieving a compromise that would provide for a period of transition, but would assure black autonomy and majority government within a "reasonably" spaced future. There were conferences in Salisbury to which Wilson journeyed, conferences in London to which Smith brought his grim-faced delegation, conferences on a warship off Gibraltar. Smith undoubtedly had already made up his mind to stand firm, but he journeyed to the successive conferences to gain time to prepare Rhodesia for the impact of possible sanctions from Britain and the United Nations, and to forge stronger ties with South Africa and the Portuguese colonies.

Wilson used all his diplomatic skill to persuade Smith that since majority rule was inevitable, would it not be realistic statesmanship to prepare for it in an orderly way? But Smith refused to accept Wilson's premise of inevitability. To him, this was a problem that could not be hedged with what he called "political weasel words." It involved survival or annihilation for his people in Rhodesia, and there was no compromise in between. The whites would never open the way to ultimate engulfment by the blacks, and no one wanted the assimilation that would produce a café-au-lait society. He reminded Wilson of the price paid by the whites for black enfranchisement in the Congo and Kenya and Ghana and other black-dominated lands. He asked Wilson, man to man, how a whole people, Wilson's own kith and kin, after painfully building a cherished way of life in what had been a wilderness, could be expected to entrust themselves to an embittered eighteen to one black majority in Rhodesia.

By November 1965, since there was no meeting of minds, Smith was ready to take Rhodesia out of the British Commonwealth. It was a heartbreaking decision. He and his people were bound to Britain by every tie of blood and tradition. His very appeal for sacrificial courage used as its text the call of Shakespeare's Henry V before another momentous battle:

> ... he which hath no stomach to this fight,
> Let him depart ...
> For he to-day that sheds his blood with me
> Shall be my brother ...
> And gentlemen in England now abed
> Shall think themselves accursed they were not here ...*

Within a few months the Declaration of Independence was proclaimed and the white Rhodesians braced themselves to ward off the consequences of reprisal. It was Wilson himself who demanded the UN condemnation, and he had Britain set the example of applying sanctions on oil and other exports that, hopefully, would force Rhodesian acquiescence by throttling its economy.

* *Henry V,* Act IV, Scene iii.

Rhodesia went through several very difficult years of rationing and austerity. But it held firmly to its resolve and it was the rest of the world that capitulated. Oil came through from South Africa. Four hundred cars rolled in monthly from Portuguese Mozambique. To reach Rhodesia they had to cross the black state of Malawi, where the lure of substantial profit apparently overcame the appeal for black solidarity. Other needed imports came from Japan and Holland. West Germany announced that it would apply the voted sanctions, but it would respect the long-term contracts that were already in being; these turned up in surprising numbers. The American space program was dependent on continued supplies of lithium, almost all of which had to come from Rhodesia. Despite the eloquence of the American advocates of sanctions, the lithium somehow reached the NASA factories and plants. The delegate of Communist Yugoslavia yelled himself purple with indignation over the racist villainy of black disfranchisement. But in the first year of sanctions, Yugoslavia's trade with Rhodesia increased by 69 percent. French exports rose by 200 percent and De Gaulle took special satisfaction in noting the discomfiture of Britain. It was only a technical discomfiture, for Britain's own trade with Rhodesia in the first seven months of 1967 was twice as much as in all of 1966.

Meantime Rhodesia found ways, through transshipment, to get its tobacco and chrome to the markets of the world. Despite the sanctions voted by the UN, and the threats of the black states, Rhodesia thrived. In 1968, when Britain was in serious economic straits and had to devalue the pound, Ian Smith gleefully sent a message to Prime Minister Wilson offering "a helping hand." Smith found himself winning ever-larger majorities. To his people he was now "Good old Smithy," with popularity that matched Winston Churchill's in his war days.

As the 1970's opened, the problems of race in South Africa and Rhodesia were as far from solution as ever. In both states the dominant government had built fortresses of repression and the protests of the outside world were dismissed as the hypocrisy of liberalism. Yet the whites were a small minority and the disproportion was growing. The black work gangs swung their picks, as they labored in the sun, to the chant: "*Abalengu ngo damn, abalengu ngo dati.*"*

The critical question remained: How long could a minority of whites keep in subjugation millions of blacks? What kind of endur-

* White people be damned, white people are dirt.

ing civilization could be built where all windows were barred by the whites at night, where ferocious watch dogs stood on guard, where it was confessed that social affairs were "making merry in the belly of a fort"? Scores of African states whose strength was steadily growing shared the determination to hasten the day of vengeance. The Communist giants could be counted on too, when the time was propitious, to exploit the festering hatreds. One of Sir Walter Scott's characters says: "When I think of all my wrongs, my blood is liquid flame." By the 1970's the policies of Malan and Verwoerd and Vorster and Ian Smith, however sincere their determination to protect the privileges of their patrimony, had turned the blood of millions of blacks into liquid flame.

The realist defined a pessimist as one who believed that the debacle for the whites would come within twenty years; the optimist stretched the respite to fifty years. But that the debacle would come seemed inevitable. How it would come apparently depended on whether there would be bitter-end inflexibility or resiliency in adjusting to a world where *apartheid* had become as anachronistic as feudalism or slavery.

51

COMMUNIST CHINA
ACHIEVES WORLD
POWER

WHEN MAO TSE-TUNG SUCCEEDED IN DEFEATING THE NATIONALIST forces of Chiang Kai-shek in 1949, driving them out of the China mainland, he established the world's largest Communist state and changed the course of history in Asia. But he soon discovered, as he turned to the problems of reconstruction, that it was as difficult to consolidate as it was to win the victory itself. China had been devastated by a decade of war against the Japanese, and then the agony was extended many years as the Nationalists and the Communists fought on to inherit the future. Millions of families caught in the storm of conflict had been uprooted and now awaited resettlement. Their abandoned land had been ravaged by the marauding armies or lay neglected as the exile of their occupants lengthened. Many of the largest cities bore the terrible marks of the struggle for possession and repossession. The mines and metal working industries of Manchuria had been looted by the Russians in 1945, and were again laid waste when the Communists and Nationalists fought on for their control. The light industry of Shanghai and Tientsin had been deserted by its skilled workers as the Communists approached and it rusted in idleness. The wrecked transportation facilities required almost complete rebuilding. Mao could not turn to the outside world for aid; the great powers, except for the Soviet Union, were now enemies. The help that initially came from Russia took the form of technicians on loan, about eleven thousand experts, but it was only a minute fraction of what was needed to provide fillip for the country's recovery.

Mao was undaunted. In one of the poems of this period he wrote:

> The sky is inverted, the earth turned
> upside down.

Then he added:

> And our spirits are soaring.

He began at once with successive five-year plans and, though the goals were set at seemingly impossible levels, they were surpassed within a decade because of the evangelical fervor that he generated. The mills and the mines quadrupled the highest tonnage figures of the pre-Communist period. The factories poured out locomotives and electrical appurtenances, ships, crude oil, cotton, and light and heavy equipment that competed in the markets of the world. Shanghai grew to a population of ten million, and it was soon producing more textiles than all of Britain. Gigantic dams and hydroelectric stations were constructed to generate power and to harness the rivers. One dam tamed the always threatening Yangtze, another the mighty Yellow River, the River of Sorrows, and these had their impact on agriculture, whose crop output doubled and then doubled again. The resettlement of the millions of uprooted families offered the opportunity to relieve the congestion of the coastal areas and to build the agriculture and industry of the interior. China was still not secured from drought or famine but it was mercifully past the dread period when twenty thousand coolies could starve to death annually on the streets of Shanghai.

When Mao turned to a national program in education he found that he was in a dark cave of illiteracy. Within the decade there were a hundred million children registered in the schools and 75 percent had acquired reading knowledge. University students were offered special incentives and, by 1960, a hundred thousand were graduating annually. Since the emphasis was on science and technology, the universities were training 75 percent as many engineers as in the United States.

These would normally be proud and comforting statistics. But not for Mao, to whom neither elementary literacy nor the most sophisticated skills touched the problem that tormented him. He was convinced that traditional Chinese education was decadent and reactionary, reflective of the imperialist legacy and the influence of the whites, the Big Noses. Its marketplace efficiency set up values that were corrupting. He therefore undertook an indoctrination program that had no parallel in history. His purpose was to transform the individual, not only in the substantive data of his training, but in his very thought processes. He wrote, "I shall later raise a tidal wave to sweep the nation and touch Heaven's height."

The country was divided up into relatively small units, the people in them obligated to meet daily in commune, in school, in office, in factory—peasants, merchants, artisans, housewives, students, even prisoners. The elected leader, approved by governing officials, conducted the carefully structured question and answer sessions, and everyone was expected to speak up and to participate. There was no escape by neutrality, no freedom of silence. Since all were usually neighbors or working colleagues and knew each other, there could be no dissembling. There were official views for everything—the wisdom of Mao, the infallibility of Marxism, the treachery of Chiang Kai-shek, the predatory imperialism of the Americans, the evils of grafting, the value of communal living, the significance of obedience. When the sessions were over the slogans were repeated on loudspeakers and piped in at restaurants and hotel lobbies, at airports and railway stations, at street corners and sports events, even in public toilets. The entire population was exposed to this incessant brainwashing, month in, month out, pounded upon, manipulated, hammered into conformity.

To supplement the thought sessions, continuous indoctrination was provided for the great mass organizations, the Federation of Youth, eighteen million strong, the trade unions with ten million, the women's federations with seventy-six million, the Student League for ages fourteen to twenty-five with twelve million. The integument was provided by the Communist Party itself, four million strong in 1950, about twenty-seven million in 1970. Overall there was the pervasive presence of Mao himself, whose portrait or bust or picture was universally exhibited, in every procession, on every billboard, in schools and offices, in every home. His *Red Book* of maxims and parables soon displaced the *Analects* of Confucius and the *Three Word* classics.

The world watched in fearsome fascination the creation of a vast society of blue ants, an Orwellian nightmare. Mao was not diverted by the pejorative labels. He had perfected a reliable technique to eliminate the old Confucian passivity—family piety, the veneration of ancestors, the attachment to tradition. It was a technique that recreated a people united by an indissoluble sense of mission. This was a far cry from the frustration of Dr. Sun Yat-sen, who overthrew the Manchu dynasty in 1911 and then said, plaintively, "It's impossible to work with these people. They are loose sand, and they have no binding cohesion."

There was one brief moment of respite. In 1956 Mao imagined that he could risk a measure of frankness and spontaneity and he lifted the ban on complaint and challenge. "Let one hundred flowers bloom together," he said, "let diverse schools of thought contend." He was taken seriously by many of the scholars and teachers and by some of the party officials. The criticism that flowed was daringly uninhibited. It was leveled at the stifling of the arts, the weakness of Communist practice, the inefficiency in industry and agriculture. The infallibility of Marxism was questioned, and though Mao himself did not come under fire some of the most highly placed functionaries did. Mao was shocked that there could be so much disaffection after the years of patient tutelage. He quickly retracted the pledge that he would welcome freedom of dissent. There were severe punishments for those who had gone too far; the suspicion was inevitable that the policy had been initially planned in order to flush out the malcontents. After 1956 few critics dared to lift their heads again, and the hundred flowers withered on the stem.

Meantime, the Old Man in a Hurry was off on another breathtaking reform. He ordered a radical reorganization of peasant life on the model of the Paris Commune of 1871. The entire rural population was to be drawn into communes, each with from ten to twenty-five thousand men, women, and children. They were to live regulated, communized lives and the family unit was to be superseded. The commune would undertake living and working functions —farming, purchasing, dining, entertaining, child rearing, the care of the old. Each commune would pre-empt total ownership—land, equipment, houses, livestock—all to be managed cooperatively. By November 1958, there were twenty-six thousand communes, each with about five thousand households, and they comprised 98 percent of the farm population. Mao hailed the plan as introducing the era of the new man, the social man, freed at last of his selfish parochialism. He called it "the era of the morning sun above the broad horizon of East Asia." Perhaps he remembered that the Paris commune lasted only seventy-three days. But if he did remember, it did not dissuade him. This was an adventure to fit the scope of his imagination. He was in a laboratory with more than five hundred million lives.

Even as the communes expanded, Mao grew impatient with the tempo of industrial progress. The glowing statistics could gratify the nations that had achieved a large measure of self-sufficiency, but since China was still dependent upon foreign nations for much of its food and its essential products, decades of growth and consolidation had to be telescoped into months. He had supreme confidence in his people, believing that man can be conditioned for responsibility. He had been impressed by the psychological theories of Pavlov, and eagerly applied them to a whole nation. He wrote, "We are a gifted people. We have a proud history. But we are not even as far advanced as Belgium. We have to apply more ardor. We must do something to raise the self-confidence of our people. . . . Our principle is to learn all the strong points of other countries—in politics, economics, sciences, technology, literature, and arts. . . ."*

In February 1958 Mao announced the Great Leap Forward, a three-year plan for bypassing the laborious, step-by-step procedures that the more conservative technicians advised. If the entire nation responded, he insisted, if the objective of immediate self-sufficiency took on the compelling character of a crusade, then the increase in steel and coal production, in electric power and the other essential resources, could far surpass conventional quotas. He ordered every family to participate in this Great Leap Forward. "Steel does not have to depend on the giant mills," he cried. "Let every home do its share." By the fall, there were 600,000 backyard furnaces puffing away at the manufacture of steel. "Food doesn't have to depend only on the labor of farmers. Let every housewife and her children become partners in the planting." By the fall virtually every mile of soil was under cultivation. It was a patriotic duty, gladly undertaken, to labor twelve, fifteen, eighteen hours a day, around the calendar, to meet Mao's expectations.

The Great Leap Forward turned out to be a Great Leap Backward. There was indeed a quantitative spurt in the first year in the production of steel and coal and electric power. But all too many of the crude backyard furnaces dissolved into piles of mud and brick after a few heavy rains. The quality of the product was often completely worthless. Millions of tons that were expectantly delivered were found to be unfit for industrial use. With all the enthusiasm of the zealots it was just not possible for backyard furnaces to accomplish instant technology. Nor was it possible to rely for substantial supplementary agricultural produce on the efforts of well-meaning amateurs.

* Cited in Jerome Ch'en, ed., *Mao* (Englewood Cliffs, N.J.: Prentice-Hall, Inc., 1969), p. 84.

Many of Mao's more conservative advisers were appalled. "We wanted to reach Heaven in one leap," they said ruefully. They estimated that China had been set back a full decade by the wasted effort and the expense of the grand design, and that it would be most dangerous if any similar overambitious experiment were undertaken. They still gave fulsome homage to the old man as the revered symbol of the revolution, but they tried harder to hedge him in with restrictions so that they could circumvent his impatient zeal. They suggested that he was now too much preoccupied to continue as chief of state. Mao was not taken in by the florid tributes that extolled his wisdom. "These are the eulogies," he noted, "of a dead father at his funeral."

The first serious strain between him and some of the men who had been closest to him, and who had shared the early battles against the Japanese and the Nationalists, dated from the disappointments of this Great Leap Forward. The strain came because the technicians and the bureaucrats misinterpreted the basic objectives that concerned him. He had no wish to evaluate the revolution by the statistics of production. He was more concerned with the vitality of spirit. To him it was lamentable that revolutionists, whenever they grew older, lost passion and turned soft. Franz Kafka had written that every revolution evaporates and leaves behind only the slime of a new bureaucracy. Mao remembered how the fervor of the Kuomintang had been extinguished by sated officeholders. He had watched with contempt this kind of degradation in Russia, where, he said, Khrushchev was now compromising with the imperialists, where cheap parasitic incentives had become the obsessive national goal. He vowed that this would not happen in China. Ways must be found for each generation to go through a rebirth of the revolutionary spirit, even to sacrifice most of itself in order to achieve this rebirth. It was an eerie kind of death-and-birth cycle, almost inducing catastrophe in order to protect the élan of redemption.

As Mao prepared for the extraordinary purification process, he realized that he could not count upon the party where, he feared, "the slime of bureaucracy" had already done its work of attrition. He had little confidence in most of his colleagues in the government who, he suspected, were mainly concerned with the power and privileges of office. But he hoped that he could count on the military. There, the austerity of Spartan living had assured protective armor. He placed reliance too on the young people, the twenty million between the ages of fifteen and twenty-five, the uncorrupted generation, whose freshness and enthusiasm would provide the foundation on which to rebuild the future. If they were redeemed there need be no concern about succession, for there would be tens of millions of revolutionary successors. "To kill a snake," the Chinese adage read, "it is enough to hit at his head. But to tear up a tree, it is essential to pluck out the roots." Mao, now seventy-three and determined to outlive himself, was ready.

To lead his crusade he turned to General Lin Piao, one of his trusted younger protégés, a comrade-in-arms who had shared many of his most dangerous experiences. Lin Piao, the son of a factory owner, was trained for a soldier's career at the Whampoa Military Academy where Chiang Kai-shek had been commandant. His small, frail, slender build belied his name, the Tiger Cat, and his continuous ill-health gave little indication of the force and tenacity that were to take him to the highest military posts. He took part in the Long March, and his victories against the Japanese in September 1937, the first the Chinese had won against foreign powers, had a spectacular effect upon morale. After the Japanese invaders had been driven out in 1945, Lin remained as Mao's chief military strategist in the continuing war against Chiang Kai-shek's Nationalists, and he vindicated the confidence of his chief. In the early days of the civil war his forces were usually outnumbered and outgunned but he always had the Chinese proverb on his lips: "One spark can consume a hundred miles of prairie." His capture of Mukden netted 400,000 prisoners, including thirty-six generals and all their arsenals. When he took Peking the Nationalist cause became hopeless, and soon afterwards Chiang fled to Taiwan. In the first years of the Communist regime Lin continued to combine military and political responsibility and in 1959 he became Minister of Defense. Mao was confident that Lin Piao was his man as he moved to complete the climactic mission of his life, the Great Cultural Revolution.

Late in 1965 Mao began tilting against the scholars and the intellectuals, who were upbraided for concentrating on sterile trivia and pedantry. Nor did he spare the bureaucrats of the party and the government, who were assailed for becoming too wedded to position and power. By the autumn of the next year the attacks had reached the top officials and included the President, Liu Shao-chi, another old comrade of Mao who had for many years been regarded as his heir apparent, so chosen by Mao himself. For three decades there had been mutual trust and affectionate collaboration between the two men, in the Chinese phrase, "as close as lips and teeth." Liu had lately become increasingly apprehensive about what he interpreted as Mao's irresponsible extremism. He had tried tactfully to restrain his revered chief but the more he remonstrated, the angrier Mao became. In August 1966, Mao announced to a party conference that he no longer favored Liu as his heir and that he now preferred Lin. The announcement confirmed the suspicion of many who were privy to the developments inside the government structure, that Lin Piao had adroitly taken advantage of Mao's declining awareness to ingratiate himself, and they pointed for proof to instances of Lin's unlimited ambition. The personal factors that were now interjected added a power struggle to the ideological issues and further endangered the stability of the government.

Mao and Lin now launched the Cultural Revolution that was to dominate the life of China for the next three years. It took the form of a summons to the high-school and college youth to organize for unremitting pressure on the established cadres of national life. It was a paradoxical call, from a septuagenarian to teen-agers, to defy their elders, to cancel out the past, to repudiate authority. The response was dumbfounding. The Great Cultural Revolution sent the young people, organized as Red Guards, into every corner of the land, released from all discipline and inhibitions, to question, to challenge, to reject. In an opening rally, where a million of them gathered in the great square in Peking, Lin Piao, with a smiling Mao Tse-tung at his side, gave them their marching orders, to cultivate the revolutionary spirit by making revolution. "Strike down the bourgeois royalists," he cried. "Eradicate old ideas, old customs, old habits of the exploiting classes. Strike down the demons." Most of the youngsters may not have known what he was talking about but they cheered themselves into hysteria. In a subsequent demonstration they marched with their crimson armbands to the home of President Liu, who had been denounced by Mao in the worst possible terms as the Khrushchev of China. The raging mob demanded the dismissal of the President. Mao's wife, who had been a B-movie actress and who was now in charge of cultural revision, added to the tumult by publicly vilifying Liu Shao-chi's wife as a prostitute. The family's humiliation was complete when their own daughter signed one of the wall posters, denouncing her father as a reactionary politician.

"The little generals of disruption," as they were called, had begun with assaults on old customs, old traditions, old ways of thought. But they were quickly out of control. They went far beyond any of the original intentions of Mao, and certainly of Lin. All schools had been closed, and they remained closed for two years, the universities for three years. This gave the young people aimless leisure and they loosed chaos wherever they went. They rampaged through the crowded streets of the cities. They brought traffic to a standstill as they shouted their insults at bourgeois influence and revisionist thinking. They dragged out editors and scholars and artists and humiliated them by crowning them with huge dunce caps in a land where the loss of face was a blemish on honor. They burned books that were stigmatized as reactionary, and the music and the art of the anathematized western world. Violinists and pianists who had become famous for their classical performances had their instruments broken, and often their fingers too. The youngsters mounted wall posters that insulted the most venerable figures and they harassed foreign diplomats. They renamed streets, giving them new revolutionary identifications. They tore into stores and intimidated shopkeepers who dealt in bourgeois merchandise. They went to ludicrous extremes, changing traffic signals so that red would mean "GO," driving on the revolutionary left rather than on the reactionary right, turning eyes left when saluting reviewing officers in their parades and their processions, forcing terrified women to change their western hairdos.

It had been expected that the Cultural Revolution would be limited to rhetoric, at least at the factory gates and in the countryside, so as not to disrupt the economy. But once the genii were out of their bottles it was not possible to get them back. The demonstrations and their accompanying intimidation affected every area of national life. Even when the factories and the communes were bypassed, their essential routine was seriously crippled. The railroads, the buses, the canal boats were frequently commandeered by the junketing Red Guards, and the services of supply and distribution were snarled. There was panic buying. The streets were not safe, nor were the homes.

This was no longer a children's crusade, to be treated with affectionate indulgence. The call to exorcize had produced monsters. Hence, after more than a year of pandemonium, there was determined resistance from the peasants and the workers, from the government officials and the party functionaries, and now, too, from the army heads and the police who had been concerned from the outset about the threat to national security. There were armed clashes, with rising casualties. The final toll could not be accurately learned, but it must have reached into the tens of thousands, for every village and every city reported bloodshed. Lin Piao offered the dubious consolation that the casualties were "less than in the Civil War."

By 1968, when the army took stern action, even Lin Piao was ready to admit that the excesses of the revolution were jeopardizing national security. The students were ordered to end their demonstrations and were shipped inland, some to work in the communes, others to work in the mines and forests. The schools were reopened although the universities did not function normally until 1970. At the Congress of 1969, the end of the revolution was made official, the announcement, however, couched in language that would not embarrass Mao.

The cost of the Cultural Revolution to China was devastating. To be sure, Mao had accomplished part of his purpose. The Establishment had been shaken up. Some of the old guard had been eliminated. The lesson had been writ large that there must be no cooling of revolutionary ardor, and that continuous renewal was a sine qua non for a dynamic China. But to dramatize this lesson an exorbitant price had been paid. For more than two years there had been a steady drumbeat of attack on authority, and even when the drumbeat was finally stilled, Mao's most precious asset, his sacrosanct mystique, had been tarnished. Directives that came down from Peking to the twenty-nine provinces were often perfunctorily filed; there were continuing complaints from Peking that orders that were marked urgent were cavalierly ignored. Above all, there was now a heavy substratum of hostility in the official family. Liu Shao-chi had been demoted and humiliated, but he had many adherents still in the wings, and Mao was the first to remember that half-defeated enemies could always come back to fight another day. Lin Piao had been named by Mao as his heir-designate, but it was not at all certain that he would be able to assume responsibility, not alone because of steadily deteriorating health but also because of the residue of bitterness everywhere.

To the western world it was no comfort that China had been weakened by the Red Guard chaos. An insecure China was a dangerously erratic entity. It was now armed with nuclear power, and, though it did not yet have adequate delivery capacity seriously to challenge the nuclear giants, Mao had often enough spoken with terrifying dispassion about the expendability of manpower. He warned the West, and Russia too, that if Chinese interests were ever jeopardized, he would not hesitate to go to the limit for his deterrent. He reminded them that even if three hundred million Chinese were immolated China would still survive, but the other nations would perish in the fiery holocaust.* A China that was treated as a pariah, disrupted by internal conflict, nursing its wounded pride, was a much greater menace than a China secure and respected. It was in the long-range interest of the rest of the world to bring China's nearly one billion people into the family of nations, and to help them to achieve confidence and stability. Even Richard Nixon, who had built his political reputation on baiting the Communists, had declared, once he was confronted with presidential responsibility, "We simply cannot afford to leave China forever outside the family of nations, there to nurture its fantasies, cherish its hates, threaten its neighbors. There is no place on this small planet for a billion of its potentially most able people to live in angry isolation."

Apparently Mao felt none of the confusion or frustration that haunted his colleagues and his protégés. He had indeed suffered some grave disappointments to sadden the sunset days of his long career. The Great Leap Forward and the Cultural Revolution had mocked his most cherished hopes. But he could also feel the thrill of pride that no personality in four thousand years had left as decisive a mark upon his country as he had. He had united his people in independence, and he had clothed them with dignity, after centuries of degrading foreign control. He had modernized the economy. He had redistributed the national resources and immeasurably raised living standards. He had unlocked the secrets of nuclear power and his arsenal was now an incontrovertible deterrent. He was certain that there was no need for concern about succession; it was inconceivable for him to think in terms of *après Mao le déluge*.† If the heir was not Lin Piao, it could be Chou En-lai, the brilliant and resourceful foreign policy aide who had been at his side from the earliest days. If Chou were too old, since only five years separated him from Mao, there would be others. For the revolutionary élan had been nurtured and protected. The future was safe. Whatever the forms of government and the modes of economy that

---

* A reputable Chinese physician told a visiting German journalist that China was the mightiest nuclear power in the world. "For we are the only nation that is ready to use its atomic arsenal, instead of just talking about it." Louis Barcata, *China in the Throes of the Cultural Revolution* (New York: Hart Publishing Company, Inc., 1968), p. 17.

† The pun was in the heading of an editorial in *The Economist*, Nov. 20, 1971.

would emerge in the centuries ahead, China would never again be excluded from a major role in world affairs. It would always be a proud equal among equals.

Then, at the end of 1971, in one of the most sensational diplomatic revolutions of the half century, Mao's faith was vindicated. President Nixon who had built his political career on hard-line anti-communism decided that the time had come to end the long hostility to Red China. A détente with China would undoubtedly give the United States more effective leverage in its negotiations with the Soviet Union. It would open the way to trade relations with a nation whose population would soon reach a billion. Above all, it would end the farce of quarantine when virtually all the major powers had bowed to reality and recognized that China belonged within the family of nations.

Once the decision had been made, Nixon paid little attention to his past declarations. There was not even pause for a diplomatic acupuncture. Indeed, Nixon seemed to take special delight in discomfiting his liberal critics by appropriating their traditional political stance. A century earlier a British Tory Prime Minister, Sir Robert Peel, firmly committed to trade protection and its high tariff walls, changed sides and elicited the comment from Disraeli, "He found the Whigs bathing and stole their clothes." Nixon too had the courage of his lack of convictions. He blandly repudiated the China lobby that had for more than twenty years resisted even the most tentative overtures to Mao Tse-tung. When the 1971 vote was taken on the admission of Red China to the United Nations, Nixon instructed the American delegation to take leadership in the affirmative action. The climax came in February 1972, when the President of the United States made the long journey to Peking personally to explore with Mao Tse-tung and Chou En-lai how the two great nations, so long estranged, could resume a friendship that had been abruptly terminated in 1949 when the Communists had won mainland China.

52

RETROSPECT
AND PROSPECT

MANY HISTORIANS AND SOCIAL PHILOSOPHERS HAVE SOUGHT A THEM-
atic unity, or at least an identifying name, for the character and
significance of the period since World War I. It has been variously
labeled the Age of Conflict, the Counter-Enlightenment, the Era of
Violence. Auden called it the Age of Anxiety, Camus referred to it
as the Century of Fear. T. S. Eliot's melancholy appraisal was so
final that Malcolm Muggeridge called him a death rattle in the
throat of a dying civilization.

In truth, there is no thematic unity or even thematic coherence
in the period. It cannot be neatly categorized, except if one resorts
to the broad generalization with which Charles Dickens began *The
Tale of Two Cities*: "It was the best of times, it was the worst of
times." It witnessed remarkable achievements—science and technology that included the conquest of space and gave new meaning
to the Psalmist's boast that man was but little lower than the angels.
But it was disgraced with evidences of inhumanity that made a
mockery of the claims of progress.

It was clearly a period in which the dominant position of Europe
in the world was thoroughly undermined. For centuries Europe had
been at the center, culturally and economically, physically controlling huge sections of the rest of the world. But after two wars in
which manpower and resources were dangerously depleted, Europe
no longer had the strength to sustain its dominance. Lord Palmerston's proud assurance, *Civis romanus sum*, offering imperial protec-

tion to Englishmen anywhere in the world, seemed as far away as its Roman archetype. Mao Tse-tung's exultant cry to his victorious Chinese people, "We have stood up," was a ringing reply to the cant of the European cartels which piously pillaged with the warrant that they were breaking down "the unrighteous walls of monopoly which bar four hundred millions of men from European civilization and God's truth."*

The peoples of Africa and Asia, who had been under colonial control for centuries, now thoroughly aware of the vulnerability of the European nations, erupted, and in every continent the pace of decolonization quickened. The white intruders were ousted, some abdicating without too much resistance, some expelled after bitter conflict. A few pockets of imperialism remained, in Angola and Mozambique, where the Portuguese clung stubbornly to their possessions; in South Africa and Rhodesia, where a small minority of white settlers held down millions of blacks; in the Guiana states in Latin America, and Hong Kong in Asia. But these were merely vestigial and not likely to be long tolerated. By 1960 the great period of European imperialism that had been set in motion after the discoveries of the sixteenth and seventeenth centuries was over. This did not, and could not, mean the end of European influence. The stamp of Europe remained. It was Europe that had supplied Africa and Asia with their technology, their institutional experience, their health reforms, their capital investments, their skills, and, in many areas, their cultural heritage. But in the last decades of the twentieth century, the white man was no longer to be the arbiter of global destiny. He would have to share the privileges as well as the burdens of civilized life with peoples who claimed equality.

In this period too the capitalist economy of the western world was challenged by the emergence of a militant, evangelical communism, and the struggle for dominance was responsible for most of the threats to peace and for the turbulence that kept the peoples of the world in almost continuous tension. The audacious coup of October 1917 by twenty thousand dedicated revolutionaries in Russia triggered a worldwide reaction. It wrought permanent changes in the social structure of China and eastern Europe. It established powerful parties in the democratic states that convulsed their political life. It penetrated the western hemisphere when it won beachheads in Cuba and Chile. It almost succeeded in imposing its iron discipline on

* Cited in V. G. Kiernan, *The Lords of Human Kind* (Boston: Little, Brown, 1969), p. 153.

Ghana in Africa and Indonesia in the South Pacific. Just as in the 1930's fascism seemed to be "the wave of the future" and was so hailed by Charles Lindbergh, now communism, in its triumphant sweep, seemed to be on its inevitable way to inherit the world.

Communism however did not remain a monolithic force. Internal dissensions shattered its unity of direction and control. The schism began immediately after World War II when Tito of Yugoslavia defied Stalin and the Kremlin, and established his own nationalist brand of communism. There was continuous restlessness among the populations of Poland and Hungary, and later, of Rumania, so that the Soviet Union had to resort to repression and compromise to maintain its control. The most serious rupture came in the late fifties when Khrushchev and Mao Tse-tung had an irretrievable falling out. Togliatti, the Italian Communist leader, spoke of "the polycentric world of communism" in which the East-West rivalries of the past were now infinitely complicated by the bitter dissensions of Red China and Soviet Russia. By the end of the sixties these were as serious as any that had precipitated the Cold War. Indeed, in many of the international crises it was not uncommon to find China on one side and the Soviet Union on the other, with the United States and its democratic allies trying to act out the role of the honest broker.* Nevertheless, whether the Communist states were ranged against capitalist enemies or locked in fratricidal struggle, their emergence was the dominating factor in the history of the half century.

Hanging over the period since 1945 was the mortal threat of the atom bomb. The race to perfect it for military use was won by the scientists of the United States, and it brought the war with Japan to an instant end. There was hope that its control could thereafter pass to an international authority which would remove the danger of its use in warfare and free its power for the needs of peace. President Truman offered to yield such control to an international Atomic Commission, but he set the condition that there must be meticulous surveillance. Russia did not have the bomb, but Stalin was unwilling to permit the required inspection, and the great opportunity passed. Much earlier than expected, Russia created its own nuclear arsenal, and this ominous achievement was followed by successful tests in Britain, China, and France. There was little doubt

* In the war of 1971 between India and Pakistan, the Soviet Union lined up with India, China supported Pakistan, and the United States kept trying to obtain a cease-fire.

that other states, even the smaller ones, would soon enter the nuclear club, since the principle of the bomb was now well known and only the expenses of manufacture and delivery were the inhibiting factors. The genie would then be out of the bottle, said President Kennedy, and it would be impossible to get him back in again. All the world therefore was now under the threat of universal destruction if ever the terror were loosed. The continuity of civilized life very literally depended upon the deterrence of mutual fear. There was somber truth in the popular doggerel,

> Let not the atom bomb
> Be the final sequel
> In which all men
> Are cremated equal.

Astonishingly, though the threat was real, the world gradually resigned itself to its pervasive presence. After the shattering shock of Hiroshima and Nagasaki, the fright wore off and the world's threatened peoples adjusted to the psychology of the villagers who continued to live stolidly in the shadow of an occasionally erupting volcano. Even the nuclear tests that discharged genetic poisons into the atmosphere, after initial protests, were accepted as the inevitable price of existence in the perilous twentieth century. Every precaution was taken to protect leadership from assassination, but the possibility of the assassination of the world itself became a fact of life to be lived with.

Another terror that haunted men, less dramatic in form but equally menacing, was the steady increase in population. In the one generation between 1945 and 1965 the number grew by a billion and statisticians noted that, because the increase was geometric, more than a billion would be added in each succeeding decade. Ironically, the development came from vastly improved health standards, especially in the control of infant mortality, and from the elimination of the diseases that had ravaged the earth in earlier periods. But the growth was unplanned and virtually out of control in Africa, Latin America, India, and other teeming centers of population where the food supply and its distribution could not sustain such growth. All attempts to bring some measure of regulation through contraception and abortion met passionate resistance from the conservative religious forces. Even where this was overcome there were insoluble problems in the ignorance or the unconcern of the populations themselves. The agencies of the United Nations gave priority to the problem and, one by one, the most affected countries set up commissions to wrestle with it. But the population still mounted and the problem ticked away as ominously as did the atom bomb.

There was a curious paradox too about the world's reaction to tragedy, and it is not inaccurate to note that a major casualty of the period was the sense of compassion. The agencies of mercy—the Red Cross, the international relief programs of the League of Nations and the United Nations, the occasional actions of governments, private philanthropy—all these were better organized and more effectively administered than ever before. But the burdens of relief became too much even for the richest nations, and the very magnitude of grief scarred the world's conscience and left it insensitive to mass sorrow. Wars brought in their wake orgies of vengeance, as when Indians and Pakistanis slaughtered each other, or Indonesian Moslems massacred Communists. Stalin and Mao Tse-tung could plan ruthless economic projects and calmly dismiss the cost in lives. Millions of Jews died in concentration camps and crematoria; other millions of refugees—Arabs, Biafrans, Bengalese—uprooted and expropriated, dragged out their miserable years on the edge of starvation and hopelessness. Millions dislocated? Millions dead? All too quickly the world adjusted to the figures. They carried little sentient meaning. Byron's words took on special appropriateness: negligence and apathy and unconcern

> . . . produce ten thousand tyrants,
> Whose delegated cruelty surpasses
> The worst acts of one energetic master
> However harsh and hard in his own bearing.*

These were all obsessive problems: keeping the peace, controlling nuclear power, managing burgeoning populations, containing the hatreds spawned by conflict. The great hope was that an international authority could be created sufficiently respected to compel the subordination of individual objectives to the discipline of the common will. Or that at least such an authority would provide the cooling-off period when tensions became too threatening, so that disputes could be later settled in a mood more reasonable and conciliatory. But the League of Nations in which Wilson placed his hope was paralyzed by the unwillingness of the great powers to subordinate their own to the common will. The United Nations was constantly blocked by the same obstacles. These disappointments did not mean that the international bodies—the League and the United Nations—

* *Sardanapalus,* I, ii.

were complete failures. Many useful functions were performed by their ancillary agencies, which supplied credit and technical help to the developing countries. There were occasions when the disputes of the smaller nations were held within limits by the agreements among the big powers—the truce that brought an armistice in Palestine in 1949, the pacification of the Congo in the early 1960's. But none of the major disputes could be settled except through the deterrence of mutual fear. The compelling force of a supranational authority was still a long way off.

The very limited achievements of the international bodies moved statesmen in many countries to try for cooperation from the bottom up instead of from the top down. They concluded that if the western world was not yet ready for a League, perhaps it would respond more favorably to regional cooperation and limited objectives. Winston Churchill in 1946 had spoken in Zurich of a Europe that, by cooperation, could rise above the weakness of its fragmentation and, in union, could become a mighty power. Jean Monnet and Robert Schuman of France, Paul-Henri Spaak of Belgium, Alcide de Gasperi of Italy, and other forward-looking statesmen ardently committed to "the idea of Europe" devoted themselves to realistic programs of economic cooperation that would appeal to the self-interest of the western nations. They were all convinced that the small nation-state, functioning in isolation, was no longer viable.

Out of their efforts came the Coal and Steel Community of 1952 that pooled the coal and steel resources and the markets of France, West Germany, Italy, and the Benelux countries. In the words of its spiritual father, Jean Monnet, "it was the first expression of the Europe that is being born." The authority that was to manage it had the right to control prices, fix production quotas, and tax each ton that was produced. Its decisions were binding and did not require the unanimity that had wrecked the power of action of other international bodies. There followed Euratom (European Atomic Energy Community), a condominium of democratic nations to promote the peaceful uses of atomic energy, including coordinated research activities.

Above all, there was spectacular success in a European Economic Community, a Common Market arrangement that modified and abolished restrictive tariffs by the member nations. The preamble of the treaty that established the EEC on January 1, 1958, cited as objectives the closer cooperation of peoples even as their economic interests were to be integrated. The Common Market united 170 million vigorous, intelligent, progressive people of six nations whose volume of world trade was nearly double that of the United States. Even Britain, long reluctant to come into any European arrangement that infringed on sovereignty, now sought entrance. Its application was at first denied because of the opposition of De Gaulle. But after De Gaulle's death, most obstacles were cleared and Britain made ready to join the European partnership by 1972.

A beginning in political integration was also ventured with the creation of a symbolic European Parliament, centered in Strasbourg. It functioned modestly, quietly, primarily as a forum, with no legislative power. It was meant only to embody the hope of men that ultimately there might emerge a United States of Europe. But it remained little more than a Messianic hope. The internal battles that convulsed Europe kept the Coal and Steel Agreement, Euratom, the Common Market, and the other regional agreements very much on the periphery of genuine unity.

In summary, the record of the half century was not a proud one, despite remarkable advances in every field of thought and, for some limited parts of the world, the comforts of life. The dominant mood was deep anxiety, the loss of confidence in the capacity of the human species to survive. The plaintive cry of Macbeth seemed never more appropriate:

> But wherefore could not I pronounce 'Amen'?
> I had most need of blessing, and 'Amen'
> Stuck in my throat.*

The mood was reflected in the apparent meaninglessness in art, in the theater of the absurd, in existentialist philosophy, in the cult of "God is dead" in religion and ethics. "Alas," wrote Rilke, "the world has fallen into the hands of men." In such a mood it was easy, almost exhilarating, to turn away from the world, to take flight from responsibility.

This self-conscious nihilism, however, was unacceptable to those who, like their spiritual forebears in every generation of travail, persevered as the carriers of civilized values. They did not say then, and do not say now, "This is the end of Man." They did not deny the sorrows, neither the naturally ordained nor the man-made. But despite the loneliness and the hostility in which they functioned, they refused to swoon into defeatism. They retained their faith.

* *Macbeth*, Act II, Scene ii.

Einstein said once that the most incomprehensible thing about the universe was the fact that it was comprehensible. It was comprehensible because of man's unconquerable determination. Whatever the confusion, the disharmony, the wickedness that haunted a historical period, there was usually a reserve of inspired leadership ready to challenge it. Thrice defeated, a hundred times defeated, the challengers persisted. History was studded with examples of the decisive influence of an affirmative will that reversed what had seemed irreversible. Churchill and Roosevelt, Gandhi and Cárdenas, De Valera and Ben-Gurion were only a few of the contemporary immortals who faced the apparently inevitable and, by refusing to accept it, fashioned it to their will. William Faulkner summarized this spiritual stamina in an address when he accepted the Nobel Prize for literature. "I believe that man will not merely endure; he will prevail. He is immortal, not because he alone among creatures has an inexhaustible voice, but because he has a soul, a spirit capable of compassion and sacrifice and endurance."*

* Speech given at Stockholm, December 1950.

INDEX

A NOTE ABOUT THE AUTHOR

ABRAM LEON SACHAR is Chancellor of Brandeis University in Waltham, Massachusetts, a school which he helped to establish in 1948, on a completely nonsectarian basis, as the first corporate contribution of the Jewish community to American higher education. For twenty years he was president of that institution.

Dr. Sachar was born in New York City and reared in St. Louis. He received his undergraduate education at Washington University and at Harvard University, with Phi Beta Kappa honors. For three years he pursued his graduate studies at Cambridge University in England. Upon his return, with a Ph.D. in history for special research on the Victorian House of Lords, he joined the history faculty of the University of Illinois.

During World War II, Dr. Sachar was a commentator on contemporary affairs over WMAQ, Chicago affiliate of NBC, and over WOR, New York outlet for the Mutual Broadcasting System. He has become a familiar figure on the lecture platforms of town halls, teachers' conventions, and university convocations. His books include *A History of the Jews,* now in its fifth edition, with translations in several foreign languages. He is a fellow of the American Academy of Arts and Sciences and serves on numerous educational and philanthropic boards. President Lyndon Johnson appointed him to serve on the United States Advisory Commission in International Education and Cultural Affairs, and governors Rockefeller, Kerner, and Sargent appointed him to commissions to evaluate the private colleges and universities of New York, Illinois, and Massachusetts. Honorary degrees from twenty-three universities have been conferred upon him. His lecture series *The Course of Our Times* is telecast weekly on educational channels in most of the larger cities of the nation.

A NOTE ON THE TYPE

This book was set on the Linotype in Baskerville. Linotype Baskerville is a facsimile cutting from type cast from the original matrices of a face designed by John Baskerville. The original face was the forerunner of the "modern" group of type faces.

John Baskerville (1706-75) of Birmingham, England, a writing master with a special renown for cutting inscriptions in stone, began experimenting about 1750 with punch-cutting and making typographical material. It was not until 1757 that he published his first work, a Virgil in royal quarto, with great-primer letters. This was followed by his famous editions of Milton, the Bible, the Book of Common Prayer, and several Latin classical authors. His types, at first criticized as unnecessarily slender, delicate, and feminine, in time were recognized as both distinct and elegant, and his types as well as his printing were greatly admired. Four years after his death Baskerville's widow sold all his punches and matrices to the Société Philosophique, Littéraire et Typographique, which used some of the types for the sumptuous Kehl edition of Voltaire's works in seventy volumes.

Composed by Cherry Hill Composition, Pennsauken, New Jersey. Printed and bound by The Haddon Craftsmen, Inc., Scranton, Pennsylvania.
Typography and binding design by Andrea Clark.